Making peace with the past?

MANCHESTER
1824

Manchester University Press

Making peace with the past?

Memory, trauma and the Irish Troubles

GRAHAM DAWSON

MANCHESTER UNIVERSITY PRESS

MANCHESTER AND NEW YORK • distributed exclusively in the USA by Palgrave

The right of Graham Dawson to be identified as the editor of this work has
been asserted by her in accordance with the Copyright, Designs and Patents
Act 1988.

Published by Manchester University Press
Oxford Road, Manchester M13 9NR, UK
and Room 400, 175 Fifth Avenue, New York, NY 10010, USA
www.manchesteruniversitypress.co.uk

Distributed exclusively in the USA by
Palgrave, 175 Fifth Avenue, New York NY 10010, USA

Distributed exclusively in Canada by
UBC Press, University of British Columbia, 2029 West Mall,
Vancouver, BC, Canada V6T 1Z2

British Library Cataloguing-in-Publication Data
A catalogue record for this book is available from the British Library

Library of Congress Cataloging-in-Publication Data
A catalog record for this book is available from the Library of Congress

ISBN: 0 7190 5672 1 paperback

ISBN 13: 978 0 7190 5672 7

First published 2007 by Manchester University Press

First digital, on-demand edition produced by Lightning Source 2010

To my Mum and Dad

Frank Dawson
(3 March 1926–4 November 2000)

Kathy Dawson, née McMahon
(2 January 1925–9 April 2003)

In loving memory

Contents

Contents

Figures

Abbreviations

ANC	African National Congress
BBC	British Broadcasting Corporation
BSI	Bloody Sunday Initiative
CIRA	Continuity IRA
CRC	Community Relations Council
DARA	Derry and Raphoe Action
DUP	Democratic Unionist Party
FACT	Families Against Crimes by Terrorism
FAIR	Families Acting for Innocent Relatives
FAIT	Families Against Intimidation by Terrorists
FEAR	Fear Encouraged Abandoning Roots
HET	Historical Enquiries Team
ICPNI	Independent Commission on Policing in Northern Ireland
ILRM	International League for the Rights of Man
INCORE	Initiative on Conflict Resolution and Ethnicity
INLA	Irish National Liberation Army
IRA	Irish Republican Army
ITN	Independent Television News
MoD	Ministry of Defence
NCCL	National Council for Civil Liberties
NGO	non-governmental organization
NICRA	Northern Ireland Civil Rights Association
NITVT	Northern Ireland Terrorist Victims Together
NIVT	Northern Ireland Voluntary Trust
PFC	Pat Finucane Centre for Human Rights and Social Change
PIRA	Provisional IRA (also referred to simply as IRA)
PSNI	Police Service of Northern Ireland
PTSD	post-traumatic shock disorder
PUP	Progressive Unionist Party
REMHI	Recovery of the Historical Memory project
RIRA	Real IRA
RSF	Republican Sinn Féin
RUC	Royal Ulster Constabulary
SAS	Special Air Service

SDLP   Social Democratic and Labour Party
SLR   self-loading rifle
TRC   (South African) Truth and Reconciliation Commission
UDA   Ulster Defence Association
UDR   Ulster Defence Regiment
UFF   Ulster Freedom Fighters
UUP   Ulster Unionist Party
UVF   Ulster Volunteer Force
UYUC   Ulster Young Unionist Council
VLU   Victims Liaison Unit
WAVE   Widows/Widowers Against Violence Empower

Acknowledgements

In researching and writing this book, I have depended on many different kinds of assistance from individuals and organizations in Britain and Ireland. I am grateful for the financial support of the British Academy, the Leverhulme Trust and the Arts and Humanities Research Board (now Council), as well the Faculty of Arts and Architecture and the School of Historical and Critical Studies at the University of Brighton, without which this study would have been impossible. I thank Yvonne Murphy and all the staff of the Northern Ireland Political Collection at the Linen Hall Library, Belfast, whose invaluable guidance, both formal and informal, made my research fruitful in 1999–2001; and especially Ciaran Crossey, an unfailing source of knowledge, leads, suggestions and humour. Thanks are also due to the staff of Belfast City Library and Queen's University of Belfast Library, and to Margaret Kane of the Irish and Local History Department of Enniskillen Library. The staff of Queen's University's Common Room ensured that my periods of residence in Belfast were safe and comfortable.

I am indebted to all who granted me an interview, an informal conversation or a guided tour, and often gave generously of their time, knowledge and hospitality, in the course of my research visits to Northern Ireland. My thanks go especially to Mark Adair, Colm Barton, Brendan Bradley, Gerry Burns, Mary Butcher, Máire Cush, Barney Devine, the FACT group from Lisburn, Leslie Finlay, Arlene Foster, Willie Frazer, Claire Hackett, Tom Hartley, Maureen Hetherington, Tommy Kirkham, Jonathan Larner, Jane Leonard, Gordon Lucy, Hazlett Lynch, Darach MacDonald, Eilish McCabe, Sharon Meenan, Deirdre O'Hara, Sandra Peake, Mark Thompson and Anna Manwah Watson. My recorded interviews were transcribed by Lani Russell and Susan Hutton.

I owe particular thanks to all those who have read and commented on chapters or whole parts of the book: Mike Cronin, Anna Davin, Sue Dare, Barney Devine, Arlene Foster, Mary Hickman, John Kelly, Hazlett Lynch, Mark McGovern, Cahal McLaughlin, Carol K. Russell, Joanne O'Brien and Al Thomson. Their feedback has helped me in various ways, whether in weeding out errors, developing analyses, focusing arguments or clarifying the sense of my prose. Any remaining errors of fact, interpretation or expression are entirely my responsibility. I wish to thank Joanne O'Brien for generously allowing me to reproduce the helpful map from her book and one of her arresting photographs, Raymond Humphreys for permission to reproduce one of his photos, Jack Bryan for creating a map of the Border areas for me and Rita Duffy for agreeing to my use of her beautiful artwork on the front cover.

Working towards this book over several years, which have encompassed some major life changes, I have been sustained and supported by numerous colleagues and friends. My particular thanks go to Paddy Maguire, Head of the School of Historical and Critical Studies, Brighton University, for his unwavering practical and professional support of the project; to my colleagues in the humanities' group at Brighton, Cathy Bergin, Bob Brecher, Mark Devenney, Tom Hickey, Paul Hopper, Peter Jackson, Vicky Margree, Lekha Menon, Anita Rupprecht and Gill Scott; to the SHaCS administrative staff, Melissa Searle, Jo Woodhead, Donna Robson and Verity Clarkson; to Matthew Frost of Manchester University Press for his belief in the project and his patience and flexibility in seeing it to completion; to Al Thomson who has been my constant reference point in exploring the ideas developed in this book, as well as an unfailing source of practical advice and mateship; and to Sue Dare, who has lived the ups and downs of research and writing with me since the inception of this project, given me the benefit of her concentrated editorial engagement with my writing in the final revision of the book and been there for me in every way for the duration.

The ideas in this book have benefited from discussion and debate with colleagues in the Memory and Narrative Series editorial group, the London Cultural Memory Seminar, the EU ACUME network (Cultural Memory in European Countries), and numerous other conferences, symposia, seminars, etc. Some sections of the book have previously been published as journal articles or chapters in edited collections, and I acknowledge the editorial input of colleagues in the following cases. Chapter 2 is based on 'Trauma, memory, politics: the Irish Troubles', in Kim Lacy Rogers, Selma Leydesdorff and Graham Dawson (eds), *Trauma: Life Stories of Survivors*, New Brunswick, NJ, and London, 2004 (first published as *Trauma and Life Stories: International Perspectives*, London and New York, 1999). Some ideas in Part III first appeared in 'Trauma, place and the politics of memory: Bloody Sunday, Derry, 1972–2004', in *History Workshop Journal*, 59, spring 2005, pp. 221–50. Chapters 7 and 8 have developed out of three essays: 'Mobilising memories: Protestant and Unionist victims' groups and the politics of victimhood in the Irish peace process', in Paul Gready (ed.), *Political Transition: Politics and Cultures*, London and Sterling, VA, 2003; 'Ulster–British identity and the cultural memory of "ethnic cleansing" on the Northern Ireland Border', in Helen Brocklehurst and Robert Phillips (eds), *History, Nationhood and the Question of Britain*, Basingstoke and New York, 2004; and 'The Ulster–Irish Border, Protestant imaginative geography and cultural memory in the Irish Troubles', in Adriana Corrado and Maurizio Ascari (eds), *Sites of Exchange: European Crossroads and*

Faultlines, Amsterdam, 2006, pp. 237–50. A shorter version of chapter 10, 'Cultural memory, reconciliation and the reconstruction of the site of the Enniskillen "Poppy Day" bomb, Northern Ireland', has been published in Ástrádur Eysteinsson (ed.), *The Cultural Reconstruction of Places*, Reykjavik, 2007, pp. 44–60.

Preface

Historians and cultural analysts do not operate in a free space outside of the histories and cultures that we seek to understand. We write from particular locations and perspectives, occupying positions and inhabiting subjectivities which, even where consciously chosen, have been shaped by our own historical and cultural formation. In the words of Stuart Hall, 'agency has to . . . submit itself to the logic of what is there, to the ground it has to operate on . . . The most original statement has to be made in a language that will always carry the traces of how others have spoken.'[1]

The roots of my connection to Ireland originate within my family, formed in response to its entangled histories, multiple inheritances and complex patterns of cross-generational identification. I was born of a marriage between an English, Anglican-raised atheist and an Irish Catholic. My maternal grandparents had migrated from Newry, in Co. Down, before the First World War, severing connections with both their families as they moved first to Scotland and then to the Yorkshire coalfield. My mother grew up in an Irish migrant community that was at once integrated into, but also distinct from, the wider milieux of the northern English working class. This cultural difference figured, and had to be negotiated, in the liaison between the McMahon family and the Dawsons' secular 'Protestant' Englishness. My father remembered all his life how the local Catholic clergy had only grudgingly countenanced the wedding, insisting it took place in the Catholic church, but refusing to allow the bells to be rung in celebration. I was brought up to think of myself as indubitably English, but also, in early childhood, as a Catholic. My mother began to rediscover and assert her Irish identity after the death of her parents in the mid-1960s. As I grew up, my mother's Irishness developed into an important part of my bond with her. She shared above all with me, an avid listener, memories of her childhood and of her parents, who I remembered for their soft brogue, white hair and the smell of mothballs in their parlour; memories especially of her much-loved father, an Irish patriot and nationalist, who nevertheless, like my English grandfather, had served in the British Army during the First World War, and who, my mother told me, wanted to see a united Ireland, but did not believe it to be a cause that justified the loss of even a single drop of human blood. In these stories, my mother also transmitted to me her conviction that I was 'a McMahon' and 'half-Irish'; an idea that I embraced within my own sense of self, but whose importance ebbed and flowed, snagging on points of tension with my Englishness.

As commonly is the case, my mixed family genealogy has posed me questions of identity and belonging, given rise to contradictions within my cultural and political affiliations, and prompted a search, if not for their resolution, then at least for modes of deeper engagement with them. Seeing the Troubles depicted on the television news, I came to recognize a disturbing sense of their being something to do with me, since the Catholics who were being burned out, killed and arrested for membership of the Irish Republican Army (IRA) were in a sense *my* people, perhaps actually my relatives. But I also remember the horror, the anxiety involved in visiting the West End of London, and the practical inconveniences of the security scare at Euston and Paddington railway stations on going up to university, as the IRA brought the war to England in 1974. Both experiences involved identifications made in the imagination and mediated in *British* representations of the Troubles, with effects which nevertheless pulled in contradictory directions. As a student I had access to screenings of documentary films censored by the mainstream media, but I also imbibed Robert Kee's series for the BBC, *Ireland: A Television History* (1980–81), and the Thames TV series *The Troubles* (1981), which introduced me to the proposition that, in order to understand the conflict, it is necessary to know the history of its development. By the late 1970s, as a socialist, I was informed and concerned about the torture and ill-treatment of detainees by the Royal Ulster Constabulary (RUC), exposed by Amnesty International and the British Government's own Bennett Commission; and about the authorities' hardline response to the 'blanket' and 'dirty' protests by Republican prisoners challenging their criminalization and the conditions of their imprisonment. Holidaying in 1979 in West Cork, I remember, with some pride, the complimentary remark of an academic at University College Cork that, for an English person, I was 'unusually sympathetic' to Irish perspectives on the conflict.

Two events of the 1980s transformed these sympathies into a more engaged political analysis and activism. The Republican prisoners' hunger strikes of 1980–81, leading to the deaths of ten young men of my own age, had an emotional impact – of shock, outrage, anger and sadness – more powerful than anything I had previously experienced, prompting me to reconsider the view of Irish Republicanism that I had received from the British news media. In 1984 the IRA's bombing of the Grand Hotel in Brighton, my home town – an attack targeting the British Cabinet, including the Prime Minister, that caused five deaths and over thirty injuries, some serious, mainly among delegates to the Conservative Party's annual conference and their families – became the catalyst that pressed me into public engagement with the Troubles. Being then a member of Brighton Labour Party, I shared in the censure of the bombing expressed by the majority of Labour representatives. But I dissented from the language in which this was couched, particularly the refusal to acknowledge the context of the attack in a war in which the British State was an active protagonist and itself bore responsibility for the perpetration of terrible deeds and the perpetuation of the conflict. In making this argument within the local Labour Party in the aftermath of the bomb, I encountered the deep-seated resistance in English culture to serious, critical discussion of the Troubles, and the way this was closed down by the polarizing ideological discourse of terrorism. In these circumstances I became a co-founder of the Brighton branch of the Labour Committee on Ireland (LCI), and worked for the next four years at both national and local levels (alongside the Brighton Women and Ireland Group and the Troops Out Movement) to break the political silence about Britain's war in Ireland.

In 1986, as secretary of the local LCI, I organized a Brighton Labour Party fact-finding delegation to Northern Ireland and accompanied some two dozen party members on the four-day visit to Belfast, Derry and South Armagh. We were hosted by nationalist families (I stayed in the Ardoyne and in Newry), met nearly thirty organizations ranging across a wide spectrum of views, from the Ulster Defence Association (UDA) to Sinn Féin, and from the Derry Trades Council to the North Belfast Community Resource Centre, and were given guided tours of the local areas. For me, this visit was formative: a journey of cultural discovery that laid down reference points and generated questions that have informed my thinking about the Troubles ever since. We encountered realities of everyday existence in a war zone under military occupation that were inconceivable in England, heard voices and stories that were never heard back home and through this encounter with the conflicting viewpoints of participants, gained some insight into the complexities of the situation. It is also the case that, being based exclusively within nationalist areas (a decision imposed by considerations of security, our own but also our hosts'), we were able to form stronger impressions of the circumstances and viewpoints of nationalists than of Unionists, and I returned to England more strongly identified with Republican perspectives – and memories.

The Brighton bomb and its aftermath also brought about my engagement with the Troubles as a researcher, writer and educationalist. I began serious reading on the history of Northern Ireland, analyses of the Troubles, and the imaginative literature of the conflict; contributed to the development in 1986–87 of one of the first Irish Studies degrees in the country, at the Polytechnic of North London; and began to introduce Irish themes into my teaching of cultural studies and literature. In 1993, having completed a book about popular memory, national identity and the soldier as hero in war stories of the British Empire, I began to research popular memories and amnesias in Britain and Ireland related to the Irish revolution of 1916–23, as an example of those British wars of twentieth-century decolonization that were not representable in terms of heroic adventure; and proposed the idea of *trauma* as a means to investigate the relevance of unresolved past conflict to the ongoing war in Northern Ireland. Begun in autumn 1993, a moment of escalating violence which included the IRA's Shankill bomb and the loyalist reprisal killings at Greysteel, this was initially conceived as a study of fiction: an investigation of themes of violence, trauma and memory in the historical novels and short stories of William Trevor.

In 1996, researching my proposed book on Trevor, I travelled to Cork, Dublin, and – for only the second time – Belfast, and encountered the different ways in which the peace process was affecting reassessment, debate and conflict over memory and the past, either side of the Border. The visit to Belfast in particular prompted a re-orientation of my project, as I realized that, at least in the North, the peace process provided the present-day context in which memories of the Troubles – and of the 1920s and earlier episodes of conflict – were now being framed; and that my investigation of the themes of violence, trauma and memory was opening up important and fascinating issues which could not be contained within a study concentrated on fiction. I began to write directly about these more compelling concerns in early 1997, in an essay published under the title 'Trauma, memory, politics: the Irish Troubles'; and by April 1998, a few days before the signing of the Good Friday Agreement, I had formulated my original conception for this book.

The project continued to evolve in sometimes unexpected ways. My primary research for the book took place between July 1999 and August 2001 in the course of nine visits to Northern Ireland and one to the Republic. This was a period of intense political activity focused on the struggle to implement the Agreement, and during my visits to the North I witnessed a number of key events and their impact, including the publication of the Patten Report into the reform of the RUC, the suspension of the new Northern Ireland Assembly, the public opening of the Saville Inquiry into the events of Bloody Sunday, and the early release of the final group of paramilitary prisoners. This was also a period of extraordinary proliferation in public history-making and commemorative activity concerned with the Troubles, which attained unprecedented public visibility and attention as work begun in the period immediately after the ceasefires was completed and published, while new projects – developed with the economic support of substantial 'peace and reconciliation' funding or in response to the politics of the peace process and its contestation – mushroomed in a plethora of new practices and forms.

By tapping into the resources of local libraries and collections, and also collecting new material circulating more widely in the public domain, I was able to build up a textual archive of current interventions as well as their historical antecedents, comprising books, newspapers and magazines, press cuttings, reports, pamphlets, posters, leaflets and other street literature, videos and ephemera. But I was also in a position to pursue new lines of inquiry as these opened up, by means of field work that brought me into direct contact with those involved in the generation, collection and representation of memories of the Troubles. This developed into an increasingly important element of the research, as I realized the value of such visits to meet 'memory workers' – including community activists, writers, local government officials, the organizers of local history projects, museum curators, voluntary sector professionals and people working in the heritage industry – and began to interview them for their insights into the local contexts and circumstances in which memories were now being produced, and about the genesis, development and value of their particular work in relation to the difficulties and conflicts of the unfolding peace process.

Most interestingly, given their invisibility in England, I encountered a growing network of local self-help groups of victims (or survivors) of the Troubles, which were clearly providing an important new form of agency for the articulation of memories of the recent war and longer cultural memories of the conflict. In exploring this development, I interviewed civil servants from local government and the Victims' Liaison Unit of the Northern Ireland Office at Stormont, participated in a conference organized by the Northern Ireland Voluntary Trust to develop the 'victims' lobby' established under the terms of the Agreement, and met with co-ordinators, spokespersons and ordinary members of a number of victims' groups from various locations. The formation of these groups (in the majority of cases, since the ceasefires), their aims and activities, and their complex relationship to the politics of the Good Friday Agreement, became a central theme of my research.

In my original conception of this study, I had decided that it was not to be an oral-history project. This was partly for practical reasons, partly due to my aversion to intruding unnecessarily, as a researcher from outside Northern Ireland, into personal lives in a society described by John Whyte as possibly, 'in proportion to size . . . the most heavily researched area on earth'.[2] Instead I was committed to using personal testimonies and life-stories that were already in the public domain, and considering the processes that put them there, as well as what they had to say; a strategy that is evident throughout this book. Through the interviews that I conducted with memory workers, however, an oral-history dimension to the research began to evolve. In undertaking these interviews, I was engaged not simply in the gathering and recording of information about an organization, its activity and its context, as I had originally supposed, but also in an active production of memory that was itself evidence of broader cultural frameworks of meaning, of an encounter between different perspectives, and of the terms of current debate about these matters. Also, frequently, while discussing a project or the work of a group, my interviewees would change register and begin to tell me stories of their own personal experiences or those of their close family, either to illustrate a point or to account for the tenor of their own involvement. Like other researchers doing field work on the Troubles, I found an unexpected willingness to talk about personal experiences among the people I spoke to, many of whom appeared to welcome the listening offered by an interested and sympathetic outsider, as well as the potential for acknowledgement and validation of their experience by an academic, and the opportunity to use a researcher as a conduit to gain access to the public domain. For my part, the personal contact, engagement and dialogue that I enjoyed with people from a broad range of backgrounds, locations and perspectives was eye-opening and inspirational. While much of this work is not detailed in this book for reasons of focus and scale, it has fundamentally altered the way I have encountered, thought about and treated its themes, in three main respects.

Firstly, personal contact, albeit on a limited scale, strengthened my commitment to understanding, and treating with due care and sensitivity, the psychic and emotional realities of my subjects' lives. As a result of field work, my research underwent a re-orientation towards understanding the cultural politics, with strong local variations, concerned with the articulation and contestation of memories of the Troubles in the context of the shift from war to peace, as lived out by actual human subjects.

Secondly, it developed my sense of place, in a growing awareness of and interest in the specificities of locations and their histories. In order to meet my interviewees or to visit particular sites of memory, I travelled all around Northern Ireland, from Newtownards in the east to Castlederg in the west, and from Derry on the north coast to the South Armagh Border. On a number of visits, I was taken on a guided 'memory tour' of the local area, and was able to photograph memorials, murals and other sites and symbols, as well as the impact of the war – and the peace – on urban and rural landscapes. The lull in violent hostilities during the research period meant that it was also possible for me to walk alone in relative safety around all areas of Belfast, where I was based, up until my final visit in summer 2001. This coincided with the eruption of serious rioting on the Crumlin Road interface of North Belfast, which curtailed my explorations for the first and only time.

Thirdly, entering into a relationship with those whose lives and memories are the object of my research, but who are also active agents of meaning in their own right, has given rise to ethical considerations which necessarily press upon, and have brought me to revise, my own perspectives and interpretations in the course of dialogue both real and imagined. This book has been researched and written from a position of dissident Englishness. As I have travelled around Northern Ireland, observing, asking questions, listening to stories and reconstructing the histories that help to explain present-day realities, I have identified myself as a historian from England, and been recognized and accepted as such. Being an outsider, I have had the freedom to move about physically, to cross borders that are geographical, cultural and psychological, and to speak to anyone – jumping in a taxi outside the Falls Road Women's Centre, for example, in order to keep an appointment in the House of Orange library ten minutes across town – without incurring the kinds of fears and suspicions that tend to bear on and restrict local people in their dealings with one another. Seeking to establish trust with those I met or interviewed, I did not assert my own politics and was never asked about them, but did voice my own views on current or past events in the course of discussion, guided by my judgement about their likely impact on my interlocutors and what could or could not usefully be said and shared, in, say, a loyalist pub in Scarva. I have tried to maintain this dialogic approach in my writing, as a way of resolving the ethical issues that have reappeared there as a question of representation: how to do justice to values and perspectives that were unfamiliar or antithetical to my own – particularly those of some Unionists and loyalists – by treating them with fairness, accuracy and respect for their integrity, while remaining true to my own understandings and analyses?

This problem, I have come to realize, is a microcosm of the peace process in general. Ethical research and critical inquiry, too, require a personal 'decommissioning' of the mind: a commitment to undoing the habits of violence and division inscribed within our language, our cultural orientation, our own subjectivity, in order to engage with those we may disagree with, across the divided formations of memory. In negotiating these painful and conflicted pasts, resources for reparative remembering may perhaps be drawn from personal experiences of loss and mourning, extended through identification to others. This book is dedicated to my English father and my Irish mother, both of whom died while I was researching and writing it, and is offered in a spirit of openness to the past. Despite or, perhaps, because of loss, memory has the capacity to enrich and dignify the way we live our lives now, generating renewed commitment to our most cherished values and prompting a reaching out to others – what Rita Duffy has called 'the essential gesture'[3] – strong in the sense that we know who we are and what we have gone through.

Notes to Preface

1 Stuart Hall, interviewed by Laurie Taylor, *New Humanist*, 6/3/2006.
2 Whyte, p. viii.
3 Duffy.

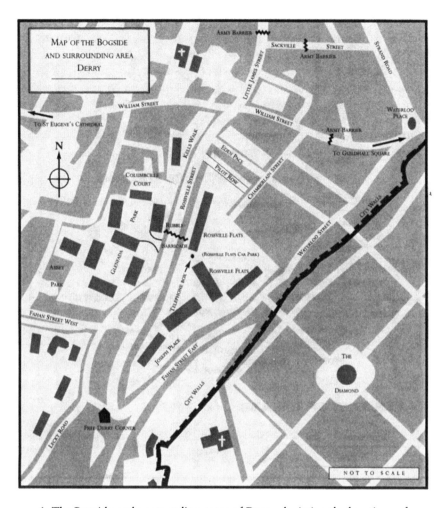

1 The Bogside and surrounding areas of Derry, depicting the locations of Bloody Sunday discussed in Part II (map drawn by Tony Murray, reproduced from Joanne O'Brien, *A Matter of Minutes*, 2002, by kind permission of the author).

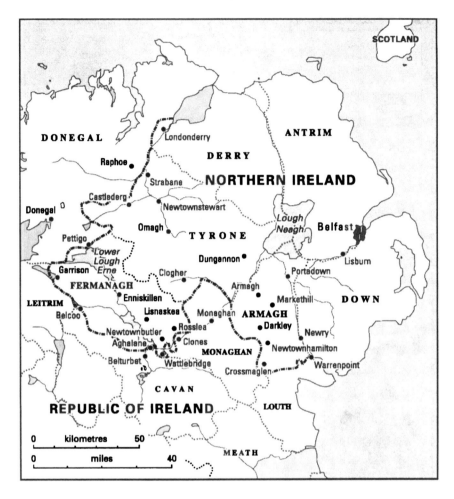

2 The Border counties of Northern Ireland and the Irish Republic, depicting the
locations of the Troubles along the Border discussed in Part III (map drawn
by Jack Bryan).

Introduction: political transition, peace-making and the past

Since the paramilitary ceasefires of 1994, the centre of 'post-conflict' Belfast, between the City Hall and the River Lagan, has been a site of redevelopment and modernization. Through the construction of new buildings like the Waterside Centre and the Hilton Hotel, the regeneration of the old, largely derelict commercial district and the opening-up of riverside walkways, the proliferation of new shops, bars and restaurants, and the promotion of Belfast's unique cultural heritage, visitors have been drawn into the city and the 'normality' of free-market capitalism has been restored. Amid this confident, future-oriented projection of Belfast as a twenty-first-century metropolis, there are few visible signs of the war that shattered the fabric and way of life in this city in the years following the eruption of violence in 1969; or indeed of the longer history of conflict that shaped its particular development and configuration since its foundation as a plantation town during the colonization of Ulster early in the seventeenth century. Yet, while the city centre may give the impression of a place looking to leave its past behind, within comfortable walking distance of this zone of affluence are locations where a sense of the troubled past is palpably present.

To walk, for example, westwards out of the city centre across the Westlink road and along Peters Hill, as I did in February 2004, is to enter the cultural world of Ulster loyalism as expressed in the commemorative landscape in and around the Shankill Road. The boundary of this world is signalled first by murals depicting the Union Jack and emblems of the loyalist paramilitary organization the Ulster Defence Association (UDA), and its *nom-de-guerre*, the Ulster Freedom Fighters, that identify this as 'British' (and claim it as UDA) territory. Along the Shankill Road itself, interspersed among the food stores and bookmakers, the clubs and pubs, and the offices of local community organizations and political parties, more murals establish powerful visual symbols representing and commemorating significant aspects of the past that has been lived here, and testifying to its compelling hold on present-day life. These include murals dedicated to the Ulster Volunteer Force (UVF) of 1912, formed to fight against Irish Home Rule, and to those local people who died fighting for its successor organization, the UVF of the current Troubles; to the loyalist volunteers who joined the 36th Ulster Division of the British Army and suffered devastating losses on the first day of the battle

1 'Indiscriminate Slaughter By So-Called Non-Sectarian Irish Freedom Fighters':
mural on the Shankill Road, West Belfast.

of the Somme in 1916 in a sacrifice for King, Country and Empire; and to
'30 Years of Indiscriminate Slaughter By So-Called Non-Sectarian Irish
Freedom Fighters', a mural of composite images representing fatal bomb
attacks by Irish Republicans that killed civilians on the Shankill, from the
Four Steps Inn and the Balmoral Furnishing Store in 1971, to Frizzell's Fish
Shop in 1993 (see figure 1).[1] In the Shankill Memorial Gardens, created to
commemorate the patriotic British dead of two world wars, an old street
lamp has been installed in memory of the nine Protestant civilians, including
two children, who died in the Fish Shop, or 'Shankill bomb' as it has become
known.

A short distance beyond the Memorial Gardens, a left turn takes you south
along Lanark Way, one of only two routes across the interface between the
Shankill and the nationalist Beechmount and Falls area. To traverse this
road, lined on either side by ten-foot-high fencing, and pass through the
material residues of what was until recently an electronic monitoring and
control barrier operated by the Royal Ulster Constabulary (RUC), is to enter
another cultural world, another commemorative landscape, equally compelling, but opposed in fundamental respects to that of the Shankill. In these
nationalist streets, the murals celebrate the contribution made by the
'women soldiers' of *Cumann na mBan* to the Easter Rising of 1916; commemorate the ten Republicans who died on hunger strike in the Maze Prison
in 1981 to secure their status as political prisoners-of-war rather than the
criminals the British State deemed them to be; and honour the names of the
local Falls volunteers of the Provisional Irish Republican Army (IRA) killed

on active service fighting to 'free Ireland' from the shackles of British rule, topped by imagery of the phoenix rising from the flames of the Northern Ireland Parliament building at Stormont. On Beechmount Avenue, most of a gable-end wall has been covered in dozens of posters bearing the names and photographs of nationalists killed by 'Unionist gunmen' suspected of being in 'collusion' with British intelligence and security forces, together with a mural alleging links to the highest levels of the British political establishment. Among these names may be those of the seven Catholics shot dead between 1987 and 1990 in or near their homes in the streets close to Lanark Way, prompting a campaign for the road to be sealed off on the grounds that '[m]any of these murders were perpetrated by gunmen driving effortlessly along Lanark Way from the direction of the Shankill Road and returning in a matter of minutes to where they came from on their errand of death'.[2]

These two worlds have been physically divided since the early 1970s by the thirty-foot edifice of concrete, corrugated steel and razor wire that forms the so-called 'peace-line' wall along Cupar Way. One of sixteen such walls erected by the British security forces during the Troubles, mostly in North and West Belfast where nationalist and loyalist communities are most closely intermingled (and often in response to pressure from local residents), the Cupar Way peace-line is the biggest and one of the oldest, having first been built to protect nationalists in the Clonard and Falls areas from the armed loyalist assault on the streets where they lived, which precipitated the beginning of the war in 1969.[3] According to the theorist of the Algerian Revolution Frantz Fanon, violent political conflict of this kind creates, for those caught up in it, 'a world cut in two' and 'divided into two compartments . . . two zones . . . inhabited by two different species', within which people are positioned according to 'the fact of belonging to, or not belonging to', one zone or the other.[4] Reality is constructed differently, in both its social and psychic dimensions, so that things look and feel different, on either side of the peace-line wall. Here, grief and mourning, as well as politics, have been split in two, polarized across the axis of violence. Reflecting this, the two cultures of commemoration on either side of the divide have also been formed in a relation of antagonism; each angling its own displays in opposition to those of the other; each articulating a partial and highly selective narrative focused on what the *other* side have done to *us*, what *we* have suffered and how *our* people have fought back. Through the highly public visual expression of these competing narratives, in the form of the murals, the representation of the past is enlisted to mark out conflicting and ongoing claims on the territory, and to provide 'anchors for the identity' that serve the needs of the present.[5] This is rooted, if in complex and highly mediated fashion, in the network of stories lying mostly beneath the surface of public visibility; stories about what has happened on either side of the Cupar Way wall in the recent past, recalled in the living memory of those who were targeted by, and those who perpetrated, the violence that has characterized the war in West Belfast.

In circumstances of war, memories, recalling what is at stake in a conflict and what has been perpetrated and suffered, structure the identities of participants, provide justifications for their use of organized violence, and underpin their broader political aspirations in respect of a settlement. To resolve a conflict, then, is it necessary to make peace with the past? Questions about divided and conflicting memories, with their silences and amnesias, are increasingly recognized as being central to the theory and practice of conflict resolution. Can – and should – past conflict be forgotten, and, if not, how is it best remembered? What part ought memories and histories to play in promoting what US Senator George Mitchell, in his work towards disarmament in Ireland, famously described as 'the decommissioning of mind-sets'?[6] How, in circumstances of conflict resolution, is the politics of memory affected by its psychic and emotional aspects, particularly those produced by the impact of the horrors, losses and traumas inflicted by violent conflict? What are the longer-term psychic consequences of the traumatic past and how are they to be addressed? This book explores the ways in which, in locations scarred over decades by the war that we have come to know as the Irish Troubles, memories of events 'in the past' have motivated but also complicated efforts towards the establishment of peace, justice and a lasting political settlement. In considering why this should be the case, it opens up an investigation into a number of associated questions, concerning the relationship of past to present, the mutual imbrications of personal and collective memories, and the way we understand the interweaving of the realms of the psyche, of culture and of politics. It inquires into the ways in which memories of war are generated out of antagonisms, violences and sufferings, and traces how they have been consolidated, disseminated, adapted, reproduced and also remade for and by new generations, within social circles ranging from the family and civic and political organizations, to the institutions of the State. It examines the politics underlying their clashes with competing memories, those of the other side, the enemy; and wonders about the conditions under which they might be transformed, from symbols articulating the effects of enmity, violation and damage, into vehicles of amity, recognition and reparation, open to the transformations of a hoped-for future, free of the painful and often poisonous legacies of violence. These questions and concerns take their bearing, and this book its particular focus, from the conflict-resolution initiative begun in 1993–94, that is commonly referred to as the Irish peace process.

Political transition and the problem of the past

In the late twentieth and early twenty-first centuries, debates about whether, to what extent and how those engaged in conflict resolution ought to encounter and attempt to deal with a problematic and conflictual past, have become pervasive features of public discourse in those societies and cultures undergoing what Paul Gready describes as 'political transition'. This he defines as 'a change in political regime and culture towards greater democ-ratization, post-repression, post-colonialism, post-war'; a process recently or currently underway, if under widely divergent conditions, in states such as South Africa, Rwanda, Argentina, Chile, Guatemala, Germany, and those formed from the former Yugoslavia, as well as Northern Ireland.[7] In all such cases, transition poses questions about how the past plays out in the present conjuncture, in relation to a historic break heralding the transformation from one condition of society to another, commonly involving change at the level of a state – whether through reform or revolution, the ending of a par-tition or an occupation – and corresponding shifts in the relation between state and civil society. Transition, argues Gready, is

> a contested and intrinsically incomplete process, shot through with considera-tions of politics and power, mobilised as a demand and a promise, and charac-terised by continuity as well as multi-faceted and uneven change. Patterns from the past are often reconfigured rather than radically altered in the present.[8]

The building of a new future requires, then, a necessary engagement and reckoning with the past. This takes various forms, according to local and national circumstances, but tends to involve two distinct though inter-related strands: firstly, the attempt to resolve the underlying causes of divi-sion and conflict by establishing the basis for peaceful co-operation and the securing of social justice; and, secondly, the attempt to address the damag-ing effects of violence inflicted and undergone in the course of conflict, whether through state repression and its resistance, war or civil strife. These concerns become intertwined, and their complex ramifications ensure that the effort to engage and reckon with the past is fraught with ambivalence, paradox and contradiction.

The desire to put an end to violence and to create a new and better future, characterized by social arrangements that differ from those of the past in being free from conflict or in channelling it into non-violent and democratic forms, motivates conflict-resolution initiatives. Yet, in such circumstances, a medley of attachments to the past are also in play, manifesting, for example, in grieving for loved ones and comrades who have lost their lives to a war; in a sense of continuing commitment to a superseded regime or to the social movements and military organizations party to a conflict; in the psychologi-cal effects of trauma, evidence of the powerful hold exercised by the past within the unconscious levels of the psyche; in nostalgia for the security of a known and lost world, or for the solidarities and intensities of armed combat; in the need to uncover and know the truth about events of deep personal or social import that remain obscure and continue to haunt the imagination; and in impulses to shape present or future actions to make good what has been lost or repair what has been destroyed in the course of conflict. These and other attachments to the past have both intra- and inter-generational effects: as in cases where the wish to keep faith with and do right by the members of previous generations who sacrificed their lives for a political cause inspires

dedication to that cause in their successor generations; or when the desire to
step out of the shadow of the past so as to embrace a new future is expressed
in terms of a commitment to the children of today and the unborn generations. Ambivalence about this relation of the past to the present and the
future is reflected in the number and variety of ways available in the English
language to describe it. A plethora of terms suggests the range of different
kinds of relations that may be established with the conflicted past in order to
transform its purchase within the present. We talk of reconciliation with the
past and of healing its wounds; of coming to terms with it; of drawing a line
in the sand in order to leave the past behind; of stepping out of its shadow,
laying it to rest, letting it go; of moving on, or forward; and, as the currently
fashionable term has it, of establishing 'closure' on the past. The common
impulse behind these various metaphors of mastery is, as Gready puts it,
'a need to liberate the present and future from the burden of the past that
threatens to overwhelm them'.[9]

How have such paradoxes and ambivalences manifested in the Irish
conflict? The past in Ireland is often seen as peculiarly problematic and
intractable. Discourse on the Troubles frequently situates current conflict as
the inevitable outcome of a long prior history, notoriously complex and
reaching back as far as the twelfth century, when a papal bull 'donating'
Ireland to King Henry II, and the subsequent Norman invasion, first placed
Irish affairs under the influence of 'England'.[10] The particular complexities
that characterize the Irish past derive from the history of the State and its
contestation in modern Ireland during three main epochs, in the course of
which political domination, subordination and resistance also became structured in terms of national and religious difference.[11] In the first epoch, from
the sixteenth until the beginning of the nineteenth century, an English colonial State was established, consolidated and preserved in Ireland by war and
conquest, the plantation of settlers, and the repression of the conquered and
the resistant. This process was begun by the Tudor armies, completed in the
decade of Cromwellian rule, established by military force in 1649, and
underwritten by the Williamite victories in the War of Succession (1688–91),
which confirmed the Protestant character of the British State and the subordination of its Irish colony. Following the suppression of the most serious
subsequent threat to the colonial State, by the armed rebellion of the United
Irishmen in 1798, which sought to 'break the connection with England'[12]
and establish a democratic Irish Republic inspired by the American and
French Revolutions, Ireland became the only British colony to be incorporated into the metropolitan imperial State itself, through the creation of the
United Kingdom of Great Britain and Ireland (UK) by the Act of Union of
1800.

During the second major epoch, contestation was characterized by the
'national question' and the development of modern Irish Unionist and Irish
nationalist politics, defined – and, especially after the conflicts over Home
Rule from the mid-1880s, polarized – by their opposing positions regarding

the form, authority and legitimacy of this integrated United Kingdom State. This situation culminated in the period of revolutionary conflict and war of 1912–23, when the very existence of British state control in Ireland was challenged and partially eradicated. The result was the partition of the country and the establishment of an independent Irish Free State, which later became the Republic of Ireland, and a Unionist-dominated statelet in six northern counties, which retained its constitutional status as an integral part of what had now become the United Kingdom of Great Britain and Northern Ireland.

In the third, and current epoch, conflict has centred on this two-state solution instituted by the UK Parliament's Government of Ireland Act in 1920 and reiterated in the Anglo-Irish Treaty ending the War of Irish Independence in 1921. The legitimacy of both the Irish Free State and Northern Ireland was disputed by those Irish nationalists and Republicans who refused to accept the continuation of British influence and control over Irish affairs; but after partition, conflict over the State and perceptions of an unresolved national question, or 'unfinished revolution', have taken different forms in 'the North' and 'the South'.

Although from 1937 the constitution of the Southern Irish State laid nominal claim to the six-county North 'pending the reintegration of the national territory',[13] in practice, since the conclusion of the Civil War between pro- and anti-Treaty forces in 1923, the conflictual repercussions of partition have manifested most acutely in Northern Ireland. This was a state secured by armed force, sustained by repressive emergency powers and institutionalized discrimination directed against its Irish nationalist and Catholic minority, and prone to regular outbreaks of sectarian and political violence. When attempts at democratic renewal eventually materialized in the 1960s but proved unable to win a consensus, and the movement for nationalist civil rights encountered state-sanctioned violence in 1968–69, the conflict known as the Troubles (a euphemism previously used to describe the prior phase of conflict in 1919–23) exploded into a war in which the legitimacy of partition and the existence of the British State in Northern Ireland were called into question. This war – with its origins, firstly, in the 'national question' of the nineteenth century (itself grafted onto prior colonial conflict) and, secondly, in the contested attempt by the UK Government to resolve this by partition – was perpetuated into the 1990s and continues to reverberate in the first decade of the twenty-first century.

This long history of conflict in Ireland is widely held to have an important, even a direct, bearing on present-day circumstances and possibilities, both in the sense of a repetition, or 'recurrence of older patterns of conflict', and because, as Ian McBride puts it:

> In Ireland . . . the interpretation of the past has always been at the heart of national conflict.
> . . . [P]erhaps more than in other cultures, collective groups have expressed their values and assumptions through their representations of the past.[14]

Many varieties of historical explanation have emphasised the intransigence of this inheritance, whether conceived as the malign influence of 'the ghosts of history' or as a ' "legacy of bitterness" ' causing 'the playing out of historical wrongs as if [the conflict] had been frozen in historical stasis since the plantation'.[15] The currency, centrality and weight of the problematic past have indeed been perceived as a 'burden', excessive and inescapable, exercising a determining influence over the present and promoting an inappropriate backward-looking mentality or fixation. To be fixated on or obsessed by the past also carries the further connotation of being embroiled in irresoluble violent conflict, sometimes envisaged as a centuries-old feud, or ethnic war. In such scenarios, 'the Irish are prisoners of their past, impelled towards violent confrontation by their atavistic passions', or trapped by their 'seemingly irreconcilable cultures, unable to live together or to live apart, caught inextricably in the web of their tragic history'.[16] Such views have provoked reactions like that of the novelist Dermot Bolger, writing exasperatedly from the safety of Dublin, who has deplored how the Irish are now held to be 'so bizarrely entangled with history that we must go back three centuries to explain any fight outside a chip shop'.[17] The wish to escape such entanglements, or to cast off the weight of the past and establish what might be considered a more 'normal' relationship to it, has fuelled much of the 'revisionist history' that preoccupied public debate in the Republic of Ireland in the 1980s and 1990s.[18] It has also motivated some commentators in the North, like the historian and political scientist Brian Walker, who has condemned what he calls 'the abuse of history', meaning 'the past being used to account for or to explain away many present-day problems' and for the provision of 'historic grievances for contemporary consumption'.[19]

Exasperation, like Bolger's, at the imprisoning power of the Irish past is understandable but not necessarily helpful. There are good reasons why the past continues to exercise pressure on the present in societies like those in still-partitioned Ireland where political, cultural and psychic landscapes continue to be shaped and polarized along lines inherited from an unresolved history of conflict. In Northern Ireland this conflict is not in the distant past but exists within the living memory of all except younger children. Since 1969, a brutal but unwinnable war was fought largely within Northern Ireland, extending also, on a much smaller scale, into the Republic of Ireland, numerous towns and cities in England, and a handful of locations in Europe. While subject to fluctuations throughout its duration, armed conflict has had two main interlocking dimensions: one involving the British Army and state security forces in fighting against Irish Republican paramilitary groups, the most important being the Provisional IRA; and the second pitting Republican forces against pro-British loyalist paramilitary groups, most notably the UVF and the UDA.

The human legacy of this war centres on the loss of 3,637 lives in 'Troubles-related' incidents up to the end of July 1999 (by which time violence leading to fatal casualties had been substantially reduced),[20] of which

Republicans were responsible for 56 per cent, loyalists 27 per cent, and the British State's forces (primarily the army) 11 per cent.[21] Most of these fatalities – all but 260, thus some 93 per cent – have occurred within the six-county territory itself,[22] an area of only 14,160 square miles, smaller than the English county of Yorkshire, extending some eighty-five miles from north to south and 110 miles east to west, with a population of 1.75 million. Some idea of the impact of this scale of loss may be conveyed by extrapolation to the UK as a whole, where the same ratio of killings to the total population of 58 million would have left over 130,000 dead.[23] The war in Northern Ireland was characterized by systematic and sustained abuses of human rights by the British State, and a systematic blurring, by all protagonists of violence, of the categories of *armed combatants* and *unarmed civilians*.[24] Among those killed in the Troubles, the great majority – roughly 2,000 – were civilians, of whom over 1,200 were Catholics (forming the largest single category of fatalities) and nearly 700 Protestants. The responsibility for these civilian deaths lay primarily with loyalist paramilitaries (roughly 850), the IRA (between 600 and 700, including both Catholics and Protestants), and the British Army (160, of whom 138 were Catholics); in all cases, civilians formed their 'biggest single category of victim'.[25] Among the armed combatants, some 1,000 soldiers and police were killed serving the British State, half of whom were from the British Army and half members of the security forces locally recruited from Northern Ireland's Unionist communities; while among paramilitary groups, roughly 390 Republicans and 140 loyalists were killed.[26] Among these deaths, a very high proportion – some 2,000 cases in 2006 – have yet to be properly investigated, and remain 'unsolved' in the sense that the circumstances of death have not been clarified and the individual agents responsible have not been identified or called to account.[27] In addition to these fatalities, an estimated 40,000 to 50,000 people suffered serious injuries during the Troubles.[28]

This violence has left economic, political, psychic and social legacies. Its economic legacies include 'damaged property/infrastructure and job loss', disincentives to inward investment and the 'diseconomies of conflict', such as 'inefficient labour and housing markets generated by intimidation and community division'.[29] Political legacies include increasingly polarized identities, defined in opposition to the other who is perceived to be responsible for the violence; together with the malign and brutalizing effects of military occupation and the surveillance state, and the demoralizing impact of political disenfranchisement (in a 'province' of the UK ruled since 1972 directly by the British Government from London). The psychic legacies of the war include what Fanon described as the pathologies of violence[30] that manifest in a gamut of heightened emotional states encompassing anger, loss, disorientation, hatred, mistrust, insecurity, fear and humiliation, and the psychic disturbances nowadays described in terms of 'trauma'. However, these legacies of the Troubles have not impacted evenly across Northern Irish society. The conflict has been characterized by different patterns of violence in rural and urban areas and its particular concentration in certain locations. Nearly half of the total number of killings within Northern Ireland occurred in Belfast, and three-quarters of these were in the north and west of the city, which also suffered the highest death rates, followed by parts of Derry City and of the rural areas along the Border.[31] There is a correlation between areas with a high incidence of fatalities and those with high indices of social deprivation, mostly working-class areas with 'concentrations of low income and poverty'. Here, the 'severely negative consequences' for the Northern Ireland economy of thirty years of violence manifest in particularly acute ways.[32] Economic, political and psychic factors have also intersected to produce social legacies. These have manifested most evidently in the lasting effects of significant movements of population, the tendency being to abandon mixed areas for those inhabited by more homogeneous nationalist and loyalist communities. This has inscribed the polarization of identities even more deeply into the spaces of everyday life and heightened friction along the interfaces between the two zones – for example, along the Falls–Shankill interface in West Belfast or the patchwork of interface communities that makes up North Belfast.[33]

The 'present past' and memory in Northern Ireland

In locations such as these, as Michael Ignatieff has remarked of comparable conflict zones in the former Yugoslavia, Rwanda and South Africa, 'the past continues to torment because it is *not* past': it is not 'over', 'finished', 'completed', but permeates the social and psychic realities of everyday life in the present. 'These places are not living in a serial order of time', argues Ignatieff, 'but a simultaneous one, in which the past and the present are . . . continuous' and 'yesterday and today [are] the same'.[34] For those whose lives are conducted within the temporal frame of what I call the 'present past', its influence is not easy to understand, nor can it be readily shrugged off.

Consider, for example, the case of North Belfast, 'a heterogeneous mixture of small groups of streets, each with a distinct identity', that form 'a mosaic of ethnic territories', a 'highly segregated area, in which many residents live in enclaves that are almost exclusively Catholic or Protestant'.[35] This area was 'the site of some of the most sustained and intensive sectarian killing', where 548 people lost their lives (15 per cent of all Troubles-related deaths), of whom 396 were civilians.[36] In just one small section of that mosaic, Ardoyne, 'an overwhelmingly nationalist/republican area of around eleven thousand people, surrounded on three sides by unionist/loyalist areas', ninety-nine residents were killed. The residents of Ardoyne died at the hands of all combatant parties, 'the RUC, the British army, loyalist paramilitaries and Irish republicans'.[37] One local man, Brendan Bradley, a co-founder in 1995 of Survivors of Trauma, a support group representing victims of violence from the area, has described how, in the early 1970s, he 'had three brothers shot and injured by the British Army'; then in 1975 a younger brother went into town and got blew up by a bomb, and killed. In 1994 I had a sister who was shot dead. In 1994 I had an uncle who was killed in an explosion and a gun attack. In 1995 I had a nephew shot dead and in 1996 I had another nephew shot dead.

These members of the Bradley family were 'killed by . . . all different sides, claiming they had the right to kill for their cause', including the IRA and the Irish National Liberation Army (INLA), as well as the loyalist Protestant Action Force (PAF) and the Ulster Freedom Fighters (UFF).[38] A 'nationalist island in a loyalist sea', and vulnerable throughout the Troubles to several overlapping patterns of violence, Ardoyne has endured a permanent condition of isolation and tension, fear and loss, the effects of which have pervaded a community grappling simultaneously with constant surveillance and harassment at the hands of the police and the British Army, as well as large-scale unemployment and economic hardship, the pressures of life lived 'off the brew' (or social security benefit), the consequences of public neglect of a range of social needs in the area and the effects of urban environmental blight.[39] In this charged atmosphere, a 'fight outside a chip shop' is likely to be a rather different kind of confrontation than it would be in Dermot Bolger's Dublin. In their local chip shop, run by the Catholic Fusco family and situated on the dangerous Crumlin Road interface, Ardoyne residents would encounter loyalists from the neighbouring Woodvale area. During the 1970s, '[s]hots had been fired into the chip shop . . . on a number of occasions' by loyalist gunmen, who in 1976 also carried out a sectarian attack on the Fuscos in their home across the road.[40] Ten years later, visitors to the area would be told the stories of these attacks (and others in the vicinity, including those of the gruesome loyalist gang the Shankill Butchers), as if they had occurred yesterday or were always happening; which in a sense they were for nationalists who, in 1986, lived in daily fear of attack and with the understanding that 'we could get killed walking home from here tonight'.[41]

Local stories such as these, about what happened or happens 'here', play an important part in shaping a living sense of local identity. In North Belfast this operates in relation to the sectarian divide but also differentiates one nationalist or loyalist enclave from another; each has 'its own distinctive sense of history and place in the mosaic of territories . . . a place unto itself with its own sense of identity'.[42] The Ardoyne Commemoration Project has argued that, while 'to be from Ardoyne usually means to have been born and grown up in certain streets . . . to share a certain sense of place and belonging and to live that out in the contacts, actions and institutions that make up everyday life', it also involves this sense of a shared and binding history, including the stories about those from the area who died in the Troubles. Such stories are 'the personal memories of those who knew and loved [the dead]', but they are also 'a key component of a collective memory through which a shared identity takes shape'.[43] However, the stories located in those streets also reach back beyond the start of the current Troubles and link today's residents of Ardoyne to the cultural world of their predecessor generations.

Gerry Adams, the President of Sinn Féin, has recalled that, when Catholic civilians were first killed by armed loyalists in 1966 and nationalist areas along Belfast's interfaces, including Ardoyne, came under attack from the RUC three years later, 'we heard some of the older people say that this kind of thing had happened before'.[44] Ardoyne's Hooker Street, Herbert Street and Butler Street, where 'RUC men, "B Specials" [the Unionist state militia] and a mob of several hundred loyalists' mounted an attack on the area on the night of 14 August 1969 – first with batons and petrol bombs, later with guns and the support of 'armoured cars mounted with heavy machine guns'[45] – were the same streets where, in the war to secure the partition and establish the new northern State in 1921–22, one Catholic resident was shot dead by loyalist gunmen, another was abducted and killed by a police 'reprisal team', and six schoolchildren were badly injured in an 'Orange bomb' attack, an incident which left 'local people in Ardoyne . . . outraged'.[46]

The older people of the 1920s would themselves have remembered, and heard stories from their own parents and grandparents about, the nineteenth-century formation of Belfast's Catholic ghettoes, when migrants were drawn into the expanding industrial city from an impoverished countryside. This process was punctuated by regular outbreaks of rioting, 'especially along the frontier zone between the main Protestant and Catholic enclaves', already described in 1914 as 'the seismic area of the city'.[47] These increased in ferocity from 1857, to the extent that major outbreaks of inter-community violence in 1864, 1872 and 1886 'resulted in more deaths than all the nationalist uprisings of the nineteenth century put together'.[48] According to A.C. Hepburn: 'Rioting, the fear of it, and the bitter memories associated with it, have been the main determinant of community relations in the city';[49] a remark that also points, like the Ardoyne Commemoration Project, to the salience of the concept of memory as a means to understanding how the past permeates the present in conflict zones like North Belfast.

In recent work in cultural history and critical theory, *memory* has been fashioned into a critical concept which offers an increasingly subtle and nuanced analytical tool for addressing the issues, problems and questions raised in this book. This proliferating new field of 'memory studies' is characterized by a number of different theoretical and methodological approaches based on various alternative conceptions of the object of study, ranging from *social* memory and *collective* memory to *popular* memory and *cultural* memory.[50] In my use of the term, 'cultural memory' refers to the representation by a social group of processes, events or experiences that have taken place or are believed to have taken place in its past; that articulates its sense of a lived connection between past and present, and the meanings it makes of that connection. Considered in this way, memory is an element in the ideological repertoire of a society, its narratives and images forming an indispensable part of the cultural maps of meaning that enable people to live in a particular environment and make sense of their personal and social experience. It is also central to the cultural construction of subjectivities and senses of belonging, and is among the factors that constitute collective identities, in the form of imagined communities of memory whose members share a sense of a common past and a set of remembered reference points encapsulating their key values. Conceptions of who 'we' are, where we come from, how our way of life has evolved here, who the others are and how we differ from them are given form in representations of the past that establish its importance and significance in and for our shared life in the present. As a tool for understanding these ideological processes, the critical theory of cultural memory prompts fresh ways of thinking about the familiar psychological processes of remembering and forgetting in everyday life.

Thus, *personal* memory always involves something more than an individual's psychological processing of personal experience, but is bound up in a reciprocal relation with these social and collective representations of the past, which both draw on the personal memories of individuals and are incorporated back within them. The theory of *cultural* memory also points to a two-way interaction at work between past and present. The legacy of the past imposes itself on and could even be said to structure how we experience ourselves and our lives. But as active agents of remembrance, we work to recall, understand and make sense of this legacy in particular ways, fashioning cultural representations that may confirm or redefine the current relevance of past experience, and organize the social relation between past and present in new, as well as traditional, configurations. This ensures that meanings concerning the legacy of the past are never simply *transmitted* from one generation to another, but are subject to a set of social and cultural conditions peculiar to any particular present. Thus, there is never any single meaning, but rather a plurality constructed through the telling of different stories that make differing interpretations and draw differing conclusions. Questions may then be posed about these agents of remembering and forgetting, and about the material processes of cultural production involved in the making of memories, as these intermesh with and are determined by wider social contexts and sets of social relations.

How, then, should we understand the material workings of memory and memory's relationship to constructions of identity and senses of place in Northern Ireland, both within the lifetime of a living generation and across such extensive duration? How are we to explain the social and cultural processes of meaning-making, but also the psychic processes of identification, at work in what the Irish historian A.T.Q. Stewart calls the 'mysterious form of transmission from generation to generation'?[51] One way in which memories are made, circulated, shared and handed on is certainly through the stories about the past told within families and the social networks of local communities. But which stories are told, under what circumstances and for what reasons? How are they listened to, understood and adapted in their handing on? Moreover, cross-generational transmission is by no means guaranteed, as Gerry Adams suggests when he describes the initial reactions of the new generation of Republican activists to the memories of 1921–22

voiced by older people: 'we were young and like most young people . . .
believed that the lessons of the past were of little enough relevance to the
immediacy of the present'.[52] The Argentinian sociologist Elizabeth Jelin,
reflecting on memories of the recent military dictatorships in a number of
South American countries, proposes:

> Inter-cohort differences – among those who lived through repression at differ-
> ent times in their personal lives, between them and the very young who do not
> have personal memories of repression – and the relationships and dialogues
> between generations produce a distinct societal dynamics [of memory].

The further question then arises of 'which new interpretations and meanings
will be given, both at the individual and group levels'?[53]

As well as through interpersonal storytelling, the present past is articulated and given meaningful form in public commemorative cultures. In
Ireland, these are of exceptional longevity and passion. In Ardoyne, as elsewhere in the North, local nationalists and Republicans have participated in
the tradition of parading and symbolic decoration of the streets to mark
important events and dates in the commemorative calendar: for example, the
150th anniversary of the rebellion of Robert Emmet in 1953, and the 50th
anniversary of the 1916 Easter Rising in 1966, as well as the more recent
Republican prisoners' hunger strikes of 1980–81. Across the Crumlin Road,
in Woodvale, Glencairn and the Shankill, the Orange parading tradition –
established in the 1790s, consolidated at the core of Ulster Unionist identity
in the 1880s and augmented since 1908 by commemorative murals as well
as the decorating of streets with arches, banners, bunting and painted kerb-
stones – celebrates the lifting of the Siege of Derry in 1689 and the victory
of King William III of Orange over the Catholic King James at the battle of
the Boyne in 1690.[54] The representation of 'the past' in these opposed commemorative traditions is mobilized to figure identities, needs and aspirations
current in any particular present. As Estyn Evans pointed out in 1951:
' "Remember 1690" – one of those crisp Ulster wall slogans – is not the
motto of an historical cult . . . so much as the reminder of present day threats
to the Ulsterman's security and independence'.[55] Nearly fifty years later, in
1995 and 1996, the loyalist politician Ian Paisley Junior, reflecting on the
violent confrontations centred on the Portadown District Orange Lodge's
'right to march' through a nationalist enclave on its 'traditional' return route
along the Garvaghy Road from the church at Drumcree, observed: 'Over the
past years the Loyalists of Ulster have watched the deliberate devaluation of
their history, culture and British identity. . . . The past is to a large degree
our present politics because the battles of the past are still going on around
us unresolved.'[56] Ian McBride notes that, in Ireland,

> commemorative rituals have become historic forces in their own right . . . When
> the 'armed struggle' was renewed in the 1970s, the Provisional IRA mounted
> attacks to coincide with key dates in the republican calendar such as Easter or
> the anniversary of internment . . . The right to march on Orange anniversaries

has been a source of inter-communal conflict for 200 years . . . [T]he fiftieth anniversary of the Easter Rising spawned a new generation of republicans in Belfast, rekindling the fears of loyalist extremists who took for themselves another commemorative name, the Ulster Volunteer Force.[57]

Reflecting on the similar politicization of commemorative dates and anniversaries in those countries of South America undergoing transition from dictatorship to democracy in the 1980s and 1990s, Elizabeth Jelin wonders: 'Are the events and activities that are carried out "really" commemorations of past events? . . . Can past and present be separated? Is it possible . . . that the original [meaning of a date] becomes only a "pre-text" for political and social struggles that are *always* anchored in the present?'[58] These questions also have a bearing on how we are to understand the 'societal dynamics' centred on personal storytelling and its relation to this politics of commemoration.

The concept of memory, then, opens a number of useful perspectives on the present past and its various modes of existence within cultures imbricated in conflict. In such locations, where 'the past' is 'a convenient quarry which provides ammunition to use against enemies in the present',[59] memories of war tend to become weapons in a war over memory. However, the past also intrudes into the present in ways less amenable to conscious agency. As Gready puts it: 'The politics of memory is interwoven with the repetition and recasting of past divisions and conflicts, as the past continues to influence, sometimes literally exploding into, ongoing societal disputation.'[60] In pointing to the existence of a dangerous, 'explosive' energy capable of reigniting current disputes in unlooked-for repetitions of past conflict, Gready's formulation indicates that factors beyond conscious awareness may be at work, and that actions may be driven by powerful psychic impulses and emotions, in the course of which scripts or narratives established in the past come to be acted out in new circumstances. Psychoanalytic perspectives on this 'unconscious' repetition of the past centre on the important determining role of 'ego defences' activated to preserve the self in response to the divisions and conflicts within the internal world of the psyche. The latter correlate with social and political divisions via well-established 'psychic pathways' that fix relations between the self and its others according to familiar cultural narratives, '[f]acilitated by constant use'.[61] This seems a particularly apt way to describe the repetitions of violent conflict along Belfast's 'seismic' interface zone, where the same social actors confronted one another in 1969 in the same streets as in 1921–22, irrespective of whether those actors remembered the earlier events or not.

Repetitions of this kind have continued to flare up in these same locations in the years since the paramilitary ceasefires of 1994 ostensibly put an end to the war. Some of the fiercest rioting in Northern Ireland since 1969, involving inter-community confrontation, large-scale loyalist assault on nationalist schools, streets and houses, and fighting between nationalists and riot police supported by the British Army, featuring petrol and pipe bombs and guns, as well as less lethal weaponry, erupted on Ardoyne's Crumlin Road interface between June 2001 and January 2002. These disturbances centred on the blockade of the Holy Cross Catholic primary school for girls, which serves Ardoyne but is situated in the neighbouring loyalist enclave of Glenbryn, by loyalist protesters who subjected the children and their parents to such a degree of physical intimidation and verbal abuse, on their way to and from school, that their safety could only be guaranteed by the presence of '[h]undreds of heavily armed, mostly masked, RUC officers in full riot gear and British soldiers carrying semi-automatic weapons and prepared for combat'.[62]

The context in which these poisonous events developed was one of persistent tension and routine violence on both sides of the Ardoyne–Glenbryn interface, with reports also emerging of Protestants being driven from the area by Republican intimidation, explictly linked by some residents to memories of the IRA campaign in the early years of the Troubles.[63] As in previous instances of rioting in the area, the Orange Order's annual Twelfth of July parade along the Crumlin Road past Ardoyne again provided the '*pretext*' for confrontation in 2001 (and has done so again since). However, the violence associated with the Holy Cross blockade was also part of a more systematic and widespread pattern of attacks on nationalist people and property throughout 2001 orchestrated by the paramilitary UDA to manifest its rejection of the peace agreement.[64] Unconscious psychic energies may be evoked and harnessed for conscious political ends, while politics becomes infused with the psychic realities of the present past.

Such events extend the psychic repercussions of conflict into the era of conflict resolution, and implicate new generations in the experiences and legacies of violence. The Holy Cross blockade and the broader pattern of interface violence of which it is a part has had traumatic psychological effects on children as young as four, while in recent years North and West Belfast, in general, and Ardoyne, in particular, have suffered from a high incidence of teenage depression and a soaring suicide rate among young people that is among the highest in Europe.[65] Violence has remained 'a relative and constant feature of Northern Irish society since the ceasefires', with, according to Shirlow and Murtagh, a significant increase in sectarian attacks after the 1998 Agreement.[66] In September 2004, a report by the Northern Ireland Housing Executive suggested that 1,245 people had been forced to abandon their homes in the previous year due to violent attacks, including petrol bombings and the firing of bullets, 'amid a climate of heightened fear on both sides of the sectarian divide'.[67] Racially motivated attacks on ethnic minorities have mushroomed. Controversy over the violence endemic to both Republican and loyalist paramilitarisms, and its malign influence over the communities they control, has been a constant theme of public debate, from the protests against punishment beatings which continued long after the declaration of the ceasefires in 1994, mounted by FAIT (Families Against Intimidation by Terrorists), through to the campaign of the McCartney sisters to bring to justice the killers of their brother Robert in 2005. Conditions of pervasive violence have produced the kind of psychic rage that could drive one loyalist youth in South Armagh, according to a story I heard told in March 2000, to respond to sectarian taunting by an older Republican man in their local chip shop by attempting to plunge him into a frier full of boiling oil.[68] To understand this rage, or the psychic realities of teenaged suicides, it might well be necessary to recognize the long-term as well as the recent history which have created the conditions for such violence, and find ways of explaining the continuing reproduction of that 'past' within the 'present' period and process of conflict resolution.

'Dealing with the past' in strategies of conflict resolution

If the past 'lives on' in different temporal rhythms in locations such as North Belfast and South Armagh, and has different modes of existence there, both conscious and unconscious, from those of Dublin or London, then what effect does this have on the processes and strategies of conflict resolution? What does it mean to 'address', or 'resolve' or otherwise 'deal with' a society's relation to its past in such a context? How is a sense of the past that has been shaped in this way by a history of war and conflict to be transformed or accommodated in peacetime conditions? In what ways might the present past be seen to motivate, but also to complicate, the search for a just and peaceful settlement to violent conflict? In work on post-conflict reconstruction, 'backwards-looking' approaches to peace-making see justice as centrally concerned with righting the wrongs of the past, whilst 'forward-looking' approaches seek to leave these aside in the interests of future-oriented goals.[69]

   In those transitional societies where initiatives to deal with with the past have been established, advocates of the view that 'any society coming out of violence *should remember*' also have to reckon with the complex 'interplay between remembering, forgetting and moving on after decades of violence', and may like Nelson Mandela find it necessary to make contradictory calls, both to face up to the unresolved legacy of the struggle against apartheid, and to 'forget the past' and 'build our country'.[70] Brandon Hamber, from his experience at the Johannesburg Centre for the Study of Violence and Reconciliation and later with the Initiative on Conflict Resolution and Ethnicity (INCORE) in Northern Ireland, has argued that the merit of these alternative positions 'remains debatable' and that there is 'no easy answer' to the problem; for example, 'despite growing research' it is 'not clear how forgetting the past, or alternatively, remembering the past, actually avoids or provokes political violence in the future'.[71] Nevertheless, argues Hamber, Northern Ireland 'has no choice but to accept that the past has to be dealt with in one way or another'.[72]

   Social strategies concerned with memory as a means with which to deal with the past commonly focus on the discovery and communication of the *truth* about what happened, understood as a process of *uncovering* what has been hidden or denied, both in the course of conflict and during its aftermath. This may take many forms, including 'formal truth commissions or commissions of inquiry' and the 'documentation of victims' stories in the form of books, archives, poetry, writing, theatre and song, as well as more structured truth telling processes, ranging from counselling to commemoration through monuments and rituals'.[73] For Hamber, this kind of remembering is 'a dangerous, difficult and often fraught task', both 'arduous and painful', involving the 'dirty business' of 'acknowledging responsibility and even finger pointing', revealing 'that we are all complicit (to varying degrees) in the violence of the past', and opening up a scenario 'of multiple and contradictory truths. One unified narrative, or version of the past, can never be uncovered. The past will remain a contested debate.'[74] Elizabeth Jelin, writing of the Central and South American experience of transition, corroborates this view:

> After periods of high political conflict and of repression or state terrorism, there is an active political struggle about meaning, about the meaning of what went on and also about the meaning of memory itself. In this arena, the struggle is not one of 'memory against oblivion' or silence, but rather between opposing memories, each of them with its own silences and voids.[75]

Such debate and struggle centre on the institutions, mechanisms, agencies and discourses constructed as the vehicles of conflict resolution. These shape the terms of engagement between competing 'forces of denial and acknowledgement'[76] as they fight over the meaning of the past, thereby realigning political conflict in relation to their own workings. One fundamental distinction here is that between state-centred processes that work from the top down, such as the Truth and Reconciliation Commission (TRC) instituted by South Africa's new democratic Government in 1995, or the Commission for Historical Clarification (CEH) established in 1997 in Guatemala under the terms of the Peace Accords of 1994–96; and initiatives emerging from civil society and working from the grassroots upwards, as in the case of the Guatemalan Recovery of the Historical Memory (REMHI) project set up in 1995 to counter the perceived weaknesses of the official Truth Commission, or the Mothers of Plaza de Mayo and other human rights groups established at the height of state terrorism following the 1976 military coup in Argentina.[77] State organizations are likely to differ fundamentally from those developed in civil society as 'platforms for voice', that provide and structure social opportunities for testimony to be recounted, heard and acknowledged, according to differing conceptions of 'the ethics and politics of public testimony and its dissemination'.[78] Such platforms, or arenas, not only enable the telling of personal memories but help to constitute them, by determining their mode of entry into the public domain and shaping their relation to wider social frameworks of remembrance.

Consider, for example, the most influential of all recent conflict-resolution initiatives, South Africa's TRC. This placed 'the process of story telling . . . [by] both victims and perpetrators' at the heart of its project to document 'gross violations of human rights' (defined as 'killing, torture, abduction, or severe ill-treatment') committed between 1960 and 1994, to make recommendations on reparations and to grant amnesty.[79] Over 20,000 victims of violence, their families and friends and witnesses submitted statements (concerning nearly 38,000 cases) to the TRC's Committee on Human Rights Violations, and some 10 per cent of these were invited to testify in seventy-six public hearings that were given extensive media coverage in 1996–97.[80] In this, as Fiona Ross argues, the TRC provided a '*public* form of bearing witness,' a forum, and 'a particular discourse within which to place, describe and understand the violence of the recent past'.[81] The TRC discourse promoted the telling of stories not only as a means of uncovering the hidden truth about the past but for its 'healing potential' in relation to the psychic wounds and scars left by the conflict, described in its final report as being both personal and public: 'People came to the Commission to tell their stories in an attempt to facilitate not only their own individual healing process, but also a healing process for the entire nation.'[82]

In its practical functioning, the TRC instituted a number of definitions and assumptions – about the character of the past to be uncovered, about the content of the testimonies to be elicited, and about the value (personal and social) of recounting the stories of the victims of violence. For Ross, the most striking, and mistaken, assumption made by the TRC concerned 'the relationship between "experience" and "testimony"'; that 'the narration of experience was . . . a simple act, a release of "stories" of pain that already existed intact within those who had experienced violations. All that was apparently required was a forum through which the "stories" could be released and channelled.'[83] On the contrary, Ross argues, 'the recounting of stories of harm is not simple' and in this case depended on the 'testimonial practices' constructed by the TRC's discourse and procedure, which enabled the voicing of certain experiences but also contributed to the silence around others, notably in the paucity of testimonies by women concerning women's experiences of violence.[84]

The experience of the TRC also demonstrates that the psychic needs of traumatized or grieving individuals do not necessarily align straightforwardly with political exigencies, in this case those of a process designed specifically to foster national unity, reconciliation and reconstruction based on the constitution of the new democratic South Africa. In particular, 'considerable anger is directed by victims and survivors towards the concept of amnesty', whereby those who had committed human rights violations were granted immunity from prosecution on condition that they would 'engage in full disclosure, prove that their crimes were political in nature . . . and demonstrate that the manner in which the offences were carried out had not displayed sadism or personal gain . . . No one had to apologise.'[85] Amnesty, as Michael Ignatieff points out, was 'the precondition for a peaceful transition of power'; yet 'the amnesty provisions were asking a society of victims to display a scarcely human forebearance',[86] and 'individuals' rights have

been sacrificed for the good of the nation'.[87] Ntsiki Biko, the widow of the
Black Consciousness leader Steve Biko, who was killed in 1977 while in
police custody, is among those critical of the TRC for failing to make perpetrators accountable or to secure justice for the families, and thus 'just
opening the wounds for nothing', when 'all that is needed is to have the
perpetrators taken to a proper court of justice'.[88]

The South African TRC, as 'the most ambitious and far-reaching' among
recent efforts to deal with the past in a process of conflict resolution, is
widely discussed as a template or 'model for other societies seeking to rebuild
their ethical order and . . . seek healing and justice after periods of war or
tyranny'.[89] In Ireland, too, it has provided an influential reference point in
the peace process.[90] Yet it represents a particular and by no means unprob-
lematic attempt, tailored to the specific conditions of post-apartheid South
Africa, to resolve the paradoxes and contradictions inherent in any society's
endeavour to make peace with its past. While undoubtedly much can be
learned from comparative analysis of such endeavours across different societies in transition, Brandon Hamber has warned against use of the South
African model of the TRC as the starting point in Ireland, pointing to fundamental differences in the political context of the two countries, and
thus the importance of developing a 'home grown strategy (or strategies)'
grounded in the political realities of transition in Northern Ireland.[91] The
crucial difference concerns the balance of political forces in relation to the
State. In South Africa, the achievement of political consensus and the transition to a new democratic dispensation and state structure had been accomplished prior to the TRC initiative towards dealing with the conflicted past.
With the African National Congress (ANC) in power, the 'dominant new
ANC hegemony' required that analysis of the political violence began with
its 'root causes' in the apartheid system, with the activities of those who supported it or colluded with it, and with the liberation struggle to end it, rather
than with the mere quantification of deaths and the attribution of responsibility. This ensured, firstly, that no equation could be made between the
'legitimate' violence of the resistance movement (notwithstanding its own
human rights violations which the TRC addressed on a case-by-case basis)
and 'the oppression of the National Party'; and, secondly, that the political
complexity of the violence (that included 'intra- or inter-community conflict'
and fighting between the ANC and the Inkatha National Party) was acknowledged and addressed. 'This could only happen', Hamber argues,
'because the ANC is in the driving seat.'[92]

This situation is in marked contrast to other contexts such as Guatemala,
Argentina or Chile, where new democratic governments in the 1980s and
1990s were limited in their scope to overturn amnesty laws passed by the
juntas of the 1970s and to hold to account those responsible for human
rights abuses committed under military rule, due to the continuing power of
the military and the fragility of the transition.[93] It also contrasts with the
balance of forces shaping conflict resolution in Ireland, characterized by

Hamber as a 'power-sharing arrangement . . . in which [both] parties [are] represented equally, and [. . . have] relatively equal amounts of public support', while 'the British government, and the Irish government to some extent, are seen as the guardians of peace . . . and their complicity in the violence over the last 30 years is . . . downplayed in the mainstream media'.[94] Speaking in February 1999, four-and-a-half years after the first IRA ceasefire, Hamber posed the question: 'to what degree is the current balance of forces [in Northern Ireland] shaping the discussions on the questions of truth, justice and the moralities of violence'?[95]

The Irish peace process

The peace process established in 1993–94 was the first serious and sustained attempt to resolve the Irish Troubles in twenty years. Since 1969, successive British governments had attempted to manage the conflict by seeking to build a middle-ground consensus between the 'moderate' currents within both Irish nationalism and Ulster Unionism, to the exclusion of the 'extremist' elements on both sides which were opposed to a negotiated compromise settlement. However, since the collapse of the power-sharing executive instituted by the Sunningdale Agreement of 1973, the politics of the conflict was polarized between two incompatible goals: on one hand, maintenance of Northern Ireland as a distinct political entity, either as part of the UK or as an independent sovereign state; and, on the other, its dissolution, leading to the reunification of Ireland in the form of a thirty-two-county Irish Republic. Further attempts at building the middle ground proved abortive in the context of the continuing Republican insurgency and the deployment of British armed forces to quell this. Throughout, the British State represented its own role as that of the 'honest broker' seeking to 'keep the peace' and facilitate agreement between two warring factions.

The peace initiative of the early 1990s broke new ground in seeking an inclusive settlement involving all parties to the conflict, including those previously excluded due to their close connection to paramilitary organizations. It was launched by the Joint Declaration on Peace – the 'Downing Street Declaration' – signed in December 1993 by the British Prime Minister, John Major, and the Irish *Taoiseach*, Albert Reynolds. This signalled the beginning of an inclusive effort 'to remove the causes of conflict, to overcome the legacy of history and to heal the divisions which have resulted'. New arrangements would 'lay the foundations for a more peaceful and harmonious future devoid of the violence and bitter divisions which have scarred the past generation'. This outcome, it suggests, could come about 'only through the agreement and co-operation of the people, North and South, representing both traditions in Ireland'. The role of the British Government is defined as being 'to encourage, facilitate and enable the achievement of such agreement . . . through a process of dialogue and co-operation based on full respect for the rights and identities of both traditions'.[96]

The Joint Declaration was the outcome of three strands of diplomacy, each conducted over several years: a co-operative strategy for conflict resolution developed by the two governments on the basis of the Anglo-Irish Agreement of 1985; understandings reached in the course of secret, mediated exchanges between the British Government's officials and the IRA; and the principles of the Hume–Adams peace strategy negotiated between the leaders of the 'constitutional' nationalist Social Democratic and Labour Party (SDLP) and the Republican party, Sinn Féin, which supported the IRA's armed struggle. It created the political basis for the IRA ceasefire declared on 31 August 1994 and its reciprocation by the Combined Loyalist Military Command in October, and for the two governments' Framework Document of February 1995 setting out the conditions for inclusive, all-party, talks on the future of Northern Ireland. Talks did not begin until June 1996 and 'substantive negotiations' were further delayed, due first to British and Ulster Unionist objections to the participation of Sinn Féin while the IRA retained its weaponry, and then to the temporary resumption of the IRA's armed campaign, in response to the slow rate of political progress, from February 1996 until July 1997. When Sinn Féin eventually joined the talks in September 1997, both the Democratic Unionist Party and the United Kingdom Unionist Party withdrew in protest. What were now multi-party negotiations culminated in the Belfast 'Good Friday' Agreement of April 1998 between the two governments, the SDLP and Sinn Féin, the Ulster Unionist Party, two smaller parties linked to the main loyalist paramilitary organizations (the Progressive Unionist Party, associated with the UVF, and the Ulster Democratic Party with the UDA), together with the cross-community Alliance Party and the Northern Ireland Women's Coalition. Thus, the Agreement was supported by a significant majority right across the political spectrum in the North, including political representatives in touch with the views of both Republican and loyalist paramilitaries. In May 1998 the Agreement was endorsed by huge majorities in popular referenda held simultaneously in Northern Ireland and the Irish Republic.[97]

In essence, the Good Friday Agreement consists of three main elements. Firstly, it affirms a 'commitment to exclusively democratic and peaceful means of resolving differences on political issues' and 'our opposition to any use or threat of force . . . for any political purpose'. It outlines measures for demilitarization to establish 'a normal peaceful society' in Northern Ireland, involving the dismantling of the State's security apparatus and its emergency powers, and 'the total disarmament of all paramilitary organisations'; and for dealing with the legacy of armed conflict in respect of the victims of violence and political prisoners.

Secondly, it creates the framework for an 'internal' political settlement within Northern Ireland, based on the principles of 'respect for, and equality of, civil, political, social and cultural rights, of freedom from discrimination for all citizens, and of parity of esteem and of just and equal treatment for the identity, ethos, and aspirations of both communities'. This is underpinned by the blueprint for a reformed state centred on the new democratic political institutions of a devolved Northern Ireland Assembly and Executive, operating according to safeguards to ensure effective power-sharing and cross-community collaboration, and reinforced by legislative commitments and new institutional mechanisms to guarantee respect for human rights and equality of opportunity. Thirdly, it seeks to resolve the national question – as to whether Northern Ireland and its people belong within the British polity as part of the UK, or within a united Ireland – by answering: 'both'. While affirming the existing constitutional position that the status of Northern Ireland depends on 'the consent of a majority of its people', and acknowledging that 'the present wish of [the] majority . . . is to maintain the Union', the Agreement also recognizes 'the legitimate wish of the majority of the people of the island of Ireland for a united Ireland', and that this wish is shared by 'a substantial section of the people of Northern Ireland'. Should this latter wish be expressed by majorities in both parts of Ireland in the future, the Agreement affirms that both governments would be under a 'binding obligation' to introduce legislation to that effect. In the meantime, the Agreement embeds Northern Ireland simultaneously in new institutional relations with the Republic (through the North–South Ministerial Council) and with the other regions of the UK (through the British–Irish Council), as well as new structures for co-operation between the two governments. The people of Northern Ireland may choose to become citizens of either, or both, of the two national states.[98]

The Good Friday Agreement is a complex balancing act that attempts to reconcile fundamentally antithetical political demands of the Unionist and nationalist constituencies with respect to all three of its elements. In negotiating the Agreement, all parties had their major demands recognized and incorporated within it, but equally, all had 'bitter pills to swallow'.[99] The 'constructive ambiguity' of this elaborate political compromise meant that Unionists and nationalists were free to interpret the British Government's strategic intentions regarding the constitutional question and partition, each in its own way, to assess the merits and disadvantages of the blueprint for their constituencies, and to campaign accordingly. As a result, parties to the Agreement, including the British Government, quickly became involved in fighting their own corners with respect to its implementation, rather than becoming genuine 'partners for peace'.

Issues that developed into major focal points of conflict over the implementation of the Agreement have included the 'decommissioning' of paramilitary weapons in relation to demilitarization by the British State; the relation between this process of 'taking the gun out of Irish politics' and the establishment of the new political institutions; the definition of 'victims of violence' and its implication for public modes of redress; the early release of prisoners convicted for Troubles-related offences; and the transformation of the police and judicial system so as to win cross-community support.

As a result, progress in implementing the Agreement has been slow and precarious, to the extent that the peculiarly protracted character of efforts to achieve political transition to a new agreed dispensation has become one of the defining features of the Irish peace process. In April 2007, over twelve years after the ceasefires first created the space for a negotiated settlement and eight years after the Agreement, new political institutions have yet to be established successfully and on a permanent basis. Meanwhile, the British State has continued to govern Northern Ireland (as it has done since 1972) by quasi-colonial Direct Rule from Westminster, and to engage in ideological as well as political management of the peace process, perhaps most significantly when British Secretaries of State at the Northern Ireland Office took decisions to suspend the new Assembly and Executive, bringing to an end brief periods of devolved government (December 1999–February 2000, May 2000–July 2001, and October 2001–October 2002).[100]

This ongoing political contestation over implementation of the Good Friday Agreement has ensured that in Ireland dealing with the past has been differently complex than it has in South Africa. Indeed, one manifestation of this contestation has been the tenacious and vigorous promotion within the political arena of competing narratives articulating antithetical versions of the causes, conduct and meaning of the conflict. These are narratives that remember the Troubles in distinctive and incompatible ways, and in so doing stake out the terms of current conflict over the shape of the peace, the new political dispensation and the new society coming into being. Memories formed on the ideological terrain of the war have thus continued to be voiced during the 'long peace'[101] with respect to all the major sticking-points over implementation. To give one brief example: debate over the question of police reform has been significantly influenced by powerfully emotive memories of the RUC. In nationalist and Republican memory, the RUC is synonymous with the subordination and oppression of nationalists by the Unionist State, and a feared and hated enemy in the war. In Unionist and loyalist memory, the RUC has generally been revered as the upholder of law and order whose officers sacrificed their own safety – and lives – to defend decent people against the threat of Republican terrorism (though such memories have been compromised for some by the RUC's role in policing loyalist protest at Drumcree and elsewhere during the peace process). Unlike in South Africa, the detail of police reform in Northern Ireland – whether concerning the change of name to the Police Service of Northern Ireland or the proposal to allow local communities to elect members to serve on their local policing board – has had to be negotiated in an ideological context in which each of these opposing memories claim to be the most valid. Here, dealing with the past is not something that happens after the conflict is over, but is bound up with the very attempt to bring conflict to an end.

This contestation of the peace settlement at the level of the State has also had a profound effect on initiatives towards conflict resolution arising from within civil society in Northern Ireland. Since the 1994 ceasefires, the peace process has stimulated widespread public debate on questions of conflict resolution, involving community activists and voluntary sector professionals, human rights advocates and local council officers, academic researchers and artists, politicians and educationalists, trades unionists and the clergy. Debate has often linked to grassroots initiatives, and has frequently drawn on experiences from other societies in transition.[102] It has also given rise to a flowering of practices of history-making, remembrance and commemoration concerned with the legacy of the Troubles. Much of this work has built on cultural initiatives undertaken while armed conflict continued, through, for example, the fostering of projects concerned with 'cultural traditions', heritage and identity under the auspices of the state-funded Community Relations Council formed in 1990; local commemorations telling the story of the Troubles and marking the impact of particular events within a particular area; and the wider public reflection on the trajectory of the conflict generated by events such as the twenty-fifth anniversary, in August 1994, of the introduction of British troops to the streets of Northern Ireland's cities and towns. Continuities with the divided and conflicting memories produced during wartime are clearly evident in much of this activity. However, the ceasefires also created new spaces for reflection on the recent past and its effects upon individuals, families, and local communities. While such grassroots activity, including oral-history and life-story publications, historical exhibitions and community history projects, has largely arisen out of and been developed specifically to address the historical experience of particular communities, it has also created opportunities for encountering other perspectives and narratives. Some initiatives were developed specifically to do this, as for example, in the innovative outreach work involving local communities from all across Northern Ireland associated with the curating and touring of the Ulster Museum's exhibition *War and Conflict in 20th Century Ireland* in 2000–1.[103] A further development in civil society made possible by the ceasefires was the emergence of wide public debate over and social engagement with the question of the victims of violence, the formation of numbers of local victims' self-help and support groups addressing the traumatic legacy of violence, and the recovery and public representation on a pervasive scale of stories recalling those who lost their lives. In some cases, such as the Ardoyne Commemoration Project, the local history of the Troubles came to be written in terms of such recovery and remembrance.[104]

Driven by local needs and dynamics, and occupying spaces that tend to allow wider room for manoeuvre and greater flexibility of response than is usual in the political arena in and around the State, these initiatives from within civil society have developed according to their own rhythms and pace, in relative autonomy from the political process. They have nevertheless been responsive to its ebbs and flows and overall trajectory. Developments in the political sphere affect the expansion and contraction of spaces for dialogue and debate within civil society, and particularly since the signing of the Agreement have reinforced and even galvanized antagonisms expressed in the war over memory at local level. This interaction has been reciprocal, as developments from below have given momentum to the peace process during periods when political progress has faltered, and the articulation of needs, interests and memories within civil society has influenced the negotiating positions of political leaderships. The organizations of civil society have also been influential in linking debates and initiatives over dealing with the past in Northern Ireland with work on conflict resolution underway in the Irish Republic.[105] Outside Ireland, far less public attention is paid to such developments, and they are mostly unknown in England, where little comparable activity has taken place, even in those localities most severely affected by the IRA's 'mainland' bombing campaign. Indeed, in Britain generally, the peace process in Irish civil society has not attracted anything like the degree of critical attention as its high-level political drama, either from the public media or from academic research.

The book

Making Peace with the Past? is a study of the complex interrelations between violence, trauma and memory in the Irish Troubles and peace process. It aims to tease out and analyse the paradoxical and contradictory implications of cultural memory during this transition from violent conflict to peaceful settlement. Reflecting on ways in which the past lives in the present, the book investigates continuities and changes in the articulation and mobilization of memories of the Troubles, before and after the ceasefires of 1994, in order to consider, on the one hand, the impact of the peace process on existing formations of memory and, on the other, ways in which such formations have continued to provide frameworks of remembrance which impact in turn on the peace process. In tracing this trajectory, the book charts what Ian MacBride has called 'a social and cultural history of remembering'.[106] At the same time, the study reflects on and aims to illuminate the kinds of cultural and political processes that are involved in the formation, reproduction and contestation of these memories in war and peace, distinguishing a number of different levels at which they operate. Who are the agents of memory and amnesia in this context? How are their identities constructed through these processes? How do the processes themselves work? How and why do some narratives come to be adopted as defining the experience of whole communities?

The particular focus of the book is on agency emerging from below, out of local communities and organizations in civil society: the grassroots activity that is such an important but under-studied aspect of the Irish peace process.[107] By attending to voices that speak on the basis of personal and local knowledge about the roots of conflict, the circumstances of war, what people have endured in the past and how they understand their relation to others, the book explores how agents of memory are positioned – and have their room for manoeuvre circumscribed – by established formations of memory, yet may nevertheless seek to make new meanings that begin to transform the relationship between past and present. To that end, the book considers the emergence of new cultural spaces, debates and narratives in the post-ceasefire period. It explores the fashioning of public voices by and for the victims of violence, linked to increasing public recognition of the effects of trauma on social groups and whole communities as well as individuals; and it traces the impact of this 'politics of victimhood' on conflicts over truth, justice and redress, and on efforts to implement the Good Friday Agreement.

A central concern of the book is the interrelation of *personal* and *collective* memories, as represented in a wide variety of forms and media. These include parades and other public commemorative events with their accompanying pamphlets and posters; monuments and war memorials; political speeches and sermons; media reportage; published community histories, exhibitions, and websites; murals and songs; personal testimonies, and oral- and life-history narratives. While existing studies have tended to focus on a particular form or medium considered in relation to its political and cultural context, this book seeks to develop a more integrative mode of analysis capable of tracing the movement of narratives and images, motifs and themes, across and between the different forms, media and occasions of their articulation. This is particularly important with respect to personal testimonies and life-stories, which have flourished in practices of popular and grassroots remembrance since the ceasefires, but have yet to receive sustained critical attention as complex texts mediated by collective ideologies and diverse conditions of cultural production. This investigation of interrelations between the personal domain and collective cultural forms is further developed through the book's focus on the psychic dimensions of memory and subjectivity as these interact with social determinants of meaning and identity. It aims to elucidate the emotional repercussions of political violence especially for its victims and survivors, but also in its impact on political and civic discourse and on community relations. This critical engagement with the psychic realities of life and death in a conflict zone is informed by psychoanalytic approaches, crucially to the issue of *trauma* but also to the ways in which processes of remembering and forgetting operate within the internal world of imagination.

Finally, the book addresses the spatial embodiment of memory as well as its temporal dimension, by investigating relations of past and present within particular locations of the Troubles in Northern Ireland. As Kate Darian-Smith and Paula Hamilton have argued, 'Memories link us to place, to time and to nation: they enable us . . . to inhabit our own country'.[108] Local cultural landscapes that constitute the familiar territory of belonging and structure the characteristic perspectives on the world beyond shared by their inhabitants have been fashioned historically and are saturated with particular memories which have soaked into the land, the buildings, the everyday material world. Yet in Northern Ireland, a contested *national* territory lies at the root of the conflict, and its cultural landscapes have been shaped by a corresponding local, communal and sectarian geography, above all in those areas most affected by the war. Local variability in the form and intensity of violent conflict during the Troubles, together with the marked distinctiveness of local cultures and identities within Northern Ireland, mean that careful attention must be paid to the locatedness of cultural memories formed in the course of the war. To make sense of this important relationship between memory and place, I have drawn on the work of cultural geographers and social anthropologists to fashion a method of inquiry focused on the traumatic micro-histories of particular locations. Close examination of the Troubles in particular areas promotes an awareness of how the members of local communities have come to be positioned in relation to one another within this nexus of past, present and place, as well as how they live out the legacy of the past in their different ways. These places of trauma, where contested memories continue to clash within the conflict-resolution process, are also the places where the work of peace-building and reparation is most urgently required and, often, most vigorously pursued.

The book has a three-part structure. Part I establishes its conceptual framework based on theories of war memory and trauma, developed in relation to a number of existing arguments concerned with 'the past' in the Irish Troubles. Parts II and III then present extended case studies of the interrelation of trauma, memory and politics in two key locations of the Troubles. Part II focuses on Derry City, where the nationalist and Republican communities of the Bogside and the Creggan are still dealing with the legacy of Bloody Sunday, one of the most significant events of the Troubles, when the British Army shot dead fourteen unarmed nationalist civilians during a civil rights demonstration. Part III is concerned with the Border areas of Counties Tyrone, Fermanagh and Armagh, where the IRA's Border campaign, waged over decades, has had a sustained traumatic impact on the loyalist and Unionist communities of the region. The case-study approach allows for detailed investigation of specific agents, processes and narratives of remembrance situated in the context of particular local histories. Moreover, these two instances, involving the making and remaking of contrasting and competing cultural memories of the Troubles, epitomize the politics of memory promoted by Irish nationalism and Republicanism, and of Ulster Unionism and loyalism, during and after the war. Both are cases where local events have been represented as central to *national* narratives of the conflict: Bloody Sunday is commonly understood as a microcosm of the more widespread Irish nationalist experience of repression by forces of the British State, while the experience of the Border Protestants has been fashioned into a symbol of the threat from Republican terrorism endured by Unionists in Northern Ireland as a whole. Their further function here, then, is as paradigm cases that bring into focus the concerns of these wider cultures of memory. While each of these two remembered pasts is explored in its own terms, the case-study approach also enables examination of their modes of antagonism, of differences in their content, formation and conditions of existence (especially in relation to the British State's narratives), and of often unremarked similarities between them, as they grapple with the common human realities of war and peace in Ireland. By addressing both cultures, charting the terms of their polarization during the conflict but also holding them together within a single framework of understanding, the book opens up a space for acknowledgement of the experiences and realities of the other, and for the discovery of resonances and parallels across the divide.

Part I

Cultural memory, trauma and conflict in the Irish Troubles

You have no power over the death but you do have power over the story.
(Virginia Ironside, *'You'll Get Over It': The Rage of Bereavement*, 1997)

1

Memory, myth and tradition: concepts of the past in the Irish Troubles

The conflicted terrain of the Irish past is occupied by two powerful grand narratives, one loyalist and Protestant, the other nationalist and Catholic. These furnish different and mutually antagonistic ways of telling the story of Ireland: two competing constructions of the 'same' history. They have also shaped dominant conceptions of the past–present relationship, that is, the way in which a society existing at any particular temporal moment orients itself in respect of its own antecedents, defining and instituting notions concerning the relevance and value, as well as the current significance, of what is 'past'. There is no pure form of these two stories, which exist only in the range of their actual tellings and re-tellings, with numerous variations and differences of emphasis and nuance, across a variety of modes and media of representation, from the murals painted in Northern Irish housing estates to the accounts produced by professional historians, and from the stories told in drama, film and fiction to the rituals of the commemorative parade.

The nationalist narrative tells a story of the suffering and oppression inflicted on the native, Catholic, Irish people by English (later British) colonialism over 800 years, and of Irish endurance and resistance throughout that time. It focuses in particular on the violent colonizations of the late sixteenth and seventeeth centuries, in which land was seized by the English Crown and planted with incoming English and Scottish settlers, and on Irish resistance, which included armed revolt against the harsh, anti-Irish, economic, political, religious and cultural system imposed by the colonists – most notably in the wars of the 1640s, the 1798 United Irishmen's revolt, the Fenian campaign of the 1860s and the Land League mobilization of 1879–82. The story tells of the eventual heroic overthrow of British imperialism in Ireland, by the Republican revolution which began with the Easter Rising and Proclamation of the Republic of Ireland in 1916, followed by the establishment of an independent government, *Dáil Éireann*, based on Sinn Féin's popular mandate won at the 1918 UK General Election. This Republican Government and its claims to sovereignty over the island of Ireland were then defended against the British counter-revolution by the IRA in the War of Independence of 1919–21. While achieving British recognition of an independent Irish Free State with jurisdiction over twenty-six of Ireland's thirty-two counties (which claimed the name 'Republic of Ireland' in 1949), the partial and incomplete success of this revolution was manifest in its failure to encompass within the jurisdiction of the new State the six counties in the North-East of the country, partitioned from the rest by the British in 1920 as the separate statelet of 'Northern Ireland', which remained within the UK. The nationalist story of this 'unfinished revolution' informed a politics of reunification and the achievement of full national sovereignty, that was enshrined from 1937 in Articles 2 and 3 of the Irish Constitution until their removal under the terms of the Good Friday Agreement in 1999. For many, this is the story which inspired the resurgence of armed, revolutionary Republicanism in Ireland, particularly in the North, from 1969.

The loyalist narrative of Ireland tells a contrary story, of how the legitimate settlement of Ireland in the late sixteenth and seventeenth centuries, under the legal auspices of the English Crown, was met with hostility and extreme violence from a native Irish population inflamed by their superstitious Roman Catholic creed. This story tells of the long struggle by the loyalist people to remain loyal to the Crown in Ireland, and to their Protestant religion and British identity. These were linked in that the defence of their 'civil and religious liberties' depended on maintenance of the political connection to Britain, enabling loyalists to withstand the threat of engulfment and destruction by an alien and feared Irish Catholic culture and the anticipated nationalist tyranny of an independent Irish state. The determination of the Protestant people (seen as a single united community) to defend these principles was embodied in the establishment, first, of the Orange Order, a popular movement formed in 1795 to defend and promote Protestant and loyalist interests against the United Irishmen; and, second, by the Ulster Unionist Movement, formed in the 1880s to guard against the threat of Home Rule for Ireland. By 1912, the threatened imminence of Home Rule led to the formation of the UVF, a paramilitary organization that mobilized a popular loyalist will to armed resistance to Home Rule by Protestants of all denominations and classes, particularly in the north-eastern part of Ulster where loyalism was strongest.

The loyalist narrative tells also of how Ulster Protestant loyalty to the British Crown as symbol of the Union was demonstrated on the outbreak of the First World War in 1914 in the wholesale enlistment of the UVF in the British Army as the 36th (Ulster) Division; and how this loyalty translated into 'Ulster's great sacrifice' at the Somme on the Western Front, on 1 July 1916, when 5,000 Ulstermen died on one day. 'Ulster', so the story goes, was rewarded for this sacrifice by the 1920 Government of Ireland Act which partitioned the country, creating a distinct jurisdiction of Northern Ireland with its own Parliament in Belfast – famously described in 1934 by the Unionist leader Lord Craigavon as 'a Protestant parliament for a Protestant people'.[1] According to the loyalist narrative, Northern Ireland has been plagued since its inception by the presence within its borders of a 'disloyal' nationalist–Catholic minority with allegiance to the 'foreign' Irish Free State rather than to the UK, and always therefore potentially 'traitorous' and liable to be intimidated or manipulated by Republicans into protest and insurrection against the State, its representatives and the loyalist people in general. 'Lessons of the past' derived from this narrative – primarily, the lesson of the continuing necessity for loyalists to be alert and energetic in their own self-interest and self-defence – are often said to inform loyalist intransigence and continuing militant, including paramilitary, hostility to Irish nationalism, especially in its Republican forms.

In the context of the Troubles since 1969, a wide critical and historical literature has developed, concerned with the problem of 'the past' in Ireland and its continuing influence in and on the present. Analysis of these competing narratives and their role in reflecting or fomenting conflict, along with the possibilities for their transformation or supersession in the interests of cultural reconciliation and political rapprochement, has been central to much of this work. Within this field, two paradigms have been predominant. The first conceptualizes the problem of the past and its resolution in terms of a dichotomy between the misconceptions of 'mythology' and the scientific truths of 'history'. The second examines the past–present relationship as an effect of distinct 'cultural traditions', each with its own partisan and selective historical consciousness and its own lacunae, but each also equally valid and deserving of respect and recognition. In recent years a third paradigm has emerged to challenge these two long-established approaches by introducing a framework of inquiry based on the concept of collective memory. My own work, as an interdisciplinary cultural historian formed by the 'British' or 'Birmingham' school of cultural studies, and drawing on international debates about what I prefer to call 'cultural memory', aims to contribute to the further critical development of this third paradigm. This first chapter begins with a theoretical critique of the problems and limitations of, in turn, the 'myth' and 'history' and the 'cultural traditions' paradigms, and goes on to establish the theoretical basis and key conceptual co-ordinates informing the study of cultural memory in the Irish Troubles and peace process developed in this book.

Myth and history

The first of these paradigms, dominant particularly in historical studies of the significance of the past in the Irish conflict, has tended to conceptualize the issue in terms of a questionable dichotomy between mythology and history. 'Myth' is understood to mean damaging misconceptions and falsehoods about the past, embedded in popular consciousness, which fuel the atavistic political identities of Ulster Unionism and Irish nationalism, and stir up political violence; while 'history' is used to refer to the more objective and truthful knowledge about the past produced by apparently disinterested professional historians, whose task is to challenge and deconstruct those myths. Originating in the 'Irish Historical Studies' project begun in the 1930s, this paradigm was given explicit exposition by T.W. Moody in his essay 'Irish history and Irish mythology' (1977). Responding to 'a recent televised debate in Northern Ireland on the theme that "Irish history will be the death of us" ', Moody argues that 'it is not Irish history but Irish mythology that has been ruinous to us and may prove even more lethal'.[2] Myth, in Moody's definition, consists of 'received views' that 'derive . . . from popular traditions, transmitted orally, in writing and through institutions', and functions to provide nations with 'consciousness of their past'. History, on the other hand, furnishes 'knowledge' arrived at by 'the application of scientific methods to . . . evidence'.[3] According to Moody, whereas myth fosters 'obsession' and 'perpetuates the closed mind', being 'a way of refusing to face the historical facts', the 'study of history' promotes the facing of those facts, 'enlarges truth' and 'opens the mind'. Thus 'the historian', while admittedly 'included' and 'involved' in the 'living present' from which mythology emerges, is construed as freed from its entrapments in order to fight '[t]he mental war of liberation from servitude to the myth'.[4]

Moody commences battle with a historical analysis of a number of current themes in 'Irish mythology', key component elements in those two grand narratives of the Irish past sketched above. His method is to historicize the emergence of each of these myths and identify its main tenets, before exposing the discrepancies between these claims and the account provided by scholarly historical research. Moody's analysis of what he calls 'Protestant mythology' includes a critique of 'the 1641 horror story' which tells of the massacre of tens of thousands of Protestant settlers by native Irish rebels, and its use to demonstrate 'the wickedness and savagery of Irish Catholics'.[5] He also critiques the 'rich and many-sided mythology' of Orangeism, which heralds the Orange Order as an international champion of Protestant 'civil and religious liberty' against Roman Catholic tyranny and political absolutism;[6] and he challenges the Ulster Protestant 'myth of unique, unwavering, and absolute loyalty to the British crown'.[7] That loyalty, he argues, has in practice been 'conditional upon [Ulster loyalists] being satisfied that their vital interests were adequately protected', and during the Troubles it has proved compatible with 'intransigence' against reforms proposed by the British, and even with calls for 'total independence' for Northern Ireland.[8]

In analysing the mythology of modern Irish nationalism, Moody takes issue with 'the "catholic-separatist" myth . . . that being an Irish catholic was incompatible with loyalty to the English crown',[9] forged during early seventeenth-century resistance to the Elizabethan conquest; and with a 'crop of strong and bitter myths' concerned with the terrible sufferings and hardships endured by the Irish under British rule during the nineteenth-century Union. Moody's most explicit connection of the current Troubles with these mythologies of the past is his critique of 'the "predestinate nation" myth', which 'identifies the democratic Irish nation of the nineteenth century with pre-conquest Ireland, incorporates the concept of [an 800-year] struggle with England as the central theme of Irish history, and sees the achievement of independence in 1922 as the partial fulfilment of a destiny that requires the extinction of British authority in Northern Ireland to complete itself'.[10] This myth 'has been revived by the Provisional IRA in its irredentist war to abolish partition . . . Whatever the cost in human suffering, demoralisation and destruction, and in material damage, they see their campaign in Northern Ireland as justified by their own infallible interpretation of Ireland's past.'[11] The politics behind this critique emerges here and in Moody's identification of two associated IRA myths – what he calls 'the most fantastic element in the Provisionals' mythology[:] . . . that they are waging war not on the protestant people of Northern Ireland but only on Great Britain'; and 'the myth, widely cherished in the Republic till recently, that partition was wholly the creation of Great Britain and that only a British army of occupation prevented the fraternal reunion of the six separated counties with the rest of Ireland'.[12]

Moody's critical argument, his hostility to both loyalist and nationalist (but especially nationalist) mythologies as currently mobilized within the Troubles, and his genealogy of their key episodes, established a 'demythologising'[13] project of historical study for a generation of Irish historians. His binary opposition between mythic falsehood and scientific truth provided a critical framework that continued to define the terms of debate about the social value and political uses of 'Irish history' throughout the 'historical revisionism' controversy of the late 1980s and 1990s, and into the new epoch ushered in by the ceasefires.[14] Discussing Irish cultural identities in 1989, for example, the historian and educationalist Jack Magee argued that the 'Irish are not preoccupied with history but obsessed with divisive and largely sectarian mythologies acquired as part of their political or religious experience'.[15] The rich debate in the Irish and British press sparked by Neil Jordan's film *Michael Collins* (1996) was concerned largely with the film's historical (in)accuracy and the extent to which it recycled myths about the politics and violence of the revolutionary years following the 1916 Easter Rising.[16]

The application of Moody's ideas to the politics of Northern Ireland and the Troubles can clearly be seen in the work of the political scientist and historian Brian Walker, whose book *Dancing to History's Tune* is indicative of a more widespread stance. Walker identifies and challenges a tendency in Irish public life, and in perceptions of Ireland by other cultures, 'to see our current conflicts as the result of a long, deterministic history or to believe that we have a unique history which ties us in a special way to the remote past'. This belief, he argues, has also informed the rhetoric of the Irish peace process ever since the reference in the Downing Street Declaration to the need 'to overcome the legacy of history'.[17] Following Moody, Walker argues that it is not 'history' but 'the myths of our history that influence our actions'.[18] While acknowledging a positive role to myths as 'a part of a sense of history, containing truths and half-truths, which a group or community can create for itself, in response to contemporary challenges and pressures', Walker is more concerned with their negative effects as 'popular misconceptions', which it is the job of the critical commentator to 'challenge' and dispel.[19] Their 'uncritical acceptance' serves particular political purposes in the present and has 'prevented us from seeing our situation and problems in a realistic light and from appreciating the real impact of our past'.[20] Indeed, Irish people 'kill the enemy' due to these 'widely held but false' notions.[21] Furthermore in Ireland, as in other circumstances of inter-community conflict, 'arguments over history often create a dead locked [sic] situation as one side can always counter the other side's historical grievances with grievances of their own'.[22] Published in 1996, Walker's analysis resonates here with current frustrations at the slow progress and apparent deadlock between protagonists in the peace process.

While analyses conducted on the basis of the 'myth and history' paradigm identify a connection between 'mythological' consciousness of the past and political conflict in the present, this approach is limited in its ability to explain how such consciousness comes about or why its adherents should subscribe to it. Its capacity to intervene in and change the condition that it diagnoses appears to rest on the assumption that when the historian speaks the truth will out and misconceptions will fall away under the powerful influence of enlightenment. These limitations are underpinned by two main theoretical weaknesses in what may be described as a liberal–rationalist critical framework. First, such approaches have nothing to say about the processes of cultural production through which these narratives about the past are brought into existence in particular forms of representation; put into circulation within particular social milieux; recreated and retained – or, it may be, rejected and replaced, or reworked and transformed – from one generation to the next; and reproduced in new political circumstances, in which they are affirmed as 'our' past and a resource in present-day struggles. Second, these approaches are unable to explain the purchase that such narratives establish within the consciousness or psyche of those who adopt them as their own, identify with them, and *feel* them to be 'our' and 'my' history. No account is offered of the processes of identification involved here, in which historical narratives contribute to the constituting of specific subjectivities and social identities. In the absence of a theory of subjectivity, contradictory assumptions about the relationship between 'mythic' histories and those who subscribe to them are left unexamined. On the one hand, various rational agents from social and political movements to individuals are assumed to be fully in control of the meanings they make of 'the past', and to be consciously manipulating it to express and promote their particular worldview. On the other hand, individuals and social groups are held to be trapped in the misconceptions of myth, as when, for example, Republican volunteers are described as having an unhealthy 'obsession' with the nationalist version of history[23] – an image that evokes an emotional intensity and fervour more akin to religious experience than amenable to liberal reason.

The subjective power of these so-called mythic narratives, including their centrality to self-identification and a sense of belonging, and the contradictory emotional repercussions that may result when they are called into question have been vividly evoked by the novelist Colm Tóibín. Speaking in a televised debate on Irish history and the peace process in January 1994, a few weeks after the signing of the Downing Street Declaration, Tóibín told a personal story about his own relationship to the 'Irish past':

> I was brought up in a small town [Wexford] in the south-east of Ireland which rose up in the 1916 Rising, which also was famous for 1798, where one of the last battles was fought in the hill above the town; and I was brought up with all that lore. My grandfather fought in 1916, my father taught history in secondary school. It was all vitally important. The names of the places were the vital names in Irish history. My father started a museum and people brought in pikes from 1798 as though they were local things that were part of all our lives.
>
> I remember being in the library at University College, Dublin, at the beginning of [historical] revisionism, reading one of the central revisionist essays by Joe Lee pointing out that a thing called Gratton's parliament, in the 1780s, wasn't Gratton's parliament at all: Gratton [an Irish political reformer associated with winning greater control over home affairs for the Irish parliament in Dublin] had no power in it. And I remember thinking, if the whole martyrology, the whole business of Irish history, the story of Ireland beginning with the invasion by the English – 700 years of gallant struggle by our wonderful people, brave and true: just say this wasn't true? Just say the Famine [of the 1840s, in which over 1 million Irish died] happened in pockets rather than all over Ireland. Just say the Famine wasn't caused by England. Just say 1916 wasn't heroic. And I felt a strange liberation: hey, we're free: we can actually live in our country without being borne down by these half-truths.
>
> But when, after this period of liberation, I went to read [some key revisionist books] and came across, say, Catholics being described in the 1798 Rising (of which I was so proud: I know all the songs) as 'the mob', I said 'Ugh!' It hits me. I want it. I feel Ireland is wide open for the whole story to be retold in any number of ways. It's been constructed; let's tear it asunder. But when the words are on the page: 'Hey, you can't do that!' And I suddenly moved from being the guy in the library to being my grandfather's grandson.[24]

In this account, the disruption of old fixities is felt to be at once exciting yet unsettling. For Tóibín, the master narrative of Irish resistance and rebellion evoked by the bare dates 1798 and 1916 is not a matter of mere words on a page, but is 'vital', a 'part of all our lives', with an intense local resonance. It has also always been there, as taken-for-granted as the rising of the sun: an ideological narrative that works to naturalize the cultural meanings that make a world, and make the self. To be brought up in this particular location, Wexford, with its particular history, is to come to know oneself as formed by and located within a cultural geography of places, names and stories through which the present is connected to the past. This vital connection is remade for a new generation through a range of interlocking cultural practices and representations: school history, local 'lore', the grandfather's personal memories and the material culture of the area, including historical artefacts 'brought in' from the private spaces of family history to be shared in the public space of the museum.

Responding to the 'strangely liberating' new possibilities opened up by revisionist historical scholarship is felt to be a dynamic and emotive process, not a calmly rational one. It involves oscillations and internal conflicts between different positions within subjectivity, different facets of identity. Tóibín moves from being 'the guy in the library' – the intellectual free-thinker, eager for new perspectives and for waging Moody's 'mental war of liberation from servitude to the myth' – to being 'my grandfather's grand-son', identified once again as a member of the cross-generational community defined and constructed by the traditional narrative, the national imaginary. Crucially in Tóibín's account, this 'reactivation' of a subjective identification that he believed himself to have superseded stems from an encounter with the hostile misrecognition of the other: the representation of Catholic rebels as 'the mob'. One of the most important functions of the heroic narrative of Irish nationalist history was precisely to combat such hostility and denigra-tion, by generating a countervailing subjective pride to empower – psychi-cally and politically – those who 'knew all the songs'. The unwonted pull of a familiar identification described here is not something peculiar to Tóibín: it is the way that subjectivity works.

Tóibín's story helps to explain why those who remain in the grip of 'popular misconceptions' often fail to be suitably enlightened by 'objective' historical scholarship. As Moody himself acknowledged: 'Irish history has made great and unprecedented advances in the past forty years [since the launch of the *Irish Historical Review* in 1938], but the effect on the public mind appears to be disappointingly slow.'[25] However, it is also the case that historians and their scholarship are also constructed subjectively in relation to accounts of the past, and do not inhabit an entirely rational and objective space outside of these complex cross-currents and identifications, but are themselves partisan – often explicitly so. Take, for example, Moody's con-clusion, in his critique of Orange 'mythology': 'The discrepancies between orangeism as viewed by a historian and as presented by orange spokesmen are both obvious and profound, and are of the essence of the Ulster predi-cament.'[26] But what, in that case, are we to make of a figure such as David Jones? Jones briefly became famous as the press officer for Portadown District Orange Lodge during the 'Drumcree stand-off' of July 1998, when the world's news media witnessed a week-long violent confrontation between the British Army and RUC, and thousands of loyalists intent on forcing a banned Orange Order parade through the nationalist Garvaghy Road area in Portadown, sparking sustained loyalist violence against Catholics through-out Northern Ireland.[27]

Jones was also a co-author of *The Orange Citadel: A History of Orangeism in Portadown*, a 110–page booklet published in 1996 to com-memorate the bicentenary of the founding of the first Orange lodge in the district, which provides a carefully researched account of the development and changing fortunes of the Order situated in the context of political and cultural conflict in the local area.[28] As well as being both an Orange activist and a historian, Jones is, like Colm Tóibín, his 'grandfather's grandson'. Interviewed in June 1998, at the height of the build-up to the contested Drumcree parade, he explained its personal significance by telling his own boyhood memories of walking behind his father, who was caretaker at Carleton Orange Hall for forty-two years and took part every year, while local residents shouted greetings: 'No-one was much bothered then. People used to come out and watch us. There was no trouble. But Sinn Féin has got hold of it now. It is orchestrating the opposition, and residents are intimidated into demonstrating against us.'[29] Jones, however, was not the only Orange protester interviewed at Drumcree to remember in this way. Eighteen-year-old Richard Abernathy gave a similar explanation: 'My grandfather's father was in the Loyal Orange Lodge, my grandfather was in it, and so am I. All in the same Lodge. It's like a family, so it is.'[30] Jones's past–present comparison was echoed by others, including the Reverend William McCrea, who also 'remembered':

> This march has been going on for 200 years. It's amazing that only since 1995 . . . has it become confrontational. I was brought up in an area where there has always been a majority of the Roman Catholic community. The Roman Catholics came and watched the parade. Now they are not allowed to. The IRA threatens them.[31]

While such claims about peaceful parades are not borne out by the archival research that informs *The Orange Citadel*, which tells a long history of violent confrontations triggered by the loyalist marching season, Jones's personal memories are articulated in terms of a shared, collective, loyalist 'mythology' of the recent past. Nevertheless, the historical subjectivity evinced in his case is woven from various strands and aspects of being, such that the grandfather's grandson, the partisan activist and the historical researcher coexist with and feed into one another, despite the tensions and contradictions between them.

Nor is partisanship the provenance exclusively of historians grounded on so-called 'extremist' political positions, like Orangeism. Despite the claims made by liberal–rationalist 'revisionist' historians working within the myth–history paradigm – such as Joseph Lee, who has argued that the Irish Historical Society 'took history out of politics'[32] – their idea of history, and the kinds of narratives as well as critiques that they produce, do have a politics. For both Moody and Walker, for example, the 'realistic' view recommended by 'objective' historical research is to accept the 'historical fact' of partition. The political aspiration to end partition, remove the border and create a new, sovereign, 'united Ireland' is reduced by Moody to a myth of 'absolute predestinarian nationalism'; the implication being that there is no rational, historically-informed basis for that aspiration. Similarly, Walker identifies the anti-partitionist views expressed in 1993 by the Irish *Taioseach* and Fianna Fáil leader Albert Reynolds – that 'history has created a border in Ireland which has outlived its usefulness' and which constitutes a 'last residual problem in Anglo-Irish relations derived from history'[33] – as an instance of the 'narrow' and 'obsessive' use of the past associated with myth, lacking any grasp of the realities of the early 1990s.[34]

The belief of Unionist politicians that 'the struggle between the two major groups in Northern Ireland has been continuous since early times' is also criticized by Walker as promoting a view that makes it 'difficult to see a resolution to our problems: either they will continue for ever, or there will be a complete victory of one side or the other'; which 'leaves little room for compromise'.[35] The compromise that Walker prefers is, presumably, a peaceful settlement within Northern Ireland that preserves partition. The main obstacle to this is seen as 'the paramilitaries, Orange and Green', on whom the 'influence of the past is especially strong'.[36] However, Walker's own use of history also serves a political project, that of weakening the narratives which inform these positions, and offering alternatives to them. It also leads him to embrace the initiation of the peace process towards the end of 1993 as 'the beginning of a movement away from the past';[37] as if it were possible, in the words of the British Secretary of State for Northern Ireland Sir Patrick Mayhew, to 'turn the key upon history and go forward into new uplands free from the burdens of the history of the past'.[38] Walker's reluctance to acknowledge the politics of his own historical practice stems directly from the basic assumptions of the myth–history dichotomy.

Cultural traditions

The second of the two main paradigms shaping recent understandings of the past–present relation within the Irish conflict is the 'cultural traditions' model. This has been predominant particularly in the arena of cultural policy in Northern Ireland, with its strong connection to the British and Irish Governments' strategies for conflict resolution and political peace-making; and in the arena of media coverage of the conflict in Britain and Ireland. This centrality can be traced back to the shift in Irish nationalist political thinking during the early 1980s, articulated in the report of the New Ireland Forum of 1984–85, which acknowledged the existence and validity of Unionist and British culture and identity in the North as a distinct 'tradition' warranting respect and recognition. The Forum promoted the idea of 'parity of esteem' between the 'two traditions' of Unionism and Irish nationalism, advocating by this a liberal politics of mutual recognition and the tolerance – even celebration – of cultural difference (later termed 'diversity') as the basis for dialogue to resolve disagreement and conflict. This way of thinking also furnished the Irish Government with the intellectual and political framework within which demands could be made for reciprocal recognition from the British Government (and the Unionists) of the 'cultural traditions', including the national symbols, modes of expression and political aspirations, of Northern nationalists. This language, and the developing consensus it facilitated between the two governments on the desirability of fostering mutual coexistence between the 'two traditions', was formalized in the Anglo-Irish Agreement of 1985, which granted the Irish Government an input into the affairs of Northern Ireland for the first time and consolidated a process of inter-governmental co-operation on which the peace process was built.

The concept of 'cultural tradition' used in these developments was informed by critical debates in Northern Ireland in the 1970s and early 1980s among educationalists, cultural practitioners and policy-makers who sought solutions to communal division, polarization and sectarianism through cultural intervention. Among them was the history teacher Jack Magee, a pioneering advocate of reform in the teaching of history in Irish schools so as to provide pupils with the critical capacity to question the 'view of past history' that they had 'acquired as part of their political and religious experience'.[39] Writing in 1970, Magee argued that, in shying away from Irish history 'as to some extent a subversive activity', schools in the North left unchallenged the 'national or sectarian prejudices' of

> two groups of people who were prisoners of history: two groups whose present attitudes were motivated by a vision of the past in which they were nearly always in conflict, and in which their interests rarely, if ever, seemed to coin-cide . . . Protestants and Catholics, unionists and nationalists . . . had a com-pletely unbalanced view of the past, and because of the manner in which their mythology had been acquired, had no knowledge at all of the historical basis of each other's point of view.[40]

While Magee's analysis was grounded in the myth–history paradigm, three emphases in this early paper point towards the rather different 'cultural tra-ditions' approach. Firstly, his interest in 'the manner in which their mythol-ogy had been acquired' drew attention to the 'variety of sources' of popular historical knowledge out of which those myths had been constructed, per-petuated and made available to young people. Secondly, he construes the role of 'history' in developing a more critical consciousness, not in terms of estab-lishing a singular truthful narrative from which the partial and 'unbalanced' mythologies may be judged, but as a process of dialogue between different perspectives informed by different narratives, thereby nurturing the real-ization that 'there is generally more than one side to an argument', and that 'those from whom they differ are the products of their environment as they themselves are conditioned by their own'.[41] Thirdly, Magee advo-cated (quoting Kenneth Jamison, then director of the Northern Ireland Arts Council) 'a rediscovery rather than continuing rejection of Ulster's tradi-tional culture' to give 'a real sense of identity. . . [and] unity . . . to Ulster people', such that, as Magee himself puts it, 'young people . . . will be made conscious of the contributions which all groups have made to its history'.[42]

From the later 1970s, the concept of 'culture' became increasingly influ-ential as a way of conceptualizing differences between social groups as the outcome of practices – like religious upbringing, schooling, rural customs, the production of television programmes – through which particular kinds of consciousnesses and identities were created. One influential formulation of the relation between culture and politics in Ireland was that of F.S.L. Lyons, who argued in a series of lectures given in 1978 that the conflict stemmed ultimately from 'a diversity of ways of life which are deeply embedded in the past and of which the much-advertised political differences are but the outward and visible sign'.[43] 'Tradition' was the term used to underline the centrality of the past–present relationship within cultural processes. In 1983, the Two Traditions Group, launching a 'debate on the role of cultural traditions in Northern Ireland's political problems',[44] connected these ideas to notions of collective identity:

> A major factor in the continuing violence and instability in Northern Ireland is the existence of two traditions, two cultures in Ireland, both of which have failed to accept the legitimacy of the other's cultural, social and religious identity. In part the problem in Northern Ireland is a question of identity: one group, the Ulster–British, who feel British as well as Irish, is intent on keeping the constitutional link with Great Britain; the other, the Ulster–Irish, aspire to participate fully in a culture and society which are Irish and which find political expression in an Irish state. Reinforcing this question of identity is a difference in religion . . . Dialogue between the groups is impeded because neither has recognised the legitimacy of the other's point of view: compromise is thus impossible, and continuing violence . . . has simply reinforced established attitudes.[45]

Anticipating the formulations of the New Ireland Forum, the Two Traditions Group advocated the development of a 'multicultural society' enabling peaceful coexistence, based on 'acceptance of the legitimacy of these distinctive traditions and cultures', the fostering of 'respect and tolerance for each other', and the 'search for . . . understanding and comprehension of both traditions and cultures (their affinities and differences)'.[46]

Such thinking chimed with parallel debates in the field of 'community relations' which led to the creation in 1987 of a new Central Community Relations Unit attached to the office of the British Secretary of State for Northern Ireland, to spearhead initiatives for improving relations between the 'two communities' as an element in the Government's strategy for conflict resolution.[47] Indeed, from the late 1980s, 'traditions', 'cultures' and 'communities'[48] became almost interchangeable terms in a pluralist discourse institutionalized in the close relationship between officers and civil servants of the British administration and a range of leading Northern Irish academics and cultural professionals. In 1988 these links issued in the formation of the Cultural Traditions Group as a forum for critical and historical debate, and for the development of new practical initiatives and opportunities for exchange, dialogue and education across the 'communal divide', based on 'a general acceptance of the validity of all cultural traditions, the importance of tradition in the creation of a sense of identity, [and] the importance of group identity as a means of self-fulfilment'.[49] To that end, in 1989 and 1990 the Group organized two conferences, 'Varieties of

Irishness' and 'Varieties of Britishness', which set about deconstructing the simple binary stereotypes shaping reductionist and essentialist conceptions of identity, by demonstrating the internal complexity and 'variety' within each of the main 'cultural traditions', and the identities constituted by them. This was itself a historical project involving the recovery of forgotten or marginalized 'traditions' that also opened up questions about the 'plural' and 'hybrid' formation of identities.[50]

While acknowledging difference and diversity 'in a non-threatening way', however, the ethos of the Cultural Traditions Group was not entirely inclusive. The challenge it faced was expressed as a question by its first Chair, James Hawthorne: 'Can we set aside the militant, the vilifiers, the violent and the bigoted so ordinary decent people can accept pluralism?'[51] The deployment of ideological categories of this kind points to the role envisaged for such work in constructing a political space for cross-community recognition and reconciliation on the basis of particular terms of inclusion and exclusion. By 1990, the Group had been incorporated into the new Community Relations Council (CRC), a publicly funded but 'independent organization, to promote better community relations and the recognition of cultural diversity in Northern Ireland. The CRC has no view on what form a political solution should take but regards the development of tolerance and mutual understanding within the community as a fundamental part of the process leading to a solution.'[52] Its primary function was to act as a conduit for British government funding to projects and organizations, especially at local level, judged to have a contribution to make to this agenda, and thus to the goals of reconciliation and conflict resolution between the 'two warring communities'. Interestingly, funding has been available through the CRC for 'single tradition' as well as 'cross-community' historical projects, on the argument that discovering and representing the history and traditions of one's own community, within this overarching framework, is a means of promoting 'self-esteem' in people and communities scarred by violence.[53] In this, the work of the CRC has extended into the peace process since 1994, on the basis that conflict rooted in social divisions, including violent conflict, will continue during the period of conflict resolution and that its eradication requires a concentration of effort on those 'feeling forgotten, abandoned and powerless'.[54]

During the 1990s the cultural traditions agenda widened out from its original focus on *two* traditions to encompass diversity. As Paul Sweeney of the Cultural Traditions Group put it: '[I]t's too narrow to say there are two communities in Northern Ireland. My own experience is that there are literally hundreds, maybe thousands of communities, all with their own definition of their own community and their own sense of place.'[55] Nevertheless, such moves towards pluralism are rooted in efforts to reduce the effects of sectarian polarization so as to *manage* conflict and its resolution. In this sense, the cultural traditions paradigm has been and remains closely related to the long-standing ideological stance on Northern Ireland promoted by the

British State since the earliest years of the Troubles, in which the conflict is represented as the result of ages-old ethnic antagonism between two polarized communities – Protestant and Catholic – each fuelled by atavistic religious passions and enmities. These two 'tribes' are held equally to blame for the repeated eruption of violence – 'each side is as bad as the other' – with the role of the British State and its armed forces constructed as that of the honest broker, holding the ground between them in an attempt to keep the peace and resolve the conflict.

The 'two tribes' ideology is a product of the longer history of British rule in Ireland. It can be traced back to the early years of the Union when the new State of the UK, having made use of Orange Volunteers to suppress the United Irishmen's rebellion of 1798, turned against the Orange Order in the 1820s for disturbing the peace, and attempted, through legislation regulating processions, to outlaw 'sectarian' activity by both Protestant and Catholic organizations. A similar strategy of representation justified the intervention of the British Army on the streets of Northern Ireland in August 1969 and, once installed, its activities as support to the civil authorities in their efforts to keep the peace. This representation of the conflict disguised the fact that the primary concern of the British armed forces was to quell the nationalist – and, increasingly, Republican – insurgency against the Unionist-run Northern Ireland statelet. The 'two tribes' narrative furnished the British State with a powerful ideological weapon that instituted and furthered its particular definition of Irish *realpolitik*, while obscuring in its own interest a more informed understanding of the political and social realities of conflict on the ground.

It is on this same basis that renewed efforts at conflict resolution were made from the mid-1980s, complemented now by the cultural traditions agenda promoted by the Irish Government. There is evident continuity between the language of the New Ireland Forum report and of the Anglo-Irish Agreement in 1984–85, and that of the Downing Street Declaration, establishing the principles on which a peace process would be conducted, in December 1993. The Declaration speaks of 'the ending of divisions [which] can come about only through the agreement and co-operation of the people, North and South, representing both traditions in Ireland'; and defines the role of the British Government as being 'to encourage, facilitate and enable the achievement of such agreement . . . through a process of dialogue and co-operation based on full respect for the rights and identities of both traditions'.[56]

The 'two tribes' narrative has also provided the dominant paradigm in news and current affairs coverage of the Troubles from the early days of the conflict right through the peace process. This is due partly to its intersection with the professional ethos of journalists committed to an ideology of 'balanced reporting' as the cornerstone of liberal media practice, but is primarily an effect of over thirty years of the propaganda war conducted by the British military and (after the imposition of Direct Rule from London in 1972) by the Northern Ireland Office of the British Government, for which the media has been a key arena in the 'battle for hearts and minds'.[57]

As a framework for understanding how the past–present relationship functions in the Irish conflict, the cultural traditions approach is open to three main criticisms. Firstly, in its emphasis on communal relations and forms of cultural expression in Northern Ireland, it defines the conflict in a way that makes no reference to the British State as one – some would say, the main – active participant. In theoretical terms, this paradigm lacks an analysis both of the effects of state power in structuring the field of representations of the past, and of the spaces in which alternative narratives may be articulated and mobilized.[58] Secondly, it tends to naturalize, as a 'tradition' to be recognized and validated, what historians like Moody and Walker see as 'myths' to be deconstructed. If all 'traditions' are equally legitimate and their representations of the past equally valid, we find ourselves in a postmodern world of relativism in which any notion of historical truth or ethical discrimination has been abandoned. Furthermore, in its general acceptance of the perspectives and understandings promoted within any particular cultural tradition, this paradigm also tends to validate traditional claims that the past–present relationship is one of continuity, rather than to question the cultural processes through which such claims are advanced by agents who are actively constructing a particular sense of the past to further present-day concerns. As Raymond Williams argued, all traditions are in practice 'selective traditions', formed by the drawing and redrawing of genealogical lines to this rather than that ancestor and involving active reinterpretations of meaning from one generation to the next; a process characterized not by the handing-on of authorized conceptions from the past to the present, but by conflicting understandings of that past derived from ideological contestation of a present-day social order.[59] Arguably, two-traditions thinking may, as a result of this naturalization of 'tradition', have contributed to fostering and stimulating the very cultures of sectarianism that it ostensibly seeks to eradicate, by entrenching a 'two tribes' ethos that gave rise to the 'culture wars' of the 1980s. Thirdly, although the cultural traditions paradigm does address the importance of 'the past' to the formation of collective identity, it shares the limitations of the myth–history paradigm regarding questions of subjectivity, and similarly provides no critical account of the reasons for, and processes by which, individuals and social groups identify themselves with particular narratives of the past.

Cultural studies and the theory of memory

A growing literature now addresses the past–present relationship in the Irish conflict from the perspective of memory. These works constitutes an emergent third paradigm, part of the general turn towards 'memory studies' that has taken place across the humanities and the social sciences since the late 1980s. In Ireland, the earliest uses of the term 'popular memory', by Irish historians such as Brendan Bradshaw and Alvin Jackson, tended to see it as a synonym for 'myth', and as such reflected a lack of conceptual clarification and theoretical rigour about how cultural processes work in the formation of a popular memory.[60] This was also the case in the media debate about Jordan's film *Michael Collins*, referred to above, in which notions of 'popular memory' were used, for example, by Joe Lee to discuss the relation between history-teaching in schools and the transmission of – or failure to transmit – a sense of the national past in the culture of the Irish Republic.[61]

During the 1990s, Irish memory studies was stimulated by controversy over the failure of the Irish State to organize a national commemoration marking the seventy-fifth anniversary of the Easter Rising. In a collection of essays, *Revising the Rising* (1991), leading cultural critics, including Seamus Deane, Declan Kiberd and Edna Longley, launched a debate about the relationship between commemorative events, the politics of popular memory and the national question.[62] Further critical reflection on these issues accompanied major popular–cultural commemorations, in 1995, marking the passage of 150 years since the onset of the Great Famine and, in 1998, the bicentenary of the 1798 United Irishmen's Rebellion.[63] Some of this work has tapped into the rich vein of Irish folk studies, drawing on models for understanding the production and transmission of collective memory in the historical anthropology of oral culture.[64] Further important work on the politics of public commemoration has addressed the histories of particular events, and traditions and their role in the construction of social identities and in sectarian conflict: notably, Jane Leonard's studies of Great War commemoration; Ian McBride's investigation of the Great Siege of Derry; and the essays in McBride's edited collection *History and Memory in Modern Ireland* (2001).[65] The conflicts of the 1990s over controversial Orange parades, most notably at Drumcree, have stimulated anthropological studies by Neil Jarman and Dominic Bryan of parading ritual and its reproduction of memory, which have challenged Orange claims about the unbroken continuity of tradition and its fixed, homogeneous significance for participants.[66]

Much of this work over the last decade has been based on the concept of 'collective memory' developed by the French sociologist Maurice Halbwachs. This shifts attention away from the psychological memory of individuals to focus on the collective frameworks of remembrance established by social groups to formulate, preserve and transmit common understandings about their significant past. For Halbwachs, such frameworks structure the personal recollections of individuals.[67] In Irish memory studies, however, it is his emphasis on the collective dimensions of memory which has predominated, in critical analyses concerned primarily with public forms of commemoration and remembrance. Little critical attention has been paid to the dimension of personal memory, one notable exception being Leonard's investigation of the remembered experiences of Irish Volunteers returning home from the British Army after the Armistice in 1918, and their exclusion from public cultures of commemoration as these polarized under the onset of the Irish War of Independence.[68] This lacuna has remained despite the proliferation since 1994 of personal stories of the current Troubles, mostly in the form of collections published without accompanying critical reflection, conceived as contributions to peace-making in their own right.[69]

The theory of memory used in this book explicitly addresses questions of subjectivity, the interrelations between the personal and the collective, and the central role in memory formation played by the national state as it interacts with forms of remembrance emerging from civil society. My thinking about these issues is grounded on concepts of 'popular memory' and 'war memory' developed in my previous work, in relation to wider debates about oral history and the relationship of personal life stories to broader public cultures. These debates have incorporated perspectives from British cultural studies, from the international oral history movement, and from the emergent field of memory studies.[70] The theory of popular memory was developed initially by the Popular Memory Group at the Birmingham Centre for Contemporary Cultural Studies, of which I was a member, during the 1980s.[71] It was shaped by the Centre's characteristic theoretical concerns with cultural representation, conflicting ideologies and the historical construction of subjectivities, and laid emphasis on the popular cultural politics whereby collective and personal meanings of the past, in its relation to the present, have been produced and contested.[72] Competing discourses and forms of representation are understood to mediate popular memory according to their various conventions, constituting a diverse range of memory texts. These are opened to investigation by methods of formal textual interpretation to establish how they structure the significance of the past–present relation, and construct a subjective position of intelligibility from which sense can be made of the 'past' by readers, viewers and participants. Analysis is concerned also with the ways in which these productions of memory are organized and circulated socially, and with their interactions within a whole cultural field of representations of the past, as structured by relations of power.

These ideas originated in the Group's essay 'Popular memory: theory, politics, method' (1982), which connected two previously separate debates: one concerned with oral history and popular, community-based, autobiographical writing; the other with media representations of the past, especially in film and on television. While the Group reads both as constructions of popular memory, the visibility and familiarity of their narratives differ considerably. These differences are theorized in terms of a distinction between 'public representations' and 'private memory'. The former term refers to those representations of the past that 'win access to' and 'achieve centrality' within the public domain, where their institutional propagation by the national and the local state, the culture industries or the public media ensure their scope to make public meanings for vast audiences.[73] Private memory, by contrast, refers to 'the more privatized sense of the past which is generated within a lived culture' and circulates among particular social groups 'in the course of everyday life'.[74] The dynamic interaction between *public* and *private* aspects of popular memory is understood in Gramscian–Marxist terms as a hegemonic process of ideological domination, resistance and contestation through which 'dominant memory' and its 'oppositional forms' are produced: 'Private memories cannot . . . be readily unscrambled from the effects of dominant historical discourses. It is often these that supply the very terms by which a private history is thought through.'[75] By the same token, the power of dominant memories depends not simply on their public visibility but also on their capacity to connect with and articulate publicly those existing popular memories which currently organize a sense of the 'collective and shared' past within lived culture; giving public representation to particular popular conceptions, while actively silencing, marginalizing and holding 'to the level of private remembrance' those meanings which are to be subordinated or excluded.[76] Cultural contestation between competing memories occurs as an element in ideological conflict centred on discontents and aspirations in the present, and at the level of subjectivity, in securing the sense of continuity between past and present necessary to both collective and personal identities.

The explanatory potential of popular memory theory as a basis for the study of war memory was demonstrated and developed by the Australian oral historian Alistair Thomson in *Anzac Memories* (1994). This draws on the ideas of the Popular Memory Group to study the hegemonic power of the Anzac legend, that founding myth of the forging of white Australian nationhood in the 'baptism of fire' undergone by the Australian and New Zealand Army Corps during the First World War. Based on oral history interviews with Great War veterans, and initially conceived as an 'oppositional history' of working-class experiences excluded from and forgotten in public memory, Thomson's study explores the complex 'entanglement' of their private and personal memories with the public legend made of their lives.[77] The personal memories of the veterans are understood as in process, rather than as immutably fixed, and grasped in relation both to the shifting forms and meanings of the public legend and to the shifting identities of the men themselves at different stages of their lives' course. By demonstrating that veterans of varying political affiliations 'had adopted and used the Anzac legend because it was resonant and useful in their own remembering',[78] Thomson shows how individual subjectivity is negotiated in relation to public memory. In detailed life-story work with three particular individuals, he explores how, as each 'has struggled to compose memories of their war . . . they have drawn upon public narratives of Anzac that have helped them to articulate experience in particular ways'.[79] While these 'negotiations between public and private sense' worked differently for each individual, to the extent that the public narratives 'have recognised key aspects of the diggers' experience', the 'Anzac legend has . . . helped many veterans to compose a past that they can live with'.[80] By the same token, 'experiences and understandings that are not recognised and that cannot be articulated through the public narratives are displaced or marginalised within individual memory', resulting in alienation, silence and 'internalised trauma'.[81] The subjective purchase of these dominant public narratives, as widely recognized and validated constructions of Australian identity, have offered particular forms of personal identity – including masculinity – not only to the veterans themselves, but also to those who welcomed their return, mourned their loss and commemorated their contribution to the story of Australia.

My own subsequent work within the popular memory paradigm complements Thomson's understanding of the subjective processes of identification, and extends his use of the concept of 'composure' which establishes a link between the composing or fashioning of narratives and efforts to secure a stable sense of self. In my book *Soldier Heroes: British Adventure, Empire and the Imagining of Masculinities* (1994), the Popular Memory Group's emphasis on the cognitive power of national, public memory is extended into an investigation of the emotional and psychic purchase of its forms. Use is made of psychoanalytic concepts to theorize the existence of a psychic dimension to remembering and forgetting, located in the internal world of the psyche, which both affects and is affected by cultural formations of memory. I argue that the soldiers' stories centred on British military heroes, stories that were among the most widely circulating and powerful cultural narratives of the nineteenth and twentieth centuries, provide masculine figures for identification that are 'subjectively entered into' and may become internalized within the psyche as the basis for the composure and social recognition of personal identities.[82] When internalized in this way, 'the national past lives on . . . in the psychic lives of succeeding generations', providing 'latent sources of psychic energy' which may be tapped subsequently by political mobilizations, as in British national–popular support for wars ranging from the suppression of the Indian Mutiny to the Second World War, the Falklands–Malvinas conflict and the Gulf War of 1991.[83]

My understanding of popular memory has been further developed through collaborative work with T.G. Ashplant and Michael Roper. In our essay 'The politics of war memory and commemoration', we argue that, in international debates in this field,

> the most compelling 'academic' research . . . [has] engage[d] critical theory and analysis in a . . . dialogue with 'living memory'; that is, with cultural producers, political and civil rights activists, and those who have perpetrated military violence and been affected by it; for all of whom the remembering and forgetting of war is not an object of disinterested enquiry but a burning issue at the very core of present-day conflicts over forms of the state, social relations, and subjectivity.[84]

In developing a model to explain how the remembering and commemoration of war is organized and contested in the cultural politics of any specific context, Ashplant, Dawson and Roper integrate popular memory theory and approaches from two other major paradigms within which the historical study of war memory has been framed. On the one hand, the 'state-centred approach', associated with Eric Hobsbawm's concept of 'invented traditions' and Benedict Anderson's idea of the nation as an 'imagined community', has been concerned primarily with 'the role of war commemoration within the political project of the nation-state', as a means of 'binding its citizens into a collective national identity'. On the other, the 'social agency approach', epitomized in Jay Winter's work on cultural responses to the First World War, emphasizes, by contrast, 'the work of remembrance performed by the agencies of civil society' and is primarily interested in 'the role of . . . [war] commemoration in translating individual grief into public mourning for the dead', stimulated by 'desire for psychological reparation of loss, in response to the traumatic impact of death in war'.[85]

Ashplant et al. propose a combination of perspectives from all three paradigms, so as to create 'a more complex, integrated account of the interacting processes that link the individual, civil society, and the state':

> This requires a redefinition of what constitutes the 'politics' of war memory and commemoration . . . [which is] capable of embracing the operations of power in civil society as well as in the state; of recognizing the existence of a cultural politics surrounding representation and meaning-making; and of tracing the effects of these processes and conflicts from the social domain into that of the psyche, where they constitute a politics of subjectivity.[86]

This has proved particularly useful in developing the analyses in my two case studies of memory in the Irish Troubles in Parts II and III of this book – concerned with Bloody Sunday and the cultural memory of the Border Protestants – since it allows distinctions to be made between the multiple levels at which remembering and forgetting are at work, while bringing into focus their complicated interactions and effects; thereby grasping more fully the complexity of memory formation during the conflict and in the conflict resolution process.

In this model, the making, circulating and contesting of the collective narratives of war memory are seen as a complex hegemonic process that operates within distinct 'socio-political spaces', or 'social arenas', each constituting a different type of collectivity:

> These range, in social breadth and political importance, from the networks of families or kinship groups, through those of communities of geography or interest, to the public sphere of nation-states and transnational power blocs.[87]

These various types of collectivity are distinguished in terms of their relative scope: 'The articulation of memory involves struggles to extend, or alternatively to limit, the arenas within which specific memories are able to circulate, and hence make claims for recognition.'[88] Within the more intimate face-to-face groupings ('ranging from family and kinship networks and gatherings of old comrades to local communities and interest groups'), individuals who have undergone a common or comparable experience – like the survivors of Bloody Sunday, or the Unionists subjected to the IRA's campaign of terror on the Border – exchange personal stories and 'begin to formulate a shared language and identify common themes'. In this process, certain aspects of the personal remembering of individuals such as Leslie Finlay from the Border area near Castlederg, Co. Tyrone, or Kay Duddy from the Bogside in Derry – particularly those which resonate with the collective experience of their community – come to be recognized, articulated and represented; while other aspects of personal memory may be excluded or suppressed from the collective story, and 'may never be articulated in any wider arena' or achieve social expression and recognition.[89]

The 'shared/common memories'[90] of such a group circulate within relatively *private* social arenas, and recognition remains restricted and contained within the group itself. In order to secure more extensive *public* recognition, group members must create agencies capable of recasting its narratives into a new, integrated, collective form and projecting this into a 'public arena' where it speaks to others beyond the immediate circle of memory.[91] Such agencies include grassroots organizations such as the Border victims' group West Tyrone Voice, the Portadown District Orange Lodge, the Bloody Sunday Justice Campaign and the Ardoyne Commemoration Project. Shared or common memories 'enter the public arena when they are articulated in some cultural or artistic form, or into a political narrative'. This may either be aligned 'within the existing framework of official memory' – in Northern Ireland, a construct of the British State – or fashion a public alternative to it, as a subordinated, marginalized or (in the case of Irish Republicanism) directly oppositional 'sectional memory'. As in the making of common/shared, memory, a process of selection, representation and transformation is at work here. A public narrative of collective memory 'shapes the individual and common/shared memories from which it is composed, selecting some and excluding others, highlighting key themes and framing them within its preferred narrative tropes. Only when memories have been woven together into a narrative which is both widely held and publicly expressed do they have the potential to secure political effects', through the competing political narratives of Irish nationalism and Unionism.[92]

For Ashplant et al., a politics of war memory and commemoration operates within all of these arenas, both private and public, as 'a diverse range of social groups, as well as individuals'[93] struggle to produce or rework narratives of collective remembrance. Tensions, contradictions and the potential for conflicts between existing and emergent collective narratives exist at each stage of the articulation process. At the apex of power, overarching and exerting influence within this whole, complex process of remembrance and commemoration, is the 'dominant national narrative' that articulates 'official memory' at the level of the state:[94] in partitioned Ireland, that of the British State in the North and the Republic of Ireland in the South. The making of war memories 'requires a constant engagement – whether negotiation or contestation – with the nation-state, its agencies and its

narratives'.[95] These function to subordinate alternative public memories
of war, but in so doing they may 'have the effect of accommodating,
constraining, reshaping or silencing [not only] sectional, [but also]
shared/common and even individual memories'.[96] The subjective and
psychic implications of these narratives range from their 'capacity to touch
off popular identifications' and channel 'individual psychic investments' into
forms of collective mobilization,[97] to their emotional efficacy with respect to
mourning and their role in the cross-generational transmission of cultural
memories to younger people without direct personal experience of the
remembered events.

The model of war memory that emerges out of this synthesis of paradigms
enables analysis of the social production of particular representations of the
past, of their determining factors in specific ideological and political conditions and of their complex effects. The strength of this approach lies in its
capacity to grasp the hegemonic contestation that occurs within and between
these various forms and practices, through which particular memories are
installed at the centre of a cultural world at the expense of others which are
marginalized and forgotten; and to illuminate the profound psychic and cultural purchase of these narratives about the past. It recognizes the power of
memory to construct our deepest senses of ourselves, our world and our relations with others; and to mobilize and legitimize the most intense social and
political energies, irrespective of whether its constructions of the past are
true in an objective and verifiable sense. It suggests that memories are not
simply *myths*, to be dispelled or transformed by the reasoning of historians;
and indeed that historians themselves are necessarily implicated in, rather
than detached from, these processes. This is not to imply that the sense of a
past is always or necessarily fixed, determined by existing commemorative
traditions and collective narratives. These cultural formations of memory
themselves undergo transformation, as shifting products of the very processes of change that they register and recall.

The understanding of the contested memories of the Troubles developed
in this book derives from these theories of popular memory and the politics
of war memory. This work provides the theoretical framework shaping my
empirical inquiry into the various agencies (those of the State, civil society,
'private' social groups and individuals) involved in articulating memories of
the Troubles from above and from below; the narratives in which competing memories are represented; the hegemonic transactions and negotiations
that occur in the contest between them; the arenas in which they seek recognition for their memories; and the master narratives (of British imperialism,
Ulster Unionism and Irish nationalism) that legitimize their voices.
Theoretical emphasis on the State brings into focus the effects of partition
on formations of memory in Ireland, where the competing narratives of
nationalism and Unionism each became instituted as hegemonic official
memories in the Irish Free State and Republic and Northern Ireland, respectively, which have continued to clash with each other, while in each case

becoming the focus of internal contestation by counter-memories arising from within their very differently organized civil societies. While the book's primary concern is with the Northern Ireland State, its analysis of memory in the Troubles is located within the shaping context of these partitioned pasts in Ireland as a whole. In examining the activities of various agents of memory in Northern Irish civil society, the book investigates the orientation of their memory work in relation to the ideological field of force centred on the State. The personal memories of individuals are read both for their congruence with themes derived from the frameworks of collective memory and for their divergence from them. The alignment of the personal with the collective is understood to be the result of an effective politics of memory as it shapes and mobilizes forms of collective identity within the conflict.

These processes of contestation over the memory of the Troubles also have a geographical dimension. As Colm Tóibín's account of popular memory in Wexford demonstrates, shared, communal remembering continues to be located within 'communities of geography',[98] all of which, as Paul Sweeney remarks, have 'their own sense of place' and spatial identity.[99] Critical understanding of conflicts over the remembered past may be further deepened, then, by integrating theories and methods developed by social anthropologists and cultural geographers to investigate the subjective identities, meanings and memories that become attached to, and invested in, the objective physical spaces of the social world. What Edward Said described as 'imaginative geography' involves the setting up of 'boundaries in our own minds' designating . . . a familiar space which is "ours" and an unfamiliar space beyond "ours" which is "theirs" '[100] – a process intrinsic to the formation of collective identities defined in opposition to others. According to the Australian cultural geographer and historian Peter Read, spatial identities, based on 'senses of belonging' in a place, develop over time as 'layers of meaning' and remembered associations accrue to a location in the course of everyday life.[101] The 'identifiable sites' formed in this way are shaped by the emotional investments made in them, but also by 'wider issues of power, group dynamics, conflicting ideologies and institutions', that affect 'both the physical appearance of places . . . and the way they are conceptualised';[102] giving rise to disputes over the possession of territory and to what Read calls 'contested attachments' to the same place.[103]

The concept of imaginative geography points to the interconnections between these cultural and political processes and the psychic and emotional dimensions of attachment and identification. Anthropologists Stewart and Strathern offer a useful conceptual clarification of these interconnected aspects when they distinguish between a 'place', that is, a 'socially meaningful and identifiable' material environment and its characteristic spaces and sites, 'to which a historical dimension is attached' through social activity; a 'cultural landscape', referring to the 'creative and imaginative' meanings and associations that are attached to a place through storytelling or practices of remembrance, enabling a community of people to orient themselves within and inhabit that place; and the 'inner landscape of the mind', an internalized sense of place formed from personal memory interwoven with elements of cultural landscape introjected within the psyche.[104]

The spatial concepts just referred to are used to inform my investigation of local, place-based forms of memory and commemoration in key locations of the Troubles, developed in Parts II and III of the book. First, though, further consideration is given to this notion of psychic 'landscapes of the mind' and their particular formation within the cultural landscapes of a conflict zone. In chapter 2, these issues are addressed in terms of the concept of *trauma*. This offers a means of theorizing the psychic dimensions of the conflict and the effects of its violence on cultural memories.

2

Trauma, memory, politics: paradoxes of the Irish peace process

Conflict resolution is a psychic as well as a political process. The profound, ongoing, emotional and psychological aftermath of the war over Northern Ireland has impacted in various complex ways on the survivors, witnesses and perpetrators of violent injury or bereavement, torture and other human rights violations, in Ireland and England. This impact is felt not only by the individuals whose internal psychic worlds have been disturbed or devastated, but also at the level of family groups, social networks and whole communities – particularly in Northern Ireland, but also, less visibly, in England and the Irish Republic. These psychic realities, and their paradoxical and problematic implications for the politics of peace-making, may be brought into focus by the concept of 'trauma'. Cultural memories are always shaped by impulses towards subjective composure involving psychic defences, as well as by political imperatives. In order to understand the workings of cultural memory in the Irish Troubles, it is necessary to investigate the painful endeavour of traumatized individuals and communities to make sense of and 'come to terms with' the shocking and horrific experiences they have undergone in the course of the conflict; to reflect on the resources – and obstacles – to that endeavour afforded by existing frameworks of memory; and to examine the effects of trauma on the collective memories which articulate the political significance of the conflict.

This chapter addresses the paradoxical entwining of the psychic and the political aspects of memory in the Irish peace process. It begins by considering some of the theoretical issues involved in the use of the term 'trauma', with its insistence on the necessary interconnection between processes and effects at the level of the internal world of the psyche (such as splitting and disavowal, integration and reparation) and the social world where meanings are made or refused, stories listened to or silenced and social recognition of subjective experiences extended or denied. It goes on to examine various forms of public and personal remembering about the Irish Troubles as cultural responses to trauma, focusing on the psychic ambivalence inherent in telling and listening to traumatic narratives, the contradictory impulses to remember and to forget, as these operate within individuals and communities, and the ways in which these quandaries are exacerbated in the context of an ongoing armed conflict, where commemoration has become deeply politicized. Here, the analysis untangles the complex relations between the psychic needs of the traumatized and the politics of commemoration. This involves considering the interplay of selective recognition (of *our* trauma) and denial (of *their* trauma) apparent in the 'politics of suffering' promoted by loyalism and Republicanism in the North. Throughout, the chapter investigates the role of what may be described as state-organized forgetting within the British and Irish Governments' efforts towards 'reconciliation' and a political settlement. It concludes with a discussion of the necessary interconnection between the fullest public acknowledgement (in Britain and Ireland) of the truth about the traumatic past, a viable process of reparative remembering, and the achievement of a just and peaceful settlement to the conflict.

Trauma, reconciliation and the Irish past

The Irish historical past is often described as 'traumatic'. The sixteenth-century plantations, the 1641 Rebellion, the Union with Britain, the Famine, the Great War, the War of Independence and the Civil War have all been referred to as traumas,[1] as have the Troubles since 1969. In nationalist history-writing and popular memory, from the nineteenth century down to the present, the experience of trauma has defined the essence of the story of Ireland as a narrative of oppression and suffering inflicted on the Irish people by English and British colonialism over eight centuries.[2] This interpretation of Ireland's past is less often recognized in England; nor is it common to see its account of a traumatic history as one that embraces Britain, too. The possibility of recognizing a traumatic element in the imperial mission was largely precluded by British colonial discourse which construed the narrative of Empire as an heroic adventure to civilize the world.[3] The imperial narrative denied the validity of the nationalist historical perspective: in Ireland as elsewhere, palpable suffering – during the Famine, for example – was held to be the responsibility of the colonized people themselves rather than of those who governed them. Where incontestable evidence of the brutality of British rule did surface, condemnation of state actions tended to start from (rather than call into question) 'traditional assumptions that Britain stood for justice, righteousness and good laws'.[4]

This tradition of British liberalism nevertheless provided a basis for naming the traumas inflicted on others to secure the British Empire. During the Irish War of Independence (1919–21), anti-Republican reprisals directed against Irish homesteads and communities by the Black and Tans and the Auxiliaries – a vivid collective memory in Ireland to this day, as public reactions to Ken Loach's film *The Wind That Shakes The Barley* (2006) demonstrated[5] – also provoked a broadly constituted and vociferous public campaign of protest in England. A Labour Party Commission sent to investigate the condition of Ireland in November 1920 reported that 'things are being done in the name of Britain which must make her name stink in the nostrils of the whole world';[6] while in the Peace with Ireland Council, Conservatives and socialists joined with Liberals to publicize and condemn the British 'terror' and to call for an end to the conflict.[7] Among its supporters, the radical, liberal historian and journalist J.L. Hammond demanded a public enquiry into the reprisals 'on the grounds of justice to the British people' as well as to the Irish. Attempting to convey, in his reports from Ireland, his sense of the reciprocal damage caused to English civil and political culture by this war waged by the imperial State, Hammond endorsed the truth of a comment made to him by an Irishman: 'This is a tragedy . . . but it is your tragedy, not ours'.[8]

However, this has never been a popular perception of Irish history in England. When in June 1921 the Dublin Castle official Sir John Anderson wrote to the Chief Secretary for Ireland, Sir Hamar Greenwood, advocating treaty negotiations to resolve the conflict, his assessment of the public mood in England was that 'their one instinctive desire in relation to Ireland is to forget'.[9] The political settlement of 1922, granting an independent Free State in twenty-six counties while maintaining partition and the Unionist-dominated six-county statelet of Northern Ireland, created the conditions for precisely such a historical forgetting. In the post-1945 period, this tendency to forget significant dimensions of Britain's own imperial history has been exacerbated by the problematical impact on British national culture and identity of decolonization (begun in Ireland) and the loss of Empire. Metaphors of an English cultural 'amnesia' regarding the causes and development of the current Troubles are indeed widespread among Irish commentators.[10] Small wonder, in such a cultural context, that the reciprocal impact – of *Ireland's* traumatic past – on England is barely considered or understood, or that historical films like *Michael Collins* (1996) and *The Wind That Shakes The Barley* received a hostile, critical reception in the British right-wing press.

On the surface, the Downing Street Declaration that launched the peace process in December 1993, signed by British Prime Minister John Major and Irish *Taoiseach* Albert Reynolds appeared to buck this historical trend. It stated that:

> The most urgent and important issue facing the people of Ireland, North and South, and the British and Irish governments together, is to remove the causes of conflict, to overcome the legacy of history and to heal the divisions which have resulted, recognizing that the absence of a lasting and satisfactory settlement of relationships between the peoples of both islands has contributed to continuing tragedy and suffering.[11]

The Declaration tapped into a deep desire for peace in Northern Ireland and (albeit less urgently experienced) in the Irish Republic and in Britain, too. It appeared to recognize the full complexity of relations involved in the conflict, and it spoke the language of healing: 'the violence and bitter divisions which have scarred the past generation' would be ended by a process of reconciliation and agreement that would 'remove the causes of conflict' and 'overcome the legacy of history'.[12] This latter phrase, however, should give pause for thought. How was this 'legacy of history' to be understood, and how were the two governments envisaging its 'overcoming'? Closer scrutiny of statements made by the Irish and British leaders in the months leading up to and immediately following the Declaration suggests that, far from grounding the proposed settlement on a sound grasp of the magnitude and character of that historical 'tragedy and suffering', what was being advocated was, rather, a wholesale abandonment of Irish nationalist popular memory, sanctioned by the Irish Government. The Foreign Minister, Dick Spring, speaking at the Irish Labour Party conference in April 1993, argued: 'Let us be prepared to cast off the chains of history, to stop being prisoners of our upbringing.'[13] A few weeks after this, *Taoiseach* Albert Reynolds suggested: 'We are not tied up in our past. We want to move forward, to look at the changes required to ensure that both communities can live together.' In November, Reynolds echoed Spring even more closely: 'We must not be the prisoners of history.'[14] Here, the dynamic metaphor of liberation (of casting off chains, of breaking free) is detached from its traditional reference – to Irish national liberation from the historical shackles of British imperialism – and turned against that very aspiration. The nationalist narrative of liberation itself becomes the chain of bondage, while reconciliation is offered as the key to freedom.

The strategic utility of 'overcoming the legacy of history' in this way was revealed by John Major writing in the Belfast-based nationalist newspaper *Irish News* in February 1994: 'We cannot live in the past. Dreadful deeds have been done by all sides in past centuries. We should all regret that, but those of us alive today are not responsible for them. Our generation must look to the future.'[15] By consigning 'dreadful deeds' firmly to the distant past, this rhetorical appeal obscured the reality that some 3,500 people had died as a direct result of the Troubles by the time the peace process was launched. Their families and friends continue to bear the psychic scars of these deaths. Many of those responsible were not only alive as Major made his speech but were serving sentences for terrorist offences in British and Irish prisons. (These prisoners, both Republican and loyalist, were instrumental in securing political agreement to the ceasefires within their communities.) Others – like the British soldiers and their military and political superiors responsible for shooting dead fourteen unarmed Catholic civilians in Derry in January 1972, or the IRA volunteers responsible for the Enniskillen bombing that killed twelve (mostly civilian) Protestants in November 1987 – have never been called to account.

The politics of reconciliation promoted by the two governments at the beginning of the peace process was designed primarily to take the IRA out of Irish politics and to stabilize the Northern Ireland State, laying the basis for a permanent political settlement in the mutual interests of capital and state security in both the Irish Republic and Britain. In furthering this, they sought initially to ground this settlement on what may be called, borrowing Heather Goodall's phrases, an 'institutional amnesia', that is, a practice of 'state-organized forgetting' concerning the causes and consequences of the conflict.[16] If this strategy has a long history in Britain, its deployment in the Irish Republic coincides with the backlash against militant Republicanism beginning in 1972, the most violent year of the conflict, as the death toll in the North escalated. In the 1970s and 1980s, an assault on nationalist popular memory was launched in the public media, promoted by 'powerfully organized cadres within the Irish intelligentsia' and underpinned by the work of revisionist historians.[17]

This 'anti-nationalist revisionism'[18] laid the ideological foundations for a political rapprochement between the British and Irish Governments, eventually formalized in the Anglo-Irish Agreement of 1985, which sought to bring official Irish and British narratives concerning the past, the present and the future into a common alignment. Reconciliation between the communities in conflict in Northern Ireland was to be established on this basis. According to the leading revisionist historian Paul Bew, for example, the 'rejectionist culture' opposed to the principles of the Declaration was 'partly fuelled by a view of Irish history which is based in an intense degree on a sense of grievance and trauma'.[19] However, when the language of reconciliation demands a forgetting of the past, this amounts to a denial of the psychic and political realities of those communities most affected by the war. In such a situation – where violent conflict has only recently ended, remains fresh in living memory, and is liable to break out again (as happened with the ending of the IRA's ceasefire in February 1996) – the psychic and political legacies of history are not 'overcome' quite so readily. That which the language of reconciliation would smooth over, and even erase, the language of trauma insists upon. It names the ongoing legacies of the Troubles as traumatic and points to the necessity of remembering in order to go forward to any viable alternative future, while acknowledging that traumas are remembered only in the face of powerful pressures to forget.

Survivor memory and the theory of trauma

'Trauma', a word popular in everyday use, refers to the psychological impact of some violent or otherwise shocking event, producing deep-rooted effects which are difficult for those individuals affected to come to terms with. Etymology reminds us that this popular usage rests on a more specific psychoanalytic concept that in turn draws from and redefines a term in pathology derived from the Greek: since at least the mid-seventeenth century, 'trauma' referred to 'a wound, or external bodily injury; also, the condition [of shock] caused by this'. Psychoanalysis extended this to psychopathology, redefining trauma as 'a disturbing experience which affects the mind or nerves of a person so as to induce hysteria or "psychic" conditions'; and, after 1916, as 'a mental shock'.[20] In the development of Freud's thinking, the concept appears initially in his work on female hysteria, with the discovery that '[h]ysterics suffer mainly from reminiscences' of traumatic events in childhood, repressed into the unconscious.[21] During the First World War, Freud developed the concept to explain the phenomenon of 'shell-shock' or 'war neurosis', and proposed the idea of a 'repetition compulsion' operating as a means of psychic defence against the traumatic memory.[22] For Freud, repression functions to prevent the psychic trace of the determining event, and the emotional charge or 'cathexis' provoked by it, from attaining symbolization, assimilation or integration within the psyche. This 'memory' nevertheless persists in a state of disconnection within the unconscious, while the emotional cathexis associated with it finds displaced, and often delayed, symbolic expression in a range of physical symptoms, hallucinations and dreams, forms of compulsive behaviour and disturbances of speech and memory.[23]

In recent years, as the language of trauma has permeated the vocabularies of journalism, political discourse and history-writing, 'trauma' has had its reference extended to encompass psychic processes that impact on whole communities and cultures. Such usage poses the theoretical problem of how a concept developed to explain the effects of corporeal and psychic shock on the individual might be applied to a social group while avoiding the danger of ascribing to that group a collective psyche (as in, for example, 'the Catholic psyche' or 'the emotional psyche of the Unionist tradition'), as if it were *like* an individual.[24] As Michael Ignatieff has argued with respect to 'wounded' nations: 'It is perilous to extrapolate from traumatised individuals to whole societies.'[25] However, certain traumatic events do affect groups of people as such, posing threats to 'group survivorship' and compounding individual psychic distress with reactions to the distress of others similarly affected.[26] Wars, along with natural catastrophes and social disasters that give rise to large-scale loss, are a common cause of such events. In this book, 'trauma' is used as a conceptual tool to identify and describe psychic effects at the level of the individual, while also providing a means to identify and analyse collective processes for which no other language exists. My concept of the 'traumatized community' involves three proposals about the past. Firstly, it indicates a psychic dimension to the conflicts of history; a sense that profound suffering has been inflicted on and endured by a community, a people or a nation, and that both the suffering and the response to it are integral to the historical record. Secondly, the term connotes the persistence into the present of a harmful social past with disturbing legacies that remain difficult to grasp or acknowledge. Thirdly, collective trauma involves a relation of memory whereby the suffering of the past is remembered, often incompletely, by a community, in forms of cultural representation and commemoration; or, alternatively, is forgotten, rendered invisible or unspeakable by a process of cultural (as well as individual) amnesia.

Since the late 1980s, trauma has become a central category in critical analysis right across the humanities and in media discourse on world events past and present.[27] The concept of trauma underpinning much of this thinking departs from psychoanalytical theory and is grounded instead on the clinical description and treatment of 'post-traumatic shock disorder' (PTSD), a term which emerged in the USA in relation to the treatment of Vietnam war veterans and the victims of sexual abuse, first used in the American Psychiatric Association's influential handbook *Diagnostic and Statistical Manual of Mental Disorders (DSM III, 1980)*.[28] As defined here and in the subsequent edition, *DSM IV* (1994), PTSD manifests in numerous forms of psychological and bodily distress accompanied by disturbances of memory; responses to an experience of helplessness and fear induced by 'an event out of the range of ordinary human experience in which one's life or the lives of one's family are endangered'.[29] While the event occurred in the *past*, its impact has delayed, persistent and long-term psychic effects, producing symptoms that characteristically involve 'mental reliving of the trauma, the numbing of general responsiveness to the external world, and paradoxically, a state of "high arousal" or hyper-alertness to certain stimuli, particularly those which evoke reminders of the original trauma'.[30] These affect the very processes of remembering. According to a second influential model, the integrated psychological and neurological approach of Bessel van der Kolk et al., traumatic memories differ from those of ordinarily stressful events in that they may involve 'extremes of retention and forgetting'.[31]

Drawing on these ideas, life-historians Selma Leydesdorff et al. have described traumatic memories as being 'unusually vivid and unusually fragmented'.[32] Like the Holocaust survivor Primo Levi, the survivor of trauma may find that 'memory of the offense persists, as though carved in stone . . . as if at that time my mind had gone though a period of exalted receptivity, during which not a detail was lost'.[33] But they are, simultaneously, likely to find themselves subject to amnesias that may last for years, in which whole episodes of the original experience have left no memory trace that can be accessed by consciousness. This fragmentation manifests as gaps and silences in personal memory narratives, understood by some life-historians in psychoanalytical terms as corresponding to a fragmentation of the psyche; an effect of the defences of the traumatized self as it represses or disavows the knowledge of painful or disturbing feelings aroused by the traumatic event, in order to survive. That which is split off in this way is experienced as being 'difficult or impossible to make sense of, assimilate, or integrate with the "ordinary" sense of oneself'.[34] It is felt to lie outside of ordinary experience, even to exist in another temporal dimension, as something 'timeless' or 'frozen in time'.[35] Such psychic discontinuities and divisions can be read in the life stories of survivors, which 'relate what is conscious and can be narrated, and provide insight into that which is subconscious and often remains unverbalized and unintegrated' in the history of the self.[36]

As Susannah Radstone has argued, where psychoanalytic theories are abandoned in favour of psychiatric models of PTSD, undue emphasis comes to be placed on

the effects upon the inner world of unassimilable external events . . . which, due
to [their] shocking and possibly incomprehensible nature, [prompt] a shutdown
in normal processes of assimilating or 'digesting' experience. In such cases, this
undigested experience is understood to occupy a walled-off area of the
memory.[37]

Critical analysis then concentrates on elucidating 'the "toxicity" of the
event, and the difficulties and costs of the struggle to confine this event
within a separated-off part of the memory', at the expense of examining 'the
inner world's *mediation* of the external world'.[38] Traumatic memory thus
comes to be seen as fixed, unbearably painful and resistant to representation.
My own understanding of traumatic splitting is informed by the more fluid,
relational and contingent conception of the internal psychic world found in
the writings of Melanie Klein and the Kleinian school of psychoanalysis.[39]

Kleinian theory posits an inner world of 'phantasy', governed by both
psychic and social determinants, which is distinct from the outer world of
social relationships and cultural identity yet complexly connected to it. The
mutual interpenetration of social and psychic worlds occurs through a spiralling, dialectical circuit of psychic exchanges involving processes of 'projection', whereby the self invests in the social world its own impulses and
feelings originating within the psyche, and 'introjection', in which it incorporates and internalizes aspects of the social world back within the psyche,
as parts of its own subjectivity.[40] Klein conceives the inner world established
through these processes as peopled by internal phantasy figures, or 'imagos'.
These are imaginative constructs which mediate the psychic and the social:
composite forms derived partly from identifications with the various qualities and aspects of the social world, partly from conflicting internal impulses
(of aggression and attraction, hate and love). The diverse and fragmentary
quality of these various identifications and impulses engenders incompati-
bility and leads to psychic conflict. Under 'normal' as well as 'traumatic' conditions, the self attempts to reconcile and resolve this conflict in an endless
endeavour 'to form a whole out of these various identifications'.[41] Internal
life in the Kleinian account thus centres on a dramatic struggle for coherence, unconscious in the first instance, in which the self strives to compose a
narrative capable of reconciling psychic conflict and integrating different
identifications.

This struggle for integration occurs in the face of a countervailing tendency to fragmentation, which Klein terms 'psychic splitting'. Chief among
the factors that provoke splitting of the self and its imagos are the disinte-
grating effects of anxiety and the defences developed in self-protection
against it. The Kleinian account therefore distinguishes between a more
open, integrative mode of subjective composure and the more defensive
mode enabled by psychic splitting, in which the self achieves a degree of
coherence based on a denial of destructive and painful aspects of its own
experience, and of the anxieties to which these give rise. Refusing its own
conflicts, it assumes a defensive formation where imagos that embody these

aspects and threaten its composure are expelled beyond tightly policed borders. The existence of these sharply-contrasting imagos produced by psychic splitting provokes 'phantasies of internal warfare', so that 'we cannot be at peace with ourselves'; and the contours of the split internal landscape are repeatedly likened by Klein to a battlefield.[42] However, various other alignments of the self and its imagos are possible, each involving characteristic configurations of anxiety and the defensive strategies used to contain it. Triumphalist phantasies, of wreaking a deserved destruction on imagos felt to be worthless, occur where the self idealizes and identifies itself with, rather than disavows, its own aggressive impulses. In depressive phantasies, the self internalizes and identifies with this destructiveness and assumes responsibility for its consequences, exposing itself to the full brunt of guilt and loss, and experiencing its own internal world in pieces: a psychic landscape of broken ruins and mutilated bodies. In reparative phantasies, the self seeks to repair this damage and 'put together what has been destroyed, to create and recreate', so as to restore a sense of fullness and coherence in the internal world, and allow the self to live at peace with itself.[43]

These psychic processes affect the investment of significance in the social world, including the way real other people are experienced and remembered. Klein's analyses explore how subjective composure is always established on the basis of an imaginative positioning of others: as they are drawn into the internal psychic world and allotted parts in the narrative phantasies that are played out within it, our sense of relatedness in social life becomes imbued with attractions and repulsions, fears and desires, that neither self nor other can fully control. In Kleinian theory, however, anxieties and fears are understood to originate both in the internal world and in social conflicts that impact on psychic splitting and integration, and are carried into the depths of the psyche by introjective processes that must use whatever is available from social life as resources for composure. Thus, it becomes possible to see how the full range of complex, conflictual, social relations – including those obtaining in an armed conflict – exist in dynamic interaction with the struggle for greater psychic wholeness and integrity. These narratives are not only shaped by imaginative investments derived from the psyche, but are forms of representation, socially and culturally determined. Their analysis must involve a double movement, following their traces inwards along the 'psychic pathways' that traverse the landscape of the internal world,[44] and outwards into the cultural discourses (including the stories of collective memory) which map the social world, invest it with imaginative significance and represent the identities of those who inhabit it.

From this perspective, trauma is not an immutable psychic state formed in the same manner in all contexts, but an ongoing psychic process characterized by countervailing impulses: on one hand to dissociate and defend against, but on the other hand to narrate and integrate, deeply shocking and painful experience, the outcome of which may be influenced by changing cultural and historical circumstances, but also varies according to internal psychic factors. In psychic reparation, traumatic splits and divisions within the internal world, derived from or exacerbated by the emotional impacts of extreme violence, may be overcome through a process of psychological binding and integration. This occurs (or not) in relation to the material places where everyday life is lived in the social world, social conflicts are fought out or resolved, and social relationships polarized or reconciled. Conflict resolution, and the reconciliation of social and political divisions, both require and also help to promote psychic reparation in a reciprocal dynamic, or circuit of exchanges, between the psychic and the social worlds. These psychic processes of splitting and integration often centre on particular places and the cultural landscapes suffusing them. Memories of traumatic events commonly focus on, and return in imagination to, the sites where they 'took place'. Those who have suffered a traumatic episode remain attached to an internal landscape formed in the past, and the difficulties experienced in integrating it psychically involve the construction of a defensive border that divides one part of the psyche from another to preserve 'a safer space, a retreat'.[45] In this process, psychic 'sites of trauma' are formed within the internal landscape that are derived from, and remain imaginatively linked to, the material sites of violence within social environments. Psychic discontinuities, once projected back into the social world, invest emotional significance into the meanings and memorial markers that constitute cultural landscapes of violence, horror and mourning.

Reflecting on his work with survivors of the Holocaust, the psychoanalyst Dori Laub has argued: 'Trauma survivors live not with memories of the past, but with an event that could not and did not proceed through to its completion . . . and therefore, as far as its survivors are concerned, continues into the present and is current in every respect'. For Laub, the traumatic event, 'although real, took place outside the parameters of "normal" reality', and is preserved in a psychic space that is split off from 'the range of associatively linked experiences'.[46] Laub identifies the effects of trauma as an 'entrapment' in a reality which eludes grasping and assimilation, but is 'relive[d] as haunting memory' in 'ceaseless repetitions and reenactments', charged with 'the fear that fate will strike again'.[47] If the survivor is to 'undo the entrapment' and 'reclaim both his life and his past', he or she must become involved in a social process of storytelling; that is, 'a process of constructing a narrative, reconstructing a history and, essentially, of *re-externalizing* the event'.[48] This necessarily involves the 'renegotiation of one's identity',[49] and an encounter with ambivalent and contradictory impulses: what Judith Herman has described as 'the conflict between the will to deny horrible events and the will to proclaim them aloud'.[50]

For survivors to speak at all about the experience is to engage in a struggle to shape the traumatic event into narrative form, to integrate it with their world of meaning, to fashion words that are in some way adequate to the dislocation and the horror. But they are also seeking recognition of that pain, disturbance, dislocation and horror from others. In Klein's concept of 'reparation', social recognition of these emotional realities occurs through the exercise of 'containment', a holding function whereby the presence of another, who is able to tolerate exposure to anxiety and painful feelings, helps the self to contain and bear them, without recourse to disavowal.[51] Thus, the survivor's narrative demands 'a reciprocal willingness on the part of others to listen, bear witness and . . . to "share the burden of pain" '.[52] This is necessary, according to Laub, to enable the survivor 'to reassert the veracity of the past and to build anew its linkage to, and assimilation into, present-day life'.[53] For Laub, this listening and holding function may take different social forms, from the private psychoanalytical encounter to the public process of 'historical witnessing' by means of the collecting of auto-biographical testimonies, as at the Fortunoff Video Archive for Holocaust Testimonies at Yale University in the USA.[54] The remembering and forgetting of trauma, then, is necessarily a communal process centred upon a struggle for social recognition.[55] It requires the fashioning within a cultural arena of what can best be described as a 'listening space', where the language of trauma may be spoken, attended to, reflected on and absorbed; and where a different kind of remembering may emerge.[56]

Trauma and the paradoxes of memory in the Irish Troubles

Despite, or perhaps because of, the devastating scale and human effects of the violence in Northern Ireland from 1969, a discourse seriously addressing its ongoing traumatic impact began to emerge only in the late 1980s, and became central to social and political debate only after the initiation of the peace process. Prior to this, sporadic attempts to identify and address the psychic effects of the conflict occurred, particularly during the early years when the contrast with pre-war conditions remained palpable. In August 1972, for example, one correspondent to the *Irish News* raised the difficulties of making an adequate public response 'now that every week in Northern Ireland brings its quota of killings', and suggested that 'some wider recognition for those killed' was necessary, 'to be accorded to all the dead', including ('for me, the hardest bit') members of the IRA.[57] However, such thinking was not reflected in representations of the violence and its effects in mainstream media reportage. These were predominantly structured by a news agenda that corresponded to the ideological imperatives of the British State, whereby certain killings received more attention (and condemnation) than others. The journalist Roy Greenslade analysed the resulting 'hierarchy of death':

> In the first rank – getting the most prominent coverage – were British people killed in Britain; in the second, members of the security forces, whether army or RUC; in the third, civilian victims of republicans, including prison officers; in the fourth were members of the IRA or Sinn Fein, killed either by the security forces or loyalist paramilitaries; and in the fifth rank, garnering the least coverage of all, were the innocent victims of loyalist paramilitaries.[58]

The proponents of the 'propaganda war' assumed more general control over the stories of the dead, survivors, and the bereaved, with the Northern Ireland Office's anti-Republican campaign centred on representations of 'IRA brutality and the suffering of victims' (particularly children), while nationalist and Unionist organizations, including the Republican and loyalist paramilitary groups, produced representations of their own suffering communities.[59] There was a general lack of support services to address the needs of the victims of violence at community level, though some support for locally recruited members of the security forces and their families was provided by the Ulster Defence Regiment (UDR) and RUC Benevolence Funds, and by the Disabled Police Officers Association.[60] This lack was exacerbated by a culture of silence, in which the existence of ongoing and widespread psychic trauma was neither publicly acknowledged nor discussed.[61] Early in the conflict, research on the 'psychic damage brought on by the political, military, and social violence' by the psychologist Rona Fields had been published by Penguin Books.[62] But this 'pathbreaking work' – it has been compared to Fanon's studies of mental health in circumstances of colonial conflict, and included material on British soldiers, on internees in Long Kesh, and on women and children – was censored, and then withdrawn, with unsold copies pulped, after 'a massive effort on the part of the governments involved to suppress my findings'.[63] The voices of those directly affected by violence, as such, were rarely granted a public platform.[64]

The beginning of a shift towards wider recognition of the short- and long-term psychic damage stemming from the violence of the Troubles can be traced in the public response to the IRA's Enniskillen bomb in November 1987. This occurred in the context of a series of disasters in the United Kingdom which brought the concept of PTSD into public awareness in Britain and Ireland during the late 1980s.[65] The utility of this concept in identifying the needs of the victims of violence during the Troubles was demonstrated in local support work in Enniskillen, and reinforced by a psychological study of twenty-six survivors of the bomb presented by doctors from the Mater Hospital in Belfast to the first European Conference on Traumatic Stress in September 1988. This found that that half of the sample were suffering from PTSD ten months after the explosion; and while the 'close-knit community in Enniskillen had helped to protect victims against psychological wounds, . . . the invisible damage wrought by the bomb was real and lasting'.[66] A more general study of 'Post-traumatic stress in Northern Ireland' argued that: 'PTSD may be a more useful term in describing psychological reaction to violence than the term "nervous shock" used by the courts.'[67] News coverage of Enniskillen, and the wider spread of public discourse on trauma, opened up possibilities for others suffering the effects of Troubles-related violence to describe their own experiences and identify their own needs in these terms. One key moment was the founding in 1991 of WAVE (Widows/Widowers Against Violence Empower), initially formed by eight women from North and West Belfast as a cross-community 'befriending' and mutual support group for 'innocent victims of sectarian murder'. This developed into an extensive counselling network open to anyone bereaved or otherwise traumatized by the war, and secured the first state funding for victims' support work in 1995.[68] Another was the formation of the Bloody Sunday Justice Campaign, in 1992, by relatives of the dead who sought their own recovery, after twenty years of traumatized silence, in a movement for truth and justice.

The initiation of the peace process created the conditions for a significant expansion of the listening space in Northern Ireland. The paramilitary cease-fires of 1994 ameliorated the climate of fear, and as the psychological pressure of dealing with the unremitting and compounding impact of violence abated, bereaved people finally found time to mourn losses, often sustained years or even decades earlier, when 'grief was suspended' or suppressed in order to cope.[69] The opening up of spaces for reflection and remembrance stimulated widespread telling of personal stories of loss, trauma and survival, and also a new public receptivity to such stories as representations of a collective experience. Among the major projects contributing in this way to public acknowledgement and understanding of the impact of violent conflict were *An Crann*/The Tree, launched in December 1994 by the writer Damian Gorman to commission and collect thousands of personal written accounts, conceived initially as the core of a new 'storytelling museum' about the Troubles; the Cost of the Troubles Study, a Belfast-based charity formed by a group of bereaved and injured people, that undertook extensive research including personal interviews with victims, issuing in a number of exhibitions and publications; and *Lost Lives*, a 1,600–page book recording the names, circumstances, and stories of all those killed during the conflict, which became a popular bestseller on its publication in 1999.[70]

Each of these initiatives generated intense interest and debate that helped to establish the victims and survivors at the centre of public awareness. Grassroots initiatives for victims' support at local level were further stimulated by the European Union's Special Support Programme for Peace and Reconciliation, first announced in December 1994, which injected into Northern Ireland and the Border areas of the Republic some £240 million over three years (subsequently extended in 1997 and 2000), and specified the victims of violence as a special target group suffering 'social exclusion' as a result of the Troubles.[71]

In describing the impact of this social process of belated remembering and mourning, counsellors such as Sandra Peake of the WAVE Trauma Centre in Belfast have used the metaphor of 'frozen time' to evoke the arresting of psychic development and the fixing of memories 'in the past' that has proved to be among the most widespread psychic legacies of the war. Speaking in 2000, Peake suggested that, '[if] the Troubles . . . in the North have been at the mass a block of ice', then 'there are many people still in the centre of that, frozen in . . . not being able to address what's happened'.[72] This image of the 'freezing' of ordinary processes of remembering and forgetting recurs throughout the critical literature on trauma in evoking the experience of feeling 'stuck' and unable to 'move on' psychically, as a result of defensive splitting. Peake also extends the metaphor to talk about a condition of collective trauma when she observes that, since 1994, 'our change of political environment has caused a bit of defrosting around the edges', but that WAVE and other counselling networks were still 'only getting the tip of the iceberg'.[73] This symbolism has also been explored by the Belfast-based artist Rita Duffy in an exhibition of paintings and film *Contemplating an Iceberg* (2005) that evoke the strange fascination exerted by the massive form and destructive potential of these alien and only partly visible objects; and in her proposal to tow an iceberg from the Arctic into Belfast Harbour for it to melt there, as a living sculpture.[74] For Duffy: 'The iceberg is a figure of fear', and of 'a certain type of madness in Northern Ireland society, a denial of what has happened to us', while its thawing and melting symbolizes a reparative process of re-opening to the past that holds out the hope of catharsis.[75]

This process of reparation not only takes time, as Duffy's iceberg metaphor suggests, but also meets with obstacles. To understand why, when survivors of the Troubles make efforts to remember and to tell a story about their traumatic experiences, they encounter internal resistances and pressures to forget, it is useful to begin with a reminder of the disturbing content of many such memories, and the challenges of imagination they pose to tellers and listeners alike. Early in 1997 the journalist Mary Holland, reporting on the archive collected by *An Crann*/The Tree, illustrated these challenges with examples from a couple of the stories, including this:

> A woman writes many years after her father's death: 'You lived for 11 days after the bomb. They say your arms and legs fell off when you died. I was 12 years old and very frightened. Frightened to look at your charred face, your badly swollen lips and eyes, the tubes in your throat. Amazingly, I remember a few jokes you tried to tell me before the end. I think you must have known how scared I was. The smell of burning flesh never really goes away. God, what you must have felt, knowing that your own child, the little girl you used to hold in your arms, was afraid to hug you, even to be left alone with you.' Only now, with children of her own, can she tell her father how angry she felt that his death left her mother and family on their own.[76]

There are immense difficulties in speaking and writing about such memories. Remembering a traumatic event is a process riven with ambivalence. Is it good to remember? Does the attempt to represent the traumatic past help a survivor to come to terms with it, perhaps to bear the pain? Or is it risking too much, ploughing up things too painful or disturbing to remember, things that are best buried, consigned to silence, forgotten? According to its founder, Damian Gorman, the primary aim of the *An Crann* project, when it was first launched within a few weeks of the 1994 ceasefires, was to 'recover the story of what happened to us' during the war: '[E]verybody's personal history is part of a shared history . . . Obviously there are very many people who have suffered. And the idea is to piece all those testimonies together as parts of a mosaic.'[77] The psychic struggle waged by the individual survivor to integrate traumatic memory within viable maps of meaning is given a social correlate in this effort to read and understand personal testimonies as elements in a larger, collective history. Responding to the point that 'some might say the project is opening old wounds that maybe would be better healed over', Gorman's response was:

> Some people do . . . say to me that the best thing to do is to bury it as deeply as possible . . . In a lot of people's lives things come up and they fold them away as if there is some reinforced concrete chamber of the human heart into which these things can be put, and there isn't. These things pulse away, and they distort, and they do harm. They can seep out into the rest of your life. And just as I believe that is the case for an individual, so it is the case for a community and there are an awful lot of things that we need to hear.

A second aim quickly emerged from the process of meeting and talking with people: to cultivate 'the practice of listening . . . to just make a space into which people can say their piece, [because] it's in spaces like that where important things can take root, like tolerance and forgiveness'.[78] With this, *An Crann* became an endeavour not only to record but to heal the traumatic past, working on the connections between the psychic and the social, the individual and the communal, telling and listening. Contrary to the practice of 'state-organized forgetting', with its impulsion to 'overthrow' and 'cast off' the past, *An Crann* called for more remembering. This is a necessary condition of authentic reconciliation, since the buried past will otherwise continue to exert a malign influence in a range of morbid symptoms, silences and emotional reactions.

However, this necessary process confronts the profound difficulties involved not only in telling, but in reading, listening and bearing witness to traumatic memories. We struggle to relate ourselves, imaginatively and emotionally, to the traumas of others. Antjie Krog, a South African poet covering for radio news the investigations of the TRC, has written very powerfully about the harrowing process of listening, day after day, to testimonies of trauma. By the second week of the hearings, while answering questions on an actuality broadcast, 'I stammer. I freeze. I am without language.' A counsellor from the TRC tells the journalists, 'You will experience the same symptoms as the victims. You will find yourself powerless, without help, without words.'

> [R]eporting on the truth commission has indeed left most of us physically exhausted and mentally frayed . . . Water covers the cheeks and we cannot type. Or think. And this was how we often ended up at the daily press conference – bewildered and close to tears at the feet of Archbishop Tutu. By the end of the four weeks they were no longer press conferences – he was comforting us . . . Every week we are stretched thinner and thinner over different pitches of grief . . . how many people can one see crying, how much torn-loose sorrow can one accomodate?[79]

Accounts like this support the psychoanalytical theory of transference which suggests that traumatic events are transmitted from one psyche to another. Disturbance, pain, and horror, remembered and represented to another, enter the listener by introjection and may reproduce themselves there – as embodiments, or perhaps evocations, of psychic scenarios buried deeply within the internal world of each of us. There they encounter (or, better, call into being) the many forms of a necessary psychic defence – whether resistance, denial and disavowal or the anaesthetic of emotional exhaustion – mobilized to split off these painful and destructive feelings from the self. This expulsion of unwanted elements from the self tends to be accomplished by their imaginative projection into people, places and objects in the social world, which thereby become the bearers of violence, of death and of loss, that return to haunt the self from the outside, as a threatening external *other*. Memories of trauma are produced through this encounter with psychic defence and denial. If those remembering must exert their telling to push through their own resistances, often they confront those of their listeners as well. To relate to the trauma of another is to risk undoing the work of psychic defence, on which the ordinary world of the self appears to be based, and admitting the traumatic. Helping a survivor bear and detoxify the effects of traumatic experience involves a psychic openness to, and an ability to tolerate, one's own pain, fear and disturbance. Defensive disavowal, on the other hand, offers the phantasy of sealing the traumatic into the zone of the other, safely split off – both psychically and socially – behind a secure border of demarcation.

This psychoanalytical account of psychic defence against trauma, as a means to preserve a less painful normality, may illuminate certain cultural responses in Britain and the Republic to the conflict 'in' Northern Ireland. Its hostile representation as an atavistic tribal war between primitives, each side being 'as bad as the other' and beyond the pale of civilized concern; the contemptuous and dismissive wish to 'leave them to it'; the fear that poisonous influences from 'up there' might pervade and contaminate normal life 'here' – these can be understood as so many cultural manifestations of psychic denial and disavowal. Damian Gorman, speaking during the temporary peace of the first IRA ceasefire (31 August 1994–9 February 1996), identified this process at work within Northern Ireland itself when he remarked:

> With the *Crann* I have been aware of the fear in people whose relatives have been killed that they will be left behind, because there is such a yearning among society at large to get away from that time. They feel they will inevitably be side-lined, because they are living, pulsing reminders of that time of death and sectarian murder. The view is that we cannot take those people with us, for if we do we can never forget all of that.[80]

State-organized forgetting, with its seductive offer to cast off the chains of history, appeals to precisely this yearning to 'forget all that', while actively

exacerbating the difficulties of social recognition and the fears of abandonment – of being left to deal with the past alone – experienced by the bereaved
in the North. A comparable 'leaving behind' has affected those bereaved and
injured by the IRA's bombing campaign in England. In a BBC documentary
in 1994 investigating the long-term psychological after-effects of the
Birmingham pub bombings – which killed twenty-one people and injured
162, many seriously, in November 1974 – a number of the survivors spoke
publicly for the first time to explain that 'they feel their story has been forgotten'.[81] Although the atrocity had 'shattered' their lives and frequently
their 'peace of mind', and continues to 'cast a shadow over us' twenty years
later, there had been no civic commemoration, and the official attitude
appeared to be that 'it's an embarrassment': 'they don't want to remember'.[82]
Similarly, Sharon Smith, a resident of the Barkantine Housing Estate devastated by the Docklands bomb that temporarily ended the IRA ceasefire in
February 1996, has condemned governmental neglect of its psychological
impact: 'No-one seems to care, they've just left us here to cope with it.'[83]
Gorman saw *An Crann* as a challenge to this tendency of the wider public,
particularly those in Northern Ireland intent on embracing the promise of a
peaceful future, 'to detach from the whole process': the voices of the survivors constituted, for Gorman, a communal resource for confronting and
representing a shared history in which all are implicated.[84]

There is, of course, more than one way of construing that shared history.
If Gorman rightly emphasizes the broader collective value and significance
of survivors' stories, it is also the case that the difficulties inherent in remembering and witnessing trauma are compounded in the context of a war,
where political antagonism is continually fuelled by – and in turn helps to
reproduce – the bitternesses and hatreds of violent conflict. In August 1995
a documentary entitled *The Trouble With Peace*, broadcast to mark the first
anniversary of the IRA ceasefire, included an interview with a Protestant
woman, Sandra Rock, whose brother Sammy had been killed by the Irish
National Liberation Army in 1993, in the mistaken belief that he was a
member of the UDA. She said:

> Why the peace made me angry was because I don't want the ones who murdered
> my brother to get off scot-free. I really wanted the ones that murdered my
> brother murdered. I want thems to be dead. And I want their families to go
> through what I've been going through . . . A lot of these people are saying, 'I
> forgive them, I forgive them.' I can't find it in my heart to forgive the ones that
> murdered my brother and I never will. And I hate those people. Hate them. And
> I do wish thems dead. That's why I hate peace.[85]

This is a chilling repudiation of the language of reconciliation, and provides
a powerful illustration of the inadequacy of state-organized forgetting as a
response to the realities of the war. The wish expressed here, to push back
onto the other the suffering that the other has placed on you, as if the lost
loved one could thereby be made to live on, regularly manifested during the

Troubles in spiralling cycles of violence, known as tit-for-tat killings.[86] But
the revenge phantasies given expression in such actions, and in support for
them, were far more widespread.[87] In the aftermath of the IRA's Shankill
Road bomb in October 1993, for example, one loyalist mourner, Margaret
Martin, stated: 'I just think they are IRA scum . . . I just hope the UVF and
the UFF go in and get them sorted. If I had a gun myself I would go out
and shoot them.'[88] For Rock and Martin, and others like them in Ireland and
Britain, it is not possible simply to 'shake off' the loss, anger and hatred generated by violent bereavement, or the impulse to mitigate the psychic distress
and alleviate the pressure of suffering through revenge. These are emotional
realities whose transformation must be worked for psychically, a process
aided by their cultural representation and social recognition. If handled sen-
sitively, media reportage itself is capable of providing a listening space where
the amelioration of painful and disturbing memories may begin. Later in *The
Trouble With Peace*, Sandra Rock describes how the very process of talking
about the killing of her brother in the interview recorded for the programme
has given some relief to the bitter feelings expressed there, so that, by the end
of her involvement in the documentary, she no longer felt quite so vengeful.

Social recognition of these psychic realities has been more readily available in Northern Ireland within those local, mainly working-class, communities – whether loyalist or Republican, Unionist or nationalist – which were
most deeply and routinely enmeshed in the war. The language of suffering
and, since 1987, the specific language of trauma have been deployed in the
public commemoration of the war dead within these communities. By relating to and representing collective memories of traumatic events, war commemoration has contributed to the development of a politics of suffering in
which political identity has been strengthened through communal bonding,
while also providing a means of social engagement with the psychic needs of
the survivors of violence. In this way, if not in every case, the personal suffering and mourning of the survivors could be publicly recognized, affirmed,
and given dignity and meaning, through its incorporation into a more
general Unionist–loyalist or nationalist–Republican political narrative about
past, present and future. When placed within a broader narrative framework
in this way, an event is invested with significance as an episode in a longer
communal history. This can be seen, for example, in loyalist responses the
1993 Shankill bomb, when nine members of the local community (including
two children) were killed in a no-warning attack on Frizzell's Fish Shop on
the Shankill Road. Under the headline 'We Will Remember Them', an editorial
in the *Shankill People* newspaper praised 'the bravery and humanity [of]
those who dived into the blasted ruins . . . to search for the victims, oblivi-
ous to their own safety', as 'worthy of their forefathers on the Somme'.[89]
Here, the spirit of self-sacrifice manifest in the embattled Shankill community of 1993 is both measured and ennobled by association with the loyalist
volunteers of the Ulster Division during the the First World War, some 5,000
of whom were killed serving their country on the first day of the battle of the

Somme, 1 July 1916. In naming the events of 30 January 1972 in Derry 'Bloody Sunday', when fourteen unarmed civilians were shot dead by the British Army, the nationalist community was both recalling and drawing a direct parallel with a previous 'Bloody Sunday': in Dublin on 21 November 1920, during the War of Independence, twelve civilians were killed by British forces firing into the crowd at a Gaelic football match in reprisal for a series of assassinations by the IRA.[90] The very naming locates the significance of the Derry atrocity within the longer history of the Irish struggle for national liberation from British imperial rule; thereby assimilating into a narrative of hope the event remembered by the Derry MP and SDLP leader John Hume as 'the most traumatic day in the lifetime of every citizen of this city and certainly of mine as their representative'.[91]

Those affected by trauma do not react uniformly, nor do all survivors of the Troubles identify with these politicized narratives of memory. Indeed, as Sandra Peake points out, 'the conflict within communities . . . [sometimes] can be as great as the conflict between communities'.[92] Shared communal memories have to be negotiated between those who may have significantly different personal experiences of the war, and this 'can be very difficult for people to deal with'.[93] For example, both the psychic experience of violent bereavement and its social recognition within a community may vary according to the identity of the perpetrator:

> Hurt . . . [might more readily be] accepted if their loved one had been killed by a member of the other community . . . but to be killed by a member of their own community, it's slightly different, and . . . the support might not be there to as great a degree.[94]

The narrative of 'our community' and its suffering is constructed on the basis of communal taboos about, and policing of, what may and may not be spoken. As a result, 'some people have felt censored for years within their communities and within their families'. This was the case for the relatives of 'the disappeared', fourteen people who were abducted, killed and secretly buried without trace during the 1970s, mainly by the IRA.

> [T]he community's ways of responding to the disappearance . . . was to deny that it had happened . . . There's rumours going on [suggesting that those missing were informers] . . . So those families are left for quite a number of years having to deal with their loved ones disappearance and suspected murder and burial. It was only with the ceasefires in 1994 that people were able . . . to address what had happened . . . and that the stories of the disappearances came out.[95]

The silencing of voices critical of IRA activity from within the nationalist community made it impossible for the relatives 'to talk about what had happened in their family and the pain and the implications for the family's welfare'. After the campaign group Families of the Disappeared was launched in 1994, the family of its co-founder Helen McKendry was ostracized and attacked by Republicans in their community of Poleglass in West

Belfast.[96] For many of those attending a WAVE trauma centre, its provision of a space free from the fear of such pressure is a necessary condition of any re-engagement with the past.

However, for those members of the embattled communities who do identify with them, these political narratives of memory have furnished important psychic resources of strength, hope and resilience, providing collective cultural means to combat the disintegration and withdrawal of the self that so often marks the presence of the traumatic. At the same time, in empowering the survivors, who thereby cease to be passive *victims*, they have energized the political will. They promise that redemption of suffering is possible and that it will be made ultimately meaningful through the achievement of the political demands of the community. And they ensure that the dead 'have not died in vain', that they live on as a touchstone and inspiration for those who have survived them and who continue their struggle. In thus underpinning and mobilizing psychic energy on behalf of the communities locked in antagonism, this politicization of memory has generated a further paradox.

Public commemoration itself has turned into a battlefield where selective, discrepant and antagonistic narratives of the past clash and compete. When, for example, Republicans remember that crucial year, 1916, they commemorate the heroic martyrs of the Easter Rising who gave their lives in a doomed revolt which nevertheless began the revolution leading to an independent Irish State. In so doing, they forget the Irish dead of the the First World War – seen as Britain's imperialist war – which is the exclusive focus of loyalist remembering of 1916.[97] The commemoration of one traumatic event has been precisely the amnesia of the other. While remembering and offering public recognition for the traumas of *our* community, politicized communal memories thus tended to withhold recognition, to forget and to deny the traumas of *the other* – since recognition of the trauma is felt to imply recognition of the political narrative that articulates its significance. Many Unionists in Derry, for instance, dispute Hume's suggestion that 'every citizen of this city' felt the trauma of Bloody Sunday. To deny social recognition to trauma, however, is not to ignore but to entrench it. In this way, the hostilities of armed conflict rebound on mourning and commemoration – a process made most overt in the common phenomenon in Northern Ireland of violent attacks on commemorative events, funerals, gravestones and memorials.[98]

Psychoanalyst Rob Weatherill has argued that when we allow no 'place for death in our own lives', when we respond to it by 'the denial of death, [by] our refusal to take it on board', then it returns in our lives as 'a trauma that comes from the *outside*', a 'radically excluded Other, which arises as if from another universe'.[99] When, on 22 February 1972, the Official IRA planted a bomb at the Parachute Regiment's HQ in Aldershot, in a revenge attack for Bloody Sunday, killing six civilian workers and a Catholic chaplain, the traumas of the Irish war indeed *returned* – were brought home – to England in this way. The English people have had no equivalent to the politicized collective memories of Northern Ireland as resources for making sense of the traumas of this war. Survivors of IRA bombings in English towns and cities have often spoken of them as 'senseless'.[100] This has been the price of longstanding English cultural amnesia about the historical suffering inflicted on Northern Irish nationalist communities by British state policy operating 'in our name'. This history became 'our tragedy', too, with the onset of the Republican bombing campaign in England.[101] Yet, over twenty years later, following the bomb in Warrington on 20 March 1993 that killed 3-year-old Johnathan Ball and 12-year-old Tim Parry, a counsellor, Jo Robertshaw, suggested that, for the children of Warrington traumatized by this attack, 'the overwhelming difficulty was the question why'. Barry Chambers, a deputy-head teacher, noticed that in 'the weeks following the bomb, the kids were saying "what is it about?" We realized there was a gap.' Significantly, one year after the bomb, many children now wished, in the words of 16-year-old Stephen Anderson, 'to find out why it happened and why it has been happening for so long'. Steps had been taken to introduce Irish history into the curriculum of Warrington's St Thomas Boteler School, and the Warrington Project had been formed to establish contacts and exchanges with schools and communities in Ireland.[102] Here, the perception of a link between *our* suffering and *their* suffering, together with a need to recover and make sense of a lost past, generated an alternative response to trauma. A strategy of remembering for reparation replaced denial, disavowal and amnesia.

Here, then, a conceptual distinction may be made, based on Kleinian categories, between 'defensive' and 'reparative' remembering in the Troubles. In defensive remembering, composure is predicated on psychic splitting. This works to seal traumatic histories into Radstone's 'walled off area of the memory', which becomes associated, through projection into the social world, with the zone and identity of the threatening other. Forgetting in this mode is a means of disavowal, of dealing with unresolved conflicts by 'putting them behind us', placing them *in* the past. In reparative remembering, composure is sought on the basis of psychic reparation that works to undo defensive splits. This involves opening emotionally to the disavowed past, connecting and integrating traumatic histories, and engaging with the memory world of the other. In this mode, forgetting allows experiences to be absorbed and incorporated psychically, so that life may continue along fresh paths.

Remembering, recognition and reparation: the cultural politics of peace

Talk of 'overcoming the legacy of the past' in the Irish conflict by drawing a line under it and 'moving on', is problematic for at least two reasons. It colludes with, and reproduces, the historical British denial of responsibility for the traumas of colonialism in Ireland; and it leaves intact deep sources of grief, grievance and antagonism that are rooted in the recent history of the Troubles. An alternative perspective was articulated early in the peace process by Martin Finucane of the Irish Campaign for Truth (launched in

January 1995): 'If we are to overcome our past, we must come to terms with it and we can only do that if we know the truth about it.'[103] In a conflict zone, however, there is always more than one truth, and more than one conception of justice. These differences will be accommodated only through a process of dialogue; but such dialogue cannot be exclusively rational. Coming to terms with the past has, I have argued, a psychic as well as a political dimension, both of which need to be addressed and understood in their complex interaction. Real tensions and difficulties, both theoretical and practical in kind, are involved in holding together these two dimensions and integrating them into a coherent analysis. The relations between trauma and cultural processes of remembering and forgetting are characterized by an inherent ambivalence even without the further complications, contradictions and paradoxes that accrue through the politics of an armed conflict. If the difficulties of dealing with a traumatic past in the face of psychic defence and resistance are profound in whatever circumstance, they are greatly aggravated by the intense pressures of a war zone.

Conceptual difficulties in making sense of the interrelations between the psychic and the political are compounded by the danger of reductionism, whereby the importance of one dimension is asserted either without reference to, or in explicit negation of, the other. Thus, in gatherings of the politically minded, talk of 'the psyche' – of mourning, mental distress, emotional realities, phantasy – can be dismissed as a distraction from the serious political issues; while among those concerned with the psychic dimension, there is a tendency to define and explore these issues in terms of the personal, the individual and the human in contradistinction to social and political processes, which are reduced, oversimplified and allowed no constitutive role in bringing about the many different kinds of traumatic experience.[104] Despite these difficulties, the language of trauma nevertheless brings into focus the realities of psychic damage within the cultural, historical and political relations in which the Irish and British peoples are mutually entwined and implicated. It challenges the strategies of containment manifest in the amnesias, silences and lacunae that characterize much of the cultural and political discourse on 'the national past' – and the current conflict – in both Britain and Ireland. It insists that there is a psychic as well as a cultural dynamic to remembering and forgetting, threaded through efforts at a political settlement capable of realigning past, present and future. And it confronts the problem of whether, and how, it is possible to further the difficult process of psychic reparation necessary to any genuine reconciliation of deep-rooted and violent conflict; of whether, and how, it is possible to undo the plethora of psychic defences erected, like so many internal 'peace-lines', in defence against the traumas of the war.

There is no easy solution to these problems – no magic remedy to heal the traumatic past. However, at the core of any worthwhile cultural project of reparative remembering must be initiatives that extend social and public recognition of trauma. At the most fundamental level, the public acknowledgement of a violent death, and the naming and calling-to-account of those responsible, establishes an objective foundation without which it may be impossible to lay the dead to rest. Public recognition of the individuality of the dead and the particular circumstances of their death also supports the emotional work of mourning, which mobilizes profound desires to keep alive the name and value of the deceased in memory, thereby 'repairing' the damage wreaked within the inner world of the psyche.[105] Early in the peace process, evidence of this widespread desire for public recognition was afforded by the unexpected success of *Bear in Mind These Dead* (1994), a booklet which simply recorded chronologically the names of all who have died in the current Troubles, with their age, the place and manner of death, and those responsible. The publisher was astonished when the entire print-run of 1,200 copies sold out with demand still high, and likened the function served by the booklet to that of the Vietnam memorial wall in Washington DC.[106] This initiative and the more ambitious *Lost Lives* project telling the stories of these deaths are among the very few instances when *all* the dead of the Troubles are gathered together in a single, inclusive, commemorative frame. However, this impetus has also created a paradox. Protests have been made about these publications by those who do not wish (and did not sanction) the loss of their loved ones to be linked or equated with the deaths of their enemies; or who objected to the greater weight of detail provided about certain cases in comparison to the meagreness of others; or who were upset at mistakes, or the repetition of unsubstantiated rumours or of the claims (of membership of a paramilitary organization, for example) originally used to justify a killing.[107]

The social recognition of trauma may be particularly valuable when it is extended to others across the communal and national divides, in a symbolic attempt to undo or reverse the reproduction of antagonism and hatred. One striking instance of this stemmed from the assassination by an IRA sniper of Lance-Bombardier Stephen Restorick at an Army checkpoint in South Armagh in February 1997, one year into the eighteen-month period during which the IRA resumed armed activity in reaction to the continuing exclusion of Sinn Féin from peace talks. A witness to the killing, local resident Lorraine McElroy, who was wounded by the same bullet and accepted the family's invitation to the funeral in Peterborough, told the press: 'People ask me if I'm nervous, as a[n Irish] Catholic, of going to a British soldier's funeral. But I'm not going to a British soldier's funeral. I'm going to the funeral of a young man who died in front of me.'[108] (In the event, Mrs McElroy was prevented from attending due to the onset of symptoms identified as those of PTSD.)[109] Hopes were expressed at the service 'that [Stephen Restorick's] death will be a catalyst to restart the peace process and bring both sides together to talk';[110] and his mother, Rita Restorick, 'out of a need to make some sense of her son's death', wrote to Gerry Adams appealing for the IRA ceasefire to be restored, and to other political leaders in Northern Ireland urging them to negotiate with Sinn Féin.[111] As the

Warrington Project demonstrates, such initiatives may be broadened into a genuinely cross-community practice of reparative remembering.

One potent form in which social recognition may be extended across the frontiers of conflict is that of an acknowledgement and apology to the victims of a particular traumatic event by those responsible for it, either directly as perpetrators or indirectly as political representatives. When the Combined Loyalist Military Command announced its ceasefire on 13 October 1994, its statement continued: 'In all sincerity we offer the loved ones of all innocent victims over the past twenty-five years abject and true remorse. No words of ours will compensate for the intolerable suffering they have undergone during the conflict.'[112] Sinn Féin leaders have made repeated apologies for IRA actions. Gerry Adams, for example, described the Shankill bombing as 'wrong' and a 'great tragedy, a devastating tragedy', offering 'my complete and absolute sympathy';[113] and in response to Rita Restorick's letter, 'gave his condolences and apologized for the grief that has been caused'.[114] In July 2002, to mark the thirtieth anniversary of 'Bloody Friday' when its members killed nine people and injured hundreds more in a series of co-ordinated bomb attacks in Belfast, the IRA issued a statement acknowledging 'all of the deaths and injuries of non-combatants caused by us', accepting responsibility for what it described as the unintentional consequences of its operations, and offering 'our sincere apologies and condolences to their families'.[115] Statements of this kind are frequently maligned as hypocritical and self-serving (especially whilst the violence continues), or as tokenistic or inadequate. Yet these expressions of recognition and apology from both sides of the political divide may represent serious attempts to undo the workings of defensive disavowal, hatred and revenge, and to grapple with the contradictions of embroilment within an armed conflict. Besides their immediate value for those survivors to whom they are acceptable (Rita Restorick, for example, expressed herself 'pleased' at Adams's letter) the effectiveness of such gestures lies in their potential to elicit mutual recognition across the political divide. Ultimately, the quality of such exchanges will be judged by their contribution to ending hostilities, and facilitating a just and lasting political settlement. The latter, in turn, is a condition of any thorough-going process of reconciliation. However, there is no guarantee that the social recognition of trauma will be placed at the centre of a political settlement. Here, the will of the State to help or hinder reparative remembering is crucial.

Efforts to push 'truth and justice' onto the political agenda in a manner that involves the British State are fundamental to the project of reparation. Sinn Féin and nationalist relatives' groups, before and during the peace process, have consistently argued against the selective condemnation of violence, whereby the IRA is demonized as solely responsible for the deaths and suffering, while any action by the British military and the RUC is justified as a legitimate response to terrorism by the forces of law and order, and their collusion with the sectarian loyalist paramilitary groups (throughout the era of the Unionist State ruled from Stormont, and continuing under Direct Rule from London) is denied and covered up. Speaking at the 1995 Bloody Sunday commemoration, Adams argued:

> There cannot be a healing process, a process of reconciliation unless all of us address honestly and openly the hurts we have caused. But everyone must do this – republicans and unionists and loyalists, and especially the British government. If John Major is genuinely committed to peace in this country, he should make a start by apologising to the people of Derry for the atrocity of Bloody Sunday.[116]

The calls from throughout Ireland for an official apology for Bloody Sunday, for the reopening of the public inquiry, and for a calling to account of the British soldiers and politicians responsible, had wider implications in that they demanded 'acknowledgement of the truth that the British state has committed human rights violations'.[117] This required a major shift in stance, away from the State's ideological self-representation as the honest broker and towards an admission of its role as an active party to the conflict. Bill Rolston observes: 'There is something particularly offensive about the human rights violations of the state . . . One can always hope that the state can identify and bring to trial or detention someone from a non-state organisation who has abused one's human rights. But who guards the guards?'[118] The importance of truth-telling and acknowledgement of responsibility for human rights violations by non-state organizations must not be underestimated, but Rolston is right to suggest that there is a particular onus upon, and need for, public recognition by the State of traumas inflicted on its behalf.

Notwithstanding the talk of 'reconciliation' and 'healing' in the Downing Street Declaration, John Major's Conservative Government proved unresponsive to the calls for justice and redress emanating from Ireland. This prompted the formation of the Irish Campaign for Truth and its demand (following some fifteen international precedents between 1974 and 1994) for the establishment of an official, state-sponsored truth commission to investigate human rights violations in Ireland.[119] Discussing this proposal in 1996, Rolston identified two problems: 'the dilemma . . . in seeking justice while the offending regime is still in power'; and the lack of popular pressure from below, capable of pushing the question of human rights abuses into the forefront of political debate.[120] Under these circumstances, he judged there to be little prospect of willing collaboration by the British State – whether to make apology, to release information on security force activities or to facilitate 'the prosecution of state personnel for past human rights abuses' – under any new political arrangements that might be achieved in Ireland as a result of the peace process.[121]

However, with the election in early summer 1997 of the new Labour Government in the UK and the new Fianna Fáil-led Coalition Government in the Republic of Ireland, a new phase in the peace process began, in which questions of truth, human rights and the effects of trauma on the victims of violence were now placed at the centre of the political agenda. The restoration of the Provisional IRA's ceasefire in July 1997 was followed shortly after by the opening of inclusive multi-party talks on the future of Northern Ireland, culminating in the Good Friday Agreement of April 1998. In November 1997, in the context of these political negotiations, the British Government established the Northern Ireland Victims Commission (headed by Sir Kenneth Bloomfield, the former head of Britain's Civil Service in the North) 'to examine the feasibility of providing greater recognition for those who have become victims in the last thirty years as a consequence of events in Northern Ireland'.[122] The Bloomfield Commission's report, *We Will Remember Them* (April 1998), defined the category of 'victim' as including all 'the surviving injured and those who care for them, together with those close relatives who mourn their dead'.[123] Prefaced by a Declaration of Support in which the parties pledged 'never [to] forget those who have died or been injured, and their families', the Agreement itself affirmed that 'it is essential to acknowledge and address the suffering of the victims of violence as a necessary element of reconciliation', and recognized that 'victims have a right to remember as well as to contribute to a changed society'.[124] A commitment was made to allocate British government resources to 'community-based initiatives . . . that are supportive and sensitive to the needs of victims', and to this end a permanent Victims Liaison Unit (VLU) was established within the Northern Ireland Office of the British Government at Stormont.[125] (With the establishment of the new Northern Ireland Assembly, a separate Victims' Unit was instituted in June 2000 in the Office of the First Minister and Deputy First Minister.)

These developments created a new framework for representation and recognition of victims of the Troubles and the ongoing difficulties they face, and new possibilities for reparation or redress. In response, there was a flowering from below of victims' groups representing – and usually composed of – victims from particular local communities or those having some other grounds of shared experience. Alongside these developments, in an unprecedented move in January 1998, the British Government announced the opening of a new judicial inquiry into the events of Bloody Sunday;[126] while in the Agreement provision was made for new Human Rights Commissions to be established north and south of the Border (and for their representatives to meet in a joint committee), to ensure that there could be no return to the discrimination and abuse of state power which had triggered the conflict nearly thirty years earlier.

While the victims' issue has been placed centrally within the framework of an inclusive process of conflict resolution, it has also figured within the strategy adopted by the British Government for hegemonic leadership of that process from above. Through the Bloomfield Commission and the VLU, the State sought to lead and direct the developing victims' movement by constructing a single, integrated, victims' lobby, that would function as a conduit for funding and speak with a consensual voice about the needs of victims within the overarching political framework of the Agreement. Within this strategy, the British State has continued to represent itself as a neutral arbiter (rather than as a participant in the conflict): as holding the ring and encouraging dialogue, reconciliation and consensus-building between the two warring factions, in the arena of the victims of violence as also in those of community relations and political conflict itself. Those victims' groups or their members which did not embrace this agenda – whether nationalist and Republican groups mainly addressing the legacy of state violence or loyalist and Unionist groups concerned primarily with the legacy and continuing threat of Republican paramilitary violence – found themselves engaged in a struggle to make their own voices heard while resisting incorporation into the state-sponsored consensus and the particular version of the past (and the future) that it promotes. Through the various victims' groups' support for, or resistance to, the State's victims' strategy, a new politics of victimhood was generated, in which the discourse concerned with the victims of violence was appropriated and articulated from a number of different ideological positions.[127] This rapidly became intertwined psychically and politically with conflicts over the implementation of the Agreement, especially those aspects that touched directly on victims' experiences, such as demilitarization, the early release of paramilitary prisoners and reform of the RUC.

At the same time, the British Government has declined to institute a formal and inclusive framework for addressing questions of truth and justice within the conflict-resolution process. This is despite the evident scale and intensity of demands for the truth to be established with regard to innumerable events of the unresolved past, including renewed calls for the establishment of a truth commission backed by, among others, the Chief Constable of the new Police Service of Northern Ireland.[128] On the contrary, the Government has continued to place obstacles in the way of a full, independent, public inquiry – as demanded by relatives, human rights organizations and Sinn Féin – into the most serious allegations of collusion between members of the British security forces and loyalist paramilitaries, in many cases where civilians were killed. Concessions on this issue were made during negotiations over the implementation of the Agreement which led to the appointment in May 2002 of the Canadian judge Peter Cory to investigate three of the most controversial of such cases, those of the solicitors Pat Finucane and Rosemary Nelson, and of Robert Hamill; as well as (out of considerations of balance) the killing by Republicans of the imprisoned loyalist Billy Wright, and (on behalf of the Irish Government) two further cases involving allegations of collusion between the *Garda* and Republican paramilitaries. When, in October 2003, the Cory reports found evidence of collusion and recommended that full public inquiries be established in all cases, the British Government delayed publication and censored their findings, before acceding to the recommendations in April 2004.

In the most sensitive case, that of Pat Finucane, the proposed public inquiry was first postponed and then became subject to new statutory limits on its powers of investigation, introduced in the Inquiries Act 2005. The Act constrains the capacity of an inquiry to hold government to public account by reducing its judicial independence from executive interference, hitherto guaranteed by the Tribunals of Inquiry (Evidence) Act 1921. It gives government extensive powers 'to exclude the public from all or part of an inquiry, to control publication of the final report, to restrict the publication of documents, to insist on the omission of crucial evidence from the final report "in the public interest", and even to sack the chairman or a member of the inquiry panel'. According to Amnesty International: 'By proposing to hold an inquiry into the Finucane case under the Inquiries Act 2005, the UK government is trying to eliminate independent scrutiny of the actions of its agents.'[129] In this context, where truth continues to be systematically concealed by the State, initiatives for reparative remembering have tended to emerge piecemeal from below, often in the form of campaigns focused on particular events and interests, in which psychic imperatives have continued to shape and be shaped by existing political affiliations. In the Irish peace process after the Good Friday Agreement, the terrain of the past has remained a battlefield.

At the centre of this continuing war over memory are some fundamental disagreements: over the causes of the violence; over who bears responsibility for its escalation during the early 1970s; and over the legitimacy of the IRA's armed struggle. The outcome of this contest has implications not only in Ireland, but in Britain, too, where a veil of official secrecy (reinforced by the current 'war on terror' following the attacks on the USA of 11 September 2001) continues to obscure the past, and to impede a necessary reassessment of the State's role in the Irish conflict, and its impact politically, culturally and psychically. Receptivity to initiatives that aim to unlock the fixities of the remembered past was also boosted in Britain by the ceasefires of 1994, during which the anti-terrorist broadcasting ban was lifted and new cultural spaces opened up. However, the extending of reparative remembering here, involving the rediscovery of Ireland's traumatic past as indeed a part of 'British history', is dependent on initiatives from below emerging in dialogue with developments in Ireland. In Northern Ireland, efforts to deal with the recent past in the context of the peace process have tended to be conducted within rather than between the two political communities, while the clash of competing memories continues to pose challenges and set limits to the possibilities of reparation. The formation of these memories in relation to each other and to the British State's counter-insurgency and conflict-resolution strategies, as well as the possibilities and limits of reparation within the peace process, are explored in the case studies on Bloody Sunday and the war along the Border, in the chapters that follow.

Whatever the political context, there are limits to any 'healing' of psychic damage. The psychotherapist Susie Orbach, reflecting on the South African process of truth and reconciliation, points out:

[A]s the Truth Commission openly acknowledges, it would be naive to think that it can wipe away the emotional pain of the individuals whose lives have been marked by acts perpetrated under apartheid. Those wounds never completely heal . . . The trauma is never fully in the past, but lives on in the present. Perhaps the most we can hope for is that if the wrongdoing and trauma are recognised in the present, future generations will experience the repercussions as their history rather than as their present.[130]

Reparation may not always be possible for the generations marked by collective trauma, and can be reproduced through family relationships into the following generation.[131] Trauma persists – but reparation is about mobilizing the resources of hope, so that living can go on in its wake.

Part II

Remembering Bloody Sunday

I think I was very lucky. I was left to tell my own story, but the poor people lying in the cemetery can't tell theirs at all. (Damien Donaghy, shot on Bloody Sunday, in Joanne O'Brien, *A Matter of Minutes*, 2002)

3

Public arenas, personal testimonies: the institution and contestation of British official memory of Bloody Sunday

In January 1972, British soldiers shot dead thirteen unarmed Irish nationalist civilians and seriously wounded fifteen others (one of whom subsequently died) on the occasion of a civil rights demonstration held in the city of Derry to protest against the inequalities, structural discrimination and state repression suffered by Northern Ireland's Catholic minority. This event, subsequently remembered around the world as 'Bloody Sunday', is the most important single case of the abuse of state power perpetrated by the British Army in the course of its long counter-insurgency campaign in Northern Ireland.[1] As such, Bloody Sunday occupies a pivotal position in the unfolding history of the Troubles. Throughout the war it was situated at the very centre of the politics of memory, and the repercussions of its unresolved 'contested past'[2] – at once political, cultural and psychic – have continued to reverberate more than three decades later, within the ongoing conflict over the vision and direction of the peace process.

'War memory . . . is first of all the possession of those individuals, military or civilian, who have experienced war' and lived to tell their story.[3] However, the cultural frameworks which shape the representation of wars are also the intimate concern of nation-states and their governing elites. The collective memory of selected episodes of armed conflict in the past is a central component in the symbolic repertoire, or national imaginary, through which popular identification with the nation and the politics of the national interest is secured. When war is a present-day reality, a state's ability to construct and install a narrative justifying the legitimacy of its own resort to violence – a narrative fundamental to both its political authority and its capacity to deploy military force effectively – centres on its efforts to control the meaning and memory of unfolding events. As Ashplant et al. have argued, the war memories of individuals are necessarily bound up in a complex social process involving agencies of the State, and also of civil society, in the making, circulating and contesting of such narratives. The 'dominant national narrative', which organizes and articulates what they term 'official memory',

operates so as to 'frame' war memories articulated from below, in forms which serve the interests of that nation-state. Such framing establishes horizons and structures which condition the meanings assigned to any particular war.

These meanings 'impact on all other agencies, reaching down to the very process of memory-formation by individuals and within families'.

> This hegemonic framing of memory is a selective process in which the nation-state exercises its power to recognize and incorporate within its national narrative only certain war memories, whilst others are officially marginalized or forgotten.[4]

State strategies, and 'the regimes of official memory and forgetting which they institute', vary according to '[d]ifferent kinds of state power'.[5] In liberal-democratic states subject to public scrutiny and accountability, like the UK, contests over the meaning and memory of war are fought out in democratic public arenas, exposing official memory to ideological challenges which the State sets out to master and defuse. Where strategies aimed at 'constraining, reshaping or silencing' memories from below are adopted,[6] these may work, paradoxically, 'not to disperse but to intensify efforts to remember and record, undertaken now by agencies in civil society representing victims or their families', thereby helping to constitute alternative public memories of war.[7]

The formation of memories of Bloody Sunday has been a process shaped in this way, both from below, as survivors articulated the stories of their own experiences of the massacre and its aftermath, and from above, as agencies of the British State – the Government, the army and the judiciary – moved to discredit and marginalize the view from below by installing a state-sanctioned official memory. This legitimized the violence perpetrated by its forces and sought to blame those killed for their own deaths. British soldiers were exonerated of any wrongdoing at the Public Inquiry set up by the British Government to investigate the killings in their immediate aftermath, conducted by the Lord Chief Justice, Lord Widgery. The Widgery Report endorsed the army's narrative of events – that British soldiers fired only at identifiable targets in self-defence, having come under sustained attack from the IRA, which was held responsible for initiating the violence – and failed to clear the names of the dead from unfounded army allegations that they were gunmen and nail-bombers.[8] The Report instituted an official memory of Bloody Sunday, substantially adopted by Northern Irish Unionists as well as majority public opinion in Britain, that served the interests of the British military and political establishment as it conducted its 'propaganda war' in Northern Ireland.[9]

Such denial of responsibility by state institutions, for abuses of power and injustices committed by its agents, is not only a strategy of legitimation but functions as a weapon of psychological warfare.[10] It works to 'silence and marginalize' the voices of its opponents, which are 'held to the level of private remembrance' – that is, actively kept private, or privatized – under the 'extreme pressures' exerted by hegemonic official memory supported by the material resources of the State.[11] Survivor memory of Bloody Sunday was formed in opposition to this narrative imposed from above, and from a matter of hours after the attack was mobilized publicly to insist on the innocence of the victims and to demand justice for them. In the years since 1972, Irish nationalists and Republicans developed and sustained an annual Bloody Sunday commemoration in Derry as a public arena from which to challenge this official memory, through the articulation of an oppositional narrative, or counter-memory, that asserts the innocence of the victims, seeks to expose the strategies deployed against them, and denounces both the violence and the injustice inherent in the British military occupation of Northern Ireland. In 1992, as the Irish war continued unabated, Derry's local human rights organization the Bloody Sunday Initiative described the atrocity as

> a microcosm, a symbol of what Britain does in Ireland. The British state and its agencies still kill people, deliberately, as a matter of policy without any compunction, often with no regret. It kills as a first step not as a last resort. It systematically manipulates the judicial processes of the courts or inquests in order that the law becomes an instrument to exonerate the state for its actions . . . It deliberately feeds false information against those it has killed . . . It establishes inquiries to conceal what has happened and to exonerate those responsible. It censors and distorts the view of those who disagree with it.[12]

These competing narratives have defined the politics of memory in the case of Bloody Sunday. By studying this particular case, the second part of the book brings into focus the central themes and dynamics of a more general confrontation between the official memory of the Troubles as promoted by the British State, and the counter-memory of Irish nationalism and Republicanism.

This chapter begins by establishing the contexts of Bloody Sunday in the contested cultural landscape of Derry, the character and purpose of the British Army's intervention there, and the resulting crisis of legitimation as its activities came to be questioned and challenged. It goes on to investigate the institution and contestation of an official memory of Bloody Sunday in three public arenas where civilian eyewitnesses took issue with the official narrative developed by agencies of the State: firstly, in the arena of the mass media with its news coverage of the shootings; secondly, in the arena of British political debate centred on the House of Commons; and thirdly, in the judicial arena of the British Tribunal of Inquiry chaired by Lord Chief Justice Widgery. The analysis investigates the scope for public articulation, from below, of eyewitness memories within these arenas, which establish terms of entry to the public sphere according to their own particular conventions, procedures and authority. These regulate who is able to speak in public, what can be said and the mode of its expression, and determine its status in relation to powerful state narratives. The chapter traces how an official narrative of Bloody Sunday was constructed through the strategies deployed against eyewitness opponents within these arenas, culminating in the representation of Bloody Sunday developed in the Widgery Report setting out the findings of the Tribunal. This consolidated and instituted the official memory of those events, which predominated for twenty-six years until the re-opening of the Inquiry under Lord Saville, announced in January 1998 by Prime Minister Blair, and which has yet to relinquish its hegemonic power even after the conclusion of Saville's investigation. (As I write, the long-overdue Saville Report is still awaited.) The chapter concludes by analysing the profound political and psychic effects of the Widgery Tribunal on the civilian eyewitnesses, the injured, the families of the bereaved and the nationalist community in Derry and beyond.

Contested space and the legitimation of state violence: Derry/Londonderry, 1968–72

The Bloody Sunday massacre occurred in a place constructed through a long history of contested attachments. The city known in Irish nationalist culture as 'Derry', in Ulster Unionist culture as 'Londonderry', and in the discourse of liberal tolerance as 'Derry/Londonderry', is a place where walls and barricades, borders and boundaries are inscribed into the physical and imaginative geography of the city, structuring the ways in which the past is felt to 'live on' in the present.[13] The Catholic ghetto of the Bogside, the location of Bloody Sunday, was formed by a geographical segregation of religious, or 'ethnic', communities, originating in the establishment of the loyalist and Protestant city of Londonderry during the colonial settlement of Ulster in the early seventeenth century.[14] Throughout its modern history, the city has been shaped by violent and traumatic conflict focused on the spatial imposition and contestation of state power, remembered in highly politicized cultures of public commemoration. Its walled citadel became a refuge for Protestant settlers fleeing the native Irish insurgency of 1641, and a defensive bastion for Protestant supporters of King William III during the wars of 1688–91, that secured both the Protestant succession to the British Crown and the Protestant ascendancy in Ireland. Having withstood the Great Siege of Derry in 1688–89, the city was transformed into a mythical place, 'forever memorable as an impregnable bulwark of British Protestantism, of civil and religious liberty'.[15] Keeping alive the memory of the great siege has been the mission of the Loyal Order of the Apprentice Boys of Derry, which parades the Derry Walls every 12 August in commemoration. This ritual parading functioned to drive 'home the point that, despite the Catholic majority [established since 1891], Derry would remain a Protestant city'.[16] In the popular memory of Derry's Catholics, loyalist commemoration of the siege made Derry City and its Walls a symbol of Protestant domination and of their own second-class status. Overlooking the Bogside from their commanding position on the impregnable Walls, the loyalist parades exuded provocation and threat, while the nationalists' own smaller commemorative parades, to mark the 1916 Easter Rising, were contained in the Bogside ghetto by 'a rigid, unwritten law that Catholics could not march within the city walls', enforced with violence by the police.[17]

During the independence struggle of 1919–22, the British Army in alliance with local loyalist paramilitaries and the new, almost exclusively Protestant, Ulster Special Constabulary, defeated the original IRA in Derry, ensuring that the city remained within Northern Ireland, cut off from the Irish Free State by the Border running some four miles to its west.[18] As the Northern State was consolidated politically after 1922, the spatial manipulation of gerrymandered electoral boundaries secured permanent political dominance for the Unionist electorate in a city where, by 1966, Catholics formed two-thirds of the population. Systematic discrimination in housing and employment, and a battery of draconian special powers legislation retained from the 1920s, kept Catholics 'in a position of permanent and hopeless inferiority'.[19] Thus, the Catholics of Derry found themselves caught in a double exclusion: as a powerless majority hemmed in to a ghetto in their own city; and also as a powerless minority trapped by partition within 'a state run by their enemies'.[20] The existence of the Border reinforced the historical divisions within the contested space of the city, heightening its 'internal borders', manifest 'in the slash mark between the names Derry/Londonderry; in the sectarian housing estates; in the old walled architecture of the town and in the competing histories of its development'.[21]

The Northern Ireland civil rights movement launched in 1968 was an attempt to break the immurement of Catholics within these internal borders by means of protest and civil disobedience. The campaign for equality of citizenship implicitly confronted the spatial organization of segregation and containment upheld by the Unionist State. This challenge to symbolic space was made explicit when Derry was chosen as the focal point for demonstrations that defied the ban on Catholic parades entering the walled city, and were met with brutal violence by Northern Ireland's militarized Special Constabulary. In a repetition of events of the 1920s,[22] police reprisals against the protest movement took the form of violent assaults on the physical and symbolic space of the Catholic ghetto. In 1969, in response to a series of such attacks, nationalists blocked the main entrances to the Bogside with defensive barricades and declared a 'no-go' area from which police were barred, known as Free Derry.

This geographical confrontation, centred on the assertion of state control over all parts of the city and its transgression by popular nationalist resistance, reached an apogee in August 1969 with the 'battle of the Bogside', a pivotal event in the escalation of the Troubles, which was sparked by an Apprentice Boys' parade. Armed police joined loyalists in an attempted invasion of the ghetto, while nationalists, fearing a pogrom, successfully defended their area with petrol bombs in forty-eight hours of fierce fighting centred on Rossville Street, causing British troops to be brought onto the streets of Derry 'to restore law and order'.[23] This dialectic of spatial contestation was intensified by the British military presence. The repressive power of the State was increasingly brought to bear on the Bogside and the adjacent Creggan and Brandywell districts, by the establishment in 1970 of a

British Army Observation Post on Derry Walls to monitor all movement of people in and out of the ghetto,[24] by the introduction in August 1971 of the controversial legal weapon of internment without trial and by the use of the British Army, including its elite battlefield troops such as the Parachute Regiment, to police the nationalist 'communities in revolt'.[25] Repression provoked an intensification of popular resistance focused on the imaginative geography of the Free Derry no-go area. This was declared independent of the civil authority, barricaded-off from the rest of the city· and defended by a citizens' militia, which developed into a re-emergent IRA waging an increasingly effective guerrilla campaign, with enthusiastic local support, against the British military occupation.[26] These competing imaginative geographies of control and resistance, transforming the material territory into a cultural landscape formed on the pattern of the conflicted past, constituted the contested space within which the British Army's narrative of legitimation was deployed, and where the civil rights march and ensuing massacre took place on Bloody Sunday.

When the British Army was reintroduced onto the streets of Derry and Belfast in August 1969, it entered the conflict zone with well-established strategies of legitimation, honed by extensive experience of colonial counter-insurgency warfare, designed to install an official narrative of events and secure its reproduction as the dominant memory. The British State represented its military involvement in Northern Ireland as a narrative about 'keeping the peace' between 'two warring tribes', and 'restoring law and order': its soldiers were virtuous and benevolent, unlike the 'troublemakers' and 'extremists' from both communities who incited and carried out unnecessary and undemocratic acts of violence. This was emphatically not 'a war' but a policing operation in support of the civil authorities.[27] According to the British State's discourse, the legitimate use of force was deployed only in response to civil disorder, and with restraint conditioned by a legal framework that determined the army's rules of engagement. The British Army's 'Code no. 70771: Instructions for opening fire in Northern Ireland' was formulated by the Ministry of Defence in consultation with the Army Legal Service and the Treasury Solicitor (a body of solicitors working full-time as civil servants to give legal advice and support to British government departments), and was carried by all British soldiers on duty in the form of the so-called 'Yellow Card'. In its original version issued in September 1969, shortly after the deployment of troops, the Yellow Card established that 'soldiers had a common-law duty, no different from the ordinary citizen, to aid the civil power in restoring law and order, by force if necessary', and 'a similar duty to help prevent crime and effect lawful arrests, using "reasonable force" '.[28] Based on the principle that firearms 'must only be used as a last resort',[29] it authorized soldiers to open fire either under orders from an officer on the spot or on their individual initiative 'at anyone carrying a firearm who was thought to be about to use it and refused to halt, or at a person throwing a petrol bomb'.[30] The Yellow Card stipulated that aimed shots could be fired only against a person whose actions were 'likely to endanger life and [where] there is no other way to prevent the danger'.[31]

Relative to other colonial counter-insurgency campaigns fought by the British Army as the Empire disintegrated in the 1950s and 1960s, the Yellow Card did provide some constraint on the exercise of military force. One soldier, who had served in Aden prior to the withdrawal of 1967, before going to Belfast two years later, recalls:

> We weren't governed by the same rules that we were in Ireland. The lads over there [in Aden] could be a lot rougher . . . because we never had the newspapers there . . . or anyone else who could actually see what we were doing. It made a lot of difference because you were given a freer hand right across the board, from commanding officers right down to the corporals in charge of the men on the ground. You could just be . . . a lot more ruthless.[32]

The Yellow Card defines how the State is to conduct warfare under conditions of public scrutiny where concerns about witnessing and representation must be taken into account. In Northern Ireland, as armed conflict unexpectedly escalated and the army entered into confrontation with rioters armed with petrol bombs and with gunmen (initially in loyalist areas like the Shankill, but from July 1970 increasingly in nationalist areas too), justification had to be made for the killing of the first unarmed civilians by British soldiers. Whereas, famously, British troops had been welcomed by nationalist communities in Belfast and Derry as protection against loyalist attacks, their killing of unarmed Catholics, often in disputed circumstances, led to a rapid deterioration in confidence, to popular protests and to the first public allegations that the British Army was operating an indiscriminate 'shoot-to-kill' policy.[33]

Following the killing of a teenager, Daniel O'Hagan, by an army marksman in Belfast in late July 1970, 'around 1,000 women marched to an army base to protest at the shooting', while at the inquest local eyewitnesses contested the army's story, that O'Hagan was fired on while lighting the fuse of a petrol-bomb after a warning had been given that petrol-bombers would be shot.[34] Sinn Féin's President, Gerry Adams, recalls that for young nationalists in West Belfast, 'the killing of Danny O'Hagan came as a dreadful confirmation . . . that what had started as a peaceful campaign for civil rights was now resolving itself into a violent confrontation between the armed forces and the ordinary people . . . Now it seemed we were heading inexorably towards war.'[35] In adjudicating on this confrontation, however, the British press 'had no qualms in accepting the army's word that the victim was a "petrol bomber" or "gunman" . . . Even journalists who believed themselves to be sceptical tended unquestioningly to accept the army's version, unless they had personally witnessed the event.'[36]

The issuing of a revised Yellow Card in January 1971 – a direct result of the challenges to the army in the O'Hagan case[37] – functioned to strengthen this claim to legitimacy in the exercise of military force. The revised code stipulated that a 'challenge must be given before opening fire',[38] except in circumstances 'when hostile firing is taking place in your area, and a warning is impracticable, or when any delay could lead to a death or serious injury to people whom it is your duty to protect or to yourself'.[39] As the conflict between the British Army and Irish nationalists escalated throughout 1971, with increased momentum after the introduction of internment without trial that August, the Yellow Card provided the legal underpinning for the army's narrative of events, and the terms in which individual soldiers couched their own testimonies concerning the mortal shooting of civilians. According to one Welsh officer, 'any active soldier with his wits about him can use the yellow card to defend firing his rifle at a Catholic in virtually any situation'.[40]

In his account of a final briefing given to soldiers beginning a tour of duty in the North in the mid-1970s, former Paratrooper A.F.N. Clarke, recalls being told: 'If you can see them, you can shoot them. Just remember, you are still bound by the conditions of the yellow card. That means whatever happens, they always shoot first. Whether they actually do or not, nobody will ever know. Get my meaning?'[41] Where eyewitnesses were present, however, soldiers' stories were always open to contestation. Under these circumstances, the assessment made in early January 1972 by the Commander of Land Forces for Northern Ireland, Major-General Robert Ford, that existing 'minimum force' regulations were hindering soldiers' ability to pacify the Free Derry no-go area (especially the activities of the so-called 'Derry Young Hooligans', whose daily rioting 'undermines our ability to deal with the gunmen and bombers and threatens what is left of law and order on the west bank' of the city), signalled a dangerous change in strategy for the army.[42] Ford's proposal 'to shoot selected ringleaders among the DYH, after clear warnings have been issued',[43] implied an abandoning of Yellow Card rules of engagement that offered some protection to unarmed civilians, and a reversion to colonial methods, 'in front of an increasingly watchful media and a proliferation of human rights groups'.[44]

On Bloody Sunday, unarmed nationalist civilians were exposed to British military fire-power in an unprecedented manner and degree, after some 20,000 men, women, and children joined a march organized by the Northern Ireland Civil Rights Association (NICRA) in protest against internment, and set off to walk from Creggan down through the Bogside to a rally at the Guildhall in the city-centre (see map 1). En route, it encountered British Army barriers erected, as Liam Wray remembers, to prevent entry into 'the sacred territory of the unionists' and 'to confine us to the ghetto'.[45] While the obstruction provoked the usual ritualistic rioting by a section of nationalist youth, the main body of the march turned away to hold a rally at the symbolic landmark of Free Derry Corner on Rossville Street. Before this rally could begin, an attack, described by the army as an 'arrest operation' against leading rioters, was launched through the barriers by soldiers from the Parachute Regiment. They assaulted and arrested not only rioters running away from the barrier but marchers, milling around prior to the meeting, and local residents; and as the frightened crowd fled, in a stampede south down

Rossville Street in the direction of Free Derry Corner, the soldiers opened fire into it using standard NATO self-loading rifles (SLRs), powerful battlefield weapons with a range of two to three miles.[46] During the next ten minutes, 'the Paras fired 108 rounds of 7.62[mm] live ammunition, an average of one every six seconds from different positions in a confined space little larger than a football pitch'.[47] Within this space, overlooked from the city's Walls where other soldiers were firing down into the crowd, the shooting – fatal and near-fatal – of unarmed civilians, including people who were running or crawling away, lying wounded on the ground, waving handkerchiefs as white flags, and going to the aid of the wounded and the dying, took place in four locations: in a car park on the northern side of Rossville Flats; in a forecourt on their southern side; on a rubble barricade, part of the Free Derry defences across Rossville Street from the flats to the gable wall of Glenfada Park; and in a courtyard of Glenfada Park and the alley leading to Abbey Park.[48] These 'sites of trauma' recur repeatedly in memories of the atrocity. If controversies like that over the killing of Daniel O'Hagan offered a challenge to the army's narrative of its conduct in Northern Ireland, Bloody Sunday threw that narrative into crisis, and exceptional measures were required to re-establish the hegemony of official memory.

Contested memories in the media and political arenas

The public arena where the contest between competing narratives of Bloody Sunday first emerged was that of the mass media: specifically, press and broadcast news. As Tricia Ziff notes, Bloody Sunday was 'an atrocity committed in the full view of the world's media', with journalists, press photographers and television film-cameramen present in Derry 'in large numbers' to report on the march.[49] Within hours of the shootings, news interviews with civilian witnesses were being broadcast which directly contradicted statements made by representatives of the British Army about what had happened. One of the first, John Berman's interview for the BBC with the local Catholic priest Father (later, Bishop) Edward Daly, who had witnessed the shooting and death of 17-year-old Jack Duddy, and had himself come under fire, was recorded while the army assault was still in progress, with both of them in deep shock.[50] In such interviews, the first survivor memories of Bloody Sunday entered a public arena in the form of eyewitness testimony – 'the "factual" account of lived experiences'[51] – told to bear witness to the truth about events and to set the record straight. The earliest accounts, broadcast in news bulletins from late afternoon and throughout the evening, pointed to the perpetration of a massacre of unarmed civilians by the British Army, and prompted immediate and sustained denunciations of the army's conduct by Catholic and nationalist leaders, including the Bishop of Derry, the Primate of All Ireland and the Republic of Ireland's *Taoiseach*.[52]

The earliest interviews given by soldiers were ineffectual in rebuffing these allegations of an army shoot-to-kill operation targeting civilians. General

Ford himself, in an 'off-the-cuff account of the situation' given to the BBC within an hour of the operation, proved to be misinformed when he stated that the army had fired three shots, killing two people, after coming under fire, only to be corrected by a journalist with the information that there were at least three dead. The Paras' commander on the ground, Colonel Wilford, interviewed for the ITN *News at Ten*, also claimed that the army 'came under fire', and was also petrol-bombed and attacked with acid from 'the flats', after which 'three gunmen were hit'; but he then indicated that five casualties had been inflicted by British soldiers (implying that two had not been armed), described these as 'unfortunate' and the number 'quite large in these circumstances', but nevertheless expressed his satisfaction with the conduct of the operation. In another televised interview, one of the Paratroopers said: 'We don't deny' reports of civilians having been shot in the back, 'but who is to say that it was not a ricochet?'[53]

In response to this early failure to provide a legitimizing narrative of the operation, a damage-limitation exercise to counter civilian eyewitness reports was launched by General Ford's 'special advisor on information policy', Colonel Maurice Tugwell, in a midnight interview for BBC radio news aimed at catching the Monday-morning newspapers. Tugwell insisted that soldiers had fired shots 'only at identifiable gunmen and bombers: all of those killed were males of "arms-carrying age", one of whom had nail bombs in his pockets . . . [and] four of the dead had been on the army's wanted list'.[54] This account of events was repeated at media briefings in London by the Ministry of Defence and in New York by the British Information Service during the two days following.[55] It asserted the legitimacy of the army's action within the terms of its rules of engagement, by making counter-allegations representing its victims as illegal combatants who posed a threat to life. This laid the foundation for the British State's official memory of Bloody Sunday, thereby ensuring a battle between the army's narrative and the memories of the wounded, of other survivors and of the witnessing community to establish the truth about the shootings.

This battle was played out both in the news media and in the political arena of the House of Commons. On the day after Bloody Sunday, the Conservative Home Secretary Reginald Maudling made a statement in the House about the 'disturbances in Londonderry yesterday', about which he expressed neither regret nor sympathy, but merely 'anxiety that a number of people were killed and injured'.[56] His brief account of events was based entirely on the report of General Tuzo, the General Officer Commanding Northern Ireland, thereby reinforcing the emergent official memory:

> [W]hen the Army advanced to make arrests among the trouble-makers they came under fire from a block of flats and other quarters. At this stage the members of the orderly, although illegal, march were no longer in the near vicinity. The Army returned fire directed at them with aimed shots and inflicted a number of casualties on those who were attacking them with firearms and with bombs.[57]

Announcing the Government's intention to establish 'an independent inquiry into the circumstances of the march and the incidents leading up to the casualties which resulted', Maudling indicated that this was necessary '[i]n view of the statements that have been made which publicly dispute this account'.[58] The Home Secretary agreed with the Labour Opposition that 'the inquiry should be impartial, judicial and should proceed with speed'. But he immediately went on to pre-empt its findings by stating: 'The Army was acting under normal instructions, which is to deal with breaches of the law, to apprehend lawbreakers, and to do both with the minimum force necessary.'[59]

One voice 'publicly disputing this account' was raised in the House in response to this announcement, that of the MP for Mid-Ulster, Bernadette Devlin. As a platform speaker at the civil rights rally on Bloody Sunday, Devlin claimed the right to speak in the Commons debate as 'the only representative in this House who was an eye-witness . . . present yesterday'. Despite her claim to eyewitness authority, the record of the debate in *Hansard* reveals the difficulty involved in articulating Irish nationalist survivor memory in this hostile arena, where Devlin was subjected to silencing and disparagement from some members of the British political establishment, who used the procedures and protocols of the Commons against her. Having twice called Maudling a liar ('Nobody shot at the paratroops, but someone will shortly'), and after her repeated efforts on points of order 'to ask a question of that murdering hypocrite' had been disregarded by the Speaker, who refused to call her while taking questions from eleven other MPs (all of whom were men), Devlin crossed the floor to the government front bench and struck the Home Secretary, causing uproar and her removal from the chamber.[60] When eventually she was granted the opportunity to speak, during the longer Commons debate on Bloody Sunday on 1 February, Devlin criticised government ministers who 'put forward the Army's point of view as fact',[61] and pointed to evidence that contradicted this account, in the face of derisive heckling from some backbenchers:

> Major-General Ford was heard and seen by millions watching television last night to say that 200 shots were fired on the British Army before the British Army opened fire. We shall hear from the reporters of newspapers and sound radio and from civil liberties observers – (*Laughter.*) (HON. MEMBERS: 'Do not laugh.') . . . We shall hear from the BBC that there were no 200 shots fired and we shall see that on that newsreel.[62]

Under these circumstances, Devlin 'made no apology for putting my side of the story beside the story of the people who took part in the march and for questioning a number of the facts put forward by the Minister [of State for Defence] today'.[63] Her testimony to the House was: 'There were no shots fired at the Army . . . the Parachute Regiment . . . fired into a crowd of unarmed civilians and thousands lay there.'[64] She questioned the army's claim to have 'fired only at identifiable . . . targets', asking: 'If those people were all snipers as the Minister for Defence says, or people throwing petrol bombs at the British Army, how does it come about that the majority happen to be shot in the back or in the back of the head?'[65] She read out the names of the thirteen dead and challenged the Minister to establish who of them were the four said to be on the British Army's wanted list.[66] She also placed Bloody Sunday in the context of a wider official strategy of representation, exposing how other innocent civilians killed by British soldiers had then been slandered by an army public relations campaign: 'We remember Barney Watt, Annette McGavigan and Eamonn McDevitt. The list goes on for ever of people who have been accused after their death. After accusations have been blazoned in the newspapers they have been found innocent but never cleared.'[67]

The nationalist counter-memory articulated in the news media and in the Commons provoked sympathetic anger or disquiet among sections of the British public, though much of this was misinformed and readily channelled into support for the Government's inquiry. Labour's Shadow Home Secretary Merlyn Rees, for example, expressed 'our sympathy with all the families of all the victims killed and injured, civilian and military, as a result of yesterday's events', when no British soldiers were killed or seriously injured on Bloody Sunday. Welcoming the Government's announcement of an inquiry, Rees called for an impartial and independent investigation focused on several key questions:

> Where did the fire come from? At the bar of world opinion it is important to know the facts . . . Was the decision to go into the Bogside a reaction to events, or was it the planned disposition of security forces? Who decided this? Was it . . . with the full knowledge of . . . the Government?[68]

These are the questions that a public inquiry might have been expected to answer, yet they remained unresolved thirty years later. The immediate effect of the announcement was to channel and draw off wider public debate in Britain about Bloody Sunday, limiting the spaces where such questions could be posed, and closing down the democratic arena of the media where critical investigation of the army operation was already actively underway.

This was conducted most thoroughly and systematically by the *Sunday Times*' highly regarded 'Insight' team.[69] On the night of 30 January the paper's editor, Harold Evans, had sent to Derry two of the team's most experienced members: war correspondent Murray Sayle and Derek Humphry who had extensive experience of covering the Troubles in the city with 'many contacts on both sides, particularly in the . . . Bogside'.[70] The two journalists conducted an intensive three-day investigation of 'primary sources (eyewitnesses, photos taken on the day, the bullet marks and other evidence still visible on the ground, and above all the ground itself)'.[71] On this basis they constructed a map, drawn up by an artist, John Butterworth, which plotted the positions of the dead bodies and of the wounded when they were hit.[72] They also produced a report, filed by telephone on 3 February, which derived a hypothesis about the army operation consistent both with this evidence and with 'lines of thinking' current in British counter-insurgency circles, then strongly influenced by the ideas of Brigadier Frank Kitson.[73]

According to Sayle and Humphry, the military plan guiding the operation sought to flush out not young hooligans but 'about eighty hard-core militants' believed by military intelligence to constitute the IRA in the Bogside (which, unlike in Belfast, had hitherto resisted effective containment by the Parachute Regiment).[74] By firing live shots at the civil rights march – those which wounded Damien Donaghy and John Johnston in William Street some twenty minutes before the main assault began – the IRA would be provoked into returning firing, and thereby drawn into an ambush. Sayle and Humphry wrote: 'If the IRA gunmen could be induced to stand and fight while other demonstrators fled, a [large] snatch squad . . . would be able to kill them or take them in', and 'the IRA problem would be, according to the [intelligence] reports, as good as over'.[75] Their account of the operation itself sought to demonstrate its logical consistency and its conformity to standard operational procedures, as the execution of such a plan 'to ambush the supposed concentration of IRA men' in the area around the Rossville Flats:

> The Saracens took up rehearsed blocking positions along Rossville Street and next to Rossville Flats. Paratroopers wearing combat and not anti-riot gear jumped out and dropped into standard British Army firing positions in spots clearly selected in advance . . . Executing the normal fire-and-movement tactic taught to British infantry . . . the Paratroopers cleared the barricades in Rossville Street by shooting everyone on it or near it [sic] . . . A section of Paratroopers running through the Little Diamond to link up with their comrades at the barricade got behind it . . . and began laying down a field of fire behind Rossville Street Flats . . . Paratroopers leading [this] pincer movement ran into Glenfada courtyard . . . and began shooting – a normal street-fighting tactic when entering a possible ambush area . . . and continued through to Abbey Park and repeated the clearing fire . . . Paratroopers burst into a house at the end of Chamberlain Street . . . and arrested 22 men . . . a part of the mass round-up of 'IRA militants'.[76]

Drawing on 'unanimous' eyewitness testimony from Catholics, including 'priests and doctors, supporters of both wings of the IRA and people opposed in varying degrees of vehemence to the IRA', Sayle and Humphry went on to point out the major flaw in the execution of this plan: the soldiers were not shooting at the IRA, who 'played no part whatsoever in provoking the Army operation or fighting back'.[77] This, they concluded, was 'a Parachute Regiment special operation that went disastrously wrong'.[78]

The establishment on 1 February of the Tribunal of Inquiry under Chief Justice Lord Widgery had the effect of the rapid closing down of further investigation and reportage about Bloody Sunday in the British media, after the Downing Street Press Office issued a statement claiming that any coverage 'which anticipated the Tribunal's findings' would be *sub judice* and open to legal proceedings for contempt of court.[79] Although there was no precedent for the use of contempt laws 'to stop the media investigating a matter of public concern just because a tribunal had been set up', the intended purpose of the laws being rather to guard against any improper attempt at influencing its outcome,[80] Sayle and Humphry were informed on 4 February that their report would not be published. The justification by the *Sunday Times* stated: 'The law is that until the Lord Chief Justice completes his inquiry nobody may offer to the British public any consecutive account of the events in Derry last weekend.'[81] Another major investigative report due to be published by the *Observer* was also withdrawn, and a documentary film by Thames Television significantly amended and reduced in scope, with the overall effect that 'accounts . . . which would have been very damaging to the army's case [were] suppressed'.[82] Henceforth, the contest over the truth about what had occurred in Derry on 30 January 1972, between the legitimizing narrative of the British Army and the testimonies of civilian eyewitnesses, would be adjudicated according to the procedures and proto-cols of a judicial arena operating under the leadership of the most senior judge in the UK, and any subsequent 'consecutive account of events' would have to reckon with its authority.

Contested memories in the judicial arena of the Widgery Tribunal

The Widgery Tribunal was the response of the British Government to the 'torrent of international criticism' that greeted the news of Bloody Sunday.[83] It was established by the British and Northern Irish Parliaments under the terms of the Tribunals of Inquiry (Evidence) Act of 1921 for the purpose of 'inquiring into a definite matter of urgent public importance, namely the events on Sunday 30 January which led to loss of life in connection with the procession in Londonderry on that day'.[84] Dermot Walsh, the barrister whose critical analysis of the Widgery Tribunal was instrumental in per-suading the British Government to open a second public inquiry into these events in 1998, notes that such Tribunals had been defined by the Salmon Report of 1966 as exceptional measures reserved for 'those rare occasions when the purity and integrity of public life has been threatened by a crisis of public confidence'.[85] Sitting in public, and invested by the Act with 'all the powers, rights and privileges of the High Court or a judge of the High Court in respect of compelling witnesses to attend and submit to examination and compelling the production of documents', a Tribunal of Inquiry differed fun-damentally from the High Court in that its remit was 'not to establish the guilt or innocence of the parties allegedly involved, but to establish the truth, if any, behind the allegations'.[86] In exercising this 'inquisitorial' function,[87] a Tribunal was not restricted to making a final judgment based on the evi-dence gathered, presented and challenged by the opposing parties in a case, but was envisaged as itself actively conducting the investigation. It was free to establish its own procedures and rules of evidence in order to ensure full legal representation and safeguards for all witnesses and interested parties.[88] Through the exercise of its power to inquire into the truth by collecting and investigating all the available evidence, the Tribunal's task was 'to persuade the public that the full facts have been established', thereby acting as an instrument in 'restoring public confidence in the integrity of government'.[89]

In the case of the Widgery Tribunal, argues Walsh, the 'crisis in public confidence' stemmed from 'the most serious allegations that had ever been made in peace time concerning the activities of the modern British Army within the United Kingdom'. The allegations had 'rocked public confidence in the state to the core' in Britain, Ireland and throughout the democratic world. Restoration of public confidence in the State and its institutions depended, firstly, on the truth being established by an investigation which was independent 'in both substance and appearance'; and secondly, in the event of the Tribunal finding that 'the deaths and injuries were unlawful or could have been avoided', on those who were culpable being held publicly to account.[90]

While the announcement of the Inquiry under Lord Widgery was broadly welcomed by public opinion in Britain, it was greeted with suspicion by Derry nationalists of all hues, who doubted the impartiality of any investigation sponsored by the British Government, but especially one conducted by a law lord who was himself a former British Army officer.[91] As Eamonn McCann points out, the question for local people, thousands of whom had witnessed the atrocity at first hand, 'was not, what truth would Widgery find? but whether Widgery could be trusted to tell this truth, and whether, in light of that, local people should give evidence to his inquiry'.[92] Initially, leaders of the 'constitutional' Nationalist Party and the SDLP, as well as Republicans and leftists, called for a popular boycott of the proceedings. Their demand was for an international tribunal, established and conducted under an authority entirely independent of the British State.[93] Some nationalists opposed or abandoned their boycott out of concern about the effects of their self-exclusion from what now appeared to be 'the only constitutional mechanism on offer for dealing with the fraught aftermath of the massacre'.[94]

Significant nationalist involvement was finally secured only on the evening of 21 February, after lawyers from the British National Council for Civil Liberties (NCCL) and the International League for the Rights of Man (ILRM), having studied Widgery's procedures and observed the first full session of the Tribunal that day, reported back to the families at a private meeting in Derry on 'the kind of forum the Inquiry would provide for the Catholic community'.[95] Voicing their view that 'the procedures adopted by Lord Widgery would provide the families of the dead and wounded and civilian eyewitnesses with a fair opportunity to present their own testimony in an open hearing, attended by the press of the world, and to permit their counsel to fully cross-examine the army witnesses', the observers recommended that they should end their boycott and 'actively participate'. According to Eamonn McCann, what swayed Derry citizens towards taking part in the Inquiry was a sense that 'the British Army's story had begun to come apart' already, and 'a feeling which gradually hardened in the area in the days after the killings that the truth was so obvious and the issues so clear-cut that no fudging or cover-up would prove plausible'.[96]

Until the involvement of these civilian witnesses and their legal representatives in the proceedings, the Tribunal could not claim to be conducting a proper investigation. As Widgery himself wrote: 'I wished to hear evidence from people who supported each of the versions of the events of 30 January which had been given currency.'[97] However, far from constituting a public arena in which critical nationalist voices from below would receive due hearing and the army's story would be discredited, the Widgery Tribunal instituted instead a hegemonic strategy of containment, whereby those critical voices were incorporated, marginalized or themselves discredited, by a newly consolidated official memory of Bloody Sunday. The Tribunal was designed to give the impression of being an impartial and *balanced* investigation into the alleged abuses of the rule of law by state forces, while in practice fulfilling a contrary political purpose. Dermot Walsh, in his analysis and evaluation of Widgery's conduct of the Inquiry, concludes that it was flawed throughout by actual 'bias' and the appearance of bias 'in favour of the party whose actions were the primary subject matter of its investigation, namely the soldiers involved in the Bloody Sunday operation';[98] and against those parties 'making allegations critical of the army'.[99] Furthermore, Widgery's handling of the proceedings and his treatment of evidence 'conveys the impression . . . that the tribunal was unduly concerned to build a case against the deceased and injured and thereby cast a more favourable light on the army's actions', in order to exonerate it from blame.[100] In practice, the Tribunal functioned 'to protect the role and activities of the army against damaging analysis', and 'served the interests of the army' (and of its political directors) by corroborating and validating its narrative, at the expense of its victims.[101] Walsh's analysis enables us to understand exactly how the judicial arena of the Tribunal functioned to counter allegations of an army shoot-to-kill operation targeting civilians, by producing an official narrative which questioned the innocence of those killed and affirmed the innocence of their killers.

The construction of the Widgery Tribunal as a judicial arena
This strategy of the State is evident in the political orchestration of the Tribunal from the moment of its foundation. For Walsh, this 'smacks of the British legal and political establishments engaging in a conspiracy to pervert the course of justice in order to protect the political and security establishments'.[102] Confidential minutes of a meeting held at Downing Street on 31 January 1972 between Lord Widgery, Prime Minister Edward Heath and the Lord Chancellor, Lord Hailsham, record their discussion about how Widgery would conduct the Inquiry.[103] The Prime Minister pointed out that '[t]he Inquiry would be operating in a military situation, with Troops coming and going and required for operational duties'.[104] This 'underlined the importance of speed' in commencing and concluding it, and made it 'necessary to bear in mind the possible risk to members of the armed forces,

and even the others, who give evidence', posed by the IRA.[105] Heath also impressed on Widgery: 'It had to be remembered that we were in Northern Ireland fighting not only a military war but a propaganda war.'[106] A number of 'procedural points' were discussed, including the composition of the Tribunal, its location, whether it should sit in public and the appointment of its legal team of solicitors and counsel.

In all cases, procedures favourable to the British Army were pressed and adopted. Contrary to the urging of the leaders of the two main opposition parties in Britain, Widgery departed from customary practice by declining to appoint two other judges to the Tribunal to assist him, preferring to sit alone – 'a former British soldier investigating very serious allegations against British soldiers'.[107] Widgery's view that the Tribunal ought to be 'held in Londonderry, so that people were not inhibited in giving evidence to it' conflicted with that of Heath, who told him that 'the Guildhall, which was the obvious place, might be thought to be on the wrong side of the River Foyle' and suggested that an alternative venue be found 'a little distance away' from the city.[108] The 'wrong side' of the Foyle figures an imaginative geography centred in the predominantly Unionist east bank of the river that bisects the city, reflecting its perspective on the predominantly nationalist west bank, the location of the Bogside where most of the civilian eyewitnesses lived. It also reflects the security concerns of the army, which recommended the eventual location, Coleraine, as Widgery acknowledged in an early draft of his Report, where he refers (in a phrase omitted from the published text) to the advice of 'Army commanders'.[109] Unlike the approach adopted by the earlier Scarman Tribunal into the violence and civil disturbances occurring in parts of Northern Ireland in 1969, which sat in a number of locations, including Derry, 'to facilitate the submission of oral evidence from civilian parties', Widgery clearly succumbed to 'both political and military pressure' to locate his Tribunal outside of Derry, 'to convenience the army and . . . to inconvenience those witnesses from the Bogside and the Creggan who were critical of the army'.[110] Military sensitivities also lay behind the discussion between Widgery, Heath and Hailsham on 'whether the Inquiry should be held in public or in private' – the latter suggestion being in direct contravention of the terms of the 1921 Act.[111] On this point the Prime Minister advised Widgery to 'wait, and see what the Army proposed in this regard',[112] a course of action that eventually resulted in Widgery permitting thirty-five soldiers to testify publicly but anonymously, identified only by a letter or a number.

Political orchestration of the judiciary also resulted in Widgery's limited interpretation of the Tribunal's terms of reference, thereby severely restricting the potential scope of the investigations from the outset. The justification for what he himself called the 'narrowness of the confines of the Inquiry' was that its value 'would largely depend on its being conducted and concluded expeditiously' (as the Prime Minister had wished),[113] ostensibily to address MPs' concerns that a protracted Inquiry might be used to relegate

Bloody Sunday to the backburner.[114] Proceedings were completed with extraordinary haste. A mere seventeen public sessions were held in Coleraine between 21 February and 14 March 1972, followed by three further sessions to hear the closing speeches of the three counsels held in London from 16–20 March,[115] after which the Tribunal concluded, submitting its Report to the Home Secretary, Reginald Maudling, on 10 April, just ten weeks after Bloody Sunday.[116] This contrasts with the two-and-a-half years' duration[117] of the Scarman Inquiry, and with the Saville Inquiry which sat for nearly four years. Widgery announced his interpretation of the Inquiry's remit at its preliminary sitting on 14 February:

> The limits of the Inquiry in space were the streets of Londonderry in which the disturbances and the shootings took place; in time, the period beginning with the moment when the march first became involved in violence and ending with the deaths of the deceased and the conclusion of the affair.[118]

These spatial and temporal restrictions effectively excluded consideration of army activity elsewhere in Derry that Sunday (including the Walls overlooking the Bogside, where army snipers were stationed), and of whether the Paras had been carrying out a planned operation. After intense criticism of this remit, Widgery conceded that the operational plans and orders given by army officers before the march – but not 'the political and military thinking behind those orders' – would be considered.[119] 'Moral judgements' were also excluded from the remit.[120] These and other restrictions ensured that the Inquiry would not investigate the key questions of political or military culpability for the killings, whether the legal constraints on the use of armed force by the State had been flouted, and whether 'a political decision [had been] taken to use the march as an excuse to restore the hegemony of the security forces' in the no-go area of the Bogside.[121]

The political purpose of the Tribunal was also furthered by its constitution as a judicial arena governed by particular procedures for eliciting and interrogating evidence, including the crucial witness statements. In the four weeks immediately after Bloody Sunday, some 700 eyewitness testimonies were collected by NICRA on behalf of the Committee for the Administration of Justice in London and by the NCCL.[122] These individual accounts originated in the exchange of stories within the private arenas of the Catholic ghetto. Don Mullan recalls how his decision to make a sworn public statement stemmed from 'retelling the story of my experience at the rubble barricade [where five young men were killed] to my friend Shaunie and our mutual friend, Murray Gormley . . . [who] had listened intently. Murray was in his mid-twenties, wiser and more experienced. After I had finished my story, he told me . . . that he felt I should, based on my experience, make a statement.'[123] Their collection, in the Holy Child Primary School's hall, in the dispensary on Central Drive, Creggan, and in the front room of NICRA leader Bridget Bond,[124] was stimulated by the announcement of the Tribunal on 1 February 1972, and they were presented as evidence to Widgery in early March.

In form, these personal narratives were shaped by the requirements of the judicial arena in which, it was anticipated, they would be read and their truth recognized. In order not to compromise the necessary objectivity, the statements concentrate almost entirely on the empirical details of personal movements, activities and locations within the killing zones, and what was seen and heard of the attack. One sensory impression that seared itself into the memories of eyewitnesses and runs through countless testimonies was, inevitably, the sight of blood – on the pavement, in the road, saturating clothes, pouring from bullet wounds, emerging from mouths and noses, covering the hands of those who tried to help the injured and dying.[125] Consider, for example, the testimony of Sean McDermott, an 18-year-old apprentice mechanic, who, witnessing the shooting of Hugh Gilmour, 'got hold of him and assisted him around the corner of the Flats on the side nearest Free Derry Corner'. Attending to his injury, McDermott saw

> a narrow hole on the left side of his body and an exit on the right side from which his innards protruded . . . blood and matter came from the narrow wound. My mate began to give Hugh Gilmore [*sic*] the kiss of life, but blood started to come from the injured man's mouth . . . I looked around then and saw Bernard McGuigan . . . further out in the Square [towards St Joseph's Place]. I saw him put his hands in the air as a gesture of peace and a bullet hit him in the right eye. I think the soldiers were over in Glenfada Park. He fell to the ground, blood pumping out of his head. I and my friend ran behind the wall beside the phone box near the shops and took cover there. Bernard McGuigan was at this time lying dead about two yards in front of us.[126]

Most witnesses, like McDermott, were themselves survivors whose own lives had been endangered. Despite – or perhaps because of – the exclusion or reduction to a bare fact of all subjective and emotional responses to the horrific scenes that they describe, these testimonies make chilling reading. Many ended with a solemn oath, like that of William McL: 'I swear to God there was no nail bombs, petrol bombs or shooting from civilians that day';[127] or a formal affirmation of its status, like Teresa Cassidy's: 'This is a true statement of what I saw on Sunday 30 January 1972. I grant permission for [it] to be used in any enquiry into the events of the day.'[128]

Having deposited their statements for consideration within the judicial arena, eyewitnesses would expect to be called to testify at a public hearing where their evidence would be subjected to examination and cross-examination by lawyers representing the Tribunal and the various parties involved, in order to establish its worth as a contribution to determining the truth about events. In the 'inquisitorial' process undertaken by tribunals, establishing the truth involved the procuring of reliable information from a range of sources and its integration into the fullest possible explanatory narrative. In the case of the Widgery Tribunal, Walsh finds evidence of further political orchestration, influencing the arrangements for legal representation and the conduct of proceedings. Widgery's construction of the judicial arena of the Tribunal was based on three fundamental points of procedure, each of which minimized its capacity to establish the truth.

Firstly, Widgery downgraded the active, investigative function of the Inquiry by curtailing the important role of Counsel for the Tribunal. Usually performed by the Attorney General, this carried the formal responsibility to represent the Tribunal and conduct its examination of witnesses. This appointment was discussed at the Downing Street meeting, where Widgery argued that the role 'might well be less important in this instance than in some previous Tribunals', so that a 'competent Queen's counsel could undertake the duties'.[129] John Stocker QC was duly appointed.

Secondly, in thus departing from the inquisitorial character of tribunals' investigation as identified by Salmon, Widgery instead conducted his Inquiry as an 'adversarial' contest between two 'opposing' parties, with each side making opening and concluding statements, presenting evidence and calling, examining and cross-examining witnesses.[130] This entailed Widgery's granting of legal representation, not separately to each of the multiplicity of parties involved as envisaged by Salmon – that is, to the British Army as the organization responsible for the actions of its soldiers, and to each individual wounded and to the next of kin of each individual killed by those soldiers – but instead to the army, on one hand, and to the families of the deceased, as a collective, on the other. Counsel for the Deceased was also required to represent the wounded, who were denied specific legal representation in their own right, and 'the citizens of Londonderry generally'.[131] This arrangement necessarily resulted in inadequate legal representation for all the individual clients,[132] particularly the bereaved families, each of whose relatives had been killed in singular circumstances requiring detailed and separate investigation. However, the arrangement did serve the purpose identified by Widgery at the Downing Street meeting, of co-ordinating the presentation of 'the "other side" of the case from the Army['s] . . . so as to make the handling of the Inquiry manageable'.[133] By instituting an adversarial form of proceedings on this basis, Widgery structured the judicial arena of the Inquiry as the site of a two-sided contest between the British Army, on the one hand, and the deceased, the wounded and the nationalist community in Derry more widely, on the other. In this way, Widgery also achieved his 'highly desirable' objective of ensuring that 'cross-examination of the Army witnesses should not devolve on Counsel for the Tribunal alone',[134] but rather, became the main responsibility of the 'opposing' counsel.

Thirdly, Widgery dispensed with the procedure, usually adopted under the terms of the 1921 Act, for the appointment of a team of solicitors to conduct the preliminary interviewing of witnesses and deposition of other evidence for presentation to the Tribunal.[135] In discussion at Downing Street, Widgery agreed with the Prime Minister that this procedure would be overly 'long and cumbersome', and a proposal by the Lord Chancellor was adopted that the services of the Treasury Solicitor be utilized instead.[136] This established a serious conflict of interests, one with 'sinister implications',[137] since the Ministry of Defence (MoD) was among the government departments regularly serviced by the Treasury Solicitor: 'Indeed the Treasury Solicitor had acted for the ministry in civil actions arising out of the fatal shooting of civilians by soldiers in Northern Ireland.'[138] The undermining of the Tribunal's independence implicit in this conflation of its legal representatives with those of the army and the MoD was underlined by the Lord Chancellor's further suggestion during the meeting, that 'the Treasury Solicitor would need to brief counsel for the Army'[139] – that is, 'counsel for the very party whose actions were supposed to be investigated by the tribunal'.[140] These arrangements establishing the judicial arena of the Tribunal ensured that its capacity to seek the truth was compromised, and that its procurement and examination of evidence worked in the army's favour.

The procurement and examination of evidence by the Tribunal
Widgery's eventual finding in favour of the soldiers' narrative was underpinned by the Tribunal's failure both to procure and consider all the available evidence and to ensure a suitably critical treatment of the evidence that was presented. In the event, 114 witnesses were heard and cross-examined during the public sessions, classified by Widgery into six 'main groups: priests; other people from Londonderry; press and television reporters, photographers, cameramen and sound recordists; soldiers, including the relevant officers; police officers; doctors, forensic experts and pathologists'.[141] The majority – seven priests and thirty 'other people from Londonderry', including relatives of the dead and the wounded, and forty soldiers – were members of the competing parties. The Tribunal also claimed to have considered a range of other evidence, including over 200 statements prepared specifically for the Inquiry, the original statements made by soldiers to the Military Police, a large number of photographs, various material exhibits, medical reports and forensic-test results on guns, clothing and the bodies of the dead.[142] Some of this material was elicited by a public appeal for evidence by the Tribunal, but due to the adoption of an adversarial approach and the relatively passive role played by the Counsel for the Tribunal, much of the evidence – including the witness statements – was identified and secured by the opposing counsels as a means for each to further its own case.[143]

The Tribunal's procurement and presentation of evidence worked in favour of the soldiers' case in several respects. Firstly, it failed to seek out key evidence that was potentially detrimental to the soldiers. Whereas the journalist Murray Sayle walked the ground where the killings occurred on ten occasions in order to test his hypothesis about the army's planned tactics against the realities of the physical terrain,[144] and even carried out his own impromptu measurement of the angle and trajectory of particular bullets,[145] the Tribunal conducted no investigations of the terrain (Widgery himself visited the scene once, for a public relations walkabout), and commissioned no Engineers' reports into the scenes of the shootings.[146] Nor did the Tribunal seek to obtain the army records and any criminal records or police files on the soldiers involved in the Bloody Sunday shootings, a clear signal that the Inquiry would not be treating the deaths as potential cases of murder.[147]

Secondly, the Tribunal concealed the existence of statements given to the Military Police by '[a]ll of the soldiers who opened fire in Derry' on the night of 30 January and the supplementary statements made by a number of those soldiers in the days following.[148] Those statements emerged into the public domain only in 1996, when they were among thirteen sets of documents, classified as 'closed', that were released by the Public Records Office (see p. 186 below). Don Mullan found in these statements testimony from soldiers indicating that shots were fired from the vicinity of the old Walls of Derry, and revealing that army snipers were operating from nearby derelict buildings[149] – an issue ignored by Widgery. After detailed analysis of these statements, Walsh concludes that

> for almost every soldier who fired one or more shots there were substantial discrepancies between the account offered in the statement made on the night of 30–31 January and the version given in oral testimony to the tribunal. The nature and extent of these discrepancies are sufficient in themselves to raise a serious doubt about the credibility and reliability of the testimony given by these soldiers.[150]

Further 'fundamental' discrepancies existed between individual soldiers' accounts where these ostensibly described the same events. These discrepancies were ironed out in supplementary statements given to the Military Police and in written statements presented to the Treasury Solicitor, whose lawyers in many cases changed details suggesting an unlawful or reckless shooting to give the appearance of a justifiable one.[151] Not only did the Tribunal neglect to pass any of these statements to the Counsel for the Deceased and Injured, but it also was actively involved in amending the testimonies 'to show the army in a more favourable light'. In evidence given to the Saville Inquiry in 2002, one former Paratrooper, identified as Soldier 027, recalled not only how the statement he had given to the Military Police was 'fabricated to suggest he saw a sniper and heard shots from terrorists' but also how, when he gave a statement to 'a lawyer from the Widgery tribunal' describing instances of the killing of civilians by his colleagues for which there was no justification, 'the lawyer said, "We can't have that, can we, private?" and took his statement out of the room where it was changed'.[152]

Thirdly, the Tribunal excluded from consideration relevant evidence 'offered on behalf of the deceased',[153] most notably in its handling of civilian eyewitness testimony. It declined, without explanation, to call a number of key witnesses to testify.[154] Among these witnesses were seven of those wounded, at least four of whom had made statements to the Tribunal, and Dr Raymond McClean, 'one of the only two medically qualified persons on the spot. I had examined and treated the first two casualties shot, I had examined four of the dead "on the scene of the crime", and had been appointed by Cardinal Conway [Catholic Primate of Ireland] to represent him at the post mortem', being present at eleven of the thirteen cases.[155] Having made a 'reluctant decision to put forward my evidence to the Widgery enquiry', McClean presented his prepared statement only to be told by officials 'that my presence would not be required at the enquiry'.[156] McClean's consequent unease about the purpose of the Tribunal was borne out when Widgery's Report was published without 'any consideration of the concrete forensic evidence produced by the post-mortem examinations, and of whether this . . . was consistent or otherwise with eyewitness accounts of the incidents'.[157] It was not until 1997, when he first saw copies of the official post-mortems, that McClean realized 'there were differences between my notes and the official reports'.[158] Walsh describes McClean as 'a potentially vital witness . . . excluded because his evidence on several critical matters contradicted the official version being offered by the army'.[159] Also excluded from consideration were the testimonies collected in Derry by NICRA and NCCL.[160] These were deposited with the Treasury Solicitor's office in London on 3 March and were seen by Widgery on 9 March, five days before he drew investigative proceedings to a close.[161]

The attitudes of Widgery, his civil servants and the Counsel for the Tribunal towards these '700 or so' statements are recorded in an official memorandum, dated 10 March, from the secretary to the Tribunal.[162] Noting that '[m]uch publicity has been given [to the statements] during the Tribunal – and indeed before it opened', the memorandum summarily denigrates their value with the assertion: 'A very large number of these are in fact of no use.'[163] A mere fifteen had been selected as 'worthwhile' and shown to Widgery, who disagreed on the grounds that 'he did not think the people who wrote them could bring any new element to the proceedings of the Tribunal'.[164] Widgery also took the view that 'the statements, which must surely have been ready for some little time, had been submitted at this late stage to cause him maximum embarrassment', and that it was now too late for them to be considered.[165] Walsh points out that the statements had been deposited with the Inquiry a mere eleven days after the start of proceedings and were only 'late' because of Widgery's 'inappropriate haste' to conclude and report, which constituted no grounds for a refusal to hear evidence allowable under the 1921 Act.[166] When read carefully by Don Mullan after their rediscovery in 1995, 'statement after statement' corroborated other excluded evidence 'that the British Army . . . was also firing live ammunition from the vicinity of the Derry Walls'.[167]

In addition to excluding important evidence from public consideration, Widgery's conduct of proceedings militated against a full, critical examination of the evidence that was presented. While Counsel for the Tribunal played some part in the examination and cross-examination of witnesses, Widgery's adoption of an adversarial process enabled it to take a back seat, leaving the main responsibility for this to Counsel for the Army, and Counsel for the Deceased and Injured. This was of decisive importance, since it made an already over-stretched Counsel for the Deceased and Injured responsible for the complex and 'most critical aspect' of the investigation, the cross-examination of the soldiers.[168] In this, Counsel for the Tribunal 'hardly featured at all',[169] and made no attempt to cross-examine the soldiers about the discrepancies between their statements prior to the Inquiry and their testimony given to the Tribunal from the witness box.[170] For its part, Counsel for the Deceased and Injured was in no position to expose the soldiers' testimony to rigorous cross-examination, since vital information about the existence of these original statements, their subsequent amendment and, thus, the revision of the soldiers' 'memories' for presentation in the judicial arena, had been withheld from it by the Tribunal.[171] In this way, the soldiers were shielded from the kind of rigorous investigation of their evidence to which they ought to have been subjected by the Counsel for the Tribunal, deploying the full resources available to the Inquiry.[172]

Evidence casting serious doubt on the soldiers' stories was heard at the Tribunal. Despite the public arena of the Widgery Inquiry having been constructed in such a way as to favour the army's case, eyewitness testimony given by civilians from a wide range of backgrounds directly and unanimously contradicted the testimony given by every soldier 'who admitted shooting at and hitting a civilian . . . that he fired an aimed shot at a person who was about to shoot at him or who was about to throw a nail bomb or a petrol bomb'.[173] Testimony regarding the shooting dead of Jack Duddy, the first casualty of the day, may serve as an illustration. Duddy was killed and four more civilians seriously injured by bullets in the first of the four killing grounds of Bloody Sunday, the car park and waste ground on the northern side of Rossville Flats (referred to by Widgery as the Flats' 'courtyard'), where some hundreds of people were gathered when the Paratroopers launched their arrest operation. In their testimony to the Tribunal, seven soldiers admitted firing shots in this area. Despite serious inconsistencies and contradictions between their respective accounts,[174] all were agreed that, as they disembarked from their vehicles, 'they had come under sustained gunfire from several gunmen', located in and around the Rossville Flats, 'nail bombing from several nail bombers, acid bombs from the flats, at least one petrol bomb and other missiles'.[175] For example, Sergeant O, 'with 10 years' experience in the Parachute Regiment',[176] told the Tribunal that: 'It was the most intensive fire I have experienced in Northern Ireland', estimating this at some eighty shots over two to three minutes, including high velocity rounds.[177]

In their testimony, each of the soldiers gave an account of every bullet he had fired in response. However, as Widgery points out, 'No shot described by a soldier precisely fits Duddy's case. The nearest is one described by Soldier V who spoke of firing at a man in a white shirt in the act of throwing a petrol bomb.'[178] Lance-Corporal V testified that 'he had the butt of his rifle at his shoulder when he fired, that the man was 50 or 60 metres away, and that he shot to kill. "My sight picture of the man was filled with the part of the man I was aiming at." . . . [T]he man was directly facing him . . . he was in no doubt that he had hit the man he had aimed at.'[179] After seeing his shot hit its target, Lance-Corporal V had noticed a burning fuse some distance away, which he assumed had become detached as the man threw the bomb.[180] Lance-Corporal V also told the Tribunal that 'he went on observing the man he had shot after seeing him fall, and had watched as the man was carried away by a group of people, including [the local priest] Fr Daly' – information which permits identification of 'the man' as Jack Duddy.[181] It was not disclosed during the Tribunal's proceedings that Lance-Corporal V's testimony – based on a statement he had given to the Treasury Solicitor – was 'substantially different' from his original statement made to the Military Police, in which he said that 'he had seen a person throw a bottle with a fuse attached to it. The bottle had hit the ground but had not exploded. V had then fired one shot at the bottle thrower.' This latter statement provided grounds for a charge of murder or attempted murder, since the firing of the fatal shot was held to have occurred after the alleged throwing of the petrol bomb, when the man no longer posed a threat to life, contrary to Yellow Card regulations. The alteration of the statement suggests to Walsh that V 'had been advised to revise [it] in order to protect himself from the threat of criminal proceedings'.[182]

The shooting of Jack Duddy was also described to the Tribunal by a number of civilian eyewitnesses who testified and were cross-examined in the public hearings. Fr Daly, who was 'running away' from the Paras' assault, 'like the rest of the crowd', remembered 'coming level' with Duddy, 'hearing the first shot, and simultaneously the young boy . . . grunt or gasp', and seeing him fall to the ground.[183] Observing the scene from balconies in Block Two of the Flats, Mrs Isabella Duffy and Mrs Mary Bonner both witnessed the crowd fleeing as the Paras drove into the carpark, jumped out of their armoured vehicles and immediately began shooting towards the crowd.[184] Duffy saw one paratrooper emerge from his vehicle, kneel down, point his rifle and shoot twice at the running Duddy, who fell at the second shot with blood covering his back. She 'shouted at the soldiers and one of them fired at me', the bullet taking a chunk out of the iron balcony.[185] Bonner also saw the soldiers begin firing as soon as they had jumped from their vehicles, including a soldier who assumed a firing position while kneeling, but, unlike Duffy, believed Duddy to have been shot by a soldier firing from the waist, hit from behind as he turned to look around. A fourth eyewitness, Derrick Tucker, an Englishman with sixteen years of service in the Royal Navy and RAF, also witnessed the shooting of Duddy from his bedroom overlooking the carpark, and corroborated Duffy's and Bonner's statements that the Paras had fired immediately after disembarking. He also saw Duddy hit from behind while running away, but was prevented from testifying to the details of what he had seen 'because Lord Widgery stated that he had already heard enough concerning this incident' from the previous testimonies.[186] All agreed that Duddy had not been carrying any weapon.[187]

These and other eyewitnesses also testified that the army had not come under attack prior to the soldiers opening fire, as the latter claimed. Daly, in his written evidence to the Tribunal, made it clear that he 'did not hear any shots' between the distinctive crack of army SLRs in William Street earlier until the shot that hit Jack Duddy, which was followed by a 'dreadful fusillade of gunfire . . . from . . . behind us, from the direction of the soldiers'.[188] He also stated 'categorically' that he 'never once heard a nail bomb explode during that whole afternoon'.[189] Tucker testified that during the short interval, lasting perhaps thirty seconds to two minutes, 'between the soldiers getting out of their vehicles and starting to fire . . . he heard no explosions nor any firing directed at the soldiers'.[190] The *Guardian* journalist Simon Winchester, Joseph Doherty from the Creggan and a Derry schoolteacher, Francis Dunne, all of whom were among the large crowd on the open ground north of the Flats that began to run away as the army vehicles swept up Rossville Street, also testified that they neither heard nor saw gunfire or explosions directed against the soldiers in this area before or during the period of army fire.[191]

Besides being internally consistent, the testimony of these and other eyewitnesses was also consistent with other evidence examined by the Tribunal. 'Some remarkable photographs of the crowd of people running from the APCs into the funnel of the Rossville Flats', including one that particularly impressed Widgery, were taken by Derrick Tucker;[192] and another photograph clearly showed the shooting of another man, the unarmed Michael Bridge.[193] The forensic test applied to Duddy's body, as to the bodies of all the dead, with the aim of determining whether or not they had fired a gun prior to being killed, showed negative.[194] Medical evidence from the postmortem examination showed that the bullet had entered at the right shoulder and passed through the upper chest from right to left, a description which is consistent with testimony that Duddy was looking back over his shoulder as he ran.[195] 'A bullet fired in the direction of where Duddy was running by a paratrooper, standing near the end of Block 1 of the Rossville Flats, would have made such a path through Duddy's body.'[196] A similar pattern of eyewitness testimony, consistent on the essential issues and largely corroborated by photographic and medical evidence, was given to the Tribunal in respect of the other twelve victims who were shot dead.

Those civilians who testified at the Tribunal's public hearings were able to present a substantial body of eyewitness testimony challenging the army's narrative and to provide compelling grounds for finding the alternative account of the killings – 'that the Paras had opened fire without having been fired upon first'[197] – to be the more plausible. However, the Tribunal 'failed to expose the inherent untrustworthiness of the soldiers' testimony',[198] despite this being so pervasive that, in Walsh's judgement, 'it would not be safe to rely on the army's version in virtually any instance where there was credible and cogent evidence to the contrary'.[199] Neither the unreliability of the soldiers' testimony nor the integrity of the civilian testimony, and the implications to be drawn from it concerning the truth about Bloody Sunday, were reflected in Widgery's Report on the findings of the Inquiry. Thus, while the Tribunal did offer a space for testimonies to be voiced which exposed the army's story, it did so in order for those testimonies to be incorporated and defused within a newly hegemonic narrative that restored legitimacy to the army operation.

Instituting official memory: the Widgery Report

The Report of the Widgery Tribunal, one of the key memory-texts of the Troubles, is notorious for having found in favour of 'the self-serving testimonies of the soldiers'[200] and for having 'based its conclusions on the army's version of events'.[201] Leaked to right-wing London newspapers on 16 April, it was published officially two days later.[202] Only thirty-nine pages long,[203] it drew no conclusions about the decision-making of the British political establishment and military high command, and exonerated the soldiers of the Parachute Regiment who had fired their guns on Bloody Sunday from any serious blame: 'The soldiers' training . . . required them to act individually . . . and no breach of discipline was thereby involved'.[204] 'Each soldier was his own judge of whether he had identified a gunman', and that 'some showed greater restraint in opening fire than others', according to individual 'temperament and character', was to be expected.[205] Thus, while some soldiers 'showed a high degree of responsibility', others were found to have engaged in 'firing bordering on the reckless',[206] 'notably in Glenfada Park', the area where 30 per cent of the total number of shots had been fired, killing four civilians and wounding three. Widgery finds the entirety of these shots to have been 'fired without justification'; the testimony of the soldiers is regarded as questionable – 'highly improbable' in Soldier H's case.[207] However, he suggests, in such a situation, 'where soldiers are required to engage gunmen who are in close proximity to innocent civilians . . . it is not remarkable that mistakes were made and some innocent civilians hit'.[208] While a number of 'infringements of the rules of the Yellow Card' were identified in the Report, Widgery found that 'they do not seem to point to a breakdown of discipline or to require censure',[209] concluding: 'The individual soldier ought not to have to bear the burden of deciding whether to open fire in confusion such as prevailed on 30 January.'[210]

In exonerating the British Army, the Report laid responsibility for Bloody Sunday at the door of NICRA: 'There would have been no deaths in Londonderry on 30 January if those who organised the illegal march had not thereby created a highly dangerous situation in which a clash between *demonstrators* and the security forces was almost inevitable' (my emphasis).[211] By implication it also held the IRA responsible – although the organization is mentioned by name only once in the body of the Report, which prefers to talk of 'gunmen' and 'civilians . . . armed with firearms'[212] – since the IRA's attack on the army's arrest operation is identified as the catalyst that provoked fire from the soldiers. Widgery's conclusions regarding the soldiers rest on the Report's answer to what he identified as the 'vital'

question, 'Who fired first?', being not the army but the IRA.[213] In support of
this finding, Widgery makes detailed use of what he describes as 'a considerable body of civilian evidence about the presence of gunmen in the Bogside
that afternoon, including some to the effect that they were the first to open
fire'.[214] Here, civilian testimonies are raided for evidence selected to support
the official narrative, and distorted by decontextualization; as in the case of
Fr Daly, who witnessed a sole civilian firing a handgun at soldiers, but only
in response to a 'fusillade' of bullets coming *first* from the soldiers, a detail
which Widgery omits from mention; thereby implying disingenuously that
Daly believed civilian gunmen to have begun the shooting.[215] On this basis,
Widgery concludes that: 'Civilian, as well as Army, evidence makes it clear
that there was a substantial number of civilians in the area who were armed
with firearms. I would not be surprised if in the relevant half hour as many
rounds were fired at the troops as were fired by them';[216] and 'I am entirely
satisfied that the first firing in the courtyard [the car park of the Rossville
Flats] was directed at the soldiers'.[217]

The Report also implicated in this attack those killed and wounded. In its
conclusion, Widgery finds that: 'None of the deceased or wounded is proved
to have been shot whilst handling a firearm or bomb. Some are wholly
acquitted of complicity in such action; but there is a strong suspicion that
some others had been firing weapons or handling bombs in the course of the
afternoon and that yet others had been closely supporting them.'[218] The language of 'acquittal' used here in relation to the victims suggests that they,
rather than the soldiers who killed them, were the ones undergoing investigation, indeed a form of trial before the law. In finding that 'none of the
deceased or wounded is *proved* to have been shot whilst handling a firearm
or bomb' (my emphasis), the Report at once acknowledges the absence of
hard evidence to support the army's case – 'that each of these shots [fired by
soldiers on 30 January] was an aimed shot fired at a civilian holding or using
a bomb or firearm' – but refuses nonetheless to reject that case unequivocally; implying instead that the deceased and wounded may well have been
shot while handling a firearm or bomb, even though this cannot be proved.
Because Widgery fails to make clear who of the deceased or wounded have
been 'wholly acquitted of complicity in such action' – with the single exception of John Johnston, wounded in the first army shots fired in William
Street, and described as 'obviously an *innocent* passer-by going about his
own business in Londonderry that afternoon' (my emphasis)[219] – the 'strong
suspicion' that 'some others had been firing weapons or handling bombs in
the course of the afternoon and that yet others had been closely supporting
them' is a suspicion that necessarily adheres to them all. With the exception
of Johnston, the Report gives no consideration whatsoever to the evidence
as to whether or not any of the known wounded had been firing weapons or
handling bombs; indeed, five of them are not even mentioned except as
names in the official list of the injured.[220] In respect of the thirteen dead, none
of them is unequivocally 'acquitted' as 'innocent' in the manner of John

Johnston. In the case of Jack Duddy, for example, Widgery simply states: 'I accept that [he] was not carrying a bomb or firearm'.[221] Thus, each of the deceased is exposed, whether directly or by association, to the suspicion that he was not innocent, and that the army's claims, while not proven, may well be true.

In addressing a second, 'impossible', task which he sets himself in the Report – that of identifying the soldier who was 'most likely to have fired the fatal shot in each case' – Widgery proceeds by attempting to match-up the medical evidence that charts the likely trajectory of each fatal bullet through the body, with the accounts given by each soldier of the shots he had fired.[222] Only in the two cases where bullets remained in the body does the Report establish any certain conclusion about this. Widgery finds that '[n]o shot fired by a soldier precisely fits Duddy's case', thereby accepting at face value Soldier V's description of his victim as wearing a white shirt and being about to throw a bomb, and concluding on this basis that V's victim could not have been Duddy, since 'Duddy was wearing a red shirt and there is no evidence of his having a bomb'.[223] Indeed, Widgery finds that he is unable to match V's account of the man he aimed at and shot with any of the known casualties.[224] He thinks it 'probable' that Soldier F and Soldier K were responsible for one fatality each,[225] but in the other nine cases he is content merely to identify a number of possible shots which could have caused the deaths.[226] In his findings on the reasons for death, Widgery exploits this uncertainty in order to avoid arriving at any clear verdict in half of the cases. By Widgery's own account, only in two cases – those of John Young and William Nash – was there any suggestion that the victim was actually using a firearm at the time of his death; while the four deaths in Glenfada Park are the only ones found to have been caused by shots fired 'without justification'.[227] Widgery claims that Duddy was shot by 'a bullet intended for someone else',[228] an explanation 'which not even the Paras themselves had suggested was the truth'.[229]

As Eamonn McCann has demonstrated, the Widgery Report is full of 'internal inconsistencies' and 'anomalies', and 'its narration and line of argument are frequently hard to follow', making it 'difficult to relate Widgery's conclusions to the body of the Report'.[230] These weaknesses of reasoning and representation, argues McCann, stem from 'a politically motivated unwillingness to tell the truth'.[231] Various strategies of representation are deployed in the Report to produce its confusions and displacements, their chief effect being to avoid any consideration of the relative merits of the soldiers' and the civilians' testimonies. When addressing the killings in Glenfada Park, for example, Widgery finds 'the evidence too confused and too contradictory to make separate consideration [of each death] possible'.[232] However, the civilian testimony in these cases was quite clear about the shooting dead of unarmed and even wounded men as they tried to escape from the soldiers who were firing at them. Only the soldiers' testimonies were inconsistent and unreliable, but this is never evaluated in relation to the civilians' testimonies;

indeed, the only reference to the latter concerns a 'conflict of evidence' between eyewitnesses as to where the dead were shot and had fallen.[233] The opposing narratives are brought into direct and detailed confrontation in only one section of the Report, the 'narrative of events' in the Rossville Flats' courtyard, where Widgery concludes: 'I am entirely satisfied that the first firing . . . was directed at the soldiers'.[234] Here, too, 'Widgery does not compare the two conflicting stories. He makes no attempt to argue that the military version is more plausible.'[235] Instead· he justifies his endorsement of the testimony of the soldiers over that of the civilians, here and in the conclusion to the Report, by reference to 'the demeanour of witnesses under cross-examination':[236]

> Those accustomed to listening to witnesses could not fail to be impressed by the demeanor of the soldiers of 1 Para. They gave their evidence with confidence and without hesitation or prevarication and withstood a rigorous cross-examination without contradicting themselves or each other. With one or two exceptions I accept that they were telling the truth as they remembered it.[237]

Widgery stops short of concluding that the civilian witnesses who contradicted the soldiers' story were not 'telling the truth as they remembered it'. Indeed, he argues, to prefer the 'demeanour' of the soldiers 'does not mean that witnesses who spoke in the opposite sense were not doing their best to be truthful. On the contrary I was much impressed by the care with which *many* of them, *particularly* the newspaper reporters, television men and photographers, gave evidence' (my emphases).[238] But these are back-handed compliments that demean as they appear to praise: the soldiers tell the truth while the others can only 'do their best' to tell the truth; the media workers give evidence carefully, while the other civilians – evinced by their absence from mention – presumably are not so careful.

Widgery's claim here is not borne out by the record of the Inquiry. According to Samuel Dash, an American lawyer who prepared an independent report on the proceedings for the ILRM in 1972, civilian witnesses, including those from nationalist Derry, provided 'clear testimony, which was subjected to rigorous cross-examination from counsel for the Army'.[239] Indeed, in a number of cases, most notably those of Geraldine Richmond and James Chapman, the Tribunal went to some length to discredit civilian testimonies as mistaken, inaccurate or unreliable.[240] Richmond 'stood firmly by her account through lengthy and hostile cross-examination by counsel for the British Army'.[241] In the fight between two competing and contradictory bodies of eyewitness testimony, however, the Widgery Report ensured that the soldiers' story was the one upheld as the authoritative truth about Bloody Sunday.

'Living with the lie': the effects of Widgery

The Widgery Tribunal's public hearings were, and are still remembered as having been, a difficult experience – for the eyewitnesses who had agreed to participate in the Inquiry, for the relatives of the dead and for the wider nationalist community in Derry. All were still reeling from shock and emotional devastation during the sittings in Coleraine, which began just three weeks after Bloody Sunday. Some relatives refused to have anything to with them, like John Young's father, who also forbade his surviving children to attend; but the Inquiry nevertheless made public investigation into, and drew conclusions about, the death of his son, which could not simply be ignored.[242] Others put up with the inconvenience of the sixty-mile round trip to Coleraine to attend the hearings, but found that the public gallery was overcrowded and often full, that there were difficulties regarding security and that the form of proceedings was alien and frequently mystifying; all of which added to the deeply disturbing matter under investigation, creating what some found to be an intolerable atmosphere.[243] Of those who had overcome doubts and made the decision to offer evidence, thirty were called to testify and be cross-examined at the public hearings. A number of these witnesses felt that their evidence was traduced and discounted, including James (Jack) Chapman, a Welshman who had served in the British Army during the Second World War, then living in Derry, who recalled in 1997:

> When both Bishop Daly and myself were called to Coleraine for the Widgery Inquiry I thought that they would believe our version of events. What had a respected priest and a British Army war veteran to gain from lying? We told the truth yet they totally rejected out of hand our submissions and made us feel like dirt. I shall never forget it.[244]

Some witnesses had their testimony cut short or were directed to focus on issues that Widgery rather than they wished to pursue.[245] Other witnesses, for instance Geraldine Richmond and Ita McKinney, were subject to hostile, insensitive cross-examination.[246] Even those treated with more civility and sympathy could be left feeling bitter. The speed with which Widgery conducted proceedings meant that numerous people were not called, leaving them with the sense that their testimony had been rejected and that their experience was not recognized to be important. [247] Frank Curran, who travelled to Coleraine every day during the public hearings, was not alone in describing proceedings as a 'travesty'.[248]

The Widgery Report had a devastating impact upon these people. The traumatic impact of the shootings and deaths was compounded by its exoneration of the soldiers and slandering of their victims as gunmen and nail-bombers. This was understood in the Bogside, and throughout nationalist Ireland and its international diaspora, to be a blatant denial of justice instituted by a judicial 'whitewash'.[249] After Bloody Sunday, no nationalist in Northern Ireland could expect the State to be held accountable for any abuse of power committed by its agents. The failure of the Inquiry to investigate the truth about the British Army's operation had paradoxical long-term effects on the Northern nationalist community. It strengthened Irish national identifications defined in opposition to Britain and stimulated recruitment to the IRA, escalating and prolonging the war;[250] while for survivors and for relatives of the dead, who have had to live with 'being lied to for thirty years',[251] it compounded the original trauma of violence and loss, prolonging their effects and blocking psychic recovery.[252]

The Report's findings, in authorizing an official memory of Bloody Sunday, instituted a damaging ideological misrepresentation of the Bogside–Creggan community. This functioned to legitimize the systematic and prolonged harassment of the bereaved families – now officially 'IRA families' – by the British Army and by loyalists, which further compounded the horror and despair of their circumstances.[253] The instituting of official memory also had wider effects beyond the local community. In the public arena of the media, it restored the army's legitimizing narrative, allowing the British press to claim that 'Widgery clears paratroops for Bloody Sunday' (*Daily Telegraph*), and even that 'Widgery blames IRA' (*Daily Express*).[254] After the Tribunal, this official narrative informed history books and mainstream debate in the media,[255] and for many years was reproduced rather than questioned in Britain, through censorship and denial of alternative perspectives. In 1978, for example, a BBC film about Derry, *A City On The Border*, 'showed a mother putting flowers on her son's grave, which bore the words, "Murdered by British Paratroopers on Bloody Sunday". The woman laying her bunch of flowers on the grave stayed in: but the shot of the tombstone was cut on the instruction of the Controller of BBC1. The British public was not to know the significance of her action.'[256] This orchestrated official memory was predicated on what can best be described as an official amnesia, which concealed (kept private) the political significance of Bloody Sunday for nationalists in the North of Ireland, preventing the wider public articulation of their memories of injustice. Critical investigation of Bloody Sunday was also forestalled by the Widgery Report, a situation not seriously breached for twenty years.[257] Sayle and Humphry's report on behalf of the *Sunday Times*' Insight team, due to be published on the weekend following the atrocity, was pulled by the editor under the threat of legal action by the State, and then disappeared for twenty-six years. Sayle, who had discarded his original draft after filing the report by telephone, was unable to find a copy either in the *Sunday Times*' office or in the Public Record Office once the Tribunal had reported and closed.[258] The civilian testimonies and other evidence neglected by Widgery similarly disappeared and were forgotten until their rediscovery by human rights activists in the mid-1990s (see pp. 186–8).

The nationalists of the Bogside and Creggan have had both to contend with the official amnesia of the British State and to negotiate the denial of their narrative in Protestant and loyalist culture. This denial has taken various forms, from simple lack of acknowledgement in local Protestant schools, to the assertion that 'the victims had all been gunmen' made in some Protestant churches,[259] and to the lyrics of triumphalist sectarian songs sung in the playground or on loyalist parades, such as this one from the UDA's *Detainee Song Book* (1974):

Went to Derry not on a hunch,
Knew I'd get a taig [Catholic] before lunch,
Bang, Bang, Bang, Bloody Sunday,
This is my, my, my beautiful day.[260]

Urban myths have circulated in loyalist areas of the city, expressing the belief that 'there was nobody shot in Derry that day. The bodies that were laid out in the morgue that night were taken out of deep freezes. They were IRA men who had been killed in previous gunbattles.'[261] While there have always been some Protestants and Unionists sympathetic to the suffering and injustice endured on and after Bloody Sunday,[262] for many years this was given no effective public voice. Recognition of the atrocity by mainstream Protestant culture and by Unionist politicians has been at best grudging. Their difficulty in 'sympathis[ing] with the relatives of the victims' stems from a perception that the killings had 'become so bound up in republican propaganda'.[263] Not until 1997 did a more generous spirit emerge, in an editorial statement in the Unionist newspaper the *News Letter* condemning the shootings as 'unforgiveable' and an 'appalling over-reaction' by the Paratroopers, who 'opened fire indiscriminately with scant regard for the lives of others who were guilty of nothing'. The editorial called for 'a heartfelt, unambiguous apology from the highest possible source' to 'those who lost innocent loved ones',[264] provoking a flood of readers' letters expressing a range of views, but the majority rejecting its sentiment.[265]

The instituting of official memory after 'the Widgery whitewash', however, also had an unanticipated ramification: it ensured that the atrocity entered nationalist popular memory as a potent symbol of the fundamental injustice and violence of British rule in Ireland. Under these circumstances, the commemoration of the dead of Bloody Sunday necessarily became a political act – an instance of what the Palestinian–American writer and activist Edward Said called 'speaking truth to power'.[266] Widgery politicized the memory of Bloody Sunday, so that the annual commemoration in Derry – initiated in 1973 and held every year since – became the focus for the articulation of a public counter-memory contesting the official narrative, which has been sustained for over three decades. This would eventually secure the discrediting of the Widgery Tribunal and the displacement of its Report from the centre of British official memory, forcing the British Government to reopen its investigation into the events of 30 January 1972 as a fundamental aspect of its conflict-resolution strategy pursued since 1997. The official memory constructed in 1972 has nevertheless continued to shape the British State's responses to Irish demands for justice throughout the process of establishing and conducting the Saville Inquiry. Bloody Sunday, then, remains a contested past. These themes of trauma, memory, political commemoration and the fight for justice – in their manifestations both before and during the peace process – are explored in the three chapters that follow.

4

Trauma and life-stories: survivor memories of Bloody Sunday

Survivor memory of Bloody Sunday first entered the public arena in the form of individual eyewitness testimony told to establish the truth about the events, so as to counter the legitimizing narrative of the British State and set the record straight. The juridical form required of eyewitness statements presented to the Widgery Tribunal precluded their representation of the traumatic effects of the attack. Nevertheless, the rejection of these testimonies from below by the Tribunal meant that the survivors of Bloody Sunday remained embroiled in a profoundly disturbed psychic reality, produced first by the shootings and then compounded by the injustices perpetrated through their unsatisfactory investigation. This counter-memory contesting British official memory remained firmly rooted in the truth authorized by the personal testimony of the survivors, and platform speakers have regularly made reference to their own experiences on the day. However, in an unlooked-for consequence of this focus on the eyewitness, the complexity of personal remembering about Bloody Sunday and its aftermath tended to become subsumed by the mobilization of testimony within the campaign of resistance to the British military occupation in Northern Ireland. Dealing with the unresolved past centred on the fight against continuing injustice, not least in the implication to be drawn from official memory that the dead of Bloody Sunday (and other nationalist victims of the British Army) were not 'innocent', and even deserved to die. Speaking at the twenty-fifth anniversary commemoration in 1997, Kay Duddy, a founder-member of the Bloody Sunday Justice Campaign and a sister of Jack Duddy, expressed the hope: 'Perhaps when we have had their names cleared we can come to terms with it and finally lay them to rest.'[1] This chapter explores the personal memories that are both suggested in and concealed by this statement.

Writing about the 'labours of memory' through which 'people incorporate in their own lives the experiences of dictatorship in Argentina',[2] Elizabeth Jelin and Susana Kaufman have argued: 'There is no single or easy connecting line between public memory sites and commemorations and personal memory and forgetting.'[3] In personal remembering, 'traces and marks of that past emerge in the development of the life course and in the everyday experiences of people':

Insofar as reality is complex, multiple and contradictory, and that subjective inscriptions of experiences are never a direct mirror-like reflection of public events, one should not expect an 'integration' or 'gelling' of individual and public memories, or the presence of a single memory. There are contradictions, tensions, silences, conflicts, gaps, disjunctions, as well as 'integration'. Social reality is contradictory, full of tensions and conflicts. Memory is not an exception.[4]

Nor should it be assumed that personal memory in itself is singular and coherent. Jelin and Kaufman identify 'various layers', or 'strata', within subjectivity, where memories exist as 'fragmented and contradictory' feelings, thoughts and reflections, as well as relatively worked-up narratives.[5] This means that, for the survivors of dictatorship, repression or war, 'the construction of memory takes on different forms':[6] it exists not only as factual eyewitness testimony of what happened, but 'as feelings that are remembered now . . . as thoughts and reflections about what one has experienced, considering the moment in the life course when this happened, and one's current thoughts about that past; [and] as reflections about one's place in the world, about one's own social responsibility'.[7] However, the possibility of any individual articulating his or her own account of this multifaceted, subjective relationship to the past depends on a relationship with others, who listen, bring to bear memories of their own, and interpret and reinterpret the meanings that are made: it is, necessarily, 'a collective, intersubjective affair'.[8]

Jelin and Kaufman's argument – about the need to distinguish analytically these personal memory-narratives from forms of public remembrance, to recognize their complexity and to consider the inter-subjective relations in which they are articulated, including that of the life-history interview – is relevant to understanding the processes of remembering that have occurred in the aftermath of Bloody Sunday. The politics of Bloody Sunday commemoration rested on a largely hidden history of individual and familial grief and loss, remembered in the private life stories of relatives and survivors. Such stories circulated within the local community and were fashioned into forms of 'shared or common', local memory, as people pooled their stories, helped each other to fill out the gaps and silences in their own recollections, and endeavoured to piece together a more complete and adequate narrative of the truths behind the traumatic events. But as Ashplant et al. make clear, some 'individual memories may never be articulated in any wider arena', including those recalling experiences that 'may be (or seem) singular', and others that are 'too painful to bear, even when they are consonant with public narratives'. These tend to be 'withheld from articulation and become isolated'.[9] An isolating process of this kind appears to have affected the relatives of the Bloody Sunday dead during the 1970s and 1980s.

The painful and disjointed stories of those who have had to live with the memories engendered by loss, horror and the devastating psychic impact of the Bloody Sunday massacre over the years and decades have never been easy to listen to or absorb, and were only sporadically granted any wider public space. The photojournalist Joanne O'Brien, a Dublin teenager in 1972, has recalled a visit north that she made on the massacre's tenth anniversary to interview James Wray, the father of Jim Wray who was shot dead in Glenfada Park, for a Dublin-based newspaper: 'It was hard to take in what James Wray said of his son's death. He held up the coat Jim had been wearing and showed us the three bullet holes at the back. The *Irish Press* duly published the piece and there was no interest in a follow up. The tenth anniversary was over.'[10] Occasional attention to a traumatic reality that was painful to witness and hard to integrate psychically remained the norm in cultural responses to Bloody Sunday for another ten years.

The experiences concealed within the privacy of family life began to be identified and given public voice only in the early 1990s, when researchers collecting memories of the dead for Eamonn McCann's 1992 book *Bloody Sunday in Derry* discovered the extent and character of long-term psychic damage and ongoing traumatic effects among their close relatives and friends. Interviews were conducted, not by journalists from outside but by the local community and cultural activist Maureen Shiels and by Bridie Hannigan from the Bogside, as part of a community history project by the grassroots Derry Women's Living History Circle.[11] According to Tony Doherty, the son of Bloody Sunday victim Paddy Doherty and a leading figure in the Commemoration Committee and the evolving Justice Campaign since the late 1980s: 'People were badly traumatised by Bloody Sunday and they were very badly treated by the Widgery Tribunal.' This research, however, found that the

> families hadn't spoken collectively about this for years and years and you could see there was evidently quite a lot of raw emotion there, when people were speaking about their loss. It still was very deep: it hadn't healed. One could also detect a sense of resignation at that stage – that it had gone on unchanged for years that they were always going to carry the burden . . . they felt very much on their own.[12]

The personal life-stories published in McCann's book gave public representation for the first time to the complexity of the families' emotional lives and conflicts, acknowledged the extent of their suffering from the effects of trauma and made those effects central to understanding the significance of Bloody Sunday. In this way, McCann's book extended opportunities for social recognition in the arenas of the local community, the city and wider national publics, and contributed directly to the emergence of the Justice Campaign, in which the bereaved families have played a central part. Its publication also marked an important shift in the form of the personal memory narrative, freeing it from the restrictions of the eyewitness account (which nevertheless remained of central importance, especially within the reconvened judicial arena of the Saville Inquiry) and enabled the telling of more reflective memories that articulate the traumatic effects of the atrocity and explore its impact within the life-stories of the survivors.

The impact of this shift can be seen in the publication, to mark the twenty-fifth anniversary commemoration in 1997 of a special Bloody Sunday Supplement in the local newspaper the *Derry Journal*, containing, alongside eyewitness testimonies, photographs and political analysis, some two dozen written statements of 'personal views' exploring a diverse range of experiences and memories.[13] That same year Joanne O'Brien launched her project to investigate the stories of the Bloody Sunday relatives. O'Brien was reminded of her interview with James Wray by reading extracts from the eyewitness statements excluded by Widgery, which had recently been rediscovered and published:

> My eye fell on an account of Jim Wray's last moments: 'Jim Wray fell close to the alleyway, immobilised by a gunshot wound in the back [. . .] to the horror of eyewitnesses, Wray was approached by a Para who shot him again in the back, at very close range. . . It was the execution of an already wounded man.' [. . .] I found myself groaning aloud and sat in shock as I read further accounts and wondered how people had coped after witnessing such scenes. I thought of those closest to the dead, their families, and wondered how they lived with the terrible memories. I resolved to go to Derry and find out.[14]

Haunted by the image of Wray's death, O'Brien felt compelled 'to do something'. Having conceived a project 'to photograph each of [the relatives] in the place where their loved one had been shot', O'Brien found that 'when we went there, the effect on them was incredible. Some got hugely emotional. Others talked and talked'.[15] The project expanded as she found herself, first, 'swapping my notebook for a tape-recorder as I listened to the memories and stories',[16] and then interviewing the wounded and other survivors as well. 'Each recalled their memories of the day, their treatment by the authorities and their feelings now. Some had never spoken publicly before.'[17] The project lasted three years, generating 50,000 words of interviews: 'The sheer variety and wealth of perspectives that I encountered amongst those who spoke to me was what kept me working at times.'[18] Being interviewed and photographed were distressing experiences for many of the survivors – and, in a different way, for O'Brien herself: 'if you're sitting opposite someone who's grieving for something that happened 28 years ago as though it were yesterday, you can't just turn the channel. Their grief becomes your grief, their story is yours to tell, and that can be a terrible burden.'[19] Moreover, the 'words of the people in this story evoked dreadful scenes in my minds eye',[20] as the journalist or historian who plays a 'role in gathering, interpreting and giving an audience to survivor memory'[21] makes her own imaginative identifications with, and investments in, the figures and situations of what is always a present psychic scenario as well as a remembered past.

These survivors' memories, articulated for the 1992 and 1997 anniversary commemorations and developed in the years immediately following, open up a hidden history largely concealed since 1972. They provide a rich and potent source for exploring the traumatic legacy of the atrocity, and of its denial, on individual survivors, friends and relatives of the dead, and the wider community in Derry's nationalist ghetto, within the domain of the personal and the private. The concept of trauma provides a productive frame for this investigation, not least because its language has entered the vocabulary of some (though by no means all) survivors themselves, offering a way of making sense of their experiences that was not available in 1972. Then, the medical talk was of 'nervous shock', and treatment relied more on tranquillizers than on talk. Twenty-five years later, the medical concept of PTSD had contributed to a widespread and growing awareness in Northern Ireland of the persistence of psychic scars created by the violence of the Troubles, and associated notions of the importance of storytelling as a means of mastering, or coming to terms with, these intractable psychic realities. However, these psychic dimensions of violent conflict are complexly intertwined with its political dynamics, in mutually determining ways, which are not yet widely appreciated or fully understood. In this chapter, I first draw on the published personal narratives of Bloody Sunday survivors to examine the psychic consequences of the massacre, investigating the interrelations of trauma, memory and storytelling, and tracing both the immediate and the long-term struggle of those affected to find ways of living with and responding to its aftershocks, for the most part in the context of continuing military occupation and war. There follows an analysis of the collective dimension of that experience, exploring the psychic dynamics within what I describe as the 'traumatized community', the formation of 'shared or common' local memories, and the interaction of the trauma of Bloody Sunday and the politics of resistance that flourished in its wake.

The traumatic impact of Bloody Sunday

Thousands of Derry nationalists were directly affected by the army attack on Bloody Sunday and its aftermath. Besides the fourteen who were killed, a further fourteen marchers suffered serious personal injuries, all but one by army bullets, and dozens of others were beaten with rifle-butts, or shot by rubber bullets, or tortured and abused in detention following their arrest. Some 5,000 people, gathered in Rossville Street prior to the rally at Free Derry Corner, experienced the fear and horror unleashed by the attack, ran in panic to escape the Paras, witnessed the violence and death erupting around them and, in many cases, were themselves shot at. Residents in the killing zones watched the shootings from their windows and offered the sanctuary of their homes to frightened marchers, while others took in the dead, dying and injured. Other people – including those some way away from the killing zones – heard rather than saw what was happening. The attack also had repercussions on the families and friends of all these people, with shock spreading as the news circulated through the city by word of mouth and media reporting.[22] To estimate on the basis of information about living relatives available in the published accounts, in the immediate families of the dead, nineteen children lost their father, ninety-eight siblings lost a brother, eighteen parents lost a son, and four wives lost their husband. To these must be added the loss of a loved one sustained by their extended families. In Patrick Hayes's late 1990s study of trauma in the families of those killed, one of his interviewees told him:

> We have cousins, aunts, nephews, nieces, like it affects everybody. Whoever that fella, whoever he happened to be, shot (brother's name) that day, he didn't only affect the one person, he affected hundreds and hundreds of people, just in my one family alone . . . there's that many nieces and nephews, brother-in-laws, uncles, aunts . . . They may have shot one person but they done a lot of damage to a lot of people just with that one particular person.[23]

The close-knit character of the Bogside, Brandywell and Creggan – densely populated communities of large and intertwined extended families, home to three-quarters of Derry's 20,000 Catholic adults[24] – meant that every household was touched, and countless numbers of people knew one or more of the dead and injured. Many people experienced multiple bereavements; like Geraldine Richmond, who knew seven of the young men killed, including Hugh Gilmour who died with his head on her knee, and her 'great friend' Jack Duddy – 'we all used to go to dances. Our age group lost a lot that day.'[25]

These people were exposed to a number of trauma-inducing events in the course of the massacre and its immediate aftermath. For those in the vicinity of the killing zones, the shootings had a deeply traumatic impact, engendering profound shock, fear and horror. Hearing the news that a loved one had been shot dead, and visiting Altnagelvin Hospital, where the bodies had been taken, in search of a missing relative or to identify the remains, were further traumatic events that had a devastating impact on those exposed to them. For many, the wakes (Geraldine Richmond could cope with attending only two and then 'went home and curled up and wouldn't go out for days'[26]) and the mass funeral for twelve of the dead, attended by a vast crowd (for Jean Hegarty, 'probably the most horrible day I ever remember'[27]), were also occasions of devastation and alienation. The traumatic intensity of these experiences is associated in memory with the locations where they occurred. Thus, for example, the four sites where fatal shootings took place – the Rossville Flats car park, the forecourt to Joseph Place at the back of the Flats, the rubble barricade across Rossville Street and the Glenfada Park courtyard and alley leading to Abbey Park (see map 1) – became places of memory within a transformed cultural landscape, and psychic sites of trauma frozen in time within the interior landscape of witnesses, survivors and the relatives of the dead. McCann records: 'The next morning there were groups of people standing around in Rossville Street, staring at the spots where it had happened.'[28] These are the places recorded in documentary photographs and film images of the events of Bloody Sunday, and in the eyewitness testimonies collected in its immediate aftermath. But these locations, the events associated with them and the personal repercussions of these events also feature repeatedly in the personal memories of survivors and witnesses many years later. Their psychic impact can be traced in terms of three major factors contributing to traumatic splitting: the incomprehensibility of the traumatic event; the acute sense of personal fear and vulnerability generated by it; and feelings of powerlessness.[29]

One pervasive reaction, shared alike by those caught up in the massacre and those who heard about it later, was a sense of disbelief at what the soldiers were doing. Liam Wray, a brother of Jim Wray, remembers: 'In 1971–1972, I really didn't believe that a soldier would shoot somebody who was unarmed. My eyes were brutally opened.'[30] For eyewitness Eamonn MacDermott, one of his 'abiding impressions' of Bloody Sunday was 'incomprehensibility':

> It was just too much to believe that they could really be firing live rounds into a crowd that big. My eyes and ears were telling me that these soldiers were standing there firing at us. We had all become too well accustomed to the different sounds made by different guns not to immediately recognise the distinctive crack of the SLR. But my brain would not accept it. There had been many marches and riots in the past but they had never ended like this, this was no gun battle this was all one way traffic.[31]

For those exposed to this lethal military force, a second trauma-inducing experience on Bloody Sunday was that of acute personal fear and vulnerability. Fear for personal safety could be indistinguishably bound up with the horror of witnessing the injury or death of another, giving rise to memories that retain an exceptional cathexis, or psychic charge, twenty-five years or more after the event. Conal McFeely, an 18-year-old on the day and now a member of the Bloody Sunday Trust, articulates this lucidly:

> I remember Bloody Sunday vividly. It remains the most terrifying experience of my life – a day when I honestly thought I was going to die. I was among the scores of people trapped at the back of the Rossville Flats. I can still hear the shots, the screaming and the crying; I can still remember the fear I felt, as I lay on the ground, too frightened to move and too frightened not to move. And I can still see, in my mind, the prostrate body of Barney McGuigan, lying dead on the ground, in a literal pool of blood. It was the first time I'd ever been so close to someone who'd been killed.[32]

What made the army's attack on defenceless civilians so acutely terrifying was the impossibility of knowing with any certainty where to find safety. The memories of Charles Morrison, a 26-year-old NICRA activist in 1972, convey the intensifying of fear through the disorientation of safe and dangerous space:

> I was very close to the Army when they came into the Bogside; I saw a soldier drop down and fire from the hip and I remember pulling off my steward's armband because I thought I would be a target. Terrified, I ran into the courtyard at the back of the Rossville Flats and tried to get away through the entrance

there. There were so many people it was like a cork, I couldn't get through. So I crawled on my knees down to the other entrance, but it was every bit as bad. At that stage I was in total confusion because the soldiers were all panning out as they were firing. I crawled back again to the first entrance and got out towards St Joseph's Place. People over at Free Derry Corner were shouting warnings – 'They're firing from the walls!' – so I crouched down for a long time under a walkway there.[33]

The humiliation of overpowering fear derives from its irresistible undercutting of the self's control and rational agency, generating behaviours that may run counter to deeply held values and principles, calling into question the foundation of personal identity. Remembering twenty-five years later the fear he felt at being unable to escape the killing zone, Morrison admits: 'One thing that haunts me, I would have physically assaulted somebody to get away. That's an awful emotion; I've thought about it often, and never want again to feel I would hurt another human being to save my own neck.'[34] Wounded in this way, the psyche may dwell on the incident over years, worrying at its memory like a scab.

The implanting within the psyche of fear, with all its corrosive effects, was not restricted to those with personal experience of British Army violence on Bloody Sunday. Fear radiated out in shockwaves emanating from the epicentre in the killing grounds of the Bogside. In the aftermath of this psychical earthquake, no nationalist in Derry, or indeed in Northern Ireland, could feel safe again. The paratrooper – and by association the British soldier per se – was transformed into a sinister and petrifying *imago*, whose phantastical power to threaten and destroy was confirmed by experience of the real; a situation which, in psychoanalytic terms, hinders the moderation and 'binding' of anxiety in the internal world, and thus exacerbates psychic splitting. This was perhaps especially acute for children. Siobhan McEleney recalls how, as a 13-year-old, she had been 'allowed to march from Creggan to William Street Baths' (a location that her parents presumably believed to be at a safe distance from 'Aggro Corner' where the usual rioting was expected), and was safely back at her home a short distance from the Bogside when she heard the shooting, and recognized 'the sharp, shrill sound of SLRs which you knew belonged to the British Army'. Her initial fear was for the safety of her family, though the safe return of her father removed that anxiety. But McEleney goes on to recall a more boundless fear, far more difficult to allay:

I remember the feelings of terror as darkness and an eerie silence fell. I don't think Derry slept that night. I have vivid recollections of being afraid to go to sleep in case the Paras would shoot us in our beds. I experienced fear like that only once before – it was just before the British Army arrived on the streets of the North and people genuinely feared they would be massacred by the B Specials.[35]

The association of memories here is important: the image of the Paratroopers – that morning 'just another bunch of British soldiers', members of the army

that had been welcomed by Liam Wray's mother and many others as the pro-
tectors of Northern nationalists against the armed supporters of the Unionist
State – is now coalesced together with that of the B Specials, and with it the
collective memory of fifty years of fear and harassment.

The experience of powerlessness in the face of brutal violence and personal bereavement, endemic on Bloody Sunday, is a third major contributing factor in traumatic splitting, and recognized as central in the aetiology
of PTSD.[36] Feelings of powerlessness are indelibly marked in the memories
of many survivors, for a variety of reasons. Primarily, this was an effect of
subjection to military power. Bernadette McAliskey (formerly Devlin) understands the inculcation of fear to be an intentional political lesson, designed
to cow and humiliate: 'On the day we knew real fear for the first time. When
the bullets were fired, people dived to the ground and crawled away like dogs
in fear of their masters.'[37] If some were stirred to anger rather than fear by
what they witnessed, the shooting of Micky Bradley demonstrated the futil-
ity of protest. Enraged by the sight of his friend Jack Duddy lying shot on
the ground in the Flats' carpark, Bradley was seen to jump to his feet and
run a few steps towards the soldiers: 'He spread his arms out wide and he
shouted in the direction of the troops at the corner of Rossville Street flats.'[38]
Bradley recalls: 'I shouted over to the soldiers, really bitter, "Come on, you
hateful bastards; come on, fucking shoot me!" All of a sudden, I felt this mer-
ciful heavy thud and I thought, Jesus, what hit me?' He received a near-fatal
bullet wound to the abdomen, and spent three months in hospital.[39]

For some relatives, the memory of their proximity to the death of a loved
one whom they were unable to reach is also infused with feelings of powerlessness focused on regret about the contact that was never made and the
help that was never given. For Kathleen Kelly, the mother of Michael Kelly
who was shot on the rubble barricade, the memory of seeing her son alive
for the last time is coloured by a tragic sense of her lost opportunity to intervene: 'I saw him before he was killed from my sister's house in Kells Walk.
There was shooting below her window, so I ran out and Michael was standing against the garages. I called to him, "Come on up, come on up." . . . But
the next time I looked he was away.' Another of her sons, John, retells her
story and points the moral: 'If he had heard her, it might have been a different story.'[40] Maura Young, sister to John Young who also died on the barricade, finds herself twenty-five years later replaying in imagination the scene
that she never witnessed in reality, but now invested with a wish-fulfilling
phantasy of her own power to save his life: 'In Rossville Street, standing in
the place that John was shot, you try to put yourself beside him to try to stop
what happened. It's a strange feeling.'[41]

A third experience of powerlessness, often intercut with sheer disbelief,
followed on hearing the news that a loved one had been shot dead. This had
a devastating impact on individual family members and was a decisive factor
in its own right leading to 'entrapment' in trauma. Many bereaved family
members tell the story of this moment, and many remember the shock of

hearing the news and the precise circumstances in which this occurred, vividly and in detail. Michael McKinney, for example, had been on the march and gathered that 'there were five and six dead down at the barricade on Rossville Street':

> Later, I went to Mass and I remember Fr Rooney speaking about the terrible events. I didn't know about Willie [his brother] . . . I went home to let my mother know that I was OK. I remember seeing Fr McLaughlin's car parked close by and thinking there must be something wrong with one of my neighbours. I went in and our house was crowded with people; my mother was sitting, crying. My father came to me and he said: 'Willie is dead.' I broke down.[42]

Not all the bereaved had Michael McKinney's experience of being told clearly and unambiguously, in his own home surrounded by his family, within hours of the shootings. The earliest news circulated in the form of rumours, and many of the relatives heard the news from people they did not know well, or from children, which made it difficult to know whether to believe what they were saying.[43] Relatives of anyone who had not returned from the march had to endure hours of anxiety and uncertainty, as accounting for the missing was complicated by the army's withholding of the names of those under arrest: this ensured that 'some families would only discover their loss in the most harrowing circumstances'.[44] One such was the family of Michael McDaid, who were twice told in error that he was not on the hospital's list of casualties, due to mistaken identification, before they discovered the truth late that evening.[45]

A fourth factor determining a traumatic sense of powerlessness, and a further nodal point of memory that surfaces again and again in survivors' stories, was their encounter with security forces' triumphalism at the killings and denigration of the dead and the bereaved. This manifested in numerous ways. One was the army's neglect of and contempt for the bodies of the injured and the dying as well as the dead. Jim Wray, the story of whose death had so disturbed Joanne O'Brien, was shot in the back as he lay seriously injured from a previous bullet.[46] James Chapman, who testified at the Widgery Tribunal, witnessed the soldiers' treatment of the bodies of William Nash, John Young and Michael McDaid: 'Troops got out of the Saracen and lifted the bodies by the hair of the head and [by the] legs and threw them into the Saracen.'[47] When they were delivered to the morgue at Altnagelvin Hospital some two hours later, Jim McLaughlin, who was helping with the identification of the bodies, recalled that the dead men were 'piled in like lumps of meat', though the bodies were unloaded more respectfully by the soldiers while civilian witnesses were present; but Fr Irwin, examining them on arrival, found that Michael McDaid's corpse was still warm, suggesting that he had still been alive in the Saracen.[48] The lives of a number of other victims might have been saved by prompt medical attention denied them by the army. This knowledge haunted Gerard Donaghey's sister, Mary, for example, who remembers:

The doctor said if they could get him to hospital, there would be a chance of him living. So Raymond Rogan and Leo Young put him into the back seat of a car. But they were stopped by the Army and arrested. I always think about what was going through his mind, him dying on his own. They left him lying alone in the car until he drew his last breath. It makes me very angry. To think that he died in an Army post when they knew that they could have saved his life.[49]

Leo Young tells how in

Barrack Street we were stopped at an army barricade and pulled out of the car. I said to the soldier, 'What about the dying young fellow?' and he said, 'Let the bastard die.' I said, 'You are just an animal.' He then put me up against some railings, pointed his gun at me and told me that if I blinked he would blow my head off.[50]

Donaghey was left in the car for two hours, after which time he was dead. In one of the most notorious episodes on Bloody Sunday, while in military custody his body was planted with four nail bombs, probably by the RUC, to fabricate his 'guilt'.[51] For Mary Donaghey, the immediate effect of this was that '[w]e couldn't get his body. My husband went over to the hospital and came back and said there was no sign of his body.' Later, they discovered that it had been taken to the Foyle Road army camp and photographed, before being delivered to the hospital where identification by the family finally took place later that evening.[52]

Another form of denigration involved the army's targeting and abuse of those trying to tend the injured and the dying. Five men were shot, three fatally, while trying to reach or tend the injured, and Knights of Malta first-aiders were also shot at, as well as vilified, beaten and arrested.[53] An inherent part of the systematic military operation, in contravention of the Geneva Convention, and thus a further source of disbelief among witnesses, was the abuse of injured civilians, and the obstruction, harassment and intimidation of medical workers. The movement of ambulances was hindered, and in at least one case an ambulance was fired on.[54] When Anna Nelis, anxiously awaiting an ambulance she had called for the badly wounded Peggy Deery and for Michael Bridge, asked two Paratroopers directly outside her house to radio for an ambulance, one told her: ' "Let the whore bleed to death" ' and ' "Let them all die." '[55] Alice Long, who worked as a first-aider with the Knights of Malta on Bloody Sunday, remembers:

I told the Army that I needed ambulances for the injured. One of the soldiers laughed and said, 'Why do you need ambulances? The Paras shoot to kill, not maim.' They sent me off in the wrong direction. As I came running back, the shooting had stopped. I heard them making jokes, 'How many did you get?' And how they were going to celebrate that night. Some officer was shouting, 'Well done, boys. Well done.'[56]

A triumphalism infused soldiers' attitudes towards the victims of their violence, and was also manifest in the callousness of official procedures for 'processing' the remains and dealing with grieving relatives. Fr Terence O'Keeffe was among those 'appalled by the paratroopers' jubilant mood: they were boasting that they must have killed at least fifty people'[57] – boasts to which some of the bereaved were subjected. Leo Young heard the news of his brother John's death from an RUC man as he was released from a night under arrest in Strand Barracks, a story retold by his sister, Maura Duffy: 'He came out as far as the gate and there was a big policeman and he said, "How many brothers have you?" and Leo said "Two. Why?" "Well, you have only one now because the other was shot yesterday", and the policeman shut the gate and left him standing on the Strand Road.'[58] An atmosphere of triumphalism, menace and abuse also infected Altnagelvin Hospital, compounding the horror and humiliation of the many relatives and friends who went there to seek news of the missing or to identify the dead.[59] The widespread anger at such treatment, as well as the resentment and frustration at feeling powerless to give it vent, help to explain impulses to join the IRA experienced by many survivors of Bloody Sunday.

Trauma, storytelling and personal memory

The survivors' memories discussed thus far in this chapter provide evidence that the events of Bloody Sunday created the conditions for traumatic disturbance and defensive splitting of the psyche on a large scale. As Hayes demonstrates, these multiple determinants of trauma brought about a wide range of acute symptoms in the immediate aftermath of Bloody Sunday, some of which persisted for years and even decades, that nowadays would be recognizable as features of 'chronic PTSD'.[60] In 1972 these effects of trauma were not widely understood, but with the passing of time, a certain degree of recovery and the increasing popular awareness of these issues, survivors themselves are now able to reflect on the psychical affects produced in them as a result of their experiences. Geraldine Richmond, for example, who had a teenaged boy die in her arms and witnessed another man shot in the head as he went to help another dying man (and who was herself subjected to hostile cross-examination at the Widgery Tribunal), states:

> For months afterwards, I had panic attacks – I didn't want to tell anybody because I thought I was going cuckoo. I had flashbacks for about three years. I'd start to sweat and my heart would pound and it would all come back. There was nobody you could tell – you couldn't really talk to the families, because you felt that bad about how they were feeling. And I wasn't shot or injured. People expected you to go back to being normal and you were never normal again.[61]

In Mary Donaghey's case, 'I started to go blind for spells. When I found it coming on, I used to put my son, Denis, in the playpen. I would sit until it would leave me. This lasted for five years.'[62] Her doctor diagnosed her symptoms as 'delayed shock', and 'gave me tablets. I was on tablets for six or seven years. Then I took very bad, and I was afraid to go out of the house, and I was put on a stronger tablet.'[63]

These stories are coherent accounts, constructed retrospectively twenty years or more after the events, when their traumatic impact had to some extent been absorbed and integrated into a narrative that achieves some degree of subjective composure. This form of memory, the outcome of a long process of reparative remembering, can be contrasted with memories of the traumatic event articulated at a time when the psychic shocks remain unintegrated and resistant to narrative representation. This can be seen in the transcript of a conversation with Alex Nash, recorded within three weeks of Bloody Sunday and published in Fulvio Grimaldo and Susan North's *Blood in the Street* (1972), in which Nash describes witnessing his son William shot dead on the rubble barricade, how he himself was shot when he went to William, and then watched helplessly as soldiers threw his son's body with the others into the back of an army Saracen and drove away. (Bracketed ellipses indicate breaks in the text; Nash's pauses are non-bracketed.)

> I walked across the street at the wee barricade, there, you know, the wee flats, Glenfada Park. So I was going across, you know, when you heard banging . . . (*voice descends to a whisper*) . . . I looked round . . . you know the shooting . . . and I looked round and I saw the wee fellow of mine . . . I say that's Willy . . . and I've seen . . . So, as fast as I could get over, I run like . . . I run across. There is some banging then, you see. I run across the street then, you know, to get Willy. But I knew . . . that he was gone. . . I knew it. . . I knew it. And I put my hand up like that . . . as I put my hand up there, they give it me in here, and then here . . . two like, two, aye. See, when I jumped down like that, they kept on pumping at me, you see. [. . .]
>
> I've seen Willy . . . the young fellow was there . . . while I was there . . . my own body was laying there . . . three bodies laying there . . . like that. He got it in the temple. Willy was in the middle, the son of mine, you see. He was laying face down, but his face was laying out that way . . . but there was no breath coming out. So I touched him and I said 'Willy', like that, there . . . and they kept pumping . . . and I got him like that there. . . his shirt was right up, you know, he's a right big fellow, isn't he, he's pretty big for his age . . . And I just touched him like that and I said 'Willy'. And I couldn't do nothing for him. [. . .]
>
> I was wounded, you see, they knew I was wounded, seen the blood pumping out of me. I thought they'd finish me off there and then, you see. But this boy (soldier) said, they just left me sitting, 'three more bodies' . . . and I say to this big fella, I say 'see, that's my son there' . . . Just dragged them in the dirt . . . one boy on top of the others . . . I thought they were going to finish me.[64]

Here, Alex Nash struggles to convey both what he saw happen around him and what was done to him, and also something of the horror, terror and outrage that forms his subjective experience. His account unfolds in fragmented images, as one point trails off or jumps to another. It circles back repetitively to particular moments: 'I just touched him like that and I said "Willy" ', a moment connected to the experience of parental helplessness ('I couldn't do nothing for him'); and 'I thought they were going to finish me', a moment centred on personal fear. And it veers away from the actual shooting of his son, which remains unverbalized: 'So I say that's Willy. . . and I've seen . . .'.

For many years afterwards, survivor memory may be subject to a variety of disturbances and difficulties in grasping or absorbing the traumatic event and integrating it into a coherent personal memory narrative. In his analysis of life-story interviews conducted with a wide network of anonymous 'first generation' relatives of the Bloody Sunday dead, Hayes discovered:

> These narratives revealed a significant amount of PTS symptoms within exquisitely detailed accounts of [their] experience of what transpired on Bloody Sunday . . . First generation narratives detailed the events prior to the traumatic event, the immediate reaction to the event, the funeral and its aftermath with photographic images and dramatic examples of the capacity of a traumatic event to make indelible marks on the psyche.[65]

These psychic marks are revealed not only in what the first generation remember and are willing and able to tell about their emotional experience, but also in how they remember and tell their stories. As discussed in chapter 2, this always involves an attempt to *process* that event emotionally, so as to internalize and integrate its affects within a less divided and damaged self. The shocking and intense emotional cathexis of the traumatic event, together with the profound difficulties it interposes in the way of absorbing and 'coming to terms with' its reality, produce a variety of mnemonic disturbances. These tend to undermine the ability of survivors to control their own life-stories, and thus their sense of agency.

At one end of the spectrum, memory is experienced as excessive, uncontrollable and overwhelming. For one of Hayes's respondents, a boy aged eight in 1972, his 'last memory of his brother' – watching him going off to the march, and being left behind himself – 'replays like a film strip . . . frame by frame'.[66] Another of Hayes's unnamed respondents explained how, during periods where there was an upsurge of violence, she would be troubled by intrusive thoughts about Bloody Sunday, so that 'I can't get it out of my head', and it became her 'only conversation'.[67] Maura Young describes 'a strange feeling; it's not constant. But if you're talking about it, something happens: flashbacks of the funeral – very vivid. It takes a few hours to go away.'[68] A vulnerability to the unwanted return of these 'flashback memories' is a typical feature in remembering marked by trauma. It may be triggered involuntarily by an association of ideas, by an image or sensory impression, or by the ritual, representation and discussion that surrounds the annual anniversary commemoration of Bloody Sunday. In 1997, Alex Nash's daughter, Linda Roddy, told Joanne O'Brien: 'My father has been traumatised since 1972, and coming up to the anniversaries his mind is hell. He thinks everybody is a Paratrooper and that they are out to kill him. It is terrible to watch.'[69]

At the other end of the spectrum of mnemonic disturbance lies amnesia. Many Bloody Sunday survivors suffered, and some continue to suffer, from loss of memory affecting periods of time ranging from minutes to years, most commonly after hearing news of the death of a loved one, and of the three-day period of wakes and funerals that followed. Some of those affected by amnesia now understand this to have been a form of involuntary psychic self-defence against being overwhelmed by the reality of what was happening.[70] In the case of Alice Long, the young first-aider with the Knights of Malta, who came under fire herself on Bloody Sunday and 'hardly treated anyone that day because they were all dead', forgetting was a conscious strategy. She recalls:

> The shock only really hit me that night and the next day. Afterwards, I prom-
> ised myself that I was going to lose all memory of it, and worked hard at trying
> to forget. I had nightmares for a couple of months; throughout the years they
> gradually wore off. It took a long time.[71]

Here, the memories expelled from consciousness are re-presented by the unconscious dreamwork of the psyche, producing nightmares, 'a form of intrusive recollections'.[72]

Hayes reads lost memory as a function of psychic denial of the event, stem-ming from an inability to 'take it in' emotionally, which manifests as a 'vac-illation' between 'intense rushes of feeling' and 'numbing, clouded perceptions', accompanied by an 'impaired capacity to relate to others'.[73] His study points to the way Bloody Sunday survivors use the language of 'blurring', 'blankness' and 'numbness' to describe their internal state in the immediate aftermath of the shootings.[74] For one man among Hayes's inter-viewees, who cannot remember 'the funerals . . . the Mass . . . going up to St Mary's to view the coffin or anything like that', but knows that 'I did do it . . . I was part of it', this 'blank' is associated with the memory of emo-tional repression, of having 'cried only once':

> I went into the bathroom and locked myself in. I don't know. Maybe I felt I had
> to be the strongest or whatever because my sisters couldn't handle it. My mother
> couldn't handle it. My Da was too busy trying to kill it . . . kill the emotion of
> it [original ellipsis].[75]

This 'killing of emotion' in response to the killing of the loved brother and son is a vivid and chilling metaphor for processes of psychic resistance to internalizing, or 'taking in', the death, that is one of the most damaging after-effects of the army's violence on Bloody Sunday. For other interviewees, gaps in memory were spaces in between 'the chaos and sadness and tears and dis-belief, crying, screaming and roaring and whatever'.[76] Jean Hegarty, the sister of Kevin McElhinney, who travelled over from Canada for his funeral, vividly evokes this experience of living in a daze, of feeling disoriented from ordinary life and dislocated from reality, seen by theorists of trauma as a form of dis-sociation whereby the victim of violent bereavement splits herself in two in order to safeguard one part, at least, from the damage: 'When I think back on it now, it was nearly like being on drugs. I was looking on at all these events – they just didn't seem real. It almost seemed like I wasn't there. The trip home was just like being outside yourself looking on.'[77] If, for some sur-vivors of trauma, memories of the real were transformed into nightmares, for others the 'unreal' world of waking life itself is remembered as having become 'just like a dream' or 'just like a nightmare'.[78]

The narratives composed by survivors, in their endeavour to integrate the memory of Bloody Sunday into a coherent life-history capable of assimiliating its emotional repercussions, must necessarily grapple with these various effects of traumatic disturbance. One particularly vivid example of the peculiar formation of personal memory under the pressure of trauma is Kathleen Kelly's story, told in 1992, of the day her son Michael was shot dead. She unfolds a detailed sequence of events, from seeing her son and witnessing the shooting up until the moment she hears the news of his death later at home. Her story represents the remembered bewilderment and disorientation of the day from the perspective of hindsight twenty years later, allowing the incorporation of information that would have been pieced together and interpreted retrospectively, when it had assumed a significance not grasped at the time:

> After the shooting was over, I didn't know that Michael had been shot. I said to a crowd of people, 'What's wrong, what's wrong?' and they said that there is so many dead. I said, 'God bless us.' I thought it was rubber bullets they were firing, because they fired one through the flat that I was in. But the people told me it was live bullets. When I asked who it was, they said they didn't know.
>
> I was walking around looking and I tried to get into the first house where he was, where people had taken him, but at that stage I didn't know he was in there. Somebody must have told Fr McLaughlin I was trying to get into the house. He came over to me . . . and I said, 'God, father, I believe there are some of them dead.' 'Aye,' he said. "Now are you going home? There's a man here who will take you up in a taxi.'
>
> I said, 'That's grand, father, because my Michael is on that march the day, and by God when I go home he will never be on a march again.' 'No,' he said, 'that's right. Now come on and this man will take you up home.'

Kathleen Kelly's account of the journey home up to the Creggan dwells on a number of incidental, disjointed but detailed memories and reads like one of Freud's descriptions of a dream: she gets out of the car to help an hysterical girl, meets a sexton and has a conversation about a lost wallet, walks up a crowded street, and exchanges words with her daughter – 'God, I'll never look at another cowboy picture again. I saw enough shooting today to finish me' – that assume a prophetic significance in the light of the news to come.

> When I came into the house it was packed. I asked what was wrong and the husband said, 'Michael was hit in the leg, that's the word we got.' I went into hysterics. 'Jesus, Mary and Joseph,' I said, 'they will take him to Long Kesh when he gets better.' Then the brother next door came in, and knelt down beside me and I said, 'Ah Jamesie, they are going to take him to Long Kesh.' He said, 'Naw, they wont take him to Long Kesh, they'll take him to the cemetery. He's dead.'
>
> I knew nothing for four or five years after that.[79]

In its skilful fashioning of the story – making use of everyday storytelling techniques of detailed reporting, contrast and irony to point to her own lack of understanding of what had happened, and other people's care to protect her, leading up to the denouement, the brutal moment of truth – Mrs Kelly's account exemplifies the effort of the survivor to shape the traumatic event into narrative form, to give it meaning and represent it for the recognition of others. In its contrast between this well-worked and detailed elaboration of clearly remembered incidents, movements and conversations, and the sudden and prolonged absence of any recollection at all – Mrs Kelly suffered the most serious prolonged amnesia of any of the grieving relatives – it also graphically illustrates the 'unusually vivid and unusually fragmented' quality of traumatic memory,[80] and the way amnesia itself may be worked into a life-story.

As Kathleen Kelly's amnesia demonstrates, loss and grief complicated by trauma were lived in very individual ways according to the different psychologies of those affected. The quality of traumatic experience also differed between families according to the varying conditions in which death and the bereavement process occurred. This point is exemplified most clearly by the case of the family of Barney McGuigan, killed by a shot through the eye, for whom the return of the body in a sealed coffin, intended to protect them from the sight of his horrific injuries, disrupted the funeral ritual and interfered with the grieving process.[81] Individually, the Bloody Sunday survivors and relatives continue to struggle with the psychic aftershocks of their particular experiences. However, all share the difficulty of accepting the reality of violent death under the abnormal circumstances of Bloody Sunday, expressed by Floyd Gilmour, who lost his brother: 'I remember the day twenty-five years ago, I remember everything. My mother and father have died since, and you accept a natural death. Whereas, twenty-five years on, I still can't accept Hugh dying.'[82] These difficulties are closely related to the families' common sense of the persisting injustice instituted by the Widgery Inquiry, as described by Linda Roddy: 'Normally, when a person dies, you're told what happened, you grieve and you get on with the rest of your life. I have been lied to for thirty years – it's hard to take. Legally, it's still on the record that William was a gunman. The British Army will not take responsibility for his murder'.[83]

Meanwhile, the invisible work of psychic reparation must continue as best it can. Reflecting on the process of recovery after nearly thirty years, Maura Young comments: 'It's very hard. But the more you talk about it, the better; it shaves a wee bit off, the more you do.'[84] These life-stories are literally that: stories that affirm life and make living possible, by telling and retelling the deaths. Since the South African TRC, this mode of 'healing through telling' tends to be associated with formal, state-centred mechanisms of inquiry into the violent past. However, in the Bogside and the Creggan after the Widgery Tribunal, the listening space had to be developed within the local community, among and between the traumatized survivors.

The traumatized community and the social life of stories

Bloody Sunday was experienced and has been remembered in collective terms as well as individually. Consider, for example, Don Mullan's story, composed from memory in 1996, about what had happened to him when, as a 15-year-old on his first civil rights march, he came under fire on the rubble barricade across Rossville Street: 'I distinctly remember a youth clutching his stomach a short distance away, his cry filling the air with despair and disbelief. For a moment we were stunned. People ran to his aid while others, including myself, sheltered behind the barricade. Suddenly the air was filled with what seemed like a thunderstorm of bullets.'[85] Like many other survivor narratives of Bloody Sunday, Mullan's story concerns more than a merely individual experience: the attack is remembered both personally and collectively, as something that happened *to us*, and to which *we* responded. As the shooting began, '[o]ur nervous systems reacted simultaneously, as though a high-voltage electric shock had been unleashed. Absolute panic ensued as we turned and ran. Doors and alleyways choked as waves of terrified adults and children tried to reach safety. "Jesus! They're going to kill us!" ' Mullan further identifies an explicitly collective dimension to the impact of the attack as he remembers the atmosphere in the city later that day: 'I had never before experienced collective shock on this scale. The entire west bank of Derry was deeply traumatised by the attack. It must be something akin to the aftermath of an earthquake. I shall never forget the silence that descended upon my native town.'[86] Others share Mullan's memory of a traumatized collective 'silence'.[87]

The character of collective shock and disturbance alluded to here, and in other personal testimonies of Bloody Sunday, produces what can best be described as a 'traumatized community'. I use this concept to refer to the effect of some thousands of people having undergone, more or less simultaneously, the same or a similar traumatic experience, and of their having been affected by, and having responded to, this experience as a social group. It also points to a particular quality of pervasive collective emotion compounded of shock, grief, fear and anger, stemming from the concentrated psychic impact of violent death on such a scale within a particular location – a phenomenon described by Frantz Fanon, writing of the Algerian independence struggle against French colonialism, as a 'pathology of atmosphere'.[88] In collective trauma on such a scale, individuals are affected with a further compounding of their own disturbed emotional states. Relatives attending the Altnagelvin Hospital in Derry on the evening of 30 January 1972 found the anguish and horror of the occasion to be intensified by the haunting presence of so many of the dead, and also by the sheer numbers of people, many of whom were known to each other, in similarly profound distress.[89] After Bloody Sunday, to know others who were also shocked and grieving was not always a source of comfort and support. Maura Young remembers, when her family visited the parents of Willie McKinney, who 'lived just down the street from us', how 'Mr McKinney opened the door and I said, "We are the Youngs, our John was shot too, Mr McKinney," and he started to squeal and roar. It must have been just the realization. Like you might wake up and say, "Is this nightmare over yet?" And it's not.'[90]

Within the traumatized community, others' sympathy as well as their grief trigger further emotional reactions and may generate additional emotional burdens. Hayes reports one woman's memory of how 'her traumatized family . . . could not leave the house in the days and weeks following "Bloody Sunday" because they wanted to hide away from everyone and everything that could remind them of the death. They . . . did not want to see people because they did not want to hear constant condolences.' When, after some months, her mother did go out to the shops for the first time, and met people who 'had not seen her since her son's death and did express sympathy', she 'could not cope with this so the daughters had to take her home and wait longer'.[91]

A further symptom of the pathology of atmosphere was '[s]urvivor guilt – a big thing in this town, without a doubt'.[92] Guilt may prompt associated feelings and concerns, that 'he should have lived', that 'I did not do what I could have done to save him' and even that 'I should have died in his place'. People who themselves were badly injured on Bloody Sunday are among those who experienced this. Alana Burke – seriously disabled by damage to her lower back and legs, and experiencing feelings of withdrawal and worthlessness, as well as nightmares – remembers: 'For years afterwards I felt guilty somehow that I survived when so many had been killed that day. I felt bad when I met the Wrays, for example. We all did Irish dancing together and were quite friendly. But their brother had been killed and I was still alive.'[93]

These conflicting emotional cross-currents, eddying through the traumatized community, were concentrated in their most intense and complex ways within families, particularly the immediate families of the dead (or 'the Bloody Sunday families', as they have come to be called), which provided bereaved individuals with their primary support network, but where the death, physical injury or trauma of one family member touched all others simultaneously, in a shared experience of horror and loss that made each of them the witness as well as the subject of traumatic experience. Michael McKinney, who had wept on hearing about the death of his brother William, remembers that 'the following morning, my father wakened me with his crying. George . . . the next eldest to Willie, was sitting with him, saying, you have still five sons, trying to console him. And my father crying his eyes out saying why couldn't they wound him instead of killing him. It broke his heart.'[94]

Such witnessing of the effects of trauma on loved ones works to compound an individual's own emotional responses with their reactions to the emotions of others. This could produce powerful traumatic effects in its own right. One of the brothers of Michael Kelly, whose mother, Kathleen, was among the most severely traumatized of all the Bloody Sunday family members, and retained as personal memorial objects all of her dead son's clothes and even a Mars Bar found in his pocket, suggests that the impact on close relatives could be as emotionally devastating as their own bereavement: 'I am very, very, very bitter. The bitterness stems not only from not having [Michael] but also what happened to my mother and my family . . . When it affected my mother, it affected me deeply . . . By watching how she reacted to it, and by watching what happened to her over the years, that's what really affected me.'[95]

The compounding of emotional affects within a 'traumatized family'[96] appears to have occurred most potently in circumstances where children witnessed the transformation of their parents and experienced the loss of their emotional support and guidance. One woman, a young teenager in 1972, remembers how her own self-confidence, stemming from the stability of her large, secure family, had been undermined by the emotional deterioration of her parents: 'Then overnight, my mother and father changed so I hadn't got the security of them anymore. They had turned into angry, bitter people. I actually witnessed my mother being violent to soldiers. I never did see violence at home and I began to feel it emotionally, my mother being violent and angry words. I didn't see this before.'[97] Children and young adults in the Bloody Sunday families could find themselves called on to assume a parent-like responsibility in looking after one another and sometimes their devastated parents. One 16-year-old boy tells how 'he changed in twenty-four hours "from a boy to a man"' after his father was killed.[98] Under pressures of such intensity, a family could rally round for support and try to ensure, like the Kellys, that '[e]verybody in the family pulled together'.[99] But it was also likely to find, with the Dohertys, that 'our family kind of fell apart . . . we were always close, but there was a lot of blackness there and we were fighting to understand it in our own way. Each of us . . . has dealt with it in our own way'.[100]

Emotional dynamics of this kind affect the composing of memories, since both the experiences themselves and the stories told about them are mediated through modes of cultural representation and exchange that make the personal remembering of individuals an inherently social and *collective* process. Through practices of storytelling within families and communities, individuals contribute to the formation of collective memory from below, a process producing fluid narratives, constantly shifting and evolving, that exist and take different forms within diverse social arenas. As Jelin and Kaufman have argued, narrated memories are never purely individual productions, but are generated through a collective practice of 'intersubjective' telling, listening, witnessing and exchanging of stories, which enables psychological remembering to assume a social existence.[101] In the process, personal stories are adapted and transformed by their dialogical relationship both to the needs and receptivities of listeners, and also, in the more Bakhtinian sense, to the personal memory narratives of others; even taking in elements of these other memories as their own.[102]

2 Kay Duddy, a founder-member of the Bloody Sunday Justice Campaign.

Such borrowings may be attributed, as relayings of the clearly demarcated stories of other people. But they may also, in Salman Rushdie's striking phrase, 'leak' psychically across the permeable boundaries of the self, from one person to another.[103] In either case, they give rise to 'strangely composite' formations, characteristic, according to Antonio Gramsci, of popular 'common sense'.[104] It is therefore necessary to examine the intersubjective and cultural mediation of personal memories, to trace their absorption of stories and images from the domain of public representations; and to analyse the formation of what Ashplant et al. term 'shared or common memories' that emerge as those who have undergone the same or a directly cognate experience (such as, for example, 'the survivors of a single campaign or massacre') begin to 'express and compare' their memories, and to 'formulate a shared language and identify common themes'.[105] As personal storytelling feeds into shared or common memories, and in turn becomes infused with them, the stories of others become a part of one's own remembering.

Consider, for example, the stories told by Kay Duddy, an elder sister of Jack Duddy and since 1992 a prominent activist in the Justice Campaign (see figure 2), who has described her own personal experience of Bloody Sunday in several published accounts.[106] Her memories feature a number of key episodes that recur constantly in the narratives of the bereaved families: receiving news of the death; identification of the body; and participation in the wake and funeral. These are focal points of intense emotional distress and the manifestation of psychic effects associated with traumatic disturbance, that each family and its individual members experienced in their own particular way, but which were also common experiences undergone – and remembered – together with others. In the case of the Duddys, a father and fourteen siblings, as well as aunts and uncles and the greater extended family suffered the shock of this bereavement. The shared experience gives rise to shared or common memories. Kay Duddy's stories are also the stories of her close relatives: her younger brother, an aunt and uncle, her father. Like Don Mullan's, her narration moves freely between the pronouns 'I' and 'we', as at some moments she recounts a shared family memory, and at others distinguishes her own individual experience. While weaving the stories of her family, friends and neighbours into her 'personal' memory narrative, she also describes moments when other people tell her story. Triggered by the shock of the news, she experienced a traumatic amnesia and has no memory of following three days, during which the wake and funeral of her brother took place. When she tried to discover whether she had even attended the funeral, by searching for her own image in photographs, it was her aunt who remembered for her: ' "No, you collapsed in the chapel and had to be taken home." '[107] We see here how fragmented personal narratives may be filled out and augmented in a process of family remembrance, in which the damaged psyches of survivors may be refurnished with stories about themselves told by others.

The Canadian anthropologist Julie Cruikshank has used the term 'the social life of stories'[108] to describe these social processes of the production, circulation, reproduction and transformation of narratives (and, it should be added, of visual images) within a particular cultural context. In the social life of stories, personal remembering also takes in, and makes its own, elements of the cultural narratives that circulate in public arenas. The news reports broadcast on television and radio on the evening of Bloody Sunday are themselves engraved in personal and family memories. They appear to have left an especially powerful imprint in the memories of children. Bernie Mullen from nearby Strabane remembers the party to celebrate his eighth birthday being cut short by the news of Bloody Sunday:

> I recall going into the living room and my parents being physically stunned at the images from Derry which flashed across our television screen that evening. It made a lasting impression on a child previously shielded from such scenes. The scale of the slaughter was shocking. Even at that relatively tender age I sensed the injustice of what was done in Derry that day . . . The sadness in that Catholic household, and the hurt, was palpable.

Reflecting on the impact that watching the news made on him, Mullen mentions two factors. One is the unreal proximity-yet-distance of the atrocity, as an event achieving the status of television news and watched on the small screen, yet occurring in a familiar nearby place: 'Unlike those in Derry that day I viewed the terrible events from a distance, in the safety of my home'; yet, as 'a child the events were made much more frightening by the fact that they took place just 14 miles from where I lived'. The second is one particular television image engrained in his memory: 'The sight of a Catholic priest, Fr Edward Daly, making his way through the Bogside holding a white handkerchief in a bid to prevent further bloodshed encapsulated the wrong which I could not verbalise until I was older.'[109] These accounts demonstrate how broadcast news is not only itself a remembered event within personal and family memory narratives of Bloody Sunday: it provides also, as in the image of Fr Daly and his white hanky, the very substance of memory for those like Mullen from outside Derry; and it supplements the fragments of information gleaned by those on the fringes of the killing zone, derived from their own sensory impressions and 'overheard conversations', with images and stories from its own *second-order* world of representations.

The visual image of Fr Daly 'waving a white handkerchief as he leads rescuers carrying Jackie Duddy, a dying victim through the still threatening bullets' has been described as 'the most remembered icon of that terrible day'.[110] Daly told his story of this incident in his statement for Widgery. This describes Duddy, whom Daly witnessed being shot while running alongside him, now 'lying on his back' in the Flats' carpark:

> I could see blood coming out over his shirt. I decided I must go to attend him . . . I took out a handkerchief and held it up and in a crouched position went to him . . . There were still bursts of gunfire from time to time, though it was not as continuous . . . I first knelt beside the boy, and held my handkerchief to his wound . . . then a young Knight of Malta whose name was Glenn came out to

the other side of the boy [. . .] After a few minutes the gunfire got worse. We both lay down beside the boy as I gave him the Last Rites of my church. I felt he was dying [. . .] After a period of time [. . .] during which there had been quite a lot of gunfire, all from one direction, in single shots and bursts, two men crawled out behind us. One of them was William Barber. They offered to help to carry the boy to a position where he could receive medical aid. They suggested that I should go in front and carry a white handkerchief and they would carry him behind me. (Original ellipses; mine in brackets.)[111]

In essence, this story is no different from those of the many other civilians who risked their own lives on Bloody Sunday in going, while under fire, to the assistance of the wounded. However, this particular moment was captured and fixed as an iconic visual memory by Fulvio Grimaldi in his famous photograph,[112] and by the BBC cameraman Cyril Cave in his film recording of the group carrying Duddy as they turned the corner from Chamberlain Street into the safety of Harvey Street,[113] broadcast on television news. Signifying the cruelty of the army's violence, and the courage and compassion of those subjected to it, this image above all others was held by many to encapsulate the meaning of Bloody Sunday. It figured an oppositional perspective questioning the official narrative, establishing in effect a memory grounded on visual representation rather than on first-hand experience, for international mass-media audiences. As the *Derry Journal* puts it: 'The image of Fr Edward Daly, crouched down and waving a white flag in front of a group of men carrying a dying teenager, which featured in media coverage all over the world, is the memory many who were not present still have of Bloody Sunday.'[114]

Indeed, these public 'media memories' generated initially by news coverage, when intercut with other elements, have also contributed to the formation of the personal memories of those who did directly experience Bloody Sunday at first hand. Bishop Daly, retelling the story that encapsulates his own memory of the events twenty years later for Peter Taylor's documentary *Remember Bloody Sunday* (1992), does so in relation to the visual image of himself as a younger man captured in Cave's film. In Don Mullan's account, his vivid memory of the terror and panic of being caught in 'a thunderstorm of bullets' on the rubble barricade is followed by total amnesia affecting his ability to recall what then transpired:

I escaped through Glenfada Park, but there are several minutes of that afternoon of which I have absolutely no memory. Five young men died at the barricade and four between Glenfada Park and Abbey Park. A further six were wounded in these locations. What I saw is somewhere hidden in my subconscious.[115]

During these lost minutes, a 'primeval instinct' had returned him safely to the family home in the Creggan Estate. Once there, however, his remembered experience has a striking similarity to that of Bernie Mullen:

The rest of the evening was spent with my family, listening to the radio and watching an old black and white television set for bulletin updates. The pictures of Fr Edward Daly from the Cathedral parish, waving a white bloodstained handkerchief as he led a group of men carrying the limp body of a teenager, was very distressing. There was something surreal about watching television coverage of a bloodbath I had just escaped, at the bottom of the local hill. This was something that happened in Sharpeville or Soweto, but not in Derry. Certainly not to neighbours and friends.[116]

For Don Mullan, an eyewitness and a direct survivor of the attack, the paradox of a local event appearing on the news and the strange spatial dislocation effected by public media coverage are heightened from unreal to *surreal*, as Derry – now, unimaginably, the scene of a bloodbath – undergoes a category shift to become a 'Sharpeville' or a 'Soweto', one of the places where something like this *could* happen. But those images captured on film, not directly witnessed but mediated through the technology of broadcast sound and vision, also shaped his survivor memory in ways that, in certain respects, resemble the entirely mediated memory of Bernie Mullen, who 'viewed the terrible events from a distance, in the safety of my home'. For Don Mullan, too, the visual image of Fr Daly, Jackie Duddy and the white handkerchief was 'very distressing' and remained vividly in personal memory for twenty-five years. In his case, though, it is sedimented together with horrific fragments of memory about his own bodily, sensory and emotional experience, and the bits of stories told by others, as one among a number of elements that make up the compound memory of the survivor.

In all the Bloody Sunday bereaved families, fuller and more coherent versions of events (denied them by Widgery) emerged only once several members were able to pool their own stories and gain access – directly or via the public media – to the accounts of eyewitnesses of their relative's death, and other evidence.[117] Kay Duddy, who was playing cards in her kitchen at the time, did not witness the gunshot that knocked her beloved brother to the ground; nor Father Daly tending to him and administering the last rites; nor Willy Barber, Charlie Glenn, Liam Bradley and another man who came to help, carrying him away along Chamberlain Street and Harvey Street as far as McHugh's shop, led by the priest with his white hanky; nor his death 'somewhere on that journey'.[118] But she learned about what had happened from those who were present, and from the photographs and television film, absorbing these representations into her personal memory of the events of 30 January 1972:

> The bishop was with Jackie when it happened. We see it all the time when there is a programme about the Troubles in Northern Ireland, the bishop – he was only Fr Daly at the time – waving the white hanky. He told us how he started to run and ran so fast he passed Jackie, even though Jackie was so fit from training.[119]

Inevitably, the public icon of the white hanky enters the memories even of the close family, who are confronted with it 'all the time' as a stock media image of 'the Troubles in Northern Ireland'. Fr Daly, however, also tells his personal story in the private and more supportive context of face-to-face communication with the Duddy family, in which motifs already in the public domain take on new and interpersonal significance (like the image of the priest overtaking the running teenager), while further, more intimate, information may also be exchanged:

> The bishop was able to give [Jackie] the last rites, and to talk to him before he died. He told us he said, 'Don't tell my mammy,' which was strange, because my mammy was dead. It ought to have been my daddy that he was worried about, who had told him he wasn't to be on the march. But then maybe at that moment that's what would come into his mind, that's who he would think of.[120]

Their shared memories of the shooting of Jack Duddy formed the basis for what Bishop Daly has described as his 'special relationship with the Duddy family, with whom he meets frequently'[121] – a connection symbolized by his gift to the family of the handkerchief, wielded in gestures of healing and protection many years earlier.[122] However, as well as enabling reparative remembering within the private arena, between those 'adoptive' or 'fictive kin' who have bonded in mutual support,[123] shared memories of this kind also underpin the formation of collective political identity.

Trauma and the politics of resistance

The psychic atmosphere within traumatized families and in the traumatized community more widely also had a major impact in terms of nationalist politics, including the armed resistance to the British occupation. The political impact of Bloody Sunday on Irish nationalists in Derry cannot be reduced to an effect of collective trauma, but it is an important constitutive factor. Two aspects of the relationship between trauma and nationalist politics may be distinguished. In the first place, Bloody Sunday brought about a fundamental rupture in the social and political consciousness of Northern Irish nationalists. This break is marked by the memories of incomprehension and disbelief at witnessing soldiers firing live rounds into a crowd of unarmed people, given expression by Eamonn MacDermott and Liam Wray (discussed above). The shootings overturned the known world and the terms in which it was knowable, causing the breakdown of an existing framework of meaning and belief, that is one of the hallmarks of trauma. After Bloody Sunday, for nationalists the world was no longer as it had seemed to be before, but had been totally transformed.

Life-historians Selma Leydesdorff et al. have written:

> Stories and life histories of traumatized individuals rarely reflect continuity: typically they are structured in terms of a 'before' and an 'after', hinging on one or several ruptures that have permanently affected these lives. In this respect a trauma is not an isolated event in a life story but may in itself often play a decisive role in a person's perception of life afterwards, interpretations of subsequent events, and consequently, memories of preceding experiences.[124]

Along with thousands of other nationalists of his generation, Liam Wray now recalls the era before Bloody Sunday – the era of the civil rights movement, when his mother could welcome the arrival of the British troops on the streets of Derry in August 1969 'with a tray and tea in her best cups' – as a bygone age.[125] Drawing on a resonant theme in the collective memory of Bloody Sunday, Wray describes this world in terms of lost innocence: 'We had this naive dream that we could change the world by peaceful protest. We believed that Protestant and Catholic could live together in peace and harmony, that people could walk hand-in-hand together into a new tomorrow singing "We Shall Overcome". Bloody Sunday was the day that innocence was slaughtered in Derry.'[126] In this respect, Bloody Sunday destroyed not only the civil rights movement, but also the subjectivity of the civil-righter, as its narrative lost its power to frame and organize the lives and identities of supporters.

The rupture in consciousness, then, involved also a break in identity. Derry Catholics shifted away from an often ambivalent identification with Britain towards a more overtly oppositional identification as Irish targets, and victims, of British military power; heightening affiliations to Irish national identity and causing alienation from the British basis of the State in Northern Ireland. Like many Derry Catholics, Joe Friel, who survived being shot in the chest on Bloody Sunday, came from a British Army family, and his father, grandfather and great-uncles had all been soldiers. Friel remembers not having 'a political thought in his head' when he went on the civil rights march – 'for the *craic*'. The conclusion he draws is that 'it just shows you, anybody could have been shot'.[127] Or take the case of Nigel Cooke, 'a relatively quiet, never-in-trouble Derry Catholic boy' who remembers playing at soldiers as a boy in the early to mid-1960s and thinking of the British troops stationed in Derry simply as 'the army'. While he did not come from a particularly Nationalist family, in his mid-teens Cooke became involved in the civil rights movement and went on the marches, but remembers: 'I still retained a healthy regard for the army, as representing a "higher authority" in Britain, which I was morally obliged by my religion and upbringing to have due respect for. I also felt a little sympathy for the soldiers.' For Cooke, then,

the impact of Bloody Sunday upon me was profound . . . Something life-changing dawned upon me that terrible day. It was the realisation that the army – and accordingly its masters – did not give a toss for my life. It could have been me lying there on my own streets in my own blood, for I fitted the apparent standard profile of the dead. I was no different from them. We simply did not matter, or count as individuals. We were mere rifle fodder, expendable. This was no 'security force' of mine. This force tried to kill me as I stood peacefully listening to a Member of Parliament at Free Derry Corner. 'My' army, the legitimate forces of law and order in 'my' state, had opened fire on me! If there was a defining moment when I ceased to think of myself as somehow British, this was it. For I recognised immediately that such an atrocity would never have been contemplated on 'the mainland'. English, Welsh or Scottish citizens could never have been indiscriminately classed as 'the enemy' by the British Army. Only the Irish could fill that role.

After Bloody Sunday, Cooke 'no longer considered this army as my own, representing my interests or my people', but identified himself in national terms as Irish and took out Irish citizenship. 'On Bloody Sunday, and many times over since, my faith in British justice was gunned down.'[128] Here, the 'defining moment' of army gunfire splits the self into a *before* and *after* along the fault-line of violence, and consigns to the past that self who was 'somehow British', respectful of 'the legitimate forces of law and order' and an innocent supporter of peaceful protest.

These ruptures in identity, and other traumatic consequences of this breakdown of meaning, posed profound psychic difficulties for the nationalist 'survivor generation' who lived through it.[129] Reflecting on this in the context of the twenty-fifth anniversary commemoration, and developing her thoughts about its significance for the 'successor generation', too, Bernadette McAliskey has remarked:

> Bloody Sunday has been described as the day that innocence died and it was undoubtedly the event that marked the end of innocence for all of us who lived through it and perhaps most tragically for future generations that were yet to be born. When I turned up to speak at that rally I never expected, suspected or even thought that such a thing could happen and when it did we all realized that it was a massive and tragic turning point for our own and our children's futures . . . For those of us who were there something in all of us died along with the fourteen who were shot dead that day. We had no comprehension of such brutality and we realized then that we would have to get used to it.[130]

'Getting used to it' is one way of describing the emotional as well as cognitive work of resistance required of nationalists individually and collectively as they struggled to address the traumatic effects of Bloody Sunday, and to make the necessary subjective adjustment to the *new* reality that existed afterwards. But for many nationalists, McAliskey among them, this process also contributed to a political consciousness-raising, grounded on a clear conception of the power and willingness of the State to enforce its authority over dissident citizens by the bullet if needs be; out of which emerged a stronger identification with an Irish identity defined in terms of militant resistance to British rule.

In examining the relationship between collective trauma and nationalist politics, then, the second aspect to be considered is the powerful impetus provided by Bloody Sunday towards Northern nationalist recruitment to the IRA. This was itself a manifestation of the new political consciousness. But it was also an effect of the pathology of atmosphere, one of the defining characteristics of a traumatized community, in the aftermath of Bloody Sunday. This included a further ingredient to those discussed above: intense anger and the emergence of collective wishes to hit back, or to gain revenge. Feelings of revenge and anger are 'common responses to man-made trauma';[131] and there

is certainly evidence that these feelings contributed to the atmosphere in
Derry after Bloody Sunday. Paul Coyle, a friend of Kevin McElhinney who
was killed near the rubble barricade, remembers that following the funerals:
'There was a very bad atmosphere about afterwards. People were out looking
for blood, revenge. I felt it myself: bitterness, anger, resentment, a lot of
fear.'[132] So, too, did some relatives of the dead. Betty Walker, sister of Michael
McDaid, recalls: 'There was a time after Michael's death that I hated everything English. If a soldier was killed, I used to say, "So?" '[133] A wave of collective anger swept Ireland. In Dublin, the British Embassy was burned down.
In Derry, this collective anger manifested in an immediate increase in young
men joining the IRA. As Liam Wray recalls:

> The day after the funerals there was an open table at the end of Rossville Street
> where people were joining the Provisional IRA – that's how they became so
> strong. As open as that, hundreds were coming and putting their names down.
> I am not just on about teenagers, there were men in their twenties and early thir-
> ties . . . there is many a young man who decided from what he had seen that
> day that there is only one way to bring justice, and that's take up a gun.[134]

Others joined after the Widgery Inquiry. It would be mistaken either to
reduce this recruitment and the wider popular support for the IRA's armed
resistance to a pathology or to ignore or downplay the rational understanding and channelling of emotions by Republican political ideology.
Nevertheless, the recourse to political violence did have a psychic and emotional content. Martin McGuinness, testifying to the Saville Inquiry, insisted
that there had been no IRA activity in Derry at any time on the day of the
march. On realizing that British soldiers had killed civilians, however, the
IRA was 'very angry and emotional'. His own 'gut reaction . . . was to get a
gun and shoot back', though it was agreed not to engage immediately as this
would 'see us fall into a trap'.[135] The senior Derry Republican Raymond
McCartney, who later became the leader of the IRA prisoners in the Maze
and took part in their first hunger strike in 1980, remembers:

> In the aftermath of Bloody Sunday, my doubts and fears that I had about com-
> mitting myself to the IRA disappeared. I remember expressing that thought to
> a very senior member of the IRA at the time and he told me – obviously having
> experienced a lot of people at that particular time expressing the same wish to
> him – not to allow emotion to influence what was a very important decision.
> He asked me to go away and reflect on it and take a couple of months before
> making up my mind. I did eventually make that decision and I joined the IRA.[136]

The military response to the atrocity, initially by both the Official and
Provisional wings of the IRA,[137] was to intensify their own armed campaign
while diversifying their methods and targets, including the revenge attack by
the Officials on the Parachute Regiment base at Aldershot in February 1972;
the PIRA's 'Bloody Friday' terror-bombings of civilians in Belfast city-centre
in July; and the campaign to destabilize the Border.[138] Altogether, there

would be a higher number of Troubles-related deaths in 1972 than in any other single year of the conflict.[139] As the armed conflict escalated, the use of repressive force by the State against the armed resistance increased, leading to the criminalization, surveillance and repression of entire nationalist communities in the North: an already brutal occupation worsened, and remained in place for a generation. The Widgery Report confirmed to nationalists that they were under the heel of a fundamentally unjust and repressive State. For Republicans, the destruction of the civil rights movement appeared to leave no viable alternative to the situation but armed struggle. With the British State intent on defeating or, at least, containing the IRA militarily, and ruling out any possibility of conflict resolution involving engagement with Republican aspirations to achieve a sovereign, united Ireland, Northern Ireland became stitched into twenty-two further years of war.

Profound divisions existed, however, within nationalism either side of the Border over the moral legitimacy and political expediency of armed struggle. In the North, this took the political form of the contest – and antagonism – between the constitutional nationalist SDLP, which sought a united Ireland by peaceful means, and the Republican movement, represented by Sinn Féin, which supported the armed resistance of the IRA to the British military occupation. In Derry as within Irish nationalism more generally, the response to Bloody Sunday, in both psychic and political terms, was complex and varied rather than uniform. In terms of psychic responses, the atmosphere of anger and revenge, and the popular turn to armed resistance, were countered by other emotional currents within the community, most strikingly among parents, especially mothers, who had just lost a husband or son on Bloody Sunday. One man in his forties, reflecting on the reaction of his younger self, recalls:

> I was sixteen and a half and obviously my first feelings were of revenge but that was never to be. My mother, on the exact same day that my father was killed made me get down in front of her and the holy picture and she made me swear that I would never get involved in anything. I would never do the same type of thing that those people had done to her. I swore that I would never become involved in anything and I never did.[140]

In Maura Young's case, falling out with a priest who had been urging forgiveness provoked a talking-to by her mother, who asked: 'If I gave you a gun now and I lined up all the soldiers in Brooke Park and you went down and shot them, is that going to bring John walking across the Green to me tonight?' She went on: 'I don't want to see any other woman sitting the way I am sitting this day without my son.'[141] Psychically, a number of different currents of feeling run through these responses. They stem partly from the depths of personal sorrow and the (often impossible) wish to guard against further loss of loved ones within one's own family, and partly from identification with the suffering, or potential suffering, of mothers *from the other side*; an impulse that strives to resist the psychic and political polarizations generated by armed conflict. Here, reparative remembering is centred on the struggle for reconciliation, not with the enemy, but within the self, and within one's own family and community, beginning at the very moment of loss.

Unsettling and unresolved emotions remained attached to these survivor memories, troubling the composure of the witnesses and bereaved families. Individual survivors, like Bishop Daly and the Duddy family, continue to grapple with personal memories that remain for the most part necessarily private, outside of and invisible from the arenas of public representation and commemoration. While the narratives of memory created, circulated and negotiated within the private arenas of shared and common memory differ in significant respects from those within wider public arenas, these two domains are linked. Interviewed in his study beside a framed photograph of Jack Duddy and 'visibly upset as he recalled the horrific events', Daly has affirmed his sense of moral obligation, or duty, to speak out publicly on behalf of the Bloody Sunday dead: 'A person's good name is important. I was at the side of some of them after they were shot and I know, beyond any doubt whatsoever, they were totally and completely innocent. I feel it as a moral responsibility to proclaim their innocence. Once that has been established I would want to let go of it.'[142] Ashplant et al. locate the politics of war memory in this transition from private to public: 'Only when memories have been woven together into a narrative which is both widely held and publicly expressed do they have the power to secure political effects.'[143] The collective memory woven by the Bloody Sunday Justice Campaign, expressed and enacted by thousands at the annual commemorations of the 1990s, is a public narrative of this kind. Its power rests on a complex, rich and fluid infrastructure of shared and common memories. It speaks across the many differences of experience among the survivor generation, and across the generational differences between the survivors and their successor generations, to articulate a collective counter-memory of injustice with which all nationalists are able to identify. The formation of this narrative, and of the Bloody Sunday Justice Campaign as its agent, are explored in the next chapter.

5

Widening the circle of memory: human rights and the politics of Bloody Sunday commemoration

Every year since Bloody Sunday, its anniversary has been marked, on the weekend closest to 30 January, by a commemorative march following the route of the original civil rights march from Creggan to rally in the Bogside. The continuity of this long-standing commemorative tradition has been made possible by the peculiar social history and cultural geography of nationalist Derry since 1972. One crucial condition has been the continuing existence in their traditional location, over thirty years and more, of the tight-knit, largely working-class, nationalist communities of the Bogside and Creggan. These are based still on interlinked networks of extended families, many of which are the same families whose sons, husbands, brothers and uncles were shot dead on Bloody Sunday; not to mention the families of the thousands of other demonstrators and local residents who came under attack that day. A second factor has been these nationalist communities' creative, mutually supportive and independent traditions of self-help and community activism from below, born out of the history of the Catholic ghetto and its culture of resistance against the Unionist and then the British state machines. The third important factor has been the persistence in Northern Ireland during those thirty-odd years, and despite the initiation of the peace process, of conditions of inequality, injustice and anti-Catholic violence endured by the nationalist minority, comparable to (if not identical with) those against which the marchers on Bloody Sunday were protesting. These factors have interacted to keep alive a public commemorative tradition for over three decades since Bloody Sunday. However, over that time, significant developments have altered the character of the annual commemoration.

For the first anniversary, thousands of people participated in a series of commemorative events on 28 January 1973, organized by NICRA. These events began with a packed requiem mass at St Mary's Chapel, attended by civil rights leaders, among them John Hume and Ivan Cooper. Later, relatives laid wreaths on the graves at a ceremony in the Creggan's cemetery. Speaking at the interdenominational church service alongside Rev. Terence McGaughey, the Presbyterian chaplain of Trinity College, the 'handkerchief priest' Fr Edward Daly told the congregation:

> At this time, on this Sunday last year, we had a massacre of innocents. Those of us who witnessed it and the families of the dead and injured will never forget

the horror of that day. Now, one year on, we are gathered to commemorate that event, to pray for those who died and for the families, to pray for our city and country, to pray for the just peace for which all of us yearn.

Peace-campaigner Lord Fenner Brockway cut the first sod at the site designated for the memorial. In the afternoon, a crowd estimated at 15,000 took part in a march, organized by Sinn Féin, from Creggan to a rally in Celtic Park. At the rally there was a recitation by Vanessa Redgrave and local school children of Thomas Kinsella's poem 'Butcher's Dozen'. Bernadette Devlin spoke about the 'death, destruction and violence' unleashed in response to a demand for civil rights, and praised the 'discipline' of the IRA in ensuring that more did not die during the army's assault on the Bogside, and the Republican leader Sean Keenan described Bloody Sunday as 'the saddest day in the history of our country'. Intercutting the sadness was anger: rioting followed the ceremonies.[1]

The elegaic and inclusive atmosphere on this first anniversary was not sustained in later years. Despite its role in creating a memorial monument in Rossville Street, unveiled for the 1974 anniversary – an unadorned obelisk inscribed with the names of the dead 'murdered by British paratroopers on Bloody Sunday 30th January 1972', and the text 'Their epitaph is in the continuing struggle for democracy' – the civil rights movement failed to survive the violence unleashed in 1972. Nationalist politics polarized around the issue of the IRA's campaign of resistance to British rule in Ireland, centred on armed struggle. In this context, the public commemoration of Bloody Sunday became a key event in Republican resistance culture; a symbol of injustice likened to other events – Amritsar, Sharpeville, Mi Lai – that had exposed the violent, repressive power of imperialism, and a potent weapon in the ideological war against the British State. The annual anniversary commemoration itself became the object of surveillance, harassment and intimidation by the British Army and the RUC, so that saturation policing, the din of army helicopters circling overhead and the continual threat of – if not actual – violent assault on participants became the norm on the commemorative march and rally.[2] For these and for more personal reasons, the anniversaries of Bloody Sunday became deeply ambivalent occasions for many of the relatives, and the initial widespread involvement in the commemoration tailed off. Bloody Sunday had become, according to Tony Doherty – who had lost his father on Bloody Sunday and joined the IRA in response – 'a republican issue';[3] its memory at once sustained and also limited by Sinn Féin's support and commitment, and contained within a resistance culture that was marginalized and under pressure. Bloody Sunday was becoming a *historical* event of the past rather than a living memory with real relevance for current politics.[4]

It was not until the advent in the late 1980s of a new grassroots movement, emerging out of the Republican culture of resistance in Derry but developing fresh thinking about its strategic objectives and campaigning tactics, that the Bloody Sunday commemoration was reinvigorated at the centre of a campaign which drew energy from the memory of injustices to inspire work towards a new future. The new grouping called itself, simply enough, the Bloody Sunday Initiative (BSI). Formed by relatives of the dead intent on 'doing something . . . about Bloody Sunday', to ensure that 'the unfinished business . . . at last be righted and that we should finally seek justice for those killed and injured', the BSI created a civil agency capable of recasting memories articulated in private forms into a new, integrated, collective form and projecting this effectively into a public arena to appeal to wider constituencies. Through reinvigorating the annual commemoration, the BSI constructed what Ashplant et al. term a 'sectional memory', directly oppositional to the dominant 'official memory' articulated by the State (see pp. 52–4).[5] According to this theory, a process of transformation and representation is at work in this making public of collective memory. The new, sectional public narrative 'shapes the individual and common/shared memories from which it is composed, selecting some and excluding others, highlighting key themes and framing them within its preferred narrative tropes', as a form is sought with the power to stake an overt political challenge.[6] The narrative developed by the BSI for this purpose used the language of human rights. This enabled campaigners in Derry to reframe local memories of the unresolved injustices of Bloody Sunday on a more inclusive and *popular* basis, thereby linking with, and contributing to, the development of a broader nationalist politics of memory, to which Bloody Sunday became pivotal. An investigation of the political commemoration of Bloody Sunday, then, is at once an inquiry into the challenge to the official memory of the British State and its representation of this specific event, and a means of illuminating the wider currents in Irish nationalist collective memory of the Troubles that pressed for public recognition and redress during the closing years of the war.

This chapter begins by tracing the emergence of the BSI and its adoption of a narrative focused on human rights to mobilize renewed interest in Bloody Sunday, in the context of a broader framework of ideas within nationalist culture of the late 1980s and early 1990s that linked historical consciousness, democratic politics and the struggle for peace and justice in Ireland and worldwide. It goes on to analyse the transformation of the annual Bloody Sunday commemoration as a vehicle for the new politics, fuelled by 'the desire to widen the circle of memory'[7] beyond its traditional base, to embrace supporters from across Ireland and around the world; including, crucially, an influx of young people from the successor generation born since 30 January 1972, whose participation ensured that the events of Bloody Sunday would not be forgotten. Finally, the chapter examines the emergence, out of this renewed culture of commemoration, of the Bloody Sunday Justice Campaign, through which relatives of the dead and their local supporters mounted a sustained challenge to the findings of the Widgery Report and to the British official memory grounded on it. While this chapter is concerned largely with developments in the period 1989–92, while the war continued, the chapter that follows will trace the interaction of this new politics of memory with the emerging Irish peace process.

The BSI and the narrative of human rights

The beginnings of a shift in political emphasis towards 'doing something on a more serious level about Bloody Sunday' began in 1988–89 in local discussions about the organization of the annual commemorative march and rally.[8] Discussions led to the formation in Derry in summer 1990 of the BSI, introduced in a public statement by two founder-members and relatives of the dead, Alex Wray and Tony Doherty, as 'a new and independent group'[9] which 'includes relatives of those killed as well as a wide range of other interested people, such as students, trade unionists, radical Christians, artists and community activists'.[10] The BSI aimed to widen participation in the annual public commemoration of Bloody Sunday, opening it outwards to involve new and broader constituencies, and renewing its significance by turning it into the focus of a live campaigning movement. According to Doherty's analysis, by the late 1980s 'the commemoration . . . was becoming . . . historical, in the past and while it was still a live political issue for many people, it really wasn't a campaigning or live human rights issue'.[11] The work of the BSI was founded on the belief that in order to inject new life into the commemoration and recover its living past–present connection – a connection that would be symbolized by the involvement of new people, including the generation that had grown up since 1972 – the political energies fixated on marking the traumatic past needed to be unlocked and transformed into a hopeful project to build a better future.

This redefinition was sketched in Doherty and Wray's first public statement: the BSI had been set up 'to encourage creative action around the future of Ireland. Our aim is to commemorate the lives of those who died in Derry on Bloody Sunday', but the Initiative 'is not a backward looking group. Our focus is the future; helping to work for British withdrawal and to build an independent, pluralistic [and] democratic Ireland'.[12] Formulated in this way, the aims of the BSI were consistent with the language of both a constitutional nationalist as well as Republican political vision, though the group made clear that it was 'committed to non-violent action', as well as 'totally rejecting bigotry and sectarianism'.[13] Indeed, the wider context for this fresh thinking was the political debate within Irish nationalism in the North concerning strategies for conflict resolution, stimulated by Sinn Féin's discussion document *Scenario for Peace* (1987) and the dialogue between Sinn Féin and the SDLP launched in 1988 by the contacts between the leaders of the parties, Gerry Adams and John Hume.[14] By 1992 this political ground had been given more pointed definition with the publication of a further Sinn Féin document, *Towards a Lasting Peace in Ireland* (1992). While repeating traditional Republican demands for British political and military withdrawal from Ireland, it also called for 'a process of national reconciliation, a constructive dialogue and debate', to replace 'the long-standing [and often bloody] conflict between Irish Nationalism and Unionism'.[15]

Such thinking was echoed in the BSI's strengthened commitment, set out in January 1992, to building a 'non-sectarian' Ireland, 'a society in which all of us, whether Catholic or Protestant, can start to fashion for ourselves the political, social and economic institutions which meet our fundamental needs and aspirations, free from the blight of outside interference and control'. The BSI insisted that it had 'no links with any political party', and its 'membership is open to anyone who wishes to work for the political goals which the Initiative seeks to achieve'.[16] This inclusivity was further extended by widening out the group's initial focus on the commemoration of the Bloody Sunday victims, to include 'the lives of all those other civilians killed in our city because of their opposition to British rule in Ireland' (though this, of course, marked it as an exclusively nationalist organization). The BSI also signalled an even wider remit (and an ambitious new frame in which to set the memory of Bloody Sunday) in seeking 'to promote respect for human rights, dignity and justice within Ireland and internationally'.[17] To that end, early in 1992 it established the Pat Finucane Centre for Human Rights and Social Change. In this, the BSI was informed by the recent emergence of a number of grassroots campaigns for justice launched by the relatives of nationalists killed by the British Army, including the representative group Relatives for Justice, and the single-issue Cullyhanna Justice Group, both formed in 1991.[18]

The Justice Group represented the family of Fergal Caraher, a Sinn Féin member from South Armagh who was shot dead (and his brother Mícheál who was seriously injured) by Royal Marines in December 1990, in disputed circumstances that had the hallmarks of a shoot-to-kill operation.[19] Since, as Archbishop Cahal Daly pointed out, many people were 'completely unconvinced by the accounts given so far by the British Army',[20] the Justice Group organized an unofficial public inquiry into the incident. Chaired by Michael Mansfield, the English barrister closely associated with human rights cases, the inquiry 'heard evidence from local people . . . [before] calling for the soldiers involved to be prosecuted'.[21] In suggesting the possibility of using a quasi-legal arena as a critical space in which an official narrative could be publicly contested and an alternative history constructed out of local testimony, the Cullyhanna Justice Group pointed the way to a politics of memory and human rights that would feed in to the evolving strategy of the BSI.

This reframing of the significance of the Bloody Sunday commemoration, shifting its emphasis away from the celebration of anti-colonial armed resistance and onto the assertion of fundamental human rights and the demand for justice, proved to be an important and innovative development that established the desired 'broader platform'.[22] As Doherty explains it, the BSI had to find a way to 'reinvent [the] campaign in terms of [public relations] and profile . . . You have to find different ways of reproducing the same story.'[23] During the post-Cold War decade of the 1990s, the BSI was not alone in grounding its retelling of an old story on the narrative of human rights.[24] A product of 'the attempt to construct a new post-Cold War ordering of international relations based on the "democratic norms" of the Western powers',[25] this narrative frames the significance of war memories in terms of the agenda of universal human rights established by international law and promoted by juridical and quasi-juridical institutions and agencies. The 'growth in importance and power of the narrative of human rights' during the 1990s has been explained partly as the result of an intensifying of efforts to forge effective instruments, increasingly operating within the transnational arena, capable of regulating and containing within limits the political violence practised by nation states, whose legitimacy has come to depend on their formal embrace of the principles and practice of human rights. Ashplant et al. argue that this process has resulted in 'a strengthening of the transnational arena, as a domain where war memories previously unrecognised in the arena of the nation state may be articulated',[26] and where 'the legitimacy of a state's practice of violence – and thus, its official memory – may be established or challenged'.[27] The exertion of pressure from *outside* or *above* a particular state may in turn shift 'the internal balance of power in favour of the marginalised and the repressed', creating opportunities for social movements from below 'to articulate war memories previously unrecognised by the state', by 'revisiting' and 'reframing' them within the terms of the human rights narrative:[28]

> In cases where a state incorporates these principles [of international human rights legislation] into its own national laws, war memories articulated in terms of the human rights narrative are able to seek recognition within the national arena. [. . .]
>   Where a state is prepared to embrace the human rights agenda in tackling a legacy of war, war memories become publicly recognizable in these terms. This in turn encourages survivors and their successors to use a human rights narrative to frame their own war memories, and to develop new civil agencies to articulate these politically. The human rights narrative is thus proving capable of bestowing a particular form of empowerment on civil groupings that are prepared to couch their own memories in its terms.[29]

In the circumstances of the 1990s, when movements for social justice motivated by socialist or anti-imperialist politics had been largely defeated or contained around the world, the narrative of human rights also provided a resonant language with global currency on which political demands could be recast in such a way as to constitute new democratic alliances against the power of repressive states. Crucially, its call for a social order grounded on fundamental principles of humanity found echoes among younger generations as well as among survivors of the wars and conflicts of the 1960s–80s. It provided the basis for what Jelin and Kaufman, examining the campaign for truth and justice concerning the state terror exercised by the military junta in Argentina, have called 'a broadening of the "we", the active subjects of reminiscing'.[30]

In Derry, the mobilizing of a non-violent nationalist politics of justice, democracy and human rights was not so much a new departure as a return to the local politics killed off on Bloody Sunday: that of the mass protest movement for civil rights launched in 1968, now reactivated and re-imagined for the 1990s. These continuities were made explicit in the first public bulletin of the BSI which recalled the campaigns by the civil rights movement for equality of access to housing and employment.[31] Noting the formulation of its demands in the now-archaic 'sexist language of the late sixties' – as in slogans such as 'One Man One Job, One Man One House' – the BSI pointed out that these 'basic demands for the equality of society within the Six-County State' had exposed the interconnections of politics, economics and the social order, forming a systematic structure of discrimination, unemployment and social injustice: 'the whole of Northern nationalist society had to be manipulated in the interests of unionist power'. A campaign for equal rights was held to be relevant in current circumstances due to British government policies which had maintained high levels of nationalist unemployment and emigration, especially of young people, and ensured continuing homelessness, poverty and hardship linked to changes in welfare provision. 'This litany of social injustice is what sustains our present quest for full national rights and social justice . . . the twin tracks for freedom'. This traditional nationalist story of the fundamental injustice of the 'Six-County State' is framed by the narrative of universal human rights: 'Since 1920, we have been denied any semblance of rights as enshrined in international law and the various charters and conventions on Human Rights and obligations such as the UN Charter and the European Convention on Human Rights.'[32]

The arguments advanced by this BSI bulletin were designed to feed into the forthcoming annual march and rally, and stimulate a particular political debate and historical awareness. The established commemorative event, which the BSI had assumed responsibility for organizing in 1990, provided the focus for its renewal of the nationalist politics of memory. Founder-member Tony Doherty recalls: 'Since 1989, we built upon the Bloody Sunday march and weekend itself, broadened out the events, looked at the issue in a broad and international context and organised events accordingly.'[33] Doherty himself helped provide continuity as well as fresh thinking, as a Sinn Féin member who had chaired the rally at Free Derry Corner during the 1980s, and did so again, in 1990, as representative of the Bloody Sunday Commemoration Committee.[34] This event was themed to draw parallels between Bloody Sunday and other, currently topical, instances of human rights violations committed by the British State in the conduct of its war in Ireland during the 1970s: the cases of the Maguire Seven, the Guildford Four and the Birmingham Six. These cases all concerned wrongful imprisonment of Irish men and women convicted for IRA pub bombings, in Guildford, Woolwich and Birmingham in October and November 1974, on the basis of forced confessions and evidence fabricated by the police, amid circumstances in Britain of popular hysteria and intense public pressure to secure convictions. The Guildford Four and the

Birmingham Six became worldwide *causes célebres* as a result of sustained campaigns during the 1980s protesting the judicial verdict in each case to have been a miscarriage of justice. This was eventually recognized to have been the case in the eventual overturning of the judgments by the Court of Appeal, resulting in the highly publicized release of the Guildford Four towards the end of 1989 and the Birmingham Six in March 1991, and damaging the reputation of the British legal system.[35]

The eighteenth Bloody Sunday commemoration that took place in Derry on 28 January 1990 under the theme 'Free the Birmingham Six',[36] occurred at a time of intense activity and renewed optimism buoyed by the recent success of the Guildford Four campaign. At the rally, emotional links were established when Paul Hill of the Guildford Four read out a letter from John Walker, one of the Birmingham Six, who was from Derry, thanking the people of the city for their support, a 'tearful' Joanne Walker, his daughter, recited the names of the Bloody Sunday dead, and an *uileann* piper played an Irish air dedicated to both sets of victims of British injustice.[37] Paul Hill also spoke of the 'sense of hope' now emerging for the release of the Six after their years of unjust imprisonment,[38] before denouncing the 'state violence' inflicted on himself and others by the repressive legal apparatus of the British State, including the Prevention of Terrorism Act that had been rushed through in December 1974, in the wake of the Birmingham pub bombing. (Introducing the bill in the House of Commons, the otherwise liberal Home Secretary Roy Jenkins described its powers as 'Draconian', 'unprecedented in peacetime', but 'fully justified to meet the clear and present danger'.[39]) The use of the law as a political weapon was further scrutinized at the rally by the Derry journalist Eamonn McCann, who described the Birmingham Six case and other miscarriages of justice against Irish people as being 'no mistake but a deliberate policy of the British state', carried out, he argued, with the 'collaboration' of the Republic of Ireland's Government in Dublin.[40] The connection between this emerging narrative of human rights and traditional themes in Republican resistance culture was established by Sinn Féin's General Secretary Tom Hartley. Linking Bloody Sunday both to the killing of nationalist children by plastic bullets fired by the army and to the assassination by the SAS, in March 1988, of three unarmed IRA volunteers, the 'Gibraltar Three',[41] Hartley 'asked those present to remember' that these were all 'deliberately planned attacks, the real purpose of which was to intimidate people. The British, he said, "do not see these as crimes but as acts of war against the nationalist population in the Six Counties" . . . [which] are meant to "break and defeat us" '. Hartley, one the architects of Sinn Féin's new peace strategy (which had already led to secret contacts with the British Government), concluded with a paeon to the strength and vibrancy of the Republican struggle 'for freedom and justice', even after eighteen years: 'we are the generation of victory'.[42]

The BSI was launched later that year with a bulletin announcing the 1991 commemoration, whose theme, 'Towards justice: remember Bloody Sunday',

built on the 1990 event. That year's rally was addressed by leading figures in
the Irish human rights movement: Bernadette McAliskey, herself a veteran of
the Derry civil rights campaign and a platform speaker on Bloody Sunday,
and Fr Raymond Murray, one of the original pioneers in the work of monitoring, publicizing and challenging violations of human rights by the British
State in Northern Ireland. His involvement dated back to December 1971
when, as chaplain of Armagh Prison, he became aware of the ill-treatment
and torture of political prisoners in interrogation centres.[43] Begun at a time
when few organizations and individuals – NICRA, the Association for Legal
Justice, Amnesty International, NCCL and 'some concerned priests, doctors,
surgeons, and lawyers' – were actively committed to stopping such violations,
Murray's campaigning work of the 1970s extended to other issues, including
abuses by the State of emergency laws, and 'unjust killings and murder by
state security forces'.[44] This work was crucial in giving public voice to the
testimony of nationalists subjected to the repression, and in ensuring that
the British State could not disregard with impunity its obligations under
international law.

Murray fostered understanding of the wider context of state violence and
abuse of human rights that made sense of Bloody Sunday as one key event
within a widespread and systematic pattern, concealed by official memory.
In 1978, for example, Murray delivered a speech to US congressmen in
Washington, DC, and to the Ad Hoc Committee for Human Rights in
Northern Ireland in Philadelphia on the 'kill, don't question', or shoot-to-
kill, security policy of the British State.[45] He traced this back to a number of
the very earliest killings of the current Troubles, between April and August
1969, because 'it is there the rot set in':

> You could be shot dead on your own street by the British army or the police and
> nobody would be made amenable for the killing. Since that time some 60 inno-
> cent people have been killed in an unjustifiable manner by British government
> forces – 14 in Derry on 30 January 1972, 6 on the New Lodge Road, Belfast, 3
> February 1973, and so on.

Murray observed that, by these actions, the British Army had committed violations of 'the right to life, liberty and the security of the person' enshrined
in Article 3 of the Universal Declaration of Human Rights, and of 'the inherent right to life . . . protected by law', so that '[n]o one shall be arbitrarily
deprived of his life', established in Article 6 (1) of the International Covenant
of Civil and Political Rights.

In 1991, the year when he spoke at the nineteenth Bloody Sunday commemoration, Murray wrote a report, later developed as a submission for the
independent Citizen's Inquiry on Northern Ireland undertaken by the
Opsahl Commission,[46] which welcomed Amnesty International's call for 'an
independent judicial inquiry into disputed killings by security forces in
Northern Ireland . . . Amnesty "believes that such an inquiry is vital to help
prevent further unlawful killings and to ensure that all . . . are promptly

investigated and publicly clarified".'[47] By mid-1992, Murray noted, there had been 'some 150 direct administrative killings, many unjust killings and scores of indirect killings manipulated by the British intelligence system'.[48] However, making reference to the Widgery Tribunal, he pointed out: 'The British government has held inquiries before, but it is clear that they do not want to reveal the truth.'[49] Murray linked the memory of Bloody Sunday and Widgery to other major instances in which the full investigation of past incidents of suspicious state violence had been prevented in order to enable the perpetration of similar incidents in the future. These included the Stalker affair of 1984, when John Stalker, the Deputy Chief Constable of the Manchester Police, was removed from his Inquiry into the killing two years earlier of three unarmed people by undercover RUC officers;[50] and the case of the Gibraltar Three (which was eventually taken to the European Court of Human Rights in 1995, where the British Government was found guilty of 'unlawful killing' in breach of Article 2 of the European Convention of Human Rights.)[51] In January 1991, relatives of the Gibraltar Three justice campaign shared the platform with Murray and McAliskey at the Bloody Sunday commemoration rally, building connections between the various campaigns, which subsequent commemorations would further strengthen.[52]

Widening the circle: the twentieth anniversary commemoration, 1992

In developing the themes of human rights and justice, the 1991 commemoration organized by the Bloody Sunday Initiative also pioneered a new format, by introducing a programme of workshops and discussions held over the same weekend as the traditional event, on topics related to the annual theme. In launching what would in future be described as 'the Bloody Sunday Weekend', the BSI was building towards the more ambitious goal of 'a major series of events and demonstrations' to mark the twentieth anniversary in January 1992, on the theme 'One world, one struggle'.[53] This was intended to broaden the human rights frame of the commemoration beyond the British–Irish conflict by situating local issues within a global context. The commemoration was envisaged as

> an opportunity for those who are working throughout the world for democracy and human rights to demonstrate their commitment and solidarity with each other whether in South Africa, China, Eastern Europe, Latin America, Palestine or Ireland. This is because . . . our own hopes are shared by those who struggle against repression and discrimination, against racism, sexism and colonialism, against poverty and injustice wherever they may live in the world.

Activists would be invited to Derry 'to share their experiences and explore common ground through an extensive programme of workshops, exhibitions and presentations', and 'to remember what happened in Derry in January 1972'.[54] This imaginative conception gave rise to a four-day programme of events that represented a significant development of the Bloody

Sunday commemoration, in three main respects. It provided an 'internationalist' forum for debate about the importance of history and strategies for dealing with an oppressive past in the context of popular democratic empowerment; it broadened the constituency involved in the commemoration; and it transformed the ways in which Bloody Sunday itself could be remembered.

The 1992 event consolidated the commemoration as an occasion for international debate concerned with the politics of resistance to oppression, with democratic renewal and transition and with the struggle for human rights and justice.[55] International speakers on the 'One world, one struggle' theme represented South Africa's ANC, a resistance movement involved in a process of national liberation which shared an anti-imperialist analysis and well-established links with Irish Republicanism; the Neighbourhood Association in Roxbury, a black ghetto in Boston with traditions of grassroots community activism to counter discrimination and oppression; and the 500th Anniversary Committee, the organizers of an alternative commemoration to challenge official celebrations marking Christopher Columbus's so-called 'discovery' of America in 1494.

Among the common issues to emerge was the central importance of history-making within resistance cultures seeking to challenge powerful legitimizing state narratives of the past, when these were often supported by the work of historians; for, as one speaker remarked, a 'people without a history is a people without a future'.[56] Debate about Ireland focused on the question of partition and perspectives on potential reunification from both sides of the Border; the role of media in miscarriages of justice, and the relation between state censorship, specifically the then-current broadcasting ban in the UK and the Irish Republic on representatives of Sinn Féin, and human rights abuses; and 'non-violent strategies for political progress in Ireland', a debate which aired alternative perceptions about how best to counter the violence of the State, and raised the vexed question of the IRA's armed struggle and its relationship to the movement for human rights, justice and peace.[57]

Bloody Sunday itself was clearly established as the focal point of these debates. In its 'Programme' leaflet, the BSI outlined the events and their aftermath, and set out its case that 'Remembering Bloody Sunday' mattered because it 'remains a microcosm, a symbol of what Britain does in Ireland'. Pointing to the connections in 1972 between the workings of various agencies of the State to ensure that its armed force was strategically deployed, legitimation for its use was secured, and those who contested it were marginalized and suppressed (see p. 91), the BSI argued: 'Twenty years on . . . the British state still sees repression, militarism and injustice as a key element of its strategy to impose its will on Ireland and its people'.[58] To counteract this, it proposed a politics of memory that would recover and reassert both the suffering and injustice inflicted in 1972 and also the spirit of resistance and renewal demonstrated by the civil rights movement of the past – and attributed by the BSI to all the Bloody Sunday dead:

Perhaps the most important reason why we should remember Bloody Sunday is that the dead were killed because they marched as a conscious political act: to speak out against the abuse that was internment and to affirm their aspiration of an Ireland where the human rights of its citizens, Protestant and Catholic, would be guaranteed, free from the attentions of an occupying army and which was genuinely democratic and able to embrace the hopes and aspirations of all its many people.[59]

Here, the agency of past civil rights protesters is remembered in a way that identifies it with the project of the BSI in 1992, as seeking the same new Ireland. Theirs 'is a vision still worth remembering and still worth struggling to achieve'.[60]

This sense of the centrality of Bloody Sunday to the new nationalist politics of memory, which sought to recoup the past as an inspiration to building an imagined new future, was developed in different directions by two speakers at the 1992 rally: the Dublin-based Irish artist Robert Ballagh and Sinn Féin's President Gerry Adams. Ballagh had been a member of the National 75th Anniversary Committee that organized a series of events in 1991 to commemorate the 1916 Easter Rising, and had recently published a critical analysis of the 'official prevarication' towards this commemoration in the Republic of Ireland. His critique exposed efforts made by 'the southern establishment' to frustrate celebration of the seventy-fifth anniversary and to censor and intimidate those intent on such celebration.[61] Here, Ballagh identified the contribution made by official memory in the Irish Republic, as well as in Britain, to counter-insurgency strategies designed to contain and criminalize modern-day Republicanism. However, for Ballagh, hostility to the commemoration from the ruling elite and their allies in the Republic was also the manifestation of emotional discomfort 'in the face of their own history', involving 'fear . . . guilt, embarrassment and shame'.[62] This psychic dimension to the politics of commemoration in Ireland stemmed, in Ballagh's analysis, from the collective mentality of a colonized people who, lacking self-confidence, 'abandon their history, culture and traditions . . . They cannot deal with the present or project a future, because they will not face the past.' The effects of this failure to 'face the past' was evident, Ballagh argued, in 'the southern response to the North'. By actively remembering 'the vision and exhilarating ideals that inspired the Easter Rising 75 years ago', these could be reclaimed 'for today's struggle to achieve an Ireland free, just and at peace'.[63] This, for Ballagh, explained the strength of grassroots activity in 1991, involving artists and performers, local committees and councils, trades unions and other organizations across Ireland, to ensure that a national commemoration of 1916 did take place.

Speaking at the Bloody Sunday rally, Ballagh identified official hostility to the 1991 commemoration of the Rising, together with anti-Republican political censorship and the emergence of the anti-nationalist school of 'revisionist' history-making, as manifestations of an 'intellectual terrorism' fostered in the Republic since the early 1970s.[64] This, he argued, was designed to destroy the 'broad national consensus' existing at that time, 'that British imperialism was wrong and should have no place in Ireland'; a consensus expressed most forcefully in the 'massive reaction to Bloody Sunday in the 26 Counties' and which had 'terrified the establishment'. Linking the popular interest in and support for the commemoration of the seventy-fifth anniversary of the Rising with that for the commemoration of the twentieth anniversary of Bloody Sunday, Ballagh pointed to the potential interconnections of nationalist memory politics North and South of the Border, and identified the importance of contesting official narratives of the past in both jurisdictions, to the development of a progressive movement of democratic renewal and national liberation across Ireland as a whole.[65]

Gerry Adams used his speech to re-articulate the established Republican narrative of national resistance to unjust and imperialist British rule in the emerging new language of democratic transition, peace and conflict resolution. He contrasted British state policy towards Ireland with a number of recent instances where 'conflicts . . . are slowly and painfully being resolved by dialogue'. Adams cited, among other cases, the reunification of Germany, the dismantling of apartheid in South Africa and the disintegration of the Soviet Union under the impact of 'mass campaigns for democratic reform' and citizens' rights in various member states, together with the initiation in response of a 'process of democratisation', or *perestroika* from above, by the Soviet State. Evoking nationalist popular memory of the Troubles, Adams contrasted this with the experience of Northern nationalists under the UK State:

> Twenty years ago the civil rights campaign was our mass peaceful unarmed peoples' uprising against a one party regime. Britain's responsibility. Twenty years ago we defied the state police and the dictators of Stormont. Twenty years ago with demonstrations which were as large proportionally as those which recently swept through many of the eastern bloc countries, we appealed for justice. When the state collapsed under the weight of our modest demands the British government should have commenced the process of dismantling it and persuading the unionists that their future is in equality with the rest of us. If the British had done so then we would be living now in a peaceful Ireland, united in our diversity and building our own social and economic democracy.

Instead of doing this, Adams argued, the British Government 'militarised the situation and as part of that it gave us Bloody Sunday'. Throughout its violent repression of those demanding their rights in the North, the British State had been granted the support of the Catholic hierarchy in Ireland, the Dublin Government, and the leaderships of all the major political parties in the Republic and Britain, as well as the Unionists. Despite this, 'twenty years after Bloody Sunday . . . British policy in Ireland is in tatters. They cannot govern us except by force . . . The British government needs a new policy.' Yet, having failed to initiate effective strategies for conflict resolution in the early years of the Troubles, 'in Ireland the very same forces which created the need for the civil rights struggle in the 1960s are refusing to talk in the

1990s and we . . . are condemned to live with an ongoing and relentless war'.

Here, Adams evoked a sense of Northern Ireland trapped in the present–past. The dynamic movement of history has stalled, leaving an endless repetition of violence, for which the British Government – 'the political wing of the murderers of Bloody Sunday' – is held responsible: 'They insist on repeating [history] . . . condemning the people of our country to a future that is but the continuation of our past'. Making use of the commemoration to articulate Sinn Féin's evolving strategy for conflict resolution, Adams called for the establishing of political dialogue 'to start a process which could move this conflict [towards] . . . the peace that all Irish people, regardless of political allegiance, deserve'. Challenging the British to engage in this peace 'process', Adams identified the importance of the human rights narrative in bringing pressure to bear, asserted both from above, through international monitoring, and from below, through the strengthening of grassroots struggle.[66]

The second major contribution of the 1992 Weekend to the developing politics of the Bloody Sunday commemoration lay in its success in 'widening the circle of memory' by drawing increasing numbers and different people into these debates and into the public rituals of commemoration. Between 10,000 and 20,000 people were estimated to have attended the march and rally, described as 'one of the most impressive and emotional demonstrations seen in the Six Counties in the last two decades'.[67] A significant increase had been achieved in only two years: 'from a few thousand people it was becoming an event people wanted to identify with'.[68] One contributing factor was the overt encouragement to young people (always a presence on the commemorative marches, as on Bloody Sunday itself): the organizers had requested that 'all children in attendance be encouraged to bring flowers to be laid at a site in the Guildhall Square'.[69] From the platform, Bernadette McAliskey drew attention to the participation in the march, alongside the 'many . . . who had been there on Bloody Sunday itself', of 'many who were not, many who had not even been born'.[70] Its internationalist theme also enabled the 1992 Weekend to embrace visitors to Derry within the circle of Bloody Sunday memory: 'Welsh, English, Scottish, French, German, Italian and Latin American accents mingled with those of our own people from every corner of the country and from their countries of exile.'[71]

Participants were drawn not only by the political debate but also by other attractions of the Weekend. The BSI devised new forms of popular protest that heightened the symbolic drama of the commemorative march. In 1992, a number of elements, now established as traditional to the ritual re-enactment of the 1972 march, were retained: it began as always at Creggan Shops, where the 'lorry with the Civil Rights Association banner led off, just as a similar one had done on January 30th 1972', followed by relatives carrying white crosses bearing the names of the fourteen dead.[72] (A traditional ritual of another sort was enacted by the British Army helicopters surveilling the march from overhead.[73]) However, for the first time, the march continued beyond the Bogside to the Guildhall, completing the route to the intended destination of the march in 1972. It passed through the killing ground itself in silence. At a mural depicting the faces of the fourteen dead, a symbolic re-enactment of the Widgery 'whitewash' was staged by actors who painted over the images on the gable wall. As the march arrived in Guildhall Square, *Cor Cochion Caerdydd*, the Red Choir of Cardiff, sang the civil rights song made popular in the 1960s 'We Shall Overcome'. Relatives passed through the crowd 'to lay wreaths and crosses at the Guildhall steps. As the minute's silence ended the clocktower bell rang out.'[74]

'One world, one struggle' also established the commemoration as a kind of community festival. This was projected in the poster for the event, that continued the metaphorical break from the grim iconography of all previous annual commemorations, begun in 1991, with a design of fourteen oak-leaves, symbolic of the Bloody Sunday dead: a single black leaf figuring the sadness and condition of mourning always associated with the anniversary, but here contained and integrated within a broader field of thirteen brightly coloured leaves, signifying hope, creativity and the celebration of life.[75] The festival atmosphere of the Weekend – reclaiming the memory of the 'relaxed and cheerful' atmosphere in the bright January sunshine at the start of the original march[76] – was enhanced by musical events held each evening, by performers from Wales, Scotland and Bolivia, as well as local Derry bands and an Irish traditional session.[77]

In turning the Bloody Sunday commemoration into an event capable of attracting an influx of interested visitors, the BSI pioneered a form of 'polit-ical' or 'historical tourism', a phenomenon that expanded internationally during the 1990s, provoking debates about its potential to generate 'differ-ent kinds of commemorative experience and . . . imaginative relation[s] to the past'.[78] Building on the informal guided tours of the city provided for vis-iting delegations and other political visitors since the early years of the war, the BSI produced for the 'One world, one struggle' Weekend a small pam-phlet, *Political Guide to Derry*.[79] This provided a map and a key to the loca-tion of twenty-five historical sites, supported by a paragraph of information on each, selected to illustrate the history of colonialism and conflict in the city, including the causes, development, and effects of the ongoing Troubles. In the entry on the seventeenth-century city Walls, for example, the *Guide* notes:

> Because of their symbolic importance for Unionists . . . Nationalists were not allowed to march within them until November 1968 when the women workers from the Shirt Factories downed tools and began to march in and out of the city gates in open defiance of the ban. Since 1970 nobody can walk the complete Walls because of the British Army Observation Post which dominates the Walls and allows the military to monitor the movements of people living in the Bogside.[80]

Other entries identify Duke Street, the location of 'the famous civil rights march on 5 October 1968 which is universally accepted as the start of the troubles'; Aggro Corner, at the junction of William Street and Rossville Street, where 'much of the rioting occurred after the 5 October [march]' and which 'continued until after the 1981 Hunger Strikes'; Ebrington Barracks, the 'British Army "command and control centre" built in 1839' and 'currently an SAS base'; and the headquarters of the RUC, whose members 'have been involved in many incidents which confirm their continuing unacceptability to the Nationalist community. No other police force in Europe has been condemned by the European Commission of Human Rights . . . or convicted so often by the European Human Rights Court'. In this way, the *Guide* maps the geography of Unionist rule, the civil rights movement and the Troubles in the city.

At the centre of this map is the Bogside and its two commemorative sites: the Bloody Sunday Memorial and the Free Derry Wall, the most famous nationalist monument of the Troubles, standing on the site of Free Derry Corner, the rallying-point for the march on Bloody Sunday and for civil rights and Republican demonstrations both before and since. This gable-end wall, once attached to a terrace of houses demolished during redevelopment, was preserved as the symbolic location of resistance together with its iconic inscription 'You Are Now Entering Free Derry'; a slogan first painted to mark the no-go area in 1969 and repainted many times since, despite, as the *Guide* points out, it being regularly mutilated by British soldiers and the RUC. These sites are the geographical 'markers' of what it describes as 'the most important date in the recent history of Derry'. However, the *Guide* does not promote a single, unified narrative of this history. Rather, it acknowledges the existence of conflicting interpretations and their connection to the currently contested space of the city, in entries on St Columb's Cathedral, where remains are buried of Protestants who died in the Great Siege of 1689, and on the Fountain, 'a small, predominantly working-class Protestant area close to the city centre', left as a result of massive Protestant migration eastwards across the River Foyle in the course of the Troubles, as 'the only significant Protestant community on the West bank'. Here, the *Guide* prompts visitors to note the two murals ('the mural of King William by the late Bobby Jackson is the oldest in the city and particularly worth seeing'), and recommends a 'visit to the Siege Museum in Butcher Street'. In this way, the *Guide* constructs a spatial framework that enables visitors to *place* local cultural memories and encourages them to walk the city, encounter its living past and engage with the contested realities of Derry/Londonderry in the 1990s.[81] Its frame of memory remains nationalist, nevertheless: the *Guide* makes no mention of the decline of the Fountain during the 1980s, nor of the Unionist cultural memory that understands the Protestant exodus eastwards to be the result of 'ethnic cleansing' by the IRA.[82]

A third important contribution of the 1992 commemoration concerned its role in inaugurating new ways in which Bloody Sunday and its aftermath could be remembered, represented and recognized in the public domain. This was significantly enhanced by the occasion of the twentieth anniversary, which itself gave a fillip to the production and circulation of memories. Ashplant et al. note 'the increasing number and enhanced profile of anniversary commemorations to mark the beginning and the end of wars, and their key episodes', during the final quarter of the twentieth century. This, they argue, is

> fuelled and amplified by the public communications media, which seize upon forthcoming commemorative dates to stimulate cultural production of all kinds. Not only are commemorative ceremonies and other events reported in – and increasingly, staged for – the news media, but their contemporary significance is scrutinized as well as celebrated in special publications, investigative reports and documentary features in which broader cultural and political significances are given a 'human face' by survivor testimony. In this way, war commemoration is transformed into a media event.[83]

Anniversaries marking the passing of decades, quarter- and half-centuries, and centenaries are especially prone to this treatment. The anniversaries of Bloody Sunday had prompted a brief flurry of media interest in this way, as Joanne O'Brien's story (in the previous chapter) of her assignment on the tenth anniversary illustrates. In 1992 the British, Irish and international news media returned to Derry, and the 'human face' voicing the testimony of the survivor again had its moment: Jim Wray's brother Liam, for example, told the family story to the *Irish News*, while Paddy Walsh, who made one of the best-known attempts to rescue the wounded on 30 January 1972, spoke, apparently for the first time, to the *Guardian*.[84] While ephemeral in itself, anniversary reporting of this kind has an important function in placing survivor testimony on the public record, and also helps to create an atmosphere of interest in and discussion about the remembered event, with a potentially more enduring impact.

Jelin and Kaufman, in their analysis of the twentieth anniversary in 1996 of the military coup in Argentina, have pointed to 'the *process* of societal remembering (and forgetting)' that emerges under the stimulus of such commemorations:[85]

> It was an opportunity to talk and to tell what had been silenced or forgotten, an occasion where society felt the emotional impact of the testimonies and the personalized narratives, the astonishment of listening to stories unknown before, of recognizing what had been denied or moved away from consciousness. People were faced with the 'reality' of re-enacting fears and disturbing feelings, asking themselves how all that happened was possible, while everyday life seemed to go on, maintaining an appearance of normality.
>
> During such moments, the labours of memory become more inclusive and shared, invading everyday life. It is hard work for everybody, on all sides of the controversies, for all people, of different ages and experiences. Facts are reorganized, existing perspectives and schemes of interpretation are shaken, voices of new and old generations ask questions, tell stories, create spaces for interaction,

share clues about what they experienced, what they heard, what they silenced
before.[86]

As Jelin and Kaufman demonstrate, not only the survivors of state violence
but also its perpetrators become involved in this process. In the case of
Bloody Sunday, British soldiers, too, were prompted on the occasion of its
twentieth anniversary to engage in memory work, and to reflect on their own
experiences and understandings of the event they had participated in.[87] Jelin
and Kaufman suggest that anniversaries provide the occasion for a particularly rich interpenetration of public and personal '*levels* and *layers*' of
remembrance.[88] At such moments, a range of agencies become involved in
memory-making and revision, and 'societal memory [is] revived by the publication of . . . books, films and videos'.[89] These kinds of memory-texts
provide new information, insights and perspectives that individuals may
incorporate as 'part of one's own personal life and recollection'.[90]

In 1992, two significant new memory-texts dealing with Bloody Sunday
entered the public domain and provoked effects of this kind. Peter Taylor's
documentary *Remember Bloody Sunday*, broadcast by the BBC on 30
January 1992,[91] punctured the post-Widgery consensus in Britain by giving
public space to survivors' memories which afforded disquieting glimpses
into the hidden history, as well as interviews with soldiers – including
Brigadier Michael Jackson, who served as adjutant to the Parachute
Regiment on Bloody Sunday and, the film revealed, had since been promoted
to become the British Army's overall commander in Greater Belfast – which
provoked angry reactions from relatives. Eamonn McCann's book *Bloody
Sunday in Derry: What Really Happened*, launched a few days before the
Weekend at Bookworm, the local bookshop, marked a new departure in the
voicing of survivors' memories within the framework of the commemoration.[92] It was in this context that the personal stories of relatives, discussed
in the previous chapter, entered public culture and debate in the city in a way
that evoked the psychic reality of their experience. In form, the book intercut a series of essays by McCann, analysing what had occurred on and after
Bloody Sunday and its political significance, with personalized commemorative tributes to the fourteen victims, derived from interviews with their relatives and friends, and accompanied by photographs, a number of which
were donated from family albums (such as the wedding photograph of
Paddy Doherty with his bride Eileen), in contrast to the iconic portraits used
in public commemoration.[93] The interviewees spoke about the personality
of their lost loved one, his beliefs and values, his work and what he enjoyed
most; and told of the circumstances in which he had been killed, and how
his body – and his family – had been treated by the army and other authorities. The power of these portraits derived from their intimacy, but also from
the ways in which the lives and deaths of the victims were refracted through
the memories of those who loved and still mourned them. Indeed, what is
most compelling about these testimonies is the witness they bear, not only to

the fourteen lives cut short by British Army bullets in 1972, but also to the lives lived out in the long aftermath, overshadowed by the damaging effects of traumatic memory and its persistence as a reality into the 1990s. The significance of these life-stories was framed by the wider concerns of the commemoration, which constituted an array of listening spaces in public and private arenas, and in turn stimulated further personal remembering, as these now public stories were discussed and absorbed into shared memory. Among these arenas was that of the book launch itself, which brought the families together for the first time in many years. Out of this meeting, the Bloody Sunday Justice Campaign was founded.

The Bloody Sunday Justice Campaign

Bloody Sunday in Derry played a major part in opening up the public commemoration to personal remembrance and in establishing the families at its centre. In his Foreword to the book, Seamus Deane registered the important shift that it introduced in the political language of Bloody Sunday:

> To have a relative murdered is, God knows, grievous enough; to have the murder condoned by the authorities adds to the grief a sense of wrong that must be personally desolating . . . such a sense of wrong, when it is deliberately inflicted by the authorities, is also a political reality, the strength and range of which is consistently ignored or underestimated.[94]

This political reality depended, he argued, on the successful deployment by the British Government and media of 'the language of the Paras, the murderers' in their misrepresentation of 'the trouble on the streets' as being 'caused by a pack of "yobbos", "hooligans" and the like'. The soldiers

> acted in the conviction that they were not dealing with people, but with caricatures of their own propaganda machine. Lord Widgery's attitude was similar. As long as that mentality prevails, the so-called 'Troubles' will continue . . . [and] as long as justice and truth are incompatible with the retention of power, then that power will be endlessly contested by those who are the victims of it.[95]

In this contestation, misrepresentation by the State in 'the language of the Paras' would be challenged by 'the victims' themselves, in deploying the language of 'wrongfulness' to tell their own stories and those of their dead loved ones, thereby restoring their human dignity and integrity, and rediscovering their own lost agency.

The renewed awareness linked to McCann's book fed into the 1992 commemoration in a number of ways. The book launch itself was publicized in the 'Programme of events', and this widely circulating leaflet also reproduced short extracts from all fourteen life-stories.[96] Organized among the events for the first time was a public occasion for the sharing of personal memories, described as a 'Retrospective', led by the photo-journalist Fulvio Grimaldi, well known in Derry as an eyewitness and the co-author of the booklet

Blood in the Street.[97] Efforts were also made to enhance the profile of the Bloody Sunday families within the commemoration. As was traditional, they led the march and performed its central symbolic act of wreath-laying; and at this year's rally Gerry Adams 'paid special tribute' to their courage from the platform, and they were made guests of honour at the special commemorative music concert.[98] However, McCann's book also demonstrated the varied and complex character of relatives' own relationships to the annual commemoration (and other forms of public memory). Eileen Doherty, for one, identified herself and her family as committed participants, involving even the youngest grandchildren in local collective memory:

> I attend the commemoration marches. I wouldn't be afraid, ever, of marching for something that's right, not after what happened, because I know they were trying to put fear into people. It was a form of intimidation of the people of Ireland. Every Bloody Sunday some one of the children has carried the wreath on the march. Glenn has carried it for the last four years because he is the wain.[99]

Others were ambivalent or hostile. Mary Donaghey explained that, 'I don't go on the commemoration marches now' but only 'to the smaller commemorations for the families in the morning' because of the psychic distress evoked: 'It would take too much out of me to go on the march, having to walk the way he walked, thinking every step you were taking of every step he took. When I did go on the march it was painful to me.'[100] The Gilmour family had distanced itself for political reasons rooted in the feeling that the meaning of the commemoration had been taken from them. In the words of Olive Bonner (Hugh Gilmour's sister): 'I don't attend the Bloody Sunday marches. None of the family does. I don't think the marches have anything to do with Bloody Sunday anymore.'[101]

Some of these differences and tensions in relatives' responses to the annual march and rally surfaced during the 1992 commemoration, when the family of Gerald McKinney 'decided to boycott the event in protest against an invitation to Sinn Féin president Gerry Adams to address the rally'. In a statement on behalf of the BSI, Alex Wray explained that the organizers were 'non-political' (presumably meaning 'non-party-political') and represented an inclusive range of perspectives:

> There are thirteen [*sic*] different families who all have very different ideas. This march has been going on for years and sometimes a family may not go one year, maybe because they don't like who's speaking, but they go another year. Its a very personal thing for the people of Derry, the fact that 14 people were murdered on the streets. The British maligned those people, saying they were gunmen and bombers. That's not true and we're still fighting to clear their names.[102]

Here, Wray slides from recognizing differences of view among the families, which is a 'personal thing', into reasserting a collective stance, as if 'the people of Derry' all thought alike. According to Tony Doherty, McCann's

˙ book was 'the first time that the full spectrum of opinion across the families had been given representation'. In bringing out the diversity of relatives' experiences and perspectives, it also pointed to the absence of an inclusive campaigning voice that could properly articulate their collective response while still acknowledging these differences: 'What we discovered was that most of the people who had been directly affected by it – the families – hadn't really been brought into the equation.' The families 'were really shafted' by the Widgery Report, but in the 'explosion of conflict' after Bloody Sunday

> its importance as a justice issue was overshadowed by hundreds of other events that year and in subsequent years . . . The overall outcome of Bloody Sunday left a lot of people damaged. There was no impetus for people to come together over that period between 1972 and 1992 . . . There was no clear critical path there for people to identify with and so they felt very much on their own.

Bloody Sunday in Derry began to tell these stories of silence and division, and their emotional truths 'started sparking off ideas' about the potential for mobilizing political support in a new kind of campaign.[103]

The emergence of a narrative of human rights that enabled Northern nationalists to reconcile their political differences within a common framework, together with the huge popular support displayed throughout the twentieth anniversary commemoration for the BSI's cause of 'remembering Bloody Sunday', helped to generate the 'impetus for [the families] to come together', missing since 1972. The launch of McCann's book provided 'the occasion in the city when the families actually met again'. Doherty recalls that:

> A lot of [the families' members] actually would have passed one another and would have said, 'There's such-and-such; it's ten years since I saw her.' The book was a timely intervention. At its launch we rediscovered one another and found out that practically everyone felt that the issue needed to be taken up.[104]

An informal group of relatives then began to meet, initially (like the Unionist victims' groups discussed in chapter 8) to exchange stories and provide a shared form of 'self-counselling'.[105] Out of this came a decision to 'begin the process of reconvening themselves, trying to set out some strategic objective for the emergence of a new campaigning group.'[106] As Kay Duddy remembers it, after Widgery 'everybody's sort of waiting and saying, "Somebody's going to do something about this." Time went on and nothing was happening. At the twentieth anniversary, a few of the family members got together and decided, "Let's see if we can do something." '[107] Those involved 'agreed that it was time that the unfinished business of Bloody Sunday should at last be righted and that we should finally seek justice for those killed and injured'.[108] In this way, at a public meeting in April 1992 born out of the annual commemoration, the Bloody Sunday Justice Campaign was formed.[109]

The Justice Campaign was launched as 'an entirely independent group made up of relatives of those killed, the wounded, and concerned individuals',

open to 'anybody who supports our objectives irrespective of religion or pol- •
itics'. Those objectives were threefold, and have remained consistent – the
campaign aimed to secure from the British Government an unambiguous
public acknowledgement 'that all of those killed and injured were totally innocent'; a public repudiation of the Widgery Report 'in its entirety'; and the prosecution of 'those responsible for the murders and attempted murders on the
streets of Derry on 30 Jan 1972'.[110] The rationale behind these demands was
voiced in terms of a counter-memory of Bloody Sunday with three main
strands. Firstly, the Justice Campaign laid claim to the memory of the civil
rights march on 30 January 1972 as a contribution to a popular campaign of
'large scale nonviolent demonstrations' and civil disobedience, in pursuit of
legitimate political demands: namely, 'an end to political and economic discrimination within the North of Ireland and for equality of opportunity and
justice for all'. Secondly, the Campaign reasserted the nationalist popular
memory of the Parachute Regiment's brutality in the Bogside as being entirely
consistent with British state policy at that time, 'of suppressing political opposition within the North of Ireland' by draconian measures including internment without trial and military force. Thirdly, the Campaign challenged the
British Government's 'official position', still based on the conclusions of the
Widgery Report, by mobilizing a memory couched in the language of human
rights violations, as developed by campaigners such as Murray, and now for
the first time applied systematically in an analysis of 30 January 1972. Bloody
Sunday was described as 'the greatest single act of state-sponsored terrorism
committed by Britain in Ireland' since partition; an act 'sanctioned by a government which had signed international human rights conventions which
outlaw the deliberate killing of civilians'. The Widgery Tribunal was an
'appalling miscarriage of justice', and demonstrated that those responsible for
the killings are 'above the law'. The 'wrongs of that day still cry out for
justice'.[111] To complete the 'unfinished business of Bloody Sunday', the truth
was required, as,

> for too long, families shattered by the impact of losing a loved one on Bloody
> Sunday have not been able to put their lives back together, because of the
> absence of justice. It is clear that neither the dead nor the living can rest easily
> while the injustice remains.[112]

In thus framing its counter-memory as a human rights narrative underpinning calls for redress of injustice and 'lasting hurt', the Justice Campaign
based the legitimacy of its three demands – for vindication, repudiation and
prosecution – on fundamental tenets of international human rights legislation. This was a strategy designed to force the British Government to
respond to (and defend itself against) the doubly heinous charge of being
responsible for serious violations of human rights that had, furthermore,
remained unacknowledged for twenty years.[113]

Between 1992 and 1997, the Justice Campaign built a broad and successful movement supporting these demands. If the narrative of human rights

provided the necessary unifying story, the Justice Campaign, through its practical organizational structure and campaigning activities, provided the agency to promote that narrative in widening public arenas, on the inclusive basis of a rapprochement between Republicans and other nationalists in the city. The position adopted, as Tony Doherty remembers it, stemmed from the recognition that 'republicans had a right to campaign, but others should be encouraged to support the issue also . . . It was a slow process of . . . allowing support to come from the SDLP tradition as well as the Sinn Féin tradition', and from the politically non-aligned.[114] Relatives among the founder-members, and central figures in the Justice Campaign, included Doherty, John Kelly, who became its first chairperson, Kay Duddy and Mickey McKinney, who succeeded Kelly in 1999.[115] Other family members became 'involved in organising things . . . during the campaign for the Inquiry', as did Mary Donaghey,[116] or, like Betty Walker, gave their support.[117] McKinney recalls how the launch of the Campaign provided a channel for emotional as well as political expression:

> I thought I had accepted Bloody Sunday and the injustice of it, but then the Birmingham Six got out [March 1991] and, happy as I was for them, it pressed a button and I was full of anger. My first reaction was, what about the people that were killed on Bloody Sunday?
> The only people that were ever going to do anything about Bloody Sunday were the families – we had to take it on. I was involved in the campaign from when it started in 1992.[118]

For a number of the relatives, active engagement in the Justice Campaign functioned as a means of psychic reparation, in winning social recognition for trauma and injustice, and in doing right by the dead through efforts to clear their names and proclaim their innocence.[119]

Participation in the Justice Campaign set its members, many of whom had little or no experience of collective organization, public speaking or the practice of other necessary skills, on a steep learning curve, with tactics emerging ad hoc.[120] One focus of their work was the building of solidarity networks. Lobbying for support began with the failed attempt, in May 1992, to secure funding from the SDLP-led Derry City Council, which was eventually persuaded to 'support in principle' the aims of the Campaign and to circulate them to other councils throughout both parts of Ireland, making it 'a debating point in a wider arena'.[121] In the South of Ireland, 'the only people who would propose the motions were Sinn Féin councillors, which . . . demonstrated how hostile people had become towards dealing with issues from the North within the South'.[122] Popular support was also sought through a tour of Ireland collecting signatures for a petition to the British Government and by a mass-sending of postcards featuring the demands of the Campaign addressed to Prime Minister John Major.[123] Access to international networks, including powerful public advocates such as US Senator Edward Kennedy, was arranged through Bloody Sunday survivor and human rights activist Don Mullan.[124] Through Mullan, Justice Campaigners were able to develop a second strand of activity, taking their personal survivors' stories into the political arenas where national and international policy-making on the Northern Ireland question was shaped, in Dublin's *Dáil*, the US Congress, the White House and the influential Irish-American lobby.[125] In January 1994, a Justice Campaign delegation addressed MPs at Westminster and presented a new report on Bloody Sunday to the Prime Minister, in support of 'the just demand for a re-investigation into the killings and cover-up'.[126] Kay Duddy recalls the emotional demands this work placed on the relatives, but also the warm response that their stories could elicit. The personal voice of the survivor, attempting to make itself heard within the centre-most political arenas of the State, risked a potentially dissonant clash of registers; as on the occasion in 1997 when, after a meeting with the new Labour Secretary of State for Northern Ireland, Mo Mowlam, 'I walked up to [her] . . . and I set Jackie's photo down and I said, "That's what we're talking about. We're talking about human beings here." '[127]

The Justice Campaign also became involved in organizing the annual anniversary Weekend. While not on the scale of 1992, this continued over the following years to provide the focal point for commemoration of Bloody Sunday within the city, and an environment of critical debate and analysis emphasizing a forward-looking agenda, with themes such as 'Beyond injustice' (1993) and 'Just peace' (1994).[128] After 1992, relatives involved in the Justice Campaign were granted a regular space as platform-speakers at the rally, establishing the Campaign as the hub of the commemoration, building the profile of the families through their use of personal storytelling to elicit identification and support, and advancing a specifically local appeal for the support of the city. In 1994, for example, John Kelly used the public occasion to reiterate the Justice Campaign's call on the British Government 'to bring those who planned the killings to justice', weaving together the personal and the political: ' "Some people say Bloody Sunday is just history and should be forgotten. But the British Government aren't saying that they will hunt the murderers of my brother till the day they die, as they do when they refer to Irish people who kill their soldiers." '[129] The following year Gerry Duddy, brother of Jack Duddy, told the rally that:

> For 23 years I have wished for nothing else than to put the terrible memories of Bloody Sunday behind me. I would like to tell you that much has changed. I would like to say that the spirit of justice has prevailed and that we have seen gestures of atonement. But this has not happened. We demand justice. Our campaign is not to seek revenge but the truth.[130]

Here, the personal and familial trauma of the relatives is equated, through the use of the collective 'we', with that of the wider nationalist community subjected to inequality, second-class citizenship imposed by the gun, and the psychic effects of trauma and victimization deployed as a deliberate strategy of state power.[131] For many others like Gerry Duddy, the achievement of justice is felt to be necessary in order to 'put the terrible memories behind me'. Psychic reparation is felt to be contingent upon the politics. Yet, the work of campaigning, being centrally concerned with telling and listening to stories, seeking and bestowing social recognition and widening the circle of memory, provides in itself a vehicle of reparation and the integration of the traumatic past, for both the individual psyche and the traumatized community.

Throughout the mid-1990s, the nationalist and Republican cultural memory of Bloody Sunday increasingly became integrated into a unified counter-memory of injustice and the violation of human rights. This work built towards and culminated in the commemoration of the twenty-fifth anniversary in 1997, when up to 40,000 people joined the march (the largest political gathering ever seen in Derry), bringing significant pressure to bear on the British Government. By 1997, the context in which the Justice Campaign was operating had changed fundamentally from that of its inception in 1992. Two linked factors are of particular importance in this shift. One is the further development of a culture of ideas, both creative and critical, propagated out of the human rights agenda launched by the BSI. The other is the emergence of the peace process, developing out of internal debate within Irish nationalism, through the IRA's ceasefire of August 1994, into inclusive efforts towards agreeing a comprehensive resolution to conflict in Ireland. Both factors, and their implications for the memory of Bloody Sunday, are addressed in chapter 6.

6

Counter-memory, truth and justice: Bloody Sunday and the Irish peace process

In the early 1990s, the BSI signalled its intention to use the occasion of the forthcoming twentieth anniversary commemoration to establish a community resource centre that would serve as the organizational focus for the annual weekend. In the longer term, the new centre was envisaged as providing a permanent contribution to the city of Derry, 'which continues to be one of the most impoverished and marginalised in Europe and which remains the target of so much state repression and social control'.[1] This centre would house 'a long-term human rights project which will seek to monitor, highlight and build campaigns around the systematic and daily abuse of human rights in our city by the British government and by the state security forces'; but it would also 'encourage the process of dialogue and reconciliation among all the many different groupings and people whose destiny is inevitably bound up in the future of Ireland'.[2] In this, it would be 'a fitting memorial to those who died 19 years ago on our streets'.[3] However, after the formation of the Justice Campaign, and to avoid the risk of 'confus[ing] the general public with two Bloody Sunday groups', the Initiative relinquished that title to the families.[4] The new centre was instead 'named in memory' of Patrick Finucane, a human rights solicitor specializing in cases arising from the British Government's emergency legislation, who consequently was labelled by British politicians and the RUC as 'unduly sympathetic' to, or even 'working for', the IRA, and shortly afterwards, in 1989, was shot dead at home in front of his family by a loyalist death squad, in one of the most notorious cases of collusion between loyalists and the British intelligence and security establishment.[5]

The Pat Finucane Centre for Human Rights and Social Change (PFC) was duly established in 1992 as 'an independent political and community resource centre situated in Derry's Bogside . . . [which] exists to promote radical social change and respect for human rights', and offers a 'home to a number of independent education and action projects'.[6] By accepting no funding from the British, Irish or US Governments, the PFC had 'safeguarded our integrity and independence in order to be free to campaign on issues which involve state violations of human rights and repression and to promote a radical politics with a human face'. The Justice Campaign was launched at the PFC, and a number of other human rights groups were based there, including Relatives for Justice. The PFC set out 'to monitor and publicize human rights abuses and violations in Derry and Ireland as a whole while campaigning to have them ended'. Its plans included 'compiling an extensive archive'; regular educational publications about Derry, the Irish conflict, and legal and human rights; and the organization of information and education workshops for human rights campaigners, community activists and general public. It also existed 'to promote a political agenda . . . in the face of determined attempts by the state and its allies to marginalise anyone seeking to challenge the status quo. The Centre promotes a different politics which empowers ordinary people and the communities in which they live.' From its inception, then, the PFC was involved in developing 'nonviolent and creative options to building a new society'. These ranged from initiatives to rejuvenate the economy and tackle endemic poverty (Derry and nearby Strabane, it pointed out, had 'the highest levels of unemployment and deprivation in the EC'), to 'the campaign to end the militarisation of the city of Derry and the Border which divides southern and northern parts of Ireland'.[7] Here, the traditional nationalist and Republican demands for British withdrawal and the restoration of a united Ireland were connected up to forward-looking and achievable political goals designed to bring about real and immediate improvements in local conditions of life.

The PFC became both the architect of a new strategy for social change and one of the think-tanks of the emerging peace process, launching Peace 2000, 'an autonomous and radical peace project . . . emphasis[ing] the need for a process to establish a lasting peace in Ireland which is inclusive of all and which enhances the political, economic and human rights of people throughout Ireland'.[8] Peace 2000 originated in a discussion paper circulated by the BSI, 'Towards a new peace agenda', containing a proposal 'to establish a new type of peace movement in Ireland which has significantly different demands from those presently constituted'.[9] This was a contribution to the evolving debate within Northern nationalism set in train by the Hume–Adams contacts of 1988 and a Sinn Féin document, *Towards a Lasting Peace in Ireland*, in 1992.[10]

'Towards a new peace agenda' mounted a critique of recent peace initiatives supported and funded by the British and Irish Governments, identifying three 'faulty assumptions' on which they were based. The first was the 'two-traditions' analysis, which understood political conflict in the North to be 'a community relations problem . . . rooted in contemporary differences of perception of nationality, religion and identity etc. Peace is thereby achieved by increasing mutual understanding, cultural awareness and community contact.' The second, which had formed the basis of British strategy for conflict resolution from the earliest years of the Troubles, was that 'peace in Ireland can be achieved by excluding Sinn Féin and the community it represents from the peace process and from any "solutions" that might be achieved'. The third, at the core of the 'propaganda war' conducted by the

British Government's Northern Ireland Office, was that 'the central problem today in the North of Ireland is the problem of political violence, particularly that of the IRA'.[11] The BSI's paper proposed to develop an alternative strategy through the establishment of an organization, Peace 2000, with the aim of securing 'a total end to armed conflict in Ireland' by the year 2000, based on 'a historic compromise in which all sides of the conflict commit themselves to a negotiated peace, without preconditions and excluding nobody, but with a willingness to show real generosity and reciprocity'.[12] In this, Derry nationalists associated with the BSI and the PFC were helping to form the principles underlying the Hume–Adams dialogue and statements of 1993, which in turn laid the basis for nationalist and Republican participation in the peace process brokered by the British and Irish Governments. The critique of the two governments' thinking sketched in the BSI's paper continued to inform alternative, particularly Republican, perspectives within this process.

Following the IRA's ceasefire announced on 31 August 1994, and its reciprocation by the Combined Loyalist Military Command in October, a 'new political space . . . developed in the 6 Counties'.[13] In the Irish Republic, the UK and the USA, too, as 'a result of the ceasefires and steady strides towards lasting peace, a new politics was emerging, the politics of peace and possibility'.[14] This space, and the movement it enabled towards a negotiated settlement of the conflict through inclusive peace talks, transformed the context in which the struggle for justice, recognition and reparation in respect of Bloody Sunday had been conducted hitherto. This chapter examines the further development of the Bloody Sunday Justice Campaign in its utilization of the new opportunities opened up by the Irish peace process. First, it considers the role of the annual commemoration as a public arena for debates about the relation between peace and justice, and for the articulation of nationalist responses to the politics of conflict resolution conducted by the two governments. It goes on to trace the ways in which the countermemory of injustice was strengthened by archival research and historymaking conducted by human rights activists associated with the PFC. Next it turns to the intersection of these developments with psychic, cultural and political energies unlocked by the 1997 commemoration of the twenty-fifth anniversary of Bloody Sunday – an occasion characterized by powerful currents of reparative remembering and by the channelling of the countermemory of injustice into a mobilization that involved young people from the successor generation, born since 1972, as well as the survivor generation which lived through Bloody Sunday.[15] By January 1998, the Justice Campaign had secured the overturning of Lord Widgery's verdict with the announcement that the British Government was to establish a new Tribunal of Inquiry led by Lord Saville of Newdigate. The chapter concludes with some reflections about the Saville Inquiry as a specific arena of memory, and its capacity to provide effective resolution, or *reconciliation*, in respect of the conflicting narratives about Bloody Sunday.

Bloody Sunday commemoration and the Irish peace process

The Justice Campaign welcomed the new opportunities opened up by the peace process, but also found itself caught up in the machinations and complexities of that process, as the key participants manoeuvred to secure their own interests in whatever new settlement might emerge. By the same token, the Bloody Sunday commemoration became a significant occasion for the articulation of nationalist aspirations and concerns as the politics of making the peace slowly unfolded. At the 1994 commemoration, held a matter of weeks after the Downing Street Declaration heralded the possibility of a new beginning, consideration of the emerging politics of the future was interlaced with an insistence on addressing the injustices of the past as a necessary aspect of conflict resolution. Its theme, 'Just peace', explored connections between the demand for demilitarization and British withdrawal from Ireland and the campaigns for justice.[16] While the yearning to be free of the violence of a heavily militarized society lay behind the new nationalist peace strategy, Sinn Féin's Tom Hartley emphasized that Republicans want 'a permanent peace, a peace built on justice and equality and on democratic rights, including our right as a nation to self-determination'. In order to achieve a peaceful settlement through dialogue, as called for in the Declaration, he argued, the British Government would have to remove the Unionists' constitutional guarantee that made Northern Ireland's position in the UK non-negotiable, and work to encourage their participation in 'the building of a new and agreed future for all the people of this island'.[17]

Prior to the 1995 commemoration, the first after the ceasefires, Sinn Féin called on nationalists to take to the streets of Derry to demonstrate their support for the pan-nationalist peace initiative and their frustration at the tardiness of the British response: 'The Irish peace initiative and the historic IRA ceasefire has presented us with a chance not only to ensure their [*sic*] are no more Bloody Sundays but to ensure that the causes of this conflict are resolved. Do not squander this opportunity, march for Justice!'[18] In the event, a crowd of 20,000 took part in the annual march and rally. They heard Gerry Adams call on the British Government to replace its current 'war strategy . . . with a British peace strategy', in response to the 'courageous IRA initiative [which] has helped to create the potential to end conflict forever in this country'.[19] In the Republican vision articulated by Adams, the British would dismantle the militarized society by the withdrawal of the British Army 'from all nationalist areas', the repeal of repressive legislation, the disbandment of the RUC and the release of all political prisoners, prior to political 'disengagement from our country'. This would create the conditions for the people of Ireland to work together to overcome division, eradicate poverty and economic inequality within 'a new economic democracy', and guarantee full civil rights and religious liberties for all citizens.[20] Adams outlined the twin planks of Sinn Féin's politics of memory in the new space opened up by the ceasefires. Firstly, conflict resolution would

require 'a process of reconciliation' based on the full and open acknowledgement of 'the hurts we have caused', made by all parties to the armed
conflict, with a particular onus on the British Government. But, secondly, in
order for the conflict to be successfully resolved, there needed to be an accurate understanding of what had caused and sustained it, so that the underlying issues could be addressed politically rather than through armed
confrontation. On both these counts, the memory of Bloody Sunday was
absolutely central.

The impact of the peace process on the memory of Bloody Sunday, and
vice versa, can be seen most clearly in relation to the emerging debate in
Northern Ireland about those who were now known as 'the victims of violence'. The Justice Campaign was fully engaged in this from the beginning:
in January 1995, presenting its submission to the Forum for Peace and
Reconciliation, Tony Doherty wryly welcomed the appearance of this new
category, which meant that 'after 23 years, I, and many of my friends, are
now officially viewed as "victims of violence" '.[21] The Forum was established
by the Irish Government to foster 'agreement and trust between both traditions', as called for in the Downing Street Declaration.[22] Anticipating the
logic of the emerging state-sponsored discourse on victimhood, Doherty
raised a number of questions 'about the process of becoming, and being
accepted as, a victim', in relation to that other category, the 'men of violence'; and identified a double standard embedded in the ideological construction of these categories of representation. The 'men of violence' were
paramilitary terrorists, 'to be rounded up, squeezed out of society like tooth-
paste, and deprived of the oxygen of publicity'; but not the State's own security forces. The instituting of these definitions perpetuated the problem that
'successive British governments, right up to John Major's . . . have persisted
in refusing to acknowledge the enormity of the crimes committed on Bloody
Sunday, or the lasting hurt felt by the people of Derry over the cover-up
carried out by Lord Widgery'.

Identifying the continuities between current official discourse on 'the
victims of violence' and the imperatives of the British State's propaganda war
against the IRA (British soldier good, IRA terrorist bad), Doherty questioned
the personal appeal to victims implied in the language of 'forgiveness' and
'reconciliation' deployed by government in the peace process: 'should I offer
to forgive "the men of violence" as my contribution to the search for peace
and reconciliation? Do I forget about Bloody Sunday?' Pointing to the experience of conflict resolution in other societies such as Uruguay and Chile,
Doherty suggested: 'Forgiveness . . . begins with the wrong-doers accepting
culpability and apologising for their actions, with a view to reconciliation and
reform'. This, he argued, is not a matter of individual moral choice but a
social process in which the State has particular responsibilities: 'We cannot
build a new future for our society if society is unwilling or unable to acknowledge its past. An essential starting point on the path to reconciling the historic problems between Britain and Ireland is for the British [State] to come

clean on its involvement in the North since 1969.' By '[f]inally laying to rest' Bloody Sunday, it could begin 'a process of real healing'.[23] In this submission to the Forum, Doherty outlined the terms of the nationalist challenge to 'state-organized forgetting' and British policy towards the victims of violence, situating Bloody Sunday as the centrepiece. This challenge gave rise to a new 'politics of victimhood' within the peace process, and stimulated the emergence from 1995 onwards of Protestant and Unionist victims' groups which sought to reaffirm the official definitions of 'victims' and 'men of violence' contested by the Justice Campaign and other nationalist organizations.

The Bloody Sunday Weekend of 1995 became the focus for other debates, conflicts and controversies in the halting peace process immediately following the 1994 ceasefires. One example is the public meeting organized by the PFC, as a contribution to the dialogue it advocated, on the theme of 'Unionist/loyalist perspectives on the peace process'. Elected representatives of the Ulster Unionist Party (UUP), the Democratic Unionist Party (DUP) and the Progressive Unionist Party (PUP) spoke to a 'packed audience' in the Bogside. While the PUP's Billy Hutchinson, from the loyalist working-class of North Belfast, 'spoke a language working-class Bogsiders could understand', Richard Dallas of the UUP rejected all the main demands made by nationalists, and the DUP's Gregory Campbell 'demonstrated how far removed his party is from the peace process'. All three speakers were reported to have 'assert[ed] their unionism' in a meeting that provided 'plenty of friction'.[24]

A second example is provided by the invitation to play a central role in the 1995 march and rally that was extended to *Saoirse* (Freedom), an organization campaigning 'in the spirit of the ongoing peace process' for the release of all 'political prisoners' of the conflict.[25] The rally was chaired by a *Saoirse* activist, Mairéad Ní hAdhmaill, and hundreds of Republican former prisoners-of-war joined together on the march under the *Saoirse* banner, in a prime position immediately behind the relatives. Also on the platform alongside Ní hAdhmaill, Adams and Gerry Duddy of the Justice Campaign was Breige Meehan of the National Graves Association, who spoke about its campaign for the release from the yard of Crumlin Road Prison of the remains of IRA volunteer Tom Williams, to enable a proper interral in the Republican Plot in Milltown Cemetery.[26] This campaign demonstrated the still-potent memory of the criminalization of Republican political prisoners during past stages of the conflict, and its association with the Justice Campaign underlines the importance attached by nationalists to challenging official memory by celebrating the resistance and redressing the injustices of the past.[27] The early release of prisoners jailed for Troubles-related offences, successfully negotiated by Sinn Féin and the parties representing loyalist paramilitary organizations, would subsequently become one of the most controversial aspects of the Good Friday Agreement, bitterly opposed by Unionist victims' groups. The lack of reciprocity on this issue was underlined at the time of the 1995 commemoration by the campaign supported at the highest levels of the British establishment for the early release from prison of Private Lee Clegg, who was 'only the second member of the Crown Forces to be convicted of murder for any of the more than 350 killings the British army and RUC have carried out between them since 1969'.[28] Clegg's eventual release in July 1995 contributed to a growing nationalist disillusionment about the British State's commitment to the peace process, expressed by rioting in some nationalist areas of Belfast.[29]

Disillusionment increased in 1995 as a result of British and Unionist insistence on a new precondition for Sinn Féin's participation in all-party talks: the 'decommissioning' of weapons by the IRA (a euphemism for its disarmament). This was perceived by Republicans to alter unilaterally the terms on which the IRA ceasefire had been brokered, and as making a demand, tantamount to the IRA's surrender, in the knowledge that this would be unacceptable, thereby introducing a deliberate obstacle to its involvement in negotiating a settlement. In February 1996, the IRA went 'back to war' with the bombing of Canary Wharf in London's Docklands, its aim, paradoxically, being to bring the British Government into re-engagement with the peace process on the basis previously agreed.[30] The 1997 Bloody Sunday Weekend took place in the context of this tactical resumption of the 'armed struggle' by the IRA, which re-opened old divisions within the Northern nationalist community; as was evident in, for example, Bishop Hegarty's call, during a memorial service for the dead held in Creggan, both for a new inquiry into Bloody Sunday and for the 'unequivocal and permanent reinstatement of the IRA ceasefire' as the means 'to give the thrust or propulsion which is necessary to obtain a true, just and lasting peace'. In his demand, the 'era of violence must be ended', the Bishop was identifying all parties that practised war as obstacles to the peace that was generally desired.[31] The IRA's tactical return to violence in 1996 was a symptom of the Major Government's failure to take advantage of the political space opened up by the 1994 ceasefire by setting in motion a fully inclusive and comprehensive process of conflict resolution. After the Canary Wharf bomb, which signalled a renewal of the 'mainland' bombing campaign, this political space effectively closed down until the election of the new Labour Government in May 1997, when the impetus towards all-party talks was re-established.

History-making, the archive and the counter-memory of injustice

Alongside the political process, the 1994 ceasefires also opened up new cultural spaces for expression, investigation and debate focused on the history and memory of the conflict. Civil society in Northern Ireland became more receptive to the discourses of trauma and human rights, and a more open climate for the discovery and communication of new ideas stimulated fresh research on histories of the Troubles. In nationalist Derry, the PFC, with its archive (itself a kind of memory-bank of the conflict) and links to other human rights organizations, provided a locus for history-making to undermine the official story of Bloody Sunday and to build the counter-memory of injustice. In 1995, researchers connected to the PFC unearthed two major 'finds', documents that would transform the balance of power – and the fortunes of the Justice Campaign.

The first of these finds was made by Jane Winter, a founding member and the director of British–Irish Rights Watch, a non-governmental organization formed in 1992 to 'monitor the human rights dimension of the conflict in Northern Ireland' and 'to promote, by means of education and research[, their] proper observance and maintenance'.[32] In August 1995, Winter discovered in the Public Record Office in London a 'confidential minute' of the meeting held on 1 February 1972 at Downing Street between Lord Widgery, Prime Minister Heath and Lord Chancellor Hailsham to discuss the forthcoming public inquiry, which exposed the political orchestration of the Widgery Tribunal (see chapter 3, above). The contents of that document were made public in November 1995 by the chair of the Justice Campaign, John Kelly, who stated that the minute

> simply proves what many have suspected for many years; that the British Government and judiciary actively colluded to prevent any vestige of truth from emerging from this so-called fair and balanced tribunal . . . It is evident that this meeting, held 24 hours after the slaughter . . . was set up to determine the terms of reference and the outcome of the yet to be established Tribunal of Inquiry.[33]

Explaining the significance of the minute, Kelly denied that the Justice Campaign was seeking resignations or apologies, since 'British politicians don't resign over Irish affairs', and 'the time for meaningful apologies has come and gone. Various British Governments have been given ample opportunity over the years to deal effectively with the situation. An apology was always the least they could offer: even that has not come.' More important, Kelly argued, was the realization that this minute and its 'new' evidence, long kept secret and discovered by accident, 'is only the tip of the iceberg. The British Government have at their disposal reams of information which they intend to keep closed for at least 75 years.' Calling for these 'hidden files' to be released to the public, Kelly mimicked and reversed the language of the British Government and the Unionists in their demand for the disarming of the IRA:

> We demand a process of decommissioning injustice, and for cover-ups to be taken out of British and Irish politics. For the Bloody Sunday Justice Campaign and hundreds of other families who have lost relatives to the British state, the current peace process must establish and include a 'justice process' if an overall just settlement is to be reached.[34]

Profoundly embarrassing to the British Government, Winter's research strengthened the moral legitimacy of the Justice Campaign, while Kelly's term 'decommissioning injustice' was taken up as the organizing theme for the 1996 Bloody Sunday Weekend.[35]

The discovery of the Downing Street minute prompted Winter, together with Patricia Coyle of the Derry solicitors Madden & Finucane, acting for the relatives of the Bloody Sunday deceased, to seek 'access to 13 categories of documents relating to the Tribunal of Inquiry which were closed to public inspection for periods of 50–75 years. After a considerable pressure, and only after the documents had been referred to the Home Office, were the solicitors given access to 12 of the 13 categories in the Summer of 1996.'[36] Among this material were copies of the soldiers' statements about shots they had fired on Bloody Sunday, given to the Military Police that night and to the Treasury Solicitor as witness statements for the Tribunal, all of which had been withheld from Counsel for the Deceased and Wounded during the Tribunal's proceedings. Also released were the Tribunal's list of evidence, drafts of Widgery's Report and records of advice given to Widgery by his secretariat. Those documents provided the crucial 'new' evidence examined in Dermot Walsh's critical study of the Widgery Tribunal (see above, pp. 104–15). Walsh's report, presented to the Law Department at the University of Limerick and published in January 1997, breached the official narrative of Bloody Sunday installed after Widgery and provided the detail that rendered the counter-memory of injustice more plausible and effective.[37] In her later Foreword to the report, Angela Hegarty points out that, prior to Winter and Coyle having 'uncovered this evidence and brought it into the public domain for the first time . . . none of us could have known the extent to which the [Widgery] Tribunal had undermined the rule of law, because none of us knew the extent of the information which was kept from the relatives, from their lawyers and from the public'.[38]

The second find, also in 1995, would provide the basis for the single most important memory-text concerned with the massacre, Don Mullan's *Eyewitness Bloody Sunday* (1997).[39] This stemmed from a chance meeting in Rossville Street between Mullan, on a visit home to Derry, and Tony Doherty.[40] While working in the archive at the PFC in 1995, Doherty had discovered a set of the witness statements presented to the Tribunal by the NCCL and NICRA but disregarded by Widgery, and now told Mullan that he had 'happened to be reading [Mullan's] personal statement of what he had witnessed on Bloody Sunday'.[41] According to Mullan,

I had completely forgotten ever having given such a statement, but Tony's reminder unleashed a flood of memories . . . I made arrangements with the Pat Finucane Centre to see the statement. There was some initial difficulty in locating my statement and several hundred others among a sea of documents related to justice, peace and human rights issues. Eventually a well-worn plastic supermarket bag, containing the statements, was retrieved from the top drawer of an old battered filing cabinet and handed to me.

I sat at a window, overlooking the junction of Westland Street and Laburnum Terrace, along which the anti-internment march had passed on that fateful day in 1972, and there, for several hours, I was enthralled in what was to become the seed of this book.[42]

In his image of the 'well-worn plastic supermarket bag', lost in 'a sea of documents', found casually stuffed into 'an old battered filing cabinet', full of eyewitness statements more than twenty years old that evoked the atrocity with 'an immediacy and a vividness that was compelling',[43] Mullan creates a wonderful metaphor for a suppressed and dispersed memory resurfacing on the very margins of social consciousness, before sprouting into life with all the energy and impact denied it two decades earlier. Preserved as if by magic in the Creggan, the location where they were created; brought to light through a chance encounter a few hundred yards away at the site where the shooting occurred; and read in a building overlooking part of the route where the march had passed; these documents sparked for Mullan a living connection between the past and present in this location. Keeping alive that connection becomes the motive behind the book, impelled by a phantasy that the lost-and-found 'good object' – its value concealed, misrecognized as worthless – may be lost, irrevocably, again: 'Reading the statements, I had a growing unease that sometime in the future, someone might find this old bag of photocopied paper and, not realising its historical importance, dump it. At that moment I began to think about having the statements published.'[44] Encouraged by Doherty's agreement that the statements opened up 'a very important part of the hidden history' of the event and of the town, and his assurance 'that I would have the support and good wishes of the families of those killed on Bloody Sunday', Mullan discussed the possibilities with leading members of the Justice Campaign during the annual commemoration in January 1996, and it was decided to publish the statements as a book to contribute to the twenty-fifth anniversary in 1997.[45]

In its form, the book that was published in January 1997 differs from Mullan's original intention, which had been to publish all the statements.[46] With over 500 in total, this proved impracticable and unnecessary: the overriding impulse to preserve them all through publication had been mitigated by the realization that other sets 'were safely deposited' with solicitors and Public Record Offices.[47] Instead, a selection of 100 of the NCCL–NICRA statements were included, alongside thirteen statements that had been prepared especially for the Widgery Tribunal. They are all unedited, 'complete documents in themselves',[48] grouped into chapters each with an introduction by Mullan, organized 'to follow the sequence of events, to highlight particular incidents, and to offer relevant insights from specific eyewitnesses such as march stewards, ex-servicemen, para-medics and the wounded'.[49] These form the core of the book, but they are framed by a substantial Preface (by Jane Winter) and Mullan's Introduction that establish the contexts necessary to understand the significance of the testimonies themselves, their original collection and subsequent fate, and their publication 'at last',[50] in relation to the 'unfinished business' of truth and justice in Derry. This becomes most sharply pointed in the second part of Mullan's Introduction, where he explains:

During the process of reading hundreds of eyewitness testimonies, a fact began to emerge which was totally ignored by Lord Widgery in his *Tribunal of Inquiry Report* [and had not been recognised by justice campaigners subsequently]: the fact that the British Army, in addition to firing live ammunition at ground level in the vicinity of Rossville Street, was also firing live ammunition from the vicinity of the Derry Walls.[51]

With this realization, '[t]he nature of this book changed considerably',[52] as Mullan set about corroborating the eyewitness testimonies with new research into the medical, ballistic and forensic evidence, spurred on by legal advice that taken altogether this 'could very seriously undermine the findings and conclusions of the Widgery Tribunal'.[53]

Like McCann's book five years earlier, Mullan's *Eyewitness Bloody Sunday* was published to coincide with, and feed into, a major anniversary commemoration, in this case the twenty-fifth. Released in Ireland on 13 January 1997,[54] it had a remarkable impact in both personal and political terms, on a par with other great human rights texts, such as *Nunca mas* in Argentina or the REMHI Report in Guatemala.[55] McCann described the reaction as 'phenomenal', while Bishop Edward Daly judged that the book's contribution 'could not be exaggerated'.[56] The book was launched shortly before the commemoration Weekend began,[57] at a press conference addressed by Mullan, Jane Winter, John Kelly and Linda Roddy of the Justice Campaign, and Hugh Kearney, one of the eyewitnesses, organized by the publishers to highlight and discuss the issues it raised. [58] Linda Roddy, in a powerful public statement, spelled out the book's impact and importance, and drew the political conclusion that ought to follow:

> Both I and other members of the Nash family are deeply disturbed and angered by the new evidence which has come to light through the research of Don Mullan in his book *Eyewitness Bloody Sunday* and which formed the basis of the recent Channel Four News Report on Bloody Sunday. Eyewitness accounts, allied to medical and ballistic opinion (corroborated by statements of soldiers and by police and army radio transcripts), point to the very real possibility that my brother William was shot by a British Army sniper in the vicinity of Derry's Walls. This is shocking and suggests a much more sinister dimension to his murder.
>
> The Nash family, with the support of the Bloody Sunday Justice Campaign, demands a full and independent open enquiry into the circumstances of the shooting dead of my unarmed brother William . . . [The Coroner] passed an open verdict on the death of William and everyone who died in Derry's Bogside on that afternoon. New evidence has come to light. The British Government has no option but to re-open the case. Failure to do so will be unforgivable.'[59]

The book's publication, and reaction to it in Derry, generated intense interest in the news media and was widely reported in its own right as well as within media coverage of the anniversary. Most importantly, its findings were publicized, 'rigorously investigated', and endorsed in a Bloody Sunday special report by the UK Channel 4 *News*, broadcast on 17 January

1997, which in Mullan's words 'stunned the British establishment into silence'.[60] In a series of further special reports, Channel 4's news team mounted a detailed critique of the Widgery Report and presented other evidence which weakened the official narrative. The impact of *Eyewitness* both stimulated and was in turn augmented by these investigations, which, together with Walsh's report, called into question established understandings in a kind of evidential chain reaction. According to Mullan, *Eyewitness Bloody Sunday* 'fused' together with these other 'powerful ingredients . . . making it possible to tell the full story of Bloody Sunday for the first time'.[61]

What *Eyewitness* uniquely succeeded in doing was to weave the new evidence that had emerged in 1997 into a coherent and cogent counter-narrative, which could be refined and clarified as subsequent revelations emerged. The original eyewitness testimonies, now re-read and reframed by the memory politics of 1997 in the knowledge of what followed, provided the basis of that narrative. Speaking about the importance of these testimonies in March 1997 in New York, John Kelly argued that they made possible 'our first step in placing Bloody Sunday on the international human rights agenda . . . [H]ere, twenty-five years ago, the British Government, through the British Information Service, issued to the world media a web of lies and misinformation . . . It is now our turn to tell our story and thankfully, at long last, the world seems ready to listen.'[62] In their public articulation of this story – the story those who survived Bloody Sunday had in a sense 'always known' – within the transnational arena of human rights, Mullan's book and the Justice Campaign worked symbiotically. *Eyewitness* handed the campaign the counter-narrative it needed to mobilize the widest and most powerful support possible, most crucially in the South: 'In the Republic as a result of Don's work, the issue of Bloody Sunday was being looked at differently.'[63] At the same time, according to Tony Doherty, the campaign 'was the clear impetus for all of this to happen; if the campaign hadn't have been there, arguably Don would not have worked on his book, and Channel Four wouldn't have picked up on it at all'. For Doherty, this potential to bring about a 'confluence' – whereby 'one good idea will attract another' so that '[p]eople working on ideas will ultimately start collaborating with others' – is the reason 'why grass roots activity is so important'.[64]

In addition to its impact on the development of the public counter-memory, *Eyewitness Bloody Sunday* also had a profound effect on personal and shared memory among the relatives and throughout the nationalist communities of the city. Within two weeks of going on sale, the book topped the bestsellers list at Eason's all-Ireland chain of bookshops. An Eason's spokesperson described it as having done 'roaring trade' on its day of release, with steady sales maintained subsequently throughout Northern Ireland but particularly in Derry: 'We have been somewhat surprised by the books [*sic*] popularity outside Derry but in terms of the city itself it has been selling at a phenomenal and unprecedented rate', and promised to be 'among the most popular of the year'.[65] In less than two years a second edition had appeared. Readers of the book discovered it to be a deeply disturbing text with the power to shock, evoke memories, provoke debate and galvanize action.

Within the city, the book's impact was sweeping. According to Raymond McClean: 'When Don Mullan's book came out, around the twenty-fifth anniversary, it was the first time a large number of people in this town started talking about the events, and where they were and what happened.'[66] Its launch, like McCann's, provided an occasion for reunions that triggered personal memories, such as Bishop Daly's emotional meeting with Michael Bridge: 'Micky was shot beside me. It was the first time we have met in 20 years or more.'[67] Having attended the launch, Fr Joseph Carolan, a curate at St Mary's in 1972, and hitherto 'hesitant about bringing up the past because of the pain and deep bitterness it can evoke', was moved for the first time to give his own eyewitness account, struck by 'how important it was that all available evidence about what happened on Bloody Sunday should be made available'.[68] The publication provided the occasion for other events at which people could meet and memories circulate. One such event was Mullan's presentation of a copy of the book to his former principal at St Joseph's Secondary School in the Creggan: the ceremony in the school's library, photographed by the *Derry Journal*, was attended by Michael McKinney for the Justice Campaign, the current principal, two Politics A-level students at the school, and the vice-principal, Kevin McCallion, whose statement is published in the book, bearing witness that 'the soldiers on Derry Walls opened fire and continued firing while . . . we crawled on all fours behind the wall'.[69] The event provides a fascinating glimpse of the kinds of cross-generational identifications and exchanges that the book helped to generate. For the successor generation that had been born and grown up in Derry since 1972, the voices of the survivors who speak again in Mullan's book offered a powerful, and apparently direct and unmediated, connection to local experiences of Bloody Sunday. For the survivors and eye-witnesses themselves, reading *Eyewitness Bloody Sunday* could be an ambivalent, even deeply disturbing, experience. For Nell McCafferty, the journalist who 'took shelter in a house at Glenfada Park and saw Jim Wray fall to the ground outside the living room window', reading Mullan forced her to reassess her personal memory of Bloody Sunday, and created a need to establish a new basis for subjective composure:

> I always believed the man behind him, who was also shot, had died. The new evidence tells me that man survived and I would very much like to meet and talk to him about why I did not open the door. The bathroom window of the house next to mine was riddled with 15 bullets. I will be there this weekend and would love to meet him.[70]

The intimation here is of survivor guilt, provoked afresh by the new knowledge, that disturbs whatever narrative has been fashioned to compose the experience, and gives rise to a desire for a new narrative; in this case, one that can be shared with the living man to whom McCafferty feels herself newly connected.

The book also had profound effects on many of the relatives, especially those, like Betty Walker (the sister of Michael McDaid), whose personal narrative of Bloody Sunday was turned upside-down by Mullan's revelations: 'Until Don Mullan's book, we took it for granted that Michael was shot by soldiers at ground level. Now it seems he was one of the the the three young men who was hit by an Army sniper on the Derry walls overlooking the Bogside.'[71] Linda Roddy, who spoke publicly at the book launch about the Nash family's anger at what they had read, described elsewhere what this meant personally: 'Because of Don Mullan's book and the eyewitness statements, we discovered that my brother had lived for 5–10 minutes. That was hard to take. When I told my father [Alex Nash] what I had discovered, he said, "How could I have ever told your mother?" It was better that she thought he died instantly' – which she had done until her own death in 1979.[72] Roddy realized that her father had 'always kept those awful last moments from us but now we know. I go to bed at night and I can almost hear [my brother] squealing and moaning'.[73] The Indian anthropologist Veena Das has proposed the concept of 'poisonous knowledge' to describe the effects of a traumatic event that has 'brutally injured' one's being but cannot be narrated, so exists in the psyche not as a memory but as a fixed moment to which horror remains attached.[74] According to Victoria Sanford, 'public speaking of truth is a transformation of "poisonous knowledge" into a collective discourse of empowerment'.[75] However, if 'poisonous knowledge' is a fitting way to describe Alex Nash's unnarratable experience, the discovery and telling of the truth about this experience in the context of a collective campaign for justice seems in this case to be less than empowering. Rather, the new knowledge gained from the testimonies published in Mullan undercuts an existing memory narrative and the subjective composure (of whatever degree) enabled by it, generating a newly imagined scene of horror and releasing fresh painful emotions, which require further psychic work if they are to be absorbed. This is also in a sense poisonous knowledge, insofar as it ruptures the sense of a shared family narrative based on Alex Nash's silence, which protected his wife and children from its telling, but also finally exposes them, like the narrator in Seamus Deane's novel *Reading in the Dark*, to the poisonous effects of a family secret revealed.[76]

Truth that empowers politically in the public arena may also have complex and ambivalent ramifications in the private. In its duel impact – the political impetus it gave to the Justice Campaign, and its stimulus to personal, often emotionally charged, and sometimes cross-generational remembering across the city – Mullan's book, like McCann's *Remember Bloody Sunday* in relation to the 1992 event, helped to colour the mood of the commemoration of the twenty-fifth anniversary of Bloody Sunday.

The twenty-fifth anniversary commemoration and the overturning of Widgery, 1997

The 1997 Weekend secured collective identification with the counter-memory of injustice on an unprecedented scale. It began on Thursday 30 January 1997 and culminated on Sunday 2 February in a march of some 40,000 people: equivalent to nearly one-third of the entire population of Derry, and 'the biggest gathering the city has ever seen'.[77] The march set off half an hour late from Creggan Shops due to the numbers, with more people joining it en route. It stretched for one and a half miles and took two hours to reach Free Derry Corner: as the front of the march reached the Bogside Inn, its rear was still in Creggan, and the rally had to be delayed for an hour to allow the rest of the march to arrive, eventually beginning before all had reached Rossville Street. The organizing committee's estimate of numbers was based on photographs showing the size of the crowd packed close together from Free Derry Corner to Pilots Row Community Centre, double that of the 1992 march, for which figures of 15,000—20,000 were accepted.[78]

In his analysis, Tony Doherty, spokesperson for that year's Bloody Sunday commemoration rally organizing committee, identified three factors responsible for 'bringing nationalists onto the streets' in such vast numbers: firstly, the special resonance of the twenty-fifth anniversary of Bloody Sunday; secondly, the recent emergence of new evidence – centrally, as the *Derry Journal* reported, the 'publication of Don Mullan's book' – which 'meant public awareness and interest was heightened'; but also, thirdly, 'a growing disquiet among the people of Derry in relation to the mess that the British government has made of recent attempts to find peace in Ireland'.[79] A further reason may have been a sense of the political importance of nationalists establishing their presence on the streets in the context of the escalating clashes over loyalist parades, most significantly at Drumcree in 1995 and 1996, but also in Derry itself where violent confrontations had occurred between Bogside residents and the Apprentice Boys.[80] These factors had coalesced to produce that 'heightened awareness' of the political significance of Bloody Sunday envisaged by the BSI eight years earlier; a collective consciousness that had manifested itself on the streets of Derry 'in numbers reminiscent of rallies organised during the hunger strikes in the 1980s'[81] – that is, as meriting comparison with the largest and most effective political demonstrations ever organized by the nationalist community in the North of Ireland. Politically, the twenty-fifth anniversary march amounted to a public demonstration of mass popular support for the relatives' demand for a new inquiry.

However, while Doherty emphasizes the altered political consciousness manifest at the event and culminating in the mass rally, the twenty-fifth anniversary weekend was also an emotionally charged event, pervaded by powerful psychic currents that not only fed into the political groundswell but were also given expression in numerous other moments and modes of remembrance. This complex of contradictory feelings, memories and reflections was recognized and acknowledged publicly by participants and commentators, many of whom drew on the language of 'trauma' and 'emotion' to reflect on what was taking place inside as well as all around them. The main speaker at the rally, Sinn Féin's Martin McGuinness, remarked that it had been 'one of the most emotional weeks for Derry since the actual shootings'.[82] That was certainly true for survivors of the attack, such as Mickey Bradley, one of the Bloody Sunday wounded, who said of the march: 'It's very emotional. It brings back so many memories.'[83] An unnamed woman told the *Belfast Telegraph* of the strength of feeling that had impelled her to take part in her first commemoration march in twenty-five years: 'This is the first time I have marched since Bloody Sunday. I had to come out today – particularly after the British government ignored the new evidence which proved what we all saw with our own eyes that day.'[84] But such emotions were not restricted to eyewitnesses and survivors of Bloody Sunday: as Michael McKinney put it, speaking from the platform on behalf of the Justice Campaign, 'the turnout showed that the sadness of the occasion could be shared with others'.[85] This sense of participating in a collective, ritual sharing of sadness, anger and hope of redress permeated not only the rally, but the whole Weekend's events, and extended beyond survivors to the younger, 'successor', generation and to visitors to the city.

One important public arena where public expression and recognition of psychic realities became possible was a meeting organized by the Weekend committee for the Saturday morning in Pilot's Row Community Centre in the Bogside, at which 'local people will remember Bloody Sunday, and give eyewitness accounts of what happened on the day'.[86] Eamonn McCann gave an introductory talk setting the political context of Bloody Sunday, and the exchange and discussion of eyewitness stories was co-ordinated by Don Mullan. The event became a channel for the powerful, emotive remembering triggered in the city by his book. This atmosphere was registered in McCann's Introduction, which analysed the military operation on Bloody Sunday as an attempt by the Unionist Government of Northern Ireland to save itself from collapse by 'clamp[ing] down on nationalist protests', and situated it within a pattern of fatal shootings of nationalists by the British Army in Derry in previous months.[87] Here, however, McCann went on to describe how 'Derry was also emotionally charged' at the time of the civil rights march, since only the week before an open verdict had been returned at the Inquest into the killing of Annette McGavigan, a 14-year-old schoolgirl shot dead by the army in September 1971 in Abbey Street,[88] a few yards from Rossville Flats, 'as she attempted to get a rubber bullet for her collection of riot souvenirs'.[89] The British Army had denied responsibility for the shooting, claimed that its soldiers had been returning fire from IRA gunmen, and blamed the IRA for McGavigan's death. The IRA had issued a statement that its volunteers in the area had thrown nailbombs at the soldiers but had not fired a bullet, and local people were adamant that the girl had been shot by a British soldier.[90] McCann, in making reference to the memory of Annette McGavigan, identified the psychic effects of the British military occupation even before Bloody Sunday, in the earliest stages of what would become the complex over-layering and compacting of trauma and grief visited on the Bogside during the Troubles. In circumstances where each and every shocking event is succeeded by another, the time and space for grieving is closed down, giving rise to the peculiarly impacted and 'frozen' formation of traumatic memory identified by counsellors such as Sandra Peake of WAVE.

In psychic terms, the overtly emotive quality of proceedings during the 1997 commemoration can be understood as a collective 'unfreezing' of feelings attached to memories of events from twenty-five years ago; a shared process of reparative remembering which Mullan's publication of the eyewitness statements, with their potent connection back across the years, played an important part in triggering. The Pilot's Row meeting of 1 February appears to have provided an arena and an occasion for exactly this kind of unlocking and opening of remembrance, effecting a transformation of the fixed and the inaccessible into something fluid and expressible. 'Beginning with the gathering at Bishop's Field different people told of their experiences on the day', in what the *Derry Journal* reported as 'a moving and poignant discussion':[91]

> At times the meeting was charged with emotion as eyewitnesses recounted the deaths of the various victims of Bloody Sunday. Some of the accounts had never been told publicly before and some of those who tended the dying and the injured told in graphic detail what they had experienced. One of the organizers said afterwards: 'It was almost as if people had been afraid to start talking about what happened to them that day in case they couldn't stop.'[92]

In contributing to this exchange, participants may have been motivated, as was Fr Carolan, by a desire to contibute in their own small way to establishing the truth about Bloody Sunday, following in the footsteps of those original eyewitnesses. Indeed, a 'video voice box' was set up throughout the afternoon in the community centre 'to allow people to record their memories . . . [to] be added to the Bloody Sunday archive which is being collected'.[93] But deep psychic needs were also being addressed through this practice, as increasing numbers of the traumatized community seized the opportunity to tell their personal story, articulate their feelings, and secure public recognition and affirmation in a safe space where many different experiences and relationships to the events of the day were able to be validated. The *Journal*'s report of eyewitnesses' detailed recall of traumatic scenes, the fact that some were speaking publicly for the first time and, above all, the image of floodgates of memory opening, in a release from fears of being overwhelmed or swept away on an unstoppable wave of talk all point towards the event as a 'space to grieve'; as if collective mourning had been unleashed after twenty-five years of containment.

The 1997 commemoration not only released such psychic energies but, in doing so, simultaneously channelled them politically into the campaign for human rights and justice. This, indeed, was the very condition of the release.

The Justice Campaign offered the means to *detoxify* memories of fear, horror and loss, transforming them into hope for justice, redress and peace. This 'magical' transformation – in reality, depending on an uncompleted and fraught politics – was enacted in the dignified symbolic rituals of the commemoration, which extended the new forms of protest introduced earlier in the 1990s in increasingly imaginative directions. To mark the moment when the shooting stopped twenty-five years earlier, the relatives, borrowing the ritual form from Armistice Day commemoration, called for the observance of a two-minute silence across the city at 4.30 p.m. on 30 January, which duly took place – on the nationalist west bank.[94] The following day, utilizing the symbolism used in previous Weekends, relatives from the fourteen families each planted an oak tree (a fifteenth was planted on behalf of the wounded who had died since 1972) in a special commemorative ceremony at Creggan Reservoir officiated by the Bishop of Derry, Seamus Hegarty, and his predecessor, Bishop Edward Daly (who wore the stole that he had last worn during the Bloody Sunday collective funeral service).[95] A spokesperson for the organizers of the event, the Creggan festival committee, said: 'These oak trees symbolise hope . . . We just hope that before these small trees reach maturity, justice will have been served.' The trees were planted on part of the site of the new Creggan Country Park, envisaged as a 'living memorial to those who died', with 'a wall and seats for people in the future to reflect upon the tragedy of Bloody Sunday'.[96]

As in 1992, the march and rally were also permeated by the symbolic language of political ritual. Children and young people were prominently involved, including relatives aged from five to twenty-five who walked at the head of the march carrying named white crosses or poster-sized portraits of their dead uncle, great-uncle or grandfather, in a living image of the cross-generational extension of collective memory.[97] On arrival at Free Derry Corner – the symbolic centre of the memorial space established in the Bogside to reclaim and detoxify the sites of trauma – they lined up to display these portraits in front of the stage.[98] Other young relatives displayed portraits of the dead, each on a four-metre banner, held high on the Fahan Street embankment directly under the city's Walls from where Army snipers had fired on the marchers below at Free Derry Corner, Rossville Street and Glenfada Park, where the vast crowd now assembled.[99] In Westmoreland Street, younger and older supporters of the Justice Campaign together staged a symbolic enactment of their desire to break through the barrier to truth created by Widgery's words, overthrow his conclusions and walk into a just future by bursting through a banner bearing a reproduction of the title page of the Widgery Report.[100] For members of the ageing survivor generation, the participation of these young people was the guarantee that the killings would be remembered. Michael McKinney of the Justice Campaign, speaking from the platform, said:

> I will not let them forget their bloody murder on Derry's streets . . . Mr Mayhew [British Secretary of State for Northern Ireland] can bury his head in the sand

for as long as he likes. I can assure him that the relatives of the Bloody Sunday dead will still be here when he looks up . . . For us to forget it is to deny our own humanity.[101]

After the speeches, the rally listened to a public reading of a poem composed by two 21-year-old Bogsiders, Killian Mullan and Sharon Meenan:

I remember people happy and the confidence of that morning.
The Creggan Shops.
I remember the banner that was carried.
The gathered message.
I remember live fire.
A pool of blood on the pavement.
I remember Hugh Gilmour and Patrick Doherty.
I remember running. The Flats.
I remember Jim Wray and Michael McDaid.
I remember screaming.
English accents.
I remember William Nash and Gerald McKinney.
I remember a crazed army.
A white hanky.
I remember Michael Kelly and John Young.
I remember it black and white. But blood is always red.
I remember Jackie Duddy and Bernard McGuigan.
I remember looking for my friend from the confusion and then through the quiet.
I remember Gerald Donaghy and Kevin McElhinney.
I remember hearing the news.
I remember John Johnston and William McKinney.
I remember thirteen coffins. Black flags.
I remember a young woman with an old face.
The funerals.
I remember my father crying hot angry tears.
I remember the lies.
And I wasn't even born.[102]

The repeated refrain 'I remember' establishes a voice that speaks in the first-person singular to evoke the story of Bloody Sunday in a sequence of brief motifs representing moments and experiences of the march, the massacre and its immediate aftermath. Intercut with these fragments of memory, the 'I' of the poem also remembers the fourteen dead, calling out their names in pairs, in a ritual incantation that echoes the form of the creed in the Catholic Mass.[103] (As each name was spoken, the banner bearing that person's image was raised in the air by other relatives on the embankment above.[104]) Only in the final line does the speaker reveal that this is the voice not of personal survivor testimony, but of the not-yet-born, advancing a claim to 'remember' personally so as to reinforce the moral imperative not to forget. The poem had been published and circulated widely in the city prior to the commemoration, in the special Bloody Sunday Supplement of the *Derry Journal* and in the leaflet produced by the commemoration committee, where it was presented as evidence of the effectiveness of the counter-memory of injustice, successfully reproduced over twenty-five years, and now taken up by 'the younger generation . . . [of] people who weren't even born before January 1972', but who 'have had the collective memory of the event etched into their young consciousness'.[105] This image of 'etching', however, is an overly passive description of the subjective identification made by a successor generation with the collective memory of its predecessors.[106]

In laying claim to a personal memory of events that took place before they were born, the young poets exemplify what Marianne Hirsch has termed 'postmemory', characterizing 'the experience of those who grow up dominated by narratives that preceded their birth . . . the stories of the previous generation'.[107] For the new generations born in the Bogside and the Creggan since 30 January 1972, local collective memory of the event and its aftermath is actively taken on and made their own, in a cross-generational exchange mediated through stories, images and participation in commemorative rituals, both public and private. Unlike the case of the Holocaust families in Hirsch's work, however, the collective 'postmemory' of Bloody Sunday appears to be experienced by significant numbers of the successor generations less as a burden than as a positive identification with a living, current struggle for peace, truth and justice.[108]

Mediated by shared, private memory as well as cultural representations in public arenas, Mullan and Meenan's poem draws intertextually upon a range of motifs which feature pervasively in the social life of stories and visual images concerned with Bloody Sunday, and shape the personal remembering of individuals from the survivor as well as the successor generation. Its remembered image of 'a white hanky', for example, is derived from several different modes and channels, both public and private, through which a collective memory of Bloody Sunday has been articulated and reproduced. It is mediated through the stories of survivors: told locally and circulating within the fluid narratives of shared memory, reported publicly in media coverage like the *Derry Journal*'s Bloody Sunday Supplement, and recovered through the publication of original written testimonies, including Fr Daly's, in Mullan's book, *Eyewitness*. The 'I' of the poem remembers through these stories, but also through the visual documentary record of Fr Daly and the group carrying Jack Duddy, in photographs and film that have been endlessly recycled in broadcast news coverage, press reports and documentaries, reproduced in campaigning literature and 'plastered [on] the walls of the Bogside'.[109] These representations from public arenas have also found their way into the private arenas of the family, where they were preserved in the homes of local people: Sharon Meenan remembers one of her aunts keeping a collection of black-and-white photographs of Bloody Sunday in a scrapbook, and recalls discovering, as a child, a copy of Grimaldi and North's *Blood in the Street* – one of the earliest publications about Bloody Sunday, featuring testimonies, photographs and interviews with local people – under a bed in her grandmother's house.[110]

3 'Bloody Sunday' mural by the Bogside Artists, depicting Jack Duddy carried
from the killing ground, led by Father Daly.

The image of Fr Daly and his white hanky also occupied a prominent location at the centre of the march and rally in 1997, in the form of a huge commemorative mural to Bloody Sunday situated on the gable-end of new
housing facing into Rossville Street, adjacent to Free Derry Wall. In 1995,
the local Bogside Artists incorporated Grimaldi's famous photograph as the
centrepiece of this mural, interweaving it with other images: the civil rights
march itself, and – to the left of the central group – a threatening figure of a
paratrooper, modelled on Stanley Matchett's photograph of the encounter
between the group carrying Duddy and armed soldiers, and positioned here
as if watching his dying victim carried away (see figure 3). The mural inte-
grates these three photographic memories into a composite image, rendered
in black-and-white as if quoting the originals, but picks out in red the now-
bloodstained and crumpled civil rights banner, trampled underfoot by the
soldier. The poem's line 'I remember it black and white. But blood is always
red' acknowledges the mediated quality of its visual postmemory and the
representations that provide its source, whilst also affirming the power of the
informed imagination to bring to life these traces of the past by recreating a
link to the human realities that they embody. As the poem culminates with
the final, decisive, political point of this postmemory, 'I remember the lies',
local collective memory of the survivor generation is mobilized as a narrative for those born subsequently to appropriate, to identify with and to
promote: that of the fight for justice.

Underlying the participation of young people in the symbolic rituals of the 1997 commemoration are these practices of postmemory which produce active, imaginative identifications with the Bloody Sunday collective 'we', capable of bonding survivor and successor generations into a common mobilization. The power of the ritual march and rally in channelling these identifications, psychically and politically, into a 'sectional' collective memory 'with the potential to secure political effects'[111] is neatly encapsulated in the *Derry Journal*'s headline: '40,000 in call for justice'.[112] However, the terms 'personal memory' and 'postmemory' signify differences in the subjective relation of the survivor and successor generations to this collective memory. While both generations might share a sense of moral obligation to the dead, for survivors the imperative to remember in the form of a campaign for justice is also a response to the complex, troubled psychic and emotional repercussions of Bloody Sunday which they have suffered in their own lives and shared with others over decades.

There is a driven quality, as if internally compelled, about the commitment of the Bloody Sunday survivors to the fight for justice, which serves, together with its moral and political objectives, a reparative function, making good the damage inflicted on the internal world by this state atrocity and its cover-up. During the 1997 commemoration, Kay Duddy described how the anniversary had brought back 'terrible, terrible memories', but then went on to express the hope: 'Perhaps when we have had their names cleared we can come to terms with it and finally lay them to rest.'[113] Speaking of his own testimony to the reconvened Public Inquiry that opened in 2000 under Lord Saville, Bishop Daly commented: 'While I have my own needs to tell the story, one has to speak for a lot of people. I feel that burden very much – for Jack Duddy particularly.'[114] For members of the survivor generation, their own personal 'need to tell the story' and the 'burden' of speaking on behalf of others are perhaps indistinguishable.

Trauma, truth and justice: the war over memory and the Saville Inquiry

The emotion channelled into politics by the 1997 commemoration was focused on the call for the British Government to repudiate the Widgery Report and initiate a reinvestigation of Bloody Sunday by means of a new judicial inquiry. This was pursued formally when on 30 January, as the anniversary was marked and the Bloody Sunday Weekend commenced in Derry, the families lodged papers in the Belfast High Court seeking a judicial review based on the new evidence; while on that same day in London, John Hume tabled an early-day motion in the House of Commons calling on the Prime Minister, John Major, to initiate a new investigation into 'one of the worst atrocities' of the conflict in the light of the new evidence,[115] in order 'to exorcise the bitter memories of 25 years'.[116] Referring to a letter written to him by Major in 1992, Hume asked: 'Given that [the Prime Minister] has told me in writing that those who were killed on Bloody

Sunday should be regarded as innocent of any allegation that they were shot
while handling firearms or explosives, if that is the case could he please tell
me why they were shot and – if he doesn't know – does he not think
it requires public investigation?'[117] Over sixty-five MPs voted for the
motion.[118]

Hume's request also had cross-party support in the Irish *Dáil* and, in a
reversal of earlier official espousals of state-organized forgetting, was backed
by the *Fine Gael*–Labour Coalition Government of the Republic. Statements
followed from the *Taoiseach*, John Bruton, and from the *Tanaiste*, Dick
Spring, who described the new evidence as 'extremely significant and very
serious, and . . . certainly in conflict with the findings of the Widgery
Tribunal'.[119] The support of the Irish Government had been won by lobbying during 1996 by the Justice Campaign, which had argued that Bloody
Sunday was 'an issue that needed to be resolved and would always be a
major injustice and therefore a barrier to lasting peace' until it was resolved;
and that 'a resolution . . . would be beneficial for everyone concerned, not
just in Ireland, but in Britain'.[120] Spring had directed the compilation of the
Irish Government's own dossier, which was presented to the British
Government in 1996, summarizing the new evidence and making the case
for a new inquiry with an international dimension.[121]

Despite this pressure, and the mounting new evidence (including new testimony by British soldiers, moved by Mullan's book, concerning army
sniping from Derry's Walls, broadcast on Channel 4's *News* on 30
January), Major replied to Hume in the House of Commons on 31 January
by ruling out any re-opening of the Inquiry.[122] His grounds were that the
killings had been 'very fully investigated by the [Widgery] Tribunal', and
no 'fresh and relevant evidence' had yet been presented to the Government
for consideration.[123] Referring to *Eyewitness Bloody Sunday*, Secretary of
State Mayhew told Jeremy Corbyn, MP, 'that it was surprising that any
fresh evidence had not been submitted to the authorities before it was published in a book'.[124] The mass-demonstration at the 1997 commemoration
was in response to Major's rebuff. However, the possibilities for moving
the Justice Campaign forward were by now dependent on restarting the
stalled political peace process. From Dublin, Spring repeated his call to
investigate 'the new evidence that has been brought forward – and to do so
as quickly as possible', and Bruton announced in the *Dáil* that the Irish
Government would pursue the matter with the British authorities during
forthcoming all-party talks, 'at the highest political level'.[125] According to
Tony Doherty, in late 1996 and in 1997 Bloody Sunday became 'a recurring item on the agenda for the British–Irish inter-parliamentary council
and the Anglo-Irish secretariat in Maryfield. We also understand that it was
raised by Martin McGuinness with the British on several occasions.'[126] In
October 1997, relatives from the Justice Campaign met the new *Taoiseach*
Bertie Ahern to discuss initial response from the British Government to the
1996 dossier.[127]

Speaking from the platform at the 1997 rally, Martin McGuinness, the party's chief negotiator, reaffirmed Sinn Féin's commitment to political dialogue despite the resumption of the IRA's armed campaign: 'There are two roads before us, the road to further conflict and the road to the negotiating table. We have declared ourselves for the road to the negotiating table.'[128] Comparing the impasse in Ireland with the successful process of transition from apartheid in South Africa, McGuinness argued that leadership was required, not only from Republicans, but from Unionists and, most of all, from the British Government: 'we need a de Klerk to emerge from Number 10 Downing Street'.[129] Whether or not the Labour Prime Minister Tony Blair, elected in May 1997, fitted the billing as a British de Klerk, his new Government's energetic commitment to putting the peace process back on track led to the resumption of the IRA ceasefire in July 1997 and the opening in September of multi-party talks that included Sinn Féin. A new initiative concerned with the victims of violence followed later that year. This renewed momentum in the peace process, involving close co-operation between the two governments at the highest level, created the context in which the British Government finally conceded ground on Bloody Sunday. In January 1998, the Justice Campaign's skilful alliance-building, linked to independent historical research and critical analysis of the Widgery Report, supported by the annual commemoration attracting tens of thousands of people, bore fruit when Tony Blair's Government announced a new investigation into the events of Bloody Sunday. This would not be the independent international inquiry called for by the civil rights movement in 1972 and repeated by the Justice Campaign in 1997, but an unprecedented re-opening of its own Tribunal of Inquiry to reinvestigate the shootings, 'taking into account any new information relevant to events on that day', to sit in Derry under Lord Saville of Newdigate and two other judges from outside Britain.[130]

To have secured from a British Government this unprecedented re-opening of the Inquiry, in itself an acknowledgement of official misgivings about Lord Widgery's verdict, was an extraordinary victory for the Justice Campaign. Heralded by the Government as an expression of its serious commitment to the Irish peace process, a major contribution towards 'overcom[ing] the legacy of history and . . . heal[ing] the divisions which have resulted', the Saville Inquiry was presented by the Prime Minister as 'the way forward to the necessary reconciliation . . . to establish the truth, and close this painful chapter once and for all'.[131] Situated in the Guildhall, the symbolic former civic centre of Derry and the unattained goal of Bloody Sunday's marchers, the new Inquiry was seen by nationalists and Republicans primarily as the means to hold the British State accountable to the people of the city, in the city, for the crimes of its army perpetrated in the city, twenty-six years earlier. For Bogsiders, the desired outcome was not so much the discovery of the truth about the deaths of their loved ones as its acknowledgement, and with this a recognition of the injustice inflicted by the State on the dead, the injured and the bereaved (see figure 4).[132]

4 'Time for truth': candlelit march from the Bogside to the Derry Guildhall,
Sunday 26 March 2000.

The existence of this hard-won Tribunal of Inquiry, however, has brought into focus further important questions. One concerns the relation of *the truth* to be established and narrated in the eventual Saville Report and *the truths* articulated in other social arenas where competing versions of Derry's contested past are represented and recognized. Bloody Sunday has continued to be dismissed as Republican propaganda within Protestant and Unionist culture during the peace process.[133] In the battle over the memory of the Troubles, which since the ceasefires of 1994 has taken the form of the politics of victimhood,[134] Unionist and loyalist opposition to the Saville Inquiry – as a one-sided sop to buy nationalist and Republican support for the peace process – has been vociferous.[135] Explicit Unionist contestation of nationalist sectional memory of Bloody Sunday occurred during the Saville hearings when, for example, the former deputy-leader of the Ulster Unionist Party, John Taylor, now Lord Kilclooney, told the Inquiry, 'I believed [at the time . . .] and still do' that the thirteen dead were IRA gunmen, and claimed: 'Nationalists were drinking and celebrating because of what had happened and because they knew it would bring about the fall of the Stormont parliament.'[136] It is questionable whether the Saville Report, long expected but still unpublished in April 2007, will further acknowledgement among Ulster Protestants of the seriousness of the state violation of fundamental human rights with respect to Bloody Sunday, and of the character, extent and depth of nationalist suffering in Derry as a result.

A second set of questions concerns the character of the Saville Inquiry as a public arena constituted in terms of the discourse of the law. While Lord Saville pursued the truth with far greater alacrity and integrity than had Widgery, his Tribunal, as a judicial arena constituted under the same Tribunals of Inquiry Act, posed similar difficulties for the relatives and survivors as a forum in which they sought institutional recognition for their stories. Participation in this judicial arena has made intense emotional demands on and posed significant psychic risks for the Bloody Sunday families and those civilians who have testified before the Tribunal.[137] Many of the relatives have closely followed proceedings involving the detailed reconstruction of the circumstances in which their loved ones died, conducted in the full glare of the global media, in the course of protracted public hearings that commenced on 27 March 2000 and concluded four years later, in February 2004. Some have welcomed the way that 'people are getting the chance to tell their stories . . . denied at the Widgery farce', seen as 'equally important for the soldiers' too;[138] and the opportunities for 'learning something . . . it's like piecing together a jigsaw puzzle'.[139] Yet others, like Regina McKinney, have spoken of the anxiety and psychic conflict generated for their families by the Inquiry: 'it opens up the wound again . . . we would want to know what really happened. It's our place to know about my daddy. But we are scared to hear the truth, how he died.'[140] The emotional difficulties of sustaining an active involvement in such circumstances, especially given the length of the process and the weight of expectation and need invested in it, has been formidable; witnesses have been 'under great stress' and 'sometimes collapse[d] through reliving the emotion and trauma of seeing people being murdered before their very eyes';[141] and the new evidence has, at times, been 'overwhelming'.[142]

Such pressures and conflicts have been intensified by ordinary civilians' unfamiliarity with legal language and procedures,[143] difficulties encountered by the families and civilian eyewitnesses in securing adequate legal representation, and the approach adopted by lawyers acting for the MoD.[144] Like Widgery, these lawyers have treated the Inquiry as an adversarial arena and fought to defend the British Army and its personnel against the allegations made against them, rather than participating in a co-operative endeavour to establish the truth. Key evidence was destroyed by the MoD shortly before the new Inquiry was announced.[145] Under its pressure, the Tribunal agreed to grant anonymity to the British soldiers who testified, on grounds of risk to their security should their identities become known, despite local insistence that accountability required their open appearance as witnesses, and the fact that the identities of many of the soldiers had long been public knowledge in Derry.[146] Public Interest Immunity Certificates were used to prevent the disclosure of information by intelligence agents.[147] Most damagingly, Counsel for the British Army sought to undermine the testimony of civilian eyewitnesses by discrediting their characters[148] and engaging in hostile cross-examination, during which some were 'made out to be . . .

liar[s] on the stand'[149] and found themselves 'defending their own integrity and their own life. You'd think they were on trial for a murder charge.'[150] The sense of disempowerment experienced by relatives is best expressed by Liam Wray: 'It hurt to watch the lawyers for the Army protect the guilty, even though I knew it was their job. I am very tired, quite disillusioned, angry that the inhumanity of what happened has been lost in the legal arguments.'[151] For many of the relatives and their supporters, these experiences have compromised the integrity of the Saville Inquiry. Instead of the 'open and transparent Inquiry' promised by the British Government in January 1998, 'we've seen the Army trying to make it as difficult as possible for the Inquiry to get to the truth'.[152] Optimism and hope for the vindication of their loved ones has been replaced with scepticism and concern that the MoD has treated the Inquiry as a 'damage-limitation exercise'.[153] For many, the Tribunal's credibility was finally destroyed by Saville's decision to move the hearings in September 2002 to Westminster Central Hall, in London, in order to take evidence from some 300 British soldiers as well as senior politicians, again out of a – questionable – concern for their security;[154] thereby violating the key principle that the Inquiry would be conducted, and the British establishment held accountable, before the citizens of Derry City on their own home ground.

It remains to be seen whether the Saville Tribunal will clear the names of those killed and call to account those responsible for their deaths. Mary Donaghey is one of those who have made a powerful emotional investment in its so doing: 'Can the Army not come out and admit that they were wrong? I don't think it would hurt them. I know [Bloody Sunday] may be in the past, but until justice is done I cannot forgive anybody.'[155] Yet such statements provoke reflection about the psychic aftermath of abuses of power, committed by a state like the UK, for its living victims many years after the event; and they involve questions about the process – indeed the very possibility – of recovering from or coming to terms with its traumatic consequences. Others have doubted from the beginning that 'the new Bloody Sunday inquiry will remove . . . [t]he hurt [that] is still in the community'.[156] Even were Saville to provide a vindication of the dead, there is no guarantee that this will have beneficial psychic effects on the living survivors. Tony Doherty believes that 'the opportunity for reconciliation has been damaged for the ordinary person' by the adversarial conduct of the Inquiry. For Doherty, 'the law is an imperfect vehicle for getting at the truth, particularly when . . . dealing with historical injustice. When the time comes and we have the final report, people will have to deal in resolute terms with closing the issue.'[157] After the Saville Inquiry is closed, for the survivors of Bloody Sunday, the emotional as well as the political work of absorbing and moving on from its conclusions, will be carried out primarily where this work has always taken place: in the local cultural landscape of the Bogside and the Creggan, where life goes on in and around the invisible 'killing grounds'. The question remains open as to whether, for those who have experienced such events and then lived with their aftermath for so long, the places of atrocity and trauma can ever really be exorcized of their ghosts, whatever the success of political campaigning for commemoration, truth and justice.

In 2007, Bloody Sunday remains a marker of wider nationalist aspirations to secure a just peace, and the Saville Inquiry a test-case of the British State's willingness to undertake a fundamental reassessment of its own role in the conflict, with all the implications this would hold for transforming its relationship to Ireland, North and South. However, after Saville, memory work on Bloody Sunday will also continue in a necessary engagement with Unionist memory. This process, underway since at least 1995, was a key theme at the 2006 commemoration weekend, where debates focused on the development of inclusive acknowledgement and recognition with respect to all the victims of the war, including those of the IRA.[158] In Part III, I turn to examine Protestant and Unionist memories of the IRA's armed campaign along the Border, and consider its psychic legacies, as well as the ways in which it has featured, like Bloody Sunday, at the heart of the politics of memory in the Troubles.

Part III

'The forgotten victims'? Border Protestants and the memory of terror

Those of us who have carried the wounds and the scars of their activities have been left, still with the pain. And there didn't seem to be any justice. There was a feeling throughout the Border counties that something will have to be done in order to ensure that we as victims are not forgotten. (J.E. Hazlett Lynch, West Tyrone Voice, 2000).

7

The Troubles on the Border: Ulster–British identity and the cultural memory of 'ethnic cleansing'

Ireland today is partitioned by an international border. Established by the Government of Ireland Act of 1920 by the unitary State of the United Kingdom of Great Britain and Ireland, initially this divided the British juris-diction over Ireland as a whole into two administrative zones, each with devolved powers: a twenty-six-county 'Southern Ireland' centred on Dublin and a six-county 'Northern Ireland' centred on Belfast. The administrative boundary between these devolved jurisdictions was transformed into an international border as a result of the Anglo-Irish Treaty of 1921 which ended the Irish War of Independence (1919–21) and brought into existence the effectively independent Irish Free State (later to become the Republic of Ireland) in the 'Southern' jurisdiction. It also formalized the partition of Ireland in the form of a constitutional 'exclusion', enabling the six-county statelet of Northern Ireland, or 'Ulster', to opt out of the new Free State and remain within the UK. In 1925, following the collapse of the Boundary Commission set up under the terms of the Treaty to consider the exact loca-tion of the divide, the Border was established on a permanent basis.[1]

International borders constitute real geopolitical divisions between states and peoples. They also have powerful shaping effects on what Edward Said has termed 'imaginative geographies': those 'mental boundaries' that differ-entiate *our* space from *their* space, thereby constituting senses of identity and belonging that define and (potentially) exclude those others who are per-ceived to inhabit a different imaginative world composed of other remem-bered associations and attachments.[2] The establishment of borders demarcating the extent of territory and its human populations over which a state claims jurisdiction, and associated conflicts over nationality, sover-eignty and the rights of minorities, are thus fundamental to the formation of such 'boundaries in our own minds'.[3] However, imaginative geographies do not always correspond exactly to social and political boundaries. Read's concept of 'contested attachments' describes how 'rivals . . . dispute not only physical possession but others' rights of emotional attachment to the same place'.[4] Since its inception, the Border that split Ireland in two has generated contested attachments of this kind. The political identities of Irish national-ism and Ulster Unionism were redefined in relation to it, and their compet-ing imaginative geographies have constituted the ground of violent conflict in the first phase of the Troubles in 1919–23, and again since 1969. For Irish nationalists, the Border represented an unacceptable division of the sovereignty and territory of the newly independent Irish State. For most Ulster Unionists, the Border established a defensive bulwark guaranteeing the separation of a small section of territory and preserving its constitutional connection to Britain: the Union. Northern Ireland was constructed specifically to sustain the Union within the largest viable territory where Protestants and Unionists – a minority of 1:3 in Ireland as a whole – could establish a permanent 2:1 majority, and thereby maintain political, economic and cultural domination, over a Catholic, nationalist minority.[5] The complex patterns of local settlement prevailing throughout the north of Ireland, in which the Catholic and Protestant populations lived in a 'patchwork' of largely endogamous but 'inextricably mixed' areas, meant that the Border could not align these political communities neatly each within its preferred state.[6] Rather, it severed both of them in two. As Joe Lee puts it: 'Partition had long existed in the mind. Now it existed on the map. But what a map! The geographical boundaries did not attempt to follow the mental boundaries.'[7]

This situation has had two fundamental effects. Firstly, in dividing the original nine-county province of Ulster in order to form the new six-county Northern Ireland, partition brought about a refiguring of Ulster Unionist identity which was predicated on an unresolved history of exclusion: that of Unionists in the three counties which came under the jurisdiction of the Irish Free State. Secondly, what I described in chapter 3 as the 'immurement' of Northern nationalists in the Catholic ghettoes of the six-county Unionist state was challenged in the 1960s, initially by the civil rights movement, but ultimately by an armed insurgency contesting the partition itself. In the course of the war since 1969, the Border areas were transformed into some of the most violent locations of conflict. Armed actions by the Provisional IRA to destabilize the Border, particularly during the period 1972–76, focused on the British State's security forces and on the local Protestant and Unionist communities from which many of their members were drawn. This created a popular perception in these communities that a campaign of 'ethnic cleansing', or 'genocide', was being waged to destroy the British cultural heritage and identity in the Border region. These experiences were understood in terms of a Protestant cultural memory of ethnic war reaching back through the period of partition and revolution in the early 1920s to the United Irishmen's rebellion of 1798, and on to the conflicts generated in response to the plantations of the seventeenth century. In the process, the experience of the Border Protestant communities has been generalized into a figure of the plight of Ulster Unionists throughout Northern Ireland.

Part III of this book examines memories of terror articulated by Border Protestants and Unionists in terms of this narrative of 'ethnic cleansing', and considers its relationship to remembering centred on affirmations of good-neighbourliness and desires for reparation and reconciliation, and to the narratives of nationalist memory. Chapter 7 investigates the significance of the

Border for the Ulster Protestants, and considers its relationship to their British identity, felt to be under threat of eradication by Irish Republicanism. It explores the traumatic splitting induced by the violence of the Republican armed struggle and examines how memories couched in terms of 'ethnic cleansing' have organized and expressed a response in which psychic and political aspects are interwoven. This complex subjective compound has been a constitutive factor in the construction of an Ulster–British heritage and identity *under siege*, while the Border itself, like the walled city of Londonderry, has come to symbolize the so-called 'siege-mentality' encapsulated in the popular loyalist slogan 'No Surrender!' By investigating the genealogy of this narrative, its centrality in Ulster–British collective memory and its powerful role in shaping Protestant, Unionist and loyalist subjectivities, major difficulties involved in conflict resolution and political transition in Northern Ireland may be brought into focus. The chapter concludes by considering processes of psychic and social reparation within Border Protestant communities, motivated by the peace process begun in 1994, that engage with both the traumatic effects of the Troubles and the unresolved legacies of partition.

British identity on the Border

In a string of villages and towns along the Clogher Valley in Co. Tyrone, two to three miles from the Border demarcating the limits of the UK State and the beginning of the Republic of Ireland, Union flags and red, white and blue bunting defiantly proclaim these communities at the 'edge of the Union' to be British territory: places with allegiance to the jurisdiction of the UK State, places of British identity.[8] Despite these public affirmations of affiliation and belonging, visible throughout the Border regions, the British-in-Ulster – perhaps especially those who live close to the Border – have a complicated relation to Britain and Britishness. Raymond Ferguson, former leader of the Co. Fermanagh Ulster Unionists, has argued: 'The term "British" . . . is not one with which the Protestant community is entirely comfortable. At least, not in the sense that members of that community readily and daily think of themselves as being British.'[9] For Ferguson, Britishness is a political identity that asserts Northern Ireland's constitutional connection to Britain and its separateness within Ireland as a whole, but one that lacks substantive cultural content and 'disturbingly chooses to ignore the way of life practised by Protestants in this place which is quite peculiar to itself [as] the product of centuries of living among the native Irish on this island'.[10]

Ferguson's argument points to a historical process of splitting and polarization which has produced in Ireland collective identities marked by sharply defensive assertions of difference and otherness.[11] During the era of popular imperialism, from the mid-nineteenth to the mid-twentieth centuries, Irish Unionists could share a common British identity with the component peoples of imperial Britain while maintaining a strong sense of Irishness. Since the end of the Second World War, this composite identity has fractured and both its constituent parts have been called into question. Ulster Unionist and loyalist versions of Britishness are grounded upon cultural co-ordinates once shared in common with, but now lost or eroded in, the other constituent parts of the UK.[12] At the core of such constructions are a compound of elements that, in the post-1945 world, have ceased to bind together the 'imagined community' of the nation: Protestantism; loyalty to the Crown; pride in Empire; core values grounded in the importance of absolute moral standards and the maintenance of tradition; an attachment to 'ethnic' or even explicitly racial purity; and a sense of living history connecting current generations to the 'community of ancestors' who fought and died for 'King, country and Empire'.[13] Now, at the cusp of the twentieth and twenty-first centuries, when, in 'mainland' Britain, British identity is being redefined as 'multiethnic and multinational . . . outward looking, internationalist, with a commitment to democracy and tolerance',[14] the 'Britishness' espoused by Ulster Unionists and loyalists tends to be regarded as old-fashioned, backward looking, and 'stuck in the past'.[15] The reasons behind this attachment to 'the past' are not widely understood, but they help to explain the specific form of Britishness espoused by Ulster Unionists (who are far from being entirely 'irrational, backward and deviant', as some 'mainland' commentators suggest).[16]

One set of reasons derives from the break-up of the United Kingdom of Great Britain and Ireland, and the associated partition of Ireland, in 1920–22. Partition had a profound impact on the Protestant and Unionist communities of the original nine-county province of Ulster. In the three so-called 'lost counties' of Ulster – Monaghan, Donegal and Cavan – some 70,000 Protestants constituting on average 18–25 per cent of the population (and up to 40 per cent in pockets), found themselves in 1920 divided from their co-religionists and fellow Ulster Unionists, and in 1922 incorporated into the new Irish Free State[17] (see map 2). 'Three-counties' Protestants suffered decline in their economic prosperity and political power, and in the cohesion of their culture, the loss of their British citizenship and Unionist political identity, and a profound 'sense of betrayal and desertion' at the breaking of the Solemn League and Covenant (signed in 1912 by 250,000 Ulster Protestants who pledged 'to stand by one another in defending . . . our cherished position of equal citizenship in the United Kingdom') by their colleagues on the Ulster Unionist Council.[18] In the six counties, substantial populations of Protestants living along the southern and western extremities of Counties Armagh, Fermanagh and Tyrone, and the north-west edge of Co. Londonderry, found themselves inhabitants of what had become the Border region of Northern Ireland.[19]

This complex relation of Protestants and Unionists to the Border is not widely remembered, primarily due to the latter's function as the political and ideological focal point of post-partition 'Ulster' Protestant identity. The unequivocal demand for its preservation has been the bedrock of Unionist and loyalist politics ever since the Northern State was created. This structural and institutional significance has shaped the imaginative geography of the Border as a defensive bulwark, likened at partition by British administrators to the North-West Frontier of India, that was established and fortified to defend the separate existence of Northern Ireland in the context of the armed conflict of 1919–22.[20] Over the next forty years, a form of Ulster nation-building took place in what was seen as 'a Protestant state' that maintained 'Protestant supremacy over Catholics even in predominantly Catholic areas'.[21] Predicated on the bulwark of the Border which demarcated the territory of the Irish and Catholic other, Unionists engaged in 'a retreat from a sense of Irishness and the development of a heightened sense of British identity'.[22] As McCall explains it:

> Ulster Britishness is defined largely in terms of separation rather than identification, that is, in terms of its Irish nationalist 'other' rather than its British 'self' . . . the Britishness of Ulster unionists was less a means of identification with Britain and 'mainland' Britishness and more a source of separation from the Irish nationalist identity. In effect, being British meant not being Irish.[23]

The continuing significance of the imposition of the Border at the moment of partition for identity formation among Border Protestants in Northern Ireland can be gauged from the tendency of older people to refer to the Republic of Ireland, after more than half-a-century of its existence, as 'the Free State' – which ceased to exist constitutionally in 1937. Leslie Finlay from the West Tyrone Border, whose parents were both 'born British' in Donegal, explains that 'they became Southern Irish citizens overnight by a stroke of the pen . . . Britain handed over Donegal and the other twenty-five counties – to them. To the Free State government. And we always called it the Free State . . . that was the ould people's way that's coming through.'[24] Felicity McCartney remembers:

> My mother was from South Armagh and the friends and neighbours we visited there often walked across [the Border] for cheap butter and some had farms which straddled the Border . . . I was amused at the way my mother and her cronies, County Armagh protestants, talked about people from 'away up in the Free State' as if it were a thousand miles instead of only four![25]

A further index of these complex shifts in belonging structured by the Border was the 'unprecedented flight' of Protestants from the Free State area (where the minority population declined by one-third from 1911 to 1926, due to Republican violence among other factors) and into Fortress Ulster.[26] In Co. Monaghan, a 23 per cent decline resulted from the high rate of Protestant migration into the North, particularly to the Border area of Co. Fermanagh, where numerous descendants of these migrants still live.[27] The cultural memory of this migration and the wider effects of partition on three-counties Protestants has been rendered largely private and invisible, and its history is still to be written. For the Monaghan writer Darach MacDonald, this is because 'it doesn't fit any of the constructions': these people are 'not "Southern Unionists", but Ulster Unionists cut off from Ulster'; inhabitants of a historical grey area in a context where, due to the polarizing effects of partition, historical experience is represented as 'either orange or green'.[28] The *Orange Standard*, newspaper of the Protestant Orange Order, provides one of the few arenas where the migration has been remembered publicly. Orange lodges in the North, with names like the 'Rising Sons of County Monaghan and County Cavan', were 'founded by brethren expelled from the South'. The 'fate of the Southern Unionists' is a central theme in Orange cultural memory. This contrasts the North, where the IRA was defeated by 'firm government' and the 'military presence along the border', to the South, where a 'pogrom against Protestants' took place during the 'terrible summer of 1922', forcing 'thousands of Orange and loyalist families' to flee north-wards. Orange historians interpret this 'pogrom', together with an assault on British culture and the 'symbols of British rule', as a cultural war to drive the Protestant and loyalist people out of Southern Ireland, with lessons for the North.[29] The Ulster Unionist politician Raymond Ferguson points out: 'The stories that travelled with these immigrants reinforced the Protestant folklore and bolstered the political imperative of separation from the south'; while Fermanagh Unionist Arlene Foster suggests that the decline in the Protestant population of the South is the basis of 'a fear that lives here [in Northern Ireland], especially in Border counties'.[30]

These fears were reactivated after 1969 in the war between a renascent IRA and the British State underpinning Ulster Unionism, over the continu-ing existence of Northern Ireland. Armed conflict provided a second set of reasons for the polarization in identity and the preservation of a specifically *Ulster* brand of imperial Britishness. One effect of the war has been the virtual eradication of a sense of Irishness among Ulster Protestants, and a near-doubling (to 69 per cent by 1993) of those identifying themselves as British.[31] A complex of factors have interacted in this process: the forms taken by political conflict and its attempted resolution; the armed violence through which that conflict has been fought out; the ongoing traumatic repercussions of that violence; and the narratives in which the war is remem-bered and commemorated. In an important sense, the war in and over Northern Ireland has produced and consolidated a particular construction of British identity among Ulster Protestants,[32] and a key element in this rede-finition has been the formulation of Ulster Protestant cultural memories of the war, in which the defence of the Border has been a central theme.

The war along the Border

Armed conflict during the Troubles has not followed a single, uniform pattern, but has taken different forms in different areas, giving rise to 'a mosaic of different types of conflict'.[33] Ulster Protestant war memories, that respond to a variety of specifically local circumstances and experiences, are correspondingly diverse.[34] Unlike the war in urban centres, with its 'high rate of civilian casualties . . . [and] "collateral" damage', in the Border regions of Armagh, Fermanagh and Tyrone a 'rural war' of marked intensity was fought directly between the IRA and British Crown forces.[35] Fifty-three per cent of all rural deaths from 1969–93 occurred in the southern Border areas of these three counties, with South Armagh experiencing the highest death rate outside North and West Belfast and parts of Derry City.[36] IRA operations to undermine British control in this highly symbolic region were frequently launched from, and returned to, the relatively 'safe' haven of the Irish Republic. A particular characteristic of the war along the Border was the large number and relatively high concentration of casualties suffered by the locally recruited security forces, the UDR, the RUC and the RUC Reserve, including part-time, off-duty and former officers.[37] Attacks by the IRA on members of those forces, and on the Protestant farms, businesses and cultural institutions in the Border communities where they lived and worked meant that their families and other Protestant and Unionist civilians were exposed to violence, and themselves subject to attack.[38] This has been experienced as an attack on Protestant *belongingness* in Ireland.

The fear and risk involved in living close to the Border figures prominently in Protestant cultural memory of the Troubles and in many personal life-stories, like that of 'Edward Gordon', the pseudonym of a former UDR soldier, who tells of two attacks on the family farm near Pettigo, Co. Fermanagh: 'The farm actually came down to the very Border. Along the river . . . it was so handy – that's why I was got'. Personal memories also testify to the violation of the private space of the home that often characterized these attacks. 'Mrs Gordon', who was nearly killed, recalls how 'they shot into the kitchen'. She links this personal experience to a pervasive threat to the local Protestant and Unionist community as a whole: 'It was a hard time, back then down this end of the country . . . It was all around.'[39] The Border itself became the site of particular forms of terror practised by the IRA, including the dumping of bodies of executed victims on Border roads, sometimes wired to a booby-trap bomb; and the use of 'human bombs' – kidnapped victims forced to drive vehicles loaded with explosives – to attack the British Army's Border checkpoints.[40] Such events had a powerful psychic impact on the entire Protestant local community, and significant numbers of residents responded to this atmosphere of fear and threat by moving away to safer towns, frequently just a few miles 'inland'[41] a word that captures the experience of the Border as an absolute frontier, like a coastline.

Ulster Protestant imaginative geography of the Border is infused with the qualities of this collective psychic reality, a compound of the collective fear, loss, anger and traumatic disturbance induced in Border Protestant communities by the IRA campaign. Knowledge of what has happened in the past here, at any particular site of violence, is carried, or seared, unforgettably in the living memory of those affected; as well as inscribed upon the familiar places of a local landscape. Joan Bullock was one of those Protestants who continued to live with her family throughout the Troubles in their cottage beside the bridge across the River Woodford at Aghalane, which marks the Fermanagh–Cavan Border near Belturbet. In 1997, she gave the writer Henry McDonald a 'terror tour' of incidents that occurred in the immediate vicinity of her home:

> The bridge was blown up by loyalist paramilitaries. It was used by the IRA to cross over from Cavan in the South to launch attacks in Fermanagh. Just here, 50 yards from the house, is where the IRA placed claymore mines to kill soldiers on patrol. Up there is what's left of the sign over the garage my husband Storey and his brother used to own. It was blown up after my brother-in-law spoke on the BBC about Tommy's murder.[42]

The most serious of these incidents had occurred in September 1972, when her husband's cousins were shot dead by the IRA at their home-farm at Killynick, a mile away. A neighbour, who 'saw a car full of men going towards the border', described the scene in the farmhouse as 'a shambles'.[43] Joan Bullock's son Simon, a baby at the time, remembers the stories of these events told him by his father,[44] figuring a local landscape of memory invisible to outsiders.

The sense of intense psychic disturbance evinced in the stories of horror and loss told by Border Protestants, which in many cases has persisted without dissipating over many years – 'to this day I haven't got over it and probably never will'[45] – is a hallmark of traumatic experience. The critical literature on trauma emphasises its quality of 'freezing' the ordinary processes of remembering and forgetting, so that those who have suffered a traumatic episode remain attached to an internal landscape formed in the past, and experience difficulties in integrating it psychically with other parts of the self and new circumstances.[46] Emotionally, this involves the construction of a defensive border that divides one part of the psyche from another to preserve 'a safer space, a retreat'; a process known in psychoanalysis as 'dissociation', or 'splitting'.[47] These psychic discontinuities are projected into the social world, demarcating sites of trauma from the places of everyday life. As part of her 'terror tour', Joan Bullock took McDonald to visit the nearby house where her husband's cousins were killed and which had remained 'empty and untouched'[48] ever since:

> The bullet holes over the door . . . are still there. The peeling white and flower-patterned paper clings to the wall of an upstairs bedroom. Faded copies of the *Daily Mirror*, jaundiced by years of damp, stick out of cupboards and drawers. Their reports tell of internment in Ulster and the war in Vietnam.

Because the family believed the killings to be part of an IRA strategy to drive Protestants away from Border areas, 'no-one from the family has dared move into the house'. Both the unused farmhouse itself and the memories of what happened here twenty-five years ago had been 'frozen in time'.[49]

Psychic splitting and its associated freezing of memory is both exacerbated by and contributes to the breaking of connections and links in the social and political world. For Border Protestants in the North, a sense of isolation and disconnectedness from wider social networks, of being peripheral and marginalized, has stemmed from the geography of their location. Hazlett Lynch, of the victims' group Voice, from the West Tyrone Border, describes this area (only some sixty miles from Belfast) as 'the most extreme western part of Northern Ireland . . . neglected and ignored . . . [F]olk here felt very much excluded, almost from Northern Ireland, because they were living right at the extremity of things.'[50] This sense of isolation has been heightened by the Troubles. When McDonald visited Joan Bullock in 1997, he noted how the road ended abruptly at the bridge beside her cottage. This was one of the many Border roads (fifty out of a total of fifty-eight in Co. Fermanagh alone) closed or destroyed during the war in a defensive reinforcement of partition. Closed roads and crossings, and the heavily fortified military checkpoints on the few 'approved roads', transformed stretches of the Border into a landscape comparable to the Berlin Wall or to 'No Man's Land during World War I'.[51] This further compounded the difficulties of maintaining cross-border contacts stemming from partition, since when, for example, Protestant congregations have been divided from their churches or chapels.[52] After the Aghalane bridge had been destroyed by loyalists to prevent IRA incursions in 1972, the three-mile journey to Belturbet in the Republic now took forty-five minutes, and the Bullock family became 'cut off from all the nearest neighbours'. Simon Bullock's most distinct memories of childhood concerned the family's isolation: 'It was a major mission to go and hang out with your mates.'[53] A process of cultural erosion has been further intensified by the sense of loss consequent on the decline of the Protestant population and its religious and social institutions in the Border settlements.[54] In such a situation, the breaking of connections in social space may establish a vicious circle, contributing to psychic divisions that in turn may feed into continuing social disintegration.

The cultural memory of 'ethnic cleansing'

The distinctive pattern of violence on the Border 'is not adequately reflected in death or injury data';[55] nor does it always feature in standard histories of the Troubles.[56] However, it is a key theme in Protestant and Unionist cultural memory of the conflict, both locally and throughout Northern Ireland, where it is recalled, controversially, as a form of 'ethnic cleansing'.[57] The term 'ethnic cleansing' was introduced into popular discourse by news coverage of the wars accompanying the break-up of the former Yugoslavia in the early 1990s, as a synonym for violent hatred expressed in 'an official and systematic, state-sponsored policy'[58] to eliminate from a particular region those who were considered 'ethnically different'; by killing or forcibly displacing them, and burning their homes, shops and other centres of communal life.[59] The term originates in the Serbian Chetnik policy formulated in 1941–42, 'to create and organize a homogeneous Serbia which must include all the ethnic territory inhabited by Serbs', to be achieved by 'the cleansing of the lands of all non-Serb elements'.[60] This scheme was resuscitated by the Milošević regime's 'Greater Serbia' project, in which 'ethnic cleansing' was practised against against minority populations in Croatia (1991), Bosnia–Herzegovina (1992–95) and Kosovo (1998–99), as a component of military action organized by the Serbian State and involving its armed forces, to extend or consolidate the areas under its territorial control.[61] The resulting destruction and displacement – reciprocated by Serbia's adversaries in these wars – was on a scale only possible with the use of state resources.[62] In Croatia by the end of 1991, for example, the Serbo-Croat War 'had caused 18,000 confirmed casualties . . . and some 14,000 missing, most of whom were probably also dead. Refugees numbered 703,000', over one-sixth of Croatia's pre-war population, and some 100,000 dwellings as well as over one-third of the country's infrastructure had been destroyed or damaged.[63]

The term 'ethnic cleansing' was first applied publicly to the war in Northern Ireland in summer 1992, in an article entitled 'Population shifts in Derry City': 'Ethnic cleansing is not only confined to Bosnia but close at home, where without publicity in the national press/media, fourteen thousand people had to move from the East Bank [*sic*] of that city because of "bombing and intimidation".'[64] Shortly after, the Ulster Unionist leader Sir James Molyneux exploited its emotional resonance by claiming, in a speech to the Grand Orange Lodge in New York, that Protestants in the Border areas 'had been the victims of "ethnic cleansing" for over twenty years . . . Thousands . . . have been intimidated from the border regions of Fermanagh and Armagh'.[65] The Orange Order took up the theme which, it suggested, 'provides an excellent platform to put the Unionist case across';[66] and its newspaper, the *Orange Standard*, began to deploy the term 'ethnic cleansing' to represent the complex issue of population movements during the Troubles, claiming that 'up to 100,000 Ulster Protestants have been driven from their homes during the past twenty years by IRA and other republican organisations'.[67] This narrative was deployed to reverse what had long been perceived by Unionists as the hostility and indifference of the public media (especially television) to the Ulster Protestant people, by encouraging sympathetic identification with their plight. This lack of media attention and concern – a persistent theme of the Orange Order's cultural politics since the early 1970s[68] – could be contrasted with the intense media focus on events in the former Yugoslavia: 'Unlike today's situation in Bosnia there was no mass presence of world television crews on the Ulster border, in Derry City, or on the Grosvenor, Springfield and Cliftonville Roads to show the Protestant families having to move from areas their ancestors had lived in for many years.'[69]

Having achieved currency in the latter part of 1992, the term 'ethnic cleansing' was consolidated in Protestant and Unionist responses to the release of the 1991 Census figures, which showed 'a move away from the Border in general, bringing with it a greater polarization of both Protestant and Catholic communities as they join members of their own religion in separate areas of the country. Protestants are moving "inland" . . . [and] finding safety in villages or "fortress towns" where the vast majority of the population is Protestant'.[70] Orange claims that this exodus was the result of 'ethnic cleansing' aimed at bringing about 'a re-drawing of the border'[71] were buttressed by local memory from villages along the County Fermanagh Border. According to Canon Edwy Kille, a Church of Ireland minister in Rosslea for nineteen years, the number of Protestants on the local electoral register had declined during his incumbency by 20 per cent (from 300 to 246):

> It is an elimination of the Protestant people by murder and threats. This . . . is a terrorist tactic. There has been persistent pressure, both in violent attacks and intimidation of people in the district. I am convinced that there is a quiet but determined ethnic cleansing going on in this district. It is not as [*sic*] the same rate as the situation in Yugoslavia, but it is going on.[72]

In the Orange politics of population, these 'demographic changes caused by Republican violence', taken together with 'the failure of the Government to defeat the IRA', had become 'a far greater threat' than the Catholic birth rate, since those changes implied a shrinkage in the area under Unionist political control.[73] By April 1993 the *Orange Standard* was celebrating the 'grim refusal' of 'strong Protestant communities' in Border areas such as the Clogher Valley 'to submit to the IRA and its ethnic cleansing policy'; and calling for a 'strong and realistic security policy [and] the support of Protestant and Unionist communities in . . . the safer regions of the east', to help them resist 'one of the most vile campaigns waged against a people since the Second World War'.[74]

Such claims have been rejected by Irish nationalists in the Border areas,[75] and especially by Republicans, who have always insisted that the IRA's military campaign was politically motivated and 'non-sectarian', being directed against the British State rather than against Northern Irish Protestants.[76] Thus, the war along the Border is one of the sites of intense and ongoing conflict over cultural memory of the Troubles. Indeed, the emotive resonance of 'ethnic cleansing' is such that not all Unionists and loyalists endorse the term's use, while others sometimes betray a certain equivocation or unease about its validity even as they deploy it.[77] The Orange Order's claims certainly rest on a questionable treatment of evidence. While migration, including Protestant migration, away from the Border is a reality,[78] this is due to a range of factors, including rural youth unemployment, as the Order itself has acknowledged.[79] Orange claims of a continuous, effective IRA campaign to 'eliminat[e] the Protestant people by murder and threats' are called into question by the IRA's strategic shift towards targeting the British 'mainland', and also by Canon Kille's own observation that the death toll in his area had been reduced after 1986 as the permanent Border checkpoints enabled state security forces to became increasingly effective in containing the IRA, such that, in the seven years since, only two killings had occurred.[80]

In arriving at its figure of 100,000 Protestants displaced since 1972, the *Orange Standard* compounds the relatively small number of migrations out of the rural Border areas (Reverend Ian Paisley has suggested that 1,000 Protestants left Co. Fermanagh in twenty years[81]), together with the differently determined exodus of Protestants from the urban centres of Londonderry and Belfast. Recent analyses of the victims of violence, in which deaths caused by the IRA are considered in the context of broader patterns of violence during the Troubles, contradict suggestions either that Protestant civilians have been uniquely targeted during the conflict or that the IRA has been engaged in an ethnic war by directing its armed operations uniquely against Protestants.[82] The patterning of violent death is clearly more complex than Unionist claims about 'ethnic cleansing' allow. In the course of the Troubles, Border Protestants and Unionists have been subjected to a politics of intimidation and terror, but this has not taken place on a scale, nor with the consistency of pattern, to warrant the description 'ethnic cleansing'.

The Protestant and Unionist narrative of ethnic cleansing ought nevertheless to be taken seriously as a cultural memory of the conflict, which articulates the cultural perceptions, political identifications, and psychic and emotional realities of Border Protestants exposed to the Provisional IRA's armed campaign over a period of twenty-five years prior to the 1994 ceasefire. As a public form of war memory,[83] it has structured their understandings of the significance of violent bereavement, providing a means not only of responding politically to the Republican armed campaign and critiquing the British Government's apparent willingness to 'sacrifice' Protestant lives, but of handling the horrors of the conflict and countering the psychic effects of the violence. In short, the narrative of ethnic cleansing has articulated the emotional and political stance of the imagined community of Border Protestants – and of Ulster Protestants more generally – as a community, united in its will to withstand the IRA.

The genealogy of this cultural memory can be traced back to the early years of the Troubles, when the war in the Border regions was at its most intense. For twenty years before the iconic phrase 'ethnic cleansing' became current and potent, Fermanagh Protestants had another term to describe the IRA's campaign along the Border: genocide. Claims of genocide were being voiced publicly in Enniskillen as early as September 1972, at the memorial service in Enniskillen Free Presbyterian Church for two local UDR soldiers killed by a booby-trap bomb left in an abandoned car a mile or so out of town. Noting that it 'is a tragic mark of the times that loyalists are gathering more and more around the gravesides of the sons of Ulster', Reverend Ivan Foster 'claimed the bombing was part of an overall Republican strategy of genocide against Protestants living in border areas'.[84] Ever since 1972, the memory of 'genocide' has been articulated politically by Unionist politicians, as representing a perceived threat to the entire imagined community of Ulster Protestants. On Easter Monday 1976, for example, Ernest Baird, leader of the United Ulster Unionist Movement, argued at an Apprentice Boys demonstration in Larne: 'The real purpose behind the Republican campaign is to drive Protestants out of Ulster.' This, he claimed, was leading to 'a situation where a million Protestants within a short time will become refugees. We are being slowly driven from our homes and Westminster is party to the exercise.'[85] Although this prediction proved to have been unduly alarmist, and the Protestant people were not driven *en masse* out of Northern Ireland, the term 'genocide' provided an effective call-to-arms which continued to be used. In 1984, for example, the Ulster Unionist MP for Fermanagh and South Tyrone Ken Maginnis raised in the House of Commons the case of the young farmer and ex-UDR soldier, Ronald Funston, who was shot dead by two IRA gunmen while he sat in the cab of his tractor on the family farm close to the Fermanagh Border, near Pettigo, in March that year: 'What message have you got', he asked Prime Minister Margaret Thatcher, 'for people who are likely to be victims, like Ronnie Funston, of the IRA's genocide along the frontier?'[86] The memory of ethnic cleansing, as articulated by Unionists and Orangemen in 1992, gathered up and re-presented, under a new sign with contemporary salience, this existing twenty-year-old narrative of Republican 'genocide' against the Protestant people, as in the expression coined by the Orange Order's Grand Master Reverend Martin Smyth in July 1993: 'genocide/ethnic cleaning'.[87]

That the charged term 'genocide' was felt to be appropriate is not merely a reflection of its perceived potency as a weapon of propaganda, but is a measure of the emotional pressure brought to bear on Border Protestants and Unionists exposed to a regular and intense degree of violence by the IRA. Its use expressed a psychic as well as political response to death, bereavement and fear. At the funeral service for Winston Howe, one of two RUC constables killed in February 1980 by an IRA landmine near the Fermanagh Border, Reverend Edwy Kille (the same Church of Ireland minister who thirteen years later would talk to the *Orange Standard* about 'ethnic cleansing' in the area) used his sermon at St Mark's Church, in the parish of Aghadrumsee, to recall

> the events that have happened in the parishes under my care during the last several years. That catalogue is frighteningly long. Our sexton in Clogh will well remember being blown out of the cab of his lorry . . . by an explosion on the mountain; here in this parish there is a memorial to Harry Creighton, shot in the back as he was returning home; three farms have been burned. Although the terrorists make a show of respect for the Dublin government this did not stop them from killing a senator [Billy Fox] from that administration in Clogh parish. You all know that much-loved and respected Douglas Deering was shot through the head in a most cold-blooded attack; Sylvia Crowe, a fine dedicated Christian woman, was blown to eternity last summer; Herbie Kernoghan was murdered in the grounds of the Roman Catholic primary school in Roslea; and the present explosion means that there have been four violent deaths in the parish in the last six months.[88]

While the circumstances in which these people met their deaths were varied, Reverend Kille here invites his congregation to remember them collectively as co-religionists, fellow parishioners and innocent victims, and their killing as a collective outrage.[89] As Republican attacks continued over the years, local memorial services for the Protestant dead provided public occasions at which the killings could be protested and their incremental impact, not simply on immediate families but on entire local communities, could be registered. At the funeral in 1986 of John McVitty, a Protestant RUC man who was shot dead by the IRA in front of his 12-year-old son while at work on a farm near Rosslea,

> the local Church of Ireland minister painted a picture of a community under siege, of Fermanagh Protestants driven from their lands, of eldest sons being murdered in order to sabotage the smooth transfer of Protestant property from generation to generation. He lambasted the Catholic Church for presiding over the funerals of IRA men, men known to have killed members of the congregation. Then, one by one, he read out the long, long list of the men and women killed by the IRA in Fermanagh.[90]

The memory of an ongoing genocide provided a way of explaining the continuing experience of fear and loss, that made sense of recent events in terms of a meaningful historical pattern. It shaped a response that worked both politically and emotionally.

The psychic value of this public narrative of 'genocide/ethnic cleansing' is evident in its use by individual victims of violence as a framework in which to couch their personal and family memories of the Troubles along the Border, such as the 'Gordons' and 'Mr Sidwell' (also a pseudonym). The 'Sidwells', whose farm and business at Wattlebridge was 'situated a mile from the border, by field much less', survived four IRA bomb attacks on the premises between 1977 and 1990 before finally being forced to leave the area by an overwhelmingly terrifying event:

> [T]hey surrounded the car . . . At first though I did think it was the Army and then I noticed the balaclavas . . . They hit me over the head and tied myself and my wife up. They held an electric wire to my legs and told us there was a bomb at the end of it . . . They took my son in his own van and then on to the border with a bomb. They had hammered my son's knees and he couldn't get out of the van at the [Army] checkpoint. . . . They had to pull him out . . . Luckily something went wrong for them and the bomb didn't go off properly because if it had it would have blown the place apart up to a mile or so it was that big . . . Because of what happened, my son had to leave. He won't be back.[91]

A year or so later the Sidwells sold the business and moved ten miles 'inland' to Lisnaskea. Reflecting on this horrifying experience, Mr Sidwell struggles to make sense of what was done to him and his family by drawing on the cultural memory of 'genocide/ethnic cleansing' for an explanation: the IRA

> have got everything they wanted, to get us out. They said the reason we were taken was because 'the family has connections with the security forces'. My wife worked as the canteen manageress in a police station and I suppose that's what they meant. They targeted us because we were a Protestant family and they were just on for putting you out of business . . . to get Protestants to move. The Catholic business[es] were never touched, always the Protestants'.

Twenty-five years after 'Mrs Gordon' left the Border area, her husband having survived two attacks on their home farm in 1972–73, she reflects:

> I often ask myself the question, 'why did they attack us?' Edward was one that helped them [neighbouring Catholic farmers], but someone had to set us up. Someone had to do it . . . [W]e had a neighbour on the UDR, a single man, who lived a couple of yards from the border but they came for us. It was families they wanted out – they seemed to go for families, farms, land that would be handed on.

In remembering their own displacement, the 'Gordons' dwell on numerous other incidents in the area; they ponder suspicions, never dissolved, about the possible involvement of immediate neighbours; and they reflect on still-unresolved uncertainties about who was most at risk and why. The widespread adherence of Border Protestants to the narrative of 'ethnic cleansing' stems from its *rationalization* of the widespread traumatic effects of such incidents, not only on individuals but on entire families and local communities. The narrative offers an explanation that can be lived with.

The individual and collective effects of trauma provide the ground of subjectivity on which the cultural memory of ethnic cleansing is constructed and perpetuated, the psychic condition to which it speaks and the emotional 'fuel' on which its political power of mobilization depends. The potency of this narrative derives, not from the accuracy of its analysis of the conflict, but from its interweaving of psychic and political imperatives into a compelling account of events, past and present, that makes sense, expresses deeply felt emotional realities, and empowers the will to stand firm and endure. In this, the narrative enables a particular kind of 'subjective composure': that is,

> a perspective for the self within which it endeavours to make sense . . . so that its troubling, disturbing aspects may be 'managed', worked through, contained, repressed. In this process, events themselves may become inseparably bound up with the storyteller's fantasies, becoming the site of imaginary scenarios with desired and feared outcomes, narrated 'as if' they had 'really' happened in just this way. These fantasy investments represent a range of possible selves, some powerful and effective in the world, others threatened and at risk . . . [S]torytelling . . . 'composes' a subjective orientation of the self within the social relations of the world . . . and involves a striving . . . for a version of the self that can be lived with in relative psychic comfort.[92]

In this sense, the cultural memory of 'genocide/ethnic cleansing' has worked to enable and support the composure of a particular form of Protestant and loyalist subjectivity.

Culture wars and the politics of Ulster–British memory and identity

Since the mid-1980s, a Unionist politics of British identity has been constructed on the ground of personal and communal traumatic memories of this kind, which have thus played a significant part in the constitution and cementing of a counter-Republican identity for Northern Ireland's Protestants. With its associated theme of betrayal by the British Government through the 'appeasement' of Republicanism, the cultural memory of 'genocide/ethnic cleansing' has contributed to the project of coalescing the disparate currents within Unionism and loyalism, including strong local and regional differences, behind a relatively coherent cultural as well as a political identity. Stimulated especially by the Anglo-Irish Agreement of 1985 (which granted the Republic of Ireland a formal input into the affairs of Northern Ireland for the first time),[93] much work has gone into the forging of a so-called 'Ulster–British' identity. This seeks to construct the cultural distinctiveness of 'the Protestant people of Ulster' through the assertion of difference from the Irish and Catholic other, while simultaneously maintaining its claim to Britishness in the face of the British State's perceived preparedness to weaken the Union. The crystallizing of this Ulster–British 'ethnic', as well as national, identity has rested on a politics of cultural memory, with a flowering of many kinds of historical works aimed at recovering, understanding and promoting Orange, Protestant, Unionist and British 'cultural heritage'.

In 1985, for example, the Ulster Society for the Promotion of Ulster–British Heritage and Culture was established to reverse 'the insidious erosion of the culture and ethnic national identity of the British people of Ulster', said to have occurred over 'the past decade' and now held to be 'a systematic policy', not only of 'the Provisional IRA and its fellow travellers', but of the British Government.[94] The Society's aims were to 'promote our distinctive culture and heritage in all its rich and varied forms',[95] and to create 'a new and enduring awareness of what it means to be British and live in Ulster', so as to bolster the claim that 'Ulster is a nation, separate from the rest of Ireland'.[96] A linked project was that of the Culture Committee of the Ulster Young Unionist Council (UYUC), which published a series of pamphlets – beginning in 1986 with *Cuchulain The Lost Legend, Ulster the Lost Culture* – arguing that 'we have to show that we are different from nationalists and the Republic of Ireland . . . We have neglected our [Ulster–British] culture and have failed to promote it effectively'.[97] While 'Ulster Unionists were content to say that we were British, and leave it at that',[98] Sinn Féin had meanwhile 'hijacked the so-called "Gaelic culture" ' and 'used "culture" as one of its weapons in the battle for supremacy on the island of Ireland'.[99] Now Unionists, too, the UYUC argued, must forge effective weapons in this 'culture war'.

One such weapon was the propagation of an alternative myth of origins, that appropriated the legend of the Cruthin for an ethnic Ulster–British cultural memory.[100] In pursuing this project, the UYUC adopted and promoted the argument advanced by the loyalist historian Ian Adamson, that the Cruthin were 'native' to Ulster before the arrival of the 'Gaelic' Celts, who established dominance by the sixth century AD.[101] In this narrative, the

Gaelic Celts become the people who colonized Ireland,[102] driving out the Cruthin and forcing their migration to Scotland, from whence their descendents returned as settlers in the plantations of the seventeenth century. While the Scots planters were 'members of the Cruthin race returning to the land of their birthright', many of 'the native (Catholic) dwellers in Ulster whom they joined in inhabiting the province were descendants of those Cruthin who had assimilated with the Gaelic invader'.[103] Prior to its adoption by 'respectable' Unionism and loyalism, Adamson's thesis about the Cruthin was also promoted by the paramilitary UDA as a basis for its vision of a separate cultural identity and nation-state of Ulster, independent of both Britain and the Republic of Ireland, and an agreed homeland for Ulster Catholics as well as Protestants.[104]

For the UYUC, on the other hand, as an organization affiliated to the UUP, the Cruthin legend was mobilized in support of a new integrationist stance of full incorporation of the people of Ulster within the UK, and explicitly opposed to Irish Catholic and nationalist identity. As developed by the UYUC, the Cruthin legend inverted the categories 'native' and 'colonial invader' that are central to Irish Republican constructions of Irishness and Britishness, while also asserting the 'ethnic difference' of Ulster from Ireland. The UYUC argued, in common with the Ulster Society, that the British people of Ulster have inherited a rich cultural heritage which stretches back through the plantations to pre-historic times, 'a heritage which has always incorporated the ideals of liberty, equality, and freedom of religion and expression'.[105] Both agreed that this has been 'forgotten and neglected', allowing ground to be lost to the 'deceptions and myths' of the nationalists.[106] Both drew the conclusion that, in order to 'preserve our cultural heritage for the generations that will follow us in our beloved Ulster', it must be rediscovered, promoted and defended with renewed zeal.[107]

This call to arms was also taken up by the Orange Order, the organization traditionally responsible for the commemoration and defence of 'our heritage . . . imperilled'.[108] Planning began as early as 1983, to ensure that the forthcoming tercentenary, in 1990, of the battle of the Boyne – the victory won in 1690 by King William III and commemorated annually by the Order in its Twelfth of July parades, as the key episode in loyalist cultural memory – would be seized on as an opportunity to 'present our Order and our Cause to a wider audience than ever before'.[109] The celebrations in 1990 were on an unprecedented scale. In addition to the regular annual calendar of loyalist commemorative parades – averaging nearly 2,000 each year between 1985 and 1990 during the 'marching season' from Easter to the end of August[110] – a further 285 separate events took place throughout the year 'in virtually every city, town, village and hamlet across the Province'.[111] The most successful of these, attended by tens of thousands, utilized forms of popular culture, such as the historic pageant or re-enactment, to reiterate the relevance of the 'spirit of 1690' and the importance of the old slogan 'No Surrender!' to current circumstances.[112]

At the culmination of this festival, the Belfast parade of 29 September, an estimated 70,000 Orangemen from around the world marched through the city to the applause of a crowd numbering some 100,000,[113] and were addressed at the Field after the parade by the Unionist MP and Orange leader Grand Master Reverend Martin Smyth, who condemned the betrayal of the 'bloodied but unbowed' Protestant people of Ulster by the Conservative Government of Margaret Thatcher which had undermined Northern Ireland's sovereignty with the hated Anglo-Irish Agreement of 1985. The Ulster loyalists of 1990, declaimed Smyth, must continue to stand firm in defence of those Protestant 'civil and religious liberties' first secured 300 years ago at the Boyne.[114] This exhortation to defence as well as celebration was repeated in Twelfth of July speeches and commemorative pamphlets, and in a spate of Orange Lodge commemorative histories, from all parts of Northern Ireland in the late 1980s and early 1990s.[115] To take just one example: in the Belfast County Grand Lodge's pamphlet *The Twelfth* (1994), which appeared a few weeks before the IRA's ceasefire in August, an editorial statement entitled 'No surrender?' painted a dark picture of a demoralized Ulster Protestant people, 'under siege' from the forces of Irish Republicanism that sought the destruction of their way of life and the eradication of their distinctive presence in Ireland, before calling for the spirit of resolute defence that had enabled 'our forefathers' to survive similar threats.[116]

The popular cultural memory produced and sustained by these practices of Unionist and loyalist history-making celebrates the longevity and tenacity of the Protestant and British presence and culture in the North of Ireland since the seventeenth century, but also warns of the dangers it has faced as a beleaguered culture, now under threat of destruction as the British and Irish Governments conspire to break the Union and foist on the people of Ulster a new pro-nationalist political dispensation. If it is to survive, the Ulster–British heritage is seen to require great vigilance and energy in its defence, while its past 'defenders' are idealized as heroes and invested with the potent psychic charge of triumphalist phantasy.[117] From this perspective, 'the story of Ireland' is told as the constant struggle for survival of hardworking and God-fearing British Protestants against their annihilation at the hands of the surrounding hostile and violent forces of Irish nationalism. In this longer story, 'ethnic cleansing' is simply the latest term for a process that reaches back to the Plantation itself, and the fight against it during the Troubles since 1969 echoes numerous prior episodes in history, which it is the business of the guardians of Ulster–British heritage and tradition to commemorate. In this sense, the cultural memory of 'ethnic cleansing' acquires an extraordinary historical depth and resonance, since it draws its psychic energy not simply from the traumatic experiences of the Troubles since 1969 but from the wars over Irish independence and partition of the early 1920s – themselves still, in the 1990s, within living memory – and, far beyond this, from so-called 'folk memories' reaching back to 1641. Recalling Republican pogroms against Protestants in Southern Ireland, and the subsequent migration of substantial numbers across the Border into Northern Ireland after the establishment of the Irish Free State in 1922, Orange popular memory finds resonant parallels with more recent displacements of the Protestant population in Northern Ireland, to the extent of re-describing these events of seventy years ago as themselves forms of 'ethnic cleansing'.[118]

The most powerful of all Protestant and Unionist cultural memories of threatened annihilation remains the narrative of the massacres during the 1641 Rebellion, when 'an unknown number of innocent people ('estimates . . . range from 12,000 to 100,000'), many of them women and children, perished at the hands of bloodthirsty rebels for no other crime than the fact that they were Protestants and of planter stock'.[119] T.W. Moody, writing in 1977, identified what he called 'the 1641 horror story' as one of the most influential popular 'myths' of the Irish past, characterized by 'a gross inflation of the numbers of victims' and the representation of the massacres as 'a deliberate attempt planned by the leaders of the rising to annihilate the settlers';[120] or, as the *Orange Standard* put it in 1991, 'part of a widespread plan by Roman Catholic protagonists to drive the Protestant population out of Ireland'.[121] The commemoration that year of the 350th anniversary of the massacres provided an opportunity to re-articulate and recharge the memory of the Rebellion, with thousands participating in events such as the parade in Portadown on 15 June, linked to a ritual re-enactment of one of the most notorious incidents, the massacre of some eighty men, women and children in the River Bann near the Bridge of Portadown.[122] The Orange Order's Executive Officer George Patton, taking stock of the successful tercentenary celebrations at an Ulster Unionist meeting in Portadown later in 1990, had recommended that a continuing programme of heritage commemoration should begin in this way, arguing that in 1991 it

> was essential that the 1641 anniversary should be remembered . . . had the massacres not taken place, then it is questionable as to whether there would have been a Siege of Derry. The memories of what happened at the bridge at Portadown, at the church in Loughgall, the bridge in Scarva, at Kernan Lake, and other places were still vivid among the Protestants in 1688 . . . [T]hey fled to the walled city of Londonderry for protection, and fearful of a repeat of what happened in that terrible October and November of 1641, when the English plantation in Ulster was practically wiped out.[123]

Orange historians have argued that the 'ruthless and cruel way in which the people were butchered' left a legacy of horror that has been transmitted in cultural memory for over 350 years. In those parts of Counties Armagh, Down and Tyrone settled by 'the planters of English stock who suffered most in the massacres . . . the tales have been told from generation to generation of how men, women and children were tortured and killed', ensuring that 'what had happened in 1641 was . . . vividly imprinted in their folk memory' and 'taught at their mother's knee'.[124]

This collective memory of 1641, inextricably bound together as it is with the quintessential mythology of 'No Surrender' at the Siege of Derry in 1688–89,[125] is not only significant in its own right, but provides a 'template'[126] that structures the way in which subsequent episodes of war and conflict in Ireland have been cast into memories of threat and defence. As Patton suggests, the trauma of 1641 is believed to have shaped the response of those Protestants who, at the outbreak of the Williamite War of Succession in 1688, 'rushed for the safety of the citadel cities of Londonderry and Enniskillen . . . fearing a *repetition* of the killings' by the forces of James II (my emphasis). The memory of the massacres and 'the real fear of a racial and religious pogrom *similar* to 1641' is also said to have determined the hostility of the Anglican Orangemen of Armagh to the United Irishmen's Rebellion of 1798, seen as 'a fearful campaign of extermination of Protestants and loyalists'. (my emphasis)[127] This memory template encodes both a cognitive framework for making sense of violent conflict and a psychic position of fear and the imperative of defence: the much discussed 'siege mentality' of Ulster Protestants.[128] It is reproduced culturally, in the form of the mythic stories of 1641 and 1689, but also psychically, through the subjectivities of later generations who may not themselves have directly experienced a massacre, but who have internalized the fear associated with it, as a sense of imminent threat to their own lives. As a cognitive framework, the template organizes the experience of 'similar' events in its terms, and is itself recharged by those events should they 'confirm our worst fears'; as in the sectarian slaughter of Protestants by Catholic rebels in Co. Wexford in 1798;[129] or at Kingsmills in South Armagh on 5 January 1976, when Republican gunmen stopped a minibus, carrying home from work twelve mill workers, and asked their religion, before shooting dead ten of the eleven Protestants, in one of worst Republican atrocities of the current Troubles (see figure 5).[130] Indeed, in imaginative terms, 1641, 1688, 1798, 1920–22 and the so-called 'ethnic cleansing' of the Border from 1969 through to the 1990s are not separate though *similar* events at all, but 'repetitions' of a collective 'primal scene' in which past and present are fused indistinguishably.[131]

Memory, reparation, and the peace process

Fashioned in the fearful years of the early 1970s and honed in the 'culture wars' of the 1980s and early 1990s, the collective narrative of 'ethnic cleansing' continued to underpin the psychic siege mentality of Ulster Unionists and loyalists, and to provide a frame for the articulation of Ulster–British memories of the Troubles, in the context of the peace process. This can be seen in the memory work of the grassroots support groups formed to represent the Protestant and Unionist victims of violence from the Border areas during the period of the peace talks and initial efforts to implement the Good Friday Agreement. During this period, the loyalist siege mentality has manifested in the fear, anger and distrust which has intruded into efforts at

5 Memorial at the roadside site of the Kingsmills (or Whitecross) massacre, Ballymoyer Road, South Armagh, 5 January 1976.

peace-making with Republicans, and in the powerfully emotive positions taken by some Unionists in contesting the terms of the Agreement, as well as in the aggressively defensive cultural assertions of the Right to March campaign focused on Orange Order parades, particularly the annual parade on 1 July from Drumcree to Portadown commemorating the battle of the Somme in 1916.[132] These issues are explored in chapters 8 and 9. However, the memory of ethnic cleansing also needs to be placed in the context of countervailing impulses towards reparative remembering during this same period.

Just as traumatic splitting is bound up with spatial divisions and political conflicts in the social world, so the possibility of psychic reparation is mutually intertwined with the rebuilding of social and cultural connection and exchange across historic divides, as aspects of conflict resolution set in train by the peace process. Narratives of reparation in the Border areas have focused on themes of the return to lost places and the rebuilding of damaged places. Imagery of the ruined-but-repaired (or at least reparable) building has been deployed to symbolize processes of psychic restoration, reparation and renewal emerging in response to psychic deathliness, destruction and disintegration. During summer 1997, for example, in the context of a renewed IRA ceasefire and the commencement of multi-party talks, public interest was seized by stories of the possible return of displaced Border Protestants to restore their houses and farms abandoned some twenty-five years earlier.[133]

These motifs can also be identified in respect of the charged sites where killings took place. In 1997, new economic opportunities emerging through the peace process persuaded the Bullock family to renovate its empty farmhouse and make it habitable again.[134] By 1999, as work neared completion and Joan Bullock planned imminently to move into the house, she showed around Susan McKay, who records that: 'We entered by the back door, the way the gunmen came, and she described the murders. "However", she said with a sigh, "that's in the past now. It is a beautiful place, isn't it?" '[135] According to the psychoanalyst, Dori Laub: 'Trauma survivors live not with memories of the past, but with an event that could not and did not proceed through to its completion', while psychic reparation requires survivors 'to reassert the veracity of the past and to build anew its linkage to, and assimilation into, present-day life'.[136] When Joan Bullock is able to place her relatives' killing 'in the past', the site of the 'shambles' may be restored as once again a 'beautiful place', and life there can be resumed. The restoration of the damaged house and the resumption of everyday life within it are at once the symbols of and the vehicles for a psychic reparation, in which the haunted place and the memory of the terrible events that occurred there are reintegrated into a social reality that is no longer overshadowed by them. Perhaps the most powerful symbol of reparation through restoration in the damaged cultural landscape of the Border areas was the redevelopment of the long-neglected site of the IRA's 'Poppy Day' bomb, beside the war memorial in Enniskillen, by the Higher Bridges Project of 1999–2001 (see chapter 10).

Reparative processes have also been set in motion through efforts towards the rebuilding of cross-border geographical and social links, initially by the re-opening of closed Border crossings, which has transformed the conditions of everyday living for local communities. By 2001, when I visited the Fermanagh–Cavan Border, the opening up of 'all European frontiers to free movement and trade' envisaged at the implementation of the Single European Market nine years earlier had been largely achieved. I had taken my passport to cross on the former 'approved road' from Enniskillen to Swanlinbar, but the British Army's Border post and barrier at Mullan had been dismantled and bypassed by a wide, newly tarmaced, main road, that skirted the ruins of the checkpoint hut. The Border here had vanished, to be replaced by a sign stating only 'Welcome to Co. Cavan'. Twelve miles away, a new bridge at Aghalane, built with money from the European Union's Peace and Reconciliation Fund, was opened in 1999 'to carry the European highway into Belturbet'.[137] For Simon Bullock, now able to go for a drink in the towns of Co. Cavan, the restored link to the South generated a new geographical consciousness: 'It is like as if we were living on an island and we don't know it. They speak with a different accent . . . The towns are so different too. Our towns have been bombed and wrecked and rebuilt – theirs are so old-fashioned.'[138] Emerging from the isolation of the war years to enter into new connections across the former divide, the places of everyday life appear strange and unrecognizable, bearing the marks of differential development in the communities north and south, engendered during twenty-five years of separation. However, some Protestants, like 'Doreen' from the Fermanagh–Monaghan Border near Rosslea, have a more ambivalent response to the demilitarization of the Border due to the peace process. While acknowledging that it had been ' "very inconvenient when the roads were blocked" . . . she had been happier [and "felt safer"] when there were blocked roads, barriers, checkpoints and soldiers in the army post',[139] in a visible manifestation of the Border's traditional defensive function.

A further reparative development in the course of the peace process has been the emergence of cross-border community development projects focused on the specific needs of Protestant communities. In 1995, for example, Derry and Raphoe Action (DARA) was launched to work with 'mainly rural Protestant communities in the counties of Londonderry, Tyrone and Donegal'. In 2001, DARA reported anxieties about the preservation of a distinct Protestant culture, including 'fear of assimilation . . . [and] loss of identity', among Donegal's 'silent minority' of 14,000 Protestants (now some 10 per cent of the county's population), despite their clear identification as Irish, and good relations with the Catholic majority.[140] For DARA, addressing these matters of faith, identity and community in Co. Donegal involves the strengthening of 'links between Protestants on both sides of the border', and their 'work[ing] together on social, economic, cultural and environmental issues'.[141] These forward-looking alliances also involve Protestants and their Catholic neighbours in reparative remembering, an intrinsic part of peace-building that has generated new initiatives, such as the archive established by the Raphoe Reconciliation Project to enable 'local people and visitors . . . to explore the historical roots of division and to create new bonds of friendship, reconciliation and community through discussion and dialogue'.[142]

Present-day Protestant cultural identity in the three 'lost counties' of nine-county Ulster, and in the Border counties of Northern Ireland, cannot be understood, protected or developed without an engagement with the troubled and divided histories of these Border Protestant communities, and the complexity of their neglected and privatized cultural memories. These are not comfortable histories to address, and the polarized legacy of memory and identity instituted by the Border is not easy to negotiate. For all his involvement with cross-border development work, Derek Reaney, a community worker with DARA in Co. Tyrone, whose own grandfather moved into Northern Ireland from Co. Wicklow during the partition and 'never again crossed the Border', believes that the

> Border is a symbol for the problems in this island. Two different communities, two different peoples and two different cultures . . . For those who are from a [U]nionist position, the Border is a line in the sand . . . [I]f and when it disappears, it will remain in the hearts of men and women. Today that red line on the map is not just ink, it is blood, sacrificed in the name of peace and freedom and it will simply not disappear as easily as some would wish.[143]

This is a salutary reminder that, for the Protestant people of the Border areas, cultural memories of violent conflict are not erasable, but are deeply inscribed within current imaginative geography, where subjectivities and senses of identity continue to be shaped, in often contradictory ways, by the psychic borders of partition.

8

Giving voice: Protestant and Unionist victims' groups and memories of the Troubles in the Irish peace process

Since the first ceasefires in 1994, histories and memories of the Irish Troubles have been voiced and contested throughout Northern Ireland, as individuals and communities attempt to come to terms with the traumatic legacy of the past. Powerful and often contradictory dynamics are at work here, in the interplay between the politics of peace-making and conflict resolution, on one hand, and the imperatives of remembrance, psychic and emotional as well as political, on the other. These dynamics are evident in attempts to address the needs of the victims and survivors of violence, and in the debates and conflicts surrounding this issue, which have centred on the British Government's victims' policy, a key component of its conflict-resolution strategy within the Irish peace process. Initiated by the Bloomfield Report of 1998, and implemented by the Victims Liaison Unit (VLU), attached initially to the Northern Ireland Office at Stormont, this approach has involved the channelling of central state funds into local areas to meet a range of physical, psychological and cultural needs, identified by victims of violence and their advocates as necessary to their well-being. It established a framework setting the terms on which existing advocacy and support groups within civil society could bid for state recognition of their work, and it also stimulated the emergence of new social agents of memory from those areas most affected by the armed conflict. The aims of these so-called 'victims' groups' are to represent the victims of violence, to tell their stories and to promote their interests by lobbying for financial, psychological and other kinds of support. In the process, they have been involved in organizing a new kind of public voice for the victims, which is authorized to speak from the newly empowered position of victim about previously silenced or 'forgotten' memories. In many cases, particularly where groups promote a nationalist or a Unionist political analysis of the causes and effects of the violence inflicted on them, these aims have produced memories of the Troubles which clash with the State's agenda of reconciliation and healing, and with the memories of other groups, bringing about a new *politics of victimhood*.

This chapter examines the memories of the Troubles articulated by grassroots victims' groups that have emerged in the Border regions of Northern Ireland (see map 2) and describe themselves, variously, as Protestant, British, loyalist or Unionist. Between July 1999 and April 2000 I visited three such groups to meet activists and members. FEAR Fermanagh, Ltd (FEAR being an acronym for Fear Encouraged Abandoning Roots), was formed in 1995 to campaign on behalf of Protestants from the Border areas of Co. Fermanagh 'who were displaced and forced to abandon roots, their homes [as a result of] direct intimidation or fear' of IRA violence.[1] Families Acting for Innocent Relatives (FAIR), based in Markethill, Co. Armagh, was formed in 1998 to represent the British victims of Republican violence in South Armagh. West Tyrone Voice, based in Newtownstewart, Co. Tyrone, was formed in early 1999 'as a result of needs which were identified amongst those who had been the innocent victims of paramilitary terrorism' in the western Border area of County Tyrone.[2] In order to represent the practical and emotional needs of their members, the groups assert the memory of a distinctive Protestant and Unionist experience of violence, as a counter to what they perceive as the Government's 'appeasement of Republican terrorists' and its responsiveness to nationalist campaigns on behalf of the victims of state violence, particularly by its investment of some £400 million in the Bloody Sunday Inquiry.[3] Their common aim is 'to tell our side of the story':[4] to break the silence about, and 'give voice' to, the trauma inflicted on the Protestants and Unionists living beside the Border by the IRA and other Republican paramilitary organizations during the Troubles; and to insist that this legacy of fear and suffering be recognized and redressed as a fundamental aspect of conflict resolution.

In this, the Protestant and Unionist victims' groups of the Border areas have laid claim to the cultural memory of ethnic cleansing as a means of framing the collective story of their communities' experiences of the Troubles. However, its re-articulation in the new context of the peace process also relates to a range of pressures and needs generated within Protestant and Unionist communities as they have struggled to come to terms with the traumatic aftershocks of the violent past, whil also adjusting to – and contesting their own place within – the transformed cultural and political environment after the ceasefires. The victims' groups have developed fresh and often more complex ways of remembering the violence and its effects, which have contradictory ramifications. Each has its own specific origins, aims and modes of remembering, that arise out of the particular history of the Troubles in its locality, but also in response to the political circumstances at its moment of formation.

FEAR, formed a few months after the first IRA ceasefire, gathered together a group of displaced Protestants who had left their homes and farms along the Fermanagh Border through fear of, or as a result of direct intimidation by, the IRA.[5] The group used the term 'ethnic cleansing' as the basis for its claim that there was a collective dimension to this forced displacement of Border Protestants from rural Fermanagh: that 'the experiences of republican violence of the past twenty-five years in many cases directed at security force personnel, was/is an attack on the entire Protestant/unionist community'.[6] FEAR, in laying claim to the category 'victims of violence' on behalf of the displaced individuals and families, sought acknowledgement of the material as well as psychological 'costs and losses' they had experienced,[7] but also financial support for those who wished to move back to the area and regenerate their abandoned homes and farms:

> The returning of individuals to communities they felt forced to leave surely speaks of trust and hope . . . The return and rejuvenation of homes and farms once occupied and thriving, carried out in the right spirit would make a beneficial contribution to the building of peace and reconciliation for the wider community as well as to the healing process of the individuals and families directly involved.[8]

While the FEAR group was formed in an atmosphere of relative optimism early in the peace process, the FAIR group originated in the complex and contradictory mood of the Unionist heartlands after the signing of the Good Friday Agreement in April 1998. If the wish to seize the opportunity for wider recognition opened up by the Bloomfield initiative was one motivating factor,[9] another was the widespread anger felt by many Unionists at the Agreement's provision for the early release of paramilitary prisoners: 'The insensitive early release of terrorists who caused so much grief has reopened old wounds which were never properly healed.'[10] This anger was exacerbated by the use of EU Peace and Reconciliation Fund money on support groups for ex-prisoners, who were widely felt to be receiving preferential treatment compared to their victims, in contravention of natural justice. These arguments had a particular resonance in the Unionist communities of South Armagh, where a scattered, isolated, Protestant minority felt itself to be living in a state of continuing fear of actual, not just threatened, Republican violence.[11] FAIR claimed the status of 'real victims' for those who suffered at the hands of Republican terrorists, as distinguished from those who, it believed, were not 'victims' at all, but rather 'perpetrators' of violence.[12] This link between the memory of unresolved injustices and the continuing fears and grievances of the present struck a chord, and FAIR quickly grew into one of the largest of the victims' groups, claiming forty-three activists supporting 613 'victims within the Bloomfield definition' at its formal launch in April 1999.[13]

West Tyrone Voice also emerged out of the groundswell of discontent provoked by the prisoner-release scheme, and functioned as a vehicle for the expression of Protestant and Unionist discontent with the peace process. Its formation was in part a response to the Omagh bomb, planted on 15 August 1998 by the splinter group the Real IRA, that killed twenty-nine people and injured several hundred others. This 'indirectly acted as a catalyst', in that it

> made people think again, about . . . why the folk who had suffered over thirty years [haven't] had their suffering recognized. Because . . . whilst a number of our members would have been folk who had suffered in the Omagh bomb, there were still thirty years of suffering and pain and mayhem and terrorism that hadn't seemed to have been accounted for.[14]

West Tyrone, especially the 'Castlederg Border triangle' which obtrudes into the Irish Republic, had seen intensive IRA activity as well as operations by the loyalist UFF.[15] Altogether some 200 people were killed in the area in the course of the Troubles, and many of those deaths remain unresolved. West Tyrone Voice set out 'to offer care and support in a sensitive way to anyone who has suffered trauma as a result of terrorist activity . . . and to their families'. By 'speaking and acting' on their behalf, it also aimed to 'seek justice for these victims', to 'seek formal recognition of their suffering', and to 'ensure the story of our pain and loss is never forgotten'. In this way, Voice set out to represent ' "the Disappeared" of West Tyrone. They have been ignored by our political and church leaders, and dismissed as irrelevant by national and international governments.'[16]

The politics of victimhood as practised by these three victims groups significantly overlaps with the political affiliations and identifications of Ulster Unionism, loyalism and Protestantism. Yet there is no neat fit between the collective 'we' of traditional religious and political identities and the 'we' of the 'suffering community',[17] as variously constructed by the victims' groups. The tensions that exist between these collective identifications are signalled in the contrast between FEAR's straightforward declaration as a group for victims of violence from the 'Unionist' and 'Protestant' community, and FAIR's rejection of those 'labels' – particularly 'the term "unionist" . . . that some government agencies have begun to use . . . when trying to describe a community of Ulster Protestants' – in favour of the so-called 'non-political' designation 'British'.[18] All three groups claim to be 'decidedly non-party political, and . . . not aligned to any religious body'.[19] This represents an 'anti-sectarian' gesture to encourage a more inclusive *we* based on cross-community membership – or at least, to avoid the stigma of being charged with sectarianism. Membership of Voice, for example, is open to all residents or fomer residents of the area who 'have suffered bereavement, loss or injury (physical, emotional or mental) as a result of terrorist activity', irrespective of 'religious background, political opinion or cultural practice', with the proviso only that 'you renounce ALL acts of terrorist violence'.[20] In April 2000, both FAIR and Voice claimed to have 'some Catholics in our group who have suffered the same as what the rest of us have suffered',[21] though in the case of FAIR, at least, the numbers were negligible.[22] According to FAIR worker Willie Frazer, while there had been over forty Catholics killed by the IRA in the South Armagh area, only a few had contacted the group, through fear of IRA intimidation or because they would not identify with its ethos.[23]

The ethos of these groups is indeed deeply rooted in a Protestant *moral* analysis of the Troubles.[24] Hazlett Lynch has claimed of Voice that, 'as country people and as people who were brought up within a broad Christian ethos, we do know the difference between right and wrong . . . And we try to take that high moral ground without in any way giving our stamp of approval to any political grouping.'[25] However, the black-and white moral categories that are then deployed – in the distinction between 'the lawmakers and the lawbreakers'[26] or between the 'guardians of law and order' and the 'evil terrorists'[27] – are intertwined ideologically with a historical defence of the morality of the Unionist six-county State and the practices of its security forces. Just as the BSI cast its human rights narrative within the frame of the national struggle for British withdrawal and a united Ireland, thereby excluding even liberal Unionists, so this narrative of law enforcement against terrorism is a political construction that would inevitably pose difficulties of identification for nationalists, even those who have no sympathy with (or who may themselves be the victims of) Republican paramilitarism. Even though these victims' groups appeal to plural constituencies, this political polarization limits opportunities for exchanging stories across the community divide.

Memory work is necessarily threaded through activities undertaken by all three groups to support victims of the Troubles, and can be traced in private and public arenas. In what follows, I look first at the role of the victims' groups in providing a safe, private, listening space for personal remembrance, before turning to the voicing of victims' stories within diverse public arenas. The analysis explores motivations behind the public voicing of these memories of the Troubles, that may pull in quite different directions, with contradictory and paradoxical ramifications. It also reflects on the complex intertwinings that exist between the politics of victimhood espoused by these groups, the political identity of Ulster Unionists and Protestants as shaped by the Troubles, and the psychic and emotional needs of the victims. Finally, it considers the unsettling effects of these 'awkward voices' on the established narratives of memory deployed by all the main protagonists within the peace process.

Personal memory within private arenas

Through their engagement with personal experience, the victims' groups found themselves involved in individual remembering that does not always simply reinforce the anti-Republican collective narrative of 'ethnic cleansing'. Like the Bloody Sunday Justice Campaign, all three of these victims' groups began their work in small-group meetings where personal stories could be told and shared. Since the victims of violence had had to live without adequate support hitherto, a vital task for the groups was to alter the mindset of 'just getting on with it' by helping people to identify their needs. In the process, telling and listening to personal life-stories emerged as powerful and important activities in their own right. This storytelling has posed a fundamental challenge to the culture of silence, which requires internal, psychic (as well as external, cultural and political) inhibitions against speaking out; inhibitions which, it emerged, had in many cases been self-maintained as a strategy for survival. Arlene Foster of FEAR explains: 'when people were having horrific things happening to their families and communities, it was this "stiff upper lip" mentality of, "If we don't discuss it then we're not victims of it", not wanting to be seen as victims, which is very much still a live issue'.[28] Within Protestant and Unionist communities, victims' groups have enabled the telling for the first time of stories of trauma, in some cases going back thirty years. Foster describes how the FEAR activists spoke to Border farmers in their sixties:

> [They] had left their homes and they'd never really spoken about how they felt at the time that they were forced to leave. They . . . never actually said, 'Well actually I felt terrible at that time, leaving my home which had been in my family for generations and the sense of "letting the whole side down" and moving away because I had young children and I felt it was the best for them.' . . . [W]hen they are talking about things that have happened in the past . . . a lot of the emotional hurt is only coming out now . . . like post-traumatic stress disorder. Things that happened twenty years ago are still there in the subconscious.[29]

For FAIR members, '[m]uch of the time in the early meetings was spent simply talking and sharing'.[30] Willie Frazer, the group's vice-chairperson, recalled: 'When a neighbour or a friend was murdered by Irish terrorists and you met their family at the graveside or on the street, it wasn't the time or place for talking. You gripped their hand and you said "I know . . ." That was all you needed to hear or say.'[31] S.J. Wilson, in his report on behalf the group, comments:

> A simple 'I know' was for over thirty years the extent of communication . . . For thirty years, no umbrella body or collective help existed where individuals could find a 'safe' haven for comfort, discussion of mutual needs, a place to get beyond the 'I know' and tease out in emotional terms what that knowledge had cost. FAIR meets this need.[32]

The Protestant and Unionist victims' groups have provided a safe, private space in which personal memories can be articulated, shared and recognized, and where the many differences as well as commonalities of remembered experience may be expressed and explored.[33] While the personal stories exchanged within this 'haven' are by their very nature private, a sense of the complex and disturbing qualities of these memories – and the intractable experiences that they struggle to compose – can be discerned in the transcripts of interviews conducted with members of FEAR in August 1997. These include 'Mr and Mrs Gordon' and 'Mr Sidwell', whose stories of displacement from their home-farms on the Border were discussed in the previous chapter. Their accounts provide evidence of contrasting forms of personal remembering, not reducible to the cultural memory of ethnic cleansing, as individuals work to compose a version of their past that can be lived with in the present.

The Gordons' memories of displacement in 1972, for example, remained live and troubling twenty-five years later, as they continued to revisit the events and hurts of the past, to question the causes of their traumatic experience and to reflect on their continuing effects in the present.[34] Recalling the decision to leave, Mr Gordon speaks repeatedly of how hard it had been to make, and – struggling with regret about its impact on their lives – emphasizes its over-whelming necessity:

> It was the hardest decision to move out of a home you were reared in and that was left to me. We were doing well at the time. I felt bad making this decision but the security forces couldn't guarantee our full protection as we were living in an area that was very isolated near the border. Because of having to move, I had to give up the farming, although I always thought I'd start up again. I had to get a living somehow and so I worked full-time in the UDR. It's all I could do.

The Gordons' whole life was upturned: 'It was unbelievable what we lost over the whole thing.' They received no relocation expenses, injury compensation was minimal and their only support from the authorities was 'an emergency house which I suppose we got over a list of others'. Financial difficulties followed from giving up the farm. They had to sell their cattle and farming machinery at a loss, but were made such a derisory offer for the land that they chose to hold on to it. By the time one of their sons began to consider farming again, the land had deteriorated too far, and the house had become run down. It was some years before they were able to sell the farm for a better price and buy a new house. Remembering these difficulties involves Mr Gordon in re-encountering feelings of powerlessness and defeat, as he revisits the decision that proved to be the major turning point in his own life and that of his family. He reaffirms that he had not given up easily, that ideals were compromised under duress: 'I said the first time "I'll not go".' The second time made me think again.' He describes the traumatic after-effects that continue to trouble him: 'I'd been attacked twice and my life was at stake. As a result I am very nervous. There are places I should go and I don't. I stopped going out.' Retelling his life-story, he works to reconfirm that he did what was right: 'We did loss out [sic] but I suppose I've got my life . . . We are both retired now and this suits us. But it would be helpful to have some recognition of what we have went through.'[35]

A different kind of remembering can be read in the story told to FEAR by 'Mr Sidwell' about his move from the Border into Lisnaskea in 1991, after his business premises had been blown up four times and his family kidnapped and used in a proxy bombing (described in chapter 7).[36] His narrative leaves unspoken the emotional impact of this sequence of events. Equally matter-of-fact is his recollection of the cumulative impact of the attacks on his family's livelihood and financial well-being, and his explanation of why they had been targeted: 'Each time [the business] was blown up we were worse off. And since they started blowing it up, the business went down hill, before all of that it was a good concern.' Having decided to sell up, 'I did not get good value . . . people were afraid to buy it, and sure it had been bombed out so many times. But they (the IRA) have got everything they wanted, to get us out.' The memory of the horror and its aftermath appear to be contained here by the imperative of resignation to a hard and unjust reality. Unlike Mrs Gordon, who continues to wonder 'Why did they attack us?', Mr Sidwell has achieved a way of making sense of the injustice of the attacks and their rationale; yet his memories have a muted quality about them. There is no hint in this story of any means of redress, and he discounts any possibility of return to the farm which the family still owns: 'There is no way you could go back to it.' Yet Mr Sidwell is adamant: 'I will not sell it.' At 68 years of age, his working life, he felt, was over; and anyway it was his son, the victim of the proxy bombing, who had been the farmer. What does come through the interview is a stoical determination to endure: 'Once we got out alive, you carried on the best you could.' But it is clear that this stoicism has a price. In memory, the unendurable has to be dealt with – or else banished: 'If you were to dwell on it [it] would put you round the bend. Your only hope is to forget about it.'[37]

Forgetting is one psychological strategy open to the victims of violence in their lifelong struggle to compose a version of the past they can live with. Nevertheless, however strong the desire to forget, the psyche's defences are unable to achieve complete amnesia. Like the nationalists traumatized by Bloody Sunday, the Protestant victims of the IRA have continued to be haunted by the past in the form of dreams, flashbacks and emotional distress; and to be affected by the frozen quality of traumatic memory, experiencing the numbness and reduced sense of personal agency that diminishes the capacity for life in the present.[38] The narration and social recognition of these traumatic experiences, whether in the restricted, private arena of a personal interview, or in the longer-term supportive environment of a victims' group, may make it possible for the feelings attached to them to be made conscious and their meanings explored. In the years immediately after the first ceasefires, the idea that 'recovering from' or 'coming to terms with' traumatic experience requires self-representation, through a process of telling one's own story, was introduced into the Northern Irish debate about the victims of violence, and entered popular discourse as a kind of conventional wisdom. The ability to narrate one's own story, as a means to secure recognition, has become associated with a transition from the condition of being a (passive) *victim*, subjected to the overwhelming after-effects of violence, into that of an (active) *survivor*, able to assert psychic agency by acknowledging and claiming a painful and difficult past as his or her own.[39] Victims of violence like Edward Gordon have used the term 'recognition' to express a felt need, and it became common currency within the victims' lobby organized by the VLU and the Northern Ireland Voluntary Trust (NIVT).[40]

Many victims' groups, including those of the Border Protestants, drew on this model to direct and explain the value of their own support work. Activists discovered that, for some of their members, this 'recognition' helped to bring about an increasing confidence and self-assertiveness in making sense of personal circumstances and seeking redress for them in the present. When FEAR first started and members were asked 'let's hear your story':

Initially they were almost embarrassed to be saying 'Oh, well, I had to move from my home', 'Oh, it wasn't too bad' . . . all this sort of thing. 'Oh, I know there's a lot of people worse off than me that were murdered, and at least I was lucky and I got out', was their way [of telling] it. But as they started to tell it more and more – because . . . when you're a group like that and you meet ministers from the Government or you meet people from Victims Liaison who want to hear what has actually happened – you can hear them asserting themselves more: 'Yes, it was difficult at that time, and for the children, having to move schools'; and . . . you could hear them thinking more about it.[41]

Besides unlocking emotions associated with the trauma of violent bereavement or loss, and often expressed in terms of the cultural memory of 'ethnic cleansing', the telling of these stories also evokes other memories and emotions. For example, in the case of former UDR soldier Leslie Finlay of West Tyrone Voice, remembering the losses of the Troubles also involved a difficult realization of official neglect and lack of support; a realization that may be especially acute for Unionists who have been deeply identified with, and fought to defend, the Northern Ireland State.

I look back on one of the things that brings a lot of sadness to me, that . . . at that time nobody seemed to be really interested in us. You were going out there, you buried a mate, the funeral was over, that's it, we're all alive and that, and we're continuing on again. And . . . we had no counselling, no nothing . . . In fact there was three people out of my platoon were buried and on the day we buried them we were expected to go out on duty that night after the funeral. And I look back on that now and that makes me very angry that people were so insensitive . . . they'd no care for us at all . . . we were sent out there . . . gun fodder. And it was, 'Go out there and get the job done, but don't say anything'! . . . [W]e thought somebody was looking after [the families of] these people. But it's only later on that we found out that there was nobody looking after them.[42]

Here, the memory of loss compounded by a realization of the 'insensitivity' and lack of care on the part of state authorities provokes a complex emotional reaction: Finlay talks of his shame, sadness, anger and sense of insult and betrayal. But such feelings have also fuelled a desire to right those wrongs, together with a conviction that no one else can be relied on to do so, that finds expression in the self-help ethos of a group such as West Tyrone Voice.

Work with the victims of violence also led to an increasing awareness that if one effect of the articulation of traumatic memory is a greater self-confidence and sense of agency, its corollary is likely to be a heightened emotional experience characterized by feelings of hurt, loss, fear and anger that may become overwhelming. In the debate about these issues, one concern was that the victims' groups 'haven't got the expertise to deal with' the emotions that arise.[43] Another was the worry that 'victims telling their stories from this past thirty years [is] going to bring an awful lot of hurt back into the community'.[44] This was a general concern in Northern Ireland after the 1994 ceasefires. Like other advocates of the value of victims' groups, Arlene

Foster argued: 'If the hurt's already there and not being discussed, then it's always going to be there and the bitterness is always going to be there, subconscious or otherwise.'[45] While not addressing the emotional issues in the same way as would a professional counsellor, the groups made it possible for such issues to be voiced and acknowledged, and they provided a stepping-stone to professional help, where appropriate. Above all, they helped raise awareness of the importance of providing a space that is, relatively speaking, *safe*. The effects of insecurity – and the dangers felt by the victims of violence to be inherent in any voicing of their stories – are powerfully felt, even within this private arena. However, the search for social recognition as well as redress also involved the victims' groups in memory work within the public domain, where those difficulties are intensified.

The voices of the victims in public arenas

In their formation, each of the three victims' groups was conceived as an agent for the voicing of survivors' memories within the public domain. Hazlett Lynch, co-ordinator of West Tyrone Voice, speaks of the strong local support for the formation of a group that would: 'be a voice for the victims, somebody to articulate our suffering and our pain, seek recognition, . . . seek justice for our members and for our community', and break the 'silence . . . enforced on us over the years'. Lynch identifies two agents of silencing. The first is the IRA:

> Quite a number of people would have had associations, links with the security forces, and you never wanted to let on, that your husband or your father or your brother served in the security forces. Because that in a sense was tantamount to encouraging gunmen to visit you or your home or your workplace. So you kept that very, very much a hush-hush thing.

The second is 'the pressure from the community, from some politicians, from the media, to say, "Don't get involved, keep yourself off-side [*sic*]." Even some of the security forces will tell us that.' For Lynch, the realization that 'we cannot stay silent', and the imperative to speak out publicly in order to secure recognition, redress and justice, manifested with new urgency as a result of events in 1998:

> We did suffer in silence. And hopefully the way we suffered was dignified, respectful to our loved ones who had been murdered. And yet we were holding in a pain and an ache inside that could only be contained for so long. And we contained it for almost thirty years . . . [It was only] after the early release of terrorist prisoners that we felt that we cannot keep this in any longer. We've got to come out, it's almost like your gay people, coming out.[46]

In Lynch's account, the 'coming out' of these 'closet' victims is a dynamic and liberating process, accompanied by a release of pent-up psychic energy, as the long-established strategy of containment breaks down in response to the provocative catalyst of the prisoner-release scheme. The 'coming out' metaphor also invokes a newly constructed identity shared with others, that empowers those who embrace it to tell their story of oppression, at the very moment they begin to throw off that oppression.

When the victims 'go public', then, they constitute for themselves a new collective voice and agency: a *we* on whose behalf the victims' group speaks – and acts. For as Lynch points out, 'It isn't only the talking, it's about action as well . . . the two things go hand-in-hand together, and we seek to follow what we say by the things that we do . . . And put feet onto the words that we're speaking.'[47] There are two aspects to this. Firstly, despite these victims' groups' strong self-help ethos, the need to be effective in welfare and advocacy work has promoted a desire to be represented by those who have real experience of speaking out publicly. Among members of FAIR, for example, it became clear that 'the victims wanted a champion':[48] 'We need someone to work for us, give advice, stand up for justice.' Secondly, in their pursuit of public recognition, redress and justice for this newly constructed community of 'we, the victims', the victims' groups re-present the many complex personal memories of their clients as a singular, collective narrative that tells of '*our* experiences'. Subject now to the forms and procedures of public representation, which shape the ways in which the victims' memories are produced for and enter various public arenas, this story comes to be told across a range of modes of representation, ranging from the exhibition, the pamphlet or the memorial site designed for a local area, to the formal submission to government; and from the human-interest story in the national public news media to the website reaching a 'global' public.

In the groups' work to articulate traumatic memories of the Troubles within the public domain, a number of distinct needs and desires come into play that can involve contradictory goals and effects. Three aims of the groups' public narration of memories can be distinguished: the first, to secure material redress to meet physical and psychological needs; the second, to elicit wider social recognition for victims as a damaged community; and the third, to achieve emotional catharsis in relation to the perpetrators of violence.

Remembering for material redress

One motive for public voicing has been the necessity to remember and represent the experience of victimhood in order to qualify for grants and other material support. It requires the framing of personal memories so as to lay claim to the category of 'victim', and their presentation within a collective history of unacknowledged trauma that seeks social recognition on behalf of a damaged local community. FEAR, for example, whose search for funding began before the victims' lobby system had been established by Bloomfield, was advised by Secretary of State Mo Mowlam to submit a needs' analysis in order to be considered for grant support.[49] This led, in August 1997, to a report commissioned from the community worker Ruth Moore, articulating the case for helping those who wished to return to their abandoned farms and homesteads to do so.[50] In her *Research document and development plan*, the identification of the various needs of victims was grounded on the claim that Border Protestants had been collectively victimized by 'republican terrorist violence', a claim underpinned by a historical analysis of the causes and effects of displacement, that was based largely on personal and collective memory, and leaned heavily on the narrative of 'ethnic cleansing'.[51] Noting both that funders 'appear more sympathetic to victims of violence – a recognized target group within [the] peace and reconciliation package',[52] and the lack of research on the relation between rural depopulation and IRA activities along the Fermanagh Border, Moore turned to oral history. This was used 'to engage with' these Protestant communities' experiences and perceptions of forced displacement 'in order to begin to identify what peace and reconciliation, [and] social inclusion . . . might mean for the individuals concerned, the wider community to which they belong, and the government and development agencies which also play a role'.[53]

Based on the contacts already established by FEAR, the research (undertaken in August 1997) focused on a small qualitative sample of nineteen individuals who had been 'directly affected by "the troubles" in Fermanagh'.[54] Most of them told not only their own personal stories but also those of their immediate or extended families. A four-part questionnaire (supplemented by either written notes or an informal interview) created a structured framework for personal remembering.[55] Authorized to speak as 'victims of violence', a number of whom had 'left their homes due to direct attacks, threat or fear',[56] these individuals' personal memories are framed and re-presented by the report to serve three purposes. Firstly, they corroborate the collective narrative of a systematic campaign by the IRA, over three decades, to 'clear the border'[57] in Fermanagh of Protestants: 'Republican violence has in part been experienced as "ethnic conflict" ', and is perceived by the Protestant–Unionist community as an instance of 'ethnic cleansing'.[58] Secondly, they demonstrate the 'traumatic experience of having to move under threat and fear', as in 'Mrs Gillen's' memory of how, 'when we had to leave Garrison, I was expecting. That child only lived for ten weeks. That was the stress of that time. In the time before we left, I used to have to go round the shed with a gun in my hand.'[59] Thirdly, they provide 'verbal testimony that scars remain and that individuals are still living with the social, psycholog[ical] and medical impact of being forced to move'.[60] This research laid the basis for the subsequent financial assessment of need requested by the Secretary of State, prepared by a PR consultant and presented to the Government in March 1999 (but subsequently turned down).[61]

In the case of FAIR, needs' assessment research was carried out in early 1999 by the consultant S.J. Wilson, funded by NIVT and the CRC from the EU Special Support Programme for Peace and Reconciliation.[62] This was produced in accordance with the requirements of what, by this time, had become an established victims' lobby structure with clear mechanisms and procedures for submitting applications for such funding. As with FEAR, a questionnaire was first drawn up by the group itself. This was distributed to the first 100 people on the group's list of registered victims, and achieved a 100 per cent response. The research itself stimulated wider interest and involvement in the group: 'Completion of the questionnaire became regarded as a positive experience. A chance to have one's say.'[63] Wilson followed this up with focus groups to discuss in more detail personal experiences of IRA terrorism, the effects of bereavement and injury, and the support – or lack thereof – for victims provided by state and other agencies. In Wilson's ensuing report, FAIR is shown to represent a traumatized community of hitherto invisible victims from an area that, he claims, suffered 'the worst levels of violence during the Troubles'.[64] Elsewhere, FAIR quantified this as '378 murders, 1,255 bombs, 1,158 gun attacks' claimed by or attributed to Republican paramilitary groups in what is described as 'the Circle of Death', an area within a ten-mile radius of 'the heart of South Armagh'.[65]

Wilson's report provides a historical analysis of the collective impact of this violence on the area's minority Protestant population, estimated to number as few as 5,000 (out of a total of approximately 25,000),[66] an impact 'evident in almost every Protestant household'.[67] As in the case of FEAR, this impact is represented in terms of the narrative of 'ethnic cleansing' and grounded on the personal memories of respondents. As in the Fermanagh Border areas, the 'British community in South Armagh actively supported the Crown Forces and many joined the RUC, RUC Reserve and the UDR', which they perceived 'as service to their community and as "doing something positive" to check the murders and the attacks on property'. Here, too, IRA attacks on the local security forces had been experienced and remembered as attacks on their families, not least because 'the UDR men [were seldom] killed "on duty". Often the killers would invade the home, and conduct the murder in full view of the family', children notwithstanding.[68] However, the story told by Wilson of 'ethnic cleansing' in South Armagh differs from the Fermanagh narrative in emphasizing the isolation of widely dispersed Protestant families and the corrosive effects of an atmosphere of intimidation and fear created by neighbours among whom they continued to live. Whereas for Fermanagh Protestants danger was felt to emanate from the Border itself, across which IRA attacks were launched and gunmen retreated, the 'IRA of Crossmaglen district didn't retreat anywhere . . . they simply went home, protected by the unseeing eyes of their families, friends and neighbours'.[69] Here, the local memory of the 'British community' traces the beginning of 'ethnic cleansing' to the earliest incidents of the contemporary conflict. According to 'the families of FAIR', the Troubles in South Armagh began not with the booby-trap car bomb that killed two RUC constables on 12 August 1970 in Crossmaglen – the 'received view' – but with the burning by Republicans of Protestant-owned farms and businesses in Crossmaglen and Newtownhamilton one year earlier on 16 August 1969.[70] Prior to this, South Armagh is remembered as having been 'an integrated and largely well adjusted pluralist society'.[71] Once the IRA campaign had begun in August 1970, however, 'Protestants began to sense a change in their Catholic neighbours', and a new atmosphere developed, of unease, fear and suspicion of being constantly observed and targeted for attack.[72] Wilson documents 'the constant trauma and terror of knowing that one's religion and ethnic identity identified one as a potential target',[73] and evokes the pervasive sense of threat transmitted by particularly shocking practices of the IRA, including cases (or rumours) of abduction and torture.[74] He also documents FAIR's bereaved families' memories of 'years of vindictive harassment . . . from neighbours who held Republican sympathies', ranging from verbal abuse and triumphalist taunts about 'how we got' the dead person to mockery of those carrying out funereal and commemorative rites and the destruction of memorial statues.[75] Republican neighbours were remembered as attending UDR funerals for the purpose of targeting the coffin-bearers.[76] Nor were the bereaved themselves free from attack, whether from the petrol bombs of local Republican youth or the guns of the IRA.[77]

'Serious psychological damage has been experienced by the community', the result of prolonged exposure to this violence, according to Wilson [78] The damage was most acute among those families who had suffered violent bereavement: thirty-four of Wilson's 100 survey respondents had suffered the loss through violence of a close relative between 1972 and 1991; twenty-two of them had been UDR soldiers or RUC officers, who tended to be of mature age and so left behind widows and young children.[79] The legacy of these violent bereavements included the economic deprivation of families without breadwinners, educational underachievement, loss of self-confidence and profound anxiety: 'for up to thirty years, the survivors have suffered nightmares, flashbacks, and a constant fear that the death squads would come back to finish the job'.[80] Wilson's report made the case for government support to address this psychological legacy, helping to secure grant aid from NIVT to fund several workers and a range of projects. These included outreach work to visit individuals and families in often isolated locations throughout the region, but also research into the local history of the Troubles by a historian, William Wilkinson, who contributed to a series of public representations that began to articulate an alternative cultural memory of the South Armagh region.

Remembering for social recognition and reconciliation
In making the case for government support for FAIR, Wilson's report also argued that the traumatic effects of violence on the Protestants of South Armagh had been compounded by their invisibility to the wider public. Unlike high-profile 'disasters' that have achieved a high degree of public recognition, where 'the name alone will evoke the mental image' of the events that occurred in a particular location – 'such as "Omagh", "Enniskillen" and "Bloody Sunday" ' – in South Armagh 'the incremental pattern of the suffering and the discrete nature of the community subjected to the terror' had been harder to convey and grasp, and thus did not attract

the same degree of sympathy and identification, or of practical welfare support.[81] 'For the majority of FAIR members, grief and trauma have been VERY private and personal experiences . . . [Their] common experience . . . is that as individuals they adapted their lifestyles with the raw trauma still integrated within them.'[82] For the community as a whole, the absence of public interest, acknowledgement and support has contributed to a loss of 'collective self-esteem' and produced 'a sense of disempowerment'.[83] In working to create a public voice, then, the Border Protestant victims' groups set out to represent the collective story of the 'suffering community' in the search for public recognition of the loss, trauma and 'scars' sustained by their members in the course of the Troubles.

In this endeavour, the groups were informed by the wider debate in the early years of the peace process about the important role of social recognition in the course of reparative remembering, and as a condition of reconciliation. Thus, FEAR's report expressed the call of the displaced – particularly among those who did not intend to move back to the Border – for 'symbolic recognition of their experiences' by means of research and 'public telling'.[84] Their memories, it concluded, 'need to be engaged with, and understood, if peace and reconciliation processes are to be developed'.[85] In the case of FAIR, for example, funding was sought specifically for this work of representation: Wilson's report argued that by providing Protestant victims with the means to tell their story as well as to secure other forms of practical support, the Government and the funding agencies would be engaged in 'a visible act of regeneration of the minority community' in South Armagh that 'will do much for that community's morale and self-confidence',[86] and could be a 'catalyst . . . in the peace process' both locally and more widely.[87] In their work to secure social recognition in this wider sense, the victims' groups have given voice to the memories of the victims in cultural forms and public arenas beyond those constituted by state and funding agencies. FAIR produced a website featuring personal testimonies,[88] a pamphlet, *The True Story of South Armagh* (discussed below), a video,[89] and an exhibition, *The Price*, representing the effects of the Republican armed struggle in South Armagh, the centrepiece of which was an Ordnance Survey map marking with a colour-coded sticker each of the remembered incidents in the 'Circle of Death', creating an extraordinary visual memory of the scale of Republican activity in the area.

The 'peace and reconciliation processes' signalled by both FEAR and FAIR have largely progressed within the Unionist communities that they represent, a situation paralleling that in the Bogside and the Creggan after Bloody Sunday. One important public arena utilized by these victims' groups, to propel Border Protestant memories into the awareness of wider reading and viewing publics is that of the news media. In Voice, for example, 'we encourage our people to tell their story to the media at every opportunity'.[90] However, the news media are not simply gatekeepers granting or censoring access to this arena, but are active agents in the articulation of public memory. News stories are selected, framed and developed according to the social and political agendas of journalists and their organizations, and according to news values which place a premium on the 'human interest' element. In turn, when victims' groups 'go public' in the news, they necessarily become involved in the cultural politics of news management. To best exploit the possibilities offered by sympathetic news coverage, they have publicized the personal stories of selected members, which most effectively capture and promote their collective project.

The power of personal life-stories, as mediated by news reportage, to seize the public's imagination – at once widening the scope for social recognition and creating possibilities for new understanding and dialogue, but also promoting the politics of the victims' groups – can be illustrated by the case of John McClure. In his early sixties when he joined FEAR, McClure underwent the transformation described by Arlene Foster, from one of those men 'who don't really want to talk about how they feel' into an articulate and effective public communicator.[91] In August 1997 his life-story was featured in a press release to mark the public launch of the group. At a moment of optimism, with the IRA's ceasefire newly restored and multi-party talks about to begin in earnest, his story received widespread and sympathetic coverage in Northern Ireland's main daily newspapers, including the nationalist *Irish News*, as well as in the local Fermanagh press and national papers in the Irish Republic and Britain; and was followed up throughout the autumn.[92] Formerly a part-time UDR soldier who abandoned his farm and home, on the Border near Garrison, and moved to a safer area 'inland' in 1972, McClure spoke in 1997 of how he'd 'love to come back' to the lost and empty homestead, abandoned with such haste in the fear of 1972, to re-establish his home there, apparently with the welcome of former neighbours:[93]

> Home is home, no matter where you are. With the ceasefire there isn't as great a threat anymore, and I suppose the only thing stopping me is finance. All my old Catholic neighbours would like me to return, but then it was never them I worried about when I was in the UDR. It was the people who came across the Border to shoot who were the problem.[94]

McClure's personal testimony was seized on by the media, attracted by its vividness in conveying the value of FEAR's aim 'to help Protestants who were forced to abandon isolated border farms to return to their homesteads', and in so doing 'to redress what some have described as the "ethnic cleansing" of the Border areas'.[95] Although FEAR's own research was discovering that, for some of the displaced, such a return was neither possible nor desirable, McClure briefly became the public face of the group, and his story was transformed into a symbol of the wider collective experience. In FEAR's press release introducing John McClure to the news public, Arlene Foster gave a specifically local inflection to the importance of voicing untold stories to challenge an established tendency to tell the history of the conflict as if it had taken place only in Belfast and Derry: 'Fermanagh people don't, in general, talk about their experiences. If this had been happening in Belfast we would probably have heard about it long before now.'[96] To win recognition for these stories is also to contribute to overcoming the marginalization of the Border regions by establishing their centrality both to the historical record of the Troubles and to the process of coming to terms with the past.

In subsequent interviews, sought by journalists eager for further memories of displacement, McClure told the story of the threat to his family posed by the killing of his neighbour Johnny Fletcher, of the psychological distress of the move, and of his anger that he had not received a 'single penny' to help with that move, while since 1972 he had seen his house and land deteriorate, which amounted to 'a big loss'.[97] Reflecting back on his life, McClure considers that he has paid a high price for being 'just a Protestant and a member of the UDR'.[98] Despite this, McClure displayed no signs of 'bitterness'. His memories of trauma and loss were attractive to the mainstream media because they were tempered by hope about the possibility of return, buttressed by his memories of life along the Border before the Troubles, when, he recalled, his family enjoyed good relations with their Catholic neighbours. McClure's memories of 'good-neighbourliness' are encapsulated in his account, reported by the *Irish News*, of the day the family left Garrison. McClure's wife, Ivy, had walked to the village to settle her grocery bill. The proprietor of the store, a Catholic, on hearing that the family was leaving, had 'asked if there were money problems. If there were she would be willing to help. McClure says this is typical of Catholic neighbours he lived and worked with in Garrison.'[99]

This theme was made explicit in FEAR's press release on the group's public launch, where the story of the displaced Protestant is connected to a memory of the other side: 'at the time a majority of Catholics were sympathetic and sorry to see their neighbours go'.[100] The claim was endorsed, and McClure's gesture of reconciliation publicly reciprocated, by Tommy Gallagher, the son of one of those neighbours and now a local nationalist (SDLP) councillor for the Garrison area, who lent his voice to FEAR's statement:

> The new peaceful atmosphere could help to build up the trust and confidence needed to develop good neighbourliness. Reconciliation does not happen overnight. But people returning to homesteads they had to leave are part of the rebuilding of those relationships. People who had to leave did so in order to survive because of the atmosphere of fear and tension at that time. They were not threatened in any way by the local community.[101]

Here, a further collective category – the Catholic neighbours of the displaced – is simultaneously established and spoken for by Gallagher, who represents these sympathetic neighbours and offers his personal memory as a guarantee of their understanding and recognition. While by no means endorsing claims about 'ethnic cleansing', a term pointedly missing from the coverage of McClure's story by the nationalist *Irish News*,[102] Gallagher noted that Garrison had lost some 32 per cent of its population over twenty years and emphasized the general advantages of any return:

[O]bviously it would be of benefit to our area to see people move back and I think that communities on both sides would welcome that very much. Those people that left here in the early '70s would still be treated as part of the community. They have their roots and their ties in this particular area.[103]

The return of the displaced in the peaceful times of the present is underpinned by a memory of good-neighbourliness in the harmonious local community of the past, which, being distinguished from those 'outside influences' held responsible for '[a]ny threat they felt they were under', contains the hope and promise of its restoration.[104] This hope for the reparation of damaged communities was figured in the 'symbolism of derelict buildings'[105] utilized in a number of these media stories about McClure and other displaced Border Protestants, in which journalists visited their ruined houses and abandoned farms, and evoked the possibility of their restoration, now that 'changed political times might allow [their] return'.[106] In one televised interview, another of McClure's nationalist neighbours touched a powerful chord by stating: 'We'd love to see the light going on again back in their homestead';[107] an image of the rekindling of life in the abandoned farmhouse that is resonant with a sense of homeliness and the warmth of human interconnectedness. McClure, however, did not move back.[108]

Remembering for emotional catharsis

The endeavour of the Border Protestant victims' groups 'to articulate our suffering and our pain' has also given rise to less reconciliatory narratives, motivated by the rather different desire for (as Wilson's report puts it) 'the cathartic relief of telling the story'.[109] This points to a further psychic dimension to the victims' demand for recognition, driven by powerful impulses to express and discharge the feelings associated with the experience of victimhood; not only pain, hurt and loss, but a gamut of intractable emotions, including horror, fear, anger, bitterness, revulsion and hatred. Such feelings tend to be focused primarily on those held responsible for causing the suffering: the *perpetrators* of violence, in this case the IRA and the smaller Republican organization the INLA. In the psychology of Protestant and Unionist victimhood, 'the Republican terrorist' becomes a highly charged imago within the internal psychic world, in ways comparable to the psychic significance of 'the Paras' in nationalist memory; becoming the bearer in phantasy of a threat which experience in the social world confirms to be realistic. This can be seen, for example, in the case of the child-survivor of the Darkley atrocity in 1983 (when gunmen from the INLA strafed the congregation with bullets during a Pentecostal church service), who long afterwards imagined 'where we could hide if they came to the house and sprayed it with gunfire', and was haunted by 'nightmares that they are going to come and take over the estate, like something you see in a war film'.[110] Alternatively, in phantasies that strip it of its threat, the 'Republican terrorist' may be transformed into a denigrated and vilified imago worthy of the fiercest retribution.[111]

These representations can be understood as performing a necessary psychic function, related to the psyche's defences against the potentially overwhelming effects of fear and the emotions of victimhood. If their intensity cannot be mastered internally, then the psyche makes use of processes of imaginative projection to invest these unwanted feelings in suitable *objects*, including people and places in the social world, which become the external *bearers* of threat, violence and death. As in the Bogside after Bloody Sunday, a 'pathology of atmosphere' developed in the Border areas, that is described in Wilson's report: 'To the minority British community, Crossmaglen and other Republican localities permeate a lingering stench of tension, sectarian hatred and anglophobic menace.'[112] In this imaginative geography, the place of the other becomes laden with the symbolic weight of projected internal disturbance. To the extent that the other remains resistant to mastery and control (through, for example, the failure of the security forces to break up a 'nest' of 'bad boys', as if they were poisonous vermin),[113] the internal disturbances remain unassuaged.

Ulster Protestants have tended to seek cathartic release of these emotions chiefly through the workings of the criminal justice system, by means of which the 'murderers' (seen as common criminals rather than volunteers in a politically motivated armed struggle) would be brought to account before the law and made to pay the penalty commensurate with their 'crimes'. However, confidence among Border Protestants that justice would be secured had been eroded by the low conviction rate for 'terrorist' attacks, even before the prisoner-release scheme was set up under the Good Friday Agreement. FAIR claimed in 1999, 'we have over 60 unsolved murders carried out by Republican terrorists in South Armagh. Justice therefore has never been done nor has it been seen to be done.'[114] This failure to obtain the redress of justice through the operation of the law created the conditions for revenge phantasies. The emotional catharsis sought in revenge found expression in violence against Catholic civilians by loyalist paramilitaries, but also in a willingness on the part of elements within the Protestant and Unionist communities to condone such attacks. This is not a response generally given public expression by any of the victims' groups, which emphasize the rejection of 'all acts of terrorist violence'.[115] Nevertheless, at FAIR's Stormont demonstration, when Willie Frazer was asked about the early release of loyalist paramilitary prisoners, he told the BBC: 'They should never have been locked up in first place'; adding, somewhat ambiguously, 'I'm not saying anyone has a right to kill innocent Catholics, but if the security forces had been doing their job there would never have been any need for the loyalist paramilitaries.'[116] While these are deeply controversial remarks for a victims' group representative, the wish for the catharsis of revenge is, no less than the desire for justice, a product of the psychic experience of victimhood. Indeed, the relation between the absence of formal justice and the impulse towards revenge – taking the law into your own hands – is comparable to the effect of the Widgery whitewash on nationalists. The crucial difference, clearly articulated here by Frazer, is that loyalist vengeance was sought in the name of the law, to uphold the existing State against those considered to be lawbreakers.

The desire for cathartic relief from the intensity of these disturbing and potentially poisonous and self-destructive emotions may also be satisfied symbolically by storytelling that emphasizes the emotional realities of victimhood in order to 'set the record straight', in opposition to what are felt to be misrepresentations of the perpetrators.[117] This has been the project of FAIR in *The True Story of South Armagh*: one of 'untold misery, bloodshed, and the pain of . . . [an Ulster Protestant] community who have been under siege for the past thirty years'.[118] The aim was to counter 'years of outlandish Republican propaganda' about a just anti-colonial war of national liberation, particularly in the USA where its fundraisers had been so successful, by telling a story of the horror inflicted on the area ' "in the name of Ireland", and without any moral justification by the IRA'.[119] Both in its narrative emphasis and in the mode of address adopted towards its audience, *The True Story of South Armagh* is markedly different from the measured, analytical tone of Wilson's needs' analysis report for government. Where Wilson sought to explain the *incremental* impact of the violence in the area, so much harder to evince than a high-profile atrocity such as the Enniskillen or Omagh bombings, the centrepiece of *The True Story of South Armagh* is precisely a triptych of atrocity stories, 'three of the worst massacres carried out in South Armagh during the period 1970s–1990s': at Tullyvallen Orange Hall (1975), Kingsmills (1976) and the Darkley Pentecostal Church (1983).[120] These events – the so-called 'forgotten atrocities' – are described as 'totally indiscriminate sectarian attacks which typified the fanatical nature of Republican death squads'.[121] Undoubtedly those attacks warrant description as sectarian atrocities. The Darkley attack, for example, in which three church elders died, was condemned by the leaders of the four main churches in Northern Ireland as 'an act of sectarian slaughter on a worshipping community which goes beyond any previous deed of violence'.[122] Nevertheless, they were exceptional events, not typical examples of the IRA's conduct of its armed struggle, nor indeed carried out through the IRA's chain of command, despite their representation as such by British counter-insurgency propaganda.[123]

The treatment of these horrific incidents in *The True Story of South Armagh* is shaped not simply by the need for a documentary 'record': as Michael Ignatieff remarks, 'atrocity myths about the other side . . . are held to reveal the essential identity of the peoples in whose name they are committed', and it is these essential truths that are remembered, rather than the details of actual responsibility and motivation.[124] In FAIR's account, the need to make horror imaginable and to find a form for catharsis make themselves felt in the adoption of the rhetorical register of melodrama. Intensely emotive, even vitriolic, rhetoric is deployed to express and contain the fear, anger and outrage attaching to the memory of the attacks, while simultaneously discrediting conventional Republican heroic discourse. The victims of Tullyvallen are 'innocent men', 'committed Christians and devout family men', who meet their deaths 'like lambs to the slaughter'; while the gunmen – far from being 'brave soldiers or courageous volunteers' – are 'cowardly', 'psychopathic killers' and 'bloodthirsty, evil gangsters who were faceless, gutless and heartless'.[125] The scene in Darkley Pentecostal Church is described as one of 'pandemonium'[126] – a term signifying the abode of the demons, Milton's 'high Capital of Satan and his Peers', the centre of vice and wickedness and 'a place of wild, lawless violence':[127]

> Children were screaming hysterically, calling for their mummys [*sic*] and daddies who were lying among the upturned pews, prayer books and bibles. All begged and pleaded for mercy as the gunmen stepped through the bodies and made their way outside.[128]

This is language in the tradition of Victorian British accounts of the 'massacre of innocents' at Delhi and Cawnpore by fiendish sepoys during the Indian Mutiny–Rebellion of 1857–58. Those accounts also focused on what had been done to innocent British women and children by an inhuman enemy: in that case, 'the Cruel Hindu' or 'the Mahomedan [who] is a ferocious animal, and made so by his creed . . . whose "wickedness" and "malignity" are so total as to make them "lose everything human and behave like demons" '.[129] This mode of representation 'splits the scene into a black-and-white world of absolute evil and absolute virtue'.[130] South Armagh becomes, like India in 1857, a nightmare landscape in which pure and defenceless innocence is overrun and destroyed by animals and devils, and even the 'sanctity' of sacred space and ritual – 'God's people' at worship – is violated, defiled and mocked by the killers.[131] Like the infamous Well of Cawnpore and other such episodes in the British imperial imaginary, the Tullyvallen Orange Hall, the Ballymoyer Road at Kingsmills, and the Darkley Gospel Hall become the imaginative loci of monstrous evil-doing and unbearable pathos, where the order of things is overturned and the world threatens to become meaningless and ungraspable.[132]

The rhetoric of melodrama adopted in *The True Story* both registers this overturning and works to re-impose moral order: to try to 'reverse the undeniable fact that good has now become evil and right has now become wrong by the appeasement of Republican terrorists by both British and Irish Governments'. By highlighting their most extreme atrocities, the 'evil Republican death squads' can be represented as lacking 'any moral justification', in contrast to 'the protectors of life and guardians of law and order', the UDR, and the persecuted but enduring community as a whole:

> During the past 30 years only commitment to our existence, coupled with unequalled bravery and a belief in God has resulted in the Protestant population not becoming extinct at the hands of a carefully orchestrated campaign to 'ethnic cleanse' . . . We are a constant reminder of exactly what a campaign of genocide stands for. Our aim is to ensure that the great sacrifice of the Protestant community in South Armagh will never be forgotten.[133]

In this public memory work developed by FAIR, then, catharsis was sought in a narrative shaped by extreme psychic splitting which dehumanizes the Republican enemy, holds it entirely responsible for violence and death, and idealizes the innocence of its victims. There is little scope here for reparative remembering.

Awkward voices and paradoxes of memory

Re-articulated as a memory of collective victimhood, the narrative of 'ethnic cleansing' expresses a psychic reality of pain, trauma and damage that demands recognition within the terms of the Government's new settlement for victims, as an essential component of reparation and peace-building. At the same time, this recapitulation of war memories expressing deep antagonism and enmity, and emphasizing the damage done to 'our community', tends to undercut efforts at building the cross-community understanding, dialogue and co-operation that is necessary to the process of conflict resolution.

There is a sharp paradox here. The emotive mobilization and voicing of highly selective, charged and antagonistic memories of the Troubles might be said to keep alive the hurts, grievances and suspicions of the war years, thus generating difficulties for peace-making and the transition to a just social and political settlement of the conflict. Nevertheless the memory work of these Protestant and Unionist victims' groups is indispensable to any inclusive process of conflict resolution. They constitute a new kind of voice from below in Northern Ireland which tells stories about the 'things that we need to hear'.[134] The articulation of these stories has deeply contradictory effects: inevitably so, given the history of the conflict, the depth of the damage inflicted and sustained, and the difficulties of conflict resolution. As well as reproducing the fixed positions and understandings inherited from the past through cultural memory, the voices of the Protestant and Unionist victims also speak from new positions and express new, emergent meanings that open up possibilities for reparative remembering on a number of levels.

The primary contribution made by these victims' groups lies at the personal level, in their importance and value for members; not only in practical terms, but in offering safe arenas in which it becomes possible to reflect on, feel, discuss and make sense of what has happened over the last thirty years, through personal storytelling. The testimony of former UDR soldier Leslie Finlay will resonate with many others who have joined these groups, when he speaks of sleepless nights sitting on the edge of his bed, experiencing flashbacks of 'them things [you see] every time you close your eyes', haunted by the row of UDR headstones in Castlederg graveyard where he helped to bury his mates, one after the other, and realizing that 'I need help' – which he found in West Tyrone Voice.[135]

While these personal stories may be mobilized to serve the public and political narrative of ethnic cleansing, whether advanced by a victims' group or by a political organization, they are always richer and more nuanced than this. In FEAR's research report, for example, the complexities of personal remembering, evident in the Gordon and Sidwell testimonies discussed above, are flattened out and reduced. What is the significance of Mrs Gordon admitting that, twenty-four years after being driven out, 'I often ask myself the question "why did they attack us?" ' Why were some neighbours, even in the UDR, not targeted? Why do some, like Mr Sidwell, 'hope to forget' in order to survive, while others, like 'Mr B. Gillen', lament the inadequacy of memory to present a fuller account of what is past: 'There was just that much happened, you end up forgetting the half of it'?[136] Why did sections of the Gillens' own Protestant community respond to their decision to leave the area by treating them 'like we were convicts, or criminals . . . Implying that we were cowards for leaving. But really what good are dead heroes?'[137] How do such suggestions of internal intimidation problematize the representation of a community united against the Republican enemy? While questions like these play no part in the narrative of ethnic cleansing, and were excluded from the collective memory of the Border Protestant victims constructed publicly by FEAR, privately its members were remembering such incidents and asking such questions within the context of the group. These private memories have the potential, over time, to feed into the telling of a more nuanced and complex collective narrative. In 'tell[ing] the world who we are, and what we have gone through', the former 'closet victims' may find that 'coming out' leads to a thoroughgoing reappraisal of the past, with profound as well as painful implications for their own identity, for their relationships with neighbours and to the State, and for the wider peace process.

Secondly, in terms of public politics and the State, the voices-from-below of the Protestant and Unionist victims are not neatly reducible to old political positions and lines of antagonism. They tell stories and ask questions that pose problems for all those who benefited from the silence of the victims. These are awkward voices for Republicans, who embrace an agenda of human rights and equality but resist attempts to probe for 'the truth' about IRA activities,[138] by confronting them with the human consequences of the Republican 'armed struggle' and with a moral demand that justice be served. The voices of the victims also ask difficult questions of the Republic of Ireland State, in demanding a public inquiry into the Irish Government's part in the development of the Provisional IRA in the gun-running controversy of the early 1970s and into allegations of *Garda* collusion over the years.[139] The awkward questions in this case raise unfinished business of eighty years' duration with what many Border Protestants still refer to as the Irish 'Free State'. One elderly member of a Border Protestant victims' group, speaking passionately about the gun-running and linking it to 'ethnic cleansing' and the current log-jam over the decommissioning of the IRA's arsenal, demanded that the latter be extended to include the 'decommissioning of the Free State Army'.[140]

These are awkward voices, too, for the Unionist establishment: for Protestant church leaders, for those who manage the UDR Benevolence Fund and, in particular, for Unionist politicians who, unless they themselves fall victim, are the object of deeply sceptical memories relating to their cynicism and ineffectuality in dealing with victims' issues.[141] According to Hazlett Lynch:

> Over the years . . . the only time that you would have seen politicians really would have been if there was an atrocity in the area and they were there with their entourage, with cameras and microphones and . . . press people . . . maybe on the day of the funeral, but after that you never saw them. And the impression . . . would have been that these guys were here because it was the politically correct thing for them to do. And it was a good vote-catcher for them to be seen to be where atrocities had taken place. But after that, certainly in our family . . . [and] a lot of the people that I've spoken to in West Tyrone would have said, that when you wanted a politician you could never get one. They were never there, they weren't interested in many regards.[142]

Lynch articulates a disparagement of Unionist politicians that is widespread among victims, stemming from a perception of having been failed, on two main counts: by the politicians' use of atrocities for party publicity at the expense of offering any sustained support for the relatives and survivors; and by their rhetoric about putting the terrorists 'behind bars' when security policy was manifestly unable – or unwilling – to do any such thing.[143]

Finally, and perhaps most significantly, the voices of the Protestant and Unionist victims raise uncomfortable issues for the British State and Government, since they call into question the workings of *justice* in Northern Ireland, and with it the long-standing strategy of containment which kept them safely silent. As Lynch puts it:

> Over the years, in Northern Ireland, the pro-British people would have had a fairly high degree of loyalty to their government. We're British subjects whose allegiance would have been to the British Crown . . . [I]t never would have entered our minds to . . . have openly criticised the policies of the Government, even though it would have been done by our political leaders, but the people on the ground wouldn't have openly criticised government policy because they are our government . . . they're, in a sense, our security forces, they were fighting our enemy.[144]

Keeping quiet, not getting involved, putting up with it, not openly criticising, not rocking the boat: these were the mechanisms whereby the 'pro-British people' closed ranks behind 'our security forces' and 'our government' in the war against the terrorists. The realization that the security forces 'were not allowed by the powers-that-be to apprehend known terrorist activists because it wasn't politically expedient for them to do so', and that they had been used as 'gun fodder', indeed 'were set up by the British Government, in the Castlederg area and around the Border',[145] fractures this 'British' alliance and generates a sceptical memory not only about Unionist politicians but about the workings of the State itself:

> [A]s long as the victims stayed quiet, it meant that . . . [successive British] Governments could pursue whatever policies they wanted vis-à-vis the victims

and vis-à-vis the security situation here in Northern Ireland. But as soon as [the victims] started to make their voice heard, it has complicated things for the Government.[146]

Breaking the silence subverts the framework of official memory, forcing a re-examination of the past and raising difficult questions: How and why were we mistaken in our understanding of what was happening? Why did we not feel impelled to speak out then, as we do now? What does that say about who we were and what we did then? Why was there no help for us then, and how can that be changed now?

One especially potent way in which Protestant victims of violence may problematize both official and paramilitary memories and amnesias of the Troubles, is in the search for the truth concerning the death of a loved one. Not infrequently this has required Unionist (as well as nationalist) relatives to probe into the secretive underworld of the 'dirty war': a world of masked gunmen, informers, double-agents and 'psy-ops', where little can be relied on, and memory becomes enmeshed in masquerade. Willie Frazer of FAIR, like Leslie Finlay of West Tyrone Voice, argues that the only explanation for the failure of the security forces to take effective action against the IRA along the Border, when the local volunteers 'were all known to the UDR', can be collusion: between the IRA and the *Garda* in the South, and the IRA and the British Army in the North.[147] According to Frazer, political control of the security forces meant that most of the time they were 'confined to kid-glove treatment of terrorists', while the need to protect the activities of special forces, informers and double-agents meant that local UDR men were set up for assassination: 'A few local people were seen as expendable in the "bigger picture".'[148] One of these was his own father, Robert Frazer, killed by the IRA in August 1975. Frazer believes that his father had been involved in undercover operations and was set up by Captain Robert Nairac, 'the most controversial military intelligence officer in the recent history of the troubles', whose abduction and 'disappearance' by the IRA in May 1977 sealed his 'indelible reputation as a mysterious figure'.[149]

Since his (assumed) death, Nairac has been the focus for 'persistent and unproven' allegations from both sides of the political divide.[150] Republicans have seized on claims first made in 1984 by a British Army 'whistleblower', the former undercover soldier Captain Fred Holroyd, that Nairac was involved in collusion with loyalist paramilitaries and shared responsibility for a number of killings, including the most serious incidents of the Troubles in the South, the Dublin and Monaghan bombings of 1974.[151] Loyalist counter-allegations are supported by a statement from former RUC Sergeant John Weir, in which he claims to have been told by a Republican informant of Nairac's involvement in the movement of explosives across the Border for the IRA, and that Nairac had supplied the IRA with 'the names of UDR members and others who had been working for military intelligence' – including that of Robert Frazer.[152] For Willie Frazer, the need to come to terms with and commemorate the death, over twenty-five years ago, of a loved father provokes the asking of awkward questions about what was really going on in the operations of both the local security forces and the IRA. The attempt to answer these questions is an attempt to penetrate a smokescreen of official as well as paramilitary secrecy, where little can be established with any certainty, and the all-important story can only be approximated through speculation and hypothesis. The motivation to do so has its source in the powerful personal desire to deal with the past and lay a loved one to rest, a desire evident also in the Bloody Sunday families.

The awkward voices of Frazer and others in FAIR may eventually join a broader movement to demand that a 'truth and justice' mechanism be found and a process duly established for investigating the murky undercover war waged by the British State in Ireland, as well as the secret world of the para-militaries. If this should occur, the voices of the victims may prove awkward for the loyalist paramilitaries, too, in exposing their collusion with British security forces. *The True Story of South Armagh* makes no reference to the illegal UVF and UFF, or to their interconnections with the UDR (those 'pro-tectors of life and guardians of law and order').[153] However, in cases like that of Robert McConnell – a South Armagh UDR soldier who was shot dead in 1976 in front of his 6-year-old nephew, now FAIR activist, Brian McConnell – allegations have been made of direct links with the UVF.[154] Brian McConnell has said that he has 'no way of knowing whether the claims regarding his uncle were true'.[155] Whether he would wish to find out is a moot question, and one that points again to the way in which the search for truth and justice not only cuts into the secret histories of the paramili-taries and the State, but may also disturb the psychic composure of those most intimately affected; as Seamus Deane has shown in his novel *Reading in the Dark* (1996), about the difficulties of living in the shadows of an unre-solved family history with deeply troubling personal dimensions.[156] Meanwhile, partial and incomplete memories persist, while the unfulfilled desire for truth generates an urgent fascination with the public memoirs of informers and undercover agents – such as Eamonn Collins and Sean O'Callaghan, or members of the SAS and MI5 required to negotiate the Official Secrets Act in order to publish at all – who are the ones 'in the know', capable of shining a light into muddied waters, but whose word can never be entirely trusted.[157]

Ultimately, these challenging questions raised by the Protestant and Unionist victims' groups will need to be addressed in a peace process that is formally committed to tackling the legacy of the conflict in terms of 'truth', 'justice' and 'human rights'. According to Hazlett Lynch, resistance contin-ues to the victims' voicing of these awkward questions and issues, from politicians and others who claim that it 'may well have the effect of desta-bilizing the so-called peace process'. In response Lynch argues: 'It isn't that we have any desire to destabilize the political process, but if the polit-ical process is seeking to marginalize me and my community and if the polit-ical process is attempting to belittle what we've suffered, then if it is destabilized so be it.'[158] A case can readily be made, however, that the raising of awkward questions from below is directly linked to the needs of the marginalized, and is a necessary element in deepening (rather than desta-bilizing) the process of peace-making and conflict resolution. As FEAR's research into displacement from the Border discovered, the stories of the victims raise 'questions regarding the meaning of peace and reconciliation' for the individuals concerned and for the communities they left, posing the problem of how the demoralization and social exclusion they have experienced are to be reversed.[159]

Lastly, then, the Protestant and Unionist victims' groups of the Border regions open up new possibilities for reparative remembering within their local communities, through a process that may be largely invisible to outsiders. These are traumatized communities scarred by decades of violence, the effects of which have yet to be properly addressed. They are now struggling for their own 'collective self-esteem' in the face of alienation and disillusionment, and a profound sense of threat to their British identity and heritage, posed by the new political dispensation in Northern Ireland and the transformation in the fortunes of Irish Republicanism.[160] While, for many of the Protestant and Unionist victims, it is 'too early' for reconciliation with those who remain political antagonists, victims' work can make an immediate contribution to building self-respect, confidence and reconciliation within their own communities.[161] What Willie Frazer called 'the healing process' must necessarily be cross-generational, embracing younger Protestants who continue to suffer the provocations of sectarian intimidation in their own daily lives and may respond with violence, but can also see how the older generation have suffered through the conflict, and 'ask people like me, "What have you got from it?" '.[162]

The rebuilding of 'morale and self-confidence'[163] in communities damaged by the Troubles necessarily involves them in the endeavour to make their peace with the past. This imperative applies no less to the young who are now growing up in the times of 'imperfect peace' but find themselves grappling with the postmemory of the war,[164] as it does to their elders who face the task of coming to terms with the aftershocks of a war they survived personally and reconciling its memories with the world that is slowly emerging through conflict resolution. The victims' groups provide local agencies dedicated to tackling the contradictions and difficulties inherent in this work of reparation and regeneration. Their understanding that the commemoration of those who did not survive the conflict is a fundamental part of its resolution has informed visions such as FAIR's conception of a 'Living Memorial Centre' dedicated to the victims of Republican violence in South Armagh. This is imagined as a

> resource in honour of the victims . . . to keep faith with the dead . . . They call out to be remembered in dignity, not in a bare stone or empty mausoleum, but a place that is alive with tribute, memory and affection . . . where we can recall our loved ones to memory and where strangers might come to know them.[165]

The Living Memorial Centre would also 'prevent the memory of the victims from being lost to the collective consciousness of a younger generation that may be the first to see peace'.[166]

Commemoration, however, cuts both ways. While it may allow ghosts to be laid to rest in a dignified acknowledgement of the permanence of loss, it may also keep alive the memory of the hurt inflicted on the Protestant and Unionist people of the Border areas, in a way that continues to fuel current grievances and antagonisms. The trauma affecting individuals and whole communities as a result of the war along the Border has a psychic reality which colours Ulster–British cultural memory. If the more damaged, as well as damaging, manifestations of this psychic reality are to be ameliorated, the call for engagement with the stories of the Border Protestants needs to be acknowledged and acted on over the longer term, as part of any inclusive conflict-resolution process. This involves giving public voice to these difficult memories of the Troubles and making cultural spaces – in Ireland and in Britain, and further afield – in which they can be articulated, listened to, heard and acknowledged in a necessary process of social recognition; but also explored, argued with, drawn into dialogue, critiqued, investigated for their truth and incorporated into critical histories of the conflict. Simply to reject, deny or marginalize the cultural memory of 'genocide/ethnic cleansing', as nationalists and Republicans have tended to do, is to contribute to the social exclusion, the psychic disturbance and the crisis of belonging increasingly experienced by those whom Susan McKay has dubbed 'an unsettled people',[167] as they struggle to adapt to new realities while preserving 'a past that they can live with'.[168] The challenge for the politics of victimhood in the Irish peace process lies in mobilizing the contradictory energies released by these victims' groups, both for the psychic work of reparation, and for the political work of building a peace that can be trusted. The obstacles to meeting this challenge, posed by conflicts within the unfolding peace process since 1994, are explored in chapter 9.

9

Mobilizing memories: the Unionist politics of victimhood and the Good Friday Agreement

The twenty-five-year war waged by Irish Republicans against the British State in Northern Ireland, perhaps particularly in the Border counties, has left a damaging legacy of bitterness, mistrust and fear among Protestants, that is encapsulated in the notion of a Unionist and loyalist *siege mentality*. Here, this commonly used term refers to a particular kind of defensive stance, with cultural, political and psychic ramifications, grounded on the mythic memory of the 1689 Siege of Derry. This story tells how Protestants loyal to William III, the newly proclaimed King of England, Scotland and Ireland, took refuge behind the physical defences of the walled city of Londonderry, then held it against the hostile besieging army of the rival Catholic King James II, under the rallying cry of 'No Surrender!' The imperative has become enshrined as the central lesson in the Protestant cultural memory of 'ethnic cleansing', asserting the necessity of a determined holding of one's ground and a constant vigilance, in a context of sustained threat from masked protagonists, where, as it has been said, every Catholic is a potential rebel.

The memory of 'ethnic cleansing' has continued to underpin the siege mentality of Ulster loyalists in the new circumstances of the peace process. The paramilitary ceasefires of 1994 created the conditions for the initiation of multi-party talks which eventually culminated in the Good Friday Agreement of April 1998. This affirmed the parties' 'total and absolute commitment to exclusively democratic and peaceful means of resolving differences on political issues', and established the framework for transition to a new political dispensation and social order in Northern Ireland, in the context of new relationships 'based on partnership, equality and mutual respect' both within and between the two parts of Ireland and between the islands of Ireland and Britain.[1] Cultural memories of the Troubles have played an important but contradictory role in this conflict-resolution process, affecting both the political battle to implement the Agreement, and broader social endeavours to come to terms with the past. This is for two reasons. Firstly, memories make manifest – and push into the peace process – the difficult and disturbing realities of the traumatic past, and insist that these need to be addressed if a liveable peace is to be created and sustained. But, secondly, these memories continue to shape antagonistic political identities and the positions staked out by opposing movements in the attempt to further their own interests and influence within the new dispensation; and thus risk becoming – or appearing to the other side as – propaganda narratives, and thus weapons in the continuation of the culture wars. The reassertion of the narrative of 'ethnic cleansing' in response to the unfolding peace process encapsulates the difficulties faced by Protestants and Unionists in negotiating these contradictions, which have introduced serious complications and challenges into the process of conflict resolution. They have been at the heart of political debate within the Unionist and loyalist parties, the Protestant churches and other organizations, including the loyalist paramilitaries, as well as the victims' groups themselves, about how best to repond to the IRA ceasefire, the negotiations and the ensuing Agreement; indeed, about whether to engage at all in peace-making with Republicans. They are also lodged within the subjectivities of the people who identify with those organizations and participate in that debate, for whom they pose personal, psychic dilemmas of understanding and emotional response.

This chapter begins by exploring these contradictions in loyalist subjectivity, between the siege mentality and impulses towards 'good-neighbourliness', before examining ways in which their effects can be traced in oscillating currents of hope and fear in response to the political dynamic of conflict resolution during the early stages of the peace process. It goes on to analyse how the emergence of a politics of victimhood, centred on the memory of suffering inflicted on Protestants by the IRA, fashioned powerfully emotive positions taken by Unionists on a number of issues central to the implementation of the Good Friday Agreement: firstly, their insistence on verifiable decommissioning of the IRA's arsenal as a condition of Republican participation in the devolved and inclusive political institutions created under the Agreement; secondly, their objections to the early release of 'terrorist prisoners'; thirdly, their hostility to the proposed reforms of the RUC and the creation of a new Police Service of Northern Ireland capable of winning the confidence of nationalists; and, finally, their antagonism to the memory work undertaken by nationalist victims' groups.

The siege mentality and the memory of good-neighbourliness

According to Denzil McDaniel, long-time reporter and editor of the *Impartial Reporter*, the local newspaper based in Enniskillen, Co. Fermanagh: 'The siege mentality is never more apparent than in the Protestant community living on the Border.'[2] My first encounter with the subjectivity of the Border Protestant and Unionist community occurred when, in July 1999, I met Arlene Foster to discuss the work of FEAR and the context in which it operated. The contradictory impulses, and the ensuing quandaries, encapsulated in the countervailing conceptions of the 'siege mentality', on one hand, and of 'good-neighbourliness', on the other, became manifest as she reflected on the legacy of the past in Co. Fermanagh. Foster is not only a founding member of one of the first victims' groups to be established after the ceasefires but was at that time a prominent member of the new generation of Ulster Unionist politicians and a former Chair of the Ulster Young Unionist Council who had played a part in that organization's work to promote Ulster–British heritage and identity. Her subsequent criticism and abandoning of the UUP, under the leadership of David Trimble, to join the DUP is a benchmark for the growth of a wider popular disaffection with the UUP's political strategy within the peace process, that eventually led to Trimble's defeat at the polls in 2004 and the emergence of the DUP as the voice of mainstream Unionism. While Foster's shift in allegiance would have been unthinkable in 1999, its origins can be traced both in the culture wars of the early 1990s and in the politics of victimhood developed during the early years of the peace process.

Running through Foster's reflections on the impact of the Troubles is a wish to hold on to the idea that Fermanagh people from both sides of the political divide are decent and tolerant, and not 'extreme', which exists in tension with her understanding of how the war has been conducted in the area. On one hand, she affirms the memory of good neighbourliness that featured so prominently in FEAR's project at that time, here endorsed by the intimacy and authenticity of family memory:

> In the past, I know certainly in my grandmother's generation, there was a tolerance of each other's rights and interests and culture. There's often the stories of Roman Catholics looking after Protestant farms while they were off for the Twelfth of July and they would do the same of the fifteenth of August during Hibernian parades for Roman Catholics . . . that sort of mutuality and respecting each other . . . I think there was a lot of truth in that . . . people knew that they were different. Certainly my grandmother was always very aware of who she was, but she would have had discussions with her Roman Catholic neighbours . . . [that acknowledged] the differences . . . So in that respect it wasn't something that wasn't talked about, it always was talked about.[3]

This perception of the past is often evoked by Ulster Protestants to describe the days before 'outside influences' (meaning Republicans) began seriously to disrupt the order of things in the six counties of Northern Ireland. In the late 1990s, it could frequently be heard expressed by those protesting the 'right to march' where nationalists campaigned against the use of 'traditional' routes on Orange and other Loyal Order parades: in days gone by, according to loyalist cultural memory, those parades had been accepted and even enjoyed by local Catholics, until Sinn Féin came in and stirred up objections.[4] While there may be in this notion an element of nostalgia for a mythical time when everything was all right, before it all started going bad – which Foster's generation, born since 1969, inherit as a postmemory – it also represents a present-day reality and potentiality, and expresses the wish to restore (or create) a more robust and sustainable culture of mutual respect. Arlene Foster gives this structure of feeling a specific local inflection:

> In Fermanagh there's very few disputes over parades . . . because I think a lot of them accept, 'Yes, let [loyalists] do this, because we'll be having our *fleidh* in

such and such a place' . . . this sort of mutuality. Apart from areas where there's Sinn Féin influence and . . . rousing . . . I just don't think in Fermanagh people there is this offence-taking that you see up the country . . . [f]rom a way before the Troubles . . . there was an understanding and a respect . . . [which] we lost a bit of during the Troubles, but I think it's still there with some people, and that's why there's not this extremism in Fermanagh that you find in other places.[5]

This affirmation of hope, through trust in good-neighbourliness, neverthe-less depends on a form of splitting in Protestant–Unionist representations of the Roman Catholic–nationalist other, whereby 'the good neighbour' can be distinguished from 'the terrorist'.[6] Under the conditions of the war waged by Irish Republicans against the British State in Northern Ireland, and perhaps particularly in the Border counties, this distinction has not proved straight-forward to make or sustain. The Protestant–Unionist Border communities have undergone thirty years of a war fought by masked protagonists and characterized by 'much mudding [sic] of the waters . . . [in which] it is hard to be sure' of anything.[7] This helps to explain the paradox that, despite its pervasiveness, the memory of good-neighbourliness is at the same time a pre-carious and fragile thing, vulnerable to disruption by those other, altogether darker, memories of local community relations during the Troubles, which find expression in the narrative of ethnic cleansing.

On the other hand, then, Arlene Foster's more optimistic reflections on good-neighbourliness in Fermanagh are contradicted by countervailing memories of this kind:

> [T]his is the strange thing about County Fermanagh – there is always such good relations between Roman Catholics and Protestants. So on a superficial basis, everybody gets on with their lives, shops in each other's shops, and there's never anything until the violence rears its ugly head. And there was always this idea of usurpers coming in from other areas and destroying the good community relations but, as far as I'm concerned, they [the IRA] could not have operated within Fermanagh . . . without even the acquiescence or knowledge of the local, some of the local nationalist community. Which is a hard realization to take, but it is true, especially if you look at Sinn Féin's electoral success in . . . Fermanagh. Especially during their most violent period in the Eighties when Bobby Sands was elected as MP for this area.[8]

Sands, the Officer Commanding of the IRA prisoners in the H-blocks of the Maze Prison, was elected MP for the Fermanagh and South Tyrone con-stituency in April 1981 on an 'anti-H-blocks' ticket, while on hunger strike in support of the prisoners' campaign to win 'special category' (or political) status. The election, a straight fight between Sands and a Unionist candidate, Harry West, polarized the local vote and was won by a narrow margin of just over 1,400 votes on an 86 per cent turnout. Raymond Ferguson, a UUP councillor in Enniskillen, recalls that the majority of Unionist voters, for whom Sands was merely an IRA gunman and a convicted criminal, were 'astounded that the Catholic community could come in and support Bobby

Sands . . . [His] election was a huge shock to the Unionist community'.[9] After his defeat, West told Fermanagh Unionists: 'Now we know the type of people we are living amongst.'[10] The 'damaging effect' of this election was impressed on Enniskillen's new Presbyterian minister, Reverend David Cupples, during his first years in the town:

> What people say to me is that when Bobby Sands was elected every single last person got out and voted that day. When hardy came to hardy, almost every single Catholic and Nationalist in this county went out and voted for Sinn Féin, for an IRA man, and they said that shows where their ultimate sympathy really lies. The number of times that was mentioned to me in the first few years I was here really surprised me[11]

Facing up to the depth of local support for Republican politics, when for Foster and her fellow Unionists this overlaps into the collusion of 'the local' – or 'some of the local' – nationalist community in IRA activities in the area, is understandably 'a hard realization to take'. It also shapes the perception of a fundamental contrast between community relations past and present: 'But now, the thirty years of violence . . . what it has done, the most damage it has done, is caused distrust and suspicion'.[12]

Foster's sense of this damaging legacy is, as for so many others, grounded in personal experience, in her case of the IRA's attack on the family farm, along the Border near Rosslea, in which her father was shot and seriously injured.

> That was difficult to take because . . . my father was always very much a community policeman and, if somebody had got a speeding ticket or something like that, they would have landed at his door for him to try and get them off. And he'd lived in the community all his life and was from there and his family was from there, so I think that probably hurt more than anything, the fact that he'd been obviously set up by somebody in the community.[13]

In terms of individual subjectivity, it is not difficult to understand how a condition of 'distrust and suspicion' might develop out of the hurt, the sense of betrayal and the insecurity that are among the lasting psychic effects of such an event. Reflecting on this, Arlene Foster draws out its political ramifications:

> The siege mentality definitely is there: 'You can't trust anybody', this sort of philosophy. And that's why . . . if you take it up to the politics, it's very easy for people to say, 'Oh, just trust them, just go that extra step.' But if you look back at the thirty years that we've had, it's very, very difficult to trust people who have been your neighbours for so long, but at the same time setting you up for murder.[14]

Memories of good-neighbourliness have worked to keep alive the vision and possibility of a community free from fear and suspicion, and like FEAR's project to return displaced families to their homes along the Border, were encouraged by 'a degree of trust and hope' awakened by the peace process.[15]

However, such efforts to build on the memory of good-neighbourliness in order to engender local community reconciliation – and indeed, Protestant–Unionist participation in the peace process more generally – has had to negotiate this countervailing structure of feeling, along with the deep paradox and unavoidable contradiction that it engenders. Public assertion of the memory of ethnic cleansing – of how our neighbours tried to kill us – is the means by which recognition, redress and justice are sought by the victims of IRA violence for what has been done to them. But rather than contributing to the rebuilding of trust and understanding, such memories tend rather to re-evoke the distrust and suspicion that nurture support for a harder, more uncompromising, stance within the political process.

Hope, fear and memory: psychic and political dynamics after the ceasefires

The twists and turns in the development of the wider peace process have had a critical bearing on how this paradox and contradiction has been lived and worked through in the Protestant–Unionist victims' groups, and in their communities more generally. For some members of those victims' groups, making peace with Republicans, politically, involves a shift in perception that they may be unable to make, due to an endemic distrust underpinned by the trauma of victimhood. For others, an initial optimism has been to a greater or lesser extent eroded by the loss of forward momentum in the unfolding of the peace process, and the build-up of suspicion and discontent about its dynamic that affected increasing numbers of Protestants and Unionists. With its ebbing and flowing of hope over more than ten years, the political process involving first the ceasefires, then the negotiations that culminated in the Good Friday Agreement, and subsequently the conflicts over the implementation of that Agreement, created a rapidly changing climate of expectations and possibilities. This has been the environment in which victims' memories of the Troubles have been articulated with new hope of recognition and redress, and the shifting context in which these memories have been shaped and the current significance of the past defined and understood. More than this, the dynamic of the unfolding peace process has also affected the way in which the very relation between the past and the present has been experienced by the victims. Insofar as trust and confidence have grown, that a more just and peaceful society is being brought into existence, then whatever has happened in 'the past' may be separated out from the present and the hoped-for future. However, when such trust and confidence have been missing, or have ebbed or been eroded, then 'the past' is not experienced as being 'over' and 'passed' at all, but is lived as the continuous and ongoing present-day reality.

This is especially the case with regard to two fundamentals of conflict resolution that have a particular importance for the victims of violence. Firstly, the establishment of safety and freedom from fear is now universally acknowledged in Northern Ireland to be a primary condition of reparative remembering that enables recovery from trauma. While the voicing of a victim's story in the public domain offers the prospect of social recognition by wider public audiences, under any circumstances the articulation of deeply painful personal memories in a public arena involves vulnerability and risks the denial of recognition, if not outright hostility, on the part of the other. In the context of the resolution of a conflict where personal safety has often been bought by silence, to do so may be courting psychic if not actual physical danger, which can have the effect of *re-traumatizing* the victim. In situations where victims continue to live in a climate of fear and violence, some describe their suffering, not as post-traumatic – as in PTSD – but *continuing* traumatic stress disorder, which has rather different psychic repercussions.[16] Secondly, the securing of justice for the violence inflicted on the victims is also widely understood to be a fundamental basis for the making of the new society of the future that will be free from violence and fear, and a psychic necessity if the victims are to come to terms with loss and integrate the hurt and pain of the past.[17]

These two conditions of transformation lie at the heart of conflict resolution in Ireland, as elsewhere, and they are sought by all the victims of violence. But their absence affects the Protestant and Unionist victims of the Border areas in particular ways. Interviewees for FEAR's research report, for example, expressed doubts and hesitations about moving back to the Border because of fears about the uncertain future of the peace process, particularly the possible breakdown of the ceasefires and a renewed terrorist campaign.[18] As 'Mr R. Rankin' puts it: 'We would need a more stable situation before you could venture back and you'd have to consider whether you'd be accepted back after people have put you out. There is not much encouragement to go back at the present time, with the bomb at Carrybridge. You would have to think of your life first and we would need a more stable political situation.'[19]

Such fears remained prevalent among Border Protestants years after the IRA's ceasefire of August 1994, exacerbated by what proved to be a temporary and limited resumption of the armed struggle with the bombing of London's Docklands in February 1996. Following the IRA's restoration of its ceasefire in July 1997, and with multi-party talks due to begin in September, press coverage of FEAR's launch that August made enthusiastic use of the language of 'hope', in reports that 'organizers are optimistic' of securing EU peace money,[20] and 'Protestant families from the Fermanagh Borderlands are beginning to dare to hope they may soon be able to go back'.[21] However, Arlene Foster, as spokesperson for the group, cautioned: 'They are relying on the Peace Process lasting – but it's a very tender thing to rely on',[22] adding: 'It's all about confidence, and at the moment because of the political situation and the parades issue, Protestant confidence isn't great. There is a feeling that attempts are still being made to squeeze them out of the community in which they live.'[23]

Pointing out that attacks had been carried out only the previous week on two small churches, one near the Border, she argued: 'The trouble over the summer parades may have been forgotten about, but meanwhile all this tension is simmering away in the background . . . if they do go back, will they feel comfortable?'[24] During the summer, there had been a tense stand-off for the third year running over the Parades Commission's attempt to ban the Orange Order's annual July parade to Drumcree Church. The previous year, during 'Drumcree Two', a nationalist boycott of Protestant businesses in protest against Drumcree and other Orange marches through predominantly nationalist areas had contributed to a 'really traumatic time' on the Fermanagh Border.[25] There had also been an associated increase in sectarian violence emanating from both sides of the political divide, including a number of arson attacks on small Orange halls and other forms of Protestant culture – 'targeting of halls like that causes, obviously, suspicion and fear . . . all over again. "Oh, some peace we're having!", that's the sort of thing you hear.'[26]

Foster's caution, and her warnings about the detrimental effects of ongoing violence on the possibility of return, were reiterated throughout the autumn of 1997, even while FEAR was enjoying its first meeting with the Government in early November. Sectarian intimidation had continued: in late October the windows of the Anglican church in Newtownbutler had been smashed, and 'Orange Order halls have been set alight, boycotts continue and fresh plans are being laid to oppose traditional summer parades'.[27] Foster warned that: 'In the end, whether people move back is dependent on the talks', and confidence that the talks could deliver permanent peace remained fragile.[28] While there had been 'a lot of talk from republicans and nationalists about confidence-building measures to strengthen the peace process', what Unionists really needed was 'to be sure this peace is going to last'.[29]

Although the renewed ceasefire had raised hopes and political developments were broadly welcomed, they also generated uncertainty, anxiety and suspicion within Protestant and Unionist communities. Concerns focused on the IRA's sincerity in seeking a peaceful solution to the conflict, and for many people the sudden termination of its original ceasefire appeared to call in question that sincerity. The Docklands bombing and further armed actions in Britain and the North over the following months were a response to the British Government's insistence on the *prior* decommissioning of some IRA weapons before Sinn Féin would be allowed to participate in multi-party talks: a pre-condition introduced for the first time by Conservative Secretary of State Patrick Mayhew, with Unionist support, in March 1995, in contravention of previous commitments that a lasting ceasefire would suffice.[30] The new Labour Government paved the way to the restoration of the ceasefire and Sinn Féin's involvement in the talks, when in June 1997 it reached agreement with the Irish Government on a policy of *parallel* decommissioning. Based on the principles of the Mitchell Report of January 1996, this would run alongside (rather than precede or follow) political talks.

Republican sensitivities and perceptions, that prior decommissioning would amount to an IRA surrender and was therefore impossible to countenance, cut no ice with Unionists, who argued that if the war really was over there was no further use for the weapons, and perceived the retention of those weapons as the IRA's way of hedging its bet on the outcome of the talks. Despite these concerns, the UUP, led by David Trimble, agreed to the *twin-track* approach, and Unionism split, with the DUP and the United Kingdom Unionist Party rejecting the re-established ceasefire as a tactical 'sham'.[31] Although the Good Friday Agreement that concluded the talks included a commitment by all participants to work to bring about 'the total disarmament of all paramilitary organizations' within two years,[32] no IRA decommissioning occurred until October 2001. During the intervening three-and-a-half years, the heated controversy surrounding the issue 'stalled the implementation of the Good Friday Agreement and plunged the process into crisis'.[33]

The Border Protestants' sense of a continuing threat, compounded by the experience of actual ongoing violence and intimidation, as well as the possibility of a return to full-scale armed conflict, were exacerbated both by the apparent refusal of the Provisional IRA to decommission its weapons and by the armed actions of dissident Republican paramilitary groups. The Continuity IRA (CIRA) – formed after a splinter group, Republican Sinn Féin (RSF), split from the Provisionals over their electoral politics in 1986 – chose the Fermanagh Border area as the site of its first major operation, a bomb in July 1996 that destroyed the Killyhevlin Hotel in Enniskillen. In September 1997, another CIRA bomb caused £3 million of damage to Markethill, where FAIR would later establish its office, in an attempt to destabilize multi-party talks, which included Sinn Féin, that had begun the day before.[34] 'Dissident' groups like RSF opposed the peace strategy, seeing it as a sell-out which recognized partition and betrayed the memory of those who had sacrificed their lives for a united Ireland. In 2000, the RSF office on the Falls Road prominently displayed a painting of uniformed IRA volunteers firing a tribute over a coffin draped with an Irish tricolour, below the slogan 'Remember What They died For' (see figure 6). In November 1997 the so-called 'Real IRA' (RIRA) was formed by a group of dissidents opposed to Republican involvement in the peace process, who left the Provisionals after an Extraordinary Army Convention had rejected their calls to resume the armed struggle.[35] Support for the new organization was strong in South Armagh, where 'PIRA–Real IRA co-operation' led to the resumption of attacks on the army along the Border, and a number of car-bomb attacks across the North, which began in January 1998 and culminated in Omagh on 15 August.[36] The Omagh bomb – 'the single worst atrocity in Northern Ireland since the Troubles began' – killed twenty-nine and injured over 200, including nationalists, Unionists and visitors to Ireland,[37] after which RIRA ended its armed campaign. A number of Omagh victims were to join West Tyrone Voice.[38]

For the Protestant and Unionist victims' groups of the Border areas, as for their communities more widely, distrust and suspicion of Republican intentions were reinforced by the experience of this prevailing climate of fear and

6 'Remember What They Died For': framed painting at the front of the
Republican Sinn Féin shop, Falls Road, West Belfast, July 2000.

intimidation that appeared to make a mockery of the *peace* process. In
Wilson's report (discussed in chapter 8), responses to FAIR's questionnaire,
in which 100 victims registered with the group were asked to agree or disagree with a series of statements about their own personal security and basic
human rights, showed that 94 per cent believed it to be 'not true at all' that

'I am free from threats and intimidation in South Armagh', while 84 per cent claimed it to be 'not true at all' that 'I am free from fear in South Armagh'.[39] Wilson suggested that, 'after 18 months of uneasy truce, the IRA's South Armagh Brigade has rejected *de facto* the Good Friday Agreement with regard to decommissioning'.[40] Willie Frazer of FAIR said, in March 2000, that he believed neither that the war was over nor that the IRA would ever decommission, arguing that Gerry Adams and the Sinn Féin leadership were simply unreconstructed terrorists who would return to armed struggle when the concessions they were winning politically had been exhausted.[41] FAIR described the Sinn Féin politicians at Stormont as 'unrepentent terrorists walking the corridors of power, gangsters disguised as democrats', and likened their involvement in the government of Northern Ireland to 'the mass child murderer Myra Hindley . . . sitting at 10 Downing Street briefing the Prime Minister on the Health Service or Education'.[42]

For Hazlett Lynch of West Tyrone Voice, distinctions between Republicans who were on ceasefire and committed to political negotiations, on one hand, and those who had already resumed the military campaign, on the other, were meaningless. In March 2000, Lynch suggested that 'just outside Castlederg the IRA are still training . . . in Killeter Forest. And the RUC know about it . . . But nothing has been done about it, because the IRA are untouchable.'[43] He also claimed that 'the IRA are rearming' on the West Tyrone Border: arms dumps – the locations of which were known to the security forces, who were unable to act on the information as to do so was considered politically inexpedient – were being emptied for use by CIRA and RIRA. But Lynch rejected the very idea of 'dissident Republicans': this was being done 'with the connivance of [Martin] McGuinness', the Minister of Education in the newly established Northern Ireland Executive, who, Lynch believed, had told the splinter groups 'to do it, but don't name us'. So, he argued, the Provisional IRA 'talks peace but rearms', using the splinter groups to help buttress its political demands.[44] At the victims' and survivors' conference 'Hear and now', on 29 February–1 March 2000, called to involve grassroots groups in the continuing evolution of the Government's victims' strategy, Lynch sought to impress on delegates the impossibility of seriously addressing the needs of Voice members while this situation obtained.[45] He refused to engage in discussion with any politician from a party connected to a paramilitary group, like Sinn Féin and the PUP,

> until they demonstrate that they have become bona fide democrats, and that violence and terror is no longer an option for them. But that doesn't seem to be going to happen certainly in . . . the immediate future, if ever. The [Sinn Féin] Assembly member for this area made [a statement] in *An Phoblacht* to the effect that, 'if the IRA decommissions, that will be tantamount to saying that our campaign was illegitimate, and the means that we used to prosecute our campaign were illegitimate. This we will never concede.' So there's no hint there that these guys are going to give up their 'armed struggle'.[46]

The difficulties this posed for Unionist victims was expressed in a workshop at the same conference by a member of FACT (Families Against Crimes by Terrorism), a group based in Lisburn with a small subgroup in the Border area of South Down, who asked: 'How can I sit at a table with my hands on top, when this other man might have a gun under it, and have a discussion with him on equal terms?'[47] This image of the gun under the table calls into question the moral standing of political negotiations with parties linked to paramilitary groups who have retained their arms; but it has a closer reference also, to the supposedly safe and supportive atmosphere in which discussion in the 'Hear and now' conference itself was taking place. Protestant and Unionist victims objected strongly to the presence of Republicans, whether as politicians or members of victims' groups, known to be perpetrators of violence. One FAIR delegate was said to have become deeply upset and angry on discovering the participation in the conference of a former Republican prisoner who had been convicted for killing one of her close relatives.

The 'gun' in these images of threat is not merely a metaphorical one. Stories about IRA intimidation in the course of everyday life in South Armagh continued to circulate in private arenas long after the ceasefires, like the one about the Republican who, when asked by a neighbour whether he had planning permission for a building extension, responded by showing his gun.[48] Leslie Finlay of Voice testified in late March 2000 to a renewed sense of threat along the West Tyrone Border:

> I've got my protection weapon packed away . . . I got it out a month ago, cleaned her all up and . . . carry it now, and that three lucky years there I hadn't carried it, I got away from it . . . Well, let's face it, they're still out and they're still, what we call, dickin'. They were targeting us, dickin' us, like.[49]

Lynch pointed out the image of an IRA gunman on a sign attached to a lamppost on the road from Newtownstewart in Strabane: echoing the infamous mock road signs in South Armagh warning of a 'Sniper at work', the sign carried the message, 'I'll be back', keeping alive the memory of fear.[50] Nineteen months after this conversation, and one week after the Provisional IRA announced that it had completed its first act of verifiable decommissioning to save the peace process from collapse, Charles Folliard, a Protestant and a former paramilitary prisoner once linked to the UDA, was shot dead in a street a few hundred yards from that sign, which was now accompanied by another bearing the slogan 'No Decommissioning'. Folliard, who was said to be 'putting his past behind him', had been visiting his Catholic girlfriend in a predominantly nationalist area. The killers, believed to have been members of either CIRA or RIRA, were condemned by Sinn Féin's Pat Doherty, the MP for West Tyrone, as 'enemies of the peace process and enemies of Republicanism'. The *Guardian* reported that 'in a dark echo of earlier times' all of the people it had spoken to about the killing 'were too scared to have their names published in the newspaper'.[51]

Victims' memories, IRA 'decommissioning' and the Good Friday Agreement

The persistence of fear, anger and hurt attached to the memories of past Republican violence and re-evoked by its continuation throughout 'the peace' helps to explain the intensity and tenacity of Unionist emphasis on the issue of the decommissioning of IRA guns. This in turn affected Unionist responses to the peace talks and the Good Friday Agreement itself. The Agreement signed on 10 April 1998 was an inclusive package of measures that sought to balance the demands of, and required concessions from, all the signatories. The package had been produced by 'a complex process of multi-layered deal-making'[52] – or, as those later described as 'dissident Unionists' saw it, by 'a fudge'.[53] While it was immediately acclaimed by its more enthusiastic supporters as marking 'a new beginning',[54] a historic 'opportunity to resolve our deep and tragic conflict'[55] and a 'start . . . [to] the healing process',[56] the chairperson of the talks, George Mitchell, 'warned that the Agreement might not still be in existence in eighteen months time and commented on the complete lack of trust, "a presumption of bad faith", between unionists and republicans'.[57] Clear, popular endorsement of the Agreement was expressed in the referenda held simultaneously in Northern Ireland and the Republic on 22 May: in the North, 71 per cent voted in favour, with a turnout of 81 per cent; in the Republic, 94 per cent were in favour, but with a turnout of only 56 per cent.[58] However, exit polls suggested that, while Catholics in the North were virtually unanimous in their support, 'Protestants were almost equally divided between "yes" and "no" voters'; and in elections to the new Northern Ireland Assembly on 25 June, the Unionist vote split almost evenly between the pro-Agreement UUP and PUP with thirty-one seats; and the anti-Agreement DUP and United Kingdom Unionist Party, plus three independent Unionists, with twenty-eight seats.[59]

In the conflict that developed within Unionism and loyalism between its pro- and anti-Agreement wings, the 'No' campaign, in particular, mobilized antagonistic memories of IRA violence, and made the decommissioning of the IRA's arsenal its central theme. Unionist pressure to progress decommissioning took the form of a strategy to prevent the establishment of a power-sharing Executive including Sinn Féin ministers without prior movement on IRA arms (in opposition to Republican claims that Sinn Féin's democratic mandate gave it an entitlement to seats on the executive irrespective of whether progress had been made over arms). The slogan 'No Guns, No Government' commanded support from both wings: that is, from those supportive of an inclusive settlement involving Sinn Féin provided this meant that 'the war is really over', as well as from those who would always refuse to engage with Republicans, personally or politically.[60]

On 15 July 1999, attempts to establish the Executive by the original deadline failed when its formation was boycotted by the UUP, under the First Minister Elect David Trimble, leading to a major crisis and triggering the

Mitchell Review of the implementation of the Agreement.[61] Trimble won a fierce battle against the anti-Agreement wing of his own party – including Arlene Foster, by now a 'leading dissident' associated with the hardline Unionism of Trimble's main challenger Jeffrey Donaldson[62] – when, on 27 November 1999, he persuaded the UUP Council, its ruling body, to accept the deal agreed with Sinn Féin during the Review. Trimble's victory made possible the implementation of the constitutional settlement, the transfer of power to the devolved institutions and the formation of the Executive, all of which occurred on 2 December 1999. However, the strength of feeling and suspicion among UUP Council delegates was such that they insisted on the recall of Council in February to assess progress, in effect imposing on the IRA an eleven-week deadline. A second crisis duly followed, and on 11 February 2000 the devolved institutions, including the Executive, were suspended by Secretary of State Peter Mandelson to prevent a Unionist withdrawal leading to its collapse. In March Trimble survived a challenge to his leadership of the UUP by an anti-Agreement candidate, former Grand Master of the Orange Order Reverend Martin Smyth, and on 6 May a historic commitment by the IRA 'to completely and verifiably put arms beyond use' created the conditions for the restoration of the Executive. On 27 May, after another period of fierce debate and conflict between Unionists, the UUP Council endorsed Trimble's re-entry to the Executive, and devolution was restored three days later.[63]

A third crisis over decommissioning occurred one year later when Trimble resigned as First Minister in July 2001 in protest at the continuing lack of action on the issue by the IRA.[64] This led to a second suspension of the institutions by the British Government, and to a second Review of the Agreement, before the first act of decommissioning by the IRA – the 'putting beyond use' of the contents of two arms dumps in October 2001 – temporarily established the Executive on a more stable footing.[65] Further acts of decommissioning followed over the next three years but failed to assuage Unionists' distrust, and in October 2002 devolved government was again suspended as relations between the UUP and Sinn Féin broke down amid allegations of an 'IRA spy-ring' at Stormont.[66] This presaged a major shift in the balance of power within Unionism towards the anti-Agreement wing, led by Ian Paisley's DUP, which became the most powerful party in Northern Ireland at the Assembly election held in November 2003.[67] Officially verified decommissioning of 'the totality of the IRA's arsenal' was announced on 26 September 2005,[68] but disputes over the basis for the restoration of devolved government were still continuing in April 2007.

Protestant and Unionist victims of violence, while supporting one or other side in the fight over the implementation of the Good Friday Agreement, campaigned most vociferously for the 'No' camp. This is paradoxical, given that the Agreement included measures to recognize and address the needs of the victims as a specific social group. Indeed, one of the champions of victims' issues in the political process – Monica McWilliams of the Women's Coalition – called for support for the Agreement in the name of the victims, as the way to discharge a social responsibility: 'We owe it to all those who have suffered and died over the past three decades to grasp this opportunity to build a society that will stand as a living testimonial to the victims of our Troubles.'[69] In Spring 1999 Wilson's report found that '73% of the FAIR group when surveyed, believed that the Good Friday/Belfast Agreement gives victims the opportunity to gain dignity and respect in the wider community'.[70] Nevertheless, FAIR joined a number of other victims' groups in an umbrella organization, Northern Ireland Terrorist Victims Together (NITVT), which was strongly associated with anti-Agreement Unionism.

NITVT organized a campaign for 'Protestant civil rights' in the form of a 'Long March' that took place from 24 June to 4 July 1999, starting at the Guildhall in Derry (a location steeped in associations with the campaign for nationalist civil rights and with Bloody Sunday) and ending at Drumcree, where it linked up with the Orange Order's protest, at Drumcree Church, itself a catalyst for 'No' campaigners.[71] The demands articulated through the march focused on 'a declaration by the IRA that the war is over', the disbandment of terrorist groups, the decommissioning and destruction of paramilitary weapons and an inquiry by an international tribunal into the Irish Government's role in relation to the development of the Provisional IRA in the early 1970s.[72] But the Long March, with its banner logo of an eye and an tear, also promoted the idea that Protestants and Unionists harmed by the IRA were the 'Real Victims' of the Troubles, and laid claim to being 'a voice for real justice in Northern Ireland'.[73] The marchers were joined by UUP and DUP anti-Agreement politicians.

As the debate intensified within the UUP, during the late summer of 1999, about the conditions necessary to establish an Executive that included Sinn Féin, UUP Council delegates were sent a copy of a video: *An Appeal to You from the Victims*.[74] This was an overt attempt to mobilize memories of Republican violence in order to swing Unionist political opinion against support for Sinn Féin's involvement in government. Framed by the 'Real Victims' and Long March logos, and intercut with images of various stages of the march, the video features visual memories of four notorious IRA and INLA bomb attacks (two of which took place in the Border regions): the IRA's 'Poppy Day' massacre at Enniskillen in 1987, the INLA's bombing of the Droppin Well bar in Ballykelly in 1982, the IRA's Shankill Road bomb of 1993 and its mortar attack on Newry RUC Station in 1985.[75] These visual reminders of carnage and pain provide a context in which four of the injured or bereaved voice their personal moral appeals to the UUP delegates, speaking as victims, in emotive language, direct to camera; for example:

I am Jim Dixon. I was seriously injured at the Cenotaph at Enniskillen . . . The blood of the innocent victims is still calling out from the ground. And their blood will be upon your shoulders if you are guilty of permitting Sinn Féin into government.
My name is Sylvia Callaghan, mother of the 17-year-old-and-5-months Alan

Callaghan which was murdered at the Droppin Well, Ballykelly . . . so please
don't let these IRA murderers into government nor let any more prisoners
out for it's only to kill more people and maim . . . The Lord said, 'Thou shalt
not kill.'

All four speakers are then heard in voiceover as the Sinn Féin President Gerry
Adams is shown as one of the bearers of a tricolour-draped coffin at an IRA
funeral.[76] This is a visual memory of the 'electrifying moment' at the funeral
of the Shankill bomber Thomas Begley (killed as the bomb exploded prema-
turely) when Adams took his turn to carry the coffin. Film footage and photographs of this event featured prominently in news stories calling into
question Adams's commitment to the peace process only a few weeks after the
Hume–Adams proposals had been presented to the Irish Government: 'how,
it was asked, could this man speak of peace while shouldering the coffin of a
bomber who had caused so many deaths?'[77]

Begley's funeral was remembered by Unionists and loyalists as an occasion
also of Republican indifference, and indeed triumphalism, in the face of
their own suffering: Begley was given 'a hero's send-off' by thousands of
Republican mourners in North and West Belfast, and in an incident when
insults were traded with mourners attending the funeral of one of the victims
of the bombing, horns were sounded, two men held up nine fingers, and one
was heard to shout at the Protestants, to the dismay of stewards: 'We got
nine of youse – we can't kill enough of you bastards.'[78] The significance of
these personal and collective memories was spelt out in an apocryphal conclusion to the video: a caption reading 'Time to decide' and the sound of a
church clock striking, followed by the image of an open Bible with 'God's
word' that 'governors . . . are sent by Him for the punishment of evildoers
and for the praise of them that do well (1 Peter 2:14)'. In this video, the
victims lobbying the UUP Council spoke the same language as Ian Paisley; a
language that became increasingly prevalent in Unionist political discourse
as confidence in the peace process waned.

Victims' memories, prisoner-releases and the reform of the RUC

The voices of Protestant and Unionist victims were raised in opposition not
only to the admittance to government of 'IRA terrorists', but to the implementation of two other policies at the centre of the Good Friday Agreement:
the early release of paramilitary prisoners and the reform of the RUC. The
early release of prisoners had been a major concession to keep on board Sinn
Féin, but also the smaller loyalist parties linked to paramilitary groups (the
PUP and the Ulster Democratic Party), during the negotiation of the
Agreement. It provided for the release of all 'conflict-related' violent offenders, Republican and loyalist, held in prisons in Northern Ireland, Britain and
the Irish Republic, on condition that they did not re-offend and that their
organizations remained on ceasefire.

The prisoner-release scheme was phased over two years, and by January 1999 had resulted in 238 releases.[79] A final group of seventy-six prisoners, making a total of 428, were freed over 24–28 July 2000; among them some of 'the most feared and dangerous killers' of the Troubles, such as the loyalist Michael Stone and the surviving 'Shankill bomber' Sean Kelly, whose release met with a chorus of protest which included the voices of their victims.[80] The release back into the community of 'terrorist prisoners' who had served a sentence, especially if reduced, had been a controversial issue for long before the Agreement. During the period of consultation undertaken while preparing his report, the British Government's Victims Commissioner Sir Kenneth Bloomfield noted that 'many people made the point to me that there seems to be a stronger and more effective lobby operating in the interests of prisoners or ex-prisoners than there is in the interests of victims'.[81] It was inevitable that the early-release scheme implemented under the Agreement would have a specific impact on the victims of violence in both Unionist and nationalist communities.

The imminent release of Republican 'terrorist prisoners' in particular proved to be a catalyst for the formation of a tranche of Protestant and Unionist victims' groups, including FAIR and West Tyrone Voice, in the months following the Agreement. As Hazlett Lynch describes it,

> there was the feeling that these people who plunged many people in Northern Ireland into bereavement, into loss, into trauma, suffering and pain, were now getting out, they were being in a sense rewarded by the Government for what they had done, whereas those of us who have carried the wounds and the scars of their activities have been left, still with the pain. And there didn't seem to be any justice or . . . fairness of any kind, shown to those of us whose lives had been traumatized by the activities of these guys . . . [O]ver the months after the signing of the Belfast Agreement and the accelerated release of terrorist prisoners there was a feeling, I think, throughout the Border counties of Northern Ireland, in particular, that something will have to be done in order to ensure that we as victims are not forgotten.[82]

The release of convicted terrorists had an emotional impact on victims for a number of reasons: it could reawaken memories of the incident itself and risked undoing the positive psychic effects that stemmed from the achievement of judicial retribution, returning victims to their original condition of loss and pain. Wilson's report for FAIR noted of the situation in South Armagh, where fifty-nine out of a total of sixty-eight 'murders of British residents still await justice': 'In the few cases where there has been a conviction, it is perceived as an act of callous insensitivity to release the killers – in one example, after ten years of a "life" sentence – on the actual anniversary of the murder. This has increased the trauma and distress to the families concerned . . . [and added to] the annual sorrow and sadness of that day.'[83] In this case, the family of the late RUC Reservist Constable David Sterritt from Markethill, killed on duty along with two colleagues and a civilian by an IRA landmine outside Armagh City on 24 July 1990, had learned of the release date of 24 July 2000 announced for one of his two convicted killers from a press report in January 1999, and asked the Sentence Review Commission that it be brought forward by a few days.[84] David Sterritt's father, Fred, was reported as saying:

> It's sickening. It is just rubbing salt in the wounds. How could they not realise what July 24 means to us as a family. It's a heartbreaking day. We knew that they would be due for early release and we have tried to come to terms with that, hard as it is. But to learn that they are getting out on the anniversary of David's death is agony.

The Commission declined to change the date on the grounds that all release dates were fixed by 'strict legislative procedure'.[85]

Release could also provoke fear among victims that the released terrorist would strike again or might be encountered face-to-face unexpectedly in the street, and anger that these difficult feelings were being re-inflicted on the victims: a member of one of the Border Protestant groups at the 'Hear and now' conference, who had lost a close relative to the IRA, spoke vehemently in private about 'those boyos coming out' of prison when 'they ought to have been – disappeared'.[86] Furthermore, release compounded in a particularly acute form the victims' sense of having been abandoned by the State and left to 'suffer in silence', their hurt unrecognized.

Meanwhile, the released 'perpetrators' were sometimes imagined as being carefree and cock-a-hoop, so that the victims' re-awakened sorrow 'will be heightened by the knowledge, that a few miles up the road, the killers and their families will be hosting a triumphalist celebration'.[87] Despite the principle enshrined in the Bloomfield Report, that it would be 'quite unacceptable to provide services for the benefit of those convicted of serious offences which are not matched in dealing with the victims of such crimes',[88] the perception flourished – and was expressed heatedly at at the 'Hear and now' conference, and again during my visits to meet the Protestant and Unionist victims' groups – that released prisoners were getting preferential treatment and securing a disproportionate amount of funding and recognition from the State. This was felt to be a blatant contravention of natural justice. While, on one hand, people 'were literally getting away with murder',[89] walking free, and then being rewarded for it, on the other, many of the victims felt that their own 'sentence' of suffering would last a lifetime.

This sense of injustice was extended to the Agreement as a whole, and lies behind FAIR's assertion that it represents an inversion of moral values – 'the undeniable fact that good has now become evil and right has now become wrong by the appeasement of Republican terrorists by both the British and Irish Governments'.[90] Over the summer of 1999, hostility to the prisoner-release scheme meshed with disillusionment at the lack of progress on arms decommissioning and disappointment at the failure to form an Executive, to crystallize growing opposition to the Agreement. On 9 September 1999 – three days after the start of the Mitchell Review – the launch of the Patten

Report on reform of the RUC sparked Unionist opposition to a third, deeply emotive, aspect of the Agreement, again involving questions of memory, security and justice, in which the Protestant and Unionist victims of violence played a leading role. Chris Patten's brief, as provided by the Agreement, was to establish the measures necessary to create a modern police service that would be 'depoliticized',[91] freed from its historic reputation as 'the armed wing of Unionism', and capable of securing the support of Catholics and nationalists. As well as making a series of detailed practical and operational proposals, the report, *A New Beginning*, recommended the creation of new symbols that should be 'free from any association with either the British or Irish states'.[92] This would involve changing the name of the force, redesigning its badge and doing away with the display of partisan symbols, including portraits of the Queen and the flying of the Union Jack in police stations.[93] 'We are transforming the RUC', Patten claimed, 'not disbanding it' as Republicans demanded.[94] Anticipating and attempting to defuse the emotional reaction from Protestants and Unionists that followed, he acknowledged the 'pain' these proposals would cause, and insisted that they implied no 'slight to the sacrifice in service' made by members of the RUC since its inception:

> The memorials to the sacrifices of the past should remain as they are and where they are. But the greatest memorial of all will, we believe, be a peaceful Northern Ireland with agreed institutions, including an agreed police service, with participation and support from the community as a whole.[95]

The 'sacrifices' he had in mind were the deaths of 302 RUC officers, the serious injuries to some 8,000 others, and the less serious injuries to a further 5,000, sustained in the course of the Troubles since 1968;[96] not to mention the casualties accrued in defence of the Northern Ireland State over nearly fifty years prior to that.

The Patten proposals were greeted with a chorus of highly emotional opposition from the Unionist press, Unionist political parties, the Orange Order, the Police Federation, victims' groups representing injured police officers and bereaved police families, and RUC victims themselves. The *News Letter* captured the tenor of this response in a full-page colour image of uniformed RUC men carrying the coffin – draped in the Union flag – of an off-duty policeman killed in 1997, under the banner headline: 'Betrayed'.[97] This amplified the theme of a statement by the Police Federation, representing 13,000 police officers, in which it vowed to fight the name change: 'The dropping of the name and emblems of the RUC is a betrayal of the widows of murdered officers, and of officers maimed by terrorists.'[98] The *News Letter's* editorial, while calling for 'careful and lengthy consideration' of the Patten Report, pointed to the 'disappointment', 'demoralization', 'anger and disgust', as well as the sense of betrayal, shared by 'the wider unionist community, which has become increasingly perturbed by what appears to be a never-ending assault on the things they hold dear'.[99] David Adams, spokesperson of the Ulster Democratic Party (linked to the UDA), articulated a second key theme when he described the proposed name change 'an insult to the memory of the RUC officers who gave their lives in defence of this community – and to those who were seriously injured in the furtherance of their duty . . . It is a blatant attempt to appease those responsible for the misery inflicted on them and their loved ones.'[100] The centrality of the RUC victims in contesting the 'appeasement of terrorists' was also emphasized by Arlene Foster of FEAR. Writing as a UUP spokesperson in the nationalist *Irish News*, she quotes a statement made by an RUC widow during consultation meetings with Chris Patten in late 1998: ' "I put the words Royal Ulster Constabulary on my husband's gravestone – that is what he died for – and I do not want to see that changed." '[101]

RUC victims, given a platform of their own to speak out in opposition to the Patten proposals, reiterated these themes, reinforced by emotional memories of their own loss. Bereaved family members such as Fred and Ivy Sterritt, and Alison McClean, the parents and sister of full-time RUC Reservist David Sterritt (whose dismay at the insensitive early-release date of his killer was augmented by the disbandment of the force for which he gave his life), and disabled former RUC officers, such as Bob Crozier, told their stories of trauma, recovery and the struggle to rebuild shattered lives, and linked these to Patten – and the Agreement. Several of the more detailed statements featured in the *Belfast Telegraph*, the *News Letter* and the *Irish News* were from South Armagh, suggesting that individual press releases had been organized by FAIR. Alison McClean's passionate attack on the proposed name-change as an 'insult to the memory' of the RUC dead demonstrates the emotive quality of these personal interventions:

> I think it is a total insult to the memory of all those people who have lost their lives to suggest that the name should be changed. I feel very angry and very disappointed – the Commission didn't really take into consideration people's feelings. The Royal Ulster Constabulary is the force which people like my brother gave up their lives for and that name is very important to the families of people who have died. The fact that they are going to phase out the [RUC] Reserve makes it even worse. I feel as if David died for nothing.[102]

Her father, Fred, added: 'My son was only doing his job when he was killed and never had any trouble with either side of the community. I feel sickened by what I've heard today. It's as if the police are being made out to be the scapegoats.'[103]

Two RUC widows, Margaret Turbitt from Richhill and Mary Allen from Markethill, told of how their husbands were abducted and shot in South Armagh in 1978 and 1980 respectively, and their bodies released only much later: two weeks in Wallace Allen's case, and attached to a 200lb bomb. Billy Turbitt's widow Margaret said that she had endured three weeks of 'mental anguish' after he went missing, and the pain had come 'flooding back' as a result of the public controversy over the renaming of the force he had served.[104] Mary Allen said she was still seeking 'the full truth . . . about what

happened to my husband' during those weeks in 1980, and protested that 'the
IRA has never offered any remorse or said sorry for what happened' to him.
This had clearly influenced her disbelief that the Patten Report 'would bring
peace' and her opposition to the 'insult' of the proposed reforms: 'You would
wonder if it's going to come to the point where the terrorists are policing
us.'[105] Another RUC widow, Hilda Jardine declared: 'The widows, orphans,
injured policemen, we are the forgotten people in all these changes.'[106] This
was a fear echoed by Bob Crozier, an RUC man who lost a leg following an
IRA ambush in which his colleague was killed in 1976, and whose life has
been plagued by disability and ill-health ever since: 'If the name and the badge
goes, where does that leave us [the disabled like myself]? We are ex-what? Or
do they really just want to forget about us?'[107]

For many victims, the proposed police reform was particularly objection-
able and raised suspicions about 'forgotten sacrifices' because it implied a
moral equivalence between those who had fought, and in many cases lost
their lives and health to maintain law and order over the years, and the terrorist perpetrators of violent conflict. Such an equivalence flies in the face of
that cherished and traditional Unionist principle which denies that the security forces were active agents – themselves perpetrators – of violence. But the
reform also called into question the meaning of their death. Willie Frazer of
FAIR expressed this sense in relation to the loss of his own father while
serving in the UDR. By dismantling the security forces 'which stand between
the terrorists and decent people' – first the B-Specials, then the UDR, now
the RUC – the British Government 'had insulted the memory of those who
served and died for what they believed in'. In his family this was a record of
service in the British armed forces reaching back 132 years, and 'my father
and many others of my family and friends have been buried in coffins draped
with a Union Jack. But I won't follow a coffin draped with a Union Jack
again.' To keep faith with the dead is to continue to remember, respect and
uphold their values in the face of betrayal. This requires a certain fixity of
memory in the service of tradition: 'If I go back on my opinion and change
what they believed in, I'd be degrading their memory.'[108] Thus, there can be
no accommodation to Republican terrorists. Only their defeat will suffice.
Ironically, this mirrors the exact same call to remember rather than betray
made by dissident Republican groups committed to maintaining the armed
struggle.

Peter Robinson of the DUP linked this traditional Unionist rejection of
moral equivalence to the political project of the anti-Agreement Unionists,
when he wrote of Patten:

> The general population will look at this report in the context that in this peace
> process, terrorist organizations are to remain unchallenged, will still be intact
> with no change to their command structures and can still retain their arms. Then
> they will look at the 313 [*sic*] people who have been killed protecting law and
> order in this society and see that the force they served in is being emasculated
> and destroyed with the support of those who signed the Belfast Agreement.[109]

This was not only an attack on the Patten Report but on the UUP under David Trimble, whose support for the peace process continued to expose Unionists to the threat of what the Orange Order described as 'the complete disbandment of the RUC',[110] even as they now rejected the proposals that would realize this threat. The memory of the RUC victims was a potent weapon in this battle. On the day following the launch, 'anti-Agreement Unionists stepped up their campaign against the Patten proposals' when Ian Paisley joined members of FAIR and bereaved RUC families in a special remembrance ceremony at Stormont.[111] Indeed, by the time of the crucial UUP Council meeting on 27 November 1999 to discuss entering government with Sinn Féin, it appeared that no public discussion of the major problems surrounding the implementation of the Agreement could be conducted without reference to, and contribution from, the victims of violence. A routine media report on the decommissioning debate, such as that on Channel 4's *News* on 19 November, canvassed a spectrum of views ranging from those of Bloody Sunday bereaved relative John Kelly ('everyone should decommission') to the Long March campaigner Jim Dixon ('put the decent, proper people into government, not terrorists . . . They have to be faced down. Evil men should not be allowed to live in society with people'), and including the injured RUC Constable Jim Davison, who lost a hand in an ambush in 1977 ('the IRA have done some awful jobs. They should decommission').[112]

On 23 November, Secretary of State Mandelson was able to 'recognize and honour the memory' of the RUC by announcing that the force had been awarded the George Cross for 'gallantry' by the Queen.[113] At the UUP Council meeting itself, delegates were picketed by 'No' campaigners whose banners and slogans proclaimed his strategy a betrayal of the victims of the IRA, a theme developed in the debate by delegates opposed to the leadership's recommendation to accept the Mitchell-brokered deal with Sinn Féin. Trimble himself, in a 'bravura performance', attempted to break the effective link forged between the memories of the victims and the 'No' camp, by invoking the memory of his friend and former UUP politician Edgar Graham, shot dead by the IRA in 1983; and by reading from a letter sent to him by Norah Bradford, the widow of Reverend Robert Bradford, another Unionist victim of the IRA, 'pledging her full support and urging him to keep at the difficult job'.[114]

The politics of victimhood and the war over memory

This lodging of the victims at the centre of political debate can be seen as something of a mixed blessing for them, heightening the contradictions involved in seeking recognition in the charged context of conflict resolution. For some, victims' issues had become caught up in a game of political football. Fraser Agnew, an Assembly member for the United Unionist Assembly Party, resigned from the Long March campaign at the end of September

1999, believing that 'innocent victims are being manipulated and exploited for political ends. It's almost like emotional blackmail.'[115] In addition to the danger of exploitation, victims were exposed to the ebb as well as the flow of public interest expressed by politicians and the media, a phenomenon that victims' groups across the spectrum have criticized. This exacerbated an ambivalent or even hostile relationship to politicians of all hues, expressed at the 'Hear and now' conference in February–March 2000.[116] For Hazlett Lynch, among others, the Good Friday Agreement was a top–down management exercise in which Unionist politicians had colluded while turning a blind eye to real fears and genuine concerns that directly impinged on the well-being of West Tyrone Voice members. Despite the pressure brought to bear on Trimble by the 'No' camp throughout the latter part of 1999 and early 2000, culminating in the challenge for the UUP leadership by Martin Smyth later in March, Lynch believed that the implementation of the Agreement rested on the 'disenfranchisement' of Border victims, as well as of other voters.[117] Several of the Protestant–Unionist victims at the conference claimed that anti-Agreement Unionists were being 'ostracized and harassed' for holding those views.[118] This points to a danger that, in the politicizing of victims' issues, those who support the losing position in a political contest will experience their defeat as a further public silencing and marginalizing of themselves as victims.

Yet Agnew's construction of the 'innocent victims' itself risks denying the agency of the victims of violence, and in particular the extent to which they have constituted themselves as active political agents in pursuit of their own interests. This is a complex issue with a direct bearing on the claims of the victims' groups to represent a new kind of collective voice, free from party-political affiliation. Victims themselves may, of course, be active as individuals in party politics, as in Arlene Foster's long and high-level involvement in the UUP and, latterly, the DUP, or Willie Frazer's candidature for the Ulster Independence Party in the Assembly elections of 1998.[119] Victims' groups may also establish close links with a particular political party, as with FEAR's close relationship to the UUP or FAIR's cultivation of the DUP. But political differences within Unionism and loyalism – including the divisions between pro- and anti-Agreement camps – have also been reproduced within the victims' groups, even in the case of FAIR, perceived by outsiders to be anti-Agreement due to the activities of prominent members. While each of the groups may have developed a distinct solution, all have had to address the problem of how these internal differences are to be accommodated, to enable the specific politics of victimhood to develop.

In certain respects, the politics of victimhood has found itself out of kilter with established political affiliations and working within a political space that can cut across the Unionist–nationalist divide. For example, Hazlett Lynch, who readily acknowledges that combating the culture of silence 'is political in nature', has argued that in pursuing this politics West Tyrone Voice is emphatically 'not party political': 'We don't get involved at all in party politics as a group . . . but we are involved politically in the situation and we can't do anything other than be involved politically'. While individuals from the group will have their own party-political affiliations, and some are party members, the autonomy of the group is fiercely upheld. This is the hallmark of a genuine grassroots movement. Lynch recognized that politicians 'are taking an interest in victims' issues now' because 'it's good coinage at the present time', with an election due in 2001, and will be 'a very useful card . . . to play, to catch votes'. While cautious of politicians of all parties who 'will use situations for their own purposes', Voice would work with any democratic politician who was 'prepared to identify with us and give us help'. The group steered a middle course between the major Unionist parties, and like FEAR (whose collaboration with Gerry Gallagher, the SDLP councillor for the Border area around Garrison, provided an early example of this potential) also built relationships with local nationalist elected representatives, including the SDLP Assembly member for West Tyrone and the chairman of Omagh District Council. Lynch maintains: 'I have got absolutely no problems working with nationalists, or working with Catholics . . . But we have a very, very big problem with terrorists.'[120] In this respect, the active political alliance that these groups sought to establish was not defined by traditional political affiliations alone, but also by a refusal to engage in dialogue with political representatives who remained identified with paramilitary groups, whether Republican or loyalist.

This continuing antagonism to Republican paramilitaries in particular, together with the making of an absolute moral–political distinction between 'perpetrators' of violence and 'innocent victims', have affected the responses of Protestant and Unionist victims' groups to those representing nationalist victims of violence. Both have campaigned on a similar range of issues, and have much in common. However, nationalist victims' groups do not share this categorial distinction, nor in practice do they refuse to have any dealings with 'perpetrators'. For example, *Cúnamh*, a group offering support to victims of violence in Derry, also provides a 'community healing' programme for all those affected in physical, psychological or behaviourial terms by the Troubles, including ex-prisoners – 'perpetrators', in Unionist terms – and their families. Nationalist justice campaigns represent not only the relatives of 'innocent victims' like the Bloody Sunday dead, but also the families of IRA volunteers such as the Gibraltar Three. Nationalist groups which are involved in commemorating local victims of violence, such as the Ardoyne Commemoration Project in North Belfast, do not exclude those killed on active service with a paramilitary group, but tell the stories of all the dead from the area. All these different types of group work with nationalist civilians, former IRA and INLA volunteers (and their families, who often have lived with the after-effects of a volunteer's injury or imprisonment), and the bereaved relatives of volunteers killed in the course of the conflict. This has posed difficulties of acceptance for activists and members of Protestant and Unionist victims' groups, and for their communities more generally, who, baulking at the paramilitary connections, have tended to see nationalist victims' groups as representing 'the perpetrators'.

As a result, in the politics of victimhood practised by the Protestant and Unionist victims' groups, these nationalist groups have been denied recognition of their trauma, suffering and loss, and often instead have become the focus of denigration and hostility. Indeed, the Unionist rejection of moral equivalence between those who have fought for and those who have fought against the Northern Ireland State, and insistence on a dichotomy between Unionist 'innocent victims' and Republican 'evil perpetrators', have given rise to a tendency to appropriate on behalf of their own dead the title of 'the real victims', while denying any valid use of the term in respect of IRA or INLA volunteers themselves, their relatives or nationalist groups which include or have any connection with Republican volunteers or ex-prisoners. Hazlett Lynch echoed a sentiment that had also been expressed on a number of occasions at the 'Hear and now' conference when he insisted: 'We'll never accept that perpetrators and victims are to be treated as equals, on equal ground . . . [I]t will never ever happen'.[121] Both Lynch and Leslie Finlay were outraged at how the funders of the victims' lobby could 'class us in the same vein as these people':[122] 'How NIVT and all the establishment bodies can lump us all together . . . just defies understanding so far as I'm concerned. And many many others like me. How can they do it, how have they the neck and the gall to do it?'[123] FAIR endorsed such thinking at its first conference in Portadown in August 1999. In 1998, the group had demonstrated at Stormont against a meeting between a government minister and relatives of those killed by the SAS in the Loughgall ambush of 1987. When, in November 1998, FAIR was invited to send a representative to the Touchstone Group, set up by the VLU to advise about policy-formulation on victims issues, it declined.[124] According to Eilish McCabe of Relatives for Justice in 2000, 'a big percentage of the Unionist victims' groups will not sit on it [the Touchstone Group] because we're there, because we've a representative on it . . . And they don't recognize us as victims.'[125] Such views commanded wider support among Unionists: 'When *Lost Lives*, the epic account of all those who had died to date in the Troubles, was published in 1999, callers to [BBC Radio Ulster's] *Talkback* objected to the inclusion of republicans who died in the 1981 hunger strikes.'[126]

In practice, this attitude demonizes not only the Republican paramilitaries, but nationalist families and whole communities, despite the protestations by Unionists that they have 'no difficulty in relating to ordinary, decent Catholics' or in recognizing that they had suffered and needed to commemorate their own dead.[127] In doing so, it reconstitutes traditional sectarian divisions and hampers any possibility of cross-community reconciliation. The expression of such beliefs, values and attitudes by members of the Protestant and Unionist victims' groups has been criticized by nationalists working to address victims' issues (including Tony Doherty of the Bloody Sunday Justice Campaign in his analysis presented in 1995) as establishing a 'hierarchy of victims',[128] where some deaths are held to be more important and so merit recognition more than others. Mark Thompson of Relatives for Justice describes this hierarchy as 'a league table', with the families of nationalists killed by the British security forces at the bottom of the pile: 'the whole substance of this is that over the years, in some way, they have contributed to their own circumstances, have caused their own deaths, or their community is responsible for the conditions under which they have happened'.[129] Relatives for Justice found themselves 'being marginalized and excluded out of . . . the category of victims' altogether[130] by means of a distinction between the 'acceptable and non-acceptable';[131] and 'we're still the unacceptable, the marginalized victims, and our pain is not the same as their pain, and we're not part of the victim community'.[132]

An associated tendency of some Protestant and Unionist victims is to assume that, among nationalists, only the 'deserving' – i.e. terrorists and their accomplices – have been harmed by state security forces. This leads to difficulties for some in accepting the evidence even of well-documented atrocities such as Bloody Sunday. By this refusal to acknowledge as sincere the motives of nationalist campaigns seeking the truth about state violence and justice for its victims, nationalist memories of atrocity may be dismissed by Unionists as so much Republican propaganda. Protestant and Unionist victims also have tended to respond to the success of those campaigns where some public recognition has been secured from the State – as in the establishment of the Bloody Sunday Inquiry, or the official investigations into the assassination of the leading human rights lawyers Pat Finucane and Rosemary Nelson – as a denial and exacerbation of their own communities' memories of trauma, suffering and loss. According to Wilson's report, the 'perceived favouritism shown to the family of the late Rosemary Nelson – audience with the Prime Minister and trip to Washington – adds to the trauma of being a second-class victim' for members FAIR, to whom the 'failure to bring law, order and justice to South Armagh', through the conviction of those responsible for so many unresolved terrorist murders, is of overriding importance.[133] Leslie Finlay of Voice expresses a view widely held among Protestants and Unionists:

> These big enquiries now that I hear tell about, on Bloody Sunday and Pat Finucane and Rosemary Nelson, all right, then, they can enquire as much as they like, these people, but . . . [there] were no enquiries in Castlederg . . . Over twenty murders in the Castlederg area and they couldn't get anybody out to investigate it.[134]

As one member of FACT argued, 'if there's going to be an Inquiry for Bloody Sunday, it has to be an Inquiry for everybody. If there's an Inquiry for Pat Finucane, a solicitor, Rosemary Nelson, a solicitor, there has to be an Inquiry for everybody else . . . What's different from them to somebody else?'[135] This is a call that politicians from both the DUP and the UUP have been prepared to echo.[136]

This demand is, in principle, egalitarian and fair; and its insistence that the process of establishing 'truth and justice' in relation to the Troubles of the past needs to be extended beyond a few high-profile cases is important and worthy of support. At the same time, it displays little understanding either of the role of the State in hindering, rather than advancing, a human rights agenda of this kind, especially where the actions of its own agents have been called into question, or of the immense effort that the relatives and their supporters have put over many years into building and sustaining a justice campaign like that of Bloody Sunday. In practice, far from supporting and extending this pressure with their own call for the State to show equivalent concern for 'truth and justice' in relation to the unresolved deaths of Protestants and Unionists as well as nationalists, those who make such arguments tend to be engaged in the application to victims' issues of Northern Ireland's familiar 'zero-sum' mentality. This refers to the perception that the extent of the *other* side's gain is the extent of *our* side's loss, and its corollary: that the necessary response to the telling of *their* story is not to listen, understand and acknowledge, but to deny, and then to set the record straight by telling *our* side of the story.

This attitude contributed to the emerging discourse and debate about victimhood quickly becoming a new battleground. To the extent that Protestant and Unionist victims share in this, they are engaged – in the words of Colm Barton of the Bloody Sunday Trust – in 'fighting the war by other means'.[137] By the same token, Protestant and Unionist victims have also experienced disrespect, callousness and hostility from Republicans, expressed, for example, in the INLA's giant commemorative statue of a gunman erected in Londonderry City Cemetery,[138] in the sectarian messages and accusations of bigotry posted on FAIR's website message-board[139] and in the violent blocking of the 'Love Ulster' march held in February 2006 in Dublin by Unionist victims of the IRA, as part of their campaign for an investigation into Irish state collusion with Republican terrorism.[140] In the final chapter of this book, I explore attempts to undo such polarizations, through forms of reparative remembering within and between nationalist and Unionist communities that developed in response to the IRA's 'Poppy Day' bomb at Enniskillen in 1987.

10

Remembrance, reconciliation and the reconstruction of the site of the Enniskillen 'Poppy Day' bomb

On 8 November 1987, the IRA detonated a 40lb bomb in St Michael's Reading Rooms, a building owned by the Catholic Church, adjacent to the war memorial in the market town of Enniskillen, close to the Border in Co. Fermanagh. Eleven people died (rising to twelve in 2000 with the death of Ronald Hill after thirteen years in a coma) and sixty-three people were seriously injured, nearly all civilians aged between two and seventy-five, and members of the town's Unionist–Protestant community, who were gathering before the annual British Remembrance Sunday commemoration in honour of the dead of two world wars. The place where this bombing occurred became an internationally recognized site of atrocity through its representation in news coverage that articulated almost universal condemnation from all shades of the political spectrum in Ireland, Britain and worldwide. As a result, the place-name Enniskillen and the image of its undamaged war memorial, foregrounding the ruins of the buildings destroyed by the bomb, became global icons signifying the inhumanity of the IRA's armed struggle and the suffering of its victims.[1] The widespread revulsion towards the IRA's campaign was due to the bomb's victims, the symbolic significance of the commemorative event against which it was directed, and the violation of fundamental human respect, as well as human rights, entailed in such an attack on a ceremony of this kind. The reaction to the bombing is now commonly understood to have been a turning point in the Troubles, motivating serious new efforts towards a political resolution to the conflict: the first Hume–Adams contacts in 1988, for example, occurred just a few weeks afterwards. In the Republic of Ireland, Enniskillen provoked a sustained debate about Irish attitudes to Remembrance Sunday, the historical reasons why it did not feature in the Irish nationalist commemorative calendar, and the reconciliatory potential of wearing the poppy and other forms of memorialization.[2]

This chapter considers the local impact of the Enniskillen bomb, by investigating its remembrance within the location where it took place. This remembrance involves the cultural and material reconstruction of the atrocity site; or rather, of the two linked sites, the war memorial and the destroyed building, both heavily loaded with symbolic significance as a result of the traumatic past. The reconstruction of this cultural landscape is also bound up in complex ways with the efforts made within the town of Enniskillen to come to terms with the political, cultural and psychological devastation wreaked by the bombing, through social reconciliation between its polarized communities, and through the associated struggle for psychic reparation and integration within the damaged internal world of the self. The chapter examines tensions within local memories of the bomb between impulses towards reconciliation, and impulses towards moral condemnation of the IRA, and retribution for the horrors inflicted. It traces these tensions through the involvement of local people in debates and conflicts over, firstly, the form of a redesigned war memorial, and, secondly, the redevelopment of the bombsite, particularly through the initiative known as the Higher Bridges Project launched in the new context opened up by the peace process. Finally, it analyses the attempted reconciliation, in the aesthetic design and planned function of the new Higher Bridges buildings, between acknowledgement and commemoration of the past, and a future-oriented strategy of transformation linked to peace-making and social regeneration.

Trauma, conflict and reconciliation after the bombing

The impact of the Enniskillen bomb on a small town with a population of 15,000 was devastating. All the dead and most of the worst injured – some with horrific wounds to the face, chest, pelvis and legs – were among a group of some forty civilians who had gathered to observe the Remembrance Sunday commemorative ceremony directly under the eastern gable wall of the Reading Rooms where the bomb exploded. They were trapped against a steel railing and buried by masonry as the wall collapsed after the detonation. Others were injured by the bomb's blast and flying glass across an area up to fifty yards away. The psychic impact of the blast rippled outwards from the injured survivors and others among the several-hundred-strong crowd, many of whom joined the rescuers digging in the rubble for the living and the dead; to the medical staff at the Erne District Hospital, mostly local people who recognized neighbours among those they were treating; to the bereaved families, and the friends, colleagues and associates of the dead. Children, who formed a high proportion of the participants at the Remembrance Day ceremony, figured prominently in all these categories.[3] Sammy Foster, a family-liaison worker in regular contact with twenty-nine members of the eight bereaved families and 105 injured or traumatized survivors, remembers encountering among them over the following months 'a profound sense of desolation, shock, brooding, anger, resentment, recurring waves of depression, feeling bereft and alone, severe anxiety and tremendous faith'.[4] According to a psychological study of twenty-six Enniskillen survivors, one of the earliest of its kind, all were manifesting symptoms of disturbance a year after the bomb, and half were suffering from PTSD.[5] Enniskillen was clearly a traumatized community, where the disturbed psychic states of individuals are intensified and compounded by the quality of collectively experienced trauma and its associated emotional currents.

Speaking before the tenth anniversary in 1997, Foster reflected: 'Those who still suffer from physical, emotional and psychological pain cannot easily forget the past.'[6]

Enniskillen was also a divided community, however, its population evenly split between Protestants and Catholics, and along the generally corresponding political divide between Ulster Unionists and Irish nationalists. Despite local traditions of inclusive good-neighbourliness, cross-community relations are deeply shaped by the existence of what Carlo Gébler termed a 'Glass Curtain': an 'invisible divide' separating the two communities; comparable to the Iron Curtain of the Cold War, except that, as a local headmaster explained, 'you can't see it . . . [and] you don't find out about it until you walk into it – bang! – and break your nose'.[7] In Enniskillen, as throughout Northern Ireland, this divide becomes visible in the public ceremonies of exclusive and ideologically opposed cultures of commemoration. The rituals and symbols of Remembrance Sunday, in honour of the patriotic sacrifice of life by men and women of the British services in the two world wars and other conflicts, are intimately associated with Ulster Unionism and loyalism (despite the participation, and death, of significant numbers of Irish Catholics and nationalists in Britain's armed forces).[8]

Thus, the 'Poppy Day' bombing, as it became known, was experienced by many as 'an attack on the Unionist community in general and their British way of life'.[9] Psychic internalizations of the 'glass curtain' are evident in the different emotional reactions to the bombing on both 'sides of the house' (itself a telling, local spatial metaphor for the split communities).[10] As Unionist councillor Raymond Ferguson recalled, 'in the Protestant community generally there was a lot of anger', as well as disbelief, 'about the loss they had suffered', which still persisted ten years later.[11] Even if, as McDaniel argues, 'the vast majority of Protestants held no ill-will towards their Catholic neighbours . . . [and] were able to differentiate quite clearly between the Catholic community and those who had carried out the attack',[12] in the immediate aftermath of the blast Catholics were verbally abused and there were 'angry shouts' about 'what *you've* done'.[13] Some Unionists, like Julian Armstrong, a teenager when both his parents were killed, at his side, by the bomb, were 'bitter against Catholics . . . [for] some time afterwards'.[14]

On 'the other side of the house', Enniskillen's nationalists reacted to the bombing with a complex mixture of emotions which pulled in contradictory directions. This included shock, grief, disbelief, and concern for the victims,[15] shared by those Irish Republicans who agreed with the Sinn Féin President Gerry Adams that the IRA action 'was wrong' and 'should not have occurred',[16] yet continued to affirm, as did Paul Corrigan, the Sinn Féin chair of Fermanagh District Council, 'the right of the IRA to wage military actions against the occupation forces'. Corrigan initiated a moment's silence at a special meeting of the Council in 'respect for those who have lost their lives', and offered 'sincerest sympathies' to the bereaved and the wounded, while refusing – under pressure from journalists – to 'condemn bombings in general'.[17] Immediately after the bombing, on the working-class, nationalist Kilmacormick estates on the outskirts of Enniskillen, 'there were groups of young people on the streets, and it was if their football team had won'.[18] But there was also a widespread assumption of collective guilt, a sense of being identified with the perpetrators and thus sharing the responsibility for their action.[19] Such feelings were exacerbated by reports in the international media equating nationalists as such with the IRA: 'It seemed that the bomb had come from our side.'[20] Monsignor Seán Cahill recalls how this left him and his congregation 'frightened and disturbed', and describes a wider 'sense of frustration, a sense of total hopelessness and . . . fear'.[21] One particularly sharp focus for these fears was the possibility of indiscriminate reprisal attacks against Catholics by loyalist paramilitaries. This web of psychic responses, entwining both sides of the communal and political divide in a situation that was emotionally as well as politically complex and fraught, contributed to a deterioration in local community relations which, according to David Bolton, one of the local community workers most closely concerned with the traumatic effects and local memory of the Enniskillen bombing, 'ran perilously close to disintegration'.[22]

This was the context in which impulses towards solidarity, reparation and reconciliation were given expression within the town. By far the best-known gesture is that of Gordon Wilson, whose 20-year-old daughter Marie was the youngest of those killed. In a 'heart-stopping . . . and totally unforgettable'[23] interview on the Sunday evening for the BBC, he described the last words he heard her speak as they held hands while trapped together under the rubble, before going on to say: 'I have lost my daughter, and we shall miss her. But I bear no ill will, I bear no grudge. Dirty sort of talk is not going to bring her back to life.'[24] Widely represented in the media as an act of 'forgiveness' – a term that Wilson himself did not use, believing such a judgement to 'rest with God'[25] – the interview underpinned the media construction of a mythic 'spirit of Enniskillen', in which Wilson and the grieving community as a whole were (unhelpfully) idealized as the embodiment of courage, dignity and Christian compassion.[26] His own motive, articulated in March 1993 in a public statement challenging the IRA to renounce violence, had been to deny 'the Loyalist paramilitaries any grounds for using my bereavement as a pretext for imposing suffering on Nationalists, Catholics, Republicans, or IRA members. I wanted no revenge, no bitterness and no grief for other families.'[27] While reprisal attacks – and killings – did occur, if not on the scale feared,[28] one group of loyalist paramilitaries admitted to halting their planned retaliation after hearing the broadcast.[29] Locally, according to David Bolton, Wilson's interview 'opened up the means by which the Catholic community could re-engage in sharing and acknowledging the sorrow of their Protestant and Unionist neighbours'.[30]

During the days following the bombing, this sharing of sorrow occurred in numerous personal conversations across the town, in bereaved homes and funeral parlours during the wakes, at the funerals attended by thousands of mourners from both communities and at a special Requiem Mass at St Michael's Catholic Church addressed by Cardinal Ó Fiaich, the Primate of All Ireland.[31] Other public initiatives drew people from both faith communities together in distancing themselves from the attack, in offering support and solidarity for the victims, and in efforts towards cross-community understanding and co-operation. An Enniskillen Appeal Fund, established to raise money to support the bereaved, the injured and their families, was administered by trustees including the ministers of the four major local churches, Presbyterian, Methodist, Church of Ireland and Roman Catholic, and a councillor from the nationalist Social Democratic and Labour Party (SDLP) and from the UUP.[32] Politically, pressure from local nationalists forced the SDLP to withdraw its support for the Sinn Féin chair of Fermanagh District Council in favour of an Ulster Unionist.[33] A number of vigils and meetings led to the formation of Enniskillen Together, a grassroots organization that worked to 'promote better community understanding . . . [by bringing] local people of different traditions together',[34] and encouraging them to 'reach out, understand and accept each other with a view to negotiating a better situation here'.[35] As the peace process unfolded from the mid-1990s, reparative impulses generated in the aftermath of the bombing influenced the Fermanagh District Partnership Board, the body responsible in Co. Fermanagh for administering the European Union's Special Support Programme for Peace and Reconciliation in Northern Ireland. Under the rubric, 'Remember and Change', adopted at a Partnership Board conference held in Enniskillen in October 1996, questions of future redevelopment to bring about social and economic regeneration in the locality were considered in relation to imperatives of remembrance and respectful acknowledgement of the past. The phrase was introduced by Aideen McGinley, chief executive of the District Council, in her call for local community involvement in the distribution of Fermanagh's £1.6 million peace and reconciliation budget in order to ameliorate tensions generated by that summer's Drumcree stand-off: 'As for resolving conflict, I can do no better than to quote a Canadian writer who said, "We may not forgive and forget but we must remember and change."'[36]

There were, however, conflicting perceptions among local Protestants and Unionists about how the bombing ought to be represented and remembered. Sceptical or critical responses to the public stance adopted by Gordon Wilson, and reactions against media reports suggesting that his was a position taken by all those harmed by the explosion, took the form of an ongoing debate on the emotional, theological and political implications of forgiveness.[37] One common claim was that 'there is no forgiveness without repentance'.[38] This position articulates a moral and political critique of the IRA's failure either to apologize for the Enniskillen bomb, or even, until 1995, to acknowledge that its explanation – the bomb, a radio-controlled device intended to catch patrolling security forces rather than civilians, had been triggered by British Army radio signals – was untrue.[39] It also meshes with a major source of anger and potential 'bitterness' – that no one responsible for the bombing had been brought to justice.[40] Speaking on this theme of injustice in a sermon in 1997, the Presbyterian minister Reverend David Cupples made reference to the twenty-fifth anniversary of Bloody Sunday, but his sense of a common experience across the political divide was not shared by all:

> Someone in the church said, 'There is always fury about Bloody Sunday, but they haven't got anyone for Enniskillen.' What was coming through was the feeling that the people who died here didn't matter as much because there isn't the same fuss made about it.[41]

Instead of making a 'fuss' or 'fury' and proclaiming the horror and injustice of the bombing, Wilson's position seemed to some to downplay it, thereby degrading the importance of the lost lives and capitulating in the propaganda war with Irish Republicanism.

Outright opposition to Wilson came to be epitomized by Jim Dixon, one of the most badly injured of all the bomb's victims. Castigated in some news reports as a 'bitter man' for his outspoken dissent from the media's construct of the spirit of Enniskillen, and for his publicly expressed doubt about the emotional honesty of those who professed forgiveness,[42] Dixon described himself as 'a righteous man full of righteous indignation', while asserting a Presbyterian moral perspective that demanded retribution against the IRA as the perpetrators of criminal violence: 'I believe in the law of the country and anyone that tries to destroy that law should be executed straight away.' Dixon also articulated a strong, Protestant–fundamentalist anti-ecumenicalism and hostility to Roman Catholicism, claiming that it had been responsible for 'brutal massacre [in Europe] over 600 years', and, interviewed on television after the bombing, referring to the IRA as the 'military wing of the Catholic Church'.[43] Such views were also expressed by others in the town, notably by Reverend Ivan Foster of Ian Paisley's Free Presbyterian Church, who circulated local homes with a four-page leaflet, *The Untold Story*, which blamed 'the Church of Rome . . . for the bomb not being detected' and attacked 'attempts at promoting unity through the grief caused by this massacre'.[44] The critique of the discourse of forgiveness and reconciliation resonated across Northern Ireland among other loyalists committed to the principle of 'No Surrender' to the IRA. In its magazine *Ulster,* for example, the loyalist paramilitary UDA dismissed nationalists' expressions of horror, remorse and cross-community solidarity as the same 'pious words and empty platitudes' heard many times before. The UDA argued that every Catholic who voted for Sinn Féin was

> as guilty as the rat who planted the war memorial bomb . . . The time for moderation is surely past. The psychopathic bigots in the PIRA must be exterminated. Ordinary, decent Catholics must remove themselves from the company or presence of anyone whom they suspect of being an IRA supporter or activists [*sic*]. A line must be drawn between the innocent and guilty.[45]

Such responses to the bombing tended to intensify perceptions and memories of a fundamental sectarian divide, contributed to political polarization and heightened intra-community mistrust and fear. In Enniskillen, these conflicting positions among Protestants and Unionists on questions of reconciliation, forgiveness and retribution in response to the Poppy Day bombing, also manifested in local debate and controversy over its commemoration, concerning, first, the form of a public memorial to those who died and, second, the redevelopment of the bomb site.

Memory, public commemoration and the Enniskillen war memorial

The responsibility for providing, in response to local wishes, a permanent memorial to the bombing fell to the Appeal Fund's trustees. Several possible locations were considered before the decision was made 'to erect a memorial on the site of the now demolished St Michael's Reading Rooms where the . . . bomb exploded', which the Catholic parish had agreed to release for the purpose. When that plan fell through, the trustees gave local architect Richard Pierce the brief to design the new memorial within the commemorative space where the Remembrance Sunday ceremony took place, around the existing war memorial.[46] Unveiled in 1922 as 'the Memorial of the County Fermanagh to its sons of all branches of the royal forces who fell in the Great War', it was situated on an island in the middle of Belmore Street, in 'the best position of the county town'.[47] Known locally as the Cenotaph, it took the striking form of a bronze statue of a soldier standing with rifle reversed and head bowed in the posture adopted in British military funerals, set high above the thoroughfare on a plinth of pale Portland stone, itself elevated by three stone steps, and inscribed with the names of 'Our Glorious Dead'; the 622 men from Fermanagh – both nationalist and loyalist – who died in the 1914–18 war. (In due course the dates and names of those who were killed in Second World War were added.)[48]

The powerful symbol of collective mourning was also a site of conflicting memories, having been associated with social exclusion by nationalists ever since it was 'first unveiled with the Union Jack floating over it' in 1922, when the town was polarized by armed conflict over Irish independence, the partition and the establishment of Northern Ireland.[49] The Cenotaph emerged unscathed from the explosion in 1987 to provide the most recognizable icon of the bombing, reproduced across the international news media: that of the bronze soldier-in-mourning foregrounded against the debris of the collapsed building.[50] This resonance lay behind Richard Pierce's suggestion, accepted by the trustees, not to erect a new structure but to redesign the Cenotaph so as to incorporate the commemoration of those who had been killed nearby: 'The bomb turned that bronze soldier from a provincial war memorial in a west Ulster market town into an international symbol of the triumph of ordinary decent people over cold-blooded terrorism.'[51]

As he began work on the design in March 1990, however, Pierce expressed a different vision of its significance: 'My concern is with my neighbours on both sides of the divide, and it is my hope that these eleven people did not die in vain. This addition to the war memorial has to be an act of reconciliation.' The idea was conveyed by 'eleven doves in Portland stone rising round the feet of the Unknown Soldier', symbols of peace and of the innocence of those who died. On the pedestal facing the bomb-site, Pierce added an inscription: 'In memory of our neighbours who died near this spot', with the date and their names in alphabetical order, to 'keep the husbands and wives together, which is poignant'. This wording was chosen in explicit opposition to 'people who are so embittered that they might like to have "Murdered by Catholics" or "Killed by terrorists" '.[52] By the time final plans were published by the trustees, after a year-long delay while legal issues concerning the use of the Fund were resolved,[53] Pierce's design had been modified. The statue of the soldier was now more than three feet higher, on a dark-bronze pedestal etched with the names of the dead from the two world wars and topped by a new column, around which circled the eleven doves, sculpted also in bronze. At the foot of the pedestal, which now rested on an extended Portland stone base, was a bronze plaque featuring the names of the Enniskillen victims and an inscription that read: 'In remembrance of eleven of our neighbours who were killed by a terrorist bomb at this site on Remembrance Sunday 8 November 1987'. By Remembrance Day 1991, the new memorial had been constructed to this design, installed and unveiled, at a cost of £100,000.[54]

The changes made to Pierce's original design were partly a result of his creative collaboration with the sculptor Philip Flanagan, and partly the outcome of a compromise made by the trustees in response to criticisms from a significant number of the bereaved and others who were consulted about the plans.[55] The criticisms were on two main grounds. First, a variety of objections, aesthetic, practical and principled, were raised to what one relative, James Mullan, called 'tampering with the existing war memorial'.[56] Strong disapproval focused on the (mistaken) belief that Enniskillen's would be 'the only war memorial in the United Kingdom which bears the names of civilians',[57] and on the addition of the bronze doves.[58] Aileen Quinton, for example, explained that:

> I have a problem with the fact that there were eleven of those creatures on the War Memorial and therefore one of those is meant to represent my mother [Alberta Quinton]. I think it is dreadful to have civilians on it: it is a war memorial. She would not have liked that at all. It was a lovely war memorial as it was and, to my mind, they have vandalised it. If I pass I would turn my head the other way: I try to imagine and pretend to myself that it hasn't been touched.[59]

This statement powerfully expresses a sense of violation that can be understood as stemming both from Aileen Quinton's loss of control over the representation of her mother, unwantedly given the form of a 'creature'; and from the close psychic association between the original memorial and the memory of her mother, who had served in the Women's Royal Air Force during the Second World War and participated every year in the Remembrance Sunday ceremony.[60] In the emotional intensity invested in her contrast between the loved-but-now-destroyed – 'vandalised' – original memorial, which Aileen Quinton tries to preserve 'untouched' in her imagination, and the 'dreadful' reality of its replacement, from which she turns away, it is possible to discern the symbolization of an ongoing work of mourning, in which the lost loved-one is recreated in reparative remembering, 'rediscovered, restored to the internal world and protected from further destructive activity'.[61] The trustees' decision, despite such objections, to reconstruct the memorial to Pierce's design demonstrates the difficulty of finding a public commemorative form capable of reconciling the differing needs of the bereaved, even among those on the 'same side' of the political divide.

This difficulty is evident, too, in the trustees' response to the second objection, where they sought – but failed to secure – a compromise over the wording of the inscription with critics who wanted to use less conciliatory language than Pierce's. While 'some relatives . . . feel that something like "Murdered by terrorists", for instance, would be more accurate',[62] Reverend Cupples, the Presbyterian trustee, remembers that 'there was also one family who said that if the word "murdered" appeared, their relative's name could not go on it'.[63] Cupples, explaining the thinking behind the trustees' eventual resolution of this dilemma, distinguishes between the moral judgement involved in using the word 'murder' to describe the Enniskillen bombing, with which he fully concurred, and the question of whether this was appropriate language to use on a public memorial: 'Morally [murder] is what happened. But when you have it set in stone and in memorials it seems to have an emotive connotation of anger and bitterness that I think should not be conveyed.' The inscription finally agreed by the trustees retained Pierce's use of the language of neighbourliness but replaced his deliberately bland 'died', with 'killed by a terrorist bomb'. That, according to Cupples, made it 'perfectly clear what the facts of the matter are and people can make their simple moral judgement'.[64] But for Aileen Quinton, among other of the relatives, this proved a deeply unsatisfactory resolution which 'play[ed] down the truth':

> The most important aspect is to reinforce and clarify that it was murder. If the trustees felt they couldn't cope with the word 'murder', then they should have given us the chance of veto. Nobody has ever asked our family for permission to put my mother's name on it or to have her represented by a creature. I think everybody has an obligation to show up terrorism and evil for what it is; don't pussy foot or pretend around it.[65]

While the insistence that the term 'murder' be used on the memorial has been understood by some, including Richard Pierce and Reverend Cupples, as a manifestation of embitterment, it is not necessarily so. The wish expressed here, to know and name the perpetrators and to define the act that ended the life of a loved-one, has been a common reaction of the bereaved throughout the Troubles. It has frequently found expression in the language of public memorials, like the Bloody Sunday memorial in Derry which describes the fourteen dead as having been 'murdered by British paratroopers', or other forms of public commemoration of the Enniskillen bomb victims, such as the DUP's plaque in memory of Johnny Megaw, 'murdered by the Roman Catholic IRA'.[66] Such naming articulates a moral and political response that calls to account those held responsible. The competing meanings of the conflict expressed in memorial inscriptions of this kind may well pose a challenge to post-conflict reconciliation.[67] At the same time, the impulse to name 'murder' may be experienced as a psychic necessity that helps to absorb the shock and hurt of loss, aids mourning and restores some sense of agency to those bereaved by political violence.

The controversy over the location, design and wording of the memorial to the Enniskillen victims demonstrates the sensitivities and difficulties involved in negotiating the relation between past and present, both psychically and politically, in the search for a symbolic form capable of securing consensus in a community with divergent needs of, and beliefs about, such memorialization. Whatever the language of public commemoration, the grieving will respond to it in their different ways. The emotional resonance of words means that, within the individual psyche, their value and use is always ambivalent, contingent, bound up in unpredictable ways with the long journey of bereavement. Ruth Kennedy, for example, speaking in 1997 of her grief at the loss of her parents, testifies movingly to the way the significance of language may emerge only over time, within an evolving emotional landscape: 'It was a long time before I could say they were killed and only recently I could say they were murdered. It really hasn't fully registered to this day that they are dead.'[68] In this complex situation, disjunctions inevitably occur between the language of personal and familial memory and that of public commemoration. The case of the Enniskillen memorial also shows how the competition between the conflicting imperatives of reconciliation and retribution ultimately resolves into a question of local power – here that of the trustees – to institute preferred meanings in public space. These sensitivities and difficulties can also be seen in local debate in Enniskillen concerning the bomb-site as a locus of memory, and efforts towards reconciliation focused on its redevelopment.

The Enniskillen bomb-site and the architecture of reconciliation

A further effect of the explosion was its destruction of a part of the material fabric of the town. The bomb had been placed on the first floor of a dilapidated old building, owned by the Roman Catholic Parish of St Michael's, known locally as the Reading Rooms. The blast caused the gable wall facing

7 The 'gaping wound in the streetscape': the white hoarding concealing the
Enniskillen bomb-site, to the right rear of the Cenotaph.

the war memorial to collapse outwards, bringing down the gable-end roof
and causing much of the rest of the building to cave in.[69] With the blackened
latticework of its rafters exposed and tilted grotesquely to the ground at a
jagged angle, the collapsed building was transformed by its representation
in the news media worldwide into an icon of the bombing, linked visually
and symbolically to the war memorial. Like the Ground Zero site in the
immediate aftermath of the 9/11 attack on New York in 2001, the presence
of this ruin acted as a graphic figure for the violation of life in the town. Its
central location meant that people going about their everyday business had
to pass it; as did funeral cortèges en route to the Breandrum Cemetery.[70]
Within two weeks of the explosion the ruined building had been knocked
down and 'a plywood hoarding now shields the rubble'.[71] Ten years later
McDaniel noted that the only changes were the deterioration of the hoard-
ings, and the considerable 'upset' among the bereaved that 'nothing has been
done with the bomb site'.[72] This was described locally as a 'gaping wound
in the streetscape',[73] an image casting the unreconstructed building as a
symbol of unresolved wounds within the psychic landscapes of those traumatized by the bomb (see figure 7). This symbolism is clearly evident in the
complex and ambivalent attitudes to the site expressed by survivors and the
bereaved. A familiar place, the meaning of which was now utterly transformed, some were drawn to it while others tried to avoid it. Aileen Quinton,

for example, remembers going two days after the bombing to see where her mother died, at 'a place where I had stood loads of times. There was the phone box where I used to ring up my father if I was in town and wanted a lift home. I just looked at it and thought, "Where is she?"' In contrast, Margaret Veitch, whose shop was only a few hundred yards away from the place where both of her parents died, 'found herself unable to walk on that side of the street', while Gladys Gault, who lost her husband, 'avoided it without even realising'. Ten years after the bombing, many of the bereaved continued to have strong emotional reactions to the site. Kathleen Armstrong, also widowed by the explosion, explained: 'I think that corner is just terrible. If I have to walk past it I just shudder. It brings it all back.' Stella Robinson, grieving for the loss of both her parents, still found herself unable to look at the site 'without getting angry'.[74]

Discussion about the redevelopment of the site dates back to the earliest proposal to situate a memorial there, but that had fallen through and been 'forgotten about'.[75] Over the years following, other proposals for the use of the site emerged, though nothing came to fruition.[76] Debate continued also about why nothing had been done. For some critics, including the DUP's councillor, Joe Dodds, the responsibility lay with the owners of the site, the Roman Catholic parish church, which he accused of (implicitly sectarian) insensitivity and neglect:

> Since the bomb nothing has been done at all with the site which is a harsh reminder to the grieving relatives. It is utterly disgraceful that it has been left in this way . . . There has not only been objections from some relatives of those killed in the atrocity over the Catholic Church's failure to act but I believe this is the view of them all. I blame Monsignor Cahill [the parish priest] for doing nothing.

According to Mgr Cahill, who described himself as 'dearly wish[ing] for something to be done' with the site, various obstacles stood in the way.[77] One was financial: the cost of redevelopment, estimated at between £0.75 million and £1 million, was beyond the means of parish funds. That problem was sharpened by a second: the architectural difficulty posed by the physical character of the site, which stands at the intersection of two roads and the River Erne, and is multilevel, with a sharp drop down from street level to where the basement floor of the Reading Rooms stood beside the river. R.H. Pierce Architects, the firm that eventually designed the new building constructed there, endorsed the view that this was 'a particularly difficult site to develop because there is a lot of space underground and . . . you see the building from all angles all the way around'.[78] A third reason related to the psychic charge attached to the bomb-site, and its proximity to the war memorial where the solemn commemorative ritual taking place every year on Remembrance Sunday now incorporated a tribute to those who died in the bomb. Cahill recalled, in 1997: 'It was very sensitive and we didn't want to put something there that would stir up emotions . . . It was very difficult in the light of the enormity of the tragedy to know what to do. Therefore, you might say it was a kind of paralysis – we waited and waited.'[79] Financial and architectural obstacles to redevelopment were, by this account, compounded by factors of memory, so that wishes for reparation and regeneration invested in the transformation of the site of atrocity were inhibited and 'paralysed' by an awareness of the weight of the past and a desire not to dishonour the dead; leaving the site 'frozen' in time.

By 1995, however, an ambitious and imaginative initiative was underway, one to which the Catholic Church gave its support. The origins of the Higher Bridges Project lay several years earlier in the purchase by Fermanagh District Council of the former Orange Hall, a Victorian listed building, abandoned and derelict since 1975, standing adjacent to the bomb-site on the other side of Queen Elizabeth Road as it runs over the East Bridge across the Erne onto the island of Enniskillen. Gerry Burns, chief executive of the Council, persuaded the Orange Order to sell what was '[o]nce one of the town's most imposing buildings', that had languished for the last twenty years 'in an advanced state of decay', with the intention of reconstructing it as an art gallery and improving the look of the eastern gateway to the town.[80] Having acquired the building, the Council's conception of the Orange Hall re-development shifted away from the arts towards an educational locus linked to initiatives for social and economic regeneration in the county, under the auspices of the Fermanagh University Partnership Board, made up of representatives of various adult- and higher-education providers, including the University of Ulster. From the mid-1990s, this project was widened to include plans for the reconstruction of the bomb-site. Richard Pierce was given the brief of designing what were now envisaged as two new 'campus' buildings on the linked sites once occupied by the Orange Hall and the Catholic Reading Rooms, transforming the social environment in that area while providing much-needed facilities for the benefit of the town as a whole.[81] Barney Devine, the project manager appointed in 1999 to oversee the construction process, commented: 'you couldn't get a better example of hope built upon what would be perceived as two disparate sectarian buildings [and] an event that killed twelve people'.[82]

The hope invested in the Higher Bridges Project was encouraged by the opening up of new funding opportunities for initiatives towards regeneration in the context of the peace process following the paramilitary ceasefires of 1994. Core capital funding for the development, of £5.4 million, was sought from the Millennium Commission in 1996, and eventually secured from the Heritage Lottery Fund and sixteen other organizations. The first phase of the Higher Bridges Project, the transformation of the Orange Hall into an Interactive Technology (INTEC) Centre, was launched formally in 1998, and by March 2000 the building was in use.[83] Work on the second phase began in May 2000, and by the fourteenth anniversary of the bombing in 2001, the completed new building – named the William Jefferson Clinton International Peace Centre, sponsorship having been secured from the former-President of the USA, closely involved in the Irish peace process from its inception[84] – had 'transformed the bomb site', providing 'a very definite backdrop during the annual Remembrance Sunday proceedings'.[85]

In its conception and realization, this innovative project, in which such powerful reparative desires had been invested, had to respond to, negotiate and attempt to reconcile a set of contradictory needs and pressures. The very name 'Higher Bridges' was chosen to convey a sense of the multiple connections to be generated by 'these two buildings . . . at the confluence of two bridges over the Erne'; involving a 'bridging into higher education, bridging the past to the future and bridging the communities'.[86] The funding application to the Millennium Commission in November 1996 affirmed: 'Our vision is of a new Centre in Fermanagh which spans cultural divisions as it spans the River Erne. We want to face the future together, and not the past separately.'[87] Yet the architecture of the new buildings also sought to be 'future-orientated'[88] and pointed towards peaceful regeneration without erasing the past, but rather demonstrating sensitivity towards the psychic and cultural significance of this location, and respect for its place in local memory.

The Janus-faced concept was reflected in the brief given by the University Partnership Board to R.H. Pierce (later Maxwell Pierce) Architects: to design plans for a development with, as Richard Pierce put it, 'the "wow" factor' necessary to interest and excite Millennium funders, and which would also fit into the existing architectural environment of an eighteenth-century market town, many of whose buildings were protected by a conservation area encompassing the Higher Bridges site.[89] The matter was resolved by retaining largely intact the existing facade of the Orange Hall, built in 1872 and now 'such an important part of the Enniskillen streetscape, both in terms of history and sentiment', while designing for the bomb-site an 'unreservedly modern' building 'moving towards the 21st century';[90] its southern facade of glass 'curv[ing] gently' to follow the river, reflecting the project's 'commitment to openness and communication'.[91] The two buildings are linked, physically and symbolically, by means of a new footbridge across the river under the existing East Bridge, and at street level with connecting steps and disabled access ramps, ensuring that the Clinton Centre in particular opens out onto public space and is easily accessible from different aspects and levels.[92] Both buildings are 'futuristic' in their use of state-of-the-art technologies to bring Fermanagh into the information age, and in their dedication of interior space to meet a wide range of economic, social and cultural needs in the locality and region.[93]

For the Clinton Centre, the crux of this attempted architectural reconciliation of the past and the future concerned the new structure's relationship to the surrounding built environment of the conservation area and, most importantly, its interface with the war memorial twenty yards to the east (see figure 8). According to Barney Devine this east-facing wall, erected on the spot where the gable wall of the old Reading Rooms had stood and where

8 The Cenotaph, Enniskillen, framed by the Higher Bridges buildings, July 2001.

the eleven had lost their lives, 'caused us great thought'. The guiding principle was the intention 'to commemorate what happened on the site' while
'avoiding that building being a memorial' or 'competing with the Cenotaph'.
Instead, the eastern wall was designed with awareness of how it would look
to those approaching the town centre from Belmore Street or visiting the
Cenotaph.[94] Contrary to earlier plans,[95] it was constructed without windows
or any other decorative features, and painted a uniform plum colour to echo
the bronze pedestal of the memorial and form a striking frame for the
statue.[96] According to the architect, Bill Maxwell, the wall was to be 'washed
in light' so that 'the Cenotaph would be seen to be silhouetted at night "in
a subtle and fantastic way" '.[97] The 'strong symbolic structure' of the building was heightened by the introduction of 'an inverted pitched roof', so that
'the wall goes up and then slopes off at a very sharp angle', a feature that is
repeated in two similarly angled rooves along the northern elevation,
echoing the jagged imagery of the collapsed gable wall in the iconic imagery
of the bombing. Finally, built into the new eastern wall, in the lower right-
hand corner at eye-level, '[we] put in one window in order to commemorate
and to recognize what happened there'; a small, opaque window with an
engraved inscription (written by David Bolton):[98]

> This is our purpose here.
>   To remember the past and those we knew and loved, solemnly and with fond-
> ness: to look to the future with hope: and bring us together to learn the ways of
> life, teaching war no more.
>   This is a place for sorrow's tears. And a place for the laughter of children.

In this way, a building that, according to Barney Devine, 'is not a memorial', but rather 'a living, dynamic entity', subtly marks the site of the bombing in a small, dedicated space, 'very clearly delineated to commemorate that event in the most sympathetic way that we know how'.[99]

This process of reconciliation through architectural design also, necessarily, had a social dimension. Plans for the Clinton Centre in particular were reconstituted and modified over several years and involved efforts to reconcile a number of interests in order to establish broad-based support for the project. Funding bodies, supportive of the project 'because of what happened . . . in 1987',[100] had different ideas about the form of the building to be constructed on the bomb-site, which 'had to be redesigned many times . . . according to who we thought might give us money and their aesthetic sentiments'.[101] The architect's brief was also reshaped through a structured process of consultation involving representatives of some fifty local, community organizations, whose input regarding the ethos and purposes of the building had a profound effect on the metamorphosis of Pierce's plans towards 'a building that was unashamedly modern, bright and practical'.[102] Local consultation was also directed specifically towards the bereaved families, bringing the project directly into contact with the difficulties surrounding commemoration of the bombing, including the 'antipathy and anger' of some relatives.[103] Barney Devine, who joined the project in 1999, over four years into the peace process and its various controversies over memory focused on the victims of violence and the Good Friday Agreement, describes the development team as being 'very sensitive to the victims of the bomb', and 'aware of this debate . . . about how sections of a community commemorate their dead, the type of commemorative symbol that they erect, and [how] one person's symbol is another person's insult'. Care was taken to involve the relatives of the dead (but, for logistical reasons, not those injured in the bombing) in the design and development process.[104]

Further recognition of their particular interest in the site was bestowed when representatives of the relatives joined civic, community and church leaders in a ceremony to mark the start of construction work on the bomb-site, in May 2000, described as 'an act of remembrance and an opportunity to look forward to the future'.[105] The families were also invited to a private meeting with former-president Bill Clinton on his visit to Enniskillen one year later,[106] when he unveiled the 'window of hope', attended by a large crowd of local school students, and spoke on the theme of Bolton's inscription: 'Meeting the families of the victims and seeing all the children – it painted in my mind a picture of how we have to make the future different from the past . . . They [the children] are really the ones who will have their lives saved by whether we succeed in the peace process or not.'[107] This close association of the families with the reparative symbolism of the Higher Bridges Project ensured that 'they were a part of this passing over from what happened in the past, an empty site, to the construction of a building, to the completion of the building, and to the thought processes that went into that

east elevation which was the bomb site itself'.[108] Through these efforts in
inclusive consultation, to involve local people in the Higher Bridges Project
and the regeneration promised in its reconstruction, the development team
sought to achieve a consensus in the town about the use of the site, and to
create a shared investment in the project's symbolism of bridging, linking,
connecting, across local social and political divisions. Barney Devine
believed that, while some political opposition to the project was inevitable,
'most people in Fermanagh, from . . . Unionist and nationalist, Catholic,
Protestant, loyalist, Republican persuasions, see what is happening on that
site, concur with the need for it, recognize the event which is the prime mover
for the building . . . [and] support what they think will be happening in it'.[109]

When the new building finally emerged from behind the scaffolding and
hoarding, however, it proved to be 'one of the most controversial . . . in
recent times', generating intense debate in the local newspapers.[110] While the
building had its supporters, including one correspondent who described it as
'a very clever piece of architecture which attempts to empathise with the historic nature of the site, yet at the same time seeks to encapsulate something
of the spirit of today',[111] it also provoked what one local paper called
'unprecedented public dismay'.[112] Letters to the press, vox-pop interviews
and a straw poll conducted with passers-by revealed an anti-modernist backlash against the building's startling material form, with an apparent majority voicing dissatisfaction and hostility, and the more extreme describing the
partially revealed building as 'a monstrosity'; 'a depressing and frightening
building [that] looms out and just makes you feel physically sick'; and 'an
eyesore . . . If I could get a crane big enough, I'd knock it down.'[113]
Criticisms focused on the eastern elevation, but were concerned less with
memories of the bomb or the sensitivity of the site than they were with the
wall's colour and shape, the absence of windows, and the building's 'gloomy'
and 'dreary looking' impact on the streetscape. The carefully contrived symbolism of the wall made little impact on local critics, who had their own
cheerful suggestions about how it might be improved, such as 'a few
windows at the gable end' or a 'nice bright mural on the wall, something eye-
catching'. Others called in question the entire development: 'It was a funny
choice to put it at a traffic roundabout. I know it's where the bomb was but
it's not the right place for it.'[114] One report suggested that 'the design was
bound to arouse strong emotions', and claimed that '[a]mong its severest
critics is a relative of one of those killed in the explosion'.[115]

As the controversies over the Cenotaph and the Clinton Centre demonstrate, neither reconstruction nor reconciliation is a static, achieved condition. Further divisions and conflicts emerge on the very ground where
resolution is attempted. However, not all such conflict is as damaging as a
bomb. The Higher Bridges team accepted that such criticism was a necessary
aspect of any innovative transformation of the built environment. In Richard
Pierce's view: 'That sort of building is always controversial . . . Not everybody likes it but I'm also aware that the controversy makes people talk about

it and that is healthy in a democratic society.'[116] For Barney Devine, negative criticism is part of a necessary process of adjustment to the strangeness of the unfamiliar, and it ameliorates as people begin to use, and get used to, a new or reconstructed building:

> I ran a community relations peace centre [in St Columb's Park House, in Derry/Londonderry], an old Georgian manor house, a beautiful building set in a parkland, and one year it was a ruin, the next we had refurbished it and set it up. So it was like a UFO landing in the park: 'What is this thing? Who are these people? What is it about?' I spent five years staffing it and . . . getting projects working out of it, but more importantly, getting the local people to own it.

In the case of the Higher Bridges building, Devine was optimistic that 'the ownership issue will become less contentious and not as difficult as that [peace centre]', because of the history and cultural memory of the bomb-site.[117]

Nevertheless, in his image of the new centre as 'like a UFO', something from another planet that intrudes disturbingly into the known world, Devine offers a striking metaphor for the emotional experience of strangeness that such a building may evoke; and of the process of adjustment necessary to include and embrace the unfamiliar, to absorb it into local imaginative geography, to re-orient the psyche so as to integrate the alien within the contours of an intimately known interior landscape. The metaphor can be applied also to the wider process of peace-building itself, in which familiar psychic and cultural landmarks in people's everyday maps of meaning are necessarily transformed, bringing about a disturbance and disorientation, rendering the world strange and unfamiliar. Making peace with the past also requires time for adjustment, for people to internalize the new realities of their social environment and the lives that can be lived there. This is an ongoing, though not widely acknowledged, aspect of the peace process as it continues to unfold in Northern Ireland.

Afterword

Any study of cultural memory, because concerned with examining how the past exists in the present and how its significance is shaped by and for present-day needs and interests, must face the inherent difficulty that this 'present' is not a fixed point in time but a constantly evolving movement. This means not only that cultural memory itself has a history, traceable through the changing circumstances in which memories are reworked; but also that its trajectory into the future is always uncertain, necessarily contingent on unpredictable events that may force narratives of the past to be reconfigured or even entirely recast. When the processes under investigation are so palpably incomplete, questions arise as to what it means to finish a study, and the drawing of conclusions becomes especially tricky. As this book goes to press, some twelve-and-a-half years after the ceasefires that were proclaimed at the time as 'the end' of the war in and over Northern Ireland, the Irish Troubles remain in many significant respects unresolved. While undoubtedly a landmark moment and an end of sorts, marking a significant change in the form and a reduction in the intensity of violent combat, the IRA's ceasefire of 31 August 1994 evoked competing meanings and memories, and opened a new chapter of conflict. For nationalists, an initial jubilant conviction that the war was over, and won, gave way to perceptions of British duplicity – and of a 'missed opportunity' to make peace. For Unionists, initial anxieties that a deal had been done behind their backs gave way to a determination to prevent any such development and an insistence on the IRA proving that the war was over by disarming and disbanding. When, eleven years later on 28 July 2005, the leadership of the IRA issued a public statement announcing that it 'has formally ordered an end to the armed campaign . . . [with] effect from 4p.m. this afternoon', and authorized its representative 'to complete the process to verifiably put its arms beyond use', Britain's liberal newspaper the *Guardian* ran the headline 'After 35 years of bombs and blood a quiet voice ends the IRA's war'. The right-wing *Daily Telegraph* was more circumspect: 'Only time will tell if this is the last act in the Ulster tragedy.'[1]

Even after the destruction of the IRA's entire arsenal was confirmed by the Independent International Commission on Decommissioning, on 26 September 2005, thereby opening the way to the implementation of other outstanding issues in the Good Friday Agreement, including the restoration of devolved government, further battles immediately commenced on the new terrain established by that act of decommissioning. Ian Paisley, the leader of the DUP, denounced 'the cunning tactics of a cover-up', and members of his party – now the dominant force in Ulster Unionism as a result of its criticism of the Agreement – announced that 'it could be years before they agreed to sit down at Stormont and share power with Sinn Féin'.[2] When the British Government then introduced the second reading of its Northern Ireland (Offences) Bill in the House of Commons in November 2005 – to fulfil an undertaking to Sinn Féin providing, in effect, an amnesty for paramilitary fugitives from justice (known as 'on-the-runs') once decommissioning was completed – it provoked all-party opposition, on a number of grounds.[3] In the debate, William McCrea of the DUP reportedly 'burst into tears when describing his murdered relatives',[4] and his party-leader objected that the measure was an 'insult to the victims' and 'wipes the stone clear' in the cases of a considerable number of terrorist offences, including fatal attacks on the RUC and the army, as well as incidents such as the Enniskillen bombing.[5] Both the Conservative Party and the nationalist SDLP objected additionally to the inclusion of members of the security forces in the bill's provision, the former because it placed soldiers and policemen on the same footing as terrorists, the latter because it would conceal the truth about illegal state killings and collusion with paramilitaries. Monica McWilliams, head of the Northern Ireland Human Rights Commission, criticized the bill as 'incompatible with international human rights standards'.[6] After Sinn Féin itself withdrew support, under pressure both from the SDLP and grassroots organizations such as *An Fhirinne* (The Truth) – a victims' support group campaigning to establish the truth concerning 'the hundreds of Catholics, Nationalists and Republicans, who have been murdered by Unionist death squads over the past thirty years with the knowledge and active assistance of the British Government' – the bill was withdrawn.[7]

Further conflict within Sinn Féin over its involvement in the peace process manifested at the first party conference (*Ard Fheis*) following the IRA's completion of decommissioning, in February 2006, when Gerry Adams acknowledged: 'The decisions made by the IRA were undoubtedly deeply difficult for many. There are republicans still trying to come to terms with it many months later. Indeed, there are some who believe that the IRA has made a mistake.'[8] The party's internal divisions now shifted focus onto the question of whether it should participate on Northern Ireland's Policing Board in order to demonstrate support for the new policing and criminal justice system; a condition set by the British Government for the restoration of devolved government. In a charged debate, the *Ard Fheis* rejected a motion requiring a timetable for British political and military withdrawal prior to Sinn Féin's granting recognition to the new Police Service of Northern Ireland (PSNI). This motion was proposed by delegates who argued that the party's traditional reasons for refusing to recognize the legitimacy of the RUC remained relevant in this new context: 'Republicans should not be enforcing the armed wing of British rule in this country.'[9] While moving away from this position, Sinn Féin's leadership nevertheless articulated its own negotiating stance, on the Policing Board and on the proposed involvement of MI5 in new post-9/11 arrangements for national security across the UK, in terms of nationalist collective memory of the RUC: 'The police force has been a partisan, political, protestant and paramilitary force. Republicans will not be . . . forced into accepting less than the new beginning to policing promised in the Good Friday agreement'.[10]

On the basis of the St Andrews agreement in October 2006 between the two governments and all the major parties in Northern Ireland, a Sinn Féin special conference in January 2007 finally pledged its support for the PSNI, overturning its oppositional stance of over eighty-five years. This decision opened the way for the election of a new Northern Ireland Assembly and the restoration of devolved government by 26 March, the final deadline set by British legislation for the formation of a power-sharing Executive (or, alternatively, for the terminal dissolution of the Assembly and the reinstatement on a permanent basis of Direct Rule from Westminster with increased involvement for the Government of the Republic of Ireland). On 24 March the DUP, as the Unionist party with the strongest representation in the Assembly, decided in principle to form an Executive with Sinn Féin, the strongest nationalist party, but secured the agreement of all the parties and the two governments to a six-week deferral, ostensibly to verify Sinn Féin's commitment on policing. On the day of the deadline, the first ever face-to-face talks took place between Ian Paisley and Gerry Adams, followed by a joint press conference where they announced their undertaking to share power in the restored Assembly from 8 May.[11] In April 2007, conclusive implementation of the Good Friday Agreement and the issues arising from it now appears imminent.

The evolving political contest over the terms of the peace, opened up by the ceasefires of 1994, has shaped the circumstances of 'the present' from which my investigation has taken its bearings in exploring how clashing memories of the Troubles have been voiced and contested, reproduced or reworked. The stake in this 'war over memory', in the peace process as it was at the height of the armed conflict, is the legitimacy or otherwise of armed violence exercised in pursuit of political goals, whether by state or non-state agencies. One powerful narrative of memory, in 2007 as in 1972, holds the IRA to be largely responsible for the violence and suffering of the Troubles, finds its 'armed struggle' to be unjustified and describes its activities as 'terrorism'. This narrative has structured British official memory of the Troubles, underpinned the Unionist collective memory of the ethnic cleansing of Ulster Protestants and justified the negotiating stance taken by Unionist politicians within the conflict-resolution process. In opposition to this, a narrative of human rights has been deployed by nationalists, most effectively in the case of Bloody Sunday, which focuses memory on the violations committed by state forces against legitimate nationalist protest and resistance to unjust and oppressive rule. IRA violence is remembered in this narrative as a reaction to the provocative and inhumane deployment of state power, the State is held responsible for the escalation of violent conflict, and enforcing the accountability of its agents is seen as the primary goal of human rights activism.

While much of my research was done between 1996 and the summer of 2001, the context in which this book has been completed is the vastly different global present of the USA's so-called 'war on terror', following the attacks on New York and Washington DC, on 11 September 2001. This new frame for global–political conflict has brought about fundamental reconfigurations in memories of colonial war, state repression and 'terrorism', and has altered the terrain on which the politics of memory is conducted, in Ireland and Britain, as throughout the world. The IRA's announcement in 2005 that its armed campaign had terminated was made just three weeks after the 7 July bomb attacks on London's transport system. These events evoked memories of the IRA's bombing campaign in the capital, now structured in terms of ironies, parallels and contrasts with the present threat from 'Islamist terrorists'. The *Guardian*'s commentator Jonathan Freedland noted: 'One war begins and another comes to an end . . . as the anti-terrorist branch scoured the streets of Britain looking for the new enemy – just as the old one finally stood down'.[12]

The impact on the Irish peace process made by the global 'war on terror', and its effects on the competing narratives of terrorism and human rights as deployed by Ulster Unionism and Irish nationalism, may be gauged by noting a speech made in January 2004 at the First International Congress of Terrorist Victims in Madrid, by David Trimble, the UUP's leader. Supporting the position articulated by the Vice-President of Columbia, that human rights groups were hindering the transition to democracy in his country by their criticism of anti-terrorist legislation and their defence of armed opposition groups such as Farc, Trimble argued: 'One of the great curses of this world is the human rights industry. They justify terrorist acts and end up being complicit in the murder of innocent victims.'[13] Here, the Unionist tendency to equate 'terrorism' with the IRA, and to see the defence of human rights as a politically motivated (nationalist) attack on decency and democracy, draws strength from its association with an international movement critical of human rights advocates for allegedly obstructing states in their efforts to combat 'terrorists'. Such arguments tend to collapse together different kinds of political violence without adequately discriminating between them or distinguishing the different contexts and reasons that explain their adoption. Indeed, the Madrid Congress ended with a declaration calling on human rights NGOs 'to make a commitment to defend victims of terrorism and to identify terrorist acts for what they are, regardless of their cause or pretext'.[14] The development of an effective culture of human rights in Ireland, as well as the traditional Irish Republican legitimation of anti-state violence in terms of the 'freedom struggle', have become more difficult in this new ideological climate.

In the context of Northern Ireland, the competing narratives of terrorism and human rights continues to equate to the political confrontation between Ulster Unionism and Irish nationalism. But in the process, other crucial narratives of memory have become marginalized. 'Terrorism' was practised not only by the IRA, but also by loyalist paramilitaries and state forces. The principles of human rights apply to Unionist as well as nationalist victims of state violence, and also to victims from either community subjected to paramilitary violence by the IRA and by loyalists. In this respect, one of the most significant developments in the politics of memory since the Good Friday Agreement is the report issued in January 2007 by the independent Police Ombudsman Nuala O'Loan finding reliable evidence of systematic collusion between Special Branch police officers and the UVF in ten killings in North Belfast between 1991 and 2000.[15] This rare official confirmation that long-standing allegations of such collusion have substance was made after a detailed investigation initiated at the request of Raymond McCord from the Unionist community. McCord's misgivings about the inadequacies of the police inquiry into the circumstances in which his 22-year-old son, also called Raymond, was beaten to death in 1997 caused him to approach the human-rights NGO British–Irish Rights Watch. Following its confidential report in July 2005 naming the UVF men responsible and calling for an independent investigation, which was sent to the British Government and leading figures at the United Nations and the US Congress, among others, McCord made a formal complaint to the Ombudsman's office.[16] He reflected: 'We use [*sic*] to think allegations of [police collusion] were republican propaganda but it was the truth.'[17] This development raises the possibility that, in the future, efforts to make peace with the past will increasingly break with entrenched narratives and traditions, and bring about unexpected new alliances.

I have not attempted in this book to provide an exhaustive overview of the contradictory workings-out of cultural memory in the Irish Troubles (valuable though such a study would be), but have sought instead to identify and analyse the kinds of processes involved in the formation, articulation and contestation of memories, both during the conflict and within efforts towards conflict resolution. Five broad arguments have been developed throughout. Firstly, this study demonstrates the complex and multifaceted characteristics of memory as it is articulated within and across distinct though interconnected arenas, both public and private. Memories are entirely personal only to the extent that they are not represented. As soon as they are given form as a story they become dialogic, angled towards and entering into relationship with the memories of others. Social negotiation of the remembered past and the contestation of competing narratives occur within the shared and common memories of family members or a local community, as well as in the more overt and visible clash between the politicized collective memories of Unionism and nationalism and those promoted by the British and the Irish State. Reparative remembering – that questions received narratives, engages with the memories of former adversaries and generates fresh perspectives on the past – has different conditions of existence within private and public arenas. Scope for establishing the effective listening spaces on which new kinds of remembering depend may be greater in those arenas farthest from the political peace process centred on the contestation of state power and the search for an agreed settlement. Yet the mobilizing of memories in any one arena has ramifications for that occurring in other arenas. This can clearly be seen in the case of the Glencree Centre for Peace and Reconciliation, in Co. Wicklow in the Irish Republic. There much valuable work has been undertaken in developing trustful interpersonal relationships across the communal divide in the North, fostered by participants' temporary departure from their everyday environments. Yet difficulties in translating these personal journeys of discovery into any broader collective rapprochement have emerged when the individuals concerned return to their communities and re-encounter deep-rooted suspicions and hostilities, which in turn are affected by the changing political situation.[18]

Secondly, I have argued for an understanding of the interaction and mutually determining effects of social and psychic factors within the processes of remembering and forgetting examined. Of central importance here have been the continuing effects of trauma involving varying degrees of psychic disturbance, but also the workings of unconscious phantasy in cultural and political responses to violence and in the formation of identities. My use of the concept of 'trauma' to refer to a gamut of psychic states affecting social groups as well as individuals is not unproblematical, but it does provide a language in which to describe phenomena that are otherwise hard to bring into focus. In the Kleinian approach to trauma adopted here, memory is not a single, internally unified process, but the site of often unconscious psychic conflicts involving defensive versus reparative modes of remembrance. Attention to these psychic dimensions of memory enables an understanding of subjective attachments to 'the past' as these play out within the process of conflict resolution. The desires and fears generated by a peace process are ambivalent and contradictory: aspirations to a future free of violence coexist with and are complicated by factors such as incomplete mourning, a sense of betrayal of the dead, and the fear as well as the desire to know the truth about the circumstances of their killing. Psychic attachments to the past may encode and fix a response to violent bereavement and other loss, in a way that makes life liveable thereafter at the price of becoming habitual and entrenched, especially when linked to the identities and senses of self of those remembering. This process poses obstacles to reparative remembering, which involves an opening of the psyche to those internal emotional realities which have been split-off and contained, perhaps disavowed and denied, thereby allowing 'something new to happen' within the internal world.[19]

Relations between this delicate and provisional process of internal transformation and the external world of social relationships and conflicts is, according to the Kleinian model, reciprocal. Psychic conflicts between defensive and

reparative remembering can be traced within the listening spaces that have
emerged in everyday social life, especially through the activities of grassroots
organisations dedicated to the support of victims, to the upholding of human
rights, and to the making and commemorating of local histories. However, the
social and psychic spaces of reparative remembering do not neatly coincide.
One individual's journey into 'something new' may occur at a different pace,
have a different reach and encounter different limits from those of others.

Thirdly, in the two case studies developed in Parts II and III of this book,
the same processes of memory and trauma may be found at work in Unionist
and nationalist cultures, but I have suggested that their forms differ according to the specificities of their historical formation. The public cultures of
commemoration found on either side of the Cupar Way peace-line wall along
the Shankill–Falls interface in West Belfast or in the competing political narratives of Bloody Sunday and the ethnic cleansing of Border Protestants have
been shaped by three sets of relations. Each is oriented *across* the cultural
and political divide in opposition to the other; each is oriented *downwards*
to its own far-from-homogeneous community, engaging with the private narratives of shared and common memory through which the lived experiences
of conflict are processed and articulated, selecting and reworking its tropes
and themes into a public representation of 'our' experience; and each is oriented *upwards* against the power of the British and Irish governments exercised in their endeavour to contain the conflict and establish hegemonic
leadership of the conflict-resolution process. In this sense, the public forms
of counter-memory developed by Unionists and nationalists are not simply
dialogic but, as Ziauddin Sardar puts it, 'polylogic',[20] and seek to reconcile
pressures which may pull in different directions.

These interlocking factors are over-determined by lines of force centred on
the State in Northern Ireland, itself undergoing historical transformation;
from the Unionist-dominated state of 1921–72, to Direct Rule from
Westminster involving the attempt to contain the Republican insurgency
while establishing a reformed State based on a limited form of power-
sharing, through to the shift in power relations in favour of nationalism
undertaken through the peace process, as the Blair administrations have
pursued the primary goal of ending armed conflict with the Republican
movement. As relations between the nationalist and Unionist communities
and the State have shifted since the reintroduction of British troops in 1969,
so this has affected the cultural and political dynamics internal to those
communities as well as between them. The narratives articulated in public
cultures of memory fashion responses to the changing political conditions
experienced on either side of the communal divide, and rework commemorative traditions so as to exercise ideological leverage within current circumstances. However, these cultures are not mirror images of one another.
Unionism has been unable to turn public commemoration of those killed by
the IRA into the instrument of a sectional narrative articulating collective
memory as effectively as does the nationalist narrative of Bloody Sunday,

even in the case of IRA operations that generated widespread public condemnation, such as Bloody Friday or the Enniskillen bomb. This difficulty
has been a result of the contradictory dynamics within Unionism stemming
from what Sarah Nelson has called 'the trauma of direct rule', when the
British Government's suspension of the devolved administration at Stormont
complicated Unionists' notions of loyalty and fragmented Unionist politics
into a number of alternative conceptions of Ulster and its future relationship
to the UK.[21]

Trauma, too, has been structured in different ways for nationalist and
Unionist communities according to the varying impacts (psychic, cultural
and political) made on them by the Troubles, whether key political moments
such as the introduction of Direct Rule in 1972 and the Republican hunger
strikes of 1980–81, or local experiences of violence. I have argued in this
book that the qualities of traumatic disturbance as a psychic response to
armed conflict vary according to the specific circumstances of any particular
incident, the ways that incident is seen to fit into – or to deviate from – recognizable patterns of violence, and the narratives of memory that articulate
its significance. The traumatic effects of the IRA's campaign upon Border
Protestants, for example, were the result not only of the actual violence
inflicted, but also of the consequent fear and sense of being under threat as
a community, the experience of betrayal by nationalist neighbours, and feelings of abandonment and exposure without adequate protection by the
State. In fashioning a narrative to represent this trauma, Unionists have not
had recourse to the human rights discourse which they have tended to perceive as a nationalist weapon deployed against the State, and which therefore remains, according to Arlene Foster, 'largely alien to most grassroots
members of [the Unionist] community'.[22] The traumatic impact of the
Troubles on nationalists, by contrast, has been infused with qualities derived
from the subjection of their community to the overwhelming power of the
State, and from the impossibility of recourse to the discourse of 'law and
order' deployed by Unionists. These differences have continued to affect the
social production of trauma in both communities throughout the peace
process.

This can be illustrated by contrasting the obstacles faced by Raymond
McCord Snr. in seeking justice on behalf of his dead son – including intimidation by the UVF and loyalist reluctance to make use of human rights
organizations[23] – with those encountered by the nationalist McCartney
family pressing for justice for the killing in 2005 of Robert McCartney,
allegedly by IRA volunteers, in a community that historically has been
unable to rely on the police or the criminal justice system, and where policing by the IRA has long been the norm.[24] In both cases, the desire for justice
as a response to the trauma of violent bereavement inflicted by paramilitaries
on their *own* communities in the years since the ceasefires and the peace
agreement runs up against deep-rooted psychic, cultural and political
assumptions specific to those communities about what can and cannot be

said or done by those belonging to them. Here too, as in the cases of Bloody Sunday and the Border Protestant experience of the Troubles, the relatives of the dead are the ones who take up the burden of truth-seeking, and thereby become the bearers of wider social aspirations for truth, justice and reparation regarding the violent past.

Fourthly, the study points to the importance within the Irish peace process of demands for truth and justice emerging from below, particularly through the voices and campaigning activity of victims and survivors of violence. As in other transitional societies, such as South Africa and Guatemala, a major dynamic in the politics of memory stems from the absence of accountability for many killings, and of full and reliable knowledge concerning the circumstances in which they occurred and the identities of perpetrators. In Ireland, too, memory snags on what is unknown, and desire for the truth motivates campaigns for its investigation, bringing pressure to bear on those organizations – both state and paramilitary – in which relevant information has been lost or concealed. In April 2007, a number of processes of investigation of unresolved killings are underway, based on a variety of mechanisms. The much-postponed Report of the Saville Tribunal of Inquiry into Bloody Sunday, with all that this entails with regard to British official memory of the Troubles, is still awaited over two years after its investigation closed, and will not now appear 'before the end of 2007 at the earliest'.[25] The considerable duration and cost of the Bloody Sunday Tribunal is likely to preclude further use of a full-scale public inquiry as a mechanism for establishing the truth about the Troubles. However, the hearings in the first of four, more restricted, investigations – into the killings of Patrick Finucane, Robert Hammill, Rosemary Nelson and Billy Wright, set up under the controversial Inquiries Act 2005 (discussed in chapter 2) – are due to begin in May 2007, with the others following over the next 12 months.[26] In January 2006, responding to pressure from many victims' families, PSNI Chief Constable Sir Hugh Orde secured £30 million of state funding to establish the Historical Enquiries Team (HET) with over 100 staff, including retired detectives, with a brief to investigate during the next four years all of the 3,268 Troubles-related killings committed (according to PSNI figures) over 1968–98. A special section within the HET is dedicated to cases in which allegations of collusion have been made, including a number of cross-border incidents (such as those discussed in chapter 8) which are linked to a UVF unit based near Glennane, Co. Armagh, with connections to members of the RUC and the UDR.[27]

Nationalist suspicion of such initiatives has ensured that the slow process of unpacking and documenting state collusion also involves investigative mechanisms entirely independent of the State, such as the report by international lawyers in November 2006, sponsored by the PFC, which found evidence of systematic collusion in up to seventy-four killings allegedly carried out by the so-called 'Glennane gang' and called for further investigation.[28] In 2003, an ambitious alternative model for truth recovery was proposed by the

Eolas (meaning 'information') Project, 'an informal grouping of organisations and individuals working with victims and former political prisoners in the republican and nationalist communities'. In its *Consultation Paper on Truth and Justice*,[29] Eolas proposed the formation of an independent international commission with relevant expertise, 'including international law, human rights [and] transitional justice', to work co-operatively with all combatant groups involved in the conflict, in investigating questions posed to those groups by victims of violence and local communities.[30] The question of justice – how, if at all, to make accountable those who are found in the course of any of these investigations to have been responsible for illegal killings – remains open and is set to become the focus for a further stage of debate and conflict concerning social redress for the human rights violations of the recent past.

Finally, the understanding of memory developed in this book differs from the currently widespread notion of 'closure' on the past. This expression has become common currency in Northern Ireland, and internationally, to describe the process of recovery from trauma and to identify what are believed to be its necessary social conditions; as in suggestions that finding the concealed remains of a loved one or discovering the truth about how she or he was killed will *allow closure* to occur. For example, Nichola McIlvenny, a niece of Lorraine McCausland who was killed in March 1987, allegedly by the UDA in North Belfast, used the term in welcoming the announcement that unresolved killings, including that of her aunt, would be reinvestigated by the HET: 'For us, this review is not about justice, it's about closure. We still don't know what happened that night.'[31] The yearning expressed here is to achieve psychic and emotional composure on the basis of fully revealed information, thereby effecting 'narrative closure', in the sense a literary critic might use the term to refer to the ending of a story in such a way that all loose ends are tied up and mysteries resolved.[32] Underlying this desire for closure is the wish for a line to be drawn under the now-resolved 'past' so that a new life can begin, one no longer enmeshed in the pain and difficulty of loss compounded by uncertainty and a sense of injustice, but oriented towards new aspirations. Imagining an achieved conclusion of this kind may be a necessity for those whose lives have been dedicated to the struggle for the truth concerning a loved one, and who hope in time to be free of this responsibility. It may also correspond to a real psychic shift brought about at highly charged symbolic moments when something longed for and worked for is accomplished. Such moments do offer an ending of a kind and contribute to the integration of the traumatic event within the internal world, on which any psychic peace depends. However, this is neither absolute nor permanent, but rather opens up a further stage of reappraisal of the past from a new perspective in the altered present.

Rather than a closing-off of the traumatic past, the concept 'reparative remembering' developed in this book points instead to an ongoing process of opening to that past so that the work of defensive splitting may be revealed and undone. In psychic reparation, integration of the event within the self involves a continuing engagement with the emotions and meanings associated with it, as layers of defence are dissolved or peeled away. However difficult, long-term and provisional, the psychic openness associated with this process is not entirely a matter of draining the poison of the past but also involves deepening, making more complex and enriching a living relationship with it. Reparative remembering creates the possibility of a new and fuller emotional sense of self in the present and, with this, novel perspectives from which to reinterpret one's own life-story and one's relations with others. This opening and re-engagement is an internal process occurring within the psychic world and the body, but it also has social implications, in altering the psychic co-ordinates that underpin the sense of others. In Rita Duffy's visual metaphor, the fist clenched in hurt and anger may soften into the 'essential gesture', expanding and reaching outwards open-palmed.[33]

Openness to others does not necessarily involve 'apology' and 'forgive-ness', current terms for a desired rapprochement heavily influenced by the South African TRC. These are problematic insofar as they constrain the process within normative and highly ideological forms, and may function to shut down acknowledgement of the inherent complexities, paradoxes and ambivalences rife within conflict resolution. An alternative perspective on reparation can be found in the 'journey to recover [our] humanity' under-taken together by Patrick Magee, the former IRA volunteer responsible for the bombing in 1984 of the Grand Hotel in Brighton, and Jo Berry, daughter of Sir Anthony Berry who was killed in the attack, following Magee's early release from prison in 1999 under the terms of the Good Friday Agreement.[34] In Berry's account, their 'journey of reconciliation' grew out of her own need 'somehow to understand those who had done it and bring something positive out of it', but depended on both her and Magee having the emotional courage 'to see and experience' the other 'as a human being.'[35] Speaking to Magee at a meeting in Brighton commemorating the twentieth anniversary of the bomb, Berry describes how 'together we opened up your commitment to hear even my most difficult feelings'.[36] Of her own journey, she writes:

> An inner shift is required to hear the story of the enemy. For me the question is always about whether I can let go of my need to blame and open my heart enough to hear Pat's story and understand his motives . . . [S]ometimes I can and sometimes I can't . . . I don't talk about forgiveness . . . But I can experi-ence empathy.[37]

For his part, Magee, a supporter of the peace process, continues to defend the legitimacy of the IRA's armed struggle and insists: 'I still stand by my actions.'[38] Yet, speaking of his first meeting with Berry, he describes feeling 'a real strong urge to be as open and frank as possible', and being confronted for the first time with the 'profound' and 'shattering' realization that, 'what-ever the political justification for it . . . I still killed your father'.[39] While always thereafter 'carry[ing] the burden that I harmed other human beings', Magee reflects: 'I am not seeking forgiveness. If Jo could just understand why someone like me could get involved in the armed struggle then something has been achieved.'⁴⁰ For Berry and for Magee, the reparative potential of their relationship lies in the other's willingness both to engage positively with the complex emotions triggered by their meetings, and to seek mutual understanding by tempering their own memories with stories from the other side of a shared but divided history.

While reparative remembering may enable the integration of a disturbed and painful past, this does not imply the pursuit of an ideal condition of freedom from psychic and social conflicts. In Kleinian thinking, reparation exists in inevitable tension with forms of defensive containment that seek to ground psychic composure in the certainties endorsed by familiar narratives. An example of this tension can be found in the testimony of an official for the Loyalist Association of Workers in the mid-1970s, who began to wonder, 'suppose they [Catholics] were right about Bloody Sunday?' after witnessing how 'the Paras went mad' one night on the Shankill. The idea 'put awful doubts in my mind', so that 'everything I had believed looked different then'.⁴¹ For some, such questioning of established memories may prove psychically intolerable or socially unsustainable under existing circumstances. However, reparation grounded on principles of openness has a further advantage over the concept of closure, in that it provides a stronger basis on which to resist those compromises over dealing with the past that are often held to be necessary for securing political rapprochement at the level of the state. The language of closure is particularly vulnerable to political appropriation, as in the case of the Northern Ireland Secretary Peter Hain's persistent use of the term to promote his controversial Offences Bill. Defending its proposed measures for amnesty against objections raised in the House of Commons and by the relatives of RUC officers killed in the conflict, Hain argued that the legislation was 'about the closure of a dark, awful and murderous terrorist campaign by the IRA'.⁴² This new political reference for the term was then elided with its more usual psychological meaning: 'The Bill is aimed at bringing closure and an end to the murderous IRA campaign . . . [and] closure for the victims'.⁴³ Here, Hain sought to represent what was, in effect, a mechanism for state-organized forgetting in the interests of achieving a political settlement with Republicans as being of benefit to the victims of the IRA, whereas the victims' demands were for the exact opposite – an investigation to establish the truth concerning the deaths of their loved ones and due process to hold those responsible to account; in other words, for *disclosure*. Following angry rebuttals in the House, Hain was forced to retract his ill-considered equation of the ending of the armed struggle with the psychic resolution desired by victims.⁴⁴ But the idea linking these two issues and underpinning Hain's equation – the desirability of 'drawing a line under the past' – went without comment; and Hain has continued to deploy 'closure' as a political term, as in his criticism of Sinn Féin for withdrawing its support for any amnesty that included British security forces, as well as 'on-the-run' paramilitaries: 'Closure on the past cannot be one-sided.'⁴⁵

Political transition to a democratic state and the creation of an effective civil society – in which the conflicts of the past do not cease but are reconfigured in a new context where they encounter, argue and clash with one another on different terms – have their psychic correlate in the reparative remembering undertaken by individuals and social groupings. However, these various levels at which peace-making occurs do not always work in harmony, but involve disjunctions, paradoxes and contradictions. Behind and within the current endgame over implementation of the Good Friday Agreement, nationalists and Unionists are manoeuvring for position in the longer contest over the constitutional position of Northern Ireland. Just as the settlement of 1921–22 fell apart over forty years later, so the negotiated peace grounded on the 1998 Agreement may prove incapable of establishing a permanent basis for democratic progress in Ireland and unravel at some point in the future. Whether it holds or not, the unfolding political process will continue to create a changing terrain within which the present–past makes itself felt, memories of conflict are articulated and efforts at reparative remembering are undertaken. New fissures will open, through which the psychic residues of unresolved conflict in the past will seep – or erupt – into the present-day practicalities of social and economic reconstruction, affecting both the ageing survivor generations who have direct personal experience of the Troubles and their successors born since the 1994 ceasefires, for whom the war is entirely a postmemory. As the politics of memory in the Irish peace process continues to evolve in the years to come, new strategies will emerge to acknowledge, articulate, absorb, confront and transform the legacies of violence; and to reconstruct the conflicted past in ways as yet unimagined.

Notes

Notes to Introduction

1 See Rolston, *Drawing Support 2*; Rolston, *Drawing Support 3*.
2 Bishop Cahal Daly quoted in McKittrick et al., pp. 1205–6; Rolston, *Drawing Support 3*.
3 Jarman, 'Intersecting Belfast'; Quinn.
4 Fanon, pp. 29–31.
5 Jarman, *Material Conflicts*, p. 18.
6 Quoted in McInnes, p. 78.
7 Gready, p. 2.
8 *Ibid.*
9 *Ibid.*
10 See, for example, Redmond.
11 See Foster, *Modern Ireland*; Bardon.
12 Theobald Wolfe Tone, 1791, quoted in Boylan, p. 383.
13 Foster, *Modern Ireland*, p. 545.
14 McBride, 'Memory and national identity', pp. 1–3.
15 Paul Arthur, 1980, quoted in Miller, 'Colonialism and academic representa-tions', p. 33; J. McGarry and B. O'Leary, 1995, quoted in *ibid.*, p. 6.
16 McBride, 'Memory and national identity', p. 5; F.S.L. Lyons, 1979, quoted in *ibid.*
17 Dermot Bolger, 1992, quoted in Walker, p. 62.
18 Brady.
19 Walker, pp. 61, 67.
20 McKittrick et al., p. 1477.
21 Fay et al., *Northern Ireland's Troubles*, p. 169.
22 McKittrick et al., p. 1481.
23 Bloomfield, p. 12.
24 Fay et al., *Northern Ireland's Troubles*.
25 *Ibid.*, p. 170; see also McKittrick et al., pp. 1480–4.
26 McKittrick et al., p. 1477.
27 *Guardian*, 21/1/2006.
28 Bloomfield; Fay et al., *Northern Ireland's Troubles*, p. 160.
29 Morrissey, p. 146.
30 Fanon, pp. 200–50.
31 McKittrick et al., pp. 1481–2; Fay et al., *Northern Ireland's Troubles*, pp. 141–6.

32 Morrissey, pp. 137, 145; and see Fay et al., *Northern Ireland's Troubles*, pp. 145–6.
33 O'Halloran; Hall, Michael.
34 Ignatieff, 'Articles of faith', pp. 119–21.
35 Jarman, *Material Conflicts*, p. 87; Fay et al., *Northern Ireland's Troubles*, p. 152.
36 Fay et al., *Northern Ireland's Troubles*, p. 147; see also McKittrick et al., pp. 1481–2.
37 Ardoyne Commemoration Project, pp. 8, 5.
38 Bradley, pp. 129–30; see also Ardoyne Commemoration Project, pp. 228–31, 469–71, 493–6, 517–18.
39 Ardoyne Commemoration Project, p. 8.
40 *Ibid.*, pp. 205–6.
41 Dawson, 'The nationalist communities', unpublished manuscript, pp. 5–9.
42 Ardoyne Commemoration Project, p. 8.
43 *Ibid.*, p. 7; see also Lundy and McGovern.
44 Adams, p. 20.
45 Ardoyne Commemoration Project, pp. 22–3; see pp. 24–6.
46 McDermott, pp. 84, 89, 153–4; see Hepburn, p. 5; and for locations of 'major riots' in Belfast 1857–1980, Downing, pp. 202–3.
47 Bardon, p. 306.
48 *Ibid.*; see Hepburn, pp. 4–5.
49 Hepburn, p. 11.
50 Radstone and Hodgkin; Radstone (ed.); Halbwachs; Popular Memory Group.
51 Quoted in McBride, 'Memory and national identity', p. 2.
52 Adams, p. 20.
53 Jelin, 'Contested memories', p. 66.
54 Jarman, *Material Conflicts*; Ardoyne Commemoration Project, pp. xv, 15, 524; Rolston, *Politics and Painting*.
55 Estyn Evans, 1951, quoted in Dewar, p. 7
56 Ian Paisley Junior in Lucy and McClure, pp. 125–7.
57 McBride, 'Memory and national identity', pp. 2–3.
58 Jelin, 'Contested memories', p. 66.
59 Stewart, p. 16.
60 Gready, p. 4.
61 Dawson, *Soldier Heroes*, pp. 50–1.
62 *An Phoblacht/Republican News* online, 6/9/2001, accessed 24/10/2003.
63 *Guardian*, 13/7/2001; *Guardian*, G2 section, 1/12/2003, pp. 4–5.
64 Gassman.
65 *Guardian*, 4/9/2002; 30/3/2006.
66 Shirlow and Murtagh, p. 51; see pp. 51–6, 81–95.
67 *Guardian*, 24/9/2004; Northern Ireland Housing Executive, *Annual Report 2004*, available at: www.nihe.gov.uk/publications/reports/ar2004a.asp/, p. 13.
68 Willie Frazer, FAIR, conversation with author, 24/3/2000.
69 Hellsten, p. 11.
70 Hamber, 'Past imperfect', pp. 2–6.
71 *Ibid.*, p. 3.
72 *Ibid.*, p. 2.
73 *Ibid.*, p. 4.

74 *Ibid.*, pp. 3–5.
75 Jelin, 'Contested memories', pp. 54–5.
76 Stanley Cohen, 2001, quoted in Gready, p. 8.
77 Hamber, 'Past imperfect', pp. 5–7; Burton, pp. 13–24; Cabrera, pp. 25–30; Jelin, *State Repression*, pp. 34–5.
78 Gready, pp. 10–11.
79 TRC Report 1998, quoted in Ross, p. 168; see also pp. 166–9.
80 Ross, p. 167.
81 *Ibid.*, p. 166.
82 TRC Report (1998), quoted in *ibid.*, p. 169.
83 *Ibid.*
84 *Ibid.*, pp. 169–76.
85 Burton, p. 21; Ignatieff, 'Introduction', p. 17.
86 Ignatieff, 'Introduction', p. 17.
87 Burton, p. 21.
88 Biko, pp. 67–8.
89 Ignatieff, 'Introduction', p. 15.
90 See, for example, *Reconciliation and Community*; Rolston, 'Turning the page'; Rolston, *Turning the Page*; Hamber (ed.); Mofokeng; Mhlaudi; Hamber, 'Comparing'; Rolston, 'Dealing with the past'.
91 Hamber, 'Comparing', p. 116.
92 *Ibid.*, pp. 112–13.
93 Jelin and Kaufman, pp. 91–110; Rolston, *Turning the Page*.
94 Hamber, 'Comparing', p. 113.
95 *Ibid.*, p. 116.
96 Downing Street Declaration, in Cox et al., pp. 327–8.
97 Cox et al.
98 *The Agreement*, in *ibid.*, pp. 301–25.
99 McWilliams and Fearon, p. 60.
100 Cox et al.; CAIN website: http://cain.ulst.ac.uk/issues/politics/government.htm.
101 Cox et al.
102 McCartney 'The role of civil society'; Northern Ireland Voluntary Trust.
103 Leonard and Hanna.
104 Ardoyne Commemoration Project.
105 See, for example, Irish Peace and Reconciliation Platform.
106 McBride, 'Memory and national identity', p. 42.
107 For the importance of the local, see Nash; Ardoyne Commemoration Project; Lundy and McGovern.
108 Darian-Smith and Hamilton, p. 1.

Notes to chapter 1

1 Walker, p. 50.
2 Moody, p. 86.
3 *Ibid.*, p. 71.
4 *Ibid.*, p. 86.
5 *Ibid.*, p. 74.
6 *Ibid.*, p. 75.
7 *Ibid.*, p. 78.

8 *Ibid.*, p. 80.
9 *Ibid.*, p. 72.
10 *Ibid.*, p. 84.
11 *Ibid.*, p. 85.
12 *Ibid.*
13 *Ibid.*, p. 86.
14 Ní Dhonnchadha and Dorgan; Brady; Boyce and O'Day.
15 Walker, p. 59.
16 Bennett and Paulin; Hopper; *Andersonstown News*, 9/11/1996; *Belfast Telegraph*, 7/11/1996; *Guardian*, Friday Review, 25/10/1996; *Irish Times*, 8/11/1996, 9/11/1996; *Orange Standard*, December 1996–January 1997; *Sunday Times*, 10/11/1996; *Sunday Tribune*, 3/11/1996.
17 Walker, p. vii.
18 *Ibid.*, p. xi.
19 *Ibid.*, pp. viii, ix.
20 *Ibid.*, pp. vii–viii.
21 *Ibid.*, p. viii.
22 *Ibid.*, p. 60.
23 See, for example, *Creggan*, Thames TV, 1979; entry on Thomas Begley in McKittrick et al., p. 1332.
24 Transcription from 'The new Irish history', *The Late Show*, Channel 4, broadcast January 1994.
25 Moody, p. 86.
26 *Ibid.*, p. 78.
27 Ryder and Kearney.
28 Jones et al.
29 *Guardian*, 30/6/1998.
30 *Sydney Morning Herald*, 11/7/1998.
31 *Ibid.*
32 Walker, p. 130.
33 Reynolds, 1993, quoted in *ibid.*, p. 65.
34 *Ibid.*, pp. 62–5.
35 *Ibid.*, p. 13.
36 *Ibid*, p. 67.
37 *Ibid.*, p. 72.
38 Mayhew, 1995, quoted in *ibid.*, pp. 73–4.
39 Magee, p. 1.
40 *Ibid.*, pp. 1–2.
41 *Ibid.*, p. 8.
42 *Ibid.*, p. 7.
43 Lyons, p. 177.
44 R.H. Buchanan, Chairman's Report, Cultural Traditions Group, p. 3.
45 Two Traditions Group, p. 5.
46 *Ibid.*, p. 3.
47 Cultural Traditions Group, p. 5.
48 Two Traditions Group, p. 3.
49 Hayes, *Whither Cultural Diversity?*, p. 19.
50 Crozier, *Cultural Traditions: Varieties of Irishness*; Crozier, *Cultural Traditions: Varieties of Britishness*.

51 Cultural Traditions Group, p. 7.
52 'Community Relations Council', leaflet (Jan. 1992?).
53 Adair interview.
54 Community Relations Council, *Into the Mainstream*, p. 6.
55 Cultural Traditions Group, p. 9.
56 Downing Street Declaration, paras 1, 2, 4, in Cox et al., pp. 327–8.
57 Rolston and Miller.
58 Rolston, 'What's wrong with multiculturalism?'; Miller, 'The new battleground?'
59 Williams.
60 Bradshaw; Jackson, 'Unionist myths'.
61 Lee, 'Reeling back the years'; ' "Michael Collins" '.
62 Ní Dhonnchadha and Dorgan; Deane, 'Wherever green is read', Kiberd, 'Elephant of revolutionary forgetfulness'; Longley, 'The Rising'.
63 Kinealy; Ó Ciosáin; Cullen; Whelan; Foster, 'Remembering 1798'.
64 Glassie; White, *Remembering Ahanagran*; Beiner.
65 Leonard, 'Twinge of memory'; Leonard, 'Facing "the finger of scorn" '; McBride, *History and Memory*; McBride, *Siege of Derry*.
66 Jarman, *Material Conflicts*; Bryan.
67 Halbwachs.
68 Leonard, 'Facing "the finger of scorn" '.
69 See, for example, *An Crann*/The Tree; Lindsay; O'Connor; Smyth and Fay.
70 See, for example, Evans and Lunn; Hodgkin and Radstone; Passerini; Perks and Thomson; Radstone (ed.); Thomson, 'Four paradigm transformations'; Thomson, Frisch and Hamilton; Winter and Sivan.
71 Popular Memory Group; Dawson and West; Clare and Johnson. My account of 'popular memory' theory here borrows in part from an earlier version incorporated in Ashplant et al., pp. 13–14. I am grateful to Timothy Ashplant and Michael Roper for their critical engagement with these ideas.
72 Turner; Johnson.
73 Popular Memory Group, p. 207.
74 *Ibid.*, pp. 210–11.
75 *Ibid.*, p. 211.
76 *Ibid.*, pp. 207, 210.
77 Thomson, *Anzac Memories*, pp. 7–8.
78 *Ibid.*, p. 7.
79 *Ibid.*, p. 216.
80 *Ibid.*, pp. 236, 216.
81 *Ibid.*, pp. 216, 220.
82 Dawson, *Soldier Heroes*, pp. 22–3.
83 *Ibid.*, p. 283.
84 Ashplant et al., p. 6.
85 *Ibid.*, pp. xii, 7–8; Hobsbawm; Anderson; Winter, *Sites of Memory*; Winter, 'Forms of kinship'.
86 Ashplant et al., p. 12.
87 *Ibid.*, p. 17.
88 *Ibid.*
89 *Ibid.*
90 *Ibid.*, p. 19.

91 *Ibid.*, p. 17.
92 *Ibid.*, p. 20.
93 *Ibid.*, p. 17.
94 *Ibid.*, p. 22.
95 *Ibid.*, p. 18.
96 *Ibid.*, p. 22.
97 *Ibid.*, pp. 10, 33.
98 *Ibid.*, p. 17.
99 Cultural Traditions Group, p. 9.
100 Said, *Orientalism*, pp. 54–5.
101 Read, pp. 3, 7.
102 *Ibid.*, p. 2.
103 *Ibid.*, pp. xi, 236; see also Johnson, *Ireland*, pp. 1–14.
104 Stewart and Strathern, pp. 3–6.

Notes to chapter 2

1 See Walker, p. 61; Leonard, *Culture of Commemoration*, p. 5; Boyce and O'Day, pp. 54, 63, 90, 97; 54; Longley, p. 43.
2 Bradshaw, pp. 191–216.
3 Dawson, *Soldier Heroes*.
4 Boyce, *Englishmen and Irish Troubles*, p. 99.
5 *Independent*, 24/6/2006.
6 Boyce, *Englishmen and Irish Troubles*, p. 99.
7 *Ibid.*, pp. 61–102 and 229, note 119.
8 *Ibid.*, p. 100.
9 *Ibid.*, p. 134.
10 For example, Kiberd, 'Anglo-Irish attitudes', p. 93; Kirkaldy, p. 40.
11 Downing Street Declaration, in Cox et al., p. 327.
12 *Ibid.*
13 Walker, p. 65.
14 *Ibid.*, p. 66.
15 *Irish News*, 25/2/1994.
16 Goodall, pp. 58–9.
17 Kiberd, 'The elephant', p. 5.
18 *Ibid.*, p. 8.
19 Paul Bew speaking on 'The new Irish history', *The Late Show*, Channel 4, broadcast January 1994.
20 *Chambers Twentieth-Century Dictionary*.
21 Freud and Breuer, p. 58.
22 Freud, 'Beyond the pleasure principle'.
23 Leydesdorff et al., p. 2.
24 Dudley Edwards, p. 167; McDaniel, p. 112.
25 Ignatieff, 'Articles of faith', p. 121.
26 Zinner and Williams.
27 See, for example, Leydesdorff et al.; Herman; Caruth (ed.); Caruth.
28 Hayes and Campbell, pp. 38–41; Leydesdorff et al., pp. 1–7.
29 *DSM IV*, quoted in Hayes, 'Narrative tradition', unpublished doctoral thesis, p. 157 (revised and published as Hayes and Campbell, 2005).

30 Leydesdorff et al., p. 5.
31 *Ibid.*, p. 4.
32 *Ibid.*
33 Levi quoted in *ibid.*, p. 4.
34 *Ibid.*, p. 2.
35 Rose, pp. 160–1.
36 Leydesdorff et al., p. 14.
37 Radstone, 'Screening trauma', p. 88.
38 *Ibid.*, pp. 88–9.
39 The following account draws from Dawson, 'Imaginative geography'; see also Dawson, *Soldier Heroes*, pp. 27–52; Garland.
40 Mitchell, p. 20.
41 Klein, 'Personification', p. 220.
42 Klein, 'Love, guilt and reparation', p. 114.
43 Segal, p. 75.
44 Wollheim, pp. 47–8.
45 Rose, p. 167.
46 Laub, 'Bearing witness', p. 69.
47 *Ibid.*, pp. 67, 69.
48 *Ibid.*, pp. 69–70.
49 Rose, p. 164.
50 Herman, *Trauma and Recovery*, quoted in Rose, p. 164.
51 Garland, pp. 109–12; Dawson, *Soldier Heroes*, pp. 40–3.
52 Leydesdorff et al., p. 6 (quoting from Herman, *Trauma and Recovery*).
53 Laub, 'An event without a witness', p. 76.
54 Laub, 'Bearing witness, p. 70.
55 For my concept of 'social recognition', see Dawson, *Soldier Heroes*, pp. 22–6, 205–6, 259–77.
56 Cf. the theory of the 'transitional space' in Winnicott, p. 118; and Weatherill's concept of 'potential space', pp. 41–2.
57 Bathoe Rainsford, letter to editor, *Irish News*, 23/8/1972.
58 Roy Greenslade, 'Hierarchy of death', 21/6/1999, The Victims and Survivors Trust, www.victimsandsurvivorstrust.com, visited 19/7/1999.
59 Northern Ireland Office, *The Terror* and *The Day of the Men and Women of Peace*.
60 Ryder; O'Connor.
61 Bolton, 'Welcome and introduction'.
62 Fields.
63 Miller, 'Colonialism and academic representations', pp. 34–5, quoting from Fields.
64 Exceptions include McCreary, *Survivors*; Fairweather et al.
65 McDaniel, pp. 85, 100–2.
66 *Belfast Telegraph*, 1/9/1988; see Curran et al.
67 Bell et al., pp. 166–9.
68 Interview with Sandra Peake (Director, WAVE Trauma Centre, Belfast).
69 *Ibid.*
70 Gorman; *An Crann*/The Tree; Smyth and Fay; McKittrick et al.
71 *Irish News*, 12/4/1995; European Commission; Black.
72 Peake interview.

73 *Ibid.*
74 *Contemplating an Iceberg*, an exhibition by Rita Duffy, Ulster Museum, 2005; *Guardian*, 29/3/2005; Barber.
75 Rita Duffy, quoted in *Guardian*, 29/3/2005.
76 Mary Holland; for the full story, see Kathleen in *An Crann*/The Tree, pp. 84–5.
77 Gorman, p. 40.
78 *Ibid.*
79 Krog, 'Cry, beloved country', drawn from the longer account in Krog, *Country of My Skull*, pp. 44, 48, 55, 73.
80 Gorman, p. 43.
81 Transcription from *Aftershock: The Untold Story Of The Birmingham Pub Bombings*, broadcast on BBC2, 9/11/1994.
82 *Ibid.*
83 *Guardian*, 'The Week' supplement, 15/2/1997.
84 Gorman, p. 43.
85 Transcription from *The Trouble With Peace*, broadcast on Channel 4, August 1995.
86 See, for example, the tit-for-tat cycle that began with the killing of Ronald Trainor on 15 December 1975 and led to the Kingsmills massacre on 5 January 1976: McKittrick et al., pp. 603, 606, 609–11.
87 For the psychic significance of revenge, see Dawson, *Soldier Heroes*, pp. 93–9, 112–13, 119.
88 *Guardian*, 26/10/1993.
89 *Shankill People*, Memorial Issue, November 1993.
90 Jackson, *Ireland*, pp. 248–9.
91 *Guardian*, 3/2/1997.
92 Peake interview.
93 *Ibid.*
94 *Ibid.*
95 *Ibid.*
96 McKittrick et al., pp. 301–4; McKendry.
97 Walker, pp. 87–91, 99–104.
98 See, for example, the destroyed memorials to James Cochrane (*Down Recorder*, 20/11/1996) and Bobby Sands (*Guardian*, 13/1/2004); the attacks on the funerals of Larry Marley and the Gibraltar Three (McKittrick et al., pp. 1069–70, 1117–20); and chapter 10 below; see also Leonard, 'Twinge of memory'.
99 Weatherill, pp. 80–1, 83.
100 See, for example, *Aftershock*.
101 Dillon, *Twenty-Five Years*, pp. 146–52.
102 *Guardian*, 19/3/1994.
103 Rolston, *Turning the Page*, p. 10.
104 Dawson, 'The paradox of authority'.
105 Dawson, *Soldier Heroes*, pp. 40–3, 117–20.
106 Sutton; representative of Beyond the Pale Publications in conversation with the author, 19/11/1996.
107 Peake interview; McKittrick et al., Preface to 2nd edn, 2001.
108 *Guardian*, 15/2/1997.
109 *Ibid.*, 17/2/1997.
110 *Ibid.*, 25/2/1997.

111 *Ibid.*, 12/3/1997.
112 Coogan, p. 452.
113 *Guardian*, 26/10/1993.
114 *Ibid.*, 12/3/1997.
115 IRA statement of apology, 16/7/2002, quoted in *ibid.*, 17/7/2006.
116 Rolston, *Turning the Page*, p. 7.
117 *Ibid.*, p. 38.
118 *Ibid.*, p. 20.
119 *Ibid.*, p. 17.
120 *Ibid.*, pp. 21, 48.
121 *Ibid.*, 50.
122 Bloomfield, p. 8.
123 *Ibid.*, p. 14.
124 The Belfast Agreement, in Cox et al., pp. 302, 316.
125 *Ibid*; see also *VLU Newsletter*, 2/11/1999.
126 *Guardian*, 29/1/1998.
127 Smyth, 'Remembering in Northern Ireland'; Smyth, 'The human consequences'.
128 'Ulster police admit 2,000 murders will stay unsolved', *Guardian*, 10/6/2003; 'Police chief calls for truth and reconciliation in Ulster', *ibid.*, 23/1/2004; 'Ulster truth commission planned', *ibid.*, 6/4/2004.
129 *Ibid.*, 21/4/2005; see also *ibid.*, 17/7/2001, p. 7; 'Judge reveals Ulster's one-sided, dirty war', *ibid.*, 2/4/2004; 'The Cory report', *ibid.*, 2/4/2004.
130 Orbach.
131 See, for example, Karpf; Hirsch; Burchardt; Jelin, *State Repression*, pp. 89–102.

Notes to chapter 3

1 Murray; Rolston, *Unfinished Business*.
2 Hodgkin and Radstone.
3 Ashplant et al., p. 18.
4 *Ibid.*, pp. 22, 24, 53.
5 *Ibid.*, p. 25.
6 *Ibid.*, p. 22.
7 *Ibid.*, p. 28.
8 Widgery; Walsh, *Bloody Sunday and the Rule of Law* (hereafter referred to as Walsh).
9 Prime Minister Edward Heath, recorded in 'Minutes of a meeting with Lord Widgery at Downing Street, 1 February 1972' (hereafter referred to as Downing Street Minutes), reproduced in Mullan, *Eyewitness*, Appendix 1, pp. 269–73, at 270.
10 Agger and Jensen.
11 Popular Memory Group, pp. 210–11.
12 Bloody Sunday Initiative, 'Programme of events: Bloody Sunday 1972–1992', leaflet, 1992.
13 Dawson, 'Trauma, place and the politics of memory'.
14 Lacey.
15 Rev. Hugh Hanna, quoted in Robinson, p. 20; see also McBride, *The Siege of Derry*.
16 Jarman, *Material Conflicts*, p. 78.

17 McCann, *War*, pp. 21–2.
18 Farrell, pp. 21–65; Bardon, pp. 466–95.
19 Farrell, p. 81; see pp. 81–97.
20 *Ibid.*, p. 92.
21 Seamus Deane in Logue, pp. 28–9.
22 Farrell, pp. 25–6; Bardon, pp. 468–9.
23 McCann, *War*, pp. 27–63; Bardon, pp. 666–72.
24 Bloody Sunday Initiative, *Political Guide to Derry*, leaflet, 1991; see also Pringle.
25 Fr Anthony Mulvey, quoted in Pringle and Jacobson, p. 34.
26 McCann, *War*, 63–116; Bardon, pp. 687, 692–9.
27 See Ashplant et al., pp. 54–60.
28 Pringle and Jacobson, p. 56.
29 'Army Code no. 70771: Instructions for opening fire in Northern Ireland', quoted in Rolston, *Unfinished Business*, p. 212.
30 Pringle and Jacobson, p. 56.
31 'Army Code No. 70771', quoted in Rolston, *Unfinished Business*, p. 212.
32 George, quoted in Taylor, *Brits*, p. 32; see pp. 30–2.
33 See Citizens' Defence Committee, *Law(?) and Orders: The Story of the Belfast Curfew, 3-5 July 1970* (1970) and Kader Asmal (ed.), *Shoot to Kill?* , both cited in McKittrick et al., pp. 52–3.
34 McKittrick et al., pp. 55–6.
35 Gerry Adams, *Before the Dawn*, quoted in *ibid.*, pp. 56.
36 Curtis, pp. 26–7.
37 Taylor, *Brits*, footnote 14, p. 402.
38 'Army Code no. 70771', quoted in Rolston, *Unfinished Business*, p. 212.
39 Yellow Card rule 13, quoted in Widgery, p. 87. A third version of the Yellow Card was issued in November 1971, permitting automatic weapons to be fired at identified targets 'when considered by the commander on the spot to be the minimum force necessary': quoted in Pringle and Jacobson, p. 56.
40 Contributor to Alistair Renwick (ed.), *British Soldiers Speak Out on Ireland*, quoted in Burke, p. 20 (no date given).
41 A.F.N. Clarke, *Contact* (1983), quoted in *ibid.*
42 Ford, quoted in Pringle and Jacobson, p. 55; see pp. 53–9.
43 Ford, quoted in *ibid.*, p. 56.
44 *Ibid.*, p. 57.
45 *Irish News*, 30/8/1992.
46 Pringle and Jacobson, p. 57.
47 *Ibid.*, pp. 143–4.
48 Mullan, *Eyewitness*; Pringle and Jacobson.
49 Ziff, p. 31.
50 Daly in O'Brien, *Matter of Minutes*, p. 146.
51 Jelin and Kaufman, p. 99.
52 Pringle and Jacobson, p. 285.
53 *Ibid.*, pp. 290–2.
54 *Ibid.*, p. 286.
55 *Ibid.*, pp. 286–7.
56 Maudling, *Hansard*, 31/1/1972, col. 32.
57 *Ibid.*, cols 32–3.
58 *Ibid.*, col. 33.

59 *Ibid.*, col. 34.
60 Devlin, *Hansard*, 31/1/1972, cols 33, 36–7, 41.
61 Devlin, *Hansard*, 1/2/1972, col. 292.
62 *Ibid.*, col. 296.
63 *Ibid.*, cols 292–3.
64 *Ibid.*, cols 294, 296.
65 *Ibid.*, cols 296–7.
66 *Ibid.*, col. 297.
67 *Ibid.*, col. 298.
68 Rees, *Hansard*, 31/1/1972, col. 33.
69 Pringle and Jacobson, pp. 7, 296–8, 301–2.
70 Sayle, p. 23.
71 Memo from Murray Sayle to H. Evans and others interested, 19/2/1972, reproduced in *ibid.*, p. 26.
72 Butterworth's map of Bloody Sunday is reproduced in Mullan, *Eyewitness*,
 pp. 280–1.
73 Sayle, p. 24; see Burke, pp. 8–16; British Society for Social Responsibility in
 Science, pp. 2–5.
74 Sayle and Humphry, article filed with *Sunday Times* on 3/2/1972 (previously
 unpublished), in Sayle, pp. 23–6, at 24.
75 Sayle and Humphry, p. 24.
76 *Ibid.*, pp. 25–6.
77 *Ibid.*, p. 26.
78 *Ibid.*
79 Curtis, p. 47.
80 *Ibid.*, p. 48.
81 *Sunday Times*, 6/2/1972, quoted in *ibid.*
82 *Ibid.*
83 Bew and Gillespie, p. 46.
84 Widgery, pp. 2–3.
85 Walsh, p. 55; *Report of the Royal Commission on Tribunals of Inquiry* (Salmon
 Inquiry), 1966.
86 *Ibid.*, pp. 55–6.
87 *Ibid.*, p. 56.
88 *Ibid.*, pp. 57–8.
89 *Ibid.*, p. 55.
90 *Ibid.*, p. 59.
91 *Ibid.*, pp. 62–3.
92 McCann, *Bloody Sunday in Derry* (hereafter *BSD*), p. 91.
93 *Ibid.*, pp. 91–2; Dash, p. 4.
94 *BSD*, p. 93.
95 *Ibid.*
96 *Ibid.*
97 Widgery, p. 4.
98 Walsh, pp. 60–1.
99 *Ibid.*, p. 70.
100 *Ibid.*, p. 81.
101 *Ibid.*, pp. 64–5.
102 *Ibid.*, p. 70.

103 Downing Street Minutes, 1/2/1972, reproduced in Mullan, *Eyewitness*, Appendix 1, pp. 269–73.
104 *Ibid.*, p. 269.
105 *Ibid.*, pp. 269–70.
106 *Ibid.*
107 Walsh, p. 63.
108 Downing Street Minutes, in Mullan, *Eyewitness*, pp. 270–1.
109 Walsh, p. 67.
110 *Ibid.*, pp. 67–8.
111 Downing Street Minutes, p. 272.
112 *Ibid.*; see Walsh, p. 56.
113 Widgery, p. 4.
114 Downing Street Minutes, p. 269; Walsh, p. 83.
115 Widgery, p. 6.
116 *BSD*, p. 94.
117 Walsh, p. 83.
118 Widgery, p. 5.
119 *BSD*, p. 92; Walsh, p. 63.
120 Widgery, p. 4.
121 Walsh, p. 64; see also p. 65.
122 Rolston, *Unfinished Business*, p. 3; Charles Morrison in O'Brien, *Matter of Minutes*, p. 26.
123 Mullan, 'Introduction', p. 38.
124 *Ibid.*; Charles Morrison in O'Brien, *Matter of Minutes*, p. 26; Pringle and Jacobson, p. 296.
125 See, for example, the testimonies of Sean McDermott, Patrick James Kelly, Noel Kelly and Denis McLaughlin, all in Mullan, *Eyewitness*, pp. 110–11, 125, 136–7, 145, respectively.
126 Sean McDermott testimony, in *ibid.*, pp. 110–11.
127 *Ibid.*, p. 177.
128 *Ibid.*, p. 150.
129 Downing Street Minutes, p. 271.
130 Walsh, pp. 76–7.
131 Widgery, p. 7; Walsh, pp. 71–2.
132 Walsh, p. 72.
133 Downing Street Minutes, p. 271.
134 Widgery, p. 7.
135 Walsh, p. 68.
136 Downing Street Minutes, p. 271.
137 Walsh, p. 70.
138 *Ibid.*, p. 69.
139 Downing Street Minutes, p. 271.
140 Walsh, p. 69.
141 Widgery, p. 6.
142 Walsh, pp. 55, 75; Widgery, pp. 7–8.
143 Walsh, p. 74.
144 Sayle, p. 27.
145 Sayle and Humphry, in Sayle, p. 26.
146 Walsh, p. 75.

147 *Ibid.*, p. 81.
148 *Ibid.*, p. 115.
149 Mullan, 'Introduction', p. 61; see pp. 55–61.
150 Walsh, p. 154; for Walsh's analysis of the soldiers' statements, see pp. 113–56.
151 *Ibid.*, p. 154.
152 *Ibid.*; *Guardian*, 17/10/2002.
153 Walsh, p. 77; see also Mullan, *Eyewitness*, Appendix 6, pp. 282–4.
154 Walsh, pp. 77–8.
155 McClean, p. 140; see also p. 181.
156 *Ibid.*, p. 140.
157 *Ibid.*, p. 142.
158 Raymond McClean in O'Brien, *Matter of Minutes*, p. 84.
159 Walsh, p. 78.
160 A number of those who had contributed to this body of NICRA–NCCL statements also prepared separate statements for the Widgery Tribunal: see Mullan, 'Introduction', p. 40, and the Index of *Eyewitnesses*, where thirteen such are indicated by asterisk, six of whom were called to testify at the Inquiry and appear in Widgery's list of witnesses.
161 Memorandum by the secretary to the Tribunal, 'Statements collected by the NCCL', reproduced in Mullan, *Eyewitness*, Appendix 2, pp. 274–6.
162 *Ibid.*
163 *Ibid.*, p. 274.
164 *Ibid.*, p. 275.
165 *Ibid.*, p. 274.
166 Walsh, p. 80.
167 Mullan, 'Introduction', p. 47.
168 Walsh, p. 73.
169 *Ibid.*, p. 73.
170 *Ibid.*, pp. 155–6.
171 *Ibid.*, p. 155.
172 *Ibid.*, pp. 72–3.
173 Dash, p. 27.
174 *BSD*, p. 106; see pp. 103–4 for an analysis.
175 Walsh, p. 120.
176 Widgery, p. 50.
177 Sgt O, testimony to Widgery, cited in *BSD*, p. 103.
178 Widgery, p. 72.
179 *BSD*, p. 108.
180 Walsh, p. 125.
181 *BSD*, p. 108.
182 Walsh, p. 125.
183 Daly, testimony in Mullan, *Eyewitness*, pp. 215–21.
184 Dash, pp. 30–1.
185 Duffy, testimony in Mullan, *Eyewitness*, p. 90.
186 Dash, pp. 30–1; *BSD*, p. 108.
187 Dash, p. 31.
188 Daly, testimony in Mullan, *Eyewitness*, pp. 217–18.
189 *Ibid.*, p. 217.
190 Tucker, quoted in Widgery, p. 47.

191 Widgery, pp. 45–9.
192 Dash, p. 30.
193 *Ibid.*, p. 41; see Michael Bridge in Mullan, *Eyewitness*, pp. 83–4.
194 Widgery, p. 72.
195 *Ibid.*, p. 72; McClean, p. 182.
196 Dash, p. 31.
197 *BSD*, p. 97.
198 Walsh, p. 114.
199 *Ibid.*, p. 154.
200 *Ibid.*, p. 101.
201 *Ibid.*, p. 154.
202 *BSD*, p. 94.
203 Dash, p. 5.
204 Widgery, p. 91.
205 *Ibid.*, p. 99.
206 *Ibid.*
207 *Ibid.*, p. 83.
208 *Ibid.*, p. 95.
209 *Ibid.*, p. 93.
210 *Ibid.*, p. 100.
211 *Ibid.*, p. 97.
212 *Ibid.*, p. 92.
213 *Ibid.*, p. 57.
214 *Ibid.*, p. 54; summarized, pp. 54–7.
215 Daly, in Mullan, *Eyewitness*, p. 220; referred to in Widgery, p. 54.
216 Widgery, p. 92.
217 *Ibid.*, p. 57.
218 *Ibid.*, pp. 99–100.
219 *Ibid.*, p. 36.
220 Dash, p. 42.
221 *Ibid.*, p. 72.
222 Walsh, p. 97.
223 Widgery, p. 72.
224 Walsh, p. 125.
225 Widgery, pp. 73, 80.
226 *Ibid.*, pp. 73–82.
227 *Ibid.*, p. 83.
228 *Ibid.*, p. 72.
229 *BSD*, p. 109.
230 *Ibid.*, pp. 94–5; see also Dash.
231 *BSD*, p. 139.
232 Widgery, p. 81.
233 *Ibid.*, pp. 81–3.
234 *Ibid.*, p. 57.
235 *BSD*, p. 106.
236 Widgery, p. 57.
237 *Ibid.*, p. 92.
238 *Ibid.*, p. 57.
239 Dash, p. 33.

240 Widgery, pp. 59–63; *BSD*, pp. 123–4; Dash, pp. 32–3.
241 *BSD*, p. 124.
242 Maura Duffy in *BSD*, p. 253.
243 *BSD*, p. 94; Ita McKinney in *ibid.*, p. 134.
244 Jack Chapman in *Derry Journal*, Bloody Sunday Supplement, 31/1/1997, p. 17.
245 E.g. Derrick Tucker; see Dash, pp. 30–1; *BSD*, p. 108.
246 Geraldine Richmond in O'Brien, *Matter of Minutes*, p. 136.
247 E.g. Eileen Doherty, in *BSD*, p. 225.
248 Frank Curran in *Derry Journal*, Bloody Sunday Supplement, 31/1/1997, p. 8.
249 Curtis, p. 49; Kay Duddy in Rolston, *Unfinished Business*, p. 11; *BSD*.
250 Mullan, 'Introduction', pp. 44–5; O'Brien, *Matter of Minutes*, p. 36.
251 Linda Roddy in O'Brien, *Matter of Minutes*, p. 70.
252 Hayes, 'Narrative tradition', pp. 181–3; Gartner, pp. 124–5; O'Brien, *Matter of Minutes*, p. 70.
253 O'Brien, *Matter of Minutes*, pp. 72, 80, 94, 142.
254 Quoted in Curtis, p. 50.
255 See, for example, Ruddy; Curtis, pp. 49–51.
256 Curtis, p. 51.
257 Significant interventions were made by two TV films, *Remember Bloody Sunday*, broadcast BBC2, 30 January 1992; and *Sunday, Bloody Sunday*, broadcast Channel 4, 30/1/1997.
258 Sayle.
259 McKay, p. 325.
260 Quoted in Bell, Geoffrey, p. 2.
261 Quoted in McKay, pp. 325–6.
262 McKay; Pringle and Jacobson.
263 Editorial, *News Letter*, 3/2/1997; Ken Maginnis, quoted in *Guardian*, 4/2/1997; see also Gregory Campbell, quoted in *Guardian*, 3/2/1997.
264 Editorial, *News Letter*, 3/2/1997.
265 *News Letter*, 10/2/1997.
266 'The pen and the sword': Edward Said in discussion with Jacqueline Rose at the Brighton Festival, Brighton, England, 14/5/1997.

Notes to chapter 4

1 Quoted in *Guardian*, 3/3/1997.
2 Jelin and Kaufman, pp. 105, 99.
3 *Ibid.*, p. 99.
4 *Ibid.*, p. 90.
5 *Ibid.*, pp. 105, 107.
6 *Ibid.*, p. 99.
7 *Ibid.*, p. 105.
8 *Ibid.*, p. 106.
9 Ashplant et al., pp. 18–19.
10 O'Brien, 'Back to Bloody Sunday', p. 14.
11 *BSD*, p. vii.
12 Doherty in Rolston, *Unfinished Business*, p. 16.
13 *Derry Journal*, Bloody Sunday Supplement, 31/1/1997 (hereafter referred to as DJS).

14 O'Brien, 'Back to Bloody Sunday', p. 14. Photographs and extracts from her interviews with relatives of each of the dead were first published here. These plus further photographs and interviews with the wounded and other survivors were later published in O'Brien, *A Matter of Minutes: The Enduring Legacy of Bloody Sunday* (hereafter referred to as *MM*).
15 O'Brien quoted in O'Connell.
16 *MM*, p. 19.
17 O'Brien, 'Back to Bloody Sunday', p. 13.
18 *MM*, p. 19; O'Brien quoted in O'Connell.
19 O'Brien quoted in O'Connell; see also Dawson, 'Trauma, place and the politics of memory', pp. 169–70.
20 O'Brien, 'Back to Bloody Sunday', p. 14.
21 Ashplant et al., p. 48.
22 *MM*; Pringle and Jacobson.
23 Anonymous interviewee, Hayes, 'Narrative tradition', p. 173.
24 Farrell, pp. 84–5.
25 Richmond in *MM*, pp. 136, 138.
26 *Ibid.*, p. 136.
27 Hegarty in MM, p. 38. See also pp. 94, 140.
28 McCann, *War*, p. 101.
29 See Hayes, 'Narrative tradition', pp. 128–90.
30 Wray in *MM*, p. 34.
31 MacDermott in DJS, p. 5.
32 McFeely in *ibid*.
33 Morrison in *MM*, p. 26.
34 *Ibid.*
35 McEleney in DJS, p. 13.
36 See Hayes, 'Narrative tradition', pp. 51–89, 137–42.
37 Quoted in *An Phoblacht/Republican News*, 30/1/1992.
38 Charles McLaughlin in Mullan, *Eyewitness*, p. 114.
39 Bradley in *MM*, p. 62.
40 John Kelly in *ibid.*, p. 128.
41 Maura Young in *ibid.*, p. 140.
42 McKinney in *ibid.*, p. 112.
43 *Ibid.*, pp. 46, 116.
44 Pringle and Jacobson, p. 271.
45 *BSD* p. 244; Pringle and Jacobson, pp. 276–7.
46 Pringle and Jacobson, pp. 195–6.
47 Chapman in Mullan, *Eyewitness*, p. 171.
48 Pringle and Jacobson, p. 266.
49 Donaghey in *MM*, p. 116.
50 Hugh Leo Young in Mullan, *Eyewitness*, p. 199.
51 See Pringle and Jacobson, pp. 253–6.
52 Donaghey in *BSD*, p. 75–6.
53 Mullan, *Eyewitness*, pp. 205–21; Pringle and Jacobson, pp. 172, 199–200, 207, 216, 231–41.
54 Pringle and Jacobson, pp. 262–5.
55 *Ibid.*, p. 259.
56 Long in *MM*, p. 66.

57 Pringle and Jacobson, p. 236.
58 Maura Duffy (née Young) in *BSD*, p. 252.
59 *MM*, p. 34; Pringle and Jacobson, pp. 275–6; *BSD*, p. 223.
60 Hayes, 'Narrative tradition', p. 3.
61 Richmond in *MM*, p. 136.
62 Donaghey in *ibid.*, p. 116.
63 Donaghey in *BSD*, p. 76.
64 Conversation with Alex Nash, in Grimaldi and North, pp. 52–3; see Editorial Note to 1998 edition.
65 Hayes, 'Narrative tradition', p. 129.
66 *Ibid.*, p. 131.
67 *Ibid.*, p. 159.
68 Maura Young in *MM*, p. 140.
69 Roddy in O'Brien, 'Back to Bloody Sunday', p. 18.
70 John Kelly in *MM*, p. 128; Hayes, 'Narrative tradition', pp. 152–4; see also chapter 5, this book.
71 Long in *MM*, p. 67.
72 Hayes, 'Narrative tradition', p. 163, quoting *DSM IV*, 1994.
73 Hayes, 'Narrative tradition', pp. 143, 150.
74 *Ibid.*, p. 153.
75 Anonymous respondent in *ibid.*, p. 152.
76 Anonymous respondent in *ibid.*, p. 154.
77 Hegarty in *MM*, p. 38; see also Hayes, 'Narrative tradition', p. 153.
78 Eileen Doherty and Kay Duddy in *MM*, respectively pp. 88 and 94.
79 Kathleen Kelly in *BSD*, pp. 191–2.
80 Leydesdorff et al., p. 4.
81 Margaret McGuigan in *MM*, p. 46; Hayes, 'Narrative tradition', p. 163.
82 Gilmour in *MM*, p. 58.
83 Roddy in *ibid.*, p. 70.
84 Maura Young in *ibid.*, p. 140.
85 Mullan, 'Introduction', p. 35.
86 *Ibid.*, pp. 35–6.
87 E.g. Floyd Gilmour in *MM*, p. 58.
88 Fanon, p. 345; see Davies, David, 'Frantz Fanon, colonialism, and Algeria', unpublished doctoral thesis, pp. 292–300.
89 See *BSD*, pp. 161–2; *MM*, pp. 140, 142.
90 Maura Duffy in *BSD*, p. 254.
91 Hayes, 'Narrative Tradition', p. 163.
92 Kay Duddy in *MM*, p. 96.
93 Burke in *ibid.*, p. 50.
94 McKinney in *MM*, p. 112; see also pp. 34, 50, 96, 136; Hayes, 'Narrative Tradition', pp. 163–7.
95 Anonymous interviewee in Hayes, 'Narrative Tradition', pp. 165–7. The details of the story, several of which feature in John Kelly's life-story in *MM* (pp. 127–30), clearly identify the family in question as the Kellys.
96 Hayes, 'Narrative Tradition', p. 163.
97 Anonymous interviewee in *ibid.*, p. 176.
98 Anonymous interviewee in *ibid.*, p. 168.
99 John Kelly in *MM*, p. 128.

100 Eileen Doherty in *BSD*, p. 224.
101 Jelin and Kaufman, p. 105.
102 Bakhtin.
103 Rushdie, p. 38.
104 Gramsci, pp. 324–6.
105 Ashplant et al., p. 18.
106 See *BSD*, pp. 24–9; *MM*, pp. 93–6; Rolston, *Unfinished Business*, pp. 10–14.
107 Kay Duddy in Rolston, *Unfinished Business*, p. 11; see also *MM*, p. 94; Hayes, 'Narrative Tradition', p. 152.
108 Cited in Thomson, 'Moving stories', p. 35.
109 Mullen in *DJS*, p. 16.
110 Mullan, *Eyewitness*, caption to photograph in section at pp. 192–3.
111 Daly in *ibid.*, p. 219; see Pringle and Jacobson, pp. 153–4, 256–8.
112 For Grimaldi's photograph, see *ibid.*, pp. 192–3; see also photographs by Stanley Matchett and Fred Hoare in Ziff, p. 32.
113 Pringle and Jacobson, pp. 256–7; see also pp. 118–19; Daly in *MM*, p. 146.
114 *DJS*, p. 12.
115 Mullan, 'Introduction', p. 35.
116 *Ibid.*, p. 36.
117 See, e.g., McDaid family, Pringle and Jacobson, pp. 262–76. Crucial evidence did not emerge until 1996: Mullan, 'Introduction', pp. 51–63.
118 Edward Daly in *MM*, pp. 144–5.
119 Kay Duddy in *BSD*, p. 28.
120 *Ibid.*
121 Bishop Edward Daly, quoted in DJS, p. 12.
122 *Guardian*, 26/1/2002. At 'Hanky day: a one-day symposium presenting inter-disciplinary approaches to the visual representation of the conflict in Northern Ireland', Manchester Metropolitan University, 26/11/2005, Margo Harkin, dis-cussing the making of a film about Bloody Sunday, referred to Kay Duddy's sub-sequent symbolic use of the handkerchief as a source of comfort, in a moment of distress during the Saville Inquiry hearings.
123 Winter, 'Forms of kinship', pp. 40–1.
124 Leydesdorff et al., p. 15.
125 Wray in *MM* p. 34.
126 Wray, quoted in *Irish News*, 30/8/1992.
127 Friel in *MM*, p. 98.
128 Nigel Cooke in DJS, p. 14.
129 Ashplant et al., p. 43.
130 Bernadette McAliskey in DJS, p. 9.
131 Hayes, 'Narrative tradition', p. 155.
132 Coyle in *BSD* p. 141.
133 Walker in *MM*, p. 78; see also Hayes, 'Narrative tradition', p. 196.
134 Wray in *MM*, p. 36.
135 McGuinness, quoted and reported in *Guardian*, 5/11/2003, pp. 4–5.
136 Raymond McCartney quoted in Adrian Kerr (comp.), *Perceptions: Cultures in Conflict*, Guildhall Press, Derry, 1996, extract on website: http://larkspirit.com/bloodysunday (visited 22/2/2002).
137 The Republican movement had split in 1970; the Officials ended their armed struggle in May 1972: Bew and Gillespie, pp. 25, 52.

138 See English; Taylor, *Provos*.
139 Fay et al., *Northern Ireland's Troubles*, pp. 136–8.
140 Anonymous interviewee in Hayes, 'Narrative tradition', p. 177; see also *BSD*, p. 219.
141 Maura Duffy in *BSD*, pp. 252–3.
142 Bishop Daly in DJS, p. 12; see also Daly in *MM*, p. 147, and the photograph of Daly with framed image of Duddy behind, p. 145.
143 Ashplant et al., p. 20.

Notes to chapter 5

1 DJS (drawing on *Derry Journal*, 30/1/1973).
2 See, for example, *An Phoblacht/Republican News* (hereafter *AP/RN*), 1/2/1990.
3 Doherty in Rolston, p. 17.
4 *Ibid.*, p. 15.
5 Ashplant et al., pp. 20, 22.
6 *Ibid.*, p. 20.
7 *Ibid.*, p. 45.
8 Tony Doherty in Rolston, p. 15.
9 BSI bulletin, 'Towards justice: remember Bloody Sunday', leaflet, 1991.
10 BSI, 'One world, one struggle, Jan. 20–26 1992, Derry City', leaflet, 1992.
11 Doherty in Rolston, p. 15.
12 BSI, 'Towards justice'.
13 *Ibid.*
14 Taylor, *Provos*, pp. 301–8.
15 Quoted in *Ibid.*, p. 323.
16 BSI, One world, one struggle'.
17 *Ibid.*
18 For the former see Rolston, *Unfinished Business*, pp. 213–24; for the latter see *ibid.*, pp. 225–32; Murray, pp. 206–11.
19 McKittrick et al., pp. 1221–2.
20 Daly quoted in *ibid.*, p. 1222.
21 *Ibid.*
22 Doherty in Rolston, p. 15.
23 *Ibid.*
24 Ashplant et al., p. 54.
25 *Ibid.*, p. 68.
26 *Ibid.*
27 *Ibid.*, p. 59.
28 *Ibid.*, pp. 68–9.
29 *Ibid.*, pp. 59, 69.
30 Jelin and Kaufman, p. 106.
31 BSI, 'Towards justice'; the quoted matter in the rest of this paragraph is from this bulletin.
32 *Ibid.*
33 Doherty in Rolston, pp. 15–16.
34 *AP/RN*, 1/2/1990.
35 McKittrick et al., pp. 479–82, 496–8.
36 See poster, *Troubled Images*, CD-ROM, Image ID: PPO2107.

37 *AP/RN*, 1/2/1990.
38 Walker, reported in *ibid*.
39 Quoted in Bew and Gillespie, p. 95.
40 *AP/RN*, 1/2/1990.
41 Murray, pp. 191–204.
42 Hartley reported in *AP/RN*, 1/2/1990.
43 Murray, p. 7.
44 *Ibid*.
45 *Ibid*., pp. 145–7.
46 Opsahl Report.
47 Murray, p. 174; see pp. 174–85.
48 *Ibid*., pp. 175–6.
49 *Ibid*., pp. 174–5.
50 *Ibid*., p. 175.
51 *Ibid*., pp. 191–204.
52 BSI, 'Towards justice'; Rolston, *Unfinished Business*, pp. 155–74.
53 BSI, 'Towards justice'.
54 Pat Finucane Centre, 'Introducing the Pat Finucane Centre' for Human Rights and Social Change', leaflet, (1993?).
55 BSI, 'Programme of events: Bloody Sunday 1972–1992', leaflet, 1992.
56 *AP/RN*, 30/1/1992.
57 *Ibid*.
58 BSI,'Programme of events'.
59 *Ibid*.
60 *Ibid*.
61 Ballagh.
62 *Ibid*., p. 7.
63 *Ibid*., p. 8.
64 Ballagh reported in *AP/RN*, 30/1/1992.
65 *Ibid*.
66 Adams reported in *ibid*.
67 *AP/RN*, 30/1/1992; see *Irish News*, 27/1/1992.
68 Doherty in Rolston, p. 16.
69 BSI, 'Programme of events'.
70 *AP/RN*, 30/1/1992.
71 *Ibid*.
72 *Ibid*.
73 *Irish News*, 27/1/1992.
74 *AP/RN*, 30/1/1992.
75 *Troubled Images*, CD-ROM, Image ID: PP02105, 1992.
76 Pringle and Jacobson, p. 44.
77 BSI, 'Programme of events'.
78 Ashplant et al., p. 70.
79 BSI, *Political Guide to Derry*.
80 *Ibid*.
81 *Ibid*.
82 McAuley; and see chapter 7, this book.
83 Ashplant et al., p. 4.
84 *Guardian*, 25/1/1992; *Irish News*, 30/1/1992.

85 Jelin and Kaufman, p. 89.
86 *Ibid.*, p. 96.
87 See, for example, Taylor, *Provos*, pp. 124–5; Col. Wilford reported in *AP/RN*, 30/1/1992; *Irish News*, 27/1/1992.
88 Jelin and Kaufman, p. 89.
89 *Ibid.*, p. 96.
90 *Ibid.*, p. 93.
91 *Remember Bloody Sunday*, broadcast BBC2, 30 January 1992
92 McCann, *BSD*; BSI, 'Programme of events'.
93 *BSD*, p. 221; see Ziff, pp. 13–19.
94 Deane, Foreword *BSD*, p. 12.
95 *Ibid.*, p. 13.
96 BSI, 'Programme of events'.
97 *Ibid.*; Grimaldi and North.
98 *AP/RN*, 30/1/1992.
99 *BSD*, p. 227.
100 *Ibid.*, p. 77.
101 *Ibid.*, p. 163.
102 *Irish News*, 27/1/1992.
103 Doherty in Rolston, p. 16.
104 *Ibid.*
105 John Kelly, conversation with author, 6/4/2006.
106 Doherty in Rolston, p. 16.
107 Duddy in Rolston, p. 11.
108 Bloody Sunday Justice Campaign (hereafter referred to as BSJC), 'Vindicate the victims; repudiate Widgery; prosecute the guilty', leaflet, 1994.
109 Tony Doherty interviewed in *The Times*, 30/1/1998; BSJC, 'Epilogue', p. 267.
110 BSJC, 'Vindicate the victims'.
111 *Ibid.*
112 BSJC, 'Epilogue', p. 267.
113 BSJC, 'Vindicate the victims'.
114 Doherty in Rolston, p. 17.
115 *Sunday Business Post*, 25/1/1998.
116 O'Brien, *Matter of Minutes*, p. 116.
117 O'Brien, 'Back to Bloody Sunday', p. 18.
118 O'Brien, *Matter of Minutes*, p. 112.
119 Hayes and Campbell, pp. 102–3, 125–7.
120 Duddy in Rolston, p. 11.
121 Doherty in Rolston, p. 18.
122 *Ibid.*
123 Doherty in Rolston, p. 17; Duddy in Rolston, p. 12.
124 Doherty in Rolston p. 17.
125 Duddy in Rolston, pp. 11–12.
126 BSJC, 'Epilogue', p. 267; *Irish News*, 31/1/1994.
127 Duddy in Rolston, p. 12.
128 *Irish News*, 31/1/1994, 30/1/1995.
129 Kelly reported in *Irish News*, 31/1/1994.
130 Duddy reported in *Irish News*, 30/1/1995.
131 Deane, 'Foreword'.

Notes to chapter 6

1 BSI, 'One world, one struggle, Jan. 20–26 1992 Derry City', leaflet, 1992.
2 *Ibid.*
3 BSI, 'Towards justice: remember Bloody Sunday', leaflet, 1991.
4 Martin Finucane in Rolston, *Unfinished Business*, p. 186.
5 *Ibid.*, pp. 184–5.
6 Pat Finucane Centre (hereafter referred to as PFC), 'Introducing the Pat Finucane Centre'.
7 *Ibid.*
8 *Ibid.*
9 BSI, 'Towards a new peace agenda: a discussion paper', unpublished manuscript, (1990 or 1991?).
10 Sinn Féin, *Towards a Lasting Peace*.
11 *Ibid.*, pp. 1–3.
12 *Ibid.*, pp. 4–5.
13 Bogside and Brandywell Initiative, statement of aims, objectives and strategy, on Bogside and Brandywell Initiative website: http://freederry.org/gdt/bbi.
14 Doherty in Rolston, p. 20.
15 Ashplant et al., p. 43.
16 *AP/RN*, 3/2/1994. See event poster (poster30r.jpg) on CAIN website: http://cain.ulst.ac.uk.
17 *AP/RN*, 3/2/1994.
18 Sinn Féin, 'Bloody Sunday commemoration, 29/1/95', leaflet, 1995.
19 Adams reported in *AP/RN*, 2/2/1995.
20 *Irish News*, 30/1/1995.
21 Tony Doherty, 'Bloody Sunday Justice Campaign: submission to the Forum for Peace and Reconciliation on 20 January 1995', in *AP/RN*, 26/1/1995.
22 Farren, pp. 55–6.
23 Doherty, 'Bloody Sunday Justice Campaign: submission'.
24 *AP/RN*, 2/2/1995.
25 Pat McGeown, 'Sinn Féin spokesperson on prison issues: submission to the Forum for Peace and Reconciliation on 20 January 1995', in *AP/RN*, 26/1/1995.
26 *AP/RN*, 2/2/1995.
27 See McVeigh.
28 *AP/RN*, 26/1/1995.
29 McKittrick et al., pp. 1207–10.
30 Taylor, *Provos*, pp. 349–52.
31 *Irish Independent*, 31/1/1997.
32 Mullan, *Eyewitness*, p. 7.
33 Statement from John Kelly, chair of Bloody Sunday Justice Campaign (BSJC), 10/11/1995.
34 *Ibid.*
35 BSI, 'Decommission injustice: Bloody Sunday weekend 1996', leaflet, 1996.
36 Walsh, *Bloody Sunday Tribunal*, p. 9; see Walsh, *Bloody Sunday and the Rule of Law*, pp. 114–15; Jane Winter, 'Preface', pp. 26–7.
37 Walsh, *Bloody Sunday Tribunal*, p. 9.
38 Angela Hegarty, 'Foreword' to *ibid.*, p. 6.

39 Mullan, *Eyewitness*.
40 Doherty in Rolston, p. 19; see also Mullan, *Eyewitness*, pp. 37–8.
41 Doherty in Rolston, p. 19.
42 Mullan, 'Introduction', *Eyewitness*, pp. 38–9.
43 *Ibid.*, p. 39.
44 *Ibid.*
45 *Ibid.*; Doherty in Rolston, p. 19.
46 Mullan, 'Introduction', *Eyewitness*, pp. 40–2.
47 *Ibid.*, p. 40
48 *Ibid.*
49 *Ibid.*, p. 41.
50 *Ibid.*, p. 33.
51 *Ibid.*, p. 47.
52 *Ibid.*
53 *Ibid.*, p. 49.
54 Mullan, 'Afterword', p. 300.
55 For *Nunca mas*, see Jelin and Kaufman; for the REMHI Report, see Introduction, this book.
56 Both cited in Mullan, 'Afterword', p. 300.
57 *Andersonstown News*, 25/1/1997.
58 Wolfhound Press, press release, 21/1/1997.
59 Linda Roddy (née Nash), press release, 20/1/1997.
60 Mullan, 'Afterword', pp. 300–1.
61 *Ibid.*, p. 301; see Doherty in Rolston, p. 19.
62 Kelly, quoted in Mullan, 'Afterword', p. 301.
63 Doherty in Rolston, p. 20.
64 *Ibid.*
65 *Derry Journal*, 7/2/1997.
66 McClean in O'Brien, *Matter of Minutes*, p. 85.
67 *Derry Journal*, Bloody Sunday Supplement, 31/1/1997.
68 *Derry Journal*, 21/2/1997.
69 *Derry Journal*, Bloody Sunday Supplement, 31/1/1997; McCallion in Mullan, *Eyewitness*, p. 157.
70 McCafferty in *Irish News*, 30/1/1997.
71 Walker in O'Brien, *Matter of Minutes*, p. 78.
72 Roddy in *ibid.*, p. 70.
73 Roddy in *Irish News*, 30/1/1997.
74 Das in Sanford, p. 73.
75 Sanford, p. 78.
76 Deane, *Reading in the Dark*.
77 *Derry Journal*, 4/2/1997.
78 *Ibid.*; *Irish News*, 3/2/1997.
79 Doherty in *Derry Journal*, 4/2/1997.
80 PFC, *In the Line of Fire*. I am grateful to Mark McGovern for this point.
81 Doherty in *Derry Journal*, 4/2/1997.
82 *Derry Journal*, 4/2/1997.
83 *Irish News*, 3/2/1997.
84 Anonymous interviewee, *Belfast Telegraph*, 3/2/1997.
85 *Derry Journal*, 4/2/1997.

86 PFC, 'Bloody Sunday weekend 1997: March for justice, time for truth: 25th anniversary, Thursday 30 Jan–Sunday 2 Feb 1997', leaflet.

87 *Derry Journal*, 4/2/1997.

88 *Ibid.*

89 McKittrick et al., p. 97.

90 *Ibid.*, pp. 97–8.

91 *Derry Journal*, 4/2/1997.

92 *Ibid.*

93 PFC, 'Bloody Sunday weekend 1997'.

94 *Irish News*, 31/1/1997; see also *Irish Independent*, 31/1/1997.

95 *Derry Journal*, 4/2/1997.

96 *Ibid.*

97 *Belfast Telegraph*, 3/2/1997; *Derry Journal*, 4/2/1997; Ziff, pp. 170–5.

98 Dawson, 'Trauma, place and the politics of memory', pp. 164–6.

99 *Belfast Telegraph*, 3/2/1997; *Derry Journal*, 4/2/1997.

100 *Derry Journal*, 4/2/1997

101 *Ibid.*

102 Meenan and Mullan. The poets misnamed Gerard Donaghey.

103 I am grateful to Mark McGovern for this point.

104 *Derry Journal*, 4/2/1997.

105 PFC, 'Bloody Sunday weekend 1997'.

106 Ashplant et al., pp. 43–7.

107 Hirsch, pp. 21–2.

108 See Hayes, 'Narrative tradition', unpublished doctoral thesis, pp. 232–8, 278–9.

109 Peress, p. 82.

110 Sharon Meenan, telephone conversation with the author, 26/4/2002; Grimaldi and North.

111 Ashplant et al., p. 20.

112 *Derry Journal*, 4/2/1997.

113 Kay Duddy quoted in *Guardian*, 3/2/1997.

114 Bishop Edward Daly in O'Brien, *Matter of Minutes*, p. 147.

115 *Irish Independent*, 31/1/1997.

116 *Irish News*, 30/1/1997.

117 Hume quoted in *Irish Independent*, 31/1/1997.

118 *Irish News*, 30/1/1997.

119 Spring reported in *Irish News*, 30/1/1997.

120 Doherty in Rolston, p. 20.

121 *AP/RN*, 9/10/1997, from web archive; see Rolston, *Turning the Page*.

122 *Irish News*, 30/1/1997 and 31/1/1997.

123 *Irish Independent*, 31/1/1997.

124 Mayhew reported in *Irish News*, 31/1/1997.

125 Spring and Bruton quoted in *Irish Independent*, 31/1/1997.

126 Doherty in Rolston, p. 20.

127 *AP/RN*, 9/10/1997 and 28/5/1997, from web archive.

128 McGuinness quoted in *AP/RN*, 6/2/1997, from web archive.

129 *Ibid.*

130 Mullan, 'Afterword', p. 308.

131 Downing Street Declaration, in Cox et al., pp. 327–8; Prime Minister Tony Blair's statement to the House of Commons, *Guardian*, 30/1/1998.

132 McCann, *BSD*, p. 91; Rolston, *Unfinished Business*, p. 9.

133 McKay, pp. 21, 325–7, 339.

134 Rolston, 'Introduction', *Unfinished Business*, pp. x–xiv; see also chapters 7 and 9, this book.

135 See, for example, McKay, pp. 120, 197; *Guardian*, 16/1/2002 and 9/5/2002.

136 *Guardian*, 15/3/2002.

137 McCann (ed.), *The Bloody Sunday Inquiry*; Hayes and Campbell, pp. 144–73.

138 Kay Duddy in O'Brien, *Matter of Minutes*, p. 96; see also p. 85.

139 Teresa McGowan in *ibid.*, p. 122.

140 McKinney in *ibid.*, p. 56; see also p. 46.

141 John Kelly in *ibid.*, p. 130; see also p. 96.

142 Mary Donaghey in *ibid.*, p. 116.

143 *Ibid.*, pp. 85, 116, 126.

144 McCann (ed.), *The Bloody Sunday Inquiry*.

145 Rolston, *Unfinished Business*, p. 9; *Guardian*, 26/7/2002.

146 Rolston, *Unfinished Business*, p. 6; John Kelly in O'Brien, *Matter of Minutes*, p. 130.

147 *Observer*, 9/6/2002.

148 O'Brien, *Matter of Minutes*, pp. 116, 118.

149 Michelle Walker in *ibid.*, p. 80.

150 Raymond McClean in *ibid.*, p. 85; see also pp. 91, 118, 147.

151 Wray in *ibid.*, p. 36.

152 John Kelly in *ibid.*, p. 130.

153 Michael Bridge in *ibid.*, p. 134; see also pp. 68, 130.

154 *Guardian*, 15/3/2002 and 24/9/2002.

155 Donaghey in O'Brien, *Matter of Minutes*, pp. 116–18

156 Charles Morrison in *ibid.*, p. 26.

157 Doherty in *ibid.*, p. 91; see also Doherty in Rolston, *Unfinished Business*, pp. 21–2.

158 I am grateful to Carol K. Russell for this point.

Notes to chapter 7

1 Martin.

2 Said, pp. 54–5; see Read, p. 2 and this book p. 55.

3 Said, p. 54.

4 Read, pp. xi, 236, 2.

5 Lee, *Ireland*, pp. 1–4.

6 Martin, pp. 83, 86–7.

7 Lee, *Ireland*, p. 45.

8 Bruce.

9 Ferguson, p. 41

10 *Ibid.*, p. 44.

11 Dawson, *Soldier Heroes*, pp. 34–48.

12 Robbins; Walker, pp. 113–15; McBride, 'Ulster and the British problem'; McCall; Loughlin.

13 See Anderson.

14 Gordon Brown, Chancellor of the Exchequer, 1998, quoted in McCall, p. 158.

15 Robbins; McCall, p. 164.

16 English and Walker.
17 Martin, pp. 84–5; Farrell, p. 24; Dooley, p. 11.
18 Dooley, p. 37 (and see pp. 37–40, 51–5); Foster, *Modern Ireland*, pp. 466–7; Fitzpatrick, pp. 139–40.
19 Lee, *Ireland*, p. 2; Martin, pp. 84–96.
20 Martin, p. 85; Farrell, pp. 21–80.
21 Lord Craigavon, quoted in Farrell, p. 92; Lee, *Ireland*, p. 46.
22 Walker, p. 119; see McBride, 'Ulster and the British problem', pp. 10–11; Loughlin, pp. 216–18.
23 McCall, pp. 156, 165.
24 Interview with Lesley Finlay (West Tyrone Voice).
25 Felicity McCartney, in Logue, p. 87.
26 Bowen, p. 24; and see Hart.
27 Dooley, pp. 47–8; Ferguson, p. 43.
28 Interview with Darach MacDonald; see his historical novel *The Sons of Levi*, 1998.
29 *Orange Standard*, May 1990 and August 1992; see also November 1992.
30 Ferguson, p. 43; Interview with Arlene Foster (FEAR).
31 Walker, pp. 123–4.
32 Ferguson, p. 44.
33 Fay et al., *Northern Ireland's Troubles*, p. 136.
34 See, for example, McKay.
35 Fay et al., *Northern Ireland's Troubles*, p. 133.
36 *Ibid.*, pp. 76–8; 142–3.
37 McKittrick et al., pp. 1478–9; Ryder, *The Ulster Defence Regiment*.
38 Ryder and Kearney, pp. 100–1; FEAR; *Orange Standard*, February 1993, September 1993, October 1997.
39 'Mr E. and Mrs G. Gordon' (pseudonyms), in FEAR, 'Personal stories' section (unnumbered).
40 See, for example, Harnden, pp. 197–225; McKittrick et al., p. 178; McKay, pp. 227–8.
41 *Orange Standard*, March 1993; FEAR, p. 12.
42 Quoted in McDonald, *Observer*.
43 McKittrick et al., p. 267.
44 McKay, p. 234.
45 'Mr Gordon', in FEAR.
46 Leydesdorff et al., pp. 13–14.
47 Rose, p. 167.
48 McKay, p. 235.
49 McDonald, *Observer*.
50 Interview with Hazlett Lynch (West Tyrone Voice).
51 MacBride, 'Roads to nowhere', pp. 50, 52.
52 Dooley, p. 54.
53 McKay, p. 236.
54 FEAR, p. 21.
55 Fay et al., *Northern Ireland's Troubles*, p. 147.
56 See, for example, Holland, *Hope Against History*, 2000, where it is barely mentioned; and Coogan, 1996, who makes no mention of it at all.
57 Bruce, pp. 47–8.

58 Cigar, p. 74.
59 Ahmed.
60 'Homogeneous Serbia', quoted in Malcolm, pp. 178–9.
61 Cigar, pp. 68–9, 74–6; Malcolm, pp. 234–52; Allcock, pp. 158–9.
62 'Ethnic cleansing' was also carried out by Croatian and Muslim militias fighting each other for territory as Bosnia–Herzegovina was cantoned along 'ethnic' lines; and against Serbs by the Republic of Croatia in the Krajina and by Albanian militias in Kosovo: Allcock, pp. 158–9; Malcolm, pp. 248–9. In these cases, too, 'ethnic cleansing' was a component of a military action organized or sponsored by a state.
63 Cigar, p. 79.
64 Reported in *Orange Standard*, October 1992; the writer mistakenly refers to the East Bank when meaning the West Bank.
65 'Ethnic cleansing on our own doorstep – Molyneux', *Orange Standard*, September 1992.
66 *Ibid.*
67 *Ibid.*
68 Smyth, *Indifferent to the Truth*; and see, for example, *Orange Standard*, January 1973 and February 1981.
69 *Orange Standard*, September 1992. The *Orange Standard* also cultivated an identification between Ulster loyalists and Serbs, as commonly confronting the threat of 'Roman Catholic' fascism: *ibid.*, May 1993, April 1991, October 1991 and August 1992.
70 *Orange Standard*, March 1993.
71 *Orange Standard*, April 1993.
72 *Ibid.*
73 *Ibid.*
74 *Ibid.*
75 *Counterpoint*, 'Driven from the land?', Ulster Television, broadcast 29 April 1993; McDaniel, p. 204.
76 Adams, pp. 51–2, 119–21; Harnden, pp. 137–8.
77 *Counterpoint*, 1993; FEAR, pp. 13, 16–17.
78 Kennedy, *People and Population Change*, p. 9.
79 *Orange Standard*, March 1993.
80 'In the 70s and early 80s it was an average of one every six weeks': *ibid.*
81 *Counterpoint*, 1993; FEAR, in 1997, noted that the true numbers displaced from the Fermanagh Border were not known.
82 Fay et al., *Northern Ireland's Troubles*, pp. 73–86; McKittrick et al., pp. 1473–84.
83 Ashplant et al., p. 16.
84 McKittrick et al., p. 255.
85 *Newry Reporter*, 22/4/1976.
86 McKittrick et al., p. 980; Ryder, *Ulster Defence Regiment*, pp. 123–4.
87 *Orange Standard*, July 1993.
88 McKittrick et al., p. 821. Roslea is an alternative spelling of Rosslea.
89 See *ibid.*, pp. 245, 803, 426–7, 791, 722, respectively.
90 *Sunday Tribune*, quoted in McKittrick et al., p. 1041.
91 'Mr Sidwell' (pseudonym), in FEAR, 'Personal stories' section (unnumbered).
92 Dawson, *Soldier Heroes*, pp. 22–3.

93 Bardon, pp. 753–68.
94 Founding statement quoted in 'The Ulster Society', *Orange Standard*, November 1985.
95 *Ibid.*
96 Ulster Society, 'Marketing', unpublished internal paper, 1985.
97 Hume, p. 18.
98 *Ibid.*, p. 16.
99 *Ibid.*, p. 15.
100 Arlene Foster, Foreword in Holmes, p. 5.
101 Adamson, 'The Cruthin', p. 8; see also Adamson, *Identity of Ulster*.
102 Hume, p. 11.
103 *Ibid.*
104 See, for example, *Ulster: The Voice of the UDA*, December 1986, January 1987.
105 Hume, p. 18.
106 *Ibid.*
107 *Ibid.*
108 Porter, p. 23.
109 *Orange Standard*, December 1982–January 1983.
110 Jarman, *Material Conflicts*, pp. 94–131.
111 *Orange Standard*, March 1990.
112 *Orange Standard*, August 1990, November 1990.
113 *The Boyne 1690–1990* (video), Grand Orange Lodge of Ireland, 1990; *Orange Standard*, September 1990.
114 Martin Smyth's speech, recorded excerpts in *The Boyne 1690–1990* (video), and reported in *Orange Standard*, November 1990.
115 Grand Orange Lodge of Ireland, *The Twelfth 1990*, pp. 33–4; Jones et al., p. 70; Colmer; Kennedy, *A Celebration*; Omagh District Loyal Orange Lodge no. 11.
116 Belfast County Grand Lodge, *The Twelfth*, pp. 3–5.
117 Dawson, *Soldier Heroes*.
118 *Orange Standard*, August 1992, November 1992.
119 *Orange Standard*, April 1991; see also Campbell.
120 Moody, pp. 73–4; see also Dewar, pp. 17–18.
121 *Orange Standard*, July 1991.
122 *Ibid. Orange Standard* puts the figure at 'upwards of 200' people, but see Bardon, p. 138.
123 George Patton reported in *Orange Standard*, November 1990.
124 *Orange Standard*, April 1991.
125 McBride, *Siege of Derry*, pp. 15–16.
126 Ashplant et al., pp. 34–6.
127 *Orange Standard*, April 1991.
128 McBride, *Siege of Derry*, pp. 70–82; see chapter 9, this book.
129 Jackson, *Ireland*, pp. 18–21.
130 Harnden, pp. 134–40; McKittrick et al., pp. 611–12.
131 Laplanche and Pontalis, pp. 11, 15–16.
132 Ryder and Kearney; Garvaghy Residents.
133 *Impartial Reporter*, 21/8/1997; *Irish Times*, 26/8/1997; *News Letter*, 26/8/1997; *Observer*, 2/11/97; *Irish News*, 6/11/1997.
134 McDonald, *Observer*.

135 McKay, p. 235.
136 Laub, 'Bearing witness', p. 69; Laub, 'Event without a witness', p. 76.
137 McKay, p. 235.
138 Quoted in *ibid.*, p. 237.
139 Quoted in *ibid.*, p. 227.
140 Derry and Raphoe Action, *Protestants in Community Life*; 'Donegal's silent majority', *Strabane Weekly News*, 16/8/2001, online at: www.ulsternet-ni.co.uk/str3301/spages/SMAIN.htm (visited 30/7/2004).
141 Derry and Raphoe Action page, Raphoe Reconciliation Project website: http://homepage.tinet.ie/~raprecpro/dra.htm (visited 30/7/2001).
142 Raphoe Reconciliation Project website: http://homepage.tinet.ie/~raprecpro/aims.htm (visited 30/7/2001); Derry and Raphoe Action, *Protestants and the Border*.
143 Derek Reaney, in Logue, pp. 172–4.

Notes to chapter 8

1 FEAR, p. 2.
2 West Tyrone Voice leaflet, 1998.
3 FAIR (npp); 'Bloody Sunday: full Inquiry, cost £400m. July 7 bombs: no inquiry, "too expensive"', filed 5/7/2006, *Daily Telegraph Online*: www.telegraph.co.uk/news (visited 27/9/2006). The Government's previous estimate of cost, in November 2005, was £163 million.
4 'Andrew Jackson' (pseudonym), member of FACT (Families Against Crimes by Terrorism), in conversation with the author, 1/3/2000.
5 Foster interview; FEAR.
6 FEAR, p. 2.
7 *Ibid.*, p. 4
8 *Ibid.*, p. 21.
9 Wilson, section 2.1.1.
10 Letter from FAIR to Northern Ireland Office, quoted in *Irish News*, 22/9/1998.
11 Wilson, 2.1.2.
12 *Ibid.*
13 FAIR; Wilson, 5.1.2, note 1; 5.3.1, note 6.
14 Lynch interview.
15 *Ibid.*
16 West Tyrone Voice, leaflet. By March 2000 Voice had 102 paid-up members out of 180 people associated with the group, most of whom were representative of wider families, constituting a network of some 500–600 supporters (Lynch and Finlay interviews).
17 West Tyrone Voice, leaflet.
18 Wilson, 3.2.2.
19 West Tyrone Voice, leaflet; see also Constitution (Draft III), in Wilson.
20 West Tyrone Voice, leaflet.
21 Lynch interview.
22 Wilson, 5.5.9.
23 Interview with Willie Frazer (FAIR).
24 Wilson, 3.2.2.
25 Lynch interview.

26 Frazer interview.
27 FAIR.
28 Foster interview.
29 *Ibid.*
30 Wilson, 2.1.5.
31 Frazer, in *ibid.*
32 Wilson, 2.1.5.
33 This aspect was particularly emphasized by members of another victims' group I visited, Families Against Crimes by Terrorism (FACT), Lisburn, 7/4/2000.
34 'Mr E. Gordon' (pseudonym), in FEAR, 'Personal stories' section (unnumbered).
35 *Ibid.*
36 'Mr G. Sidwell' (pseudonym), in FEAR, 'Personal stories' section (unnumbered).
37 *Ibid.*
38 See chapter 2, this book.
39 Leydesdorff et al.; McKimm.
40 Magowan and Patterson; Interview with Mary Butcher (VLU).
41 Foster interview.
42 Finlay interview.
43 Foster interview.
44 *Ibid.*
45 *Ibid.*; Cf. Damian Gorman in chapter 2, this book; see Bolton, 'Welcome and introduction', p. 8.
46 Lynch interview.
47 *Ibid.*
48 Wilson, 5.6.2.
49 Foster interview.
50 FEAR.
51 *Ibid.*, p. 4; see also pp. 3, 12–15, 17, 22.
52 *Ibid.*, p. 22.
53 *Ibid.*, pp. 7–8.
54 *Ibid.*, p. 9.
55 The questionnaire is reproduced in *ibid.*
56 *Ibid.*, p. 9.
57 'Mr C. Ford' (pseudonym), quoted in FEAR, p. 15.
58 FEAR, p. 4; see also pp. 3, 12–15.
59 'Mr B. and Mrs A. Gillen' (pseudonyms), in FEAR, 'Personal stories' section (unnumbered); also quoted on p. 19.
60 FEAR, pp. 18–19; see also 'Personal stories' section.
61 Foster interview; Arlene Foster, e-mail communication with author, 8/5/2002.
62 Wilson, 1.1.1.
63 *Ibid.*, 5.4.
64 *Ibid.*, 3.1.2; Cf. Fay et al., *Northern Ireland's Troubles.*
65 FAIR; these figures for bombings and shootings correspond with those compiled by the RUC, but FAIR's figures for murders differ from those of the RUC, which numbered them at 240: Harnden, p. 11.
66 Frazer interview.
67 FAIR.
68 Wilson, 4.1.9; 4.1.10.
69 Tim Pat Coogan, 1995, quoted in Wilson, 4.1.7.

70 Wilson, 4.1.4; see Harnden, pp. 37–44.

71 Wilson, 4.1.3.

72 *Ibid.*, 4.1.8.

73 *Ibid.*, 4.1.1; 4.1.2.

74 *Ibid.*, 4.1.12; 4.1.2, note 8; Cf. Harnden, who describes most of these torture stories as 'myths' (pp. 132, 140–1, 205).

75 Wilson, 4.1.13; 4.1.14.

76 *Ibid.*, 4.1.8.

77 *Ibid.*, 4.1.13; Harnden, p. 132.

78 Wilson, 1.2.2.

79 *Ibid.*, 5.5.10; 5.5.11.

80 *Ibid.*, 5.5.21. See also 5.5.13 – 5.5.17.

81 *Ibid.*, 4.2.2

82 *Ibid.*, 1.2.2. Here Wilson uses the term 'integration' to mean the complete opposite of the concept developed in psychoanalytic theory (see Chapter 2, this book).

83 *Ibid.*, 5.9.6; 1.2.2.

84 FEAR, p. 20.

85 *Ibid.*, p. 13.

86 Wilson, 5.9.5.

87 *Ibid.*, 5.9.6.

88 FAIR website: www.victims.org.co.uk.

89 *Families Acting for Innocent Relatives*, video, undated [1999].

90 West Tyrone Voice, leaflet.

91 McClure was interviewed for FEAR's report under the pseudonym of 'J. Doherty'.

92 *Irish News*, 12/8/1997; *Impartial Reporter*, 21/8/1997; *Irish Times*, 26/8/1997; *News Letter*, 26/8/1997; *Daily Telegraph*, 30/10/1997; *Observer*, 2/11/1997; *Irish News*, 6/11/1997.

93 McClure, quoted in *Irish News*, 6/11/1997.

94 McClure, quoted in *News Letter*, 26/8/1997.

95 *Impartial Reporter*, 21/8/1997.

96 Foster quoted in *ibid.*

97 McClure, quoted in *Irish News*, 6/11/1997.

98 McClure, quoted in *ibid.*

99 *Irish News*, 6/11/1997.

100 *Irish Times*, 26/8/1997.

101 *Ibid.*

102 *Irish News*, 12/8/1997 and 6/11/1997.

103 Gallagher, quoted in *Irish News*, 6/11/1997.

104 Gallagher, quoted in *ibid.*

105 FEAR, p. 2

106 *Irish News*, 6/11/1997; *Daily Telegraph*, 30/10/1997; see pp. 229–30, this book.

107 Foster interview; the programme referred to was 'Back To The Border', *Spotlight*, BBC, 1997.

108 Arlene Foster, e-mail communication with author, 8/5/2002.

109 Wilson, 5.5.26.

110 'Testimony of a Darkley Gospel Hall survivor', FAIR website: www.victims.org.uk/darkleytestimony.html (visited 14/9/2000).

111 See chapter 2, this book.

112 Wilson, 3.2.1.
113 Frazer, quoted in McKay, p. 197; see also pp. 324–5.
114 FAIR; see Harnden, p. 34.
115 West Tyrone Voice, leaflet.
116 Frazer, quoted in McKay, pp. 193–4.
117 Frazer interview.
118 FAIR.
119 *Ibid.*
120 *Ibid.*; see Harnden, pp. 132–40; McKittrick et al., pp. 571–3, 611–14, 963–4.
121 FAIR.
122 McKittrick et al., p. 963.
123 Nairac, p. 369.
124 Ignatieff, 'Articles of faith', pp. 115–16.
125 FAIR.
126 *Ibid.*
127 *Oxford English Dictionary.*
128 FAIR.
129 *Reynolds' News* and *The Times* (both 1857), quoted in Dawson, *Soldier Heroes*, p. 88.
130 Dawson, *Soldier Heroes*, p. 97.
131 FAIR.
132 Dawson, *Soldier Heroes*, pp. 89–94.
133 FAIR.
134 Damian Gorman, quoted p. 71, this book.
135 Leslie Finlay (West Tyrone Voice), in conversation with the author, 27/3/2000; on Castlederg cemetery, see Finlay interview.
136 'Mr B. and Mrs A. Gillen', in FEAR, 'Personal stories' section (unnumbered).
137 *Ibid.*
138 See, for example, Danny Morrison interviewed by Fergal Keane, *Resigning Issues*, broadcast on BBC Radio 4, 13/10/1998.
139 Wilson; Smyth, 'The human consequences', pp. 131–2; 'Five members of my family were murdered by the IRA. Why has the world forgotten?', *Belfast Telegraph*, 8/5/1999.
140 Unidentified FAIR member, in conversation with author, 29/2/2000; for continuing use of the term 'Free State', see above p. 213.
141 Black, p. 30; Wilson, 5.1; Frazer interview; Lynch interview; Finlay interview.
142 Lynch interview.
143 *Ibid.*
144 *Ibid.*
145 *Ibid.*
146 *Ibid.*
147 Frazer interview.
148 *Ibid.*
149 McKittrick et al., p. 722; see also Frazer interview; Harnden, pp. 211–24.
150 McKittrick et al., p. 722.
151 *Ibid.*, p. 724; see Dillon, *Dirty War*, pp. 188–208.
152 McKittrick et al., p. 724.
153 FAIR.
154 McKittrick et al., pp. 636–7.

155 Brian McConnell, 1999, quoted in *ibid.*, p. 637.
156 Deane, *Reading in the Dark* .
157 O'Callaghan; Collins.
158 Lynch interview.
159 FEAR, p. 8.
160 Wilson, 5.9.6; see also 1.2.2; McKay, pp. 187–237; Howe.
161 Frazer interview.
162 *Ibid.*
163 Wilson, 5.9.5.
164 The phrase was that of the Secretary of State, Mo Mowlam, speaking on *An Imperfect Peace*, BBC Radio 4, broadcast 3/12/2001 and 10/12/2001.
165 Wilson, 5.8.1.
166 *Ibid.*, 5.8.2.
167 McKay.
168 Thomson, *Anzac Memories*, p. 216.

Notes to chapter 9

1 *The Agreement*, 'Declaration of support', in Cox et al., p. 302.
2 McDaniel, p. 203.
3 Foster interview.
4 See chapter 1, p. 41, this book.
5 Foster interview.
6 For a theory of splitting within stereotypes, see Hall, Stuart, pp. 307–8.
7 FEAR p. 17.
8 Foster interview.
9 Ferguson, quoted in McDaniel, p. 188.
10 West, quoted in *ibid.*, p. 186.
11 Cupples, quoted in *ibid.*, p. 189.
12 Foster interview.
13 *Ibid.*
14 *Ibid.*
15 FEAR, p. 6.
16 Peake interview; Lynch interview; Kavanagh; Magowan and Patterson, pp. 34, 44, 80.
17 Bolton, 'Welcome and introduction'.
18 FEAR, pp. 20–1.
19 'R. Rankin' (pseudonym), in FEAR, 'Personal stories' section (unnumbered).
20 *Irish News*, 6/11/1997.
21 *Daily Telegraph*, 30/10/1997.
22 Foster, quoted in *Impartial Reporter*, 21/8/1997.
23 Foster, quoted in *Irish Times*, 26/8/1997.
24 *Ibid.*
25 Foster interview.
26 *Ibid.*; see also, for example, *Orange Standard*, October 1997.
27 Foster, quoted in *Daily Telegraph*, 30/10/1997.
28 *Ibid.*
29 Foster, quoted in *Observer*, 2/11/1997.
30 See chapter 6, this book.

31 McInnes, pp. 78–86.
32 *The Agreement*, 'Decommissioning', reproduced in Cox et al., pp. 217–18.
33 McInnes, p. 86.
34 Taylor, *Provos*, p. 360; see also pp. 361–2.
35 *Ibid.*, pp. 355–60.
36 Harnden, p. 313; and see pp. 309–18.
37 Fay et al., *Northern Ireland's Troubles*, p. 49.
38 Lynch interview.
39 Wilson, section 5.8, figure 5, 'Alienation of British victims in South Armagh'.
40 Wilson, 5.5.23.
41 Frazer interview.
42 FAIR.
43 Lynch interview.
44 Hazlett Lynch (West Tyrone Voice), conversation with the author, 'Hear and now' conference, 29 February–1 March 2000.
45 For conference proceedings, see Magowan and Paterson.
46 Lynch interview.
47 'Andrew Jackson' (pseudonym, FACT member), conversation with the author, 'Hear and now' conference, 29 February–1 March 2000.
48 Frazer interview.
49 Finlay interview.
50 For the South Armagh signs, see 'Sniper at work', 1994, in Rolston, *Drawing Support 2*, p. 19; 'Business as usual', 1997, in Rolston, *Drawing Support 3*, p. 17.
51 *Guardian*, 31/10/2001.
52 Bew, p. 47.
53 Unnamed 'dissident Unionist', quoted in de Bréadún, p. 211.
54 Albert Reynolds, quoted in *ibid.*, p. 141.
55 John Hume, quoted in *ibid.*, p. 140.
56 Unattributed quotation, in Ruane and Todd, p. viii.
57 Ruane and Todd, p. viii.
58 Cox et al., 'Conclusion', p. 290.
59 *Ibid.*, p. 291.
60 Aughey.
61 McInnes, p. 85.
62 de Bréadún, p. 334.
63 de Bréadún.
64 *Guardian*, 2/7/2001.
65 *Ibid.*, 24/10/2001.
66 *Ibid.*, 15/10/2002.
67 *Ibid.*, 29/11/2003.
68 *Ibid.*, 27/9/2005.
69 McWilliams, quoted in Fay et al., *Northern Ireland's Troubles*, pp. 48–9.
70 Wilson, 5.9.4.
71 Smyth, 'The human consequences', p. 131; Ryder and Kearney.
72 Smyth, 'The human consequences', pp. 131–2.
73 *An Appeal to You from the Victims*, video, no details of production (1999).
74 *Ibid.*
75 See McKittrick et al., pp. 927, 1011, 1328; and chapter 10, this book.

76 *An Appeal to You from the Victims.*
77 Eamonn Mallie and David McKittrick, 1996, quoted in McKittrick et al., p. 1332.
78 *Ibid.*
79 Page, p. 100.
80 *News Letter*, 24/7/2000; see *Guardian*, 28/7/00.
81 Bloomfield, p. 33.
82 Lynch interview.
83 Wilson, 5.7.1 and 5.7.2.
84 Wilson, 5.7.2 and note 8; McKittrick et al., p. 1203.
85 McKittrick et al., p. 1203.
86 Anonymous (to protect identity), conversation with the author, 'Hear and now' conference, 29 February–1 March 2000.
87 Wilson, 5.7.2.
88 Bloomfield, p. 33.
89 Frazer, quoted in *Belfast Telegraph*, 8/5/1999.
90 FAIR.
91 Chris Patten, quoted in *News Letter*, 10/9/1999.
92 *A New Beginning*, 'Summary of recommendations', p. 121.
93 *Ibid.*; see Dickson.
94 Patten, in *News Letter*, 10/9/1999.
95 *Ibid.*
96 *Belfast Telegraph*, 9/9/1999; see Fay et al., *Northern Ireland's Troubles*, pp. 159–60.
97 *News Letter*, 10/9/1999.
98 Police Federation, quoted in *ibid.*
99 Editorial, *ibid.*
100 Adams, quoted in *Belfast Telegraph*, 9/9/1999.
101 Foster, quoted in *Irish News*, 10/9/1999.
102 Alison McClean, quoted in *ibid.*
103 Fred Sterrit, quoted in *ibid.*
104 Turbitt, quoted in *ibid.*
105 Allen, quoted in *Belfast Telegraph*, 9/9/1999.
106 Jardine, quoted in *ibid.*
107 Crozier, quoted in *ibid.*
108 Frazer interview.
109 Robinson, in *News Letter*, 10/9/1999.
110 Orange Order, in *ibid.*
111 *Belfast Telegraph*, 10/9/1999.
112 Channel 4, *News*, 19/11/1999.
113 de Bréadún, pp. 287–8.
114 *Ibid.*, p. 290.
115 Agnew, quoted in Smyth, 'The human consequences', p. 132.
116 Magowan and Patterson.
117 Lynch, conversation with the author, 'Hear and now' conference, 29 February–1 March 2000.
118 'Andrew Jackson', conversation with the author, 'Hear and now' conference, 29 February–1 March 2000.
119 McKay, p. 195.
120 Lynch interview.

121 Lynch interview.
122 Finlay interview.
123 Lynch interview.
124 Smyth, 'The human consequences', p. 131.
125 Interviews with Mark Thompson and Eilish McCabe (Relatives for Justice).
126 McKay, p. 193.
127 Frazer interview; Lynch interview.
128 *Justice: Newsletter of Relatives for Justice*, no. 2, 2000, p. 2; Thompson and McCabe interviews; see also pp. 67, 182–3, this book.
129 Thompson interview.
130 *Ibid.*
131 McCabe interview.
132 *Ibid.*
133 Wilson, 5.7.1.
134 Finlay interview.
135 FACT, group interview.
136 See, for example, Ken Maginnis's support for an inquiry into the involvement of the Irish State with the IRA, in McKay, p. 197; Gregory Campbell's position on the Bloody Sunday Inquiry in *Irish News*, 28/3/2000.
137 Colm Barton, (Bloody Sunday Trust) conversation with the author, 26/3/2000.
138 *Belfast Telegraph*, 3/3/2000.
139 Entries posted from 17/2/2000–21/5/2000 on FAIR's Guestbook message-board, at: http://books.dreambook.com/dcz5152/guestbook.html (visited 11/4/2000 and 22/5/2000).
140 'Violent clashes in Dublin over Orange parade', filed 25/02/2006, *Daily Telegraph* online: www.telegraph.co.uk/news (visited 27/9/2006).

Notes to chapter 10

 1 McKittrick et al., pp. 1094–6.
 2 Leonard, 'Twinge of memory'.
 3 McDaniel.
 4 Foster, quoted in McDaniel, p. 135; see pp. 133–5.
 5 Curran et al.
 6 Foster, quoted in *Impartial Reporter* (hereafter, *IR*), 6/11/1997.
 7 Gébler, pp. 57–8; 54.
 8 Jarman, *Material Conflicts*, pp. 152–8; Jeffery; Johnson, *Ireland, pp. 115–18*; McDaniel, pp. 112–17.
 9 McDaniel, p. 117.
10 See, for example, Gébler, p. 60.
11 Ferguson, quoted in McDaniel, p. 125.
12 McDaniel, p. 22.
13 Gébler, p. 107; see also McDaniel, pp. 20–1, 122.
14 Armstrong, quoted in McDaniel, p. 173.
15 McDaniel, pp. 70–5.
16 Adams, quoted in McDaniel, p. 192.
17 Corrigan, quoted in *The Times*, 11/11/1987, cited in Gébler, pp. 110–11.
18 Gébler, p. 115.
19 *Ibid.*, p. 53; McDaniel p. 71.

20 Msg Séan Cahill, quoted in McDaniel, p. 71.
21 Cahill quoted in *ibid.*
22 Bolton, 'Threat to belonging', p. 210.
23 McCreary, *Gordon Wilson*, p. 52.
24 Wilson, quoted in *ibid.*, pp. 51–2.
25 Wilson, quoted in *ibid.*, p. 88.
26 McCreary, *Gordon Wilson*, pp. 48–61, 87–9; Bolton, 'Threat to belonging', p. 207; Parkinson, pp. 50–70.
27 Wilson, quoted in McCreary, *Gordon Wilson*, p. 130.
28 McKittrick et al., pp. 1098–9; *Michael Stone: Portrait of a Killer*, UTV broadcast 12/10/2000, reported in 'Michael Stone: I killed in revenge for Enniskillen', *IR* online (www.impartialreporter.com), 12/10/2000.
29 Bardon, p. 777.
30 Bolton, quoted in McCreary, *Gordon Wilson*, p. 60.
31 McDaniel, pp. 67–76; McCreary, *Gordon Wilson*, pp. 69–71.
32 McDaniel, pp. 80–1, 133–5.
33 Bew and Gillespie, p. 208.
34 Community Relations Council, *Fifth Annual Report, 1995*, p. 25.
35 Community Relations Council, *Dealing with Difference*, p. 53; see also McCreary, *Gordon Wilson*, pp. 119–21; Gébler pp. 74–9; McDaniel, pp. 140, 205–6.
36 *Fermanagh Herald* (hereafter, *FH*), 24/7/1996, p. 8; see Fermanagh District Partnership; also 'Remember and change: survivors of the conflict shaping their own future', conference proceedings in Northern Ireland Voluntary Trust.
37 McDaniel, pp. 123–5.
38 Joe Kennedy, quoted in *ibid.*, p. 124.
39 McKittrick et al., pp. 1095–6.
40 McDaniel, pp. 126, 146–8.
41 Cupples, quoted in McDaniel, p. 127.
42 See, for example, *Daily Telegraph*, 7/11/1988; McDaniel, pp. 19, 163–5.
43 Dixon, quoted in McDaniel, pp. 130–1.
44 Rev. Ivan Foster, *The Remembrance Day Massacre in Enniskillen: The Untold Story*, 1987, quoted in *ibid.*, pp. 128–9.
45 'After Enniskillen', *Ulster: The Voice of the UDA*, December 1987–January 1988, p. 13; see also 'Murder most foul!', *Young Unionist*, 8, 1988, p. 9; *Orange Standard*, December 1987–January 1988, p. 5.
46 *News Letter*, 28/11/1987; McDaniel, pp. 135–6.
47 *IR*, 26/10/1922, reproduced in *IR*, 30/10/1997.
48 McDaniel, pp. 115–16.
49 Jim Lunny, quoted in Gébler, pp. 63–4; see *IR*, 26/10/1922, reproduced in *IR*, 30/10/1997; Bardon, pp. 468–500; Gébler, pp. 121–7.
50 See, for example, *Sun*, 10/11/1987; *Irish Press*, 11/11/1987; *News Letter*, 9/6/1988.
51 Letter, Pierce to trustees, quoted in McDaniel, p. 136.
52 Pierce, quoted in Gébler, pp. 175–7.
53 Report, quoted in *FH*, 17/11/1990; see also *IR*, 7/3/1991.
54 *IR*, 7/3/1991. A twelfth name and dove were later added to mark the death in 2000 of Ronald Hill.
55 McDaniel, p. 138; see also *IR*, 7/3/1991.

56 Mullan, quoted in McDaniel, p. 138.
57 McDaniel, p. 138. The war memorials in Lampeter (Cardiganshire) and Whitchurch, near Cardiff, for example, name civilian casualties. I am grateful to David Skilton for this information.
58 According to Leonard, *Memorials*, p. 18: 'On two occasions, doves have been stolen from the memorial, possibly as an expression of non-endorsement of its new sentiments.'
59 Quinton, quoted in McDaniel, p. 138.
60 *Ibid.*, pp. 49–50; Quinton.
61 Dawson, *Soldier Heroes*, p. 40; see also p. 119.
62 Gébler, p. 218, reporting a telephone conversation with Pierce.
63 Cupples, quoted in McDaniel, p. 138; see McCreary, *Gordon Wilson*, p. 48.
64 Cupples, quoted in McDaniel, pp. 137–8.
65 Quinton, quoted in *ibid.*, p. 137.
66 *Ibid.*, p. 130.
67 Leonard, *Memorials*.
68 Kennedy, quoted in McDaniel, p. 142.
69 McDaniel, p. 106.
70 *Ibid.*, pp. 65, 156.
71 *Independent*, 23/11/1987.
72 McDaniel, p. 156.
73 *Ibid.*
74 All quoted in McDaniel, pp. 156–8.
75 Cllr Sammy Foster, quoted in *IR*, 27/7/1995.
76 *FH*, 17/11/1990; 'Poppy Day bomb site to be market', *News Letter*, 9/11/1990; *IR*, 7/3/1991; *IR*, 27/7/1995.
77 Dodds and Cahill, both quoted in *IR*, 27/7/1995.
78 Bill Maxwell, quoted in *FH*, 25/7/2001; see also *FH*, 24/4/1996.
79 Cahill, quoted in McDaniel, p. 158.
80 *IR* online (www.impartialreporter.com), 7/9/2000 (accessed 26/7/2005); interview with Gerry Burns.
81 Fermanagh University Partnership Board (hereafter FUPB), 'University Partnership' The Natural Choice, leaflet, (1993?); *FH*, 24/4/96; *IR*, 2/11/1995.
82 Interview with Barney Devine (Project manager, Higher Bridges Project); see also *IR*, 6/11/1997.
83 *IR*, 14/11/1996; 29/8/1996; 13/2/1997; 9/10/1997; *IR* online (www.impartialreporter.com), 30/3/2000 and 14/9/2000 (accessed 26/7/2005.)
84 *IR* online (www.impartialreporter.com), 24/5/2001 and 31/5/2001 (accessed 26/7/2005).
85 *Ibid.*, 15/11/2001 (accessed 26/7/2005).
86 Devine interview; see also FUPB, 'INTEC for everyone', leaflet (2000?).
87 Application to Millennium Commission, quoted in *IR*, 14/11/1996.
88 Devine interview.
89 Pierce, quoted in *IR*, 14/10/1999.
90 Richard Pierce, quoted in *FH*, 24/4/1996; Pierce, quoted in *IR* online (www.impartialreporter. com), 6/12/2001 (accessed 26/7/2005); Pierce, quoted in *IR*, 14/10/1999.
91 Application to Millennium Commission, quoted in *IR*, 14/11/1996.
92 *Ibid.*; *IR*, 14/10/1999.

93 FUPB, 'INTEC for everyone'; see also *IR* online (www.impartialreporter.com), 30/3/2000 and 14/9/2000 (accessed 26/7/2005); Devine interview.
94 Devine interview.
95 *FH*, 24/4/1996; *IR*, 14/11/1996, 14/10/1999.
96 Devine interview.
97 Bill Maxwell, quoted in *FH*, 25/7/2001.
98 Devine interview.
99 *Ibid.*
100 Devine, quoted in *FH*, 25/7/2001.
101 Pierce, quoted in *IR*, 14/10/1999.
102 Devine, quoted in *FH*, 25/7/2001.
103 Devine interview.
104 *Ibid.*
105 *IR* online (www.impartialreporter.com), 24/5/2000, and see *ibid.*, 27/1/2000 (accessed 26/7/2005); Devine interview.
106 Devine interview.
107 Clinton, quoted in *IR* online(www.impartialreporter.com), 31/5/2001 (accessed 26/7/2005).
108 Devine interview.
109 *Ibid.*
110 *IR* online (www.impartialreporter.com), 18/10/2001 (accessed 26/7/2005).
111 *Ibid.*
112 *FH*, 25/7/2001.
113 *Ibid.*; *IR* online (www.impartialreporter.com), 18/10/2001 (accessed 26/7/2005).
114 *FH*, 25/7/2001.
115 *IR*, 26/7/2001.
116 Pierce, quoted in *ibid.*
117 Devine interview.

Notes to Afterword

1 *Guardian* and *Daily Telegraph*, 29/7/2005.
2 Paisley quoted, and unnamed DUP politicians reported, in *Guardian*, 27/9/2005.
3 *Hansard*, 23/11/2005, vol. 439, columns 1528–1618; also available online at www.publications.parliament.uk.
4 *Guardian*, 24/11/2005; see *Hansard*, 23/11/2005, col. 1534.
5 Ian Paisley, in *Hansard*, 23/11/2005, col. 1534.
6 Quoted in *Guardian*, 12/1/2006.
7 *An Fhirinne* website: www.anfhirinne26.com (visited 16/2/2007); *Guardian*, 12/1/2006.
8 Quoted in *Guardian*, 20/2/2006.
9 Unnamed delegate, quoted in *Guardian*, 20/2/2006.
10 Gerry Kelly, quoted in *ibid.*; see also *Guardian*, 10/1/2007.
11 *Guardian*, 26/3/2007 and 27/3/2007.
12 *Guardian*, 29/7/2005.
13 Quoted in *Guardian*, 29/1/2004.
14 *Ibid.*
15 PONI (Police Ombudsman Northern Ireland).

16 *Guardian*, 23/1/2007; British–Irish Rights Watch, *Annual Report 2005*, available online: www.birw.org (visited 24/4/2007).

17 Quoted in *Guardian*, 23/1/2007.

18 For the activities of the Glencree Sustainable Peace Network, see Glencree Centre Website www.glencree.ie (visited 24/4/2007); and the film, *Brothers In Arms*, Fast Forward Productions, 2005.

19 Dawson, *Soldier Heroes*, p. 41.

20 Ziauddin Sardar, speaking at the 'Fundamentalisms: culture and difference' conference, University of Brighton, 20/5/2006; for the concept *polylogue*, see Sardar.

21 Nelson, p. 107.

22 Arlene Foster; see also Felner, p. 16.

23 British–Irish Rights Watch, *Annual Report 2005*, and 'Deaths since the ceasefires: cases', both at www.birw.org (visited 24/4/2007); see also Rolston, 'Dealing with the past'.

24 For the McCartney campaign, see *Guardian*, 24/2/2005; *Guardian*, 'G2', 11/3/2005.

25 Bloody Sunday Inquiry website: www.bloody-sunday-inquiry.org.uk/index2.asp?p=7 (visited 24/4/2007).

26 *Guardian*, 10/4/2007.

27 *Guardian*, 21/1/2006 and 22/1/2007; see HET pages on the PSNI website: www.psni.police.uk/index/departments/historical_enquiries_team.htm (visited 24/4/2007).

28 *Guardian*, 7/11/2006; Cassel et al.

29 *Eolas* Project, p. 1.

30 *Ibid.*, p. 26.

31 Quoted in *Guardian*, 21/1/2006.

32 See Belsey, pp. 70–82.

33 See the painting *Paxies II*, in Duffy, and on front cover of this book.

34 Jo Berry in Cantacuzino and Moody, no pps (pp. 10–11); also available on the website of the Forgiveness Project at www.theforgivenessproject.com/stories/jo-berry-pat-magee (visited 24/4/2007).

35 Berry, 'Why I am returning to Brighton'.

36 Berry speaking at a meeting with Pat Magee organized by the Forgiveness Project at St Nicholas Church, Brighton, 12/10/2004; edited transcript in *Argus*, 13/10/2004.

37 Berry in Cantacuzino and Moody, no pps (pp. 10–11).

38 Pat Magee in Cantacuzino and Moody, no pps (p. 11); also available on the website of the Forgiveness Project at www.theforgivenessproject.com/stories/jo-berry-pat-magee (visited 24/4/2007).

39 Magee speaking at a meeting with Jo Berry organized by the Forgiveness Project at St Nicholas Church, Brighton, 12/10/2004; edited transcript in *Argus*, 13/10/2004.

40 Magee in Cantacuzino and Moody, no pps (p. 11).

41 Quoted in Nelson, p. 135.

42 Hain, in *Hansard*, 23/11/2005, col. 1531.

43 *Ibid.*, col. 1530.

44 See *Hansard*, 23/11/2005, cols 1538–9.

45 Hain, speaking on *Today*, BBC Radio 4, 11/1/2006.

Bibliography

Articles, books, leaflets, pamphlets and reports

Adams, Gerry, *The Politics of Irish Freedom*, Dingle, Brandon, 1986.

Adamson, Ian, 'The Cruthin', in Holmes (ed.), *Cuchulain the Lost Legend*, pp. 7–10.

Adamson, Ian, *The Identity of Ulster: The Land, the Language and the People*, Bangor, Pretani Press, 1982.

Agger, Inger and Jensen, Søren Buus, *Trauma and Healing under State Terrorism*, London and New Jersey, Zed Books, 1996.

Ahmed, Akbar S., ' "Ethnic cleansing": a metaphor for our time', *Ethnic and Racial Studies*, 18, 1, 1995, pp. 1–25.

Allcock, John B., *Explaining Yugoslavia*, London, Hurst & Co., 2000.

An Crann/The Tree (ed.), *Bear in Mind: Stories of the Troubles*, Belfast, Lagan Press and *An Crann*/The Tree, 2000.

Anderson, Benedict, *Imagined Communities: Reflections on the Origins and Spread of Nationalism*, London, Verso, 1983.

Ardoyne Commemoration Project, *Ardoyne: The Untold Truth*, Belfast, Beyond the Pale, 2002.

Ashplant, T.G., Dawson, Graham and Roper, Michael, 'The politics of war memory and commemoration: contexts, structures and dynamics', in T.G. Ashplant, Graham Dawson and Michael Roper (eds), *Commemorating War: The Politics of Memory*, New Brunswick, NJ and London, Transaction, 2004, pp. 3–85 (first published as *The Politics of War Memory and Commemoration*, London and New York, Routledge, 2000).

Aughey, Arthur, 'The 1998 Agreement: Unionist responses', in Cox et al. (eds), *Farewell to Arms*, pp. 62–76.

Bakhtin, Mikhail, *The Dialogic Imagination*, Austin, University of Texas Press, 1981.

Ballagh, Bobby, '1916: goodbye to all that?', *Irish Reporter*, 2, 1991, pp. 6–8.

Barber, Fionna, 'An iceberg's collision with history: some recent work by Rita Duffy', catalogue essay in *The Essential Gesture: Recent Works by Rita Duffy* (?Belfast: no publisher named), 2005.

Bardon, Jonathan, *A History of Ulster*, Belfast, Blackstaff, 1992.

Beiner, Guy, *Remembering the Year of the French: Irish Folk History and Social Memory*, Madison, University of Wisconsin Press, 2006.

The Belfast Agreement, reproduced in Cox et al. (eds), *Farewell to Arms*, Appendix 2, pp. 301–25.

Belfast County Grand Lodge Publications Committee, *The Twelfth 1994*, Belfast (Grand Orange Lodge of Ireland), 1994.

Bell, Geoffrey, *The Protestants of Ulster*, London, Pluto, 1976.

Bell, P., Kee, M., Loughrey, G.C., Roddy, R.J. et al., 'Post-traumatic stress in Northern Ireland', *Acta Psychiatrica Scandinavica*, 77, 2, 1988, pp. 166–9.

Belsey, Catherine, *Critical Practice*, London and New York, Methuen, 1980.

Bennett, Ronan, and Paulin, Tom, 'Ghosts from a civil war', *Sight and Sound*, 6, 12, 1996, pp. 30–2.

Berry, Jo, 'Why I am returning to Brighton with the bomber who killed my father', *Argus*, 12/10/2004, pp. 6–7.

Bew, Paul, 'The Belfast Agreement of 1998', in Cox et al. (eds), *Farewell to Arms*, pp. 40–8.

Bew, Paul and Gillespie, Gordon, *Northern Ireland: A Chronology of the Troubles 1968–93*, Dublin, Gill & Macmillan, 1993.

Biko, Ntsiki, 'Justice first', *Index on Censorship*, 25, 5, 1996, pp. 67–8.

Black, Mary, 'Current work with victims and survivors', in Magowan and Patterson (eds), *Hear and Now*, pp. 27–33.

Bloody Sunday Initiative, *Political Guide to Derry*, leaflet, Derry, 1991.

Bloody Sunday Initiative, 'Towards justice: remember Bloody Sunday', leaflet, Derry, 1991.

Bloody Sunday Initiative, 'One world, one struggle, Jan. 20–26 1992, Derry City', leaflet, Derry, 1992.

Bloody Sunday Initiative, 'Programme of events: Bloody Sunday 1972–1992', leaflet, Derry, 1992.

Bloody Sunday Initiative, 'Decommission injustice: Bloody Sunday Weekend 1996', leaflet, Derry, 1996.

Bloody Sunday Justice Campaign, 'Epilogue', in Mullan, *Eyewitness*, pp. 267–8.

Bloody Sunday Justice Campaign, 'Vindicate the victims; repudiate Widgery; prosecute the guilty', leaflet, 1994.

Bloomfield, Sir Kenneth, *We Will Remember Them: Report of the Northern Ireland Victims Commissioner, Sir Kenneth Bloomfield*, Belfast, TSO Northern Ireland, 1998.

Bolton, David, 'The threat to belonging in Enniskillen: reflections on the Remembrance Day bombing', in Zinner and Williams (eds), *When a Community Weeps*, pp. 190–211.

Bolton, David, 'Welcome and introduction to conference participants', in Magowan and Patterson (eds), *Hear and Now*, pp. 3–10.

Bowen, Kurt, *Protestants in a Catholic State: Ireland's Privileged Minority*, Dublin, Gill & Macmillan, 1983.

Boyce, D. George, *Englishmen and Irish Troubles: British Public Opinion and the Making of Irish Policy 1918–22*, London, Cape, 1972.

Boyce, D. George and O'Day, Alan (eds), *The Making of Modern Irish History: Revisionism and the Revisionist Controversy*, London and New York, Routledge, 1996.

Boylan, Henry, *Dictionary of Irish Biography*, Dublin, Gill & Macmillan, 1988.

Bradley, Brendan, 'Survivors of trauma', in Northern Ireland Voluntary Trust, *Towards a Civil Society*, pp. 129–31.

Bradshaw, Brendan, 'Nationalism and historical scholarship', in Brady (ed.), *Interpreting Irish History*, pp. 191–216.

Brady, Ciaran (ed.), *Interpreting Irish History: The Debate on Historical Revisionism*, Dublin and Portland, OR, Irish Academic Press, 1994.

British–Irish Rights Watch, *Annual Report 2005*, available online: www.birw.org (visited 24/4/2007).

British–Irish Rights Watch, 'Deaths since the ceasefires: cases': www.birw.org (visited 24/4/2007).

British Society for Social Responsibility in Science, *The New Technology of Repression: Lessons from Ireland*, Paper 2, Nottingham, Russell Press, 1974.

Bruce, Steve, *The Edge of the Union: The Ulster Loyalist Political Vision*, Oxford, Oxford University Press, 1994.

Bryan, Dominic, *Orange Parades: The Politics of Ritual, Tradition and Control*, London, Pluto, 2000.

Burchardt, Natasha, 'Transgenerational transmission in the families of Holocaust survivors in England', in Daniel Bertaux and Paul Thompson (eds), *Between Generations: Family Models, Myths and Memories*, Oxford, Oxford University Press, 1993, pp. 121–37.

Burke, Maurice, *Britain's War Machine in Ireland*, New York, Oisin Publications, 1987.

Burton, Mary, 'The South African Truth and Reconciliation Commission: looking back, moving forward', in Hamber (ed.), *Past Imperfect*, pp. 13–24.

Cabrera, Roberto, 'Should we remember? Recovering historical memory in Guatemala', in Hamber (ed.), *Past Imperfect*, pp. 25–30.

Campbell, Alan (ed.), *Remember 1641*, pamphlet, Belfast, A. Campbell, 1991.

Cantacuzino, Marina and Moody, Brian (eds), *The F Word: Images of Forgiveness*, (exhibition booklet), London, Forgiveness Project (?2005); also available online: www.theforgivenessproject.com/stories.

Caruth, Cathy, *Unclaimed Experience: Trauma, Narrative and History*, Baltimore and London: John Hopkins University Press, 1996.

Caruth, Cathy (ed.), *Trauma: Explorations in Memory*, Baltimore, MD, and London, John Hopkins University Press, 1995.

Cassel, Douglass, Kemp, Susie, Pigou, Piers and Sawyer, Stephen, *Report of the Independent International Panel on Alleged Collusion in Sectarian Killings in Northern Ireland (October 2006)*, Notre Dame, IN, Centre for Civil and Human Rights, Notre Dame Law School, 2006, available online: http://cain.ulst.ac.uk/issues/collusion/docs/cassel061106.pdf.

Cigar, Norman, 'The Serbo-Croatian War, 1991', in Stjepan G. Meštrović (ed.), *Genocide After Emotion: The Postemotional Balkan War*, London and New York, Routledge, 1996, pp. 51–90.

Clare, Mariette, and Johnson, Richard, 'Method in our madness: identity and power in a memory work method', in Radstone (ed.), *Memory and Methodology*, pp. 197–224.

Cohen, Stanley, *States of Denial: Knowing About Atrocities and Suffering*, Cambridge, Polity, 2001.

Collins, Eamon, *Killing Rage*, London, Granta, 1997.

Colmer, Albert W.K., *In Glorious Memory: Tercentenary 1690–1990, an Historical Account of Orangeism in Lecale No. 2 District, Co. Down*, pamphlet, Downpatrick (Orange Order, 1990).

'Community Relations Council', leaflet, Belfast, CRC (?Jan. 1992).

Community Relations Council, *Fifth Annual Report*, Belfast, CRC, 1995.

Community Relations Council, *Into the Mainstream: Strategic Plan 1998–2001*, Belfast, CRC 1997.

Community Relations Council, *Dealing with Difference*, 2nd edn, CRC, Belfast, 1998.

Coogan, Tim Pat, *The Troubles: Ireland's Ordeal 1966–1996 and the Search for Peace*, London, Arrow, 1996.

Cox, Michael, Guelke, Adrian and Stephen, Fiona, 'Conclusion: closure for the Irish Question?', in Cox et al. (eds), *Farewell to Arms*, pp. 290–6.

Cox, Michael, Guelke, Adrian and Stephen, Fiona (eds), *A Farewell to Arms? From 'Long War' to Long Peace in Northern Ireland*, Manchester, Manchester University Press, 2000.

Crozier, Maurna (ed.), *Cultural Traditions in Northern Ireland: Varieties of Irishness*, Belfast, Institute of Irish Studies, Queen's University of Belfast, 1989.

Crozier, Maurna (ed.), *Cultural Traditions in Northern Ireland: Varieties of Britishness*, Belfast, Institute of Irish Studies, Queen's University of Belfast, 1990.

Cullen, Mary (ed.), *1798: 200 Years of Resonance. Essays and Contributions on the History and Relevance of the United Irishmen and the 1798 Revolution*, Dublin, Irish Reporter Publications, 1998.

Cultural Traditions Group, *Giving Voices: The Work of the Cultural Traditions Group 1990–94*, Belfast, Community Relations Council, 1994.

Curran, P.S., Bell, P., Murray, A., Loughrey, G., Roddy, R. and Rocke, L.G., 'Psychological consequences of the Enniskillen bombing', *British Journal of Psychiatry*, 156, 1990, pp. 479–82.

Curtis, Liz, *Ireland: The Propaganda War. The British Media and the Battle for Hearts and Minds*, London and Sydney, Pluto Press, 1984.

Darby, John, 'The effect of violence on the Irish peace process', in Cox et al. (eds), *Farewell to Arms*, pp. 263–74.

Darian-Smith, Kate and Hamilton, Paula, 'Introduction', in Darian-Smith and Hamilton (eds), *Memory and History in Twentieth-Century Australia*, pp. 1–6.

Darian-Smith, Kate and Hamilton, Paula (eds), *Memory and History in Twentieth-Century Australia*, Oxford and Melbourne, Oxford University Press, 1994.

Dash, Samuel, *Justice Denied: A Challenge to Lord Widgery's Report on 'Bloody Sunday'*, New York, National Council for Civil Liberties and International League for the Rights of Man, 1998 (first published 1972).

Dawson, Graham, *Soldier Heroes: British Adventure, Empire and the Imagining of Masculinities*, London and New York, Routledge, 1994.

Dawson, Graham, 'The imaginative geography of masculine adventure', *Renaissance and Modern Studies*, 39, 1996, pp. 27–45.

Dawson, Graham, 'The paradox of authority: psychoanalysis, history and cultural criticism', *Angelaki*, 2, 1996, pp. 75–102.

Dawson, Graham, 'Trauma, place and the politics of memory: Bloody Sunday, Derry, 1972–2004', *History Workshop*, 59, 2005, pp. 151–78.

Dawson, Graham and West, Bob, 'Our finest hour? Popular memory of World War Two and the struggle over British national identity', in Hurd (ed.), *National Fictions: World War Two on Television and Film*, London, British Film Institute, 1984, pp. 8–13.

Deane, Seamus, 'Wherever green is read', in Ní Dhonnchada and Dorgan (eds), *Revising the Rising*, pp. 91–105.

Deane, Seamus, 'Foreword', in McCann, *Bloody Sunday in Derry*, pp. 9–13.

Deane, Seamus, *Reading in the Dark*, London, Vintage, 1997.

Deane, Seamus, personal reflection in Logue (ed.), *The Border*, pp. 27–9.

de Bréadún, Deaglán, *The Far Side of Revenge: Making Peace in Northern Ireland*, Wilton, Cork, Collins Press, 2001.

Derry and Raphoe Action, *Protestants in Community Life: Findings from a Co. Donegal Survey*, Raphoe, Derry and Raphoe Action, June 2001.

Derry and Raphoe Action, *Protestants and the Border: Stories of Border Protestants North and South*, pamphlet, Derry and Raphoe Action (?Raphoe, 2005).

Dewar, M.W., *Why Orangeism?*, pamphlet, Belfast (Grand Orange Lodge of Ireland), 1958.

Dewar, M.W., Brown, John and Long, S.E., *Orangeism: A New Historical Appreciation*, Belfast, (Grand Orange Lodge of Ireland), 1967.

Dickson, Brice, 'Policing and human rights after the conflict', in Cox et al. (eds), *Farewell to Arms*, pp. 104–15.

Dillon, Martin, *The Dirty War*, London, Hutchinson, 1988.

Dillon, Martin, *Twenty-Five Years of Terror: The IRA's War Against the British*, London, Hutchinson, 1996.

Doherty, Tony, in Rolston (ed.), *Unfinished Business*, pp. 15–22.

Doherty, Tony, 'Bloody Sunday Justice Campaign: submission to the Forum for Peace and Reconciliation on 20 January 1995', *An Phoblacht/Republican News*, 26/1/1995.

Dooley, Terence, *The Plight of the Monaghan Protestants, 1912–26*, Dublin, Irish Academic Press, 2000.

Downing Street Minutes, confidential record of a meeting between Lord Chief Justice Widgery, Prime Minister Edward Heath and the Lord Chancellor at 10 Downing Street, 1/8/1972, reproduced in Mullan, *Eyewitness*, Appendix 1, pp. 269–73.

Downing, Taylor (ed.), *The Troubles: The Background to the Question of Northern Ireland*, London, Thames Television–MacDonald Futura, 1980.

Duddy, Kay, in Rolston (ed.), *Unfinished Business*, pp. 10–14.

Dudley Edwards, Ruth, *The Faithful Tribe: An Intimate Portrait of the Loyal Institutions*, London, HarperCollins, 1999.

Duffy, Rita, *The Essential Gesture: Recent Works by Rita Duffy* (?Belfast, no publisher), 2005.

Eolas Project, *Consultation Paper on Truth and Justice: A Discussion Document* (draft version 3), Belfast, Relatives for Justice, 2003.

English, Richard, *Armed Struggle: The History of the IRA*, London, Pan, 2004.

English, Richard and Walker, Graham (eds), *Unionism in Modern Ireland: New Perspectives on Politics and Culture*, Dublin, Gill & Macmillan, 1996.

European Commission, *Peace and Reconciliation: An Imaginative Approach to the European Programme for Northern Ireland and the Border Counties of Ireland*, Luxembourg, Office for Official Publications of the European Communities, 1998.

Evans, Martin and Lunn, Kenneth (eds), *War and Memory in the Twentieth Century*, Oxford and New York, Berg, 1997.

FAIR, *The True Story of South Armagh*, Armagh, FAIR (1999).

Fairweather, Eileen, McDonough, Roisin and McFadyean, Melanie, *Only the Rivers Run Free. Northern Ireland: The Women's War*, London and Sydney, Pluto, 1984.

Fanon, Frantz, *The Wretched of the Earth*, London, Penguin, 1990.

Farrell, Michael, *Northern Ireland: The Orange State*, London, Pluto, 1980.

Farren, Sean, 'The SDLP and the roots of the Good Friday Agreement', in Cox et al. (eds), *Farewell to Arms*, pp. 49–61.

Fay, Marie-Therese, Morrissey, Mike and Smyth, Marie, *Mapping Troubles-Related Deaths in Northern Ireland 1969–1994*, Derry, INCORE, 1997.

Fay, Marie-Therese, Morrissey, Mike and Smyth, Marie, *Northern Ireland's Troubles: The Human Costs*, London and Sterling, VA, Pluto Press, 1999.

FEAR Fermanagh, *Research document and development plan: 'People, they don't realize the hurt of having to leave what you have worked for all your life'* (np, 1997).

Felner, Eitan, 'Human rights leaders in conflict zones: a case study of the politics of "moral entrepreneurs"', Cambridge, MA, John F. Kennedy School of Government, Harvard University, available online: www.ksg.harvard.edu/cchrp/pdf/Felner.2004.pdf (visited 24/4/2007).

Ferguson, Raymond, 'Locality and political tradition', in Crozier (ed.), *Cultural Traditions in Northern Ireland: Varieties of Britishness*, pp. 40–5.

Fermanagh District Partnership, *Remember Change: Conference Papers*, a one-day conference held in the Killyhevlin Hotel, Enniskillen, 19 October 1996 (Enniskillen), Fermanagh District Partnership, 1996.

Fermanagh University Partnership Board, 'University partnership: the natural choice', leaflet, (?1993).

Fermanagh University Partnership Board, 'INTEC for everyone', leaflet (?2000).

Fields, Rona, *A Society on the Run: A Psychology of Northern Ireland*, Harmondsworth, Penguin, 1973 (republished as *Northern Ireland: Society under Siege*, New Brunswick, NJ, Transaction, 1980).

Fitzpatrick, David, *The Two Irelands 1912–1939*, Oxford, Oxford University Press, 1998.

Foster, Arlene, 'Protestants need rights explained to them', *Fortnight*, Feb. 2003, pp. 12–13.

Foster, Rev. Ivan, 'The Remembrance Day massacre in Enniskillen: the untold story', (?Kilskeery), 1987.

Foster, R.F., *Modern Ireland 1600–1972*, London, Penguin, 1989.

Foster, Roy, 'Remembering 1798', in McBride (ed.), *History and Memory*, pp. 67–94.

Freud, Sigmund, 'Beyond the pleasure principle', in *On Metapsychology* (1920), ed. A. Richards, Penguin, London, 1984.

Freud, Sigmund and Breuer, Josef, *Studies in Hysteria* (1895), ed. A. Richards, London, Penguin, 1974.

Garland, Caroline (ed.), *Understanding Trauma: A Psychoanalytical Approach*, London, Karnac, 2002.

Gartner, Joelle, 'Anger at the heel: the legacy of Bloody Sunday', in Ziff (ed.), *Hidden Truths*, pp. 117–31.

Garvaghy Residents, *Garvaghy: A Community under Siege*, Belfast, Beyond the Pale, 1999.

Gassman, Michele, 'Chronology of "pipe-bomb" attacks: July 1997 to 13 February 2001', available at CAIN website: http://cain.ulst.ac.uk/issues/violence/attacks/pipebomb.htm (visited 7/4/2003).

Gébler, Carlo, *The Glass Curtain: Inside an Ulster Community*, London, Hamish Hamilton, 1991.

Glassie, Henry, *Passing the Time in Ballymenone*, Bloomington and Indianapolis, Indiana University Press, 1995.

Goodall, Heather, 'Colonialism and catastrophe: contested memories of nuclear testing and measles' epidemics at Ernabella', in Darian-Smith and Hamilton (eds), *Memory and History in Twentieth-Century Australia*, pp. 55–76.

Gorman, Damian, 'Voices of the victims', Gary Law interviews Damian Gorman, *Causeway*, 3, 1996, pp. 39–43.

Gramsci, Antonio, *Selections from Prison Notebooks*, trans. and ed. Quinton Hoare and Geoffrey Nowell-Smith, London, Lawrence & Wishart, 1971.

Grand Orange Lodge of Ireland, *The Twelfth 1990: Tercentenary Issue*, Belfast, Grand Orange Lodge of Ireland, 1990.

Gready, Paul, 'Introduction', in Gready (ed.), *Political Transition*, pp. 1–26.

Gready, Paul (ed.), *Political Transition: Politics and Cultures*, London and Sterling, VA, Pluto, 2003.

Greenslade, Roy, 'Hierarchy of death', 21/6/1999, available at Victims and Survivors Trust website: www.victimsandsurvivorstrust.com (visited 19/7/1999).

Grimaldi, Fulvio and North, Susan, *Blood in the Street*, Derry, Guildhall Press, 1998.

Halbwachs, Maurice, *The Collective Memory*, New York, Harper & Row, 1980.

Hall, Michael (ed.), *Life on the Interface: Belfast 'Peaceline' Community Groups Confront Common Issues* (Island Pamphlets No. 1), Newtownabbey, Island, 1993.

Hall, Stuart, 'The West and the rest: discourse and power', in Stuart Hall and Bram Gieben (eds), *Formations of Modernity*, Cambridge, Polity Press, 1992.

Hamber, Brandon, 'The past imperfect: Exploring Northern Ireland, South Africa and Guatemala', in Hamber (ed.), *Past Imperfect*, pp. 1–12.

Hamber, Brandon, 'Comparing Northern Ireland and South Africa', in NIVT, *Towards a Civil Society*, pp. 112–19.

Hamber, Brandon (ed.), *Past Imperfect: Dealing with the Past in Northern Ireland and Societies in Transition*, Derry/Londonderry, INCORE, 1998.

Hansard: House of Commons Official Report, TSO, London.

Harnden, Toby, *'Bandit Country': The IRA and South Armagh*, London, Hodder & Stoughton, 1999.

Hart, Peter, 'The Protestant experience of revolution in Southern Ireland', in English and Walker (eds), *Unionism in Modern Ireland*, pp. 81–98.

Hayes, Maurice, *Whither Cultural Diversity?*, pamphlet, Belfast, Community Relations Council, 1991.

Hayes, Patrick and Campbell, Jim, *Bloody Sunday: Trauma, Pain and Politics*, London and Ann Arbor, MI, Pluto, 2005.

Hellsten, Sirkku K., 'Ethics, rhetoric and politics of post-conflict reconstruction: how can the concept of social contract help us in understanding how to make peace work?', WIDER Research Paper No. 2006/148, Helsinki, World Institute for Development Economics Research, November 2006, available at: www.wider.unu. edu/publications/rps/rps2006/rp2006-148.pdf.

Hepburn, A.C., 'A past apart: historical and literary perspectives', in A.C. Hepburn (ed.), *A Past Apart: Studies in the History of Catholic Belfast*, Belfast, Ulster Historical Foundation, 1996, pp. 1–21.

Herman, Judith, *Trauma and Recovery: From Domestic Abuse to Political Terror*, New York, Basic Books, 1992.

Hirsch, Marianne, *Family Frames: Photography, Narrative and Postmemory*, Cambridge, MA, and London, Harvard University Press, 1997.

Hobsbawm, Eric and Ranger, Terence (eds), *The Invention of Tradition*, Cambridge, Cambridge University Press, 1983.

Hodgkin, Katharine and Radstone, Susannah (eds), *Contested Pasts: The Politics of Memory*, London and New York, Routledge, 2003.

Holland, Jack, *Hope Against History: The Ulster Conflict*, London, Hodder & Stoughton, 2000.

Holland, Mary, 'The secrets of troubled minds', *Observer*, 19/1/1997.

Holmes, Richard (ed.), *Cuchulain the Lost Legend, Ulster the Lost Culture*, pamphlet, Belfast, Ulster Young Unionist Council, 1995.

Hopper, Keith, ' "Cat-calls from the cheap seats": the third meaning of Neil Jordan's *Michael Collins*', *Irish Review*, 21, 1997, pp. 1–28.

Howe, Stephen, 'Mad dogs and Ulstermen: the crisis of loyalism', available at: www.openDemocracy.net, Part 1 posted 28/9/2005, Part 2 posted 30/9/2005.

Hume, David, 'Ulster: the Lost Culture', in Holmes (ed.), *Cuchulain the Lost Legend*, pp. 11–18.

ICPNI, *A New Beginning: Policing in Northern Ireland: The Report of the Independent Commission on Policing for Northern Ireland*, London, HMSO, 1999.

Ignatieff, Michael, 'Articles of faith', *Index on Censorship*, special issue: 'Wounded nations, broken lives: truth commissions and war tribunals', 25, 5, 1996, pp. 110–22.

Ignatieff, Michael, 'Introduction', in Jillian Edelstein, *Truth and Lies: Stories from the Truth and Reconciliation Commission in South Africa*, New York, New Press, 2001, pp. 15–21.

Irish Peace and Reconciliation Platform, *Peace Building in the Republic of Ireland: Discussion Document*, Dublin, IPRP, 2000.

Jackson, Alvin, 'Unionist myths 1912–1985', *Past and Present*, 136, 1992, pp. 164–85.

Jackson, Alvin, *Ireland 1798–1998*, Oxford, Blackwell, 1999.

Jarman, Neil, 'Intersecting Belfast', in B. Bender (ed.), *Landscape, Politics and Perspectives*, Oxford, Berg, 1993.

Jarman, Neil, *Material Conflicts: Parades and Visual Displays in Northern Ireland*, Oxford and New York, Berg, 1997.

Jeffery, Keith, 'The Great War in modern Irish memory', in T.G. Fraser and Keith Jeffery (eds), *Men, Women and War*, Dublin, Lilliput Press, 1993, pp. 136–57.

Jelin, Elizabeth, 'Contested memories of repression in the Southern Cone: commemorations in a comparative perspective', in Gready (ed.), *Political Transition*, pp. 53–69.

Jelin, Elizabeth, *State Repression and the Struggles for Memory*, London, Latin America Bureau, 2003.

Jelin, Elizabeth and Kaufman, Susana G., 'Layers of memories: twenty years after in Argentina', in Ashplant et al. (eds), *Commemorating War*, pp. 89–110.

Johnson, Nuala C., *Ireland, the Great War and the Geography of Remembrance*, Cambridge and New York, Cambridge University Press, 2003.

Johnson, Richard, 'What is cultural studies anyway?', in John Storey (ed.), *What Is Cultural Studies? A Reader*, London, Arnold, 1996, pp. 75–114.

Jones, R. David, Kane, James S., Wallace, Robert, Sloan, Douglas and Courtney, Brian, *The Orange Citadel: A History of Orangeism in Portadown District*, Portadown, Portadown Cultural Heritage Committee, 1996.

Karpf, Ann, *The War After: Living with the Holocaust*, London, Minerva, 1996.

Kavanagh, Paul, 'Hopes and fears of survivors of the Troubles', in NIVT, *Towards a Civil Society*, pp. 104–11.

Keating, Thomas F. and Knight, W. Andy (eds), *Building Sustainable Peace*, New York, United Nations University Press, and Edmonton, University of Alberta Press, 2004.

Kelly, William with Kelly, Tom and Hasson, Kevin, *Murals: The Bogside Artists*, Derry, Guildhall Press, 2001; extracts posted on the Bogside Artists website http://cain.ulst.ac.uk/bogsideartists (visited 17/12/2004).

Kennedy, Billy (ed.), *A Celebration 1690–1990: The Orange Institution*, Edenderry, Grand Orange Lodge of Ireland, 1990.

Kennedy, Liam, *People and Population Change*, Co-operation North, Belfast, 1994.

Kiberd, Declan, 'Anglo-Irish attitudes', in Field Day Company (ed.), *Ireland's Field Day*, Derry, Field Day, 1985.

Kiberd, Declan, 'The elephant of revolutionary forgetfulness', in Ní Dhonnchada and Dorgan (eds), *Revising the Rising*, pp. 1–20.

Kinealy, Christine, *The Culture of Commemoration: The Great Irish Famine – A Dangerous Memory?*, pamphlet, Dublin, Cultures of Ireland, 1996.

Kirkaldy, J., 'Anglo-Irish relations: things have changed', *Irish Studies Review*, 1, 1992.

Klein, Melanie, 'Love, guilt and reparation', in Melanie Klein and Joan Riviere, *Love, Hate and Reparation*, London, Hogarth, 1937.

Klein, Melanie, 'Personification in the play of children', in *Contributions to Psychoanalysis 1921–45*, London, Hogarth, 1948.

Krog, Antjie, 'Cry, beloved country', *Guardian*, 18/1/1997.

Krog, Antjie, *Country of My Skull*, London, Vintage, 1999.

Kulle, Dorte, 'Victims and survivors: a study of the dynamics of the victims' debate in Northern Ireland', in Magowan and Patterson (eds), *Hear and Now*, pp. 79–87.

Lacey, Brian, *Siege City: The Story of Derry and Londonderry*, Belfast, Blackstaff Press, 1990.

Laplanche, Jean and Pontalis, Jean-Bertrand, 'Fantasy and the origins of sexuality', in Victor Burgin, James Donald and Cora Kaplan (eds), *Formations of Fantasy*, London and New York, Methuen, 1986, pp. 5–34.

Laub, Dori, 'Bearing witness, or the vicissitudes of listening', in Shoshana Felman and Dori Laub, *Testimony: Crises of Witnessing in Literature, Psychoanalysis and History*, New York and London, Routledge, 1992, pp. 57–74.

Laub, Dori, 'An event without a witness: truth, testimony and survival', in Shoshana Felman and Dori, Laub, *Testimony: Crises of Witnessing in Literature, Psychoanalysis and History*, New York and London, Routledge, 1992, pp. 75–92.

Lee, J.J., *Ireland 1912–85*, Cambridge, Cambridge University Press, 1989.

Lee, Joe, ' "Michael Collins" and the teaching of Irish history', *Sunday Tribune*, 17/11/1996.

Lee, Joe, 'Reeling back the years', *Sunday Tribune*, 3/11/1996.

Leonard, Jane, *The Culture of Commemoration: The Culture of War Commemoration*, pamphlet, Dublin, Cultures of Ireland, 1996.

Leonard, Jane, 'Facing "the finger of scorn": veterans memories of Ireland after the Great War', in Evans and Lunn (eds), *War and Memory*, pp. 59–72.

Leonard, Jane, *Memorials to the Casualties of Conflict: Northern Ireland 1969–1997*, Belfast, Community Relations Council, 1997.

Leonard, Jane, 'The twinge of memory: Armistice Day and Remembrance Sunday in Dublin since 1919', in English and Walker (eds), *Unionism in Modern Ireland*, pp. 99–114.

Leonard, Jane and Hanna, James, *War and Conflict in 20th-Century Ireland. A Travelling Exhibition from the Ulster Museum: Exhibition Guide*, Belfast, Ulster Museum, 2000.

Leydesdorff, Selma, Dawson, Graham, Burchardt, Natasha and Ashplant, T.G., 'Introduction: trauma and life stories', in Rogers et al. (eds), *Trauma*, pp. 1–26.

Lindsay, John (ed.), *Brits Speak Out: British Soldiers' Impressions of the Northern Ireland Conflict*, Londonderry, Guildhall, 1998.

Logue, Paddy (ed.), *The Border: Personal Reflections from Ireland, North and South*, Dublin, Oak Tree Press, 1999.

Longley, Edna, 'The Rising, the Somme and Irish memory', in Ní Dhonnchadha and Dorgan (eds), *Revising the Rising*, pp. 29–49.

Loughlin, James, *Ulster Unionism and British National Identity since 1885*, London, Pinter, 1995.

Lucy, Gordon and McClure, Elaine (eds), *The Twelfth: What it Means to Me*, Lurgan, Co. Armagh, Ulster Society, 1997.

Lundy, Patricia and McGovern, Mark, ' "You understand again": testimony and post-conflict transition in the North of Ireland', in Perks and Thomson (eds), *Oral History Reader*, pp. 531–7.

Lyons, F.S.L., *Culture and Anarchy in Ireland 1890–1939*, Oxford, Oxford University Press, 1979.

McAuley, Leon, *The Fountain: People from the Fountain*, Belfast, Arts Council of Northern Ireland–Verbal Arts Centre, 1993.

McBride, Ian, 'Ulster and the British problem', in English and Walker (eds), *Unionism in Modern Ireland*, pp. 1–18.

McBride, Ian, *The Siege of Derry in Ulster Protestant Mythology*, Dublin, Four Courts Press, 1997.

McBride, Ian, 'Memory and national identity in Modern Ireland', in McBride (ed.), *History and Memory in Modern Ireland*, pp. 1–42.

McBride, Ian (ed.), *History and Memory in Modern Ireland*, Cambridge, Cambridge University Press, 2001.

MacBride, Oistin, 'The roads to nowhere', *Irish American Magazine*, May–June 1993, pp. 50–4.

McCall, Cathal, 'The protean British identity in Britain and Northern Ireland', *Soundings*, 18, summer–autumn 2001, pp. 154–68.

McCann, Eamonn, *War and an Irish Town*, London, Pluto Press, 1980.

McCann, Eamonn, *Bloody Sunday in Derry: What Really Happened*, Dingle, Brandon, 1992.

McCann, Eamonn (ed.), *The Bloody Sunday Inquiry: The Families Speak Out*, London and Ann Arbor, MI, Pluto, 2006.

McCartney, Clem, 'The role of civil society', in McCartney (ed.), *Accord*, 8, pp. 44–9.

McCartney, Clem (ed.), *Accord*, special issue: 'Striking a balance: the Northern Ireland peace process', 8, 1999.

McCartney, Felicity, personal statement in Logue (ed.) *The Border*, pp. 86–9.

McClean, Raymond, *The Road to Bloody Sunday*, Londonderry, Guildhall Press, 1997.

McCreary, Alf, *Survivors*, Belfast, Century, 1981.

McCreary, Alf, *Gordon Wilson: An Ordinary Hero*, London, Marshall Pickering, 1996.

McDaniel, Denzil, *Enniskillen: The Remembrance Sunday Bombing*, Dublin and Niwot, CO, Wolfhound Press, 1997.

McDermott, Jim, *Northern Divisions: The Old IRA and the Belfast Pogroms 1920–22*, Belfast, Beyond the Pale, 2001.

MacDonald, Darach, *The Sons of Levi*, Monaghan, Drumlin Press, 1998.

McDonald, Henry, 'Families return to the farms of sorrow', *Observer*, 2/11/1997.

McGeown, Pat, Sinn Féin spokesperson on prison issues: submission to the Forum for Peace and Reconciliation on 20 January 1995, *An Phoblacht/Republican News*, 26/1/1995.

McInnes, Colin, 'A farewell to arms? Decommissioning and the peace process', in Cox et al. (eds), *Farewell to Arms*, pp. 78–92.

McKay, Susan, *Northern Protestants: An Unsettled People*, Belfast, Blackstaff Press, 2000.

McKendry, Helen, with Bishop, Heather, 'Disappeared: the search for my mother', *Real*, March 2004, pp. 52–5.

McKimm, Cathie, 'Narrative, imagination and a pluralist vision', in Magowan and Patterson (eds), *Hear and Now*, pp. 95–103.

McKittrick, David, Kelters, Seamus, Feeney, Brian and Thornton, Chris (eds), *Lost Lives: The Stories of the Men and Women Who Died as a Result of the Northern Ireland Troubles*, Edinburgh and London, Mainstream Publishers, 1999.

McVeigh, Jim, *Executed: Tom Williams and the IRA*, Belfast, Beyond the Pale, 1999.

McWilliams, Monica and Fearon, Kate, 'Problems of implementation', in McCartney (ed.), *Accord*, 8, pp. 60–7.

Magee, Jack, 'The teaching of Irish history in Irish schools', Belfast, Northern Ireland Community Relations Commission, 1971, mimeo, pp. 1–8 (first published in *The Northern Teacher*, winter 1970).

Magowan, James and Patterson, Norma (eds), *Hear and Now . . . and Then . . . Developments in Victims and Survivors Work*, Belfast, Northern Ireland Voluntary Trust, 2001.

Malcolm, Noel, *Bosnia: A Short History*, London, MacMillan, 1994.

Martin, Ged, 'The origins of partition', in Malcolm Anderson and Eberhard Bort (eds), *The Irish Border: History, Politics, Culture*, Liverpool, Liverpool University Press, 1999, pp. 57–111.

Meenan, Sharon and Mullan, Killian, 'I wasn't even born', *Derry Journal*, Bloody Sunday Supplement, 31/1/97, p. 4; also in Pat Finucane Centre, 'Bloody Sunday weekend 1997'.

Mhlaudi, Mbuyi, 'Working through loss and pain', in NIVT, *Towards a Civil Society*, pp. 96–99.

Miller, David, 'The new battleground? Community relations and cultural traditions', in *Planet: The Welsh Internationalist*, 102, December 1993–January 1994, pp. 74–9.

Miller, David, 'Colonialism and academic representations of the troubles', in Miller (ed.), *Rethinking Northern Ireland*, pp. 3–39.

Miller, David (ed.), *Rethinking Northern Ireland: Culture, Ideology and Colonialism*, London and New York, Longman, 1998.

Mitchell, Juliet, 'Introduction', in *The Selected Melanie Klein*, ed. Juliet Mitchell, Harmondsworth, Penguin, 1986.

Mofokeng, Tlhoki, 'Periods of transition: times of opportunity and challenge', in NIVT, *Towards a Civil Society*, pp. 49–53.

Moody, T.W., 'Irish history and Irish mythology', in Brady (ed.), *Interpreting Irish History*, pp. 71–86.

Morrissey, Mike, 'Northern Ireland: developing a post-conflict economy', in Cox et al. (eds), *Farewell to Arms*, pp. 136–52.

Mullan, Don, 'Afterword to Second Edition', Mullan, *Eyewitness*, pp. 300–10.

Mullan, Don, *Eyewitness Bloody Sunday*, 2nd edn, Dublin, Wolfhound Press, 1998.

Mullan, Don, 'Introduction' in Mullan, *Eyewitness*, pp. 33–67.

Murray, Raymond, *State Violence in Northern Ireland 1969–1997*, Cork and Dublin, Mercier, 1998.

Nairac, Captain Robert, 'Talking to People in South Armagh', British Army briefing paper, 1977, reproduced in Harnden, *'Bandit Country'*, pp. 367–72.

Nash, Catherine, 'Local histories in Northern Ireland', *History Workshop Journal*, 60, 2005, pp. 45–68.

Nelson, Sarah, *Ulster's Uncertain Defenders: Loyalists and the Northern Ireland Conflict*, Belfast and New York, Appletree Press–Syracuse University Press, 1984.

Ní Dhonnchadha, Máirín and Dorgan, Theo (eds), *Revising the Rising*, Field Day, Derry, 1991.

Northern Ireland Office, *The Terror – and the Tears: The Facts about IRA Brutality and the Suffering of Victims*, pamphlet, Belfast, NIO, 1972.

Northern Ireland Office, *The Day of the Men and Women of Peace Must Surely Come . . .*, Belfast, NIO, 1989.

Northern Ireland Voluntary Trust, *Towards a Civil Society: A Report of Conference Proceedings* ('Communities in Transition: The Challenges of Peace Building' and 'Remember and Change: Survivors of the Conflict Shaping Their Own Future', organized by NIVT and the Foundation for a Civil Society), Belfast, NIVT, 1999.

O'Brien, Joanne, 'Back to Bloody Sunday', *Sunday Business Post*, 25/1/1998, pp. 13–20.

O'Brien, Joanne, *A Matter of Minutes: The Enduring Legacy of Bloody Sunday*, Dublin, Wolfhound Press, 2002.

O'Callaghan, Sean, *The Informer*, London, Corgi, 1999.

Ó Ciosáin, Niall, 'Famine memory and the popular representation of scarcity', in McBride (ed.), *History and Memory*, pp. 95–117.

O'Connell, Jennifer, 'Bloody Sunday's legacy lives on', *Sunday Business Post* online: www.sbpost.ie (2000).

O'Connor, Stephen (ed.), *More Than a Uniform*, Kesh, O'Connor Publications, 1999.

O'Halloran, Chris, 'Interface communities and the peace process', in NIVT, *Towards a Civil Society*, pp. 17–23.

Omagh District Loyal Orange Lodge no. 11, *A Brief History: Omagh District LOL no. 11*, pamphlet, Omagh, Orange Order, 1995.

Opsahl Report, *A Citizen's Inquiry on Northern Ireland*, Dublin, Lilliput, 1993.

Orbach, Susie, 'When truth is not enough', *Guardian*, Weekend Supplement, 26/10/1996.

Page, Michael von Tangen, 'A "most difficult and unpalatable part": the release of politically motivated violent offenders', in Cox et al. (eds), *Farewell to Arms*, pp. 93–103.

Parkinson, Alan F., *Ulster Loyalism and the British Media*, Dublin and Portland, OR, Four Courts Press, 1998.

Passerini, Luisa (ed.), *Memory and Totalitarianism*, Volume 1: *International Yearbook of Oral History and Life Stories*, Oxford, Oxford University Press, 1992.

Pat Finucane Centre, 'Bloody Sunday weekend 1997: march for justice, time for truth: 25th anniversary, Thursday 30 Jan–Sunday 2 Feb 1997', leaflet, Derry, PFC.

Pat Finucane Centre, *In the Line of Fire: Report on Events in Derry Following on from the Drumcree Stand Off that Began on 7th July 1996*, Derry, PFC, 1996.

Pat Finucane Centre, 'Introducing the Pat Finucane Centre for Human Rights and Social Change', leaflet, Derry, PFC (?1993).

Peress, Gilles, 'An interview with Trisha Ziff', in Ziff (ed.), *Hidden Truths*, pp. 71–82.

Perks, Robert and Thomson, Alistair (eds), *The Oral History Reader*, 2nd edn, London and New York, Routledge, 2006.

PONI, Statement by the Police Ombudsman for Northern Ireland on her investigation into the circumstances surrounding the death of Raymond McCord Junior and related matters, (Operation Ballast), Belfast, Police Ombudsman for Northern Ireland, 22/1/2007, available at: http://cain.ulst.ac.uk/issues/police/ombudsman/poni220107.htm (visited 24/4/2007).

Popular Memory Group, 'Popular memory: politics, theory, method', in Centre for Contemporary Cultural Studies (ed.), *Making Histories: Studies in History-Writing and Politics*, London, Hutchinson, 1982, pp. 205–52 (edited extract in Perks and Thomson (eds), *Oral History Reader*, pp. 43–53.)

Porter, Rev. W. Warren, 'Here we stand: an outline of Orange principle', in Kennedy (ed.), *A Celebration*, pp. 22–5.

Pringle, Peter, 'Bloody Sunday: exorcising Widgery', in Ziff (ed.), *Hidden Truths*, pp. 52–65.

Pringle, Peter and Jacobson, Philip, *Those Are Real Bullets, Aren't They? Bloody Sunday, Derry, 30 January 1972*, London, Fourth Estate, 2002.

Quinn, F., *Interface Images: Photographs of the Belfast 'Peacelines'*, Belfast, Belfast Exposed Photography Group, 1994.

Quinton, Aileen, 'After the disaster', *Welfare World*, 1, 1996, pp. 5–9.

Radstone, Susannah, 'Screening trauma: *Forrest Gump*', in Radstone (ed.), *Memory and Methodology*, pp. 79–107.

Radstone, Susannah (ed.), *Memory and Methodology*, Oxford and New York, Berg, 2000.

Read, Peter, *Returning to Nothing: The Meaning of Lost Places*, Cambridge and Melbourne, Cambridge University Press, 1996.

Reaney, Derek, personal statement in Logue (ed.), *The Border*, pp. 172–4.

Reconciliation and Community: The Future of Peace in Northern Ireland, report of the Belfast conference, Belfast, Northern Ireland, 6–8 June 1995 (sponsored by Foundation for a Civil Society and others).

Redmond, Michael L., *A Nation's Holocaust and Betrayal: Ireland 1172–1992*, Bishop Aukland, Pentland Press, 1994.

Robbins, Keith, 'Varieties of Britishness', in Crozier (ed.), *Cultural Traditions in Northern Ireland: Varieties of Britishness*, pp. 4–18.

Robinson, Peter, *Their Cry Was 'No Surrender': An Account of the Siege of Londonderry, 1688–1689*, Belfast, Crown Publications, 1988.

Rogers, Kim Lacy, Leydesdorff, Selma and Dawson, Graham (eds), *Trauma: Life Stories of Survivors*, New Brunswick, NJ and London, Transaction, 2004 (first published as *Trauma and Life Stories: International Perspectives*, London and New York, Routledge, 1999.)

Rolston, Bill, *Politics and Painting: Murals and Conflict in Northern Ireland*, London and Toronto, Associated University Press, 1991.

Rolston, Bill, *Drawing Support 2: Murals of War and Peace*, Belfast, Beyond the Pale, 1995.

Rolston, Bill, 'Turning the page without closing the book', *Index on Censorship*, 25, 5, 1996, pp. 32–7.

Rolston, Bill, *Turning the Page Without Closing the Book: The Right to Truth in the Irish Context*, pamphlet, Dublin, Irish Reporter, 1996.

Rolston, Bill, 'What's wrong with multiculturalism? Liberalism and the Irish conflict', in Miller (ed.), *Rethinking Northern Ireland*, pp. 253–74.

Rolston, Bill (ed.), *Unfinished Business: State Killings and the Quest for Truth*, Belfast, Beyond the Pale, 2000.

Rolston, Bill, *Drawing Support 3: Murals and Transition in the North of Ireland*, Belfast, Beyond the Pale, 2003.

Rolston, Bill, 'Dealing with the past: pro-state paramilitaries, truth and transition in Northern Ireland', *Human Rights Quarterly*, 28, 3, 2006, pp. 652–75.

Rolston, Bill and Miller, David (eds), *War and Words: The Northern Ireland Media Reader*, Belfast, Beyond the Pale, 1996.

Rose, Susan, 'Naming and claiming: the integration of traumatic experience and the reconstruction of self in survivors' stories of sexual abuse', in Rogers et al. (eds), *Trauma*, pp. 160–79.

Ross, Fiona, 'The construction of voice and identity in the South African Truth and Reconciliation Commission', in Gready (ed.), *Political Transition*, pp. 165–80.

Ruane, Joseph and Todd, Jennifer (eds), *After the Good Friday Agreement: Analysing Political Change in Northern Ireland*, Dublin, University College Dublin Press, 1999.

Ruddy, Gerry, 'Peddling propaganda in the classroom', *Andersonstown News*, 20/8/1994.

Rushdie, Salman, *Midnight's Children*, London, Pan, 1982.

Ryder, Chris, *The Ulster Defence Regiment*, London, Methuen, 1991.

Ryder, Chris and Vincent Kearney, *Drumcree: The Orange Order's Last Stand*, London, Methuen, 2001.

Said, Edward, *Orientalism*, London, Penguin, 2003.

Sanford, Victoria, ' "What is written in our hearts": memory, justice, and the healing of fragmented communities', in Gready (ed.), *Political Transition*, pp. 70–89.

Sardar, Ziauddin, 'Beyond difference: cultural relations in the new century', in Ehsan Masood (ed.), *How Do You Know: Reading Ziauddin Sardar on Islam, Science and Cultural Relations*, London, Pluto Press, 2006.

Sayle, Murray, 'Murray Sayle finds his long-lost account of what happened on Bloody Sunday and returns to Northern Ireland to give evidence to the Saville Inquiry', *London Review of Books*, 11/7/2002, pp. 21–8.

Segal, Hannah, *Introduction to the Work of Melanie Klein*, London, Hogarth Press, 1973.

Shirlow, Peter and Murtagh, Brendan, *Belfast: Segregation, Violence and the City*, London and Ann Arbor, MI, Pluto Press, 2006.

Sinn Féin, 'Bloody Sunday Commemoration, 29/1/1995', leaflet, 1995.

Sinn Féin, *Towards a Lasting Peace in Ireland*, Dublin and Belfast, Sinn Féin, 1992.

Smyth, Clifford, *Indifferent to the Truth: How Media Bias Against Ulster's British and Protestant Population Has Prolonged the War and Continues to Cost Lives*, pamphlet, Belfast, Grand Orange Lodge of Ireland Education Committee, 1993.

Smyth, Marie, 'The human consequences of armed conflict: constructing "victimhood" in the context of Northern Ireland's Troubles', in Cox et al. (eds), *Farewell to Arms*, pp. 118–35.

Smyth, Marie, 'Remembering in Northern Ireland: victims, perpetrators and hierarchies of pain and responsibility', in Hamber (ed.), *Past Imperfect*, pp. 31–49.

Smyth, Marie and Fay, Marie-Therese (eds), *Personal Accounts from Northern Ireland's Troubles: Public Conflict, Private Loss*, London and Sterling, VA, Pluto, 2000.

Stanley, Jo, 'Involuntary commemorations: post-traumatic stress disorder and its relationship to war commemoration', in Ashplant et al. (eds), *Commemorating War*, pp. 240–259.

Stewart, A.T.Q., *The Narrow Ground: Aspects of Ulster 1609–1969*, London, Faber & Faber, 1977.

Stewart, Pamela J. and Strathern, Andrew, 'Introduction', in *Landscape, Memory and History: Anthropological Perspectives*, London and Sterling, VA, Pluto Press, 2003, pp. 1–15.

Sutton, M., *Bear in Mind These Dead: An Index of Deaths from the Conflict in Ireland, 1969–1993*, Belfast, Beyond the Pale, 1994.

Taylor, Peter, *Provos: The IRA and Sinn Féin*, London, Bloomsbury, 1998.

Taylor, Peter, *Brits: The War Against the IRA*, London, Bloomsbury, 2002.

Thomson, Alistair, *Anzac Memories: Living with the Legend*, Oxford and Melbourne, Oxford University Press, 1994.

Thomson, Alistair, 'Moving stories: Oral history and migration studies', *Oral History*, 27, 1, 1999, pp. 24–37.

Thomson, Alistair, 'Four paradigm transformations in oral history', *Oral History Review*, spring 2007, forthcoming.

Thomson, Alistair, Frisch, Michael and Hamilton, Paula, 'The memory and history debates: some international perspectives', *Oral History*, 22, 2, 1994, pp. 33–43.

Turner, Graeme, *British Cultural Studies: An Introduction*, 3rd edn, London, Routledge, 2002.

Two Traditions Group, *Northern Ireland and the Two Traditions in Ireland*, pamphlet, Belfast, Two Traditions Group, 1983.

Walker, Brian, *Dancing to History's Tune: History, Myth and Politics in Ireland*, Belfast, Institute of Irish Studies, Queen's University of Belfast, 1996.

Walsh, Dermot, *The Bloody Sunday Tribunal of Inquiry: A Resounding Defeat for Truth Justice and the Rule of Law*, Derry, Bloody Sunday Trust, 1999 (first published as a paper for the Law Department, University of Limerick, January 1997).

Walsh, Dermot P.J., *Bloody Sunday and the Rule of Law in Northern Ireland*, Basingstoke and London, MacMillan, 2001.

Weatherill, Rob, *Cultural Collapse*, London, 1994.

West Tyrone Voice, Information leaflet (1998).

Whelan, Kevin, 'The politics of memory', in Cullen (ed.), *1798*, pp. 143–60.

White, Richard, *Remembering Ahanagran: Storytelling in a Family's Past*, New York, Hill & Wang, 1998.

Whyte, John, *Interpreting Northern Ireland*, Oxford and New York, Oxford University Press, 1991.

Widgery, Lord Chief Justice, *Bloody Sunday 1972: Lord Widgery's Report of Events in Londonderry, Northern Ireland, on 30 January 1972*, London, TSO, 2001.

Williams, Raymond, *Marxism and Literature*, Oxford, Oxford University Press, 1977.

Wilson, S.J. and Associates, *A Needs Analysis of Families Acting for Innocent Relatives* (no place of publication, 1999).

Winnicott, D.W. *Playing and Reality*, Penguin, Harmondsworth, 1974.

Winter, Jane, 'Preface', in Mullan, *Eyewitness*, pp. 11–31.

Winter, Jay, 'Forms of kinship and remembrance in the aftermath of the Great War', in Winter and Sivan (eds), *War and Remembrance*, pp. 40–60.

Winter, Jay, *Sites of Memory, Sites of Mourning: The Great War in European Cultural History*, Cambridge, Cambridge University Press, 1995.

Winter, Jay and Sivan, Emmanuel (eds), *War and Remembrance in the Twentieth Century*, Cambridge, Cambridge University Press, 1999.

Wollheim, Richard, *Freud*, London, Fontana, 1971.

Ziff, Trisha (ed.), *Hidden Truths: Bloody Sunday 1972*, Santa Monica, CA, Smart Art Press, 1998.

Zinner, Ellen S. and Williams, Mary Beth (eds), *When a Community Weeps: Case Studies in Group Survivorship*, Philadelphia, PA, Brunner–Mazel, 1999.

Newspapers, newsletters and periodicals

Andersonstown News
An Phoblacht/Republican News
Argus
Belfast Telegraph
Causeway
Daily Telegraph
Derry Journal
Down Recorder
Fermanagh Herald
Fortnight
Guardian
Impartial Reporter
Independent
Irish American Magazine
Irish Independent.
Irish News
Irish Times
Justice: Newsletter of Relatives for Justice
London Review of Books
Newry Reporter
News Letter
Observer
Orange Standard
Shankill People
Strabane Weekly News
Sunday Business Post
Sunday Times
Sunday Tribune
Sydney Morning Herald
The Times
Ulster: The Voice of the UDA
Victims Liaison Unit (VLU) Newsletter
Young Unionist

Unpublished documents

Bloody Sunday Initiative, 'Towards a new peace agenda: a discussion paper', unpublished manuscript (?1990 or 1991), in 'Bloody Sunday' box, Northern Ireland Political Collection, Linen Hall Library, Belfast.

Davies, David, 'Frantz Fanon, colonialism, and Algeria: the historical formation of a radical discourse', unpublished Ph.D thesis, University of Brighton, 2004.

Dawson, Graham, 'The nationalist communities and Republican politics in Belfast', report on the Brighton Labour Party Delegation to Northern Ireland, June 1986, unpublished MS, 1986.

Hayes, Patrick, 'Narrative tradition, intergenerational perceptions of trauma, social identity development and general health implications among a sample of the "Bloody Sunday" families, Derry, Northern Ireland', unpublished Ph.D thesis, Queen's University of Belfast, 2000 (revised and published as Hayes and Campbell, 2005).

Ulster Society, 'Marketing', unpublished internal paper, 1985, in 'Ulster Society' box, Northern Ireland Political Collection, Linen Hall Library, Belfast.

Interviews

Adair, Mark, Cultural Traditions projects officer, Northern Ireland Community Relations Council, interviewed 30/7/1999.

Barton, Colm, projects co-ordinator, Bloody Sunday Trust, interviewed 5/4/2000.

Burns, Gerry, formerly chief executive, Fermanagh District Council, interviewed 31/7/2001.

Bradley, Brendan, co-ordinator, Survivors of Trauma, interviewed 6/4/2000.

Butcher, Mary, civil servant in the Victims Liaison Unit, Northern Ireland Office, interviewed 7/2/2000.

Devine, Barney, project manager, Higher Bridges Project, interviewed 31/7/2001.

FACT (Families Against Crimes by Terrorism), group interview 7/4/2000.

Finlay, Leslie, treasurer, West Tyrone Voice, interviewed with Hazlett Lynch, 27/3/2000.

Foster, Arlene, secretary, FEAR, interviewed 29/7/1999.

Frazer, Willie, vice-chair, FAIR, interviewed 24–25/3/2000.

Lynch, Hazlett, co-ordinator, West Tyrone Voice, interviewed with Leslie Finlay, 27/3/2000.

McCabe, Eilish, Relatives for Justice, interviewed with Mark Thompson, 4/4/2000.

MacDonald, Darach, writer, interviewed 31/7/2001.

Peake, Sandra, director, WAVE Trauma Centre, Belfast, interviewed 6/4/2000.

Thompson, Mark, co-ordinator, Relatives for Justice, interviewed with Eilish McCabe, 4/4/2000.

Radio and TV broadcasts, film, video and visual material

Aftershock: The Untold Story Of The Birmingham Pub Bombings, broadcast on BBC2, 9/11/ 1994.

An Appeal To You From The Victims, video, no production details (1999).

Brothers In Arms, Fast Forward Productions, 2005.

The Boyne 1690–1990, video, Grand Orange Lodge of Ireland, 1990.

Contemplating an Iceberg, Rita Duffy, exhibition at the Ulster Museum, 2005.
Counterpoint, 'Driven From The Land?', Ulster TV, broadcast 29/4/1993.
Creggan, Thames TV, dir. Mary Holland and Michael Whyte, 1979.
Families Acting For Innocent Relatives, FAIR video, undated (1999).
An Imperfect Peace, BBC Radio 4, broadcast 3/12/2001 and 10/12/2001.
The Late Show, 'The New Irish History', Channel 4, broadcast January 1994.
Michael Collins, dir. Neil Jordan, 1996.
Remember Bloody Sunday, dir. Peter Taylor, first broadcast BBC2, 30/1/1992.
Resigning Issues, Danny Morrison interviewed by Fergal Keane, broadcast BBC Radio 4, 13/10/1998.
Sunday, Bloody Sunday, first broadcast Channel 4, 30/1/1997.
Troubled Images: Posters and Images of the Northern Ireland Conflict from the Linen Hall Library, Belfast, CD-ROM, Belfast, Linen Hall Library, 2001.
The Trouble With Peace, broadcast Channel 4, August 1995.
Today, BBC Radio 4, 11/1/2006.

Websites

An Fhirinne: www.anfhirinne26.com (visited 16/2/2007).
An Phoblacht/Republican News web archive: www.irlnet.com/aprn/archive (visited 11/9/2003).
Bloody Sunday Inquiry: www.bloody-sunday-inquiry.org.uk (visited 24/4/2007).
Bloody Sunday Trust: www.bloodysundaytrust.org (visited 22/2/2002).
Bogside and Brandywell Initiative website: http://freederry.org (visited 26/9/2006).
British–Irish Rights Watch: www.birw.org (visited 24/4/2007).
CAIN Project (University of Ulster): http://cain.ulst.ac.uk.
Derry and Raphoe Action page, on the Raphoe Reconciliation Project website: http://homepage.tinet.ie/~raprecpro/dra.htm (visited 30/7/2001).
FAIR: www.victims.org.uk (visited 14/9/2000).
FAIR's Guestbook: http://books.dreambook.com/dcz5152/guestbook.html (visited 11/4/2000 and 22/5/2000)
Forgiveness Project: www.theforgivenessproject.com (visited 24/4/2007).
Glencree Centre for Peace and Reconciliation: www.glencree.ie (visited 24/4/2007).
Hansard: House of Commons Debates: www.publications.parliament.uk (visited 24/4/2007).
Impartial Reporter online: www.imparialreporter.com/archive (visited 12/10/2000, 26/7/2001).
John F. Kennedy School of Government, Harvard University: www.ksg.harvard.edu (visited 24/4/2007).
openDemocracy: www.openDemocracy.net.
Police Service of Northern Ireland: www.psni.police.uk (visited 24/4/2007).
Raphoe Reconciliation Project website: http://homepage.tinet.ie/~raprecpro/aims.htm (visited 30/7/2001).
'Remembering Bloody Sunday' pages, created 1997–2000, Larkspirit website: http://larkspirit.com/bloodysunday (visited 22/2/2002).
Sunday Business Post online: www.sbpost.ie.
Victims and Survivors Trust: www.victimsandsurvivorstrust.com (visited 19/7/1999).

Index

Note: 'n.' after a page number indicates the number of a note on that page. Numbers in *italic* refer to illustrations

Lightning Source UK Ltd.
Milton Keynes UK
UKOW04f0158180714

235289UK00001B/2/P